Effective Public Relations

PRENTICE-HALL, INC., Englewood Cliffs, New Jersey 07632

effective PUBLIC RELATIONS

5th edition

Scott M. Cutlip

*Dean, Henry W. Grady School of
Journalism and Mass Communication,
The University of Georgia*

Allen H. Center

*Journalism Faculty,
San Diego State University;
Formerly, Vice President, Motorola, Inc.*

Library of Congress Cataloging in Publication Data

CUTLIP, SCOTT M.
    Effective public relations.

    Includes bibliographies and index.
    1. Public relations.   I. Center, Allen H.,
joint author.   II. Title.
HM263.C78   1978   659.2   78-6039
ISBN 0-13-245035-6

Effective Public Relations, fifth edition

Scott M. Cutlip *and* **Allen H. Center**

© 1978, 1971, 1964, 1958, 1952 by Prentice-Hall, Inc.,
Englewood Cliffs, New Jersey 07632

Printed in the United States of America

10   9   8   7   6   5

PRENTICE-HALL INTERNATIONAL, INC., *London*
PRENTICE-HALL OF AUSTRALIA PTY. LIMITED, *Sydney*
PRENTICE-HALL OF CANADA, LTD., *Toronto*
PRENTICE-HALL OF INDIA PRIVATE LIMITED, *New Delhi*
PRENTICE-HALL OF JAPAN, INC., *Tokyo*
PRENTICE-HALL OF SOUTHEAST ASIA PTE. LTD., *Singapore*
WHITEHALL BOOKS LIMITED, *Wellington, New Zealand*

preface

This fifth edition carries *Effective Public Relations* into its second quarter century. First published in 1952, this book has become the most widely used textbook in this field. It has been published in Italian, Japanese, Korean, and Spanish editions and has been used around the world to introduce a full generation of practitioners to a challenging calling. The expressions of gratitude that have come to us over the years have amply rewarded our efforts.

It is our hope that this book will continue to serve as a definitive and comprehensive resource for educators, students, and careerists. Though the book has changed greatly over the years, our objective has remained constant.

When the first edition appeared, the field of public relations was mushrooming; its function was not clearly defined, and its essentiality was not fully accepted. Today, the growth has slowed to a solid, steady gait. The function has diversified, yet it is more clearly defined and more widely understood. Many of the concepts first set forth in this book have now become standard operating procedures in the practice. Today the essentiality of this function is seldom questioned in a time when the world suffers from conflicts in which confrontation all too often displaces communication. As society continues to become more massive, more impersonal, and more segmented, the need for public relations grows. The practitioners, individually and collectively, have made progress in improving their competence and in raising the ethical level of their work. This is reflected in the accreditation and institute programs of the Public Relations Society of America and the Canadian Public Relations Society. College and university teachers in public relations have had a major role in these advances. These 25 years have brought much progress in public relations; there is need for more. The authors hope that their efforts will continue to contribute to the educational undergirding.

This revision required accurate interpretation of some changing conditions peculiar to the 1970's. The calling had sustained injury to its prestige. The emphasis in certain precincts of the practice had shifted perceptibly away from programs openly bidding for popular support in favor of discreet or covert efforts aimed selectively at critical points of power and influence. The employment market has become more selective and specialized.

In response to these and other changed conditions, education for public relations became oriented more to technical skills than to concepts of persuasion or to the professionalism of the function. Public relations sequences became more segmented. Several new specialized texts appeared on the scene to serve one or another of the segments.

By itself, the segmenting of education for skills of a professional nature may be healthy. There is cause for thoughtful appraisal, however, to the extent that the segments represent a slicing of the same loaf of information and inquiry into thinner pieces simply for quicker, easier consumption. Public relations expertise cannot be learned in ten easy lessons.

Your authors decided to leave segmentation to others in favor of sustaining the substantial, comprehensive nature of this text. For new substance, a chapter on Public Relations Law was added to meet a need lacking in other texts. A canvass of the calling was conducted as a basis for the chapter on The Practitioners, Staff and Status. Obsolete material was weeded out. Practical examples of precepts were updated. The writing was tightened. More illustrative material was added. Case problems were separated to avoid interruption of mainstream reading, and to provide exercises for classroom and homework.

Structurally, we have designated a Part I and Part II. The sequence of Chapters 1 through 17 in Part I supports the lecture chronology of an introductory or overview course. Part II, Chapters 18 through 25, are positioned to provide reference reading in schools where there is but a single overview course, or to accommodate the textual need in an advanced practice course. We feel that the entire context is needed for career advancement and accreditation purposes.

We hope fervently that this edition will have the out-reach to be a creditable reflection of the remarkable progress of the calling in attaining proficiency and recognition of its social significance as well as its proven practical utility. There are a number of individuals who have earned a public salute for important contributions.

Scott Cutlip wishes to acknowledge with gratitude the help of President Alice Beeman of CASE; David Brown, founding president, Association of Government Communicators; John Cone, secretary, South Carolina School Boards Association; Fred Christenson, formerly public information director, San Diego County; Rowene Danbom, director, public information, Colorado Department of Health; James Dickson, coordinator of public information, West Virginia Department of Education; Robert J. Doyle, information officer, University of Wisconsin; Kirk Hallahan, Harshe, Rotman & Druck, Los Angeles; George Hamel, director, school-community relations, Fairfax County (Va.) Schools; Maj. Gen. L. Gordon Hill, formerly chief of information, U.S. Army; Harvey K. Jacobson, assistant to the vice president, University of Michigan; Kurt H. Krahn, director, public relations, American Family Insurance Group; Dr. William E. Lee, Post-Doctoral Fellow, University of Georgia; Gordon C. McLean, director, public relations, St. Mary's Hospital, Evansville, Ind.; Professor John T. McNelly, University of Wisconsin School of Journalism and Mass Communication; William Pruett, vice president for public relations, Coca Cola; Alan A. Rubin, director, public information, United Way of America; Assistant Dean J. Thomas Russell, University of Georgia School of Journalism and Mass Communication; Rea W. Smith, executive vice president, PRSA; David Steinberg, chief executive, PR Newswire; Roy K. Wilson, formerly executive director, National School Public Relations Association; Sanford H. Winston, public affairs officer, Department of

Health, Education and Welfare; Al Wolf, eastern public relations manager, Dow Chemical Co.; Professor Alan Wurtzel, University of Georgia School of Journalism and Mass Communication. In addition, there are my secretary, Mrs. Clara Stewart, who helped me in countless ways, and Sandra Stinespring, who did much of the typing.

Allen Center wishes to express appreciation for the cooperation of many organizations in providing illustrative materials, and for the contributions of new and updated information from colleagues, practitioners and former students. Among these are Commanders Milton S. Baker Jr. and William D. Collins, Naval public affairs; Edward M. Block, vice-president, AT&T; Ellis N. Brandt, director, business communications, Dow Chemical; Philip W. Callanan, senior vice-president, Hill and Knowlton, Inc.; Chris B. Cameris, manager, international public affairs, First National City Bank; Lee Cary, director, public relations, Badger Meter, Inc.; Thomas J. Fay, general manager, public relations department, Mobil Oil; J. Michael Mattson, development and community relations, University of Utah; Leonard J. McEnnis, Jr., office of public information, Federal Trade Commission; Michael Radock, vice-president, university relations and development, University of Michigan; Onetha Trammer, manager, Comm/Pro Program, Eaton Corporation; James B. Strenski, chairman, Public Communications Inc.; Barbara Teitscheid, San Diego State graduate student; Mary Wampler, editor, *Senior World;* R. Vincent Ward, director, public relations and public affairs, United Telecommunications Inc.; Dr. Frederick Teahan, Director of Education, and, Mary W. Wilson, director, Information Center, PRSA.

Scott Cutlip and Allen Center jointly wish to acknowledge the help rendered by Don Bates, director of special projects, PRSA; Byron DeHaan, manager, public affairs, Caterpillar Tractor Co.; George Hammond, chairman, Carl Byoir & Associates, Inc.; Thomas W. Hope, president, Hope Reports Inc.; Carl Lenz, president, Modern Talking Pictures; Frank Seymour, president, Frank M. Seymour Inc.; Alvie L. Smith, director, internal communications, General Motors; Richard Weiner, president, Richard Weiner, Inc.; Marvin C. Wilbur, executive director, The Religious Public Relations Council; Frank Wylie, director, public relations, U.S. Auto Sales, Chrysler Corp.; and, Albert J. Zack, director, public relations department, AFL-CIO. We also appreciate the importance of the cooperation extended by the editors of the *Public Relations Journal* and the *Public Relations Review,* and the publishers of *Corporate Public Issues (CPI), O'Dwyer's Newsletter, Public Relations News, Public Relations Quarterly,* and *PR Reporter.* We owe a debt of gratitude to Wallace Jamie, a counselor; Dennis L. Wilcox, coordinator PR degree program, San Jose State; Max M. Rule, University of Akron; and R. Max Wales, University of Oregon, for their helpful critiques of the fourth edition as a prelude to our revision. We have endeavored to meet their criticisms. Most of all, we recognize a large debt to our students who over the years have made many suggestions for improvements. Many of those suggestions are embedded in this edition. We are grateful for the painstaking and imaginative job by Professor Noel Griese in devising a practical teacher's manual.

Finally, for the fifth time we underscore the original dedication of this text to our wives, Erna Cutlip and Nancy Center, for their encouragement and help, and, indeed, for their forbearance through hectic periods of revision.

Scott Cutlip
Allen Center

To Erna Cutlip and Nancy Center

contents

The Principles and the Process

The process:
fact-finding and feedback-the first step 138

THE FOUR-STEP PROCESS. IMPORTANCE OF FEEDBACK. THE RESEARCH ATTITUDE.
The Listening Phase of Public Relations. The Objective Look.
Counseling and Programming Support. Uncovering Trouble Spots.
Improving Outbound Communication. Useful Intelligence from Research.
Information Center. THE RESEARCH PROCESS.
Defining the Problem and the Publics. Reaching the Audience.
THE RESEARCH TOOLS. Informal Methods. More Reliable Methods.
CASE PROBLEM.

The process:
planning and programming-
the second step 162

WHERE PLANNING MAKES THE DIFFERENCE. THE PURPOSES OF PLANNING.
A PROCEDURE FOR PLANNING. A Searching Look Backward.
A Wide Look Around. A Deep Look Inside. A Long, Long Look Ahead.
STRATEGIC THINKING. THE MOST DIFFICULT PARTS OF THE PROCESS.
Writing the Program. Budgeting. INDOCTRINATION: A CONTINUING PROCESS.
TIMING AS A KEY ELEMENT. Planning for Disasters.
THE NEED FOR A PUBLIC FACT CENTER. THE OUTLOOK.
CASE PROBLEM IN FORCED PLANNING.

The process:
action and communication-
the third step 188

THE NATURE OF COMMUNICATION. The Fundamentals.
THE TWO-STEP FLOW THEORY. THE CONCENTRIC-CIRCLE THEORY.
THE DIFFUSION PROCESS. BARRIERS AND DISTORTION.
THE ACT OF COMMUNICATING. A Few Fundamentals. STEREOTYPES.
SEMANTICS. THE PRACTITIONER AS "ANSWER MAN." HOW DO WE GO ABOUT IT?
SAY IT WITH SYMBOLS. THE 7 C'S OF COMMUNICATION. 1. Credibility.
2. Context. 3. Content. 4. Clarity. 5. Continuity and Consistency.
6. Channels. 7. Capability of Audience. CASE PROBLEM.

The process:
evaluation-the fourth step 213

MEASUREMENT BY OBJECTIVES. BEFORE AND AFTER.
THE PUBLIC RELATIONS AUDIT. PRETESTING. POSTTESTING.
MEASURING IMPACT. Evaluation Tools. Measurement of Results.
OVERALL REVIEW OF PROGRAM. CASE PROBLEM.

Public relations for business: changing emphases, priorities, and programs

THE RISE AND ROLE OF PUBLIC AFFAIRS. Lobbying: A Specialty.
Moving from Stout Defense to Stout Advocacy.
THE SEVERAL GARBS OF THE NEW ADVOCACY.
Statements of Missions and Integrity. Speeches and Reprints. Advertising.
Candor and Availability. PHILANTHROPY: AID TO EDUCATION, HEALTH, WELFARE,
AND THE ARTS. Corporate Giving: Large in Dollars, Small in Percent.
A Foremost Beneficiary, Education. Health and Welfare.
Culture and the Arts. A Few Flies in the Ointment.
CORPORATE FINANCIAL RELATIONS. Corporate Ownership.
The Responsibility and the Role. Effective Workaday Programming.
The Annual Meeting of Stockholders. Financial Analysts: A Growing Factor.
CONSUMER RELATIONS: AREA OF FOMENT. The Resurgence of Consumerism.
The Role of Public Relations in Consumer Affairs. The Outlook.
A CASE PROBLEM IN CRISIS.

The practice: trade associations, professional societies, and labor unions

ASSOCIATIONS AND SOCIETIES. Differentiation. An Epoch of Gains.
The Problem of Serving Many Masters. An Era of Change and Gain.
Some Variations in Approach.
The Growing Importance of Public Relations. The Nature of Programming.
The Relative Importance of Functions. LABOR UNIONS.
The Role of Public Relations. Tools and Media. The AFL-CIO Program.
The Problem of Strikes. A CASE STUDY IN CONSERVATION.
A CASE PROBLEM IN COMPROMISE.

The practice: voluntary agencies, hospitals, and churches

PUBLIC RELATIONS FOR WELFARE AND HEALTH AGENCIES. The Perspective.
The Program. The Problems. The Years Ahead.
PUBLIC RELATIONS FOR HOSPITALS. The Perspective. The Program.
Hospitals and the Press. Two Trends of Note.
PUBLIC RELATIONS FOR CHURCHES. The Perspective. The Program.
A Case Study in Promotion. FUND RAISING. The Big Effort.
Professional or Amateur? Costs. The Principles. CASE PROBLEM.

Effective Public Relations

Part

I

THE PRINCIPLES AND THE PROCESS

1

Public relations is the planned effort to influence opinion through good character and responsible performance, based upon mutually satisfactory two-way communication.

Introduction to Contemporary Public Relations

Two persistent questions are, "What *IS* public relations?" and "What does it *DO?*" Answering these questions is a continuing challenge. For one thing, the function is dynamic. It adapts to change as the assignments given it shift in emphasis, priority, and variety; and at the same time, the media used to communicate undergo changes in technology and effectiveness. The competition among public news media for audience is continuously intensifying. This affects news values and the acceptability of news from outside sources, including public relations people. These changes alone can frustrate efforts to achieve a simple, universal definition. But there are other factors. For instance, the views and opinions of audiences that public relations efforts seek to influence reshape themselves like passing clouds, as subjects or issues are reexamined.

The forces compelling change will be examined in Chapter Five, "The Public Relations Environment." As an introduction here, we will try to put the various definitions of public relations into a practical perspective that will be helpful to anyone who might be called on to describe the function or the people who perform it.

The problem of definition

One source of definition is whatever dictionary is at hand. One dictionary offers this definition:

> **public relations:** relations with the general public through publicity; those functions of a corporation, organization, branch of military service, etc., concerned with informing the public of its activities, policies, etc., and attempting to create favorable public opinions.[1]

This is all right as far as it goes. The emphasis here is on the one-way issuance of information. The motive is to create favorable opinion. This definition reflects

FIGURE 1-1

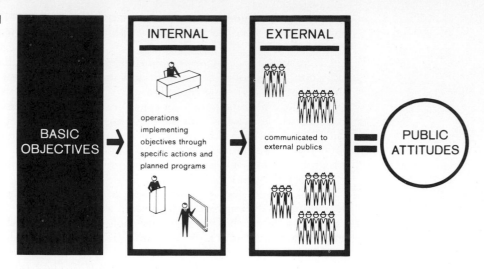

the early years of the calling, when the emphasis was almost entirely on getting publicity.

Another dictionary mentions such specific publics or audiences as customers, employees, and stockholders. It adds that the motivation of an organization is to "adapt itself to its environment and interpret itself to society." This definition introduces the fact that public groupings can be distinguished from each other and selected as targets. It broadens the motivation to embrace the adjustment of an organization to its total environment.

A third dictionary adds something else, by saying that actions are taken to "promote goodwill," a suggestion from which one can infer that understanding, empathy, and even harmony or compromise might on occasion be involved. The reader of the definition could conclude that inherent in the public relations function there is a nobility of purpose beyond self-interest. Perhaps the scanning of other dictionaries would uncover a definition that implied an ethical thrust, or standards of conduct higher than those prevailing for the general public.

Of course, these dictionary definitions do not necessarily describe the way most people actually perceive the term, the function, its practitioners. Relatively few people in the world turn to a dictionary definition of public relations. But most people do encounter the use of the function. Perhaps such an encounter would be getting a response to a product complaint letter, or reading a news item that a product has been recalled, or watching a TV talk-show guest. Student encounters may consist of reading about the resignation of a university official, the hiring of an outstanding teacher, or the acquisition of new scholarship funds; or attendance at a meeting staged by Zero Population Growth, or hearing Jane Fonda give a speech, or having a corporate or military official as guest lecturer in class. All these might have been prepared or arranged by public relations practitioners.

In actuality, the vast majority of people arrive at their impressions almost by accident: An acquaintance is a public relations practitioner and talks about the work; or a neighbor is in the news media and expresses a liking or a distaste for practitioners; or a person might be employed where there is a public relations department and be aware of its specific duties, such as editing the house

3

employee publication. Impressions may also come from seeing news events or people in them described, favorably or unfavorably, as having "public relations" motives.

Given such happenstance circumstances, it is understandable that people's individual conceptions of the term and the function vary widely, with many misconceptions and some confusion.

To some, one of the parts—for example, publicity or press-agentry—appears to be the whole. Having someone in an Indian headdress sitting by a teepee on Main Street during a Community Fund campaign, with a smoke signal spelling out "GIVE," may be good press-agentry, and also a good fund-raising tactic. But it is probably only one small part of the fund's public relations programming. It is far from the whole of it.

The skills and talents required to be a successful practitioner may seem as demanding and complex to some people as those needed for scientific opinion analysis or the teaching of social psychology. To others, what they see of the function may appear as basic as grammatical writing or as simple as tabulating.

Many misconceptions derive from the fact that employers and clients determine the makeup of the function by the nature of the tasks they assign to it. These tasks vary widely from one employer to the next. Thus, in one instance, the practice is characterized by an employer's policy of candid, open communications; in the next, by efforts to maintain a low public profile. In one situation, the strategy may be to provoke controversy, and in another, to gain a reconciliation or compromise. The assignments, to the outsider, have few patterns of consistency where concern for the public good, ultimate consequences, future recurrences, or even humanitarianism are concerned.

The world knows the public relations function more by what practitioners DO than by what practitioners aspire to BE.

As a career, the function is relatively young. The gap between assigned duties, underlying concepts of social science, and professional aspirations will remain, but will diminish gradually. Meantime, those entering the field will be confronted with making some adjustments in their preconceptions and perhaps experiencing some frustrations.

The semantics of the term

The term *public relations* is used in at least three senses: the *relationships* with those who constitute an organization's publics or constituents, the *ways and means used* to achieve favorable relationships, and the *quality or status* of the relationships. Thus the one term is used to label both *means and ends,* to name a *condition,* and to express *the conduct or actions related to that condition.*

Although singular in meaning, the term is spelled and spoken as a plural. It is often used interchangeably with *propaganda, information, communications, public affairs, advertising,* or *persuasion.*

Finally, the term is used as a noun, "How's your public relations?"; as a verb, "They really public relationed that situation"; and as a modifier, "It was a public relations triumph."

Frequently, practitioners have decried the term as a misnomer, as awkward to use, or as negative in its implications (that employers or clients have problems they can't handle in their relationships). Many employers of public relations

EXHIBIT 1-1

The Game of Definitions

For at least 50 years, practitioners, editors, and authors have sought to capture the essence of the function in a phrase, slogans, or book title that might catch on popularly and dispel misconceptions.

Among these are:

X (the deed) $+ Y$ (the way the deed is interpreted) = public attitudes

Good performance, publicly appreciated

PR = *P*erformance and *R*ecognition

Pathways to public favor

Crystallizing public opinion

The engineering of consent

The conscience of an organization

Doing good and getting credit for it

Deeds first, then words

Virtue brings its own reward

Other efforts have sought to devise a definition of sufficiently broad dimensions to accommodate variations and, by promotion, to congeal its usage. One of the most persistent efforts has been that by *Public Relations News,* one of the commercial newsletters catering to the calling. Its definition:

> Public Relations is the management function which evaluates public attitudes, identifies the policies and procedures of an individual or an organization with the public interest, and plans and executes a program of action to earn public understanding and acceptance.

A serious and scholarly effort to put a comprehensive definition on paper was made in 1976 by Dr. Rex F. Harlow, social scientist, author, and venerable practitioner. Dr. Harlow's efforts were under the sponsorship of the Foundation for Public Relations Research and Education.

Dr. Harlow's working definition:

> Public relations is a distinctive management function which helps establish and maintain mutual lines of communication, understanding, acceptance and cooperation between an organization and its publics; involves the management of problems or issues; helps management to keep informed on and responsive to public opinion; defines and emphasizes the responsibility of management to serve the public interest; helps management to keep abreast of and effectively utilize change, serving as an early warning system to help anticipate trends; and uses research and sound and ethical communication techniques as its principal tools.[2]

The game goes on. Meantime, *public relations defines itself by what it does.*

multiply the confusion by using other terms they prefer for the department performing the functions. Some of them are *Corporate Relations, University Relations, Hospital Relations, Public Information* or *Office of Information, Public Affairs, Communications, Public and Professional Affairs, Public Education,* and *Public-Sector Programs.*

The administrative and functional concepts

Much of the confusion will clear away as more and more employers come to understand the distinction between public relations as an *operating concept of administration* and public relations as a *specialized staff function serving administrators.*

The first is a set of policies, or a state of mind, that guides administrators—for example, the decision of the United Nations that "the activities of the Department of Public Information should be so organized and directed as to promote . . . an informed understanding of the work and purposes of the United Nations among the peoples of the world. . . ." This is administrative policy.

The second is the specific function for which skilled practitioners are hired. In the United Nations, administrative policy is implemented by specialists who are "equipped to analyze trends," who "provide all the services for the daily, weekly, and periodical press," and so on.

The essentiality of the second, functional concept is no longer disputed in a world bound together by instant communications but separated by the competition of values and life-styles. Acceptance of the need for the first concept is gaining rapidly in a society bound together by interdependence and pulled apart by spasms of crisis and confrontation. The coupling of the first with the second is by no means a universal approach taken by the leaders of private and public institutions. The trend, nonetheless, is clearly in a direction favorable to the public relations function.

Public relations thinking by senior management has its first influence on the performance of an organization. That is as it should be. *Responsible performance on the part of an institution is the foundation for public acceptance.* Inescapably, however, the character of the organization and the behavior of its officials are coupled in public opinion with performance. Responsible performers are expected to act in the public interest, and to be legally and morally upright. When an elected official is found to flout the public interest, to be immoral, or to misuse funds entrusted to him or her, the reputation of the whole institution comes into question.

In broad terms, public relationships are the responsibility of an organization's administrators. Staff and line specialists advise and implement policy decisions that have impact upon public opinion.

From a concern for public relationships comes this typical comment of a senior official: "At least half our time is taken up with discussing the possible repercussions of what we propose to do." Once public relations thinking is embraced at the top, it spreads out and down through an organization. An ultimate application of this is seen in the efforts of Delta Airlines to indoctrinate employees with the idea that everyone in the company is "in public relations." A public relations–mindedness catches the attention of competitors or opponents, particularly if programs springing from it are accompanied by a gain in customers, donors, members, enrollees, or voters. And what one organization attains, competitors must seek to match or surpass by the same means or by other strategy or tactics.

Impetus for the involvement of senior officials in public relations thinking has come from the focus of the general public's attention on the total role of all institutions in matters of social as well as economic concern. Business is no

6

exception. As one business spokesman put it, "We know perfectly well that business does not function by divine right, but, like any other part of society, exists with the sanction of the community as a whole. The interests of the community are, in turn, expressed through governments. . . . Today's public opinion, though it may appear as light as air, may become tomorrow's legislation—for better or worse."

His words have had many dramatic illustrations. Examples are the successful advocacy of automobile safety legislation by Ralph Nader, the thwarting of a major nuclear plant project by a citizens' group, and the increase in legal penalties that environmentalists put through for killing birds of an endangered species.[3]

For the heightened attention to social and public responsibilities on the part of administrators, public relations practitioners deserve much of the credit. They have been the interpreters of forces expressed in the marketplace, at the polling booth, and by countervailing power blocs, media, and public protests. The evaluation of this upward-moving awareness, and the heed paid to it by administrators, documents a favorable trend.

The functional concept

Today's administrators require the assistance and counsel of skilled specialists. It does not matter whether the size, nature, and scope of the organization are those of a local hospital, a federal agency, a land developer, or a resort hotel. All are faced with a complexity of laws and regulations, financial and human problems, and competitive factors too great for one person to handle.

The public relations officer, manager, or consultant is one of the specialists. His or her natural responsibility to the senior official falls in three areas:

1. To facilitate and ensure an inflow of representative opinions from the organization's constituent publics so that policies and operations may be in tune with the needs and views of these publics.
2. To counsel senior officials on ways and means of maintaining or reshaping operations or communications policies to gain maximum public acceptance.
3. To devise and carry out programs that will gain wide and favorable interpretation of the organization's policies and operations.[4]

Practitioners fulfill these responsibilities in any one, or a combination, of three setups. There is the full-time staff executive on the payroll, who, with the aid of assistants, serves the employer exclusively. There is the independent counselor who maintains his own offices and staff to serve a number of clients with nonconflicting interests. And there is the advertising agency that provides counseling and services either through a department within the agency or through a subsidiary firm.

The internal staff represents the dominant choice of employers. In some types of organizations—for example, the military services—internal staffing is mandatory. However, whether the public relations functions are provided in-house or by outside counsel, or by both, the work done is much the same.

The organized practice: its purposes and parts

The purpose of all that is labeled public relations is to influence public opinion. The power of public opinion is recognized, and it is felt everywhere. The automotive, oil, and sugar industries have felt the sting of adverse consumer public opinion when their actions ran counter to public expectations. Community governments have suffered from adverse homeowner opinion when public services were inadequate. No institution can be successful for long without public sufferance. But faith in the good common sense of the people is as fundamental in the practice of public relations as it is in politics. *An informed public is a wise public.* [5]

A sure, sensitive, and continuous reading of the changing human environment as it affects public opinion can be a practitioner's most valuable service. This is a service not available within most organizations from any functionary. That many practitioners are not positioned or expected to exercise this responsibility, and that many more simply do not measure up to it, was shown in the way institutions were caught flat-footed by the civil-rights revolution of the 1960s and again in the credibility crunch of the 1970s.

Opinion research

Opinion research is the first of the eight major activities that the practice comprises. Research, in practical terms, means doing your homework before telling an employer to leap boldly into public print or to be unavailable to a reporter. Ideally, research is the earliest of the functions leading to a program or communications decision. Research can be as elaborate as that required to oppose new federal legislation or as simple as determining whether to hire a black receptionist to show visitors that you have a "no-discrimination" employment policy. Research also has value after the fact, as a basis for evaluating an ongoing program and deciding whether to terminate it, revise it, or continue it as is.

Sophisticated forms of opinion sampling, measuring, and evaluating are largely confined to organizations where the stakes are large, a few percentage points in public opinion are critical, and the budget is ample. Examples would be in the pretesting of a new theme for corporate advertising, or in predetermining the strategy for a national political campaign. Small and nonprofit organizations usually turn to Harris, Roper, and Gallup surveys for a "feel" of the public mood on public issues. Trade associations, professional societies, and counseling firms supply their research findings to members and clients. Many questions of significance can be answered by simple polling methods.

Most practitioners, lacking formal research funds or staff, maintain a "fact file" of intelligence tidbits relevant to their function and their employer. This is updated as they scan news media, mail, books, and other sources. The intelligence is fed upward as needed to the institution's decision makers. On occasion, it becomes a factor in a decision concerning an operating policy. Fact-file intelligence is also used in preparing publicity and other informational output.

Public opinion research is growing as a specialized function requiring special training and skills. Such organizational activities as intelligence accumulation, speech research, and the functions of librarians and historians often come under its wing.

Press-agentry

In the orchestra of public relations, press-agentry represents the brass section. You find press agents (often dubbed "superflacks") pumping up circuses, motion pictures, radio and television programs and personalities, sports and political figures, and crowd events. Considerable press-agentry is involved in the staging of national political party conventions, with the aim being as much to glue a large audience to the electronic media as to nominate candidates.

Today's press agent for the circus, according to Mae Lyons, former agent for Ringling Bros., Barnum & Bailey Combined Shows, Inc., is the drumbeater who "plays all instruments in the public relations band." She adds, "There is more to circus public relations than exaggerated fibbing. There is far more to it than a story and a picture in the newspapers." Jim Moran, another well-known press agent, relates the function to public relations by saying, "It is the fun part of the job." Most practitioners whose employers or clients depend on visibility, drama, and public notice would agree. They would probably add that it is the most hectic part of the job, too.

The aim of press-agentry is more to attract attention than to gain understanding. Notoriety can be more useful than piety. It thrives in the box-office world. It adds a dimension of excitement and flamboyance, but little stature, to the public relations calling. Many press agents, in fact, seek to borrow from the stature of the calling, by assuming the title of "counselor." But this does not alter the work they do, or their no-holds-barred methods. In the candid words of a veteran, "We stoop to anything, but our stuff gets printed." And it pays off. A rock music group's earning power may be as much a tribute to the skill of its press agent as to its musical abilities.

Students of press-agentry often cite the success of the late Steve Hannagan and the legends surrounding him. He was the one who promoted the Memorial Day auto race at Indianapolis into a national event. Miami Beach and Sun Valley as internationally known resorts owe much to Hannagan's fertile imagination.[6] Most organizations venture into press-agentry on occasion. This is how Miss Tuna Fish, the Maid of Cotton, the Rose Bowl Parade, the Wild Rice Festival, and National Pickle Week came into being.[7]

Product promotion

A thin line, sometimes indistinct, separates what is done to promote a product or service in the name of public relations and what is done in the name of marketing. There is also a thin line between product promotion and press-agentry. Practitioners in competitive, consumer-oriented companies, wholesale and retail trade channels, and trade associations sometimes report directly to marketing executives. In banks, insurance companies, and other service organizations, public relations and marketing are closely allied. Among the fields that deal heavily in promotion are fashions, foods, home furnishings, autos and appliances, cosmetics, beverages, travel, and banking.

Some counseling firms specialize in product promotion and publicity. These firms also tend to provide services related to consumerism.

The sustained and appealing promotion of a meritorious product or service by public relations events and techniques has the added advantage of enhancing the reputations of the organizations behind them. Promotion has seen some impressive triumphs, such as the "coffee break" in America, and the popularity of bicycling, tennis, and skiing. Such ideas as "wall-to-wall" carpeting, "indoor-outdoor" carpeting, and the carpeting of football and baseball playing fields are tied to product promotions, as are Weight Watchers, mobile homes, and fast-food services. The list is long.

Publicity

All the information released as news to the news media by businesses, government agencies, schools, welfare and health agencies, and a host of causes, fronts, and lobbies comes under the elastic term *publicity*. The main difference between publicity and news is that with publicity, it is its sponsor that considers it newsworthy; the media receiving it may or may not agree. Examples of publicity are the sales or earnings reports of a corporation, the progress of a charity fund-raising campaign, the scientific findings in the latest space exploration, discovery of a new medicine or improvement of a surgical technique, a change in Social Security payments, the return to duty of an ailing congressman, and so on. Events usually give rise to publicity. Thus, we have ground-breakings, anniversaries, reunions, dedications, ceremonial appointments, signings and installations, and seminars, speeches, and public "appearances," all designed as news events.

The confusion of publicity with the broad practice of public relations as a whole is understandable. The practice, in substantial part, evolved from publicity. Much of contemporary practice, and the most visible part, is concerned with generating publicity. And sometimes publicity, or product promotion publicity, is in fact the whole of a public relations department's activity.

Lobbying

To some people, *lobbying* is an ugly word meaning the manipulation of government for selfish interests. This impression has been decreasing as more and more people have joined various citizens' groups that are organized to lobby.[8] Actually, the right to petition government is guaranteed by the Constitution. This prevails whether citizens are protesting an action of government itself, seeking to build or to oppose a nuclear plant, trying to get rid of guns or abortions, or attempting to have marijuana legalized.

Public relations sometimes embraces lobbying. More often, it aids lobbying as it aids the marketing, personnel, and fund-raising functions of an organization. Washington, D.C., and the state capitals are centers of lobbying. Activities of a lobbying nature at the county or municipal level usually come under the subhead of civic affairs or community relations.

Lobbying breaks down into several tasks: (1) digging out information from officials or records that ought to be known "back at headquarters"; (2) persuasively informing government officials; (3) promoting legislative or administrative action for an organization or against an adverse interest; and (4) obtaining government cooperation or sponsorship, such as in a proclamation of Fire Prevention Week. The legal aspects of lobbying are covered in Chapter Twelve.[9]

Every large organization is confronted with a great number of involvements with government. There are always regulations to be complied with. For each regulation, there may be reporting requirements. There is a continuing stream of proposed legislation to evaluate, and to oppose, support, or ignore. These involvements were once almost entirely the province of the lawyer. Today, with the views of citizens' groups being expressed more vigorously, responses by the organizations affected require skilled opinion analysis, mediation, and preparation of communications. Consequently, the responsibility is shared; the effort is a collaboration.

The lists of registered lobbyists in Washington carry the names of many public relations practitioners. Trade associations, professional societies, and organized labor are major employers of public relations specialists whose work gets into lobbying. Railroads, airlines, and buslines lobby competitively to persuade lawmakers and voters that their mode of transportation deserves preferential consideration. And so it goes in a democracy.[10]

Public affairs

Lobbying as a specialty is often confused with the general public-affairs function in industry. The two overlap, are generally coordinated, and are often headed by lawyers. However, corporate public affairs is a function that has had its greatest growth and application in only a few hundred of the nation's largest corporations and conglomerates. It is involved with an organization's total concept of corporate citizenship. This includes political education for employees, civic service by employees and managers, and cooperation in the advancement of home communities. It gets into the implementation of specific community improvement programs related to the environment, education and health facilities, employment, safety, transportation, and more. It involves the encouragement of political participation via contributions and votes, and the urging of greater civic and charitable participation by business leaders, particularly where ownership and senior management are not resident in a plant community.

Public affairs assists in the monitoring of government activities that affect a particular corporation, industry, or institution. The title *Public Affairs* is preferred to the title *Public Relations* by most of the armed services units, some of the government agencies, and some nonprofit private agencies whose activities are concentrated in a single community. This tends to create confusion, because for the most part, the functions performed are those that fall comfortably and logically under the public relations umbrella.

Fund raising and membership drives

For thousands of private health, education, and welfare agencies and for special-interest causes dependent on contributions, the function of fund raising is their lifeblood. And fund raising leans primarily on effective communications.

For thousands of trade associations, professional societies, and labor-union units, funding, usually acquired in membership dues, relies heavily on communications that portray the aims and progress of the organization. In these entities, the functions of the executive secretary or director, the public relations executive, and the in-house or outside fund-raising experts overlap and blend. The public relations people for these organizations require knowledge of direct mail and other specialized media. They must have a keen sensitivity to an organization's constituency, skill in persuasion, and an abiding faith in the worth of the undertaking. It is no place for anyone who feels, "I don't like asking people for money."

Special-event management

Every thriving institution, by its nature and doings, generates happenings calculated to catch public attention. These events may be of potential interest to only a small segment of the institution's constituency—for example, the opening of a day-care unit for children of employees—or they may be of broader potential interest—for example, the announcement of a new vaccine that prevents acne. In the former case, the principal news carrier might be a house publication. In the latter, national news media catering to youth and family might be attracted. The range of such events is vast: the groundbreaking for a new university library; the launching of a new navy vessel; the commemorative flight of a commercial airline; the opening of a new cardiac unit in a hospital.

The origination, planning, staging, timing, invitations, and almost all preparations that go into special events have become increasingly significant in the public relations scheme of things. They feed the pride, vanity, and togetherness within a sponsoring organization, and they help compete for public notice outside the organization.

The day-by-day practice

The daily practice of public relations contains a myriad of little tasks, along with a few continuing major problems. Someone has called the minor tasks, like hand-delivering news releases or tracking down the source of an obscure news item, the "nitty gritty" of public relations. Someone else has termed them the "ash and trash." By whatever name, these minor and menial tasks usually make up the initial assignment for a newcomer in the department or counseling firm.

Big task or little, each calls for common sense, courtesy, decency, and a sense of responsibility, whether it involves doing a favor, hosting a visitor, preparing a speech, or giving one. At stake can be something as important as helping administrators through a strike or protest situation, as sensitive as helping a determined newsman to get a story from a press-shy executive, as touchy as writing a letter to a parent whose daughter has been expelled from college.

Toward maturity

Several common denominators have evolved for activities carried on in the name of public relations. They bear close scrutiny.

1. There is a concern with the attitudes and behavior of certain individuals and groups. How do you measure these? How can you oppose, neutralize, or change them?
2. There is strategic thinking and planning with specific objectives, audiences, and timing in mind.
3. There is action taken that is consistent with the organization's policies and goals, and with the character, personality, and performance standards of the top officials.

EXHIBIT 1-2

Live examples from a huge reservoir

To emphasize airline progress and to help justify increased fares, Trans World Airlines marked the anniversary of nonstop transcontinental service by flying an ancient Ford trimotor airplane over the initial route. The aircraft, lumbering along at 110 mph, took 36 hours for the trip that is now made in six hours.

Dramatizing the spirit of America's Thanksgiving, the U.S. ambassador to Ecuador invited 250 workers and their families to a dinner at the YMCA in Quito. Service was by American Girl Scouts, Brownies, and Boy Scouts. The ambassador read the president's proclamation and explained the meaning in terms of America's desire to share its abundance with all peoples. The U.S. information officer arranged for rebroadcasting over Ecuador's radio stations, which were then the main channel of communications in a nation where literacy was not universal.

Allis-Chalmers dealt with problem drinkers on its payroll by rehabilitation rather than weed-out. Communication was established through a psychologist, himself a rehabilitated alcoholic, for counseling those who sought help. Supervisors were taught to understand addiction as an illness, and to coax victims toward the counselor. These actions were far more credible than speeches or advertisements on the subject would have been.

Maryland hospitals, faced with a critical shortage of trained nurses and having federal funds for training, turned to public relations for recruiting help. The list of former nurses who had dropped out was combed. A direct-mail piece offering training, higher wages, and a chance to perform a service of compassion was created and sent out. A friendly disc jockey devised and aired a musical parody, "Nurse Bailey, Won't You Please Come Home?" Some 300 nurses returned, at a direct public relations cost of just over $1 each.

Sunshine Supermarkets turned to public relations counseling for help in combatting sales decline and absenteeism. After research, the counsel recommended a course in courtesy for checkout personnel, a bonus system, frequent changes of uniform, a weekly internal magazine, a suggestion system on serving the public better, a schedule of social activities, and bonuses for store managers.

When news media reported that the commander of the Third Fleet was being reassigned as Commander, Naval Air Force, Pacific Fleet Hq., one newspaper headlined precisely the opposite, "Coogan Takes Over Third Fleet." The task for the public affairs office that day was to point out the careless mistake, get the error corrected, and explain to the admiral how these things happen.

When the Swedish Parliament changed the nation's traffic from left-hand to right-hand driving, the switch was implemented with an actual *decrease* in the rate of auto accidents. This was accomplished in great part by advance preventive public relations in the form of a $5 million advertising and news information campaign.

The fact that Bethlehem Steel encourages employees to take part in community services is pointed out to its constituents in an illustrated booklet. The content states the firm's policy and gives a range of examples, from the founding of a young peoples' choir to the tutoring of Chinese children in English, to election of an employee as a school-board director.

When a small Baptist college in California needed to raise money for new athletic equipment and uniforms, it staged a cartwheel contest in the gymnasium. Publicity produced many sponsors of contestants at rates of 1 to 5 cents

13

EXHIBIT 1-2 (CONT.)

per cartwheel. A 16-year-old girl won first prize, with 2,002 loops at intervals of two seconds. A 5-year-old girl won the hearts of the community and the local headlines with 1,645 cartwheels, leotards and all.

The nations's bicentennial provided a Roman holiday for public relations projects. Practitioners had a hand in the symbolism all the way from red, white, and blue fire hydrants and special postage stamps, to scholarly papers and forums, and solemn events seeking to rededicate Americans to the nations' founding principles. (It remains for historians and students to evaluate whether the challenge and the opportunity of the occasion were met or wasted, the objectives attained or thwarted, and the public interest served or abused.)

4. Actions taken place great emphasis on communications, whether in simple response to inquiry, as planned statement or project, or as prolonged programs.
5. In the actions, consideration is given to legal, ethical, and social implications.
6. There is some method of assessing the reactions of audiences, the results of the efforts, and the potential consequences. Assessment is the basis for continuation, modification, or termination of actions and for communication about them.

On a grand scale, practitioners can point to positive contributions. Public relations practices have deepened the sense of social and public responsibility in economic enterprises. The function has aided the administration of private and public health, welfare, and educational institutions. It has added to the variety of information available to the public and has broadened the coverage of newsworthy events by mass media. It has helped bring to public notice a balance beween the strengths and the ills, the needs and the attainments of society.

Overpromises and underdelivery

At times, the case for the essentiality and the capabilities of the function are overstated. Public relations efforts, no matter how well-intentioned, do not constitute a panacea for all the ills of an institution. No amount of well-conceived communication can change a bad performance into a good one. Neither can it compensate for lack of integrity, or persuade an audience that an unfair or selfish attitude is, in fact, fair and unselfish.

No credibility or stature is added to the public reputation of the function itself in instances when services are sold on a "free publicity guaranteed" basis, when elected officials are warned to "avoid mistakes in public relations or be voted out," when corporate executives are exhorted to improve their image to "save the private enterprise system." Practitioners do themselves no favor by contending that their magic has successfully impeded the democratic process, popularized a tax increase, or won the day for a questionable cause. An unfavorable stereotype is strengthened when a counselor says in public that he can elect any person to public office if that person "has $60,000, an IQ of 120, and can keep his mouth shut."[11]

Overstatements and overpromises followed by underdelivery—and underhanded methods, on occasion—have led to recurrent unfavorable publicity for the calling, denigration of its importance, and scorn for those identified as practitioners.

Unfortunately, preoccupation with "image" rather than substance gives credence to the impression of practitioners as "build-up boys." This is particularly evident in the promotional gimmickry that surrounds many products, events, and services of no real value. Under the headline, "Is it a Bicentennial or a Buy Centennial?" the *Wall Street Journal* pointed out that the extreme commercialism of the bicentennial produced a backlash. Making light of traditional values and virtues confers no credit on communicators.

The labeling of public relations efforts as frivolous or shallow, or as the synonym for a false front, has a long history. Thus, a columnist can borrow the term to criticize President Carter, saying that in his efforts to be a common man, to de-imperialize the presidency, he is putting on a "public relations campaign." The calling is tarred as much as the presidency. It has also long been a convenience of employers and clients to use practitioners as their whipping boys, or "fall guys," to spare officials of an organization blame or embarrassment.

The calling has sustained and survived considerable direct scorn by journalists. An editor tells his readers, "If you want to get plausible disguises for unworthy causes, hire a public relations expert." A columnist speaks of the "perversion of the language by public relations . . . an accepted form of lying to the public in order to manipulate it as the promoters wish." A newspaper labels public relations "a parasite on the press."

The calling will have to endure the labels and stings as long as there are practitioners in the field whose conduct rearms the critics and negatively affects the bystanding public. Meantime, *on the favorable side, in more and more organizations, particularly in the nonprofit sector, public relations executives are becoming the most credible spokesmen and women dealing directly with concerned publics and news media, handling inquiries without deference to "higher authority."*

Meantime also, educators in mass communications, the professional societies, and the vast majority of practitioners are aiding in the evolutionary process of maturation. The calling has developed sound educational underpinnings, a code of professional standards, a program of accreditation, grievance and punitive procedures, and research into public opinion.

Working definitions

These efforts have produced some declarative commitments for the guidance of working practitioners. The Public Relations Society of America, on behalf of its more than 8,000 members, declares that "the public relations profession in servicing the legitimate interests of clients or employers is dedicated fundamentally to the goals of better mutual understanding and cooperation among the diverse groups, institutions and elements of our modern society."

The International Public Relations Association offers this all-embracing commitment: "Public Relations is a management function, of a continuing and planned character, through which public and private organizations and institutions seek to win and retain the understanding, sympathy and support of those with whom they are or may be concerned—by evaluating public opinion about themselves, in order to correlate as far as possible their own policies and procedures, to achieve by planned and widespread information more productive cooperation and more efficient fulfillment of their common interests."

The British Institute of Public Relations defines the function as "the deliberate, planned and sustained effort to establish and maintain mutual understanding between an organization and its publics."

To all of this, we add a capsulized working definition that we feel reflects the times and predicts the future:

> Public relations is the planned effort to influence opinion through good character and responsible performance, based upon mutually satisfactory two-way communications.

ADDITIONAL READINGS

BRUCE F. ACKERMAN, "Essential to Think about Correlation between PR & FR," *Fund Raising Management,* January/February 1974.

STEVEN H. CHAFFEE and MICHAEL J. PETRICK, *Using the Mass Media: Communications Problems in American Society.* New York: McGraw-Hill, 1975.

JOHN N. CRISFORD, "Straight Thinking in Public Relations," *Public Relations Quarterly,* Winter 1973. British practitioner on defining public relations.

PAUL GARRETT, "The Four Dimensions of Public Relations," *Printers' Ink,* Vol. 203 (June 11, 1943); and his "A New Dimension in Public Relations," *Public Relations Journal,* Vol. 12 (October 1956).

ROBERT HEILBRONER, "Public Relations—The Invisible Sell," *Harper's Magazine,* Vol. 215 (June 1957).

HILL AND KNOWLTON EXECUTIVES, *Critical Issues in Public Relations.* Englewood Cliffs, N.J.: Prentice-Hall, 1975. Essays and speeches. Foreword by Max Ways, editor of *Fortune,* "Who Needs Public Rela-

tions?" deals with the essentiality of the function in modern society.

IRVING KRISTOL, *On the Democratic Idea in America.* New York; Harper & Row, 1972.

PHILIP LESLY, ed., *Public Relations Handbook,* 4th ed. Englewood Cliffs, N.J.: Prentice-Hall.

JOHN MARSTON, *The Nature of Public Relations.* New York: McGraw-Hill, 1963.

———, "What to Do When Public Relations Is More Important," *Public Relations Journal,* August 1974.

RAYMOND SIMON, *Public Relations as a Process.* Columbus, O.: Grid, 1976.

CHARLES S. STEINBERG, *The Creation of Consent.* New York: Hastings House, 1975.

RICHARD WEINER, *Professionals' Guide to Publicity.* New York: Richard Weiner, 1976.

WILLIAM WESTON, "Public Relations: Trustee of a Free Society," *Public Relations Review,* Vol. 1, No. 2 (Fall 1975).

FOOTNOTES

1. By permission, *Webster's New Twentieth Century Dictionary,* unabridged, 2nd ed. (New York: Will-Collins & World Publishing Co., Inc., 1976), p. 1456.

2. For the full text of Dr. Harlow's definition, write to Dr. Frederick Teahan, Foundation for Public Relations Research and Education, 845 Third Avenue, New York, N.Y. 10022.

3. The Nader–GM landmark case study is discussed in Dan Corditz, "The Face in the Mirror at General Motors," *Fortune,* Vol. 78 (August 1966), and in Robert L. Bishop and Jane Kilburn, "Penny Whistle of Public's Advocate," *Public Relations Quarterly,* Vol. 12 (Winter 1968). For the

book that shook an industry, see Nader's *Unsafe at Any Speed* (New York: Grossman Publishers, Inc., 1965). For a classic case of successful public opposition, see Allen H. Center, *Public Relations Practices: Case Studies* (Englewood Cliffs, N.J.: Prentice-Hall, 1975), Case No. 6, "A Community Confrontation: Nuclear Plant Opposition at Bodega Head." In the same text is a case in which environmentalists sought to protect the endangered American eagle.

4. For a detailed presentation of the manner in which large counseling firms serve clients, see "The Byoir Way," a pamphlet of Carl Byoir & Associates, Inc., New York. For an outside look at

a counseling firm, see T.A. Wise, "Hill and Knowlton's World of Images," *Fortune,* Vol. 76 (September 1967).

5. For this point of view, see William Lydgate, *What America Thinks* (New York: Thomas Y. Crowell, 1944). For the opposite view, see Nicholas Samstag, *Persuasion for Profit* (Norman, Okla.: University of Oklahoma Press, 1957).

6. For background on Hannagan, see "Steve Hannagan Is Dead," *New York Times,* February 6, 1953, p. 19; "Steve Hannagan," *Current Biography,* Vol. 5 (August 1944), 29–31; "Prince of Agents," *Colliers,* Vol. 120 (November 22, 1947), 75ff; and "For the Defense, Steve Hannagan," *Public Relations Journal,* Vol. 26 (August 1970).

7. For a recent update on Hollywood publicists, see Jack Slater, "Where the Flack Falls Thick and Fast," *Los Angeles Times,* April 5, 1976; and "Bobby Zarem, Super Flack," *Newsweek,* January 1, 1977.

8. Theodore Levitt, *The Third Sector: New Tactics For a Responsive Society* (New York: Amacom, a division of American Management Associations, 1973). A readable book, developing the concept of a "third sector" composed of all the groups that feel the other sectors are unresponsive, the use of publicity to gain their ends, and what becomes of such groups.

9. For additional discussion of lobbying, see Bert Goss, "PR Is Not Lobbying," *PR,* Vol. 1 (July 1956); Robert L.L. McCormick, "The Anatomy of Public Relations in Washington," *PR,* Vol. 2 (January 1957); Morris Victor Rosenblum, "Effective Public Relations with Washington, D.C.," *Public Relations Quarterly,* Summer 1967; and Edie Fraser, "Successful Communication in the Washington Maze," Ruder and Finn Paper No. 4, New York, 1976.

10. An excellently documented case of using public relations to influence legislation is *Noerr Motor Freight, Inc., et al.* v. *Eastern Railroad Presidents' Conference, et al.,* in *Federal Supplement,* Vol. 155 (December 23, 1957), 768–841; 273 F. 2d 218 (1959); 81 *Supreme Court Reporter,* 523, February 20, 1961. Also, for discussion of the legal aspects of lobbying, see Morton J. Simon, *Public Relations Law.* Obtainable from the Foundation for Public Relations Research and Education, 845 Third Ave., New York, N.Y. 10022.

11. Mark Richardson, *The Antitrust Bulletin,* Vol. 10 (July–August 1965), 511.

2

It is always hard to go beyond your public. If they are satisfied with cheap performance, you will not easily arrive at better.

Emerson

The Practitioners: staff, status, and functions

Counting public relations heads is a difficult business. The U.S. census, for example, contains the solitary occupational listing, "Public Relations and Publicity Writers." To practitioners, "writers" is too confining, but the census provides no other occupational breakdown for public relations. Thus, even though the census has a separate listing for "photographer," a photographer on the payroll of a public relations department or counseling firm at the time of a census might be listed as a public relations "writer."

The census and the Department of Labor estimates are helpful, however, in portraying the trend. See Table 2–1 for trend figures, and Table 2–2 for a comparison of 1970 census figures in several occupations with a familial relationship.

TABLE 2–1 Public relations employment trend

U.S. Census	Public Relations and Publicity Writers
1950	19,000
1960	31,141
1970	75,852
Dept. of Labor Estimates	
1976	115,000
1985	134,000

It may be helpful to compare the census figures for public relations with those for other occupations that are familiar but not related. The census lists 3,923,309 secretaries, stenographers, and typists. That's 50 times the number shown for public relations. There are 197,676 bartenders, 124,501 hucksters and peddlers, 35,928 funeral directors, and 34,794 airline attendants.

Sources within the public relations field have estimated its total employment to be as high as 115,000. Whatever the precise total, there is ample evidence that

TABLE 2-2 Occupational employment comparison

Occupation	Total	Male	Female
Public relations and publicity	75,852	55,698	20,154
Editors and reporters	152,984	91,501	61,483
Advertising agents & salesmen	66,903	55,698	20,154
Photographers	65,960	56,526	9,434
Proof readers	29,802	7,777	22,025
Social science teachers	12,732	10,069	2,663

Source: U.S. Department of Commerce, *Census of Population: Occupational Characteristics,* June 1973, Vol. 2, Pt. 7A.

the number is growing. And in an effort to assign a financial dimension to the calling, *Jack O'Dwyer's Newsletter* reasoned that if it comprised 40,000 persons averaging $18,000 income per year, public relations was a $2 billion calling in terms of spendable income.[1]

Over the past few decades, many separate and limited polls have been taken to measure or predict a specific aspect of the occupation. A few of those surveys have periodically retraced their steps, and these have been helpful in disclosing some benchmarks.[2] Most of the one-time surveys, however, have been concerned with one particular function or one type of employer. Consequently, they do not provide a complete profile of public relations or of the practitioner.[3]

Because of dynamic changes during the 1970s, we felt a critical need to offer educators and students a profile suitable for periodic updating nationally, and for drawing local or regional comparisons. To this end, in 1976–77 we undertook an independent canvass of 1,384 departments and counseling firms. From this mailing, 472, or 34 percent, were returned and were tabulated and analyzed. The sample represented 6 percent of the membership of the Public Relations Society of America (PRSA). The breakdown between profit-making and nonprofit organizations was 48 and 42 percent respectively, reasonably in line with the ratio of the total membership in the society.

The results of the two-part survey are woven into this chapter and at other relevant points throughout the text. For simplicity of reference, the study will be called the "C-C Survey."[4]

Size of staffs, internal and counseling

Table 2–3 shows the average (not median) number of persons in the responding internal departments, by categories of organizations, from the C-C Survey.

The averages are indicative but cannot be projected across the calling. Variations and exceptions are influenced by whatever activities are grouped together under the banner of public relations, and by whether a respondent is reporting for an entire organization, its department headquarters, or an operating branch or local unit. Further, prosperous and generously staffed departments are more prone than underbudgeted and understaffed ones to respond to surveys and to identify themselves in their response. Two or three very large departments—for example, the U.S. Air Force, or General Motors—can stretch the average upward significantly.

TABLE 2-3 Staff sizes, internal departments

No. of Respondents	Category of Dept.	Average No. in Dept.
78	Businesses over $1 billion	44.0
33	State & federal agencies & military	21.1
44	Public & private education	13.5
74	Businesses under $1 billion	9.8
59	Associations, professional societies, & unions	7.6
26	Municipal & county agencies	7.2
27	Private health & welfare agencies	6.3
24	Private causes & foundations	5.7
11	Public health & welfare local units	4.7

The employment figures for the 96 responding counseling firms and public relations departments in advertising agencies were as in Table 2–4.

TABLE 2-4 Staff sizes, counseling firms and agency departments

Number of Employees	Percent of Responding Firms
Under 10	67%
11 to 20	14
21 to 40	12
41 to 75	5
76 to 100	0
Over 100	2

Distribution of public relations employment tends to confirm the trend to bigness in all types of organizations. A few giants seem to get bigger and bigger. In *O'Dwyer's Directory,* General Motors reported a PR staff of 180, AT&T 130, Chase Manhattan Bank 95, Aetna Life 75, and Mobil 69. The Federal Energy Administration has been reported to have a staff of 112. Federal departments that identified themselves in the C-C Survey included the Departments of Transportation with a staff of 38, Treasury with 30, and Housing and Urban Development with 30. In the military, the U.S. Command headquarters in Korea had a staff of 40, and the U.S. Marine Corps at Camp Pendleton 21. In education, the University of Notre Dame reported a staff of 75 for public relations and development combined, and the U.S. Military Academy 22. The American Red Cross reported a department of 44 persons.

In the counseling and agency area, *O'Dwyer's Directory* lists the 40 largest counselors. The five largest employers in 1976 were Burson-Marsteller with 605, Hill and Knowlton 602, Carl Byoir and Associates 293, J. Walter Thompson (ad agency department) 232, and Ruder and Finn 240. The 40 largest together added up to 3,943 employees, for an average of 98.

From the available facts, some conclusions can be drawn. *First, fewer than 1,000 public relations departments and counseling firms account for as much as one-third of the 75,852 persons counted in the U.S. census. Second, the larger part of the remaining two-thirds is spread among thousands of departments and counseling firms having fewer than six employees.*

Scope and emphasis

Eight major job classifications of public relations work were developed in a vocational guidance survey conducted by the Education Committee of the Public Relations Society of America. These are:

1. *Writing.* Reports, news releases, booklet texts, radio and TV copy, speeches, film sequences, trade paper and magazine articles, product information, and technical material.
2. *Editing.* Employee publications, newsletters, shareholder reports, and other communications directed to both organization personnel and external groups.
3. *Placement.* Contacts with the press, radio, and TV, as well as with editors of magazines, Sunday supplements, and trade publications, with a view toward enlisting their interest in publishing an organization's news and features.
4. *Promotion.* Special events, such as press parties, convention exhibits, and special showings; open-house, new-facility, and anniversary celebrations; special day, week, or month observances; contests and award programs; guest relations; institutional movies; visual aids.
5. *Speaking.* Appearances before groups and the planning requisite to finding appropriate platforms. The preparation of speeches for others, organization of speakers' bureaus, and delivery of speeches.
6. *Production.* Knowledge of art and layout for the development of brochures, booklets, special reports, photographic communications, and house periodicals as required.
7. *Programming.* The determination of need, definition of goals, and recommended steps in carrying out the project. This is the highest-level job in public relations, one requiring maturity in counseling management.
8. *Institutional advertising.* Advertising a company's name and reputation through purchased space or time. Close coordination with advertising departments is maintained, and frequently the advertising–public relations responsibility is a dual one.

To this list must be added some other functions that have gained so much in importance that they predict the future of the calling. One is the gathering of *intelligence,* enabling an organization to be responsive to its natural constituency. Another is *representation* of an organization on frequent occasions in projects related to civic, social, educational, and cultural advancements. A third is the *interpretation* to government bodies and voters of an organization's interests in matters of public policy. And a fourth is the *training* of effective spokesmen for an organization. Also see Fig. 2–1.

Figure 2–2 displays the relative importance assigned to the workday functions according to the C-C Survey. The respondents were 376 public relations departments—in 152 businesses; 59 associations, societies, and unions; and 165 nonprofit organizations. The results would be different if the figures were broken down by categories of employers. For example, if only the nonprofit employers were given, the function of fund raising would rank much higher.

In the survey of 96 counseling firms, respondents rated their services to clients

Basic Skills in Public Relations
shows you how to tackle any PR problem

FIGURE 2–1   For the printed program of a five-day continuing-education refresher in public relations, the American Management Association chose this way of graphically depicting the many functional hats worn by the practitioner. Courtesy of AMA; hats courtesy of Dobbs.

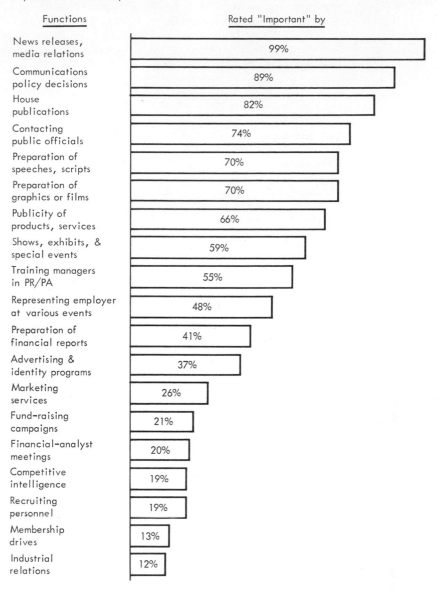

FIGURE 2-2 Emphasis in internal departments.

Functions	Rated "Important" by
News releases, media relations	99%
Communications policy decisions	89%
House publications	82%
Contacting public officials	74%
Preparation of speeches, scripts	70%
Preparation of graphics or films	70%
Publicity of products, services	66%
Shows, exhibits, & special events	59%
Training managers in PR/PA	55%
Representing employer at various events	48%
Preparation of financial reports	41%
Advertising & identity programs	37%
Marketing services	26%
Fund-raising campaigns	21%
Financial-analyst meetings	20%
Competitive intelligence	19%
Recruiting personnel	19%
Membership drives	13%
Industrial relations	12%

as in Figure 2–3 on the next page. Counselors were asked to rate the importance of their functions comparatively "1970 vs. Now." None of the functions listed lost ground during the seven-year span. The largest percentage gain was scored by "legislative intelligence." Double the number of counselors found it more important in 1977 than in 1970, owing to the generally increased attention to public affairs. At the same time, the intelligence function in public relations has had the longest way to go. In 1970, only 25 percent thought it "important." By 1977, this had nearly doubled to 49 percent.

The second largest area of increase in functional importance for counselors was "opinion research." This has been another slow bloomer. The gain was from 49 percent rating it "important" in 1970 to 73 percent in 1977. "Helping clients with meetings and special events" was next in increase, and other large gainers were "competitive intelligence" and "helping clients with booklets, brochures, and interviews."

FIGURE 2-3 Emphasis in counseling firms and agencies.

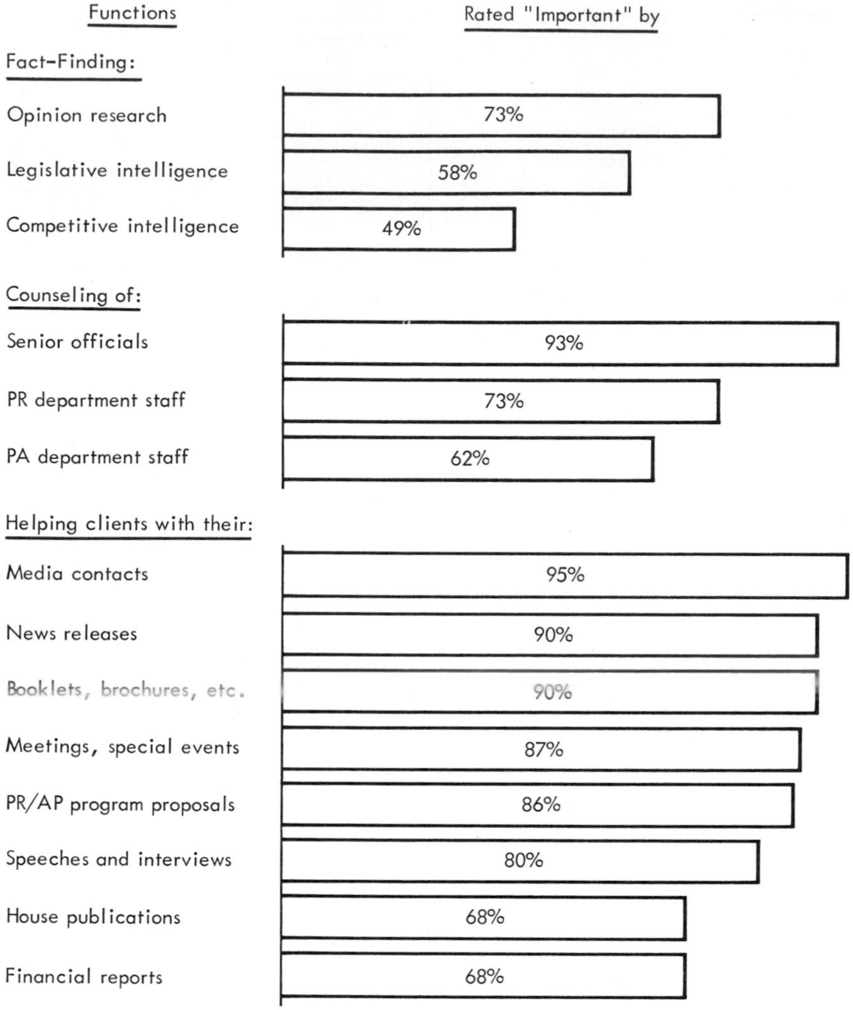

Functions   Rated "Important" by

Fact-Finding:

Opinion research   73%

Legislative intelligence   58%

Competitive intelligence   49%

Counseling of:

Senior officials   93%

PR department staff   73%

PA department staff   62%

Helping clients with their:

Media contacts   95%

News releases   90%

Booklets, brochures, etc.   90%

Meetings, special events   87%

PR/AP program proposals   86%

Speeches and interviews   80%

House publications   68%

Financial reports   68%

Audiences

In the two-part survey, staff department executives and counselors were given an opportunity to rank the *importance of their relationships* with specific publics of their clients or employers. Table 2–5 shows how that came out.

The reason investors as a public rank relatively low for staff public relations is that the survey was cross-sectional, including nonprofit as well as corporate respondents. Similarly, if only private educational institution respondents had been shown, "donors or patrons" would rank at the top and the "customers" of education—students—a close second. The common denominator of importance in the rankings is the extent to which a particular public provides the money and the support that an organization needs to succeed.

TABLE 2–5   Relative importance of publics

How Counselors Ranked the Importance of Clients' Publics		How Department Executives Ranked the Importance of Employers' Publics	
Consumers	1	Customers	1
Community	2	General voting public	2
Investors	3	Members	3
Government	4	Employees	4
Employees	5	Community	5
		Government (all levels)	6
		Donors or patrons	7
		Investors	8

One other measurement of workaday emphasis is relevant here. Counselors regard business as their most important client; trade associations, professional societies, and unions are second; private health, education, and welfare organizations are third; and government entities fourth. Between 1970 and 1977, all four gained in importance, but *government entities gained the largest percentage.*

Stature and qualifications

The positioning of the public relations function in various types of organizations will be discussed in Chapter Three. In Table 2–6, the stature is quantified according to the titles given the departments and the practitioners. Among 299 departments, the preferred titles were as shown.[5]

The matter of titles has taken on some cosmetic characteristics within public relations circles. During the 1960s, some newsworthy transgressions of a few practitioners stigmatized the label "Public Relations" in the eyes of many organizational leaders. Several government bodies, particularly the military, found "Public Affairs" more acceptable and impressive than "Public Information" to legislators and municipal officials, so they adopted it. In turn, several large businesses found virtue in "Public Affairs" or "Corporate Relations." Thus a pattern developed.

TABLE 2–6   Titles of public relations departments

Public relations	151
Public affairs	46
Public information (or office of information)	33
Communications	24
Public relations/public affairs	19
Public relations and advertising	14
Community relations	12

One of the special studies issued intermittently by Jack O'Dwyer announced, "PR Title Losing Favor at Large Companies." The point was made that only 40 of the nation's largest companies, and only seven of the largest 20, used the title "Public Relations." "Public Affairs" was in use by 24. There is no compelling reason to suppose, however, that "Public Affairs" will take over, or even survive, if the actions of many wearing the label tend to taint it.

But regardless of the label used, there are more meaningful indications of the stature of departmental and counseling executives. The main one is the working relationship between the practitioner and the top officials. This is determined by the qualifications of the practitioner to deal with and help those officials.

One of the questions asked department heads in the C-C Survey was about the title of the person to whom department heads report. The survey of counselors asked which one of four client relationships they found "most effective." Table 2–7 shows the staff departments' responses on the left and the counselors' responses on the right.

TABLE 2–7 Comparison of reporting relationships

Departmental Reporting Relationships (356 Respondents)[a]		Counselors' Preferred Relationship (109 Respondents)[b]	
To chief executive officer	56%	No firm lines; our best qualified person handles it	42%
To No. 2 executive	11%	Contacts with senior officials only	32%
To administrative staff officer	5%	One-to-one matchoff of equivalents in client organizations	18%
To others, including operating officers, adm. assts., deputies, & dept. heads for advtg., personnel, planning, marketing, legal, etc.	28%	Contact with PR/PA dept. personnel only	8%

[a]The survey was a cross-section. A single segment selected to show where reporting relationships were high or low would have been misleading. The 56 percent reporting to CEO's represents progress for the function.

[b]The discrepancy of 109 respondents occurs because several marked two first choices having equal value to them.

Practitioners in internal departments tend to be ultrasensitive about reporting relationships—and with reason. Internal reporting relationships tend to predetermine the stature they will have in dealings with outsiders—with reporters or editors, with legislators—and also the level of inside conferences in which the practitioners participate and the level of confidential information to which they are privy.

Education and in-service training

In a subscriber survey, *PR Reporter* found that 82 percent of 800 respondents held college degrees, and 21 percent held graduate degrees.[6] Both figures were higher than those in the C-C Survey, which were 73 percent with baccalaureates and 19 percent with graduate degrees. The disparity reflects a difference in the samples. In the C-C Survey, departmental headcounts included many employees with clerical and other special skills. The distribution of areas of study for bachelors' degrees was as in Table 2–8.

TABLE 2-8   Public relations practitioners' baccalaureates

Journalism	40%
Social science	11
Public relations	10
Economics/Bus. adm.	9
Marketing	3
Advertising	3
Others	24

The interest of the practitioner in advancing by career-related education and participation in peer groups is keen and persistent. Some 92 percent of the respondents to the departmental questionnaire affirmed membership in the Public Relations Society of America; 64 percent said they had taken part in some in-service training courses; 57 percent had taken extension or night courses at a nearby university; and 39 percent had attended one of the various institutes identified with PRSA. Presumably, the counseling side of the calling would echo the patterns of the internal staffs. The thrust for self-improvement and professionalism is a healthy sign of improvement in stature and qualifications.

A questionnaire, originally developed by McLeod and Hawley to measure the professional orientation of newsmen, was applied by three educators at Colorado State University to a sample of 73 respondents who were members of the Colorado Public Relations Chapter and the Denver Advertising Club, and government public information officers in the area. Of these respondents, 81 percent had gone beyond high school.[7] The Colorado practitioners rated their own stature as below that of physicians, lawyers, architects, engineers, and college professors, but above airline pilots, reporters, social workers, advertising agents, funeral directors, and retail salespersons. They professed a high degree of job satisfaction, stressing freedom from continual close supervision, opportunity for originality and initiative, enjoyment of doing what's involved in the job, and having contact with important people. When asked where professional improvement was most needed, they mentioned competence, ethical standards, keeping up to date, trustworthiness, opinion research, and rendering services.[8]

Remuneration

The information on practitioners' salary levels is piecemeal and spotty, but enough can be put together for a reasonable perception. Of first interest to interns, apprentices, or beginners is the starting pay. The Bureau of Labor Statistics lists the averages as:

Public relations practitioner	$8,250
Reporter	8,750
Advertising representative	9,000
Radio or TV announcer	9,000[9]

The *Encyclopedia of Career and Vocational Guidance* suggests that a beginner can be making $9,000 to $15,000 in three years. For a counseling-firm account executive, this would most likely be $12,000 and up. For the director of public relations in a small nonprofit enterprise, the range would be $15,000 to $20,000; in a small business, $15,000 to $30,000; and in a large company, $20,000 to $50,000.[10]

There are, of course, public relations executives earning over $100,000 annually.

The census lists medians for *all* practitioners as in Table 2–9. In 1974, the Bureau of Labor gave the following medians: for the heads of public relations, $23,000; for advertising managers, $20,000; and for reporters with five years' experience, $14,265.

TABLE 2–9 Comparison of salary medians

	Public Relations	Reportorial	Advertising
Male	$11,713	$10,618	$10,789
Female	6,133	5,530	5,024

In the effort to scan the whole calling, the C-C Survey set up four income ranges. The questionnaire provided for respondents to indicate the range fitting (1) chief executives; (2) assistant department heads; (3) media-services managers; (4) specialists in government or community affairs, in fund raising, radio or TV, graphics or films; and (5) editors or news writers. Results are shown in Table 2–10.[11]

TABLE 2–10 Distribution of salary range

Remuneration Range	152 Businesses (1,599 persons)	59 Assns., Societies, & Unions (182 persons)	165 Nonprofit undertakings (706 persons)
Under $12,000	14%	16%	23%
$12,000–$25,000	50%	56%	57%
$25,000–$40,000	27%	24%	18%
Over $40,000	9%	4%	2%

PR Reporter, in its survey, provided the information in Table 2–11 concerning median salaries for 676 of its subscribers.[12] Conclusions that emerge from the data available are that despite the setback occasioned by the recession and slow

TABLE 2–11 Median salaries and ranges

	1977	1976	Change	Range
Consumer-product companies	$31,500	$28,500	+$3,000	$16,500–78,000
Conglomerates & other industrials	32,500	32,000	+ 500	15,000–90,000
Utilities	30,000	30,000	0	16,500–49,700
Banks and insurance	26,000	25,000	+ 1,000	12,000–60,000
Trade and professional associations	23,750	25,250	− 1,500	13,200–57,000
Hospitals	20,000	17,200	+ 2,800	13,350–30,000
Government	24,400	20,000	+ 4,400	17,000–36,500
Education	24,500	23,500	+ 1,000	14,000–55,000
All U.S. organizations	27,800	27,000	+ 800	11,350–90,000
Public relations counseling executives, U.S.	39,000	38,000	+ 1,000	24,000–100,000

recovery in the mid-1970s, income levels have generally kept pace with cost-of-living increases, and in some instances raced ahead of it. Beyond that, the outlook is bright for the 1980s.

Counseling service costs

The services of a counsel or counseling firm may be obtained for a specific project or for a continuing service, reviewable and renewable at intervals.

Fees for continuing services are usually established in one of four ways:

- A fixed monthly retainer (service fee)
- A retainer plus monthly billing for actual staff time on an hourly or per diem basis
- A base fee, billed monthly, to which are added increments for services performed beyond the retainer
- Straight hourly charges[13]

Out-of-pocket expenses are generally billed at cost and are exclusive of the fee.

There are wide variations in the size of fees. One of the largest counseling firms, Hill and Knowlton, has had a minimum fee of $4,000 per month. Carl Byoir has charged a flat fee of $50,000 a year to corporate clients that had sales over $30 million. At the other end of the scale, counseling firms may provide a limited service, such as writing occasional news releases, for as little as $50–$100 each.

The average monthly retainer in 1977, for 83 firms of various sizes, was in the $750–$1,000 range, as compared to the $500–$750 range in 1970. The average hourly time charge computed for 96 firms in 1977 approached $40, up from about $30 for the same firms in 1970.[14]

Regardless of variables or averages, five elements are reflected in counseling fees and charges:

1. Cost of the staff used on the project
2. Executive time and supervision
3. Overhead costs
4. Out-of-pocket costs—for example, telephone and travel
5. A reasonable profit for doing the work

Accounting practices also vary in computing costs. For example, there are different methods used for determining the hourly rate for individuals working on accounts. Some firms use cost accounting, based on dollar salary cost per hour plus overhead and profit, determined by mathematical formulas. Some firms guess at their approximate costs and then apply an arbitrary factor for all clients. Others use different factors for different clients. There is also considerable variation in arriving at overhead costs. Some firms put time spent getting new business into overhead, others do not.

A survey of counselors in 1976 showed that prevalent practices favored (1) open-end contracts, (2) straight hourly charges, (3) hourly charges at $2\frac{1}{2}$ times salary, (4) collateral materials marked up 17.65 percent for handling, and (5) out-of-pocket expenses at cost.[15]

The workings of a department

Where there is no outside counseling, an internal department handles all four steps in the public relations process. Operating on a budget, the staff undertakes *fact finding.* It sets up public relations objectives and *plans the programs.* The staff follows through with the necessary *communications and events.* Then it *evaluates results.* Many departments vary this pattern by hiring opinion research firms to measure public opinion and to evaluate results, since some employers hold that a staff may be biased in evaluating the results of its own work.

The larger the department, the more segmented the work. Special talents are needed for international affairs, opinion analysis, speech writing, and contacts with electronic-media program directors or with backgrounders on a posture against legislation. In smaller departments, and where the function is limited to house publications or news, the staff tends to be composed of generalists, trained in journalism.

In both these setups, there may be the need to retain some outside services because either time or talent is lacking internally. For instance, where the internal staff has planned a booklet, determined its content and distribution, and written its copy, typical outside services could be the layout, artwork, printing, binding, and mailing of the booklet. Other examples might be the catering of refreshments for an open house, monitoring of press notices, cutting of tapes for radio or film for TV broadcasts, provision of a speaker for a nonprofit occasion, or mimeographing and mailing of news releases.

The department's advantages

A staff practitioner has four factors working favorably for him or her and the department:

1. Team membership
2. Knowledge of the organization
3. Economy to the organization
4. Availability to associates

Team membership is a great advantage. The confidence, trust, and support of colleagues that go with it tend to overcome or to relegate into unimportance any antagonism toward the public relations function. At the same time, the close connection between the function, the department, and the chief executive office of the organization provides first-team membership rather than marginal membership. The price of admission is loyalty.

Knowledge of the organization means an intimate, participating knowledge that comes from being insiders. The staff members know the relationships between individuals and their functions. They know the undercurrents of influence, the key people, the conservatives, the ones who put personal ambition and expedience ahead of the organization's interests, the articulate and the tongue-tied.

This kind of knowledge can be acquired by outsiders, but insiders are in a position to do most about it continuously. They can advise where needed, conciliate, and render services from within to induce attitudes and actions that will bring about harmonious relationships inside as well as outside.

Economy can result simply from residence and integration in an organization. For example, the department's bills for rent, heat, and light in a large organization do not loom large. They are expressed generally as a part of an overall cost for many departments and offices or buildings.

Similarly, for an event like a 100th anniversary, the department's activity is not a single, separate cost. It is part of a whole celebration cost. Perhaps the only separate departmental tasks would be preparation of a booklet and placement of a giant cake with 100 candles on the front lawn. Concurrently during the year, the advertising department might run special ads; the board of directors might establish a scholarship in memory of the founder; all employees might be given a holiday on the anniversary date. These activities, to the publics involved, would all be "public relations," but only two would have been charged or executed departmentally.

Availability of the staff practitioner has many facets. When things go wrong, the practitioner is only a minute away from a face-to-face meeting with the organization's officials. And as a deputy, he can be entrusted with delicate matters. If a senior executive defects in a huff, the president wants a public relations man or woman on the spot who knows the background, understands the dangers of mishandling the news, and has credibility with the news media.

Availability means being on call for all departments, divisions, decentralized units. The staff man or woman can slip into and out of committees and meetings. He belongs. He is handy for consultation. He has both acceptability and authority.

Availability to perform service functions involves the practitioner in a broad range of activities. He may be asked to handle a tour for some foreign visitors who do not speak English. He may represent his organization on a local civil-rights or fund-raising committee. He may respond for the organization on receipt of a citation. Or he may make the arrangements for the president's attendance at a charity social event.

The department's handicaps

The advantages of team membership can, however, get in the way on occasion. Availability and loyalty can become possessive bear hugs. The practitioner risks *loss of objectivity*. In supporting and being supported, he or she tends to be absorbed and compromised by group views. There is also the danger of being a "yes" man or woman. Being a team player and helping others is one thing; having one's time diverted from goals, planning, and strategy to running errands for others is another. The practice can deteriorate into *domination and subjectivity*, resulting in loss of respect for the person and the function by colleagues and employer.

The practitioner walks a narrow line between rendering services that are valuable, helpful, and appreciated, and rendering a *subservience* that is easily replaced. Walking this line successfully tends to sort out the potential staff executive from the person who can't or won't attain executive status. Detractors like to describe this in oversimplified terms as "organizational politics," or "playing the political game." There's much more to it, not only in public relations but also in professional sports or any other competitive endeavor. The key is team play, but with retention of one's individuality and objectivity. It's not easy.

The outside counselor or agency

The 1,700 or more public relations counseling firms in the United States range widely in size and scope of service. A large number of advertising agencies also offer public relations services. Of the 40 largest public relations operations, according to the Jack O'Dwyer survey, 11 are departments in advertising agencies. Among the 96 tabulated responses to the C-C Survey, 25 listed themselves as being in the combined business of public relations and advertising, and six others were departments in advertising agencies.

The majority of counseling firms are engaged in public relations work exclusively. A growing number, however, are offering advertising, graphic arts, trade association management, and sales promotion services as well. There is a discernible trend toward specialization among public relations firms. The foremost area is media relations. After that come financial relations, community relations or civic affairs, legislative affairs or lobbying, marketing, attitude surveys, political campaigns, and fund raising for purposes other than political campaigns. There is specialization in health care, religious affairs, sports, and travel and tourism. In line with this trend, one senior counselor in the Los Angeles area has created a "resource group" of specialized counselors for whom he functions as a broker for their expertise on specific client problems.[16]

Most advertising agencies have found it difficult to determine what public relations services to offer, how to effectively organize the function, and how to sustain it apart from the advertising relationship whence it derives its tonnage of dollar billings. N.W. Ayer pioneered in 1920, and Albert Frank–Guenther Law took the next step when it expanded its operations to offer a full-fledged public relations and publicity service. In the next few years, J. Walter Thompson, Young and Rubicam, and Benton & Bowles followed suit. By the mid-1940s, 75 agencies were providing publicity service for clients, according to an *Advertising Age* survey. In 1953, *Advertising Age* made another survey and concluded, "The role of the public relations department in the advertising agency is a strange one. Many topflight, multimillion dollar agencies still do not have one. Many of those that do regard it purely as a service function."

The attitude of many ad agencies continues to be one of ambivalence. Wherever public relations, advertising, and promotional services are all rendered, there is usually an effort to identify the firm as offering a "complete marketing service."

Another discernible trend in counseling firms is toward mergers and the designation of associates or affiliates. This trend stems in part from the need to offer a nationwide or multinational capability to match the scope of clients' operations, and in part from the need for cost efficiency in a field that is extremely competitive. This is not to say that the field has been taken over by a few giants. Size of counseling firms was touched on earlier. The trend toward "the big getting bigger" is an echo of what has been happening in all U.S. institutions.

How do clients and counselors get together?

Chester Burger lists six reasons why outside agencies are retained:

1. Management has not previously conducted a formal public relations program and lacks experience in organizing one.

2. Headquarters may be located away from New York City, the communications and financial center of the nation.
3. A wide range of up-to-date contacts are maintained by an agency.
4. An outside agency can provide services of experienced executives who would be unwilling to move to other cities or whose salaries could not be afforded by a single firm.
5. An organization with its own PR department may be in need of highly specialized services that it cannot afford on a permanent basis.
6. Crucial matters of overall outside policy dictate a need for the independent judgment of an outsider.

There are ethical procedures by which counseling firms seek clients they feel they can help. Sometimes the client seeks the counseling firm. The client may have a nagging problem, as government regulation of offshore drilling has been for the oil industry. Or a client may perceive an opportunity to capitalize on a situation, as happened several times when Jimmy Carter and Jerry Ford, as campaigners, seized on each other's mistakes. Or there may be an emergency, like the case when Canadian medical research appeared to link saccharin to cancer in rats, and when a potential swine flu epidemic called for mass inoculations.

In an emergency situation, the counsel has no choice. There must be immediate effort to correct existing communications problems. Either later or simultaneously, the sources of the breakdown can be investigated and preventive measures for the future suggested.

But in normal circumstances, the counsel will begin the service to a new client by exploring the health of the relationships between the client and those publics on whom the client depends. This is sometimes called a "public relations audit." The initial exploration might take months. When it is completed, one of three things can be expected to happen: (1) The counselor tells the client that he finds no problem or threat of harm in communication of a magnitude to require outside assistance; (2) he tells him that the problems disclosed by the research are in a realm other than that of his field; or (3) he tells him that there are problems that can be solved through the application of public relations techniques.

In the last case, the counsel usually arranges to make a presentation of his findings. In this presentation are exposed:

• The central core of the difficulty
• Its current status in terms of harm to the organization
• Related difficulties that must be considered
• Ultimate alternatives to be faced
• Desirable objectives
• A long-range plan toward the objectives
• An immediate program of action involving anything pertinent, even if it involves the removal of a senior official, or an aggressive published response to an allegation

Not all factors in a presentation are invariably exposed at one sitting. However, to establish a suitable working climate, the counselor must obtain an agreement over the full range before his firm's talents can be committed sincerely to the tasks.

The burden of proof for the effectiveness of advice and actions rests with the counsel. Many results are intangible or nebulous. Who can tell how many extra dollars for a charity drive came in because of the newspaper stories about the work of the charity during the year? Polls are helpful, but many of the common yardsticks are not appropriate. The counsel submits reports of progress, holds periodic meetings with key people in the client's organization, and coordinates the program.

As the counselor-client relationship matures, the shape of the client's enterprise very probably undergoes variations. Communications programs are revampd, scrapped, or replaced. New ones are activated. Special devices are "imagineered" to deal with peculiar needs.

The counselor usually functions in one of three ways with clients:

1. Provides advice, leaving the execution of plans to others
2. Provides advice and undertakes full execution of plans
3. Provides advice and collaborates with the client's staff to execute the plans

The counselor's advantages

Counselors rank their *variety of talents and skills* as their greatest advantage, compared with internal staffing. Their *objectivity,* as relatively free agents, untrammeled by the politics within an organization, ranks second. The *range of prior experience* is put third, the *geographical scope* of their operations fourth, and the *ability to reinforce and upgrade a client's internal staff* fifth.

A number of counselors emphasize the *flexibility* of their staff and their operations as a prime advantage.[17] In their shops, or no farther away than the telephone, are artists or models, copy editors, magazine-article writers or placement specialists, talk-show experts, lawyers, and home economists. A client can say what's needed or wanted *now,* and an account executive can assure attention to immediately. This is not always so with internal staff.

Flexibility is also tied to scope of operations and to range of experience. From an office in New York, Washington, or Chicago, the counselor can serve clients in Colorado, West Virginia, and Vermont. If that becomes impractical, the counselor can open branch offices in major population centers. Services can be exchanged with firms in other cities and countries. In cases of need, sandlot offices in Colorado, West Virginia, and Vermont can be installed. Reasonably intimate contact can be maintained through periodic meetings on the premises of clients. If that does not suffice, the counsel can help the client obtain a suitable staff director, or he can lend someone from his own staff. At the same time, the counselor's central location in a metropolitan communications hub permits frequent and personal contact with the press, radio, magazines, and TV—the main means of outward communication for all clients. Contacts embrace the news media in New York, Washington, Chicago, San Francisco, and Hollywood. Several firms offer publicity services on a U.S. network basis and on an international basis.

In the course of any year, a counselor will be confronted with many different communications problems. Typical would be a strike, a protest movement on skyrocketing hospital costs, the introduction of a new product, prospective unwanted legislation, and the inauguration of a university president. The range of a successful counselor's services is wide. If the agency department is a successful, substantial one, its range is equally wide. In a sense, a public relations firm is a repository of living case histories. Each project adds to its fund of knowledge. Experience and versatility of staff make this synergy possible. The counselor approaches each case bolstered by past familiarity with the type of situation and knowledge of the success or failure that attended previous encounters.

The counselor's handicaps

The foregoing may sound as though the task of the counselor is simply to arrive on the premises. The rendering of a counseling service—and this applies to almost all consultants—with rare exception, meets with some *opposition ranging from non-acceptance to antagonism.* This is, at least in theory, the counselor's most serious handicap. The *resistance to outsiders* is a natural human trait. The old guard resists change—the new idea, the new approach, the new look—as a threat to its security. This resistance is almost a certainty in organizations that have been static for years. Perhaps what they need most is a new look in public relations; but they put up resistance—probably plenty of it—and this is logical. That does not mean that a new idea is no good. Hostility comes naturally when drastic or sudden changes are proposed.

The counselor, more often than not, is in the position of having to suggest changes designed to improve relationships. And whether the changes involve policies, equipment, methods, or practices, the people originally responsible for them can be alienated by these suggestions. Their realm is being invaded; their judgment is being criticized. The offended ask, "What does this outsider know about our organization . . . our way of doing things?"

Counselors, however, do not rank this problem at the top. *They overwhelmingly cite questions of cost as the chief bugaboo with clients. They list "threat to old guard and set ways" as the second most persistent handicap. Resistance to "outside" advice comes in third,* and *fourth is unforeseen conflicts of personality or conviction.*[18]

This most recent assessment does not square off well with an earlier one made in the late 1960s by *Public Relations Quarterly.* Counselors then asked to describe their main problems in effective service said:

1. Being unable to hire the right number and kind of professional staffers, 38%
2. Having to report to client contacts of unprofessional caliber, 35%
3. Lack of direction or poor direction from client, 26%
4. Being denied suitable access to top management, 15%
5. Failing to ascertain what the client really wanted and/or needed, 13%
6. Personality conflicts, 9%
7. Failing to deliver what we originally promised, 2%

Obviously, there were some changes in problems and priorities during the 1970s.

Other problems expressed frequently by counselors are a stubborn *lack of understanding of public relations by clients, client inertia* when it comes to doing what counselors think ought to be done; and the *unavailability of clients,* presumably the decision makers, at times when counselors want decisions. This would suggest a problem of priorities.

Whatever the first stumbling block—costs, threat to the status quo, resistance to change, or inertia—others can pile up. Insiders may attempt to discredit the counselor. The anxieties of insiders and old-timers can be barriers. A finger of concern can be pointed at the cost of the proposed services or program. A question can be raised as to guarantee of return on investment. Accusations can be made of the counselor's *superficial grasp of the organization's unique problems*—the local and historical angles to the problems, the sacred cows, the "things we never talk about." Under such circumstances, it is uphill all the way for the counselor.

The division of responsibility

Regardless of staff and scope, advantages and handicaps, all practitioners share the same philosophy of service. There are several natural questions to be answered: Is the counseling firm more or less effective than the department of the advertising agency? than the internal staff? Are they all necessary? If so, in combination or separately?

Forces making public relations essential are such that the question of relationships between the outside counsel and internal staff is not critical. Each organization has to evolve a pattern suited to its changing needs. A small college in a midwestern state may need to augment its internal staff for a period of six months to raise capital funds. In this case, it is simpler to retain outside counsel for the project. A large professional society may get caught in the crunch of crisis, find its internal department deficient, and turn to outside counsel. A Rocky Mountain ski-resort company may retain a public relations agency in New York to gain more direct access to the national news media.

Whether a public relations agency or a department within an advertising agency is best is again a matter of variance. If the need is primarily product publicity, it may be feasible to use the same agency for both advertising and publicity. Generally speaking, advertising agency departments or subsidiaries are not equipped to provide broad-range counseling. Howard Chase, a counselor who served as a corporate staff director and as head of public relations for a large advertising agency, describes advertising and public relations as "unidentical twins." He asserts:

> While the target of both advertising and public relations may be a share of the human mind, the scope of advertising is limited, and will be limited, by the availability of purchasable media. There are no limitations on the scope and range of public relations. . . . It is my impression that recognition of these functional differences will gain wide acceptance at high executive levels.[19]

We have seen that the calling is expanding in numbers and diversity. Public affairs, as part of the mix, has gained authority in many large organizations that are subject to government regulation. Practitioners who know their way around Washington and the state capitals, or have the versatility to learn their way, are in demand. Whether in the name of public affairs or public relations, those in executive positions are in closer contact, more frequently, with top officials. More top officials are available as spokesmen. Not as many are timid about an aggressive newsmaking action or advocacy.[20] Such actions or advocacy now seldom wait until oxen are being gored, or a defensive reaction is sought by media or opposition. Legal considerations continue to be decisive, but public relations people and lawyers are learning to work together more effectively.

The other most visible trend in the calling is the increased prominence that women have attained. The Department of Labor puts female employment in the field at about 25 percent. Of this, an increasing proportion is at the executive level. The PRSA has had a female president. A female member of the head-

EXHIBIT 2-1

Ladies Up Front

Historically, the calling has had its share of female as well as male pioneers. The "Lowell Offering," as far back as 1840, was published by female factory workers, with Harriet Robinson its editor. In more recent times, to mention a few groundbreakers without offense to others, Lee Jaffee at the New York Port Authority made her way in what most would consider a totally male operation. Sally Dickson started the first female counseling firm, closely followed by Woodward and Flanley. Greta Murphy headed public relations for a Milwaukee engineering school in Milwaukee and was the first female chapter president in the national society. Caroline Hood established the Christmas celebration in Rockefeller Center, New York. Gertrude Bailey headed a New York public relations office for Monsanto Chemical. Melva Chesrown was consultant to major corporations.

Women figured actively in man–wife public relations teams. Among the most notable have been Edward L. Bernays and Doris Fleischman, Boston consultants; Clem Whitaker and Leone Baxter, California specialists in political work; Robert Newcomb and Marg Sammons, specialists in employee communications; and Shirley and Rea Smith, both of whom have served as the ranking staff officer of the National Public Relations Society.

quarters staff has been elevated to executive director, the top spot. The first top executive of CASE, formed by the merger of the American College Public Relations Association and the American Alumni Council, was a woman. There is an organization, Women Executives in Public Relations. Several of *Fortune's* 500 largest corporations have named women as department heads.[21] Women occupy executive-officer positions in many large counseling firms, and in private and public health and welfare institutions. Hundreds of counseling firms are headed by women. In the public arena, the conflict-of-interest problem involving women married to public officials has touched the calling at least once.

All this cannot be brushed aside as response to popular pressure. The phenomenon is not, as one business executive claimed, a case of "putting some women in highly visible positions where they can't do much harm." The simple fact is that more women are seeking careers in public relations and are demonstrating the intelligence, empathy, and skills employers want.

ADDITIONAL READINGS

ASSOCIATION OF NATIONAL ADVERTISERS, *How Public Relations and Advertising Are Working Together to Meet Company Objectives.* New York: The Association, 285 Madison Avenue, New York, N.Y. 10017.

"Budgeting in the Public Relations Agency," *Quarterly Review of Public Relations,* Vol.6 (Fall 1961).

Career in Public Relations, a booklet to help those seeking employment. Public Relations Society of America, 845 Third Avenue, New York, N.Y. 10022.

CHESTER BURGER, *Primer of Public Relations Counseling.* Prepared by Counselors Section, Public Relations Society of America, 1972.

SONDRA K. GORNEY, "Status of Women in Public Relations," *Public Relations Journal,* Vol. 31, No. 5 (May 1975), 10–13.

FARLEY MANNING, "How to Charge a Client," *Public Relations Quarterly,* (Summer 1963).

ALFRED G. PAULSON, "Cost Accounting in the Public Relations Firm," *Public Relations Quarterly.*

REA SMITH, "Women in Public Relations," *Public Relations Journal,* Vol. 24, No. 10 (October 1968).

JAMES B. STRENSKI, "Achieving Effective Client-Agency Relationships," *Public Relations Quarterly, Services of Hill and Knowlton,* a booklet describing in detail the makeup and services of the world's largest counseling firm. Available from Hill and Knowlton, Inc., 633 Third Avenue, New York, N.Y. 10017.

The Byoir Way, a booklet describing a large counseling firm's services and method of operation. Available from Carl Byoir & Associates, Inc., 380 Madison Avenue, New York, N.Y. 10017.

FOOTNOTES

1. Jack O'Dwyer, "$2 Billion Spent on Public Relations," *Advertising Age,* November 21, 1973.

2. Jack O'Dwyer, *O'Dwyer's Directory of Public Relations Firms, O'Dwyer's Directory of Corporate Communications,* and *O'Dwyer's PR Profiles* (New York: Jack O'Dwyer, 1976); also, "Annual Subscribers Survey," *PR Reporter* (Meriden, Conn: PR Publishing, 1976).

3. In this category, and no discredit to the sponsors, are The Conference Board, serving commercial and industrial interests; surveys by management consultants seeking or serving clients; and spot checks by newsletters catering to potential subscribers or flattering one segment, such as women, youth, or minorities.

4. For more particulars about the Cutlip and Center Survey of 1976, see "Canvassing the Calling," *Public Relations Journal,* Vol. 33 No. 11 (November 1977). p. 40.

5. Not all of the 376 respondents filled in this segment of the questionnaire; hence, the 299 tallied departments.

6. "Level of Education among PR Executives," *PR Reporter,* Vol. 18, No. 37 (September 15, 1975).

7. Blaine K. McKee, Oguz B. Nayman, and Dan L. Lattimore, "How PR People See Themselves," *Public Relations Journal,* November 1975.

8. An interesting and unusual inquiry was embodied in an unpublished thesis by Lt. Comm. Milton Sumner Baker, Jr., "Perceptions of Public Relations: The Practitioner as Seen by Three of His Publics," San Diego State University, 1976, with a synopsis given in *Public Relations Journal,* Vol. 33, No. 8 (August 1977). The study encompassed a survey of three "publics"—the employers of public relations, journalists, and the general public or layman.

9. U.S. Department of Labor, Bureau of Labor Statistics, Bulletin 1975, *Occupational Outlook Handbook,* 1976–77 ed.

10. *The Encyclopedia of Careers and Vocational Guidance* (Chicago: J.G. Ferguson Publishing Company, 1975).

11. A discrepancy occurs between the number of respondents in each category and the number of persons listed for each. This is because not all respondents filled in the income table. Thus, numbers of persons are less than the total numbers employed by the respondents.

12. It can be assumed that subscribers to *PR Reporter* are, for the most part, executive professionals rather than clerical or lower-income employees.

13. "Fees, Charges and Overhead in the Practice of Public Relations," a study report sponsored by the Counselors Section, PRSA. Fourth printing, 1972. (No later edition had been produced as of 1977.)

14. The averages were computed from information given in the C-C Survey.

15. Anthony M. Franco, "Counseling Fees: It's a Matter of Cost Consciousness," *Public Relations Journal,* Vol. 32, No. 8 (August 1976).

16. The Wallace Jamie Resource Group, Inc., Los Angeles, an interesting variation in counseling, to be watched for its outcome.

17. From the C-C Survey. Respondents were asked to rank five choices. The factor of "flexibility" came as a write-in.

18. From C-C Survey. Respondents were offered four choices to rank. "Costs" was one of them.

19. Howard Chase, "The Issue: Issue Inaction vs. Issue for Action," *Corporate Public Issues,* Vol. 1, No. 6 (June 30, 1976). Describes one CEO's program for speaking out on issues affecting his company.

20. *Ibid.*

21. The list includes, among others, Gulf Oil Co., Greyhound, Kraftco, Colgate-Palmolive, Celanese, Motorola, and Illinois Bell Telephone.

3

He who wishes to travel far spares his mount.

RACINE

The Function and its Employers: the working relationships

This chapter deals with the positioning of public relations, whether within an organization or as counseling from the outside. Positioning includes reporting relationships, responsibilities and authority, and working harmoniously with other departments and functions.

As a starting point, it is helpful to know some of the ways in which the function comes into being, and then evolves to accommodate special goals or needs. This can make it easier to understand why public relations practitioners and consultants may occupy positions or perform roles in or for particular organizations that seem unusual or incongruous.

For example, the function is often activated when an employer discovers a need for better communications with an important group. Perhaps an employee publication is desired in a small but growing organization. An editor is appointed or hired by the personnel manager. The publication is successful. Then the editor, being energetic and ambitious, is given—or takes on—the task of writing and issuing occasional news releases generated by material in the employee newsletter. The dual task necessitates an assistant for the editor, and a secretary for the two of them. At this point, the function might be lifted out of the personnel department, given the title of "Public Relations Department," and reassigned to the chief executive officer because he or she is the spokesman for the organization.

Other common starting points are the need for product or service publicity, or news support for national advertising, fund-raising, or membership campaigns. The genesis can be in assisting with executive speech writing; in answering letters from customers or members; in writing copy for direct mail, advertising, or booklets; in handling visitors and arranging for meetings; or in serving as an organization's ombudsman.

The beginning of a counseling relationship also can be quite simple and unpretentious. An outside agency might be asked to do a one-time project such as preparing a questionnaire, or conducting a survey of community attitudes. The results could lead to proposals to take advantage of an opportunity or to correct a public opinion problem disclosed during the initial project. This might lead to

EXHIBIT 3–1

Some actualities that call for public relations

- **An Emergency**—A group of armed Indians, calling themselves the Menominee Warriors Society, took over a vacant 64-room abbey of the Alexian Brothers that they wanted for a medical facility to serve the Menominee reservation. Farmers in the nearby Shawano community were incensed. The governor called out the Wisconsin National Guard. Guns were fired. Marlon Brando appeared on the scene. After 34 days of siege, the abbey was given to the Indians for "$1 and other considerations." Public relations counsel and communications were indicated on behalf of the Indians, the governor, the National Guard, Shawano, and Marlon Brando.

- **An Overhaul**—For years, the public relations activities of a foundation of employee relations plans had been a hit-or-miss proposition. There was a growing desire for purposeful, planned effort to enhance the foundation's standing as an educational organization and a source of employee-benefits information. An in-depth study of needs was authorized by the foundation's board. This was performed as an "audit" by an outside counseling agency.

- **A Threat**—Humane Society groups were increasing their efforts to show that the rodeo, a billion-dollar business attracting 10 million spectators, was cruel to animals. The Rodeo Cowboy Association felt it was being attacked, and retained public relations counsel to develop its defense and response.

- **Public Service**—In the early 1960s, the National Safety Council investigated the hazards of glass, and made the recommendation that only safety glazing materials, not annealed glass, be used in locations where people could be hurt by breaking glass. Definitions and standards were required, state by state. Pittsburgh Plate Glass Industries (PPG) seized the public affairs initiative, along with dozens of sponsoring organizations in organized labor, metals, chemicals, architecture, construction, and government. In less than a generation, safety glass became practically universal.

- **Causes**—Peace in the world is a constant, elusive goal; military service is an unacceptable alternative to many. In 1917, the American Friends Society, a Quaker organization, provided conscientious objectors with an alternative to military service, a "service of love in wartime." More than 60 years later, the AFS administers projects of compassion throughout the world, its main communications weapon "peace education."

- **Effecting Change**—It is national policy to convert to the metric system, but the United States lags behind several other nations in effecting the changeover. Among many communications efforts to hasten the process, the California Department of Education is teaching metric weights and measures, and a paper company has introduced "metric-cartoon" cups for children.

a continuing and expanding relationship as the full range of the agency's capabilities was brought to bear on the organization's goals.

The installation of a public relations function does not always spring from a welcome opportunity to advance the interests of the organization. In many cases, an organization is confronted with an emergency or a crisis that attracts considerable public attention, and there is no one on the staff qualified to handle the public information requirements. People brought in under such emergency conditions, whether as staffers or outside counsel, might subsequently be hired or retained on a continuing basis. Then, beyond the emergency or crisis situation, the place and the role of the function are determined and redetermined to fit

EXHIBIT 3-2

Some possibilities that would call for Public Relations

- **Promotional Opportunity**—A new company is formed to sell a new product, like a CB antenna or a shirt-pocket calculator.

- **Competitive Challenge**—A discount house moves into an area where competition has not been intense.

- **Controversy**—An old private school for girls decides to go coeducational, against the wishes of alumni and the hometown community.

- **Adverse Publicity**—A local charity staff is discovered by a reporter to be employing paroled criminals.

- **New Image**—An elderly, quiet, scholarly president of a university is replaced by a youthful, articulate, gregarious charmer noted for fund-raising success.

- **Catastrophe**—A river bridge connecting two sides of a small town collapses while under repair by a local contractor. Several lives are lost.

- **Ineffective Communication**—A survey of employees shows that they don't read or believe what's in the house publication.

- **Conflict of Interest**—The site chosen for an interceptor missile installation is a forest preserve bordered by a surburban community of expensive homes. An opposition petition is circulated. One of the residents is president of the company that builds the missiles.

- **Crisis**—Loggers working on a contract for a major paper company accidentally set fire to a 30,000-acre tract of timberland. The fire threatens four towns in the area, each of which has only one fire engine.

changing needs, problems, opportunities, and value standards as perceived and set by a succession of senior officials.

Thus, we occasionally find small departments in large institutions and over-sized departments in small ones, and reporting relationships to personnel officers and to advertising managers. We find outside counsel where internal staff seems indicated, and internal staffing where logic might dictate outside help. We sometimes find a large complement of standby public relations people in an organization that engages in the least possible public exposure or advocacy. Finally, we find understaffed units of harassed practitioners trying desperately to marshal massive public support, or neutralize well-organized public opposition. It is well to remember that *mismatches often express nothing more than a delay in adapting to change, and employers' reluctance to dismiss people of seniority, loyalty, and good intent in any manner that is inconsiderate or unappreciative of past contributions to the organization.*

Every day, in thousands of routine and special situations involving public opinion, public relations activities are initiated, changed, or otherwise involved. In one instance, the effort is to marshal an aggressive public support; in another, to obtain public understanding or neutrality; and in still another, simply to respond to public inquiry. A few real-life and potential incidents and situations are capsulized in Exhibits 3–1 and 3–2.

Establishing and structuring a flexible public relations activity is not as simple as drawing the profile of an ideal and then filling in the parts. In addition to dealing with changing public opinion moods and with the unexpected, there are rules and traditions governing employer-employee relationships, with laws protecting the interests of both. There is the factor of human chemistry, the likes and dislikes of those thrown together; and there is the state of health of an employing organization at any given time. And besides all this, there is no unanimity even among practitioners as to what would be the "best" or the "right" structural setup for continuous effectiveness of the function in various types of institutions served. Nor, is there general agreement on a "most effective" kind of working relationship between public relations and all the other functions that make up an organization. Consequently, *each public relations function must be tailor-made and must be altered to meet change.*[1]

Public relations starts with administrators

One of the few safe generalizations on this subject is that *an organization's public reputation derives in substantial part from the public voice of its senior officials. As those with administrative responsibility and authority act and speak, so go the interpretations and echoes created by the public relations function. Thus, public relations is inescapably tied, by nature and by necessity, to the administrative function.* Dr. Albert Oechl puts this precisely: "Public relations today is a function of management. . . . They have an ambivalent relationship to each other. They need each other, and they supplement each other, but they cannot represent each other mutually in all cases. The decisive point is that they always cooperate with full confidence in each other."[2]

From this platform, we can postulate that long-term success in public relations programming should have five characteristics:

1. Commitment and participation by management.
2. Competence in the public relations functionaries.
3. Centralization of policy making.
4. Communication up from constituent publics, down to them, and sideways through the organization.
5. Coordination of all efforts toward defined goals.[3]

It may seem that the burden is heaviest on senior management, but practitioners are fully involved. The first task, and a continuing one, is to earn and hold broad support for the public relations charter *within* the organization. As one veteran practitioner put it, "I find that I can afford to spend up to 75 percent of my time, if necessary, to persuade my associates as to what I do in the remaining 25 percent." Unless support is earned, there will be conflict, not coordination and cooperation. Conflict begets friction and frustration.

Although ultimate value and clearly defined purposes develop with time and a track record of achievement, practitioners have at least eight goals for the effective integration of their work:

1. Ensure the public relations–mindedness of organization officials.
2. Obtain a written definition of authority and responsibility.
3. Blend public relations goals into organizational goals.
4. Gain the confidence and cooperation of associates.
5. Indoctrinate the entire organization in principles and programs.
6. Provide service to other departments, staff and line.

7. Develop a desire and opportunities for mutual participation in the program.
8. Promote a communication philosophy of candor.

Administrators determine basic objectives; they manage by goals and objectives, long-term and short-range. Administrators set policies; they approve procedures for the guidance of everyone. In the process, they decide, at least tentatively, on the scope and the place of all staff or line, office or field functions. In doing so, intentionally or not, they determine the relationship of each to the others.

A senior official relates this to public relations bluntly: "When it is all said and done, a public relations office will only be as useful to management as management wants it to be. If management thinks of the public relations operation in a small way, then it will occupy a small place in the scheme of things, and its contribution will be small. If management thinks it is important, then it will occupy a prominent place, and its contribution will be significant." Whether management does think the function is important depends on several things, among them the yardstick the executives use to evaluate it. And this depends, in turn, on their concepts of what makes a good practitioner, what goes into the function, and what is expected to come out of it. Another factor is the shifting pressures for response to public interests.

The staff role

Public relations is a staff function, one of several that serve to advise top officials. Thus, practitioners need to understand the staff role.

The line–staff principle of management originated in the military but has been extended to most organizations of some size. In industry, the product- and profit-producing functions—engineering, production, and distribution—are *line functions. Staff functions* are those that advise and assist the line executives—finance, legal, personnel, planning, public relations, research, sales promotion, and advertising. These functions became more and more necessary as organizations increased in size and complexity. Line executives have the authority and responsibility to see that the work gets done, but they need assistance in the form of plans, advice, and suggestions from staff executives. *The job of the staff officer is to advise top officials and to support and assist the line officers.*[4]

Staff work involves the art of collaboration. Staff people justify their jobs by their total effectiveness. Robert Sampson says they need "(1) a sense of organization and operations; (2) an understanding of people, their functions, their relationships; (3) an acceptance of managers as full-scale managers; (4) a humility about their contribution in their limited role; (5) a desire to relate themselves helpfully and dynamically to the ongoing management process."[5] The counselor must keep this inviolate basic objective constantly before him: *the continuity of the organization and its survival as a healthy entity.*

Management and staff have a right to expect certain things from each other. *Management should expect from the public relations staff:*

1. Loyalty.
2. Help with the public relations aspects of decisions.
3. Skill in articulating principles and in enlarging understanding of the organization.

4. Inspiration to help all members do their best cheerfully.
5. Influence in restraining other members from saying or doing anything detrimental to the organization's welfare.

Educated, trained, and experienced practitioners, by sensitive reading of public sentiment, act as conduits. They feed information upward before major decisions are made; they feed information on decisions down and outward; and after those decisions have been carried out, they feed information upward on public reaction and response, thus forming a continuous loop.

This capability attained a milestone in 1963 when the idea of feedback was applied by President Kennedy in redefining the mission of the United States Information Agency. From its inception, the USIA had been directed "to submit evidence to peoples of other nations by means of communication . . . that the objectives and policies of the United States are in harmony with . . . their legitimate aspirations." President Kennedy added to this directive the function of *advising* the president, his representatives abroad, and the various departments on the implications of foreign opinion on present and contemplated policies of the United States.[6] (The USIA became the International Communication Agency in 1978.)

In the corporate sphere, AT&T reaffirmed the principle in 1974:

> Any executive officer worth his salt seeks public relations advice at every stage in the development of new products, programs and policies. . . . If information—both incoming and outgoing—is one basic element in the job the chief executive expects from his public relations people, professionalism is the other. . . . The division of responsibility that this suggests would seem to assign to the corporate executive the content, and to the public relations specialist the container in which it is packaged. . . . But that's not true, in my view. Public relations people must participate in shaping the content first. Then the packaging can follow.[7]

The staff should expect from management:

1. Positive public relations leadership.
2. Support of approved communications policy.
3. A definite plan embracing all policies and programs.
4. A budget to do the job that needs to be done.
5. Funds for adequate public opinion research and analysis.
6. Reasonable availability for consultation and for public exposure.

Both have the right to expect of each other standards of character and performance that will stand public scrutiny.

The perspective outlined on the preceding pages is important to remember. Management determines the ground rules. Public relations works within those rules and with other executives on matters having a strong impact on the opinions of various publics, inside and outside. Public relations may be called on for its view or help with other matters. Often matters comprise a mix of internal and external, public and private interests, selective communications and censorship. In these matters, all involved executives might participate. Final decisions are the province of the senior official. All executives have the duty to implement these decisions to the best of their ability, whether they agree or not.

That the working relationship between top officials and public relations executives has, with some exceptions, grown closer is well documented. In a 1965 survey of 182 corporations by Prof. Robert Miller, 39 percent of the public relations department heads reported to the chief executive officer. In the 1976 survey by Cutlip and Center (including 152 corporations), this had risen to 56 percent.

Management by objectives

Most organizations have in written form a statement of goals and objectives, long range and immediate. These are often paraphrased into public statements of obligations.[8] Whether these documents are kept private for competitive or security reasons, or whether they are open statements of mission, standards of conduct, or specific purposes, the resident practitioners are privy to them. In organizations where no such statement has been set down, there is an urgent need for the resident practitioner to propose one. Figure 3–1 gives some examples.

In nonprivate statements of this type, subject matter variously gives the organization's attitude in dealing with its employees, members, customers, neighbors, or donors. It acknowledges its citizenship obligations. There may be statements of posture on government regulation or environmental control, explanation of how it measures its own progress, and so on.

Those portions of the document that focus on public obligation or responsibility are very important to the public relations function, for two reasons: First, they commit the whole organization to accountability, and that means visibility or communications of some sort. And second, the attitudes expressed provide a framework in which public relations can devise its objectives and goals, shape its talents, ask for funding, and devise appropriate programs.

If the organization has a management-by-objectives plan on paper, public relations should have its long-range plan on paper. Its objectives and plans should be stated, at least briefly, in the master-plan statement. If the organization has a formalized "goals and objectives" plan, public relations should be stated as one part of it. A separate document should give guidance within the department. If the managers or general officers are periodically subject to performance review by a superior officer, the public relations manager should be reviewed equally or equivalently. If existing line departments or functions hold annual conferences to reenergize everyone, so should public relations. To attain organizational maturity, the function must be mainstream in every sense, not a side show.

It is imperative that, however simple or informal, a public relations function have goals and programs set down on paper and approved by the governors of the organization. Effective programming requires management agreement on a clearcut platform.

The following is a clearcut statement of responsibilities and functions sent around to all executives of an institution when a department of information was activated:

The responsibilities and functions shall be:

1. To serve as the central source of information about us and as the official channel of communication between us and the public.
2. To bring to public attention, through appropriate media, significant facts, opinions, and interpretations which will serve to keep the public aware of our policies and actions.

FIGURE 3-1 Public commitments. Courtesy Motorola, U.S.I.A., and Dow Chemical.

(USIA became the International Communication Agency in 1978.)

3. To coordinate activities which affect our relations with the general public or with special-public groups.
4. To collect and analyze information on the changing attitudes of key public groups toward us.
5. To plan and administer informational programs designed to fulfill most effectively the responsibilities outlined above.

In this organization, the department of information was placed under a director responsible to the president. Outside counsel retained by the organization developed the statement and worked with the internal staff.

Figure 3–2 contains excerpts from guidelines set for the public relations mission. Figure 3–3 cites the specific goals of one department in the framework of public affairs.

The New York Heart Association summarized its public relations program in terms of continuing goals and immediate specific objectives. The statements below are excerpts from a longer document:

GOAL 1: **To increase public knowledge of cardiovascular disease.**

OBJECTIVE 1: To increase time contributed by radio and TV stations by 25% by the end of fiscal year.

OBJECTIVE 2: To increase by 100% the amount of time contributed by movie theatres in spots during fiscal year.

OBJECTIVE 3: To begin to provide the public and corporate press with regularly scheduled educational articles about the different aspects of cardiovascular disease during fiscal year.

GOAL 2: **To furnish promotion and publicity support to all the departments of the New York Heart Association.**

OBJECTIVE 1: In the area of Community Programs and Education, to provide each of the program assistants with a minimum of two publicity support projects during the fiscal year.

OBJECTIVE 2: In the area of fund raising, to provide written promotion for at least four department programs or activities during the year and total media coverage for the campaign.

OBJECTIVE 3: In the area of research, to plan and carry out a minimum of three publicity support projects.

OBJECTIVE 4: In the area of Public Information, to develop two projects during the summer to increase employee awareness and acceptance of the department.

GOAL 3: **To increase public knowledge of the goals and objectives of the New York Heart Association.**

OBJECTIVE 1: To produce two informative bookets and one picture sheet about the New York Heart Association for distribution to the staff, volunteers and/or public during the year.

RELIGIOUS PUBLIC RELATIONS HANDBOOK

for local congregations of all denominatic

CORPORATE COMMUNICATIONS MISSIONS

<u>Corporate Communications Mission</u>

To initiate, develop and maintain a planned effort to obtain understanding and acceptance between the corporation and its various publics.

<u>PUBLIC RELATIONS POLICY GUIDELINES</u>

PPG's Public Relations objective, stated very broadly, is this: to plan and execute a continuing program of communication that will earn public understanding and acceptance of the corporation, its products and its services.

In order to fulfill that objective, the lines of communication must reach out to all of PPG's many publics -- employees, customers, plant communities, shareholders, the financial community, government and the general public -- and the message communicated must accomplish these additional objectives:

<u>Public Affairs Department Mission</u>

To assist United Telecom management in developing, initiating and maintaining activities to fulfill its responsibilities as a good corporate citizen in those communities in which United Telecom companies operate. Objectives support the cultural, economic, political and social development and generally improve the quality of life in those communities.

<u>Public Relations Department Mission</u>

To assist United Telecom management in initiating, developing and maintaining corporate advertising and corporate identification programs to gain and hold the favorable opinion of the publics served by the corporation, and to counsel, assist and monitor the advertising, corporate identity and public relations policies and practices of the affiliated companies.

RL "MISSION" AND POLICY GOALS

A professional medium committed to the principle of free information as embodied in the United Nations Charter and the Universal Declaration of Human Rights, Radio Liberty to the best of its ability serves the informational needs of the peoples of the Soviet Union who are denied free speech and free access to information.

CATERPILLAR TRACTOR CO.

Peoria, Illinois 61629

PUBLIC AFFAIRS OBJECTIVE

The objective of the public affairs activity is to help Caterpillar achieve the understanding and support it needs to operate a worldwide enterprise successfully. In pursuit of this objective, it is a public affairs responsibility at each operating unit to establish channels of communication with employees and other selected segments of the public, and to use those channels as effectively as possible to generate favorable attitudes toward Caterpillar's operations, goals, policies, and basic beliefs.

Seven Continuing Public Affairs Goals

I. Develop a better, truer public "impression" of Caterpillar . . . what we are, what we do, what we believe.
    1. A worldwide enterprise whose products are doing important, constructive work around the world.
    2. A strongly service-minded organization.
    3. A company placing heavy emphasis on research and engineering.
    4. A member of a highly competitive industry.
    5. A believer in high levels of integrity, achievement, and quality.
    6. A widely held company.
    7. A well-managed enterprise.
    8. A good company to work for.
    9. A good company to do business with.
    10. A believer in keeping the public informed.
    11. A responsible corporate citizen.

II. Secure better understanding of the benefits of Caterpillar operations in localities in which facilities are located.

III. Establish better understanding of Caterpillar's viewpoint on important legislative and governmental matters.

IV. Promote better understanding of the creative role of profit in contributing to a better life for employees and the public.

V. Contribute to an improved climate for business operations . . . and an improved community attitude on factors that make settlement and growth in a given country, state or locale attractive to business.

VI. Build increased community confidence in and goodwill toward the Company, its operations and its people.

VII. Inspire greater individual participation in public affairs.

OBJECTIVE 2: To report to the public by the Annual Meeting, October 19, on the Heart Association's stewardship of contributed funds.

OBJECTIVE 3: To maintain regular written communication, at least six times during the year, with all the hospital public relations directors in New York City.

GOAL 4: **To further develop cooperation between the media and the New York Heart Association for the purpose of advancing our goals and objectives.**

OBJECTIVE 1: To personally contact, during fiscal year, all media representatives in order to determine needs and attitudes in relation to us and to further develop cooperative relationships.

OBJECTIVE 2: To form an active Public Information Advisory Committee by September, which will meet a minimum of three times per year.

Just one example among many

As an example of how all this works in practice, a study was made of a small midwestern college (800 students) by a consulting firm principally qualified in cost accounting. Their conclusions were that the ideal size for a small college, in order for it to survive financially, was between 1,200 and 1,500 students. The college trustees and officers adopted the recommendation and set their long-term objective at 1,200 students. Their short-term goals were, in order, to raise money, and to add buildings, housing, faculty, and equipment needed. The responsibility assigned to the development and public relations offices was to devise fund-raising and publicity programs to help. Out of this came a five-year fund-raising campaign, titled, "A Greater Siwash." The goal was $5 million. Special publications were to report progress to alumni, donor prospects, college community, and friends. Publicity efforts were tied to each newsworthy item of progress toward the $5 million and the "ideal" small college.

Organization charts

Organization charts and job descriptions tied to statements of goals, policies, and principles serve a useful purpose: They lay the groundwork for acceptance of the function throughout the organization. The danger is that formal charts and job descriptions can be restrictive or, worse, can become shields behind which insecure people take refuge. Some practitioners become preoccupied with trying to change the charts and edit the job descriptions, as though this, with no other changes, would elevate their function. One long-standing opponent of the organization chart on principle was the late Clarence Randall, innovator in management approaches, when he was head of Inland Steel. One of his statements said, in part:

. . . To know who is to do what and to establish authority and responsibility within an institution are the basic first principles of a good administration, but this is a far cry from handing down immutable tablets of stone from the mountaintop. . . . It is not the preparation of the organization chart that I condemn, but its abuse: this blowing up of its significance to a point where guidance ceases and inhibition sets in.[9]

Organization charts are, at best, approximations, but they do clarify the role and relationships of various functions in general terms. The charts in Figure 3–4, for example, express the situations in an organization where public relations is an officership and reports directly to the CEO, and where the function reports at a lower level but has direct access to the CEO on matters of communications policy. Figures 3–5 through 3–8 demonstrate other formats.

FIGURE 3–4

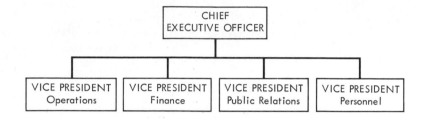

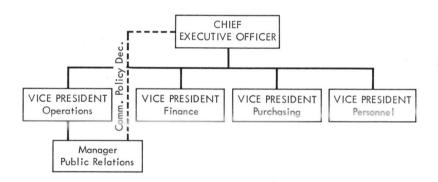

FIGURE 3–5   Basic functions and reporting relations. Courtesy the U.S. Air Force Academy.

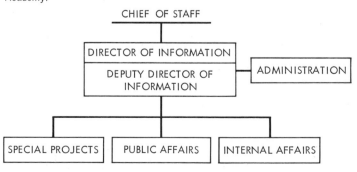

FIGURE 3-6   Courtesy Citibank Corp. public affairs department.

Public Affairs Department

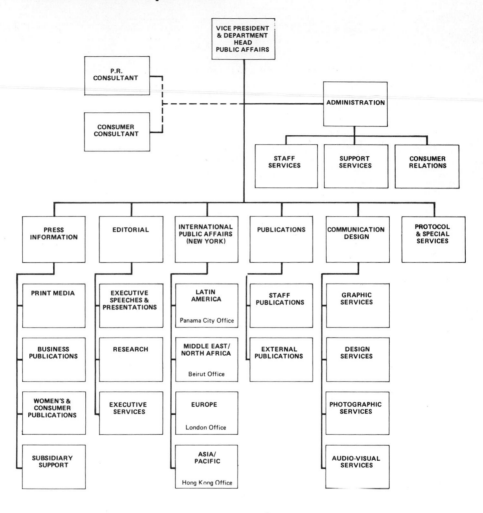

Functions of the practitioner

Intelligence

Four basic problems confront the administrator—determination of the *goals,* development of a system of *controls,* encouragement of *innovation,* and collection, collation, and interpretation of *intelligence.* The last is defined as "the problem of gathering, processing, interpreting, and communicating the technical and political information needed in the decision-making process." Wilensky elaborates:

> The more an organization is in conflict with its social environment or depends on it for the achievement of central goals, the more resources it will allocate to the

53

FIGURE 3–7   Courtesy Chrysler Corp. auto sales public relations department.

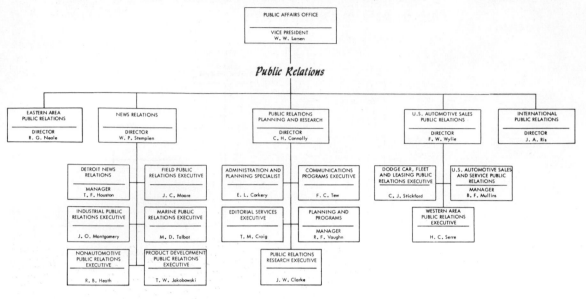

FIGURE 3–8   The director of public information for a small university diagrams her job by relevant publics and duties. Courtesy Sara Finn, APR, Director of Public Relations, University of San Diego.

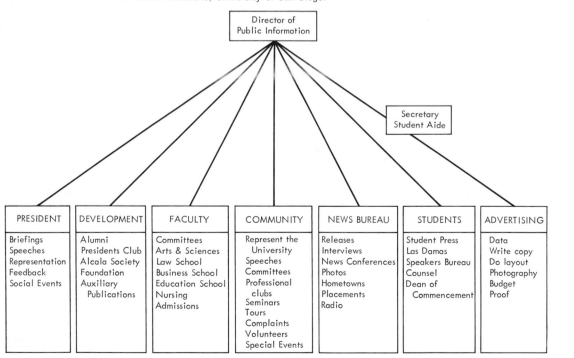

intelligence function and the more of those resources will be spent on experts whom we might call "contact men." The contact man supplies political and ideological intelligence the leader needs in order to find his way around modern society.[10]

The more useful the intelligence concerning public opinion that is fed up to administrators, the more likely it is that their decisions will take into account the interests of everyone affected by them. With all major institutions under increasing public scrutiny, the national news abounds with reports of adverse reactions that were preventable if only the involved practitioners had armed administrators with adequate intelligence about probable public reactions.

For example, a large oil producer seemed to place itself on the side of the public interest by stressing that higher consumer prices for fuel leading to larger profits would make available more funds for oil search and, ultimately, less dependence on foreign sources. Then, when higher profits materialized, the company used millions of dollars to acquire a major mass merchandising company and a container corporation, neither of them more than nominally involved in oil. The move obviously served the corporation's obligation to its shareholders, but gave the impression of deception and ignoring or flouting the public interest. A private welfare agency, in its fund-raising booklet, pointed out that much of its work was among those who were "ignorant," "illiterate," and "lacking in moral training." The pictures were entirely of one minority race. Intentionally or not, the language and its implications were tasteless and an affront to that racial public.

When a certain state had to cut its budget, a sizable amount was deducted from the funds for state universities. The word went down the line to university administrators and out from them to the academic schools and departments that were being cut back, one of which was a school of professional studies. The impression given was that too many students had been shifting into professional studies, and administrators felt they should be referred back into liberal arts. This incensed many students to whom vocationally oriented studies were more helpful than liberal arts courses in finding employment in a tight job market.

In these instances, the practitioners involved should have alerted their principals to the hazards in their actions. There is no assurance that different administrative decisions could or would have been made. Nonetheless, in rendering such counsel, there is assurance that the intelligence function of public relations is performed with maturity and professional candor, and without concern for the risk of "losing a few points" on the scoresheet of executive vanity.

Top administrators, for the most part, are not trained or skilled in reading the subtleties in the climate of public opinion. They tend to be more keenly sensitive to the *facts* dictating a course of action than to the *impressions* that their actions and decisions will make on others.

Sensitivity, translation into practical intelligence, and the upward flow of that intelligence in the decision process are responsibilities testing the skill of the practitioner.

Information

A second service to be performed by the public relations function also earns it a place among those who advise chief executives. That service is the interpretation of the organization among constituents whose approval or support is coveted. Interpretation means telling the story accurately, persuasively, and in keeping with the character, the personality, and the performance standards of the enterprise. Only actions that command a favorable response from the audience can build a solid platform for congenial relationships.

Today, people are swamped and surfeited with information to a point of resentment. They are bombarded with pleas to listen, to buy, to give, to vote, to do this or not to do that. Faster living permits less and less attention to these pleas. The demands of making a living, taking care of family chores, engaging in recreational pursuits, and fulfilling civic obligations take most of one's available time and energy. There is little time left to listen, less to read, and precious little to think. The news media are pitched to these facts of life.

Hence, the effort to tell the story of an industry or institution is born not so much of the desire for free publicity as of the need to be accurately interpreted. Unless institutions make that effort, they risk being misunderstood and misrepresented. Many misunderstandings can be traced not only to misinformation but also to the lack of information, and this can be the root of needless frictions and aggressions. *Informed support is strong, sure support.*

Thus, in the *intelligence* and *information-action* tasks, we see the fundamental place for the practitioner. He enables top officials to take actions that are at the same time responsive to public interest and beneficial to private interests.

Collaboration

Public relations staffers work most closely with the other staff functions of advertising, personnel, industrial or employee relations, legal, finance, and development. These functions intertwine and overlap in varying degrees, and sometimes the department finds itself in unavoidable conflict with another. Particular sources of internal friction are the departments of *legal counsel, personnel,* and *advertising.* Such disputes are costly to all concerned, especially to the employer. Each function needs the support and cooperation of the others if it is to discharge its obligation effectively. But with the potential for conflict inherent in the fluidity of the public relations function, practitioners should be aware, alert, and ready to mend fences.

Legal counsel: The conflict between public relations and legal counsel is an old one. In the days of the "muckrakers," corporate executives turned first to their lawyers to "fix things." Some still do. Ivy Lee felt strongly about this: "I have seen more situations which the public ought to understand, and which the public would sympathize with, spoiled by the intervention of the lawyer than in any other way. Whenever a lawyer starts to talk to the public, he shuts out the light."[11] Even today, we can expect conflict when one corporation counsel asserts, "I am prepared to defend the position that the truly competent legal counsellor to the public relations division should be expected to express his opinion not only on matters of factuality which have potential legal impact, *but even on matters of good taste, logic, honesty,* yes, even at times on the persuasiveness of your copy."[12] Conversely, a seasoned practitioner could claim that his own views and his adeptness with words could help make legal documents understandable to the layman. In doing so, he could save the organization the "costs" of being misunderstood via obscure or needlessly harsh language in touchy situations. Empathy is needed.

There are many areas in which the close coordination of legal and public relations counsel are beneficial to the employer: for instance, the area of labor contract negotiations and other legally based or explosive situations—an antitrust suit, a campus uprising, the threat of boycott, an accusation of discrimination, or a military court-martial. Additionally, there must be coordination on such matters as booklets explaining benefits to employees, announcement of new facilities, legality of advertising or publicity claims, disclosure of financial information, and so forth.[13]

Close cooperation of legal and public relations counsel, once seen mainly in the business world, is now necessary in most organizations as they deal with an ever more complex environment, threats to health or safety, urban renewal, and the expanding scope of government. In education, we have seen campus protesters frequently resort to the courts to achieve their demands or to escape punishment, posing a combined legal and public relations problem for the college. When parents go to court to protest grooming regulations or to block sex education in the schools, the situation requires collaboration by the school board's legal and public relations counsel. Similarly, such collaboration has long been required by the military in case of publicized courts-martial or antiwar protests.

Personnel or industrial relations: The relationships between public relations and personnel and/or industrial relations are many. The risk of friction is high. The fundamental problem concerns (1) whether communications in the community constitutes an extension of the employee relationship, and (2) whether the employee is a "public," calling for public relations concepts of attitude measurement and communication. Compromise comes when practitioners and personnel specialists realize that internal relationships inevitably have their echoes externally.

In the past, clashes of career ambitions and careless statements of influential bystanders have fanned embers of envy into open antagonism. One such example is this statement in a well-intentioned but overzealous commercial newsletter: "Indoctrinating the worker and equipping him to assume and discharge his citizenship responsibility intelligently are most assuredly phases of employee relations, *an established area of PR.*" Control of employee communications (not the whole of employee relations) is the most frequent bone of contention between these two functions. Increasingly, it is being allocated to public relations, which has the communications specialists on its staff.

The C-C survey in 1976 showed employee communications to be rated "important" by 91 percent of the responding 376 organizations, profit and nonprofit. In another study, a survey of American corporations showed this breakdown of specific tasks that are often bounced from one function to the other.[14]

Public relations dominant	Personnel dominant, public relations advisory
Annual reports	Employee attitude surveys
Open house, plant tours	Employee meetings
News releases on labor negotiations	Safety-promotion material
Maintenance of biographical data on key employees	

Personnel dominant, public relations not involved	Responsibility split
Suggestions systems	Employee publications
Bulletin boards	Employee newsletters
Reading racks	Liaison with civic bodies
New-employee orientation	Manpower for local fund drives—e.g.,
Exit interviews	United Fund
Service awards	Conducting career days
Recruitment programs	
Pay inserts	
Christmas parties	

Advertising (promotion, fund raising, membership): A company has three voices to the outside world—advertising, sales promotion, and public relations. The need for these voices to sing the same tune is plain, but effecting this harmony is not easy. There are many areas of potential conflict. Here the tussle is usually over control of image or advocacy advertising and over publicity of products or services. In nonprofit enterprises, the main bone of contention is usually allocation of budget or people, and methods of raising funds, recruiting members or enrollees, or educating a constituency.

Varied patterns of organizational relationships are to be found—public relations as a subfunction of advertising, advertising and sales promotion as subfunctions of marketing, combined public relations and advertising departments, and independent public relations, advertising, and marketing functions on a coordinate level.

Competition among these functions is understandable. They compete on parallel career tracks for recognition, for job advancement, and for bigger budgets. Often, both seek to control the advertising. Often, both seek to control publicity. Advertising to promote the general reputation of the company should, by its nature and goals, be supervised by the public relations department but may require the expertise of the advertising department for graphic preparation and media placement. Similarly, product advertising plans should appropriately be under marketing, but should be reviewed by the public relations department to ensure that the content will not offend the audience or otherwise damage the organization's reputation.

The growth of articulate protest groups, boycotts, petitions, investigative reporting, corrective advertising, class actions, and closer scrutiny of communications by government agencies all mandate public relations–mindedness.[15] Backlash is an ever-present potential. At least part of the auto industry's problems of credibility have stemmed from frequent changes in advertising emphasis—from speed, to large-size vehicles, to compacts, and then to "full size," all in turn said to be in response to "what the public wanted."

Control of conflict: One means of controlling conflicts is to form a communications or public relations committee, or consulting group, that includes the opponents. The public relations counselor or staff director assumes the role of coordinator, executor of decisions, or secretary to the group. Majority conclusions overcome individual oppositions, and the clash of personalities generally gets lost in the shuffle, at least for the moment.

Of course, the formation of policy groups has advantages beyond removing conflicts. There is much to recommend in the occasional bringing together of the best minds available—all the specialists—to thrash out problems affecting the whole organization. They can swap ideas, and the best solution will emerge. When all is done, everyone is committed.

A main consideration in the formation of guiding groups is to keep them small enough so they will not collapse of their own weight. Only those intimately concerned should be brought in, and only problems common to all participants in the group should be raised. For example, the treasurer of a university does not want to give an entire morning to discussion of how often the campus lawn should be mowed; nor would the superintendent of grounds relish the idea of having a subject he considers in his exclusive domain tossed on the table for the opinions of uninvolved officials. Finally, in guiding group discussions toward a decision, a coordinator should lead off with the areas of common agreement, not the points of probable conflict.

A number of the nation's major corporations, in an effort to eliminate overlap and conflict, have tried combining public relations and personnel functions into one department under one director or vice-president. The General Electric Company was the first to do this. The inherent problems are illustrated by the fact that GE has put its relations services department through several subsequent reorganizations. Other companies that combined these functions and later split them apart include General Foods, Quaker Oats, Eli Lilly, and Penn Central.

At Quaker Oats, Robert Thurston, formerly public relations director, advanced to senior vice-president, with law, public relations, personnel, and the corporate secretary's office under his wing. Thurston has said that public relations covers so many different areas that "there is no logical reporting 'fit' other than at the top." Most of those involved in this experiment agree that there is logic in combining these functions, at least in small companies and in plant operations away from corporate headquarters.

A large concern that has found having one department for public and industrial relations to be satisfactory is Texaco. Its senior vice-president, Kerryn King, comments, "There are any number of arrangements that can work satisfactorily. . . . In a company that has strong centralized labor negotiations and a high concentration of its employees, I believe it is better to have a separation of the two functions. On the other hand, where the centralized department furnishes primarily functional guidance to the operating departments of the parent company and its affiliates, there are advantages to be derived from the combination setup." Other firms have combined public relations and advertising, for the same reason. Penn Central is one example.

Getting off on the right foot

A public relations executive can be prejudged harmfully if his or her personal moral and ethical standards are lower than those he prescribes for others. Personal principles and conduct loom larger and larger in the effective integration of the function. Others are watching. A good example must be set.

The executive must gain the confidence of the thoughtful and influential people in the organization. He must learn their "language," their problems, their thinking. Respect for the practitioner and his judgment must reach from top administration down past the supervisory levels. The confidence top management has in him quite logically derives in part from the respect for him that people on down the line and in outside contacts have.

To gain respect, *the effective public relations man or woman must operate through channels, keep promises, preserve matters given in confidence, and seek no partiality. He or she must lick personal wounds privately.*

The practitioner needs a bit of the crusader's fervor. Where the function is new or young, enthusiasm coupled with results will go far toward instilling a public relations–mindedness in the organization. Goodwill, prestige, and a good press can become everybody's desire. That has been achieved adroitly in many organizations. When the president or general officer makes a speech, everybody can "prove" that what he says is right. The spirit is such that ideas for programs are volunteered; everybody wants to "get into the act."

Personal popularity is much more difficult for the outside consultant to achieve than for the staff man. The counselor is not on the premises daily to cultivate acquaintances. His visits are largely consumed in meetings with a relatively small number of people, so he must make the most of his opportunities.

Before an initial program is planned, the practitioner goes to school, so to speak. He becomes a student of the environment. He does his homework. It may be that he has research performed by outside firms, but in personal contacts, he is the researcher. He seeks out old-timers on the premises and draws them out about their experiences, about changes in attitude and policy that have taken place through the years. He studies all the departments in the organization and their relationships to each other. In the process, he learns the motivations and the insecurities that exist. Ideally, he becomes the best-informed person in the organization, *the answer man.*

The legwork is important in such personal research, but no less important is the desk work. The practitioner examines complaint letters and testimonials from outsiders; reads the files on grievances, resignations, important meetings; goes through employee handbooks, statements of policy, typical letters going out, bulletin board notices, the organization's history, financial reports, and various brochures. He digs around in the file morgue and among friendly media for the history, the legends, the lore, the skeletons or taboos, and the memorabilia.

In the search, the practitioner is, of course, looking for past or potential causes of breakdown in the communications the organization has with its publics. He is rethinking the needs for the future and informally auditing the past. The search takes him walking, around the hometown, the post, or the campus. As he goes, he listens with empathy and an open mind. He listens in the barber chair, at the corner grocery, in the bank, on the golf course, at the bus stop, and across the back fence.

The indoctrination process

The public relations executive is simultaneously a learner, an advocate, and a teacher. He or she makes tactful efforts to infuse colleagues with a public relations attitude. There are several ready-made vehicles:

1. Public opinion surveys—those commissioned by the organization, those published in newspapers or magazines, those published by other institutions—can be routed to other executives.
2. Samplings of letters from critical parents or customers, from alumni or shareholders, can be routed to all concerned.

3. Compilations of news-media comments about the organization can be routed to involved executives.

4. Clippings of news about the organization and about its competitors can be routed among department heads.

5. News stories to be sent out should be cleared with the persons and departments involved. Copies of releases to executives not involved is an appreciated courtesy.

6. Professional publications can be routed, with marginal notations for the attention of interested individuals.

7. Personal notes of congratulations and compliments can be sent concerning the civic activities of members of the organization. The same for condolences. Not only are the notes indicative of thoughtfulness, but they also serve to remind people that it is effective to do likewise.

8. Personal participation in community welfare campaigns or civic enterprises can become the internal practitioner's hobby. Again, here is an example for others.

9. The house publication can emphasize, without heavy-handed promotional techniques, that public relations is everybody's job. This is an old, well-worn theme that has endured because of its ultimate truth. After all, the contacts of the purchasing agent, salesman, soldier on leave, or student do perform a public relations job for the organization he represents. The house publication can become an effective integrating force through constant and adroit development of the idea of universal participation. In its own editorial staffing, it can include reporters appointed through the organization, a voice-of-the-people column, a column of suggestions, by-lines for contributors, and the enclosure of questionnaires sincerely seeking guidance from readers.

10. Activities can be encouraged to bring together groups having objectives and functions in common. As prototypes, there could be a Better Letter-Writing Clinic for business correspondents, a Leadership Forum for military noncoms, a Civic Council for students, a Customers' Service Panel for utility office people, a Newcomers' Welcome Committee for the Chamber of Commerce, and Outing Clubs for members of a retail association.

Rendering personal service

There are many opportunities for personal service. Minor as these services may seem, they are important to the recipients. They personalize the staff to others. This does not imply subservience, but rather a service-oriented attitude. The service approach is effective and almost limitless.

Completing the integration

A significant indication that public relations–mindedness is permeating the whole structure appears when people begin to tell each other that candor in communication is the best policy. "Those PR people know what they're doing," or, "We've got to tell the world what we're doing about pollution," and so forth. This means that public relations consciousness is gaining ground, and the employees have growing confidence that the staff will place the company in the right light publicly.

With the appearance of this important symptom, the public relations group can actually apply more candor in the communications structure, wherever it may have been lacking. The various groups sharing in the organization can be told more of what they want to know. Outsiders can be helped to get any kind of look into the organization that they want.

FIGURE 3-9 In the normal course of events, all departments or units of an organization benefit from public relations services. Here is a partial news-release list for one medium-sized company over a period of a year.

NEWS RELEASES	DEPARTMENTS MENTIONED
Announcement of spring advertising campaign	Sales, Advertising
Announcement of average wage in factory	All plant employees
Announcement of new technique in window trimming	Sales promotion
Monthly meetings of supervisory people to hear outside speakers	Factory supervisors, union officials
Visit of foreign distributors to hometown plant	Export
Results of beauty contest among girls in office and plant	Factory, Office, Sales promotion
Installation of plant safety devices	Factory management, Personnel
Company participation in local industrial exhibit	Public relations, Foremen, Beauty contest winners
Announcement of special promotion	Sales, Advertising
Announcement of company annual report	Production, Sales, Research, Finance
Attendance of engineers at industrial institute	Factory engineering
Award of product to high school valedictorian	Factory official
Bus-load of employees to neighboring festival	Factory assembly and others
Signing of a union contract	Factory management, union officials
Comparative figures on employment locally in plant	Factory employees
Visit of officials from foreign subsidiary	Management export
Announcement of new product	Sales, Advertising, Promotion, Factory, Design group
Promotion of executive	Sales, Field force
Announcement of sales meetings	Field force, Divisional sales managers
Establishment of welfare fund	All employees
Human interest—employee father of three children born same day of different years	Factory employees
Article on proper care of product	Service
Policy statement allocating merchandise	Sales, Management
Plans for convention participation	Sales
Announcement of trend to higher-priced products	All employees
Disclosure of new material used in product	Research
Article on company aircraft	Administration
New display device	Sales promotion
Factory methods	Factory management
Instructions on wrapping gift parcels for soldiers overseas	All employees, Office management
Viewpoint of Latvian employee	All employees
Retention of prominent designer	Sales, Design group

The exposure to public gaze of a clean organization, operating in the mutual interests of itself and its publics, does not mean that everything about the organization should be blurted out. In business, there is competition to think of. In the military, there are security considerations. In health institutions, there are ethical qualifications. In government agencies, there are political and regulatory factors. Everywhere there are legal pros and cons. Common sense helps.

Case problem in working relationships

You are in charge of the five-person public relations department in a community hospital. You formerly reported to the administrator, but following a major expansion, you were reassigned to a new vice-president for staff activities. He was reticent about public exposure, and he put your department under the director of personnel, who also reports to him.

A story surfaces in the local newspaper involving some of your hospital's employees in an illicit drug activity. You had been tipped off by a friend at the paper, but your immediate boss said, "Cool it. The hospital isn't responsible. The employees will be released. It will blow over." If your boss took it up with the staff VP, he didn't tell you.

However, the administrator, your old boss, ignores channels and calls you directly on the phone to verify the story. Then he says, "I can't handle everything up here. I expect all you people to get together and set it up so that I learn about any embarrassing situations in advance, and how you intend to handle all aspects of them."

At this point, what would you propose to your present boss, in structure and method, to fulfill the instruction to improve upward communications? Remember, you must avoid reflecting adversely on your supervisor's conduct or authority, and you must not bypass the staff vice-president.

ADDITIONAL READINGS

AMERICAN FOUNDATION FOR MANAGEMENT RESEARCH, *Management 2000.* New York: The Foundation, 1968. Proceedings of a symposium.

MELVIN ANSHEN, *Managing the Socially Responsible Corporation.* New York: Macmillan, 1974.

PETER F. DRUCKER, *Management: Tasks, Responsibilities, Practices.* New York: Harper & Row, 1974. A landmark tome from a prolific author.

WILLIAM P. EHLING, "Public Relations Administration, Management Science, and Purposive System," *Public Relations Review,* Vol. I, No. 2 (Fall 1975), 15–43. A scholarly examination and analysis of the function's behavior.

MILTON FAIRMAN, "The Practice of Public Relations," an address at the 15th Annual PR Institute, University of Texas, Austin, June 13, 1973. Available from Foundation for Public Relations Research and Education, New York.

JOHN W. HILL, "The Function of Public Relations in Helping to Restore Confidence in American Institutions," an address at the 16th Annual PR Institute, University of Maryland, College Park, July 10, 1974. Also available from the Public Relations Foundation.

MARSHALL C. LEWIS, "The Problem of Credibility: A Report from the Weatherman," a talk by the vice-president for communications, American Can Co., at Commercial Development Association, New York, March 19, 1975.

CHARLES H. PROUT, "How to Organize and Run a Corporate Public Relations Department," *Public Relations Journal,* Vol. 19 (February 1962).

THOMAS W. STEPHENSON, "Developing PR Managers for Their Changing Role," a talk at Golden Workshop, New York, June 19, 1975.

FOOTNOTES

1. Fact-finding audits are a common method of rethinking and restructuring staff functions. Usually regarded as confidential documents, such audits, where available, are helpful in the development of case studies and theses.
2. From a talk, *Public Relations and Management,* at the Sixth International Conference of Public Relations, Geneva, Switzerland, April 18, 1973.
3. In a letter to one of the authors, the public relations executive at Boys Town indicated that his queries of other executives showed that those who felt, "I am in charge of the image of the institution," ran centralized departments. Those who felt, "My job is to disseminate news about the institution," ran more decentralized departments.
4. Theon Wright and Henry S. Evans, *Public Relations and the Line Manager* (New York: American Management Association, 1964), p. 174.
5. Robert C. Sampson, *The Staff Role in Management* (New York: Harper & Row, 1955).
6. The background of this shift in policy is discussed in Thomas C. Sorensen, *The Word War* (New York: Harper & Row, 1968).
7. Excerpts from a talk, "Selling the Chief Executive Officer on Public Relations," by Robert D. Lilley, President, before the Public Relations Society of America, Bal Harbour, Florida, November 1974.
8. Statements for public consumption in written form are available from most large corporations and federal government departments and agencies.
9. Clarence Randall, *The Folklore of Management* (Boston: Little, Brown, 1959), p. 24.
10. Harold L. Wilensky, *Organizational Intelligence* (New York: Basic Books, 1967), p. 10.
11. Ivy Lee, *Publicity: Some of the Things It Is and Is Not* (New York: Industries Publishing Co., 1925), pp. 58 and 59.
12. William Barron, counsel for General Electric, in speech given at the PRSA Conference, Philadelphia, November 18, 1957. A common point of view, not as commonly reciprocated.
13. See Chapter 12 for several examples of relevant cases.
14. A survey conducted by Scott M. Cutlip and Leroy Johnson to ascertain trends in the patterns of organizing the public relations, personnel, and advertising functions. Questionnaires went to public relations and personnel directors in 75 firms. Some 74% responded.
15. See Chapter 12, the section dealing with the Fairness Doctrine and counteradvertising.

4

Those who cannot remember the past are condemned to repeat
it.
                                                    —GEORGE SANTAYANA

The Origins
of Public Relations:
how it all began

Studying the origins of public relations can provide helpful insight into its functions, its strengths, and its weaknesses. Published histories have usually telescoped and oversimplified a fascinating story, emphasizing novelty and a few colorful personalities. There is a great deal more than this in the story.

The history of public relations cannot be told by simply saying that it grew out of press-agentry. Nor can it be fully told in terms of the influential career of an Ivy Lee, or a John W. Hill. Efforts to communicate with others and to deal with the force of opinion go back to antiquity; only the tools, degree of specialization, breadth of knowledge, and intensity of effort required today are relatively new. The growth of the field has extended over many decades. The factors inducing its origin and development are many and complex.

The Greek theorists wrote about the importance of the public will, even though they did not specifically use the term *public opinion.* The urban culture of the later Roman Empire gave scope to the opinion process. Certain phrases and ideas in the political vocabulary of the Romans and in the writings of the medieval period are related to modern concepts of public opinion. The Romans inscribed upon their walls the slogan, "S.P.Q.R.—the Senate and the Roman People." Later, they coined the expression *vox populi, vox Dei*—"the voice of the people is the voice of God." Machiavelli wrote, in his *Discoursi,* "Not without reason is the voice of the people compared to the voice of God," and he held that the people must be either "caressed or annihilated."

The communication of information to influence viewpoints or actions can be traced from the earliest civilizations. Archeologists found a farm bulletin in Iraq that told the farmers of 1800 B.C. how to sow their crops, how to irrigate, how to deal with field mice, and how to harvest their crops—an effort not unlike today's distribution of farm bulletins by the U.S. Department of Agriculture. What is known today of ancient Egypt, Assyria, and Persia comes largely from recorded material intended to publicize and glorify the rulers of that day. Much of the literature and art of antiquity was designed to build support for kings, priests, and other leaders. Virgil's *Georgics* was written to persuade urban dwellers to move to the farms to produce food for the growing city. The walls of Pompeii were inscribed with election appeals. Caesar carefully prepared the Romans for his crossing of the Rubicon in 49 B.C. by sending reports to Rome on his epic achievements as governor of Gaul, and historians believe he wrote his *Commentaries* as propaganda for himself.

Rudimentary elements of public relations can be found in the history of ancient India. In writings of the earliest times, there is mention of the king's spies, whose functions included, besides espionage, keeping the king in touch with public opinion, championing the king in public, and spreading rumors favorable to the government.[1] Public relations was used many centuries ago in England, where the kings maintained Lords Chancellor as "Keepers of the King's Conscience." These chancellors surely offer a historical counterpart to today's practitioners. Long before the complexities of communication, there was acknowledged need for a third party to facilitate communication and adjustment between the government and the people. So it was with the church, tradesmen, and craftsmen. The word *propaganda* was born in the seventeenth century, when the Catholic Church set up its *Congregatio de propaganda,* "congregation for propagating the faith."

The American beginnings of public relations are to be found in the American Revolution, which brought the struggle for power between the patrician-led patriots and the commercial, propertied Tories. Great efforts to gain public support were made during the conflict between the trade and property interests led by Hamilton and the planter-and-farmer bloc led by Jefferson, during the struggle between Jackson's agrarian frontiersmen and the financial forces of Nicholas Biddle, and during the nation's greatest internal conflict of all, the Civil War.

The twentieth-century developments in this field are directly tied to the power struggles evoked by the political reform movements, from Theodore Roosevelt to Jimmy Carter. These movements, reflecting strong tides of protest against entrenched power groups, were the catalytic agents for much of the growth, since the jockeying of political and economic groups for dominance created the desire of each cause to have the public on its side.

Public relations has also grown in response to the need for our swiftly advancing technology to gain public acceptance and utilization. For example, when the Bell Telephone System switched to all-number telephone dialing, it ran into a storm of public opposition on the West Coast from the Anti Digit Dialing League, organized by Carl May against what he called the "cult of technology."[2]

The history of public relations is meaningful only when it is related to these power conflicts and recurring crises of change. For example, it is not mere coincidence that in the past, large business interests have taken public relations most seriously when their positions of power were challenged or threatened by the forces of labor, the farmer, the small shopkeeper, or a maturing generation. Nor is it a coincidence that labor's programs have been intensified when an adverse public reaction to labor was crystallizing in regulatory legislation. Similarly, the most intense developments in public relations within government have come in periods of crisis: World War I, the Great Depression, World War II, the Korean War, Vietnam, and the uneasy years with Russia, China, and the Middle East.

So the origins of the art and practice must be examined in their natural social and historical settings.

The american beginnings

Utilization of publicity to raise funds, promote causes, boost commercial ventures, sell land, and build box-office personalities in the United States is older than the nation. The American talent for promotion can be traced back to the first settlements on the East Coast in the sixteenth century. And probably the first systematic effort on this continent to raise funds was that sponsored by Harvard College in 1641, when that infant institution sent a trio of preachers to England on a "begging mission." Once in England, they notified Harvard that they needed a fund-raising brochure—now a standard item in a fund drive—and in response to this request came *New England's First Fruits,* largely written in Massachusetts but printed in London in 1643, the first of countless billions of public relations pamphlets and brochures.[3]

The tools and techniques of public relations have long been an important part of the weaponry in political conflict. Sustained campaigns to move and manipulate public opinion go back to the Revolutionary War and the work of Samuel Adams and his cohorts. These revolutionaries understood the importance of public support, and knew intuitively how to arouse and channel it. *They used pen, platform, pulpit, staged events, symbols, the leak, and political organization*—in a determined, imaginative, and unrelenting way. Adams worked tirelessly to first arouse and then organize public opinion, proceeding always on the assumption that "the bulk of mankind are more led by their senses than by their reason." Early on, he discerned that *public opinion results from the march of events and the way these events are seen by those active in public affairs.* He once wrote to Joseph Warren, ". . . it will be wise for us to be ready for all Events, that we may make the best improvement of them." And Adams would create events to meet a need if none were at hand to serve his purpose.[4]

Today's patterns of public relations practice have been shaped far more than most practitioners realize by innovations in mobilizing public opinion developed by Samuel Adams and his daring fellow revolutionaries. In fomenting revolt against England, these propagandists, operating largely from the shadows, developed and demonstrated the power of these techniques:

1. The necessity of an organization to implement actions made possible by a public relations campaign—e.g., the Sons of Liberty, organized in Boston in January 1766, and the Committees of Correspondence, also born in Boston, in 1772.[5]
2. The use of symbols that are easily identifiable and emotion-arousing—e.g., the Liberty Tree.
3. The use of slogans that compress complex issues into easy-to-quote, easy-to-remember stereotypes—e.g., "Taxation without representation is tyranny."
4. Staged events that catch public attention, provoke discussion, and thus crystallize unstructured public opinion—e.g., the Boston Tea Party.[6]
5. The importance of getting your side of a story to the public first, so that your interpretation of events becomes the accepted one—e.g., the Boston Massacre.[7]
6. The necessity for a sustained saturation campaign using these techniques through all available channels of communication to penetrate the public mind with a new idea or a new conviction.

The emotion-laden Revolutionary campaign set patterns for the nation's political battles that were to follow.[8]

In weak contrast to the bold, effective ways of communication developed by the revolutionists, the Tories, supporters of King George and the British Empire, relied not so much on propaganda as on legal and military pressures—to no avail. Little wonder than an exuberant Sam Adams would exult when he heard the firing at Lexington, "Oh, what a glorious morning is this!" He and his fellow propagandists had done their work well.[9]

The next landmark in public relations in the new nation came with the publication of 85 letters written to the newspapers in 1787–88 by Alexander Hamilton, John Madison, and John Jay. Later collected in book form as *The Federalist,* the letters urged ratification of the Constitution. David Truman says, "The entire effort of which *The Federalist* was a part was one of the most *skillful and important examples of pressure group activity* in American history." [Emphasis added.] Morrison and Commager hold that "unless the Federalists had been shrewd in manipulation as they were sound in theory, their arguments could not have prevailed."

Historian Allan Nevins extravagantly described these propaganda efforts as "history's finest public relations job." He wrote, "Obtaining national acceptance of the Constitution was essentially a public relations exercise, and Hamilton, with his keen instinct for public relations, took thought not only to the product but to the ready acquiescence of thoughtful people; and he imparted his views to others. . . . Once the Constitution came before the country, the rapidity with which Hamilton moved was a striking exemplification of good public relations. He knew that if a vacuum develops in popular opinion, ignorant and foolish views will fill it. No time must be lost in providing accurate facts and sound ideas."[10]

The first clear beginnings of *the public presidential campaign* and of *the presidential press secretary's function* came in the era of Andrew Jackson and in the work of Amos Kendall. In the late 1820s and early 1830s, the common man won the ballot and the free public school was started. The literacy of the public grew greatly, and its political interest was stimulated by a burgeoning, strident party press. As the people gained political power, it became necessary to campaign for their support. No longer was government the exclusive concern of the patrician few. "The new Democracy was heavily weighted with what gentlemen were pleased to call the rabble." With the rise of democracy in America came increasing rights for, and power of, the individual.[11] The ensuing power struggle produced an unsung pioneer in public relations, Amos Kendall.

As the key member of President Jackson's "Kitchen Cabinet," Kendall served Jackson as a *pollster, counselor, ghost writer, and publicist.* The "Kitchen Cabinet" was unexcelled at creating events to mold opinion. On all vital issues that arose, Jackson consulted these key advisors, most of whom, like Kendall, were former newspapermen.

Jackson, a man unlettered in political or social philosophy, could not get his ideas across with ease. Like many a modern executive, he needed a specialist to convey his ideas to Congress and the country. Jackson's political campaigns and his government policies clearly reveal the influence of Kendall's strategy, sense of public opinion, and skill as a communicator.[12]

The president of the Bank of the United States, Nicholas Biddle, and his associates were fully alert to the methods of influencing public opinion in their battle with Jackson and Kendall. In fact, banks were the first businesses to use the press for this purpose; by loans to editors and placement of advertisements, they influenced many newspapers and silenced others. John C. Calhoun asserted as early as 1816 that the banks had "in great measure, control over the press." Biddle's publicist, Mathew St. Clair Clarke, saturated the nation's press with press releases, reports, and pamphlets stating the bank's case. In 1830, the bank spent $7,000 for printing and distributing a bank report and pamphlet by Albert Gallatin. In March 1831, the bank's board authorized Biddle "to cause to be prepared and circulated such documents and papers as may communicate to the people information in regard to the nature and operations of the bank." But the pamphlets, the many articles planted in the press, the build-up of Davy Crockett, and the lobbying efforts by Biddle and his associates were unavailing against the forces of Jackson and Kendall.[13]

The middle years

The modern concept and terminology of public relations were little known in those days of the young America. There were few inducements for its full-scale development, no means of mass communication on a national basis. Group relationships were relatively simple; people were relatively self-sufficient and independent. But many of the generating forces had their origins in the nineteenth century.

Alan Raucher writes, "Three major antecedents of twentieth-century publicity can be distinguished from their sometimes shady past. One of these was press-agentry. Another was advertising. A third antecedent for publicity, rather unexpectedly, came from business critics and reformers. By the first decade of the century, those three elements, largely unnoticed by contemporaries, fused into a new compound."[14] Of the elements that formed this new compound, public relations, three merit a few words. The roots of a practice so varied, a concept so diffused, are to be found in many places.

Press-agentry

To state that public relations has evolved from press-agentry is a gross over-simplification—but the statement does contain a kernel of truth. Systematic efforts to attract or divert public attention are as old as efforts to persuade and propagandize. Much of what we define as public relations was labeled press-agentry when it was being used to promote land settlement in our unsettled West, or to build up political heroes. For example, the legend of Daniel Boone, now woven deeply in the fabric of our culture, was the creation of a landowner promoting settlement in Kentucky.

Elements of press-agentry are to be found in many public relations programs today, but not as strongly as the critics of public relations assert. Mainly, press-agentry, beginning with Phineas T. Barnum and the theatrical press agents who followed, developed as an adjunct to show business and advertising; and box-office enterprises are still the prime employers of press agents.

Amos Kendall's time brought an effective demonstration of the "buildup" when Jackson's opponents created the myth of Davy Crockett in an effort to woo the frontier vote away from Old Hickory. Crockett's press agent was Mathew St. Clair Clarke. (The Davy Crockett legend was given an intensive if short-lived revival in the 1950s, when Walt Disney featured that "yaller flower of the forest" in movies, TV programs, books, and records. Disney did not create the Crockett legend; he embellished it.[15]

But the master of them all was Phineas Taylor Barnum—and he knew it. Barnum's life span, 1810–91, covered a period of great importance in the evolution of public relations; his influence still lives today. Barnum's recent biographer, Irving Wallace, writes, "Barnum's showmanship was evident not only in a canny instinct that enabled him to give the masses what they wanted, but also in his ability to dictate to them a desire for what he thought they should want. . . . Every man has his star. Barnum's star was an exclamation mark."[16] Promoter Barnum also employed a press agent, Richard F. "Tody" Hamilton. Dexter Fellows, a latter-day circus drumbeater, said that Hamilton developed exaggeration into a fine art: "Chary as Barnum was of giving credit to anyone but himself, he has been quoted as saying that he owed more of his success to Tody Hamilton than to any other man."[17]

Success begets imitators. The showman led the way, and others followed in an ever-increasing number. During the two decades before 1900, the art infiltrated from show business into closely related enterprises. In due time, it could be found in almost every type of enterprise that needed to attract the public's attention. Book publishers, for example, found this new technique profitable in boosting book sales.

But as press agents grew in number and their exploits became more outrageous—although successful, more often than not—it was natural that they would arouse the hostility and suspicion of editors, and inevitable that the practice and its practitioners would become tainted. This inherent suspicion remains as part of public relations' heritage.

Political campaigning

Public relations has long been an essential part of the political party's apparatus. Virginian John Beckley must rank among the first of a long line of political propagandists and organizers who have made our party system work. He was a devoted aide of Thomas Jefferson in building what was then known as the Republican party but today is the Democratic party. He was Jefferson's eyes and ears, his propagandist, "one of the leading party organizers of the 1790s."[18]

However, the development of modern political campaign methods and techniques, except insofar as these have been modified by television, is largely rooted in the last decade of the nineteenth century. Increasingly, "the activities of the public relations man have become a significant influence in processes crucial to democratic government."[19] In the 1880s and 1890s, techniques used by the political party managers changed with the changing American environment, then rushing headlong toward industrialization and urbanization.

The bitter, close race in the 1876 Tilden-Hayes presidential campaign jarred party leaders. They began searching for new ways to woo the support of the voters, whose numbers were rapidly increasing because of high birthrates and immigration. The campaign of 1888 saw the introduction of *campaign literature on a mass scale and the increased use of newspapers.* These developments stemmed from improved printing technology, such as improved presses and the Linotype, the abundant supply of cheap paper, and a growing literacy—factors that were also increasing the number of newspapers.

The need seen by both parties to "educate" the new immigrants spurred the evolution of the party "literary bureau" into *a press bureau, now a standard fixture of political campaigns.*[20] For example, in Indiana alone, the GOP distributed some 300,000 pamphlets explaining General Harrison's stand on the liquor question and another 300,000 fliers refuting the charge that Harrison considered a dollar a day a fair wage. Also, 300,000 lithographed portraits of the general were sent out, along with "uncounted bushels of tin buttons." This 1888 campaign also saw the introduction of the "front-porch campaign"—a technique later used successfully by William McKinley in 1896 and Warren G. Harding in 1920. From mid-July until November, General Harrison sat on his front porch in Indianapolis and welcomed nearly 200,000 supporters.[21]

The hard-hitting Bryan-McKinley campaign of 1896 marked the first use of modern political campaigning methods, setting a pattern that served for sixty years. Both parties set up their campaign headquarters in Chicago, from whence flowed a heavy stream of pamphlets, posters, press releases, and other campaign propaganda, now a standard part of the American political campaign. The 1896 pattern of campaigning was, for the most part, repeated in 1900 and continued in subsequent campaigns with slight modification, until the introduction of radio broadcasting in the mid-1920s.

In this precedent-setting 1896 campaign, the Republicans relied primarily on a costly publicity effort and on GOP-financed pilgrimages of special groups to McKinley's front porch in Canton, Ohio. The penny-pinched Democrats relied mainly on the oratory of Bryan, who traveled across the country in the first campaign train. McKinley's Chicago headquarters spent nearly a half-million dollars for printing, and the publicity bureau, under Perry Heath, flooded the nation's press with *releases, cartoons, and boiler plate,* and the nation's homes and stores with *posters and pamphlets.* A conservative estimate placed the GOP campaign budget at $3.5 million. The Republicans even took a rudimentary public opinion poll, today a central instrument of political campaigns. The large-scale publicity bureau and the campaign train used in this contest became fixtures of national election campaigns in a nation whose electorate now stretched across a 3,000-mile continent.[22]

As the population grew, the voters became more and more out of reach of the stump speaker, and indirect methods of communication were inevitably pushed to the fore. By 1900, the manager of the political press bureau, both national and state, had assumed most of the functions that characterize today's practitioner.

Business practices

The last two decades of the nineteenth century brought the discernible beginnings of today's practice. It is here that we find the roots of a vocation that flowered in the seedbed years of 1900–17.

The fundamental force setting the stage for public relations in the twentieth century was the wild, frenzied, and bold development of industry, railroads, and utilities in America's post–Civil War era. In the 25 breathtaking years from 1875 to 1900, America doubled its population and jammed its people into cities, went into mass production and enthroned the machine, spanned the nation with rail and wire communications, developed the mass media of press and magazines, and replaced the plantation baron with the prince of industry and the versatile frontiersman with the specialized factory hand. All this laid the foundation for the mightiest industrial machine the world has yet known.

The rise of powerful monopolies, the concentration of wealth and power, and the roughshod tactics of the robber barons and their imitators were to bring a wave of protest and reform in the early 1900s. Contemporary public relations was to emerge out of the melee of the opposing forces in this period of the nation's rapid growth. Goldman observes, "Shouldering aside agriculture, large-scale commerce and industry became dominant over the life of the nation. Big business was committed to the doctrine that the less the public knew of its operations, the more efficient and profitable—even the more socially useful—the operation would be."[23] In this era of "the public be damned," the bold exploitation of the people and of the natural resources of this rich continent was bound to bring, ultimately, protest and reform once the people became aroused.

The prevailing hard-bitten attitudes of businessmen toward the public—be they employees, customers, or voters—was epitomized in the brutal methods used by Henry Clay Frick to crush a labor union in the Carnegie-Frick Steel Company's Homestead, Pennsylvania, plant in 1892. Frick directed the struggle while Carnegie indifferently viewed events from afar in his Scottish castle, seemingly unperturbed by the brutality and killings. The employees' strike was ultimately broken and the union destroyed by the use of the Pennsylvania state militia. Coldblooded might won this battle, but the employees would eventually win the war. Much of public relations history is woven into this unending struggle between employer and employee that today, fortunately, is fought with public relations men, not Pinkertons.[24]

Historian Merle Curti observes, "Corporations gradually began to realize the importance of combating hostility and courting public favor. The expert in the field of public relations was an inevitable phenomenon in view of the need for the services he could provide. As early as the 1890s, George Harvey, a newspaperman and publisher, was engaging in public relations activities for Thomas Fortune Ryan and Harry Payne Whitney, well-known promoters and financiers."[25] Even before this, in about 1888, the Mutual Life Insurance Company had employed a Charles J. Smith to manage a "species of literary bureau." According to one contemporary writer, "In ordinary times [Smith's] activities have been general and rather unimportant, but in time of emergency they are enlarged; for instance, last September when the investigation began, he turned all his strength to preparing articles calculated to counteract the reports of the investigations sent out through regular news channels."[26]

Raucher holds that advertising is one of the antecedents of public relations. Although the two functions are distinct in today's business enterprise, they have developed along parallel lines, with overlapping of function, blurring of distinctions, and confusion in the public mind. Advertising evolved to meet the needs of business; public relations evolved partly for this reason, but mainly for others. Advertising and product promotion, today intertwined and often confused, have their roots in the post–Civil War industrialization. With the introduction of mass-production methods, more and more businesses needed regional or national distribution of their soaps, foods, and other products. For example, "To break down consumer bias against eating meat that had been slaughtered weeks earlier and half a continent away, Swift turned to advertising."[27] By 1879, advertising revenue in newspapers, much of it promoting patent medicines, totaled $21 million.

The *first corporate public relations department,* in the contemporary meaning of this term, was established by George Westinghouse for his newly founded electric corporation in 1889. Westinghouse had organized his firm in 1886 to promote his then-revolutionary alternating-current system of electricity. Thomas A. Edison's Edison General Electric Company was already established, with its direct-current system of distribution. The now-famous "battle of the currents" ensued. Immediately Edison, aided by his right-hand man, the astute Samuel Insull, launched a scare campaign against the Westinghouse AC system. McDonald records, "Edison General Electric attempted to prevent the development of alternating current by unscrupulous political action and by even less savory promotional tactics. . . . The promotional activity was a series of spectacular stunts aimed at dramatizing the deadliness of high voltage alternating current, the most sensational being the development and promotion of the electric chair as a means of executing criminals."[28] The state of New York adopted electrocution in 1888, and the next year, Westinghouse realized he had to get his story to the public. He hired a Pittsburgh newspaperman, E.H. Heinrichs, who served Westinghouse as his personal press representative until the latter's death in March 1914. Heinrichs later said that he was hired not because of the "battle of the currents," but because Westinghouse, like today's executive, did not have time to deal with the press. Heinrichs was the company's main channel through which news about the company passed to the press, and he was the one who received reporters.[29] Then, as now, it took specialized skill to gain a hearing in the public forum and to deal with media demands.

Other activities

Still other threads in the fabric were first woven in the 1880s. The American fund-raising drive, an important task today, was further developed in the Civil War. Jay Cooke, "the first to understand the psychology of mass salesmanship," conceived and directed the first American fund-raising drive. "A propagandist of truly heroic proportions," Cooke sold war bonds for the Union by first selling patriotism and building a militant public opinion. Many of his techniques reappeared in the bond drives of World Wars I and II. Also by the time of the Civil War, the U.S. Marine Corps was using advertising on a regular basis to attract recruits. And in the Spanish-American War of 1898, the work of Cuban propagandists did much to arouse American sympathies for Cuba and to discredit Spain. This *junta* used press releases and mass meetings to raise funds and promote support for the Cuban cause from 1895 on.

The Association of American Railroads claims that it was the first organization to use the term *public relations*—in 1897, in the *Year Book of Railway Literature*. Railroads, born in the era of "the buccaneering orgy" and of business autonomy, have long maintained public relations departments, but few have ever achieved satisfactory public relationships. *Longevity of the public relations function does not always equate with efficacy.*

Even professional groups were taking cognizance of public opinion more than a century ago. In 1855, the American Medical Association passed a resolution "urging the secretary of the Association to offer every facility possible to the reporters of the public press to enable them to furnish full and accurate reports of the transactions." And in 1884, the AMA launched the first of its many programs to counter the attacks of the antivivisectionists. Evidence that public relations thinking is not brand new is shown in the letter of Theodore N. Vail, rare for its time, reproduced in Figure 4–1.

FIGURE 4–1

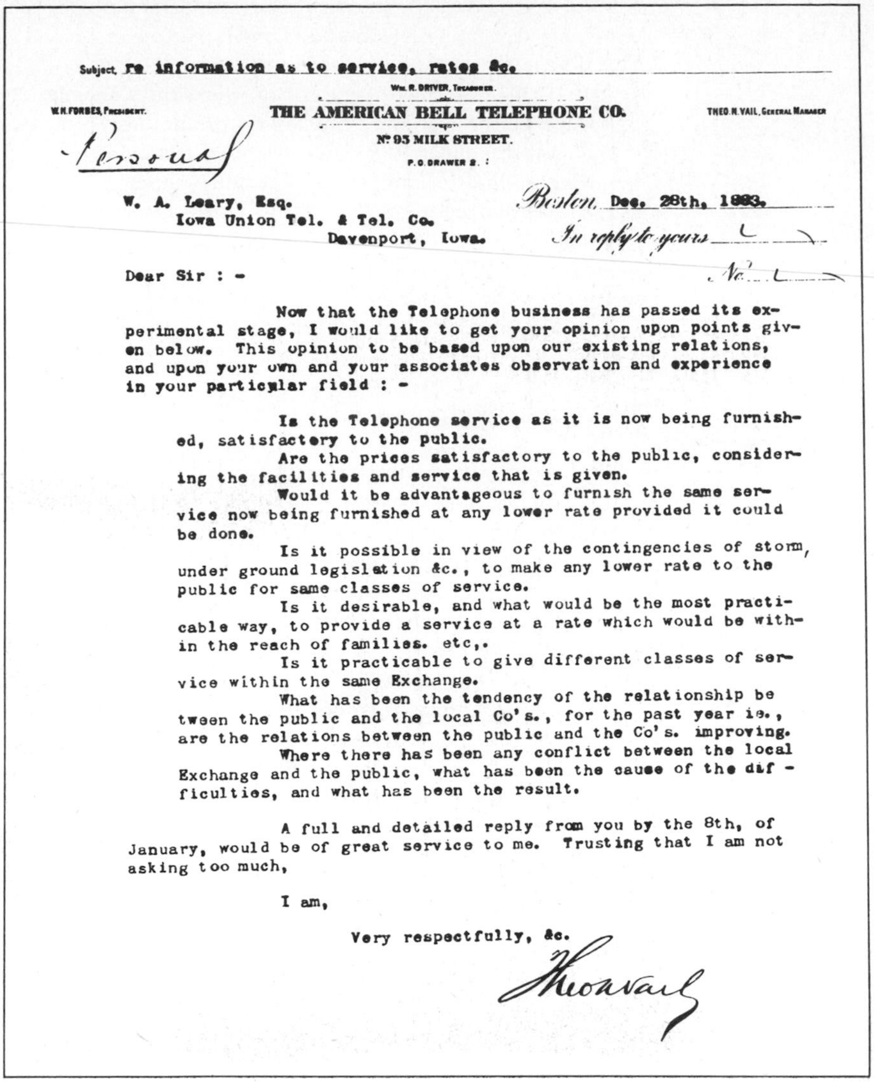

Subject, re information as to service, rates &c.

WM. R. DRIVER, TREASURER.

W.H. FORBES, PRESIDENT. THE AMERICAN BELL TELEPHONE CO. THEO. N. VAIL, GENERAL MANAGER

Nº 95 MILK STREET.

P. O. DRAWER 2.

Personal

W. A. Leary, Esq.
Iowa Union Tel. & Tel. Co.
Davenport, Iowa.

Boston, Dec. 28th, 1883.

In reply to yours ___

No. ___

Dear Sir : -

Now that the Telephone business has passed its experimental stage, I would like to get your opinion upon points given below. This opinion to be based upon our existing relations, and upon your own and your associates observation and experience in your particular field : -

Is the Telephone service as it is now being furnished, satisfactory to the public.

Are the prices satisfactory to the public, considering the facilities and service that is given.

Would it be advantageous to furnish the same service now being furnished at any lower rate provided it could be done.

Is it possible in view of the contingencies of storm, under ground legislation &c., to make any lower rate to the public for same classes of service.

Is it desirable, and what would be the most practicable way, to provide a service at a rate which would be within the reach of families. etc,.

Is it practicable to give different classes of service within the same Exchange.

What has been the tendency of the relationship between the public and the local Co's., for the past year ie., are the relations between the public and the Co's. improving.

Where there has been any conflict between the local Exchange and the public, what has been the cause of the difficulties, and what has been the result.

A full and detailed reply from you by the 8th, of January, would be of great service to me. Trusting that I am not asking too much,

I am,

Very respectfully, &c.

Theo. N. Vail

Evolution to maturity

Although the roots of today's practice lie far in the past, its *definite beginnings* date from the early 1900s, when the world entered the century that took mankind from the horse and buggy to the moon. The dividing lines may be blurred, but the growth can be traced through five main periods of development:

1. 1900–1917—Era of Muckraking Journalism countered by defensive publicity, a period of far-reaching political reforms.

2. 1917–1919—World War I, which brought dramatic demonstrations of the power of organized promotion to kindle a fervent patriotism—to sell war bonds, enlist soldiers, and raise millions for welfare work.

3. 1919–1933—Roaring Twenties Era, when the principles and practices of publicity learned in the war were put to use promoting products, earning acceptance for changes wrought by the war-accelerated technology, winning political battles, and raising millions of dollars for charitable causes.

4. 1933–1945—Roosevelt Era of the Great Depression and World War II, events profound and far-reaching in their impact, which advanced the art and extended the practice of public relations.

5. 1945–present—Postindustrial Era, which brought a tremendous boom in public relations practice, a maturing concept, and progress toward professionalism.

The muckraking era

The muckraking journalists—David Graham Phillips, Lincoln Steffens, Upton Sinclair, Ida Tarbell, and others—effectively exploited the newly developed national forums provided by the popular magazines, national press services, and feature syndicates. Regier says, "Muckraking . . . was the inevitable result of decades of indifference to the illegalities and immoralities attendant upon the industrial development of America."[30] The reform and protest period extended roughly from 1900 to 1912. The muckrakers took their case to the people and got action, a fact that perceptive observers noted. The agitation before 1900 had been primarily among farmers and laborers. Now the urban middle classes took up the cry against corruption in government and the abuses of Big Business. The little fish did not enjoy being swallowed by the big ones. These writers thundered out their denunciations in boldface in the popular magazines and metropolitan newspapers, which now had huge circulations. By 1900, there were at least 50 well-known national magazines, several with circulations of 100,000 or more. The *Ladies Home Journal,* founded only 17 years before, was approaching a circulation of 1 million. The impact of the growing mass media was beginning to be felt.[31]

The muckraker was a key figure in the Progressive movement, which found its strength in the *journalism of exposure.* "Before there could be action, there had to be information and exhortation. Grievances had to be given specific objects. These the muckraker supplied. It was muckraking that brought the diffuse malaise of the public into focus."[32] The work was dramatically begun by Thomas W. Lawson's *Frenzied Finance,* appearing as a series in *McClure's* magazine in 1903. Ida Tarbell's *History of the Standard Oil Company,* described at the time as "a fearless unmasking of moral criminality masquerading under the robes of respectability and Christianity," and Upton Sinclair's novel, *The Jungle,* exposing the foul conditions in the meat-packing industry, both produced violent public reactions. Public protest and reform brought regulatory legislation and a wave of "trust-busting." Businessmen were forced to take the defensive. The corporations, the good ones along with the ruthless ones, had lost contact with their publics. For a while they sat helplessly by, inarticulate and frustrated, waiting apprehensively for the next issue of *McClure's* magazine.

Business leaders, long accustomed to a veil of secrecy, felt the urge to speak out in self-defense but did not know how. Their first instinct was to turn to their advertising men and lawyers. In the first stages of the muckraking era, many great corporations sought to silence the attacks from the press by the judicious and calculated placement and withdrawal of advertising. Thus, the newly established advertising agency was brought into public relations early. In the wake of New York State's Armstrong Committee's exposure of wrongdoing in the insurance industry, the New York Mutual Life Insurance Company commissioned N.W. Ayer to carry out an advertising campaign to restore public confidence in the insurance business.[33]

The nation's first publicity firm, The Publicity Bureau, forerunner of today's public relations agency, was founded in Boston in mid-1900 by George V.S. Michaelis, Herbert Small, and Thomas O. Marvin "to do a general press agent business for as many clients as possible for as good pay as the traffic would bear." Michaelis, a Boston newspaperman once described by an associate as "a young man of many expedients," took the lead in organizing this new enterprise, and was with it until 1909 or thereabouts. One of the first people hired was James Drummond Ellsworth, who would later work with Theodore N. Vail in building the program of the American Telephone & Telegraph Company.[34]

The Publicity Bureau came into national prominence in 1906, when it was employed by the nation's railroads to head off adverse regulatory legislation then being pushed in Congress by President Roosevelt. Ray Stannard Baker reported: "The fountainhead of public information is the newspaper. The first concern, then, of the railroad organization was to reach the newspaper. For this purpose a firm of publicity agents, with headquarters in Boston, was chosen. . . . Immediately the firm expanded. It increased its Boston staff; it opened offices in New York, Chicago, Washington, St. Louis, Topeka, Kansas . . . and it employed agents in South Dakota, California, and elsewhere."[35] Baker records that The Publicity Bureau operated secretly, "careful not to advertise the fact that they are in any way connected with the railroads." *This firm effectively used the tools of fact-finding, publicity, and personal contact to saturate the nation's press, particularly weeklies, with the railroads' propaganda.* The campaign was to little avail, however, because the Hepburn Act, a moderately tough regulatory measure, was passed in 1906, after President Roosevelt used the nation's press and the platform to publicize a more persuasive case. Failure of their nationwide publicity effort caused railroad executives to reassess their public relations methods and, within a few years, to set up their own public relations departments. The Publicity Bureau faded into oblivion sometime after 1911.

Other industries, fighting fire with fire, turned to the specialist who could tell business's story in the public forum—the newspaperman. Thus began *the large-scale recruitment of newspapermen to serve as interpreters for corporations and other public institutions.* Some newspapermen took The Publicity Bureau's lead and organized similar firms. With waves of the popular revolt beating against Capitol Hill, the opportunity for such a firm in Washington became apparent. Willian Wolff Smith quit his job as correspondent for the *New York Sun* and the *Cincinnati Enquirer* to open a "publicity business" in the capital in 1902. A *New York Times* reporter later recalled that the Smith firm solicited "press-agent employment from anybody who had business before Congress."[36]

Smith's agency also lasted for little more than a decade. The third agency set up in this seedbed era—Parker & Lee—had an even shorter life; it lasted less than four years, but the junior partner, as we shall see, left a lasting mark on this emerging craft.

The Hamilton Wright Organization, Inc., dates from 1908 when Hamilton Mercer Wright, a free-lance journalist and publicist, opened an office in San Francisco. He moved to New York City in 1917. Wright's first publicity work was to publicize California for the California Promotion Committee. His agency's first account was the promotion of the Philippine Islands on behalf of U.S. business interests. His son and grandson, both carrying the same name, followed in the founder's footsteps by specializing in promotion of foreign countries in the United States.

The fifth agency started in this decade would, like Hamilton Wright's, endure. Pendleton Dudley, who was to become for half a century an influential figure in public relations, took his friend Ivy Lee's advice and in 1909 opened a publicity office in New York's Wall Street district. For 57 years, until he died at the age of 90, Dudley remained the active head of his firm, Dudley-Anderson-Yutzy.

The second agency organized in Washington, D.C., was that of Thomas R. Shipp.[37] Shipp, like William Wolff Smith and George R. Parker, was a native of Indiana and a former newspaperman. He set out on his own after spending six years learning the arts of publicity and politics under two experts, Theodore Roosevelt and Gifford Pinchot. Shipp opened his "publicity company" in 1914, at about the time Smith was closing his to return to law school.

Ivy Lee

Ivy Lee: For the most part, these ex-newspapermen in the employ of business countered the muckrakers with whitewash press-agentry, demonstrating little grasp of the fundamental problems in the conflict. But there were exceptions. One of these was Ivy Ledbetter Lee.

Lee, son of a Georgia minister, was a Princeton graduate who, as a reporter covering the business world, saw the possibility of earning more money in the service of private organizations who were seeking a voice. After five years as a reporter, Lee quit his poorly paid job on the *World* in 1903 to work for the Citizen's Union, an organization supporting Seth Low's campaign for mayor of New York. Lee's work in this post led to a job in the press bureau of the Democratic National Committee during the 1904 presidential campaign. Some time after the election, he teamed up with George F. Parker, former Buffalo newspaperman and veteran political publicist, to organize a public relations firm in New York City.

Parker had directed the publicity for Grover Cleveland's three campaigns for the presidency, but Cleveland was not wise enough to use him as a press secretary during his two terms as president.[38] In 1904, Parker was recalled to political battle to direct publicity for the Democratic National Committee in the futile campaign to unseat President Roosevelt, and the young Lee was hired to assist him. Out of their association during the campaign came the decision to form a partnership. However, their relationship was neither profitable nor happy, and the firm dissolved in 1908, when Ivy Lee became the Pennsylvania Railroad's first publicity agent. That year, Parker set up another partnership with C.A. Bridge, then city editor of the *New York Herald.* Presumably the Parker-Bridge partnership folded in 1913, because that was when Parker was appointed to handle publicity for the Protestant Episcopal Church, a position he held until 1919. The next year, Parker returned to politics when General Leonard Wood hired him to provide counsel on his campaign for the GOP presidential nomination.[39]

Lee, when appointed to represent George F. Baer and his associates in the anthracite coal strike, issued a *"Declaration of Principles," which was to have a profound influence on the evolution of press-agentry into publicity and of publicity into public relations.* Eric Goldman observes that this declaration "marks the emergence of a second stage of public relations. The public was no longer to be ignored, in the traditional manner of business, nor fooled, in the continuing manner of the press agent."[40] It was to be informed. Lee's declaration, mailed to all city editors, reads:

> This is not a secret press bureau. All our work is done in the open. We aim to supply news. This is not an advertising agency; if you think any of our matter ought properly to go to your business office, do not use it. Our matter is accurate. Further details on any subject treated will be supplied promptly, and any editor will be assisted most cheerfully in verifying directly any statement of fact. . . . In brief, our plan is, frankly and openly, on behalf of business concerns and public institutions, to supply to the press and public of the United States prompt and accurate information concerning subjects which it is of value and interest to the public to know about.[41]

Lee put this new approach to work in the anthracite coal strike. The work of reporters assigned to cover the strike was enormously simplified because all channels of communication were open. Although the press was not permitted to be present during the strike conferences, Lee did provide reports after each meeting. *Lee was among the first to use the "handout" system on a large scale.* His success in getting a good press for the coal operators led to the retention of Parker and Lee by the Pennsylvania Railroad in the summer of 1906. Lee handled this account.[42]

During this period, Lee was using the term *publicity* to mean what we call public relations; his concept steadily grew, and his success grew with it. In December 1914, at the suggestion of Arthur Brisbane, Lee was appointed as a personal adviser to John D. Rockefeller, Jr. At the time, the Rockefellers were being savagely attacked for the strike-breaking activities of their Colorado Fuel and Iron Company. Thus began a long career for him in the service of the Rockefellers.

Contrary to popular belief, Ivy Lee was not hired by John D. Rockefeller, Sr., nor did he originate the elder Rockefeller's practice of giving dimes to children. In fact, Rockefeller, Sr., did not approve his son's hiring of Lee, but he adhered to his long-standing promise not to interfere with the son's decisions. In his long service to the son, Lee did, in fact, provide many services to the founder of Standard Oil. Although his work for the Rockefellers is the most publicized, Lee also served a number of other clients in the years from 1919 until his death in 1934.

Ivy Lee did much to lay the groundwork for contemporary practice. Even though he did not use the term *public relations* until at least 1919, Lee contributed many of the techniques and principles that practitioners follow today. *He was among the first to realize the fallacy of publicity unsupported by good works* and to reason that performance determines the publicity a client gets. He saw the importance of humanizing business and continually stressed the human element. "I try to translate dollars and cents and stocks and dividends into terms of humanity." In his efforts to humanize wealthy businessmen and to put big business in the best possible light, Lee propelled the growth of publicity departments and trained publicity advisors in many institutions. And in his 31 years as a public relations man, Lee changed the scope of what he did from "pure agency" to serving as "a brain trust for the businesses we work with." One of the craft's most forceful spokesmen, he made an occupation of public relations by his practice and preachments. However, Raucher warns, "Ivy Lee's reputation before World War I as the outstanding publicity specialist may easily obscure the general forces which created the new occupation. Lee built his career by exploiting problems of giant corporations in the early twentieth century."[43]

Lee's record, although substantial, is not free from criticism. When he died, he was being criticized for his representation of the German Dye Trust, controlled by I.G. Farben, after Hitler came to power in Germany and the Nazis had taken control of this cartel. Although he never received pay directly from the Nazi government, Lee was paid an annual fee of $25,000 and expenses by the Farben firm from the time he was retained in 1933 until his firm resigned the account shortly after his death in 1934.[44]

Theodore Roosevelt: The part played by Theodore Roosevelt in spurring the evolution has been little noted. The colorful president was a master in the art and power of publicity, and he used his knowledge and skill to gain his political ends. Observers claimed that Roosevelt ruled the country from the newspapers' front pages. One of his first acts upon assuming the presidency was to seek an understanding with the press. Veteran newsman David S. Barry later observed that Roosevelt "knew the value and potent influence of a news paragraph written as he wanted it written and disseminated through the proper influential channels." A *Harper's Weekly* article was titled, "Theodore Roosevelt: Press Agent." Roosevelt's successful and well-publicized antitrust suit against the Northern Securities Company turned the tide against the concentration of economic power. His conservation policies, effectively promoted by Gifford Pinchot in the government's first large-scale publicity program, saved much of America's resources from gross exploitation.

With the growth of mass-circulation newspapers, Roosevelt's canny ability to dominate the front pages demonstrated a new-found power for those with causes to promote. He had a keen sense of news and knew how to stage a story so that it would get maximum attention. Using these skills, Roosevelt advertised and dramatized to the country a point of view that was new and exciting. Frederick Lewis Allen wrote that this was his "most vital contribution to American history." Not only did Roosevelt set patterns, but his skill forced those he fought to develop similar means. He fully *exploited the news media as a new and powerful tool of presidential leadership,* and he remade the laws and the presidency in the process.

Other pioneers: Businessman John D. Rockefeller never appeared to mind criticism, but Philanthropist Rockefeller was cut to his Baptist quick by the accusation that his philanthropies were a means of buying public favor. When the "tainted money" issue flared yet again in 1905, he was hurt and angered. His advisor, the Reverend Frederick T. Gates, urged him to abandon his policies of secrecy, and Rockefeller finally admitted that he needed defense in the public prints.

This led to his employment of Joseph Ignatius Constantine Clarke, colorful Irish newsman, at a then-high salary of $5,000 a year. Clarke, attached to the legal department and given a staff of one stenographer, one office boy, and a man to paste clippings, worked hard to lift the veil of secrecy from Standard Oil and its founder, and with some success. Rockefeller became more open and courteous with reporters, and, starting in October 1908, he published a series of autobiographical articles in *World's Work*. But as the legal and public attacks mounted, the company's executives quit giving Clarke information, and he resigned in frustration in 1913, the first in a long list of practitioners who have quit because of lack of administrative support.[45]

The period 1900–17 saw an intensive development of public relations skills by the railroads and the public utilities. These businesses, particularly the local transit companies, were the first to feel the heat of public anger and to be brought under public regulation. The Interstate Commerce Act had set the pattern. In a five-year period, 1908–13, more than 2,000 laws affecting railroads were enacted by state legislatures and by Congress.

From 1897 on, the term *public relations* appeared with increasing frequency in railroad literature and in speeches of railroad men. In 1909, the *Railway Age Gazette* pleaded for "better public relations" in an editorial entitled, "Wanted: A Diplomatic Corps." J. Hampton Baumgartner, another pioneer, was hired in 1910 to be "in charge of publicity and public relations of the Baltimore & Ohio Railroad." In 1913, he gave a talk to the Virginia Press Association on "The Railroads and Public Relations," explaining that, in response to agitation, railroads had "endeavored to establish closer relations with the public, chiefly through the medium of the press and with its cooperation."

As of 1909, the Illinois Central Railroad was employing an assistant manager who served in a two-way capacity, to interpret the public to the company as well as to publicize the IC. And as early as 1905, Charles S. Mellen, president of the New Haven, had told fellow New England railroad executives, "Publicity, not secrecy, will win hereafter. Corporations must come out into the open and see and be seen. They must take the public into their confidence." The failures of the Pennsylvania and New Haven railroads make it plain that it takes more than platitudes to build productive public relationships.

Henry Ford pioneered in the positive use of public relations in selling cars. His work dramatized the worth of publicity as a supplement to paid advertising. Prof. David Lewis, who has chronicled Ford's public relations story, says, "The industrialist is revealed . . . as perhaps the most astute self-advertiser in the whole history of a land that has produced its full share of promoters and showmen." From 1908 on, Ford and his associates sought publicity, in sharp contrast to their publicity-shy business contemporaries of that era.[46]

Ford sensed the value of auto-racing events in publicizing the performance of his new gas buggies. The house organ, *Ford Times*, was started in 1908 "to introduce hints among members of the Ford organization." Ford was among the first to use opinion surveys; in 1912, he had 1,000 Model T owners queried as to why they had bought Fords. As another promotional device, he organized Ford owners into clubs. And he pulled out all the publicity stops in 1914, in announcing his $5 a day for an eight-hour day, a story that was to shake the industrial community and make him a world figure.

Another businessman, Samuel Insull, was equally innovative in the expanding utility field in these years. In the late 1890s, his Chicago Edison Company relied on sales techniques, free wiring, and rate cuts to increase the use of electricity. In 1901, Insull created an advertising department to ensure specialized treatment of his many messages to the public; in 1902, he built a demonstration "Electric Cottage"; and *in 1903, he started* Chicago, The Electric City, *an external house organ, "to gain understanding and good will" of the community*. Insull began using films in

1909, *perhaps the first to use movies for public relations purposes.* He initiated "bill stuffers" in 1912, and in later years used these for political messages. He and his associates made countless public speeches, many of which were reprinted for wider distribution. Insull knew well that those identified with an institution are the prime determinants of its public reputation.[47]

The American Telephone and Telegraph Company was a pioneer in public relations as well as in communications. Although public relations got short shrift after Theodore N. Vail was forced out in 1887 until he was returned to power in 1902, *the Bell company did organize a "literary bureau" in Boston around 1890* and was one of the first clients of The Publicity Bureau. After Vail returned as a director, the policies that are today identified with AT&T began to take shape, and they were brought to the fore when Vail became president in 1907. Vail hired James Drummond Ellsworth and began a publicity program.

Efforts were undertaken to eliminate public criticism through efficient operation and consideration for the needs of subscribers. A systematic method of answering complaints was put into effect. Unlike other utilities, Bell did not fight public regulation, but accepted it as a price for monopoly. Vail and Ellsworth, in collaboration with the N.W. Ayer advertising agency, began an institutional advertising campaign that continues to this day, with the same agency handling the account. AT&T showed the way in public relations advertising.

Nonbusiness growth: In this same period, equally important public relations developments were taking place outside the business community. For instance, the seedbed years brought innovative publicity programs to colleges and universities. At Yale, Anson Phelps Stokes in 1899 converted the office of secretary into an effective alumni and public relations office. At Harvard, Charles W. Eliot, who in his inaugural address of 1869 had voiced the necessity of influencing "opinion toward advancement of learning," retained The Publicity Bureau in 1900. The University of Pennsylvania's public relations program dates from 1904, when it set up the University Bureau of Publicity. That same year, Willard G. Bleyer, pioneer journalism educator, organized a press bureau at the University of Wisconsin at the direction of public relations–minded President Charles R. Van Hise. But it was William Rainey Harper, dynamic builder of the University of Chicago, who did more than any other educator to harness the power of publicity to the cause of higher education. His methods and his resulting success were observed and copied by many others.[48]

In this era of ferment and change, churches too began to perceive the need for a public voice. One cleric wrote, "We will find that if we believe in the fruits of publicity we must believe also in the potential power of human nature to achieve goodness." Nonetheless, as in the case of business, it was the sharp attacks of critics that brought about the first programs. The Seventh Day Adventist Church, responding to public attacks on its opposition to Sunday laws, in 1912 established a publicity bureau with a former newspaperman in charge.[49] The Trinity Episcopal Church of New York City, under biting public attack since 1894 for its exploitation of renters in its church-owned tenements, in 1909 became one of the first clients of Pendleton Dudley, and thus the first church to employ an outside counselor.

The whirlwind high-pressure campaign to raise money for charitable causes was first fabricated in 1905 in Washington, D.C., by YMCA fund raisers Charles Sumner Ward and Lyman L. Pierce, in a drive to raise $350,000 for a YMCA

EXHIBIT 4–1 Proposal for a public relations bureau in AT&T in 1912, by Walter S. Allen.

> The establishment of a Public Relations Bureau in the American Telephone and Telegraph Company in which all information concerning the relations of the telephone companies to the public should be concentrated and made available for use, would serve to coordinate much of the work now done independently by various departments of that company and the operating companies.
>
> This Bureau could bring together a large amount of material at present scattered and a proper arrangement and collation of this would make it readily available and eliminate a considerable amount of duplication.
>
> It would also be able to give its attention to the trend of public opinion and the drift of legislation and by a study of these, bring to the attention of executive officers in a condensed form the broader lines of public sentiment in time to enable the telephone company to meet new phases of legislation and in many cases to forestall legislation by remedying conditions which have been the cause of trouble.
>
> By employing a central organization to collect, analyze and distribute material relating to these questions there will be a distinct saving in the time of those actually engaged in work in the field and a broader and more efficient treatment of the problems.
>
> All the available material can be brought together and everyone dealing with these questions be kept in touch with the trend of public opinion and action throughout the country. . . .

building. Here, *for the first time, a full-time publicist was used in a fund drive.* The Y's successful techniques were soon utilized in the annual appeals of churches, colleges, civic centers, and health and welfare agencies.[50]

In 1908, the first health group to appeal for public gifts, the National Tuberculosis Association, established a publicity program. That same year, the American Red Cross hired its first publicity man. The U.S. Marine Corps established a publicity bureau in Chicago in 1907 under Captain William C. Harllee, thus paving the way for today's large-scale public relations programs in our military services.

As this period neared its close, there was growing appreciation that high-pressure publicity was not the answer to good relationships with the public. In an effort to dispel public "ignorance," the American Red Cross in 1913 appointed a committee of three newspapermen to study the problem. The next year, this committee recommended creation of an information division that would gather intelligence, disseminate information to the press, answer inquiries, and build public confidence through "proper and effective publicity."

Publicity had grown to considerable dimensions in these first few years of the new century, as reflected in the growing concern of newspapermen about the "perils of publicity." Don C. Seitz, business manager of the *New York World*, reported to the 1909 convention of the American Newspaper Publishers Association that the number of press agents was growing, and that some were making $6,000 to $12,000 a year—very high pay in those years. "Everybody was employing them; even the New York Orphan Asylum was paying a publicity man $75 a month. The advertising agencies—Albert Frank and Company, Lord & Thomas, N.W. Ayer & Son, J. Walter Thompson—had set up publicity departments which took fees for their services, fees diverted from the advertiser's newspaper advertising budget. Automobile manufacturers were sending a page of material each day to the *World,* and the cement, food, insurance, utilities, and other businesses were equally busy."[51]

World War I

As we have seen, contemporary practice first emerged as a defensive measure; but World War I gave it great offensive impetus. George Creel and his Committee on Public Information demonstrated, as never before, the power of mass publicity to mobilize opinion.

The Committee on Public Information was set up by President Wilson, who was aware of the importance of public opinion and knew the value of using the agencies of communication. George Creel was made chairman. The subsequent events are well described in Creel's book, *How We Advertised America,* and by Mock and Larson in *Words That Won the War:*

> Mr. Creel assembled as brilliant and talented a group of journalists, scholars, press agents, editors, artists, and other manipulators of the symbols of public opinion as America had ever seen united for a single purpose. It was a gargantuan advertising agency, the like of which the country had never known, and the breathtaking scope of its activities was not to be equalled until the rise of the totalitarian dictatorships after the war. George Creel, Carl Byoir, Edgar Sisson, Harvey O'Higgins, Guy Stanton Ford, and their famous associates were literally public relations counselors to the United States Government, carrying first to the citizens of this country and then to those in distant lands, the ideas which gave motive power to the stupendous undertaking of 1917–1918.[52]

Creel emphasized the positive approach. The Liberty Loan drives, although based primarily on advertising techniques, taught businessmen and other executives how public relations practices could be used. This successful demonstration was to have a profound impact on the American culture. Analyzing the influence of the Creel Committee in spurring the growth of what it still termed "press agents," the *New York Times* commented in 1920:

> Essentially the species, if not a war product, is one which the war has mightily increased. Liberty Loans had to be advertised throughout the country. Publicity did that. Five times, at short intervals, the newspapers of the nation stepped into line and "put across" to the man at the breakfast table, and in his office, in the factory, in the mine—in every phase of commerce and industry, in fact, the need of digging down deep into his pocket and "coming across." It worked. Beautifully and efficiently. Not only did he have a staff of press agents working immediately under him in a central office, but Creel decentralized the system so that every type of industry in the country had its special group of publicity workers. In this manner, more than in any other, were the heads and directors of movements of every type introduced to and made cognizant of the value of concentrating on publicity in so-called "drives."[53]

To document the *Times's* point: When America entered the war, the Red Cross had a membership of 486,194 in 372 chapters scattered across the nation, and $200,000 in working funds. In September 1918, as the war neared its end, the Red Cross had 20 million members in 3,864 chapters and had raised more than

$400 million in gifts and membership dues. Another example: On May 1, 1917, there were only some 350,000 holders of U.S. bonds; six months later, after two organized publicity/sales drives for Liberty Bonds, there were 10 million bond-holders. Equally impressive was Herbert Hoover's reliance on public relations to encourage food conservation by the nation's households, hotels, restaurants, and food dealers. The Food Administration, under the public relations direction of Ben Allen, former AP correspondent, transmitted appeals about saving food to the public by every available means of communication. The nation's media donated nearly $20 million in advertising space, and an estimated 20 million people pledged their support by returning coupons inserted in publications or distributed at countless local meetings.

Little wonder that in the years after the war there emerged a general belief in the power of mass communication. A noted political scientist, Harold D. Lasswell, observed, "But when all allowances have been made, and all extravagant estimates pared to the bone, the fact remains that propaganda is one of the most powerful instrumentalities in the modern world."[54]

The Creel Committee trained a host of practitioners, who took their wartime experiences and fashioned them into a profitable calling. Among these were Carl Byoir and Edward L. Bernays. Byoir, at 28 the associate chairman of the CPI, after a decade's detour in other endeavors founded in 1930 what is today one of the large public relations firms, employing 300 people. Bernays, who had a minor role in the CPI, became the tireless advocate of public relations over the next 60 years. Their skills and success in public relations undoubtedly stemmed in large degree from their experience and the lessons they learned as World War I propagandists.

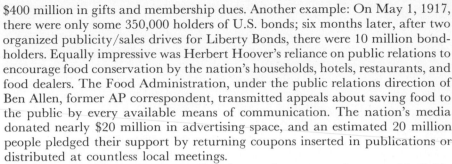

Carl Byoir

Between the wars

Vigorously nourished by wartime developments, the public relations specialty quickly spread. It showed up in government, business, the churches, social work—now burgeoning in the war's aftermath—the labor movement, and social movements. The victory of the Anti-Saloon League in achieving national prohibition, and the triumph of the women's suffrage movement, provided fresh evidence of the new-found power. And because the process of industrialization and urbanization had been pushed ahead several notches during the war, the growth and development of the practice, like much else in society, was accelerating.

With the war over and his duties with the American Red Cross ended, Ivy Lee resumed his practice in a newly organized counseling firm, Ivy Lee & Associates. Included was T.J. Ross, who joined the firm in 1919 and became an influential figure in his own right. In 1961, when Ivy's son, James, retired from his father's firm, this agency took the name of T.J. Ross and Associates. Ross died in 1975, but the firm still retains his name.

Among those vying with Ivy Lee for prominence and for business in the 1920s was Edward L. Bernays, long a central and controversial figure in this craft. Prior to World War I, Bernays had worked as a press agent, serving, among others, Enrico Caruso. When he worked for the Creel Committee during the war, his busy mind was envisioning the possibility of making a life's work of what he called "engineering public consent."[55] Bernays formally retired in 1962 but continued his role as advocate and critic for more than 15 years.

Edward L. Bernays

Bernays coined the term *public relations counsel* in his landmark *Crystallizing Public Opinion,* the first book on public relations, published in 1923. He broke more new ground the same year when he taught the first course in the subject at New York University. Bernays's book was preceded by Walter Lippmann's 1922 *Public Opinion,* a book that reflected the awakening interest in the nature and power of opinion. In all the years prior to 1917, there were only 18 books on public opinion, publicity, and public relations printed, but at least 28 titles were published between 1917 and 1925.

The scholarly interest of social scientists also dates from this period. Here began the shift of interest from the power to the nature of public opinion and the role of communication in its formation. *The work of social scientists in studying public opinion, analyzing propaganda, and observing the work of pressure groups in society has contributed much.* Although development of sound opinion-measurement methods was slow until the 1930s, market research, social surveys, and public opinion polls gained headway during the postwar years. General Foods, a market research pioneer, set up a panel of homemakers in 1926 to test recipes for jams and jellies. The Lynds' historic social survey, *Middletown,* was made in 1925. The *Literary Digest* conducted its first presidential-election poll in 1916.

Many other rapid-fire developments occurred in this postwar period. A number of new counseling firms were established alongside the existing ones of Wright, Dudley, Lee, and Bernays. In 1919, John Price Jones established his firm, which he called an "Organization and Publicity Counsel," to direct fund-raising campaigns and to provide publicity service to corporations. Over the years, until he retired in 1956, Jones made more money and gained more fame as a fund raiser than as a public relations counselor.

Harry A. Bruno was an aviation enthusiast and wartime flier. In 1923, after the airline he was working for went broke, he set up a firm in partnership with Richard Blythe. Most of Bruno's early clients were makers of airplane motors and instruments, and he aided them by promoting aviation. He gained national prominence when he and Blythe handled the press relations for young Charles A. Lindbergh's historic flight across the Atlantic in May 1927. Bruno's publicity and public relations projects did much to speed America's acceptance of the air age, and he also helped make motorboating a popular pastime. He retired in 1969.

John W. Hill

There were only six public relations firms listed in the Manhattan telephone directory in 1926. In that year, William Baldwin, after having served an apprenticeship in a shipbuilding firm and as a fund raiser, opened an agency that was to serve corporate and civic clients—many of the latter gratis—over the next 35 years. In 1927, John W. Hill, a newsman in Cleveland, started a firm in that city. In 1933, he formed a partnership with Don Knowlton, and a short time later, Hill moved to New York to found Hill & Knowlton, Inc., while Knowlton remained to run Hill and Knowlton of Cleveland. The two firms, connected only by overlapping ownership, operated independently until 1964, when Knowlton retired and the Cleveland office was sold to a successor firm. Hill died in 1977.

Two years before Hill set up shop in Cleveland, Edward D. Howard II organized a public relations agency there that celebrated its 50th anniversary in 1975. Another little-known pioneer was Glenn G. Hayes of Chicago, who established Hayes, Loeb and Company in 1921, an agency specializing in farm public relations. His partner, Sidney C. Loeb, landed Sears, Roebuck & Co. as the first big account when Sears needed a program to overcome the effects of a movement by thousands of local merchants to fight mail-order competition.

Paul Garrett

Arthur W. Page

Advertising agencies started moving into the field, as product publicity became an important aspect of marketing. A few advertising agencies had set up publicity sections prior to the war. The 1909 Seitz report noted that there were four agencies with publicity departments at that time. In the 1920s, more agencies developed this service for both advertiser clients and nonclients.

This period saw increased use of public relations advertising as a tool. The Illinois Central Railroad started a campaign in 1920 that continued for fifty years. These ads sought "promotion of a better understanding and closer relationship with the patrons of our lines." In 1922, the Metropolitan Life Insurance Company started a good-health campaign. In 1923, General Motors began to use advertising to sell GM as an institution. GM did not set up its own department until 1931, when it brought in Paul Garrett, another influential pioneer.

In 1921, the American Association of Engineers held *its first national conference on public information.* Later it published the proceedings, in a book entitled, *Publicity Methods for Engineers.*

Another development of the early 1920s was the wholesale adoption of the Creel techniques by Samuel Insull and his cohorts in the utilities industry. Insull sparked a movement, beginning in 1919, to convince the American people of the blessings of his particular private ownerships.[56] Despite the cloud that later crossed this program, it embodied some forward-looking concepts. Insull's chief lieutenant, Bernard J. Mullaney, said in 1924, "Honest and intelligent publicity effort is a most important part of a public relations program . . . but not the whole program; and not even a part of it, as 'publicity' is commonly understood. . . . 'Publicity' that seeks to 'put over' something . . . is unsound; in the long run, it defeats itself."[57] Mullaney was more prophetic than he knew.

Quick-buck promoters also grasped the lessons taught by the success of war-time promotional campaigns. The disreputable Ku Klux Klan, born during Reconstruction, had been revived in Atlanta in 1915 as a bottle club. By 1919, the club was floundering, and its promoter, William Joseph Simons, hired two publicists, Edward Y. Clarke and Bessie Tyler, who had formed the Southern Publicity Association as a firm to promote wartime fund drives. The Clarke-Tyler campaign multiplied the Klan's membership from a few thousand members in 1920 to some 3 million in three years, earning great sums for themselves at the expense of a bitter legacy to the nation.[58]

Among the pioneers shaping today's practice, Arthur W. Page stands at the summit. Page built three successful business careers, yet found time to contribute his talent to many public-service endeavors. He was a writer and editor of *World's Work Magazine* and other periodicals of Doubleday, Page & Company from 1905 until 1927. Then he accepted Walter Gifford's offer to become vice-president of American Telephone & Telegraph Co. to succeed James D. Ellsworth. At the outset, Page made it clear to Gifford that he would accept the vice-presidency only on the conditions that he was not to serve as a publicity man, that he would have a voice in policy, and that the company's performance would be the determinant of its public reputation. The next year, Gifford spelled out the Bell System policy, that "the service shall at all times be adequate, dependable and satisfactory to the user." Page's philosophy is summed up in this statement: "All business in a democratic country begins with public permission and exists by public approval. If that be true, it follows that business should be cheerfully willing to tell the public what its policies are, what it is doing, and what it hopes to do. This seems practically a duty."[59]

Page retired from AT&T in 1947 after having integrated public relations concepts and practices into the Bell System. From then until his death in 1960, he served as a consultant to many large corporations and gave much time to the service of government, higher education, and other causes; but it was Page's work for AT&T that left his lasting imprint on public relations.

It was also during this period that *a sense of identification and professionalism began to emerge in this new craft.* The first national public relations organization was established in Chicago on June 15, 1915, as a part of the Associated Advertising Clubs of the World. Seven bankers founded the new organization and called it the Financial Advertising Association, reflecting the fact that banking public relations in the era of World War I was seen as advertising—and stiff, high-collar advertising, at that. In its early years, the association was mainly an "idea exchange" for its members, but it changed its name in 1947 to the Financial Public Relations Association, in 1966 to the Bank Public Relations and Marketing Association, and again in 1970 to the Bank Marketing Association, to better express its work.

The next group to organize exemplified better the evolution of public relations. A handful of major universities and colleges had set up press bureaus prior to the war, and more did so in the early 1920s, generally as an adjunct to a capital fund-raising drive. Owing mainly to the determined efforts of T.T. Frankenberg, then publicity director for the Western College of Women in Oxford, Ohio, the Association of American College News Bureaus had been organized in April 1917. It lapsed into inactivity during the war, but came alive again in the 1920s. At the 1925 convention, the organization took on new strength, reflecting the growth of the practice in higher education. Symbolic of its growth in ensuing years, the organization's name was changed in 1930 to the American College Publicity Association, in 1964 to the American College Public Relations Association, and in 1974, after a merger with the American Alumni Council, to the Council for the Advancement and Support of Education (CASE). This merger reflected a shift in emphasis in college public relations from publicity to development and fund raising. CASE was launched under the leadership of Alice Beeman, the first woman to head a public relations association.

After World War I, the interest in and utilization of publicity techniques spilled over into the new field of social work, which had been given great impetus by the war and the dislocations it produced. As more and more money had to be raised to meet more and more needs of an urban society, recognition of the importance of publicity and of the need for trained publicists grew. Advancement of social-work publicity was spearheaded by Evart G. and Mary Swain Routzahn of the Russell Sage Foundation. The Routzahns played a key role in the birth of the National Publicity Council for welfare agencies and of a Health Education Section in the American Public Health Association in the early 1920s. What was first a committee on publicity methods in social work became, in 1922, the National Publicity Council for Welfare Services. From its inception until 1940, the council was used by the Routzahns to transport new ideas, new techniques, and missionary zeal to novices in health and welfare publicity work. This body, which attained 1,200 members, went through several reorganizations and name changes. In 1975 it became the National Communications Council for Human Services and in 1977 was merged into the Public Relations Society of America. Some of the NCC's services were continued by the PRSA to serve those in the nonprofit field. The Community Chest movement, which burgeoned after the war, also provided employment for a growing number of publicists.

More religious leaders also sensed the changing times. In 1918, the National Lutheran Council launched a strong national church-publicity program. Later that same year, a Catholic organization, the Knights of Columbus, organized a publicity bureau with John B. Kennedy as its director. The *New York Times* noted at the time, "They are quite frank in admitting that the 'biggest and most practical human lesson learned from the war is that nothing requiring organized effort can succeed without publicity and plenty of it.'" The quote was attributed to Kennedy. The YMCA and YWCA had long had publicity staffs, and they formed something of a nucleus for the spread of organized church publicity. Astute leaders everywhere were observing this "most practical human lesson from the war."

The Roosevelt era

Propelled by the wartime lessons and the changing nature of the American environment, the practice moved full speed ahead until the stock-market crash in 1929. The ensuing Great Depression marks another milestone. That economic catastrophe and Franklin D. Roosevelt's New Deal generated a fuller and broader development in many fields.

FDR combined strong leadership with consummate skill to harness the forces of protest into an effective political coalition. He won his battles on the front pages and over the radio, a new medium that he used with matchless skill. Roosevelt's adroit moves in the public arena can be credited in large part to his public relations mentor, Louis McHenry Howe. The astute, tough-minded Howe served FDR faithfully and effectively from 1912 until his death in 1936. He gave his life to being Roosevelt's right-hand man and did much to advance him to the White House.[60] FDR's success in winning public support spurred the efforts of the conservative forces, particularly the business community, to counter his appeals. But such a cataclysmic event as the depression was bound to produce a sharp readjustment of values, and a new trend set in, marked by wider acknowledgement of an institution's or industry's social responsibility. It was increasingly realized that profitable public relationships could be built only by coupling responsible performance with persuasive publicity.

Events flowing from the depression and the New Deal brought home to every group the need to build informed public support. The New Dealers soon found that this was essential to pave the way for their radical reforms, and government public relations had its greatest expansion under Franklin Roosevelt. School administrators were made to realize the dangers of an uninformed public as hard-pressed taxpayers chopped off "the frills" in education. The depression brought a tremendous expansion in social-welfare needs and agencies, whose administrators also came to realize the need for better public understanding. Military leaders, looking apprehensively at the buildup of the Nazi and Fascist war machines, began to promote support for more adequate armed forces. Colleges and universities, caught in the web of financial woes, turned more and more to public relations to win contributions and to recruit students.

Business leaders turned increasingly to public relations men for help in fighting against Roosevelt's biting criticisms and his legislative reforms. There was a marked trend away from occasional and defensive efforts, and toward more positive and continuous programs, executed by newly established departments. A growing labor movement, too, found that it had problems and needed guidance. Growth was stimulated all along the line by the social and economic upheavals of the depression.

This period brought the tool that promised more precise, more scientific measurement and assessment of public opinion. The Roper and Gallup polls, begun in the mid-1930s, won wide respect in the presidential election of 1936. Perceptive practitioners began using this new tool to advise managements and to formulate programs. The public opinion poll, with the application of new sampling methods, has steadily improved in validity and in utility.

This era also produced the forerunner of a major segment of today's practice—the political-campaign specialist. In 1933, Clem Whitaker and Leone Baxter, husband and wife, formed the first agency specializing in political campaigns, headquartered in San Francisco. California, with its heavy reliance on the initiative and referendum and its weak political party organizations, provided fertile ground for the growth of political firms. In their second year, Whitaker and Baxter played a major role in the defeat of the onetime Socialist Upton Sinclair, who was running for governor on a campaign to "end poverty in California." A quarter-century later, Whitaker admitted with some embarrassment, "It was one we hated to handle." From 1935 through 1958, the firm managed eighty major campaigns and won all but six. This agency brought a new approach to politics, including the media blitz in the final days of the campaign. Today it has many imitators. Whitaker died in 1961; his widow is still active as head of Whitaker & Baxter, International.

Leone Baxter

World War II

World War II produced more violent changes in our environment and accelerated the development of public relations. Once more the government led the way, with a breathtaking demonstration of the power of an organized informational campaign. This time the instrument was the Office of War Information, with the capable Elmer Davis as its director. Davis, veteran newsman and radio commentator, never effectively brought the warring forces in the OWI under control, nor did he play the role Creel did in counseling the president, but he and the OWI set the pace for extensive expansion of the practice in the armed forces, in industry, and in allied fields. More techniques were developed and many more practitioners trained in this gigantic program, which completely dwarfed that of the Creel Committee. In the opinion of a public relations scholar, the "OWI's greatest significance lies in its work as the predecessor of the United States Information Agency. It was the OWI which pointed out the danger in allowing distorted ideas of the United States to exist throughout the world."[61] This is a lesson other institutions learned in these tumultous years.

In industry, public relations was used primarily to spur war production by promoting productivity and combating absenteeism. But there were other, equally challenging tasks that could best be met by specialists, such as the lack of goods to sell and the need to keep the company name before the public, and these spurred the organization of new departments and the wider use of institutional advertising.

On the government front, war bonds had to be sold; materials and manpower had to be conserved; rationing had to be accepted by the public; and the morale of those at the front and those at home had to be bolstered during the long hard sacrifice of wartime. All these purposes required intensive efforts. In the expanded armed forces, thousands of men and women were trained in public relations. Everywhere, more and more people discovered the value of the art.

In World War II, practitioners were confronted with new challenges and new opportunities. That they proved their worth is indicated by the booming growth of the practice that later ensued. The accelerating developments since that time have been the most extensive yet recorded. Reasons for this growth will be underlined in the next chapter.

ADDITIONAL READINGS

ROBERT J. BERENS, *The Image of Mercy.* New York: Vantage Press, 1967. A history of public relations in the American Red Cross.

RAY A. BILLINGTON, *Words That Won the West.* New York: Foundation for Public Relations Education and Research, 1964.

ELMER E. CORNWELL, JR., *Presidential Leadership of Public Opinion.* Bloomington: Indiana University Press, 1963. Traces the presidential use of public relations to LBJ, shows PR's impact on society.

CHARLES P. CULLOP, *Confederate Propaganda in Europe: 1861–1865.* Coral Gables, Fla.: University of Miami Press, 1969.

ELMER DAVIS, "The Office of War Information, 13 June 1942–13 September 1945, Report to the President," in *Journalism Monographs,* ed. Ronald T. Farrar, No. 7, August 1968, Association for Education in Journalism.

FRED F. ENDRES, "Public Relations in the Jackson White House," *Public Relations Review,* Vol. 2 (Fall 1976), 5–12.

L.L.L. GOLDEN, *Only by Public Consent: American Corpo-* *rations' Search for Favorable Opinion.* New York: Hawthorn Books, 1968. Gives a brief history of public relations programs at AT&T, General Motors, Du Pont, and Standard Oil of N.J.

JOHN GUNTHER, *Taken at the Flood—The Story of Albert D. Lasker.* New York: Harper & Row, 1960. Biography of America's advertising pioneer who also made many public relations innovations.

JOHN W. HILL, *The Making of a Public Relations Man.* New York: David McKay & Co., 1963. Part autobiography, part philosophy by one of PR's pioneers.

JAMES W. IRWIN, "Four Decades of Public Relations," interview, *Public Relations Quarterly,* Vol. 12 (Spring 1967).

ROBERT LINDSAY, *This High Name: Public Relations and the U.S. Marine Corps.* Madison: University of Wisconsin Press, 1956.

PETER LYON, *Success Story: The Life and Times of S.S. McClure.* New York: Charles Scribner's Sons, 1963. Biography of the architect of the muckraking movement.

FOOTNOTES

1. A.L. Basham, *The Wonder That Was India* (London: Sidgwick & Jackson, 1954), p.122.

2. John Brooks, *Telephone: the First Hundred Years* (New York: Harper & Row, 1976), pp. 270–71.

3. Samuel Eliot Morison, *The Founding of Harvard College* (Cambridge, Mass.: Harvard University Press, 1935), p. 303.

4. Philip Davidson, *Propaganda and the American Revolution, 1763–1783* (Chapel Hill: University of North Carolina Press, 1941), p. 3. Now available in paperback.

5. See Cass Canfield, *Sam Adams's Revolution (1765–* *1776)* (New York: Harper & Row, 1976). A book written to give Adams his due, but one that adds little new.

6. Benjamin Woods Labaree, *The Boston Tea Party* (New York: Oxford University Press, 1966). Tells the story well.

7. For the account that imprinted the patriots' version on history, see "A Short Narrative of the Horrid Massacre in Boston," by James Bowdoin, Dr. Joseph Warren, and Samuel Pemberton, in Merrill Jensen, *Tracts of the American Revolution, 1763–1776* (New York: Bobbs Merrill, 1967).

8. William Baldwin, Jr., "Bicentennary of a Classic Campaign," *Public Relations Quarterly,* Vol. 10 (Spring 1965).

9. For the Tory side of the propaganda battle, see Carol Berkin, *Jonathan Sewall, Odyssey of an American Loyalist* (New York: Columbia University Press, 1974).

10. Allan Nevins, *The Constitution Makers and the Public, 1785–1790* (New York: Foundation for Public Relations Research and Education, 1962), p. 10.

11. T. Swann Harding, "Genesis of One 'Government Propaganda Mill,'" *Public Opinion Quarterly,* Vol. 11 (Summer 1947), 227–35. A history of public relations in the U.S. Department of Agriculture.

12. For one example of Kendall's work, see Lynn Marshall, "The Authorship of Jackson's Bank Veto Message," *Mississippi Valley Historical Review,* Vol. L (December 1963). For a further view of Kendall, see *Autobiography of Amos Kendall* (Micro-Offset Books, 1949, reprinted), and for an estimate of Kendall's influence, see Arthur M. Schlesinger, Jr., *The Age of Jackson* (Boston: Little, Brown, 1945).

13. For accounts of this epic public relations battle, see James L. Crouthamel, "Did the Second Bank of the United States Bribe the Press?" *Journalism Quarterly,* Vol. 36 (Winter 1959), and Bray Hammond, *Banks and Politics in America* (Princeton, N.J.: Princeton University Press, 1957).

14. Alan Raucher, *Public Relations and Business, 1900–1929* (Baltimore: Johns Hopkins Press, 1968). A history focused on public relations development in business.

15. For accounts of Davy's build-up, see James A. Shackford, *David Crockett, the Man and Legend* (Chapel Hill: University of North Carolina Press, 1956); Marshall Fishwick, *American Heroes: Myths and Realities* (Washington, D.C., 1954), pp. 70–71; and Vernon Parrington, *Main Currents in American Thought* (New York: Harcourt Brace Jovanovich, 1930), Vol. II, pp. 173–78.

16. Irving Wallace, *The Fabulous Showman: Life and Times of P.T. Barnum* (New York: Knopf, 1959).

17. Dexter W. Fellows and Andrew A. Freeman, *This Way to the Big Show* (New York: Viking, 1936; Halcyon House, 1938); *The Life of P.T. Barnum Written by Himself* (New York: Redfield, 1855).

18. Noble E. Cunningham, Jr., "John Beckley: An Early American Party Manager," *William and Mary Quarterly,* Vol. 13 (January 1956), 40–52.

19. Stanley Kelley, Jr., *Professional Public Relations and Political Power* (Baltimore: Johns Hopkins University Press, 1956.) One of the first books to point out the growing role of public relations in politics, it gives examples from the late forties, early fifties.

20. Luther B. Little, "The Printing Press in Politics," *Munsey's Magazine,* Vol. 23 (September 1900), 740–44.

21. Richard Jensen, *The Winning of the Midwest, 1888–1896* (Chicago: University of Chicago Press, 1971), pp. 12–13.

22. For a full account, see Stanley L. Jones, *The Presidential Election of 1896* (Madison: University of Wisconsin Press, 1964).

23. Eric F. Goldman, *Two-Way Street* (Boston: Bellman Publishing Co., 1948). A sketchy potboiler.

24. For a concise account, see Leon Wolff, *Lockout* (New York: Harper & Row, 1965).

25. Merle Curti, *The Growth of American Thought,* 3rd ed. (New York: Harper & Row, 1964), p. 634.

26. "Manufacturing Public Opinion," *McClure's Magazine,* Vol. 26 (February 1906), 450–52.

27. Ray Ginger, *The Age of Excess* (New York: Macmillan, 1965), p. 25.

28. Forrest McDonald, *Insull* (Chicago: University of Chicago Press, 1962), pp.44–45. A biography of the utility magnate who blazed many public relations trails before he crashed to his ruin.

29. "America's First Press Agent a Well-Known Pittsburgher," clipping in Westinghouse Company files, circa 1906.

30. C.C. Regier, *The Era of the Muckrakers* (Chapel Hill: University of North Carolina Press, 1932). Regier neglects the role of metropolitan newspapers in this muckraking. For a generous sampling of newspaper articles, see Arthur and Lila Weinberg, eds., *The Muckrakers* (New York: Simon & Schuster, 1961).

31. Vernon L. Parrington, *Main Currents in American Thought,* Vol. III, pp. 404–5. For details on the rise of the mass media, see Edwin Emery, *The Press and America* (Englewood Cliffs, N.J.: Prentice-Hall, 1972); Theodore Peterson, *Magazines in the Twentieth Century* (Urbana: University of Illinois Press, 1964); and James Playsted Wood, *The Story of Advertising* (New York: Ronald Press, 1958).

32. Richard Hofstadter, *The Age of Reform* (New York: Knopf, 1955), p. 185.

33. Ralph H. Hower, *The History of an Advertising Agency: N.W. Ayer & Son at Work, 1896–1939* (Cambridge, Mass.: Harvard University Press, 1939), p. 117. See also p. 95 of the 1949 revised edition.

34. For details, see Scott M. Cutlip, "The Nation's First Public Relations Firm," *Journalism Quarterly,* Vol. 43 (Summer 1966). It was in fact a publicity agency, not a public relations agency.

35. Ray Stannard Baker, "Railroads on Trial,"

McClure's Magazine, Vol. 26 (March 1906), 535–44. The story is also told in Weinbergs, *The Muckrakers.*

36. "Department Press Agents," Hearing before Committee on Rules, House of Representatives, May 21, 1912, 62nd Cong. 2nd sess. (Washington, D.C.: Government Printing Office, 1912), p. 16. Also see William Kittle, "The Making of Public Opinion," *Arena,* Vol. 41 (1909), 443–44.

37. For details of Shipp's career, see his obituary, *Washington Post,* February 11, 1952, p. 2B.

38. Gordon A. Moon II, "George F. Parker: A 'Near Miss' as First White House Press Chief," *Journalism Quarterly,* Vol. 41 (Spring 1964), 183–90.

39. Correspondence in Box 141, *General Leonard Wood Papers,* Library of Congress, suggests that the Parker & Bridge firm continued into the 1920s with Parker and Roy Mason as partners.

40. Goldman, *Two-Way Street.*

41. Quoted in Sherman Morse, "An Awakening on Wall Street," *American Magazine,* Vol. 62 (September 1906), 460.

42. *Ivy L. Lee Papers,* Princeton University Library. Lee's correspondence of 1907 includes a letter from the president of the Pennsylvania Railroad to a colleague in Southern Pacific, saying that he had concluded that the time had come to take measures to "place our case before the public."

43. Raucher, *Public Relations and Business.* For a definitive biography, see Ray Eldon Hiebert, *Courtier to the Crowd: The Story of Ivy L. Lee and the Development of Public Relations* (Ames: Iowa State University Press, 1966).

44. For testimony on this case, see *Investigation of Nazi and Other Propaganda: Public Hearings before a Subcommittee of the Committee on Un-American Activities,* Hearing Numbers 73-NY-7 (Washington, D.C.: Government Printing Office, 1934); *Trials of War Criminals before the Nurenberg Military Tribunal,* Volumes VII and VIII, Case Six, *U.S.* v. *Krauch,* "The I.G. Farben Case," (Washington, D.C.: Government Printing Office, 1963). For a contemporary closeup of this continuing problem, see *Activities of Nondiplomatic Representatives of Foreign Principals in the United States,* Hearings before Committee on Foreign Relations, U.S. Senate, Parts 1–13. (Washington, D.C.: Government Printing office, 1963).

45. For the full story, see Joseph I.C. Clarke, *My Life and Memories* (New York: Dodd, Mead, 1955); and "A New Press Agent," *Editor & Publisher,* Vol. 4 (May 12, 1906).

46. For the fascinating, instructive story of Ford's public relations, see David L. Lewis, *The Public Image of Henry Ford: An American Hero and His Company* (Detroit: Wayne State University Press, 1976).

47. Samuel Insull, *Central Station Electric Service* (Chicago, privately printed, 1915), p. 356.

48. For more on the development of public relations in higher education in the seedbed era, see Scott M. Cutlip, "'Advertising' Higher Education: The Early Years of College Public Relations," *College & University Journal,* Vol. 9 (November 1970), Part I; Vol. 10 (January 1971), Part II.

49. Howard Weeks, "The Development of Public Relations as an Organized Activity in a Protestant Denomination" (unpublished Master's thesis, American University, 1963).

50. For a full account of public relations' role in fund raising, see Scott M. Cutlip, *Fund Raising in the United States: Its Role in America's Philanthropy* (New Brunswick, N.J.: Rutgers University Press, 1965).

51. Edwin Emery, *History of American Newspaper Publishers Association* (Minneapolis: University of Minnesota Press, 1950), pp. 125–30.

52. James O. Mock and Cedric Larson, *Words That Won the War* (Princeton, N.J.: Princeton University Press, 1939), p. 4.

53. *New York Times,* February 1, 1920, p. 9, col. 1.

54. Harold D. Lasswell, *Propaganda Techniques in the World War* (New York: Knopf, 1927), 220.

55. For a detailed chronicle of his career as he saw it, see Edward L. Bernays, *Biography of an Idea: Memoirs of Public Relations Counsel Edward L. Bernays* (New York: Simon & Schuster, 1965). Still active in his eighties, Bernays received PRSA's Gold Anvil Award in 1976.

56. For this unsavory page in history, see *Utility Corporations: Efforts by Associations and Agencies of Electric and Gas Utilities to Influence Public Opinion,* a Summary Report Prepared by Federal Trade Commission, 70th Cong. 1st sess. (Senate Document 92, Part 71-A) (Washington, D.C.: Government Printing Office, 1934). A popular summary is Ernest Gruening's *The Public Pays* (New York: Vanguard, 1931). For a kinder view, see McDonald, *Insull.*

57. Speech, "Public Relations in the Public Utility Industry," given at University of Illinois, May 24, 1924. In files of Peoples Gas Company, Chicago.

58. John M. Shotwell, "Crystallizing Public Hatred: The Ku Klux Klan in the Early 1920s" (unpublished Master's thesis, University of Wisconsin–Madison, 1974).

59. George Griswold, Jr., "How AT&T Public Relations Policies Developed," *Public Relations Quarterly,* Vol. 12, (Fall 1967), p. 13. A special issue devoted to AT&T's public relations. Also see

Noel L. Griese, "Public Relations Counsel Arthur W. Page," *Public Relations Quarterly,* Vol. 21 (Fall 1976).

60. For a balanced view of Howe's contributions to FDR's career and his public relations ideas, see Alfred B. Rollins, Jr., *Roosevelt and Howe* (New York: Knopf, 1962).

61. For a quick study of the OWI, see Robert L. Bishop and LaMar S. Mackay, "Mysterious Silence, Lyrical Scream: Government Information in World War II," *Journalism Monographs,* No. 19 (May 1971), based on their Ph.D. dissertations written at the University of Wisconsin.

5

In its modern sense, public relations was brought into being by the ever-increasing complexity of the economic, social and political problems that have assailed the human race in the years since World War I. Its roots are fixed in the basic fact that public opinion . . . is the ultimate ruling force in the free world.

—JOHN W. HILL

The Public Relations Environment

Ecology, a word once used mainly in the life sciences, is somewhat overworked these days. But social scientists have found it useful in describing the interrelationships of environment and human institutions. As the interdependence and complexity of the American environment accelerate, the function of public relations continues to grow in scope and importance. Once society's needs are understood, the function's purpose and capability to help an institution adapt to a changing environment become clear. When viewed as a direct response to its environment, public relations' *essentiality* is easily understood.

Any organization is dependent upon the environment for many things—a charter to operate, personnel, funds for operating expenses and growth, freedom from undue regulation, and so on. This dependence entails constraints and some loss of autonomy. One way of reducing dependence and enlarging autonomy is to create and maintain a favorable reputation for the organization with its constituent publics.[1] In the vernacular of the chief executive, "It's public relations' job to get me the freedom I need to keep this organization growing and going."

A public enterprise—profit or nonprofit—must, to prosper and endure, (1) accept the public responsibility imposed by an increasingly interdependent society, (2) communicate, despite multiplying barriers, with publics that are physically distant and psychologically diversified, and (3) achieve integration into the total community that it was created to serve. In point (1), we find the source of *public relations thinking* in management enterprises. In point (2), we find the reason for the growth of public relations as a *specialized staff function.* In point (3), we find the *objective* of both the management philosophy and the specialized practice.

The twentieth century has brought an avalanche of change that has transformed the world beyond the wildest dreams of those who lived when the buggy was the means of local transportation and exploration of the planets a Jules Verne fantasy. America has steadily and swiftly moved from an agrarian society of small towns, small organizations, and face-to-face relationships into an industrial society of big cities, big organizations, and impersonal relationships.

For some 250 years (1620–1870), the United States was an agricultural society; over the next 90 or so, it became the mightiest industrial society in the world. *Fortune* termed this progress the "Permanent Revolution," in which a free people broke the power of capital as their master and put it to work as their servant,[2] an assertion that many dispute.

Now, as the twenty-first century looms, America has moved into a postindustrial society, a term that hardly describes the vast changes at work in an interdependent world. Daniel Bell defines this era as one in which "the economy has moved from being predominantly engaged in the production of goods to being preoccupied with services, research, education, and amenities."[3] In 1956, the United States reached a symbolic turning point; for the first time in any nation, white-collar workers outnumbered blue-collar workers. Two decades later, white-collar outnumbered blue-collar workers by 40 percent. Industry is declining as the prime motive force in our society; a new social system is emerging; and serious scholars write of the "Twilight of Capitalism."

Most of the problems confronting our society, problems that call for public relations skills, are the result of a history that began with the Industrial Revolution, gathered momentum through World War II, and has now exploded into the Technology Revolution. In a single lifetime, we have progressed from a semi-industrialized to an industrialized to a computerized economy.

The net result of these complex forces has been the creation of an affluent society, yet one in which 26 million people live below the poverty line; a fluid, mobile society of overpowering size, impersonality, and interdependence; and a society dominated by technology and troubled by conflict. Andrew Hacker, in his gloomy book, *The End of the American Era,* predicts, "The remainder of this century will witness a world in turmoil. Revolution and subversion, insurrection and instability, will continue to unsettle American sensibilities. . . . It will be difficult to be an American on such a planet."

Today's world is a world of complex organizations, big structures, and societies in scale. Increases in size change the very nature of organizations, give rise to multiple hierarchies, and introduce new problems of coordination and communication. *Too many of today's large-scale enterprises are like the dinosaur—the body has become too large for its central nervous system.* Compare, for example, the communications problems of a university of 3,000 students in 1910 with one of 40,000 students now. It is a world of escalating changes that disturb and alarm large segments of society. We have shifted in this century from simple answers, Main Street, and colonial possessions, to a complex of international communications that bring the world within instant reach of any listener or viewer, to a world in revolution. Not all institutions have made the transition successfully, and more will falter in the years ahead. These rapid-fire changes encounter stout human resistance. Helping institutions and individuals to cope with change is increasingly the task in public relations.

It is this environmental context that defines the problems and establishes the essentiality of this staff function in management. For example, drug abuse has become a serious problem. One way of treating drug victims is establishment of residential treatment centers. But location of such centers often brings angry protests from alarmed residents. Gaining neighborhood acceptance and public funding of such centers is a typical assignment. Thus, it becomes necessary to look at the relationship of the practice to its environment—its *ecology.* Here we find the compelling force.

First we shall look at the *basic trends* in society that produce change, next at the relevant *consequences* of these trends, and finally, at *how these consequences manifest themselves* in the major sectors of our society.

The basic trends

World population explosion

It took all the millennia of man's existence on earth until 1830 to produce a world population of 1 billion; by 1930, a century later, this number had doubled; and by 1960, only thirty years later, the world's population totaled 3 billion. The rate of growth began to slow in 1970, but in 1976, the population reached the 4 billion mark, twice the number living on this planet 46 years earlier. Of this 4 billion, 72 percent live in the less-developed countries, particularly in Africa, Latin America, and Asia, according to the U.S. Census Bureau.

The U.S. population passed the 200-million mark in 1968 and is expected to reach 248 million in 1985, 300 million by the year 2000. There will be substantial shifts within this population. Those under 15, who now make up roughly 30 percent of our population, will total 82 million, or 27.4 percent, by 2000. The proportion of working-age people, 15 to 64, will rise from 61 to over 63 percent by then. Those 65 and over will increase from 19 million to 25 million, remaining at 9.4 percent of the total. Such shifts require a revised definition of target publics.

Projections for world population, based on present birth and mortality rates, give us a figure of 5 billion by 1989, and more than 7 billion by the end of the century. What is more, it is estimated that more than 90 percent of this growth will take place in the less-developed countries. And all this in a world that cannot provide food, shelter, and jobs for those already alive. Obviously, political struggles over distribution of food, income, and wealth will surely intensify, both nationally and internationally.

Urbanization

The Industrial Revolution—the factory system, mechanization of farming, and speedup of transportation of goods—produced the twentieth-century phenomenon of more and more people crowded into urban complexes. These stretch down the East Coast, wrap around the Great Lakes, and blanket California. Today, two-thirds of all Americans live in urban areas. Raymond Mack estimates that "if the present rate of urbanization continues until the year 2050, more than 90 percent of the world's people will live in cities of 20,000 or more."[4] Urbanization poses one of the nation's most troublesome problems.

In 1970, according to the U.S. census, residents of the nation's suburbs became the largest sector of the population, 71 million, exceeding for the first time both central cities and the rest of the country. In the 1970s, many of those fleeing the cities moved to exurbia or smaller towns. From 1970 to 1975, the nation's metropolitan counties, those with a city of at least 50,000 people, grew less than 3 percent in population while nonmetropolitan counties gained more than 4 percent. Much of this shift was from the Northeast and Midwest to the Sunbelt states.

The "white flight" from the central cities in the nation's metropolitan areas left in its wake staggering problems in financing municipal government, welfare, education, and transportation. The proportion of the nation's population living in central cities dropped from 33.8 percent in 1960 to 29.6 percent in 1974; and median family income there, as a percentage of nationwide family income, declined from 105.1 percent to 94.2 percent. The net exodus of nearly 6 million people from central cities between 1970 and 1974 cost cities $30 million of income annually.

In Theodore White's view, "The cities of America are where the crisis of American civilization is happening. If the cities' problems cannot be solved, then the civilization goes to ruins. The old Liberal Idea of the sixties had provoked many experimental approaches to city problems . . . and most failed."[5] Surely, America's destiny in her third century will be decided in the cities.

Scientific explosion

The greatly increased amounts of manpower and money being devoted to research are producing changes in society at a far faster rate than man can accommodate to. It is estimated that 90 percent of all scientists who ever lived are living today. U.S. government investment in research has multiplied 200 times since 1940. This scientific advance has brought not only space travel but cybernation, which results in a system of almost unlimited capacity. Its principles and organization are as different from those of the industrial era as those of that era were from the agricultural era. This scientific explosion has also brought a revolution in weaponry, the inhumanity of which precludes its use in war because it can obliterate civilization. Further, half the world's scientists are engaged in military work, and defense analyst Herman Kahn thinks military technology has supplanted the "mode of production" as a major determinant of social structure.

Finally, Americans have learned that advances in science and technology alone are no guarantee of accompanying improvement in the human condition. The harsh impact of advancing technology—as in the case of the supersonic Concorde—was forcing Americans in the 1970s to redefine "progress." Nonetheless, the revolution of rising expectations rides on the revolution of technology. And the pace of technological change is being speeded by increasing investment in research and development. For example, in 1976, research and development spending in the United States totaled $38.1 billion, an increase of 8 percent over the year before.

Segregation and automation of work

Unlike earlier times, today a person's work is remote from his home and family life. Automation—machines running other machines—changes the nature of work and the requirements for jobs, and it basically alters the problems of investment capital and increases the need for steady, stable markets. Galbraith lists these imperatives of the new technology:

1. An increasing span of time separating the beginning from the completion of any task.
2. Increase in capital that must be committed to production.
3. Growth in flexibility in commitment of time and money.
4. Requirement of specialized manpower.
5. Increased importance of organization to bring work of specialists to a coherent result.
6. Necessity for planning.[6]

Industry run by managers, not owners

Ownership of industry, once in the hands of a few, became widely dispersed in the first half of the century, but it is now coming to be concentrated in pension trusts, funds, and so on. In any case, the entrepreneur has been replaced by the professional salaried manager. He manages with precision and planning, and so he needs a corps of specialists. The corporation has become a dominant force in our society, one directed by a self-perpetuating oligarchy. "This New Industrial State," as Galbraith terms it, has required a "massive growth in the apparatus of persuasion and exhortation that is associated with the sale of goods."[7]

Education explosion

At the turn of the century, most Americans left school at the age of 12 or 13. Today, a college degree is a social expectation and a requirement for more and more jobs. In 1900, there were about 200,000 students enrolled in colleges and universities; in 1950, there were 2.2 million; in 1963, 3.5 million; but by 1973, this number had swollen to 6,620,000, an increase of 87 percent in just a decade.

A slight downturn set in in the mid-1970s, due no doubt to rising tuition rates and changes in the life-style of the young; it is estimated that 6,515,000 students will be enrolled full-time in 1983, representing a decline of 2 percent over the decade. A Bureau of Labor Statistics study shows that the percentage of high school graduates going on to any college increased sharply from 1962 to 1968 and then declined to 1962 levels by 1974. Nonetheless, Education and Economic Systems, Inc., of Boulder, Colorado, predicts that national college enrollment in 1990 will be virtually the same as in 1978, despite a 24 percent decline in the enrollment base by that time.

High school enrollments, reflecting the "baby boom" that followed World War II, peaked in 1973 at 15,276,000 and will decline to 13,100,000 by 1983, a drop of 14 percent for the decade, according to the National Center for Education Statistics.

This education explosion is "middle-class-izing" our society, increasing the flow of new knowledge, and changing people's self-images. A group of opinion leaders queried on this point suggest, "The better-educated person will have more self-respect, will want to be treated more as an individual, will be far less tolerant of authoritarianism and organizational restraints, will have different and higher expectations of what he wants to put into a job and what he wants to get out of it." Andrew Hacker asserts that education "undermines the pre-conditions for patriotism and piety."

Social revolution

Alvin Toffler sees Western society caught up in a fire storm of change sweeping through highly industrialized societies at accelerating speed. "In three short decades between now and the twenty-first century, millions of ordinary, psychologically normal people will face an abrupt collision with the future."[8] This results in what he termed "future shock." If institutions are to survive in the fragile, fragmented social environment produced by this upheaval of change, they must strategically adapt to powerful, changing external forces. Prof. George D. Downing thinks the public relations practitioner is best suited to "lead the way to new managerial concepts . . . to compatibly adapt to relevant environments."[9]

For example, the demand for full human rights is now universal around the globe and particularly evident in the civil-rights and women's-rights movements. But equal treatment for all, regardless of creed, race, or sex, will be difficult to attain within the present context of society. Even when government-mandated, programs to achieve such equality will require fundamental changes in attitudes that can be brought about only with time and persuasive communications. The same communications revolution that has enabled these social demands to spread so widely and rapidly can be used to respond directly to them. The practitioner, if equipped, can play a key role in this process.

These continuing trends are bringing changes great in number and magnitude. There is growing evidence that technology is subtracting as much or more from the sum of human welfare as it is adding to it. Progress can come only through change, yet gaining acceptance of change is a difficult task. Labor's opposition to elimination of jobs by automation, students' protests against outmoded university rules, and the debates on moral imperatives are examples of the tensions that accompany change. The upheaval created by rapid-fire change and emergence of new values has brought a disintegration of the public consensus that complicates the public relations task of every institution.

James E. Webb, former NASA administrator, has been proven right in his prediction, "The thrust into space will change the ideas and lives of people more drastically than the Industrial Revolution." Arthur Schlesinger, Jr., writes, "This constant acceleration in the velocity of history means that lives alter with startling and irresistible rapidity, that inherited ideas and institutions live in constant jeopardy." Kenneth Boulding put it succinctly: "If the human race is to survive, it will have to change its ways of thinking more in the next twenty-five years than it has done in the last 25,000."

Consequences of the trends

Significant and far-reaching consequences were bound to flow from changes as profound as those just described, and these consequences have had great significance for public relations.

Increased interdependence

Our industrialization has made us small cogs in one great industrial complex. Each segment is dependent upon countless others, many unseen and remote. We all have a place on the nationwide assembly line, and a breakdown at any point along this line quickly and directly affects all who man it. A steel strike in Pittsburgh radiates its economic consequences to the automobile dealer in Phoenix or the coal miner in West Virginia. A chemical company manufactures Kepone to fight fire ants and in the process maims workers, pollutes the James River to Chesapeake Bay, and wrecks a municipal sewage system.[10] Consumers welcome the convenience of the aerosol spray can only to find that this handy gadget erodes the blanket of stratospheric ozone that protects all life from lethal doses of solar radiation. A growing population needs more electrical energy for its heating, cooking, and cooling, yet nuclear power plants pose safety and pollution problems of great magnitude to those same users. Travelers need larger airports in metropolitan areas, but the residents insist they be located "someplace else."

Arab oil producers effect a petroleum boycott against the United States, and an acute gasoline shortage results. A drought in Russia brings large wheat sales to U.S. farmers and higher bread prices to consumers.

We have moved, in a half-century, from the general store to General Motors. Interdependence can be seen in the simple example of a neighbor's blaring radio, or in an industrial plant's smoke billowing across town. Its magnitude was dramatically demonstrated when the failure of one small component in an electric power system serving Ontario and the northeast United States blacked out 80,000 square miles and left 30 million people in the dark. *Newsweek* reported, "Elevators hung immobile in their shafts. Subways ground dead in their tunnels. Streetcars froze in their tracks. Street lights and traffic signals went out. . . . Airports shut down. Mail stacked up in blacked-out post offices. Computers lost their memories. TV pictures darkened and died. Business stopped."

As the speedup in communications and transportation hastens the day of Marshall McLuhan's "global village," interdependence is swiftly spreading around the world, blurring the lines of government boundaries and the divisions between the public and private sectors. Individually, we are no longer masters of our fate. Hence, there is a compelling need for each component to be responsible to all others. If this responsibility is shirked, society ultimately finds a means of enforcing it.

Growth in the power of public opinion

That Americans are free to have opinions and to make them effective in shaping their destinies gives great force to public opinion. Using the techniques of organization and protest, small groups can catch the eye and ear of the nation with a "Hike for Hunger," a sit-in, or a police confrontation. People in urban complexes are much more easily and quickly rallied to vent their views than was a dispersed population in the days of agrarian protest. Because citizens nearly everywhere have learned how to influence government, public opinion has become the dominant force in the late twentieth century. Growth of consumerism is an example.

Public opinion can be more quickly mobilized than ever before. Yesterday's protests become today's laws. There is a larger proportion of young people than ever before, and young people tend to be action-oriented. People are better educated than ever before, and educated people tend to be impatient with the status quo. With the advent of TV, news travels faster than before, and the technique of creating media events to capture the channels of communication is known from South Boston to Wounded Knee to the carrier *Enterprise* at sea in the Pacific. The technique of organization is equally well known today. For example, there are now 40,000 local organizations across the country seriously concerned with the quality of our environment—an increase of 100 percent over 1971.[11] These groups have been able to stop expressways in Memphis and Milwaukee, block power plants on the Hudson and on Bodega Bay, divert an interstate highway from a sandhill-crane nesting area, and block U.S. construction of an SST.

Cause groups have also learned to utilize the courts to win their way. Such public-interest law firms as the Center for Law and Social Policy, the Natural Resources Defense Council, and more than a dozen others with similar names emerged in the 1970s to make the voice of protest heard in the court of law as well as in the court of public opinion. Some $40 million a year is spent in public-interest law. Max Ways sees this demand for public participation as the "second revolution." Asserting that "people want more say," he writes, "In a society where great organizations—governmental, business, educational—are central to the mode of life, a thrust for greater participation replaces the old drive for independence."[12] In the decades ahead, society will be confronted by issues turning upon participation.

Confirming this, a group of foundation-funded economists found in a study, "Strengthening Citizen Access and Governmental Accountability," that, contrary to popular myth, "citizens do not want less government involvement in the economy," that "they strongly support public responsibility, but under a modern banner which could well read, 'No regulation without citizen representation.'" The Exploratory Project for Economic Alternatives found citizens demanding a "direct role in the administrative and judicial processes which have largely excluded them."

An example of citizens' insistence upon participating in public decisions can be seen in the cancellation of the largest timber-cutting contract ever granted by the federal government. In 1968, Champion International acquired the rights to cut timber in the Tongass National Forest in Alaska. Eight years later, the contract was canceled because the Sierra Club, using legal action and a public relations campaign, had successfully blocked its implementation. A small group compelled the U.S. Forest Service to agree that no future timber sales would be made until a land-management plan had been prepared for that forest.

Another example of the dollars-and-cents consequences of changes in public opinion can be seen in the price of Ethyl Corporation stock the day before and the day after gasoline marketers, responding to public pressure, decided to remove lead from gasoline. It was the same corporation, with the same management and same resources, the day after this announcement as it had been the day before. Public opinion made the difference.

This power will grow, in the opinion of Daniel Bell, for three reasons: "We have become, for the first time, a national society . . . in which crucial decisions affecting all parts of the society simultaneously . . . are made by government, rather than through the market; in addition, we have become a *communal* society, in which many more groups now seek to establish their social rights—their claims on society—through the political order; and, third, with our increasing 'future orientation,' government will necessarily have to do more and more planning."[13]

Escalation in competition for attention

As popular opinion has grown in force and the ways of influence have multiplied, the competition for public favor has steadily escalated. And the struggle to align people on the side of one's cause, client, or company has become not only more competitive, but far more costly. When environmentalists in California got a proposition on the ballot to restrict construction of nuclear power plants, the public relations battle that ensued cost the opposing groups approximately $5 million. The high stakes in today's business and political worlds intensify this competition, making public relations efforts of *communication, persuasion,* and *adjustment* essential.

Today's citizen, equipped with education, access to information, and organizations of strength, has a considerable amount of power to enforce a public accounting on all institutions vested with a public interest—not only business, but government, social-welfare agencies, labor unions, schools, churches, and the like. This power reaches its zenith in what David Riesman has called our "other-directed" society. It is exerted with consumer dollars, investment dollars, philanthropic dollars, and votes; and most important, citizens have the means to communicate their views and thus build organized support to enforce group opinions.

Given the power, potential and demonstrated, of the mass media, access to their audiences has become the prize in a spirited struggle. In the view of one observer, "The battle now shaping up over the public's right of access to the mass media may well be the most important constitutional issue of this decade."

Loss of community

In Erich Fromm's opinion, man is suffering from his sense of alienation—"his feeling of being cut off, shut out, adrift, fragmentary." The schoolteacher in New York City, the rubber worker in Akron, the salesperson in Chicago, and the forest ranger in the Pacific Northwest share a sense of helplessness. They seek the security of belonging, the respect of personal dignity. The rapidity of our urban growth has accentuated this problem. Although we huddle together in cities or flee in droves to suburbia, we are more estranged from one another than ever before. The small town was also a neighborhood, but not today's large apartment building or urban housing project. Nor is neighborliness always found in suburbia, where today more than one-third of our people live. People there tend to meet not heart to heart, but rather at cocktail parties or the like, where the talk is superficial. The mechanization and automation of work have likewise depersonalized our society, leading to what Harvey Swados termed "the stultifying vegetativeness of the modern American work routine."

Today's citizen feels futility and frustration as he watches decisions being made for him by those beyond his reach. "There appears to be a tenuous line of communication between the governors of our society and the governed." John Cogley once asked this disturbing question: "Are our problems so vast, the technical aspects of modern life so tricky, access to the facts so slight, and the necessary knowledge so elusive that American democracy will become simply a matter of living one's private life and turning over the management of the public sector to professionals?"

A prime source of the bitter conflicts that beset our society is a lack of adequate lines of communication with institutions that appear unresponsive. Citizens are caught up in a public sense that their problems are increasingly unmanageable—with the consequence that the individual sees himself as being more and more distant from the source of power, thus becomes more reluctant to trust any institution. This helps account for the erosion of credibility all institutions have suffered over the past decade. Richard Goodwin, a writer for *The New Yorker,* thinks it is "hard to overstate the extent to which the malaise of powerlessness has eaten its way into our society, evoking an aimless unease, frustration, and fury." Blocked lines of communication and rigidity of institutions bring ghetto unrest, teacher strikes, tenant strikes, and citizen protests. People who feel they no longer control their own destinies are prone to dissent. James Reston thinks America's crisis is the feeling that the political system for dealing with our problems has broken down. Leo Rosten sums it up: "Each of us is a little lonely, deep inside, and cries to be understood. . . ."

We live in a world of fragments and factions, forever splitting off, one against another. Consequently, we retreat into the protective arms of groups where we "belong," where we can find a sense of worth, of dignity—but the result is too often not communication but groups rebounding from groups. Our relations with other human beings are conducted through organized groups—nation and nation, corporation and union, farm cooperative and market. Much of public relations work involves efforts to supply this sense of belonging and a line of communication between the leaders and the people. It can serve society by helping to restore a sense of communion to an integrated community.

Multiplying maladjustments

The swiftly accelerating pace of technology and its consequences have enormously multiplied the number of adjustments that must be effected among widely separated people and organizations. An obvious example is the proliferation of automobiles, which has brought us critical urban problems of congestion, traffic control, safety, and air pollution. It is easier to fly across the country than to drive across town. By 1976, the United States had more than 134 million cars, trucks, and buses, or 63 for every 100 people. By 1991, it is estimated, there will be 170 million vehicles, or 69 for every 100 people. The increased traffic and vehicle-storage demand will add to the congestion and costs of the city, magnify old problems, and create new ones.

The social and cultural lag caused by man's inability to adjust to such advances has long been a source of concern. A tense world cowers in fear of annihilation because scientists split the atom. Man tries frantically to erect political institutions capable of controlling the use of atomic and hydrogen warheads coupled with satellite- or submarine-launched missiles. The United Nations is one hope; the "hot line" is another. On such instruments all else depends.

The maladjustments resulting from this social lag are also seen in lesser but nonetheless critical ways—the continuing unemployment of unskilled labor, many of them school dropouts; the mounting populations in our mental and penal institutions; the decaying blight of the central city ringed by new suburbs; efforts to bring safety on the highways and in the airlanes; and countless other areas.

The swiftness of the changes has left a smaller and smaller span of time for adjustment. Our forebears had a whole lifetime to adjust to the railroad and telegraph, then another to adjust to the automobile. We whip across the ocean in a jet plane in about the time it took them to travel by car to the big city. In the span of only about a decade, America's space industry became bigger than the 75-year-old automotive industry. This generation has had to grapple with adjusting to mass communications, jet aircraft, data processing, automation, nuclear energy, earth satellites, and space travel.

Human inability to keep pace with this fast-flowing change has great implications for the function of public relations, since it brings not only the need to win acceptance of new ideas, new products, and new ways of doing things, but the need to ameliorate the harsh consequences of change.

Specialization

To perform the myriad tasks in today's highly scientific, computerized society, specialists are required. The knowledge needed to manage today's large-scale enterprises is so vast, complicated, and abstract that few have either the time or the ability to master it. Instead, each person tackles one small sector and masters that. Thus we have the specialist in data systems, personnel, planning, or fiscal management, the corporate lawyer, the nucleonic engineer, the high-energy physicist, and the public relations specialist. Each specialization has its own particular language, and this raises communication barriers. Specialists need translators of their jargon to communicate across their narrowing boundaries.

The specialty of public relations has attained its greatest impetus in periods of conflict, change, and major social progress. Discussing the increasing importance of the public relations specialist in American politics, Stanley Kelley, Jr., wrote, "It is based on a solid demand. . . . More than anything else, public relations as an occupation owes its existence to the growth of the mass media of communication. Having committed themselves to the use of the mass media of communication for propaganda purposes, politicians and interest groups have found it an exceedingly complex problem to use them in such a way as to receive wide circulation for a point of view." [14] As the costs of communication rise, the need for expertise becomes more evident. In Kevin Phillips's view, the nation's political party system has given way to a "politics of communication," a trend that gives the function new importance and power.

The communications lag

The fact that our society has become one of separateness and abrasiveness has placed a tremendous burden on the communications function. Today we are confronted by a paradox: unparalleled facilities, but increasing difficulty and complexity in communication. Men can send televised pictures from Mars to the peoples of the earth but cannot communicate across neighborhood or national boundaries. Today's policeman is equipped with radio and radar, but his squad car has cut him off from communication with the people on his beat. A thoughtful publisher, Alfred A. Knopf, doubts that the activities of today's business corporation can be made meaningful to more than a handful of its shareholders. He thinks corporations "are all operating today in fields so highly technical that the average layman cannot understand what they are doing, much less its significance, no matter how simple the language." A philosopher, Charles Frankel, expresses a despairing sense "that events are outrunning the human capacity to understand them." Laws requiring public participation in highway planning, for example, mean little if those attending public hearings are not informed.

Thus the urgent need for the communications specialist, capable of interpreting the publics to an institution's managers and, in turn, interpreting the institution to its constituent publics, becomes evident. The pressure of events is demanding someone capable of bridging the chasms created in this twentieth-century society. Your authors recognize the magnitude of the problem. This is why we believe that *the practitioner will come to be more and more the interpreter of the complexities of his organization and of the environment in which it will prosper or perish.*

EXHIBIT 5-1   America's Destiny for the 1980s, by Roy Amara, President, Institute
for the Future. Reprinted from *World,* published by Peat, Marwick,
Mitchell & Co.

Population: 230 million by 1985, based on a growth rate of only seven-tenths of 1% per year. Nevertheless, household formation will be at an all-time high in the early '80s. Why? Because the babies born between 1945 and 1965 will be 20 to 40 years old by 1985.

Women: Their presence in the labor force will increase; they'll make progress rapidly in the professions; they'll move increasingly into management positions. This might produce a male backlash in some industries.

Economic Development: Slow growth, only 3% a year in real gross national product. High unemployment. It will grow at a rate between 6 and 8% a year, as compared with the [current] rate of 7.8%. The entry of large numbers of young, unskilled workers into the job market will reduce increases in productivity to about 2% a year as compared with the customary 3%.

Freedom: Greater variety in permissible lifestyles; more toleration of deviant behavior; a reduction in some forms of regimentation.

Urban-Suburban Living: Continuing deterioration in inner cities; steady urbanization of the suburbs; some movement back to the cities in the 1980s. Beyond 1990, a steady improvement in cities.

Transportation: A long term trend toward smaller, lighter automobiles, some use of electric vehicles in late 1980s. Redesigned modes of transport to improve mass transit.

Alienation: Continuing distrust and disrespect for authority and institutions until the early 1980s; continued growth in the crime rate.

Family: The husband-wife social unit will remain dominant, but greater mobility, freedom and equality of the sexes will loosen family bonds.

Work: Growing blue and white collar alienation and disaffection due to (a) increasing education, (b) gradual disappearance of "grateful populations" who climbed from the bottom of the socio-economic ladder, and (c) the declining role of the church and family in fostering the work ethic.

Education: The proportion of the population completing one or more years of college will rise from 25 to between 30 and 35%.

Equality: Diminishing discrimination on the basis of age, family income, place of residence, and race or background.

Health: A national health insurance program is a virtual certainty, accompanied by an increase in mental health problems attributable to the accelerated pace of social and economic change.

Crime: It will increase until the mid-1980s, then, as the under-30 population drops, so will it.

Energy: High vulnerability to shortages. However, beyond 1985, growth of nuclear, solar, and coal alternatives to oil should lessen U.S. dependence on foreign supplies.

Environment: Demand for clean air and water will have to contend against the impact on jobs, productivity and cost.

The net sum of all this

These basic trends coursing through society, sweeping it along on a turbulent course and shaping it as it goes, have brought us Big Business, Big Labor, Big Agriculture, Big Government, Big Pressure Group, Big Education, Big Media—big everything. What was once a small enterprise with a few personal relationships is today the multiplant, multinational corporation, frequently part of an even larger corporate conglomerate. Big Business has, in turn, produced Big Labor. To protect themselves against the growing economic power of today's employer, corporate or public, a sizable number of the nation's employees have banded together in labor unions that have themselves grown to giant size, with millions of members and billions in pension funds. For example, the powerful Teamsters Union has nearly 2 million members and more than $1 billion invested in business enterprises.

America was born on the farm, but it moved to the city. Agriculture is no longer a way of life; it is a heavily mechanized, capitalized, computerized high-risk business with difficult problems in capitalization and marketing. Government at the turn of the century was a narrow instrument. Industrialization, accelerating technology, urbanization, and the concentration of economic and political power have combined to produce Big Government, so large and so pervasive that it is incomprehensible to the average American. In 1976, 5 million Americans, one in every 43, were on the federal government's payroll—2.9 million civilian workers in government, 2.1 million on active duty with the armed forces.

And Big Government, with its widening arc of regulation and its franchises and contracts, has brought the Big Pressure Group. To match the power of opposing groups or of the government, today's citizens are compelled to band together into trade, business, professional, interest, and cause groups to protect and promote their interests and beliefs—in short, to win public opinion to a particular group's point of view. Advancing technology, urbanization, and the rising level of education have brought Big Communications Media, which have become the common carriers of decision-making information. Gaining access to the limited space and time available in these media has become highly competitive, calling for the expertise of the specialist.

To provide the internal communication required for organizations large in size and spread over great distances to function, and to establish a two-way exchange of ideas and information between these organizations and their constituent publics, also spread over great distances, is the formidable task of public relations. The sum of today's public relations environment *makes clear the essentiality of the function and defines the tasks it must address.*

ADDITIONAL READINGS

MELVIN ANSHEN, ed., *Managing the Socially Responsible Corporation.* New York: Macmillan, 1974. A collection of speeches. Particularly pertinent is Harold Burson's essay, "The Public Relations Function in the Socially Responsible Corporation."

JAMES DEAKIN, *The Lobbyists.* Washington, D.C.: The Public Affairs Press, 1966. A look at pressure groups in the nation's capital.

FRED FERRETTI, *The Year the Big Apple Went Bust.* New York: Putnam's, 1976. The near bankruptcy of the nation's largest city dramatizes the plight of our cities.

JOHN K. GALBRAITH, *The Affluent Society,* 3rd ed. Boston: Houghton Mifflin, 1976.

PETER GILMAN, "Supersonic Bust: The Story of the Concorde," *Atlantic,* Vol. 239 (January 1977).

EDIE N. GOLDENBERG, *Making the Papers.* Lexington, Mass.: D.C. Heath, 1975. Examines efforts of "have-not" groups to gain access to metropolitan papers.

ANDREW HACKER, *The End of the American Era.* New York: Atheneum, 1970. Political scientist sees the U.S. as "embarked on its time of decline."

FLOYD W. MATSON, *The Broken Image: Man, Science and Society.* Garden City, N.Y.: Doubleday (Anchor ed.) 1966.

KEVIN P. PHILLIPS, *Mediacracy: American Parties and Politics in the Communication Age.* Garden City, N.Y.: Doubleday, 1975.

DAVID RIESMAN et al., *The Lonely Crowd.* New York: Doubleday, 1953.

LEONARD SILK and DAVID VOGEL, *Ethics and Profits: The Crisis of Confidence in American Business.* New York: Simon & Schuster, 1976.

AVA SWARTZ, "Ads for Outgroups," *Columbia Journalism Review,* March–April 1974, pp. 12–15.

FOOTNOTES

1. Charles Perrow, "Organizational Prestige: Some Functions and Dysfunctions," *American Journal of Sociology,* Vol. 66, 335–41.
2. Editors of Fortune, *USA: The Permanent Revolution* (Englewood Cliffs, N.J.: Prentice-Hall, 1952). For later views on the course of this revolution, see Robert L. Heilbroner, *Business Civilization in Decline* (New York: Norton, 1976); Daniel Bell, *The Cultural Contradictions of Capitalism* (New York: Basic Books, 1976); and Michael Harrington, *The Twilight of Capitalism* (New York: Simon & Schuster, 1976).
3. "Notes on the Post-Industrial Society (II)," *The Public Interest,* No. 7 (Spring 1967). See also Part I, in *The Public Interest,* No. 6 (Winter 1967).
4. Raymond Mack, *Transforming America: Patterns of Social Change* (New York: Random House, 1967), p. 10. A readable, useful book.
5. Theodore White, *The Making of the President 1972* (New York: Atheneum, 1973), p. 39.
6. John Kenneth Galbraith, "The Imperatives of Technology," in *The New Industrial State* (Boston: Houghton Mifflin, 1967).
7. Galbraith, *The New Industrial State,* p. 3.
8. Alvin Toffler, *Future Shock* (New York: Random House, 1970), p. 11. A best-selling book that capsuled the swiftness of change in today's world.
9. George D. Downing, "The Emerging Public Relations, a New Strategic Perspective," *Public Relations Journal,* Vol. 30 (May 1974), 14.
10. In October 1976, the Allied Chemical Company was fined $13.2 million for illegally dumping Kepone and other toxic wastes into the James River. Federal Judge Robert R. Merhige, Jr., warned the business community that those who foul the environment should no longer expect to escape with nominal penalties.
11. For lists of these spirited, influential organizations, see the *Conservation Directory,* published annually by the National Wildlife Federation; *Environmental Volunteers in America,* published by the National Technical Information Service, Springfield, Va.; and *The Challengers,* published by the Public Affairs Council, Washington, D.C.
12. Max Ways, "More Power to Everybody," *Fortune,* Vol. 81 (May 1970).
13. Bell, *Cultural Contradictions.*
14. Stanley Kelley, Jr., *Professional Public Relations and Political Power* (Baltimore: Johns Hopkins Press, 1956), p. 202. Available also in paperback. For another discussion of this development, see Leon D. Epstein, *Political Parties in Western Democracies* (New York: Praeger, 1968).

The power of public opinion must be faced, understood, and dealt with. It provides the psychological environment in which organizations prosper or perish.

Persuasion and Public Opinion

Growth in the power of public opinion, outlined in Chapter Four, has resulted in a commensurate growth of efforts to influence it, mainly through the persuasive arts of public relations and advertising. Basically, there are four means of getting people to do what you want them to do—*purchase, patronage, pressure, or persuasion.* If a woman wants a hairstyling, she pays for the service. That's *purchase.* If a governor needs a legislator's vote on a crucial bill, he agrees to appoint the legislator's friend to a state post. That's *patronage.* If a taxpayer fails to file his or her income tax return, the taxpayer is penalized. That's *pressure.* The U.S. Postal Service mounts a nationwide advertising campaign to encourage the public to write more letters and thus increase postal revenues. That's *persuasion.*

Persuasion, primarily a communications process, is an effort to convey information in such a way as to get people to revise old pictures in their heads, or form new ones, and thus change their behavior. The basic objective of most programs is either to *change or neutralize* hostile opinions, to *crystallize* unformed or latent opinions, or to *conserve* favorable opinions by reinforcing them. The last is the primary effect of most communications programs. Practitioners rely largely on the mass media to accomplish these objectives. *"Persuasive messages presented via the mass media may provide the appearance of consensus regarding orientation and action with respect to a given object or goal of persuasion."*[1] In short, the practitioner seeks to communicate information in such a way as to persuade members of target groups that the behavior the communicator desires is socially sanctioned by their group.

To illustrate: Each autumn, in cities across the nation, a charity fund drive is staged to raise large sums of money for the community's volunteer social and welfare services, under the banner of "United Way" or "United Appeal." These whirlwind campaigns to raise money in a few weeks' time bombard the public with heart-tugging appeals. Scores of volunteers are recruited to solicit funds from many times their number. The pattern has changed relatively little since it was developed by the YMCA in the early 1900s. These campaigns utilize professional practitioners at the national and local levels to provide persuasive communications that will build social pressures on citizens to give their "fair share."

FIGURE 6-1 One company's effort to deal with public opinion.

Too many people believe business doesn't give a damn about the public.

Minds are tough to change.

Times *do* change, though. And business is changing. Faster than a lot of people's attitudes toward business.

American business invests more money every year in strenuous efforts to communicate the benefits of competitive enterprise. (Including ads like this one.)

Yet survey after survey shows that public sentiment is against big business.

This suggests to us a communications problem. And a credibility problem.

It also suggests some possible corrective steps toward more effective communications with the public.

First, let's stop talking mostly to ourselves.

Let's stop resorting to one-sided arguments that thoughtful adults are no longer willing to accept on faith.

Let's stop pretending that there aren't any flaws at all in our system, and the way it works.

Instead, let's face up to our mistakes, and correct them. Admit that we're not perfect. And engage in open discourse instead of arm-twisting diatribes.

Since public opinion is ultimately the controlling force in our democracy, an informed public is really one of the costs of staying in business.

Thus there may be only one way for business to restore its credibility. And that's to level with the public.

It's definitely worth a try.

(Why not try these thoughts out on somebody who's turned off by business?)

Pennwalt Corporation, Three Parkway, Philadelphia, Pa. 19102.

For 126 years we've been making things people need—including profits.

PENNWALT
CHEMICALS ■ EQUIPMENT
HEALTH PRODUCTS

The drive is kicked off in early September with fanfare and publicity; in press conferences, news stories, and public-service announcements over the air. The amount to be raised, usually somewhat higher than the amount raised the year before, is trumpeted. The goal has been set by the organization, but the kickoff luncheon and supporting publicity make it appear to be the *community's goal,* carrying the approval of all citizens. A large thermometer, clock, or some such device is erected in the courthouse square to record the "community's progress" toward this goal. Subsequent stories in the news media, in brochures, and at "report luncheons" record progress toward the goal, building to a climax near the end to go "over the top." The persuasive communication widely publicizes the "fair share" each person is expected to give—usually a percentage of pay received—in order to make the "fair share" an *approved shared norm,* forcing givers to give in this range or else appear stingy or "unfair" in the eyes of their fellow workers or neighbors.

These drives are ostensibly led by outstanding community leaders atop the community power structure, lending the aura of prestige and endorsement, while the organization and publicity work is being done in the background by paid professionals. This persuasion is carried into offices, workplaces, and homes by fellow workers or neighbors, thus adding their pressure to that being built by the communitywide publicity. Organizational rivalries and internal pressures are used to make members of an organization—be it a college, a corporation, or an insurance agency—feel compelled to cooperate to demonstrate that their organization is a "good community citizen." Payroll pledge cards make it easy to give simply by checking an amount for payroll deductions—and make it difficult to resist the pressure to put "Our Outfit" over the top. Those who resist this pressure at the office must face that of a neighbor soliciting a pledge when they get home. Of course, no one wants to be known as the neighborhood tightwad. Thus, with the organized use of *persuasive communication, goals, socially approved norms,* and sometimes *economic pressures,* the money is raised. In this, public relations has had a major role.

Other examples:

Some years ago, a number of harsh criticisms erupted in New York State against that state's welfare programs. To allay these criticisms, the State Communities Aid Association set out to bring the critics face to face with the grim problems of poverty, illegitimacy, and illiteracy, in a modern version of citizen inspection of the poorhouses of yesteryear. The project's basic plan was simple: to let the community leaders see and talk to people living on welfare, and watch caseworkers cope with the complex problems they face every day. The pilot project was sponsored in ten New York communities and financed by a grant from the Field Foundation. Other communities later adopted the plan.

In these communities on a given day, community leaders—particularly those most vocal about "loafers," "chiselers," and "loose-living women"—are paired off with caseworkers. Critic and caseworker spend the afternoon visiting typical welfare recipients. The recipients are not tipped off in advance, but when asked if the observer may sit in, they usually grant permission. Typical households, rather than "best" or "worst," are visited. Then all visitors and welfare workers come together for a dinner and discussion of what has been seen during the day. The discussion often runs past midnight, and the critics wind up with a different opinion about those living on welfare. The State Communities Aid Association, after the pilot program, concluded, "This demonstration has proved its value in helping lift the fog of public suspicion about welfare."

Similar welfare visitation projects have been carried out in Michigan and Minnesota, there too, serving to replace hearsay with straight fact and to focus the attention of *influentials* on the broad scope of services provided by the county welfare department. These programs are planned efforts to *change hostile opinions.*

Public relations efforts to *create attitudes* where none exist were illustrated in the National Safety Council's campaign to get motorists to use seat belts. Research had indicated that universal use of seat belts would save 8,000 to 10,000 lives each year and would reduce serious injuries by one-third, but that announcement met the ingrained resistance of human habit. The Joint Seat Belt Committee, consisting of the National Safety Council, the American Medical Association, and the U.S. Public Health Service, kept up a steady barrage of persuasive communication, using films, posters, public-service advertising, news stories, TV documentaries, and spot radio announcements to get more motorists to use seat belts. Here, the effort was *to crystallize latent or unformed opinion.*

The diamond has long been a standard of ultimate value, fluctuating little more than money itself. When sales charts disclosed a trend away from the use of diamonds in engagement rings, the DeBeers Consolidated Mines did something about it. To revive the concept of a diamond as a symbol of high fashion, their publicity pointed out to readers and viewers that TV, radio, and movie stars wore diamonds when they got engaged. Fashion models were encouraged to wear diamonds with new gowns. Diamonds and St. Valentine's Day were linked in publicity. Jewelers were given special materials and booklets to use at service clubs and schools. All these efforts had the object of *conserving favorable opinion.*

The practitioner is striving constantly to start, lead, change, speed, or slow trends in public opinion. His daily tasks are created by people's differences in outlook and opinion—people who "don't understand us," who "won't cooperate," who "won't work as hard as they should," who "won't vote right," who "won't give as much as they should," and so on. Usually, the end objective is to influence the social, political, or economic actions of others.

The term *public opinion* is a slippery one. Our ability to measure it is greater than our ability to define or manipulate it. Although the concept originated in the eighteenth century, it has always been difficult to describe, elusive to define, hard to measure, impossible to see. For this reason, it is utilized less and less in the growing precision of social psychology, sociology, and political science. Some scholars doubt that there is a field of public opinion separate from the psychology of attitude formation and change.

Nonetheless, public opinion's pervasive power is easily felt; most agree that its force is perceptible, even though the concept is vague. James Russell Lowell said, "The pressure of public opinion is like the atmosphere. You can't see it, but all the same it is sixteen pounds to the square inch." Another New Englander, Samuel Bowles II, added, "Public sentiment is a capricious, intangible thing, so hard to reach, so hard to manage when it is reached." For example, it takes more than a federal court order to successfully desegregate a school system. The power must be faced, understood, and dealt with in a free country. *Public opinion provides the psychological environment in which organizations prosper or perish.*[2]

The power structure

This slippery abstraction, public opinion, finds its tangible expression in *the decisions of a power structure concerned with a particular issue.* Power, an ancient concept, is a relation among people, a capacity or ability to control others, and *power structure* describes the network of influences existing among the individuals and organizations involved in a given community's decision-making process. *The power structure, not some vague concept of "the public," must be the focus of the practitioner's work.*

There are many power structures, not just one elite group, and they vary with the type of community. This concept was first developed by sociologists C. Wright Mills and Floyd Hunter. Both developed the simplistic theory that each community is dominated by a single power group, the economic elite.[3] Another sociologist, Arnold M. Rose, took issue with Mills and Hunter by propounding a "multi-influence" hypothesis that is much more plausible. Rose wrote, "The multi-influence hypothesis depicts social reality as a far more complex conflict than does the economic-elite dominance hypothesis."[4] Rose saw the bulk of the population as consisting of integrated groups and publics, stratified with varying degrees of power, and thus not subject to control by any so-called elite, whereas Mills saw the public as an undifferentiated mass of inert individuals.

Political scientist Robert Dahl supports this pluralistic view in generalizations growing out of his study of the power structure of New Haven, Connecticut. He wrote, "Any investigation that does not take into account the possibility that different elite groups have different scopes is suspect. . . . There is no doubt that small groups of people make key decisions. It appears to be the case, however, that the small group that runs urban redevelopment is not the same small group that runs public education, and neither is quite the same as the two groups that run the two political parties."[5] Dahl sees this variation of influence in a community as a result of *dispersed inequalities.* Different citizens have different resources to influence public decisions; such resources are unequally distributed, and usually no one influence resource dominates all the others. For example, only a small proportion of low-income people participate in voluntary associations, and therefore they have little contact with those who make community decisions. This situation is beginning to change; these low-income groups are now starting to organize in order to participate in society's informal government. Organizations of welfare mothers are an example. But seldom is one influence source effective in all areas of decision making.[6]

Enlisting the support of influential leaders is one of the first steps in trying to influence public opinion. Rogers and Shoemaker define opinion leadership as the ability of an individual to informally influence other individuals' attitudes or overt behavior in a desired way with relative frequency. They identify three types: (1) *stimulator opinion leadership,* (2) *legitimizer opinion leadership,* and (3) *implementor opinion leadership.*[7]

The influential opinion leader provides legitimacy to a cause or program and thus encourages its acceptance. For example, the U.S. Civil Rights Commission found that the leadership of school administrators, school-board members, and civic leaders determined the outcome of programs to desegregate a school system. If the leaders opposed desegregation, turmoil, confusion, and sometimes violence resulted. If they supported it, desegregation came about peacefully.

Public opinion is thus expressed in the decisions flowing from the interactions *within* and *among* integrated groups making up the power structure that revolves about a particular issue. This fact becomes important when you understand that *the basic purpose of public relations is to assist managers in establishing, regulating, and maintaining satisfactory relationships between and among social units.*

A working definition

There are countless definitions of public opinion. Most scholars agree that public opinion represents a *consensus*, which emerges, over time, from all the expressed views that cluster around an issue in debate, and that this consensus exercises power. Hennessy holds that *"for any given issue, public opinion is the collection of views, measurable or inferable, held by persons who have an interest in that issue."*[8]

Each of the two words that make up the term *public opinion* is significant. A *public* is simply a collective noun for a group of individuals tied together by some common bond of interest and sharing a *sense of togetherness*. It may be a small or a large group; it may be a majority or a minority group. We talk about an "employee public," a "community public," an "alumni public," and so forth; there is an infinite number of smaller publics within the general public. John Dewey, in *The Public and Its Problems*, defined a public as a group of individuals who together are affected by a particular action or idea. Thus, *each issue, problem, or interest creates its own public.*

An *opinion* is simply the expression of an attitude on a controversial issue. *Opinion* implies controversy, whereas *fact* implies general acceptance. The law of gravity is a fact; the justice of a right-to-work law or of school busing is a matter of opinion.

The terms *attitude* and *opinion* are often used interchangeably, which leads to some confusion. They are distinctly separate concepts, although there is a continuing interaction between inwardly held attitudes and outwardly expressed opinions. An *attitude* is simply a predisposition to respond in a given way to a given issue or situation. Rokeach, who defines attitude as a relatively enduring organization of beliefs about an object or situation, suggests that "attitude change is a function not merely of attitude toward an object but also of attitude toward a situation."[9] Wiebe thinks, "Opinions adapt attitudes to the demands of social situations; but having adapted them, opinions appear to become ingredients in the constant, gradual reformulation of attitudes."[10]

The attitudes of individual citizens are the raw material out of which a consensus develops. Influencing an individual's attitudes is a prime task of the practitioner. Consequently, he must know their source, their organization as reflected in the person's value system and personality, and the processes that bring attitude change.

There are two main streams of thought with respect to the determination of man's attitudes: (1) One school assumes a person to be an irrational being with limited powers of reason and thus susceptible to emotional appeals; (2) the second assumes a person to be a rational being with strong powers of reasoning and discrimination. Advertisers who rely heavily on the power of suggestion and who exploit fear reflect a belief in the irrational person. Those who adhere to the rational model of man put their reliance on getting adequate information to people. Our educational system, for example, is based on the rational model. Practitioners who make use of two-way communication demonstrate their belief in the importance of intelligence and comprehension in the formation of opinions.

In actuality, most persons are influenced by *both* irrational and rational reasoning. A person who smokes may ignore overwhelming evidence linking cigarette smoking with lung cancer, but the same person may use reasoning in arriving at an opinion about a civic issue. Either school of thought can point to evidence that supports its assumptions and undercuts the arguments of the other. There are elements of truth in both approaches in dealing with attitude formation and change.

On the psychological level, the reasons for holding or for altering attitudes are found in the *essential functions they perform* in enabling the person to cope with his or her situation. These are the functions of adjustment, ego defense, value expression, and knowledge. Daniel Katz, social psychologist, groups these according to their motivational basis:

1. *The instrumental, adjustive, or utilitarian function. ... .* A modern expression of this approach can be found in behavioristic theory.
2. *The ego-defensive function,* in which the person protects himself from acknowledging the basic truths about himself or herself or the harsh realities in his external world. . . .
3. *The value-expressive function,* in which the individual derives satisfactions from expressing attitudes appropriate to his personal values and to his concept of himself. . . .
4. *The knowledge function,* based upon the individual's need to give adequate structure to his universe. The search for meaning, the need to understand, the trend toward better organization of perceptions and beliefs to provide clarity and consistency for the individual. . . .[11]

In sum, this functional approach is an effort to understand the reasons why persons hold the attitudes they do.

In dealing with the formation and change of attitudes, the practitioner will find Leon Festinger's theory of *cognitive dissonance* of some help. This theory is based on the fact that human beings demonstrate a great desire for consistency and congruity in their attitudes and, conversely, find conflict between what they know and what they do disturbing and discomfiting. Festinger states his theory thus:

> Any time a person has information or an opinion which considered by itself would lead him not to engage in some action, then this information or opinion is dissonant with having engaged in the action. When such dissonance exists, the person will try to reduce it either by changing his actions or by changing his beliefs and opinions. If he cannot change the action, opinion change will ensue. This psychological process, which can be called dissonance reduction, does explain the frequently observed behavior of people justifying their actions. . . . When dissonance exists, dissonance-reduction attempts do occur.[12]

Essentially, the dissonance concept says that people avoid information that is adverse to their views or situation and seek out information that is consonant with their world. The smoker will either reject antismoking information or give up the habit; he or she is not likely to live in a state of internal tension. Festinger and his associates, in the light of continued research, have narrowed the application of the theory. They now say that the information producing the dissonance must have implications for subsequent behavior; in other words, it would probably be ignored if it related only to action the person was already committed to.[13]

Much of communications-opinion research suggests that persons seek out only information pertaining to their perceived interests or to attitudes they already hold. The corollary is that the information they take in reinforces the values they hold, thus setting up a circular process that makes it difficult to change attitudes.[14] Which indeed it is.

Others dissent from this closed-circle notion. Sears and Freedman grant that "most audiences for mass communications apparently tend to overrepresent persons already sympathetic to the views being propounded, and most persons seem to be exposed disproportionately to communications that support their opinions." But, they add, "a considerable amount of experimental research has uncovered no general psychological preference for supportive information."[15] Another theoretician, Richard Carter, suggests the answer when he holds that the supportive view focuses on the *expressive* function of the person's communication behavior, but that in the second function, value *formulation*, adverse information may *not* be avoided. Sears and Freedman conclude, "Perhaps resistance to influence is accomplished most often and most successfully at the level of information evaluation, rather than at the level of selective seeking and avoiding information." These authors agree that most persons in an audience are those sympathetic with the message. Republicans attend Republican rallies, Baptists attend Baptist revivals. Schramm says, "Selective exposure is not really in doubt, but its causes are."

Recent research also suggests that much of a person's media consumption results in information gain that has no perceptible effect on attitude or behavior. Although attitudes have long been conceived as an important variable in determining the response made to a given message, scholars are beginning to question the long-standing assumption that attitude change measures the effect of communication. Schramm explains, "The trouble is that it has proved extraordinarily difficult to match attitudes with action. In family planning surveys . . . it is very common for 70 to 90 percent of the respondents to express favorable attitudes toward family planning and contraception but for only 10 to 15 percent of them to go to the clinic for treatment or materials."[16] Another example: An attitude survey conducted by the Ohio Department of Highway Safety found that 69.1 percent of 25,000 drivers interviewed favored requiring seat belts in automobiles but that only 28 percent were using them when they drove. Behind this shift of communications theory has been an accumulation of evidence that the linking of attitudes to knowledge and behavior is ambiguous. Studies in which both attitudinal and behavioral changes have been induced show low correlations between the two, and few examples of directly parallel effects.[17]

This discussion makes clear that *the opinion formation–communications process is one total multifaceted ongoing process.* Although it may be a bit arbitrary and perhaps confusing, the two components are broken apart in this book to facilitate discussion. This chapter and Chapter 9 need to be studied in tandem.

Predispositions

Human beings vary greatly in their personal-psychological organization, in their perceptions, in what messages they receive from the whirring world about them. Individual differences in personality characteristics are bound to lead to variations in the effects of messages. Each person accumulates his or her *predispositions to think or act in a certain way* from many places, many sources. His or her attitudes remain latent until an issue arises for the group to which he or she belongs. An issue arises when there is conflict, frustration, or anxiety. Thus confronted, the person forms an opinion. For example, people have widely varying views on pornography—what constitutes it and whether it should be permitted in a community. A city ordinance is passed outlawing X-rated movies and massage parlors. Patrons and civil libertarians band together to fight "censorship." A conflict ensues. These attitudes *crystallize* into opinions pro and con. The opinion a person expresses represents the sum of his or her attitudes on a specific issue in debate, tempered by his or her degree of concern for group approval of his or her *expressed* opinions.

Earlier, we took the term *public opinion* apart; now let us try to put it together. The individual opinions expressed by members of a group with a common bond—be it a fraternal organization or voters of a commonwealth—are loosely bunched under the umbrella concept, public opinion. This is not the opposite of private opinion. Rather, *public opinion is the aggregate result of individual opinions on public matters.* Public matters are those that affect groups of people, not isolated individuals. A public is a group of people affected by the same affairs. Publics cannot and do not have opinions, because a public is not an entity in itself. *Public opinion is the sum of accumulated individual opinions on an issue in public debate and affecting a group of people.*

The ultimate expression of public opinion is not an arithmetical sum of all opinions, but rather the sum of *active* opinions working through power structures or social systems. For example, the opinions of the 70 million eligible voters who sat out the 1976 election counted for little in the political decisions of that year. It is helpful to a practitioner who must deal with this force on a daily basis to understand that he or she is painting on a *broad backdrop of three categories of public opinion:*

1. Public opinion in its broadest sense is the whole way of life in the nation, the "culture" of a people. Support of the underdog and a sense of fair play are illustrations.
2. Public opinion is the prevalent mood of a people, or at least of a considerable portion of them. These moods vary from decade to decade; one decade's bonfire is another's holocaust. For example, the Vietnam War and the Watergate scandal left a residue of skepticism, distrust, and cynicism that permeated public opinion through the 1970s.
3. Public opinion is the collection of individual opinions in a group of people whose attention is directed toward a common subject, purpose, like, or dislike. For example, when a highway department announces plans for an interstate highway through rich farmland, farmers and environmentalists organize to oppose it, and public opinion lines up on both sides of the issue. The directives of public opinion tend toward generality, rather than specificity.

The tides of public opinion are forever going in and out, beating against the boulders of public issues as they ebb and flow. These tides move at slow, almost imperceptible rates, for the most part. They are propelled more by events than by publicity. In Galbraith's phrase, "The enemy of conventional wisdom is not ideas but the march of events." Events change values. The drug thalidomide causes deformed babies, and the nation passes stiffer drug laws. Disillusionment caused by Vietnam brings a rebellion against intervention in Angola. *Public opinion encompasses attitudes and supporting behavior that polarize around an issue in public debate.* When goals are accomplished, the supporting opinions tend to disappear. Public opinion on one issue can be displaced by opinion on another. The episodic nature of our news coverage facilitates this process. As issues change, so does public opinion. In this process, the practitioner plays an influential role.

The *process of opinion formation* goes something like this:

1. A number of people recognize a situation as being problematic and decide that something ought to be done about it. They explore possible solutions and do some fact-finding.
2. Alternative proposals for solving the problem emerge and are discussed back and forth.
3. A policy or a solution is agreed upon as best meeting the situation recognized as problematic. Agreement and a decision to promote its acceptance lead to group consciousness.
4. A program of action is undertaken, and it is pressed until the requisite action is obtained or the group becomes weary of the battle and its members turn to other projects and other groups.

Roots of our attitudes

Public opinion gets its power through individuals, who must be persuaded and organized. To deal effectively with this potent force, one must study it situation by situation and influence it individual by individual, group by group, starting with the individual and the source of his opinions. This requires an almost endless exploration of heredity, environments, and the motivations of human behavior. People act on the basis of "the pictures in their heads" rather than in accordance with the reality of the world outside. What a person believes is true, moral, or ethical *is true, moral, or ethical for him or her.* To understand him or her, we start by digging out the roots of these "pictures in our heads."[18] What goes into the composition of these pictures of a world out of sight, out of reach?

Personal factors

We start with the fact that each person is a bundle of conscious ideals, life goals, fears, frustrations, hates, loves, habits, fixations, prides, and prejudices. That not all of these are visible or measurable is one of the factors making prediction or assessment of human behavior risky. The individual is primarily concerned with meeting others' expectations of his performance, and he really believes in the opinions and actions he adopts. Many psychologists believe that much human behavior can be explained by the numbers, intensities, and interactions of psychological and physiological needs. Just how these interact is difficult to ascertain, because one cannot separate mind from body. This much seems agreed upon: The human personality has four primary determinants:

1. Biology or heredity.
2. Group membership, essentially one's environment.
3. Role, involving one's age, sex, social status, class, and color.
4. Situation, all the accidental things that affect people, which can make two brothers from the same environment quite different.

Environmental factors

Harwood Childs classified the environmental factors that shape a person's attitudes into two categories. The *primary factors* are of *experience,* the things we read, hear, or see—"the channels of communication and what comes through them—the ideas, reports, representations that constitute our world of verbal symbols." The *secondary factors* are those of *culture, family, religion, race, school, class, and status* in the community. Our interpretation of issues is shaped by the glasses through which we view them, our experience; but the lenses in our glasses are ground by the secondary factors of environment—where we live, how old we are, how prosperous we are, and our biological, physical, social, and psychological heritage. The primary factors are *active;* the secondary factors are *latent.*[19]

The roots of one's attitudes are many and extend in all directions to varying depths in the soil of our culture. You can dig up and examine each of these roots; but you cannot determine with any certainty the amount of vitality or degree of variation that each root contributes to the living plant. Which has the greater force on what one thinks and says—*heredity? environment? family or peers? church? political party?* The list of factors is almost endless, and the role each plays in relation to all the others is hard to calculate. It varies with each person and each situation of conflict. The "pictures in our heads"—the symbols, codes, slogans, superstitions, and stereotypes that people live by—have their origins in many places.

In most attempts to enumerate and classify, the influence of heredity as against environment is a common starting point. From there, such efforts take different pathways to answering the old question, "Why do we behave the way we do?" It is a question continually confronting the practitioner for a practical answer. Why do more people like coffee than like tea? Why do people in Boston prefer brown eggs, while people in most other parts of the nation prefer white eggs? Why do few Northerners like grits?

Culture

No man lives unto himself alone. From the crib to the casket, a person is influenced by others. The newborn child finds an elaborate civilization awaiting him; he fits into historic institutions and is molded by them. The family, play group, school, church, city, state, and nation are organized ways of entering social relations. They make possible a richer life than could be attained if individuals lived in isolation. The necessities of civilized life, in turn, compel us to maintain cordial and cooperative relations with our fellows. We group ourselves together to work, to play, to worship. Without society and its cultural heritage, man would be a beast.

These are the factors that determine a person's *mental set*—the screen upon which are cast the lights and shadows of what he *reads, sees,* or *hears* to form the pictures in his head. The basic institutions of family, church, school, and economic groupings are the determinants of how we view the world outside—of norms, standards, and values. They transmit from one generation to another what Bagehot named "the cake of custom." *Man shapes these institutions and, in turn, is shaped by them.* Public relations plays its role in this process.

There are two basic points to remember about the role of a nation's culture in shaping its opinions. First, as Cuber declares, the culture is "fundamental to the understanding of the human beings and of groups. Most of the other social science ideas grow out of it or are dependent on it." The second is that culture is *learned* from the time of birth to death. Illustrative of the cultural backdrop against which the drama of public debate takes place is what is generally accepted in the United States as the democratic creed. Two researchers found wide agreement on these propositions: "Democracy is the best form of government." "Public officials should be chosen by majority vote." "Every citizen should have an equal chance to influence government policy." "The minority should be free to criticize the majority decisions." "People in the minority should be free to try to win majority support for their opinions."[20] Nations live by their myths.

The necessity of considering varying cultural patterns has been repeatedly demonstrated in the failures of well-intentioned outsiders to help the impoverished mountaineers in Appalachia. Many have tried without success to bring change to these people. One, a minister, later commented on "the sullen and sometimes almost hostile way in which the people responded . . . when I tried to follow the procedures I had been taught . . . [and] . . . the meagre results I obtained from following the literature sent out by my church's central office. The people simply didn't see things—ordinary things—the way my colleagues and I saw them. . . . They had good points and bad points, but they were unmistakably different."

The family

The family, the germ cell of society, is the first molder of opinions. No person can escape its strong formative influences. Henry Adams was not recording a unique experience when he wrote that his father's character contributed more to his education than did the influence of any other person. In many, many ways, some overt, some subtle, the child acquires the parents' attitudes and outlook. A great many people, for example, inherit their political affiliation. For example, Butler and Stokes found, in their studies of British political behavior:

> A child is very likely to share his parents' party preference. Partisanship over the individual's lifetime has some of the quality of a photographic reproduction that deteriorates with time: it is a fairly sharp copy of the parents' original at the beginning of political awareness, but over the years it becomes somewhat blurred, although remaining easily recognizable.
>
> Within the family is to be found the germ of all those potentialities which later ripen into love and hate, work and play, obedience and revolt, reverence and agnosticism, patriotism and treason. It is the matrix which molds the human personality and gives it the initial impetus and direction determining its goal and means to its fulfillment.[21]

This influence is underscored by recent knowledge indicating that many of our principal characteristics are acquired before the age of 5. It is the family that bends the tender twig in the direction it is likely to grow.

There are, however, cautions to observe in assessing the role of the family in shaping attitudes. First, members of a family are influenced by the same environments, the same neighbors, and same neighborhoods, so one can't be sure whether a particular influence originates inside the family or in the outside neighborhood. And second, current social trends appear to diminish the influence of the family. Childs wrote, "Many factors definitely lessen the influence of parents: notably multiplication of outside diverting influences . . . stronger emotional ties to peer groups, weakened parental authority, family mobility, family instability, and the employment of women . . . outside the home."[22]

Many of our social institutions serve as reinforcing devices to reinculcate the lessons the child learned in the family circle. The neighborhood, mother's bridge-club companions, father's fellow workers, the evening paper, network newscasts, the neighbors next door, and the breadwinner's economic status—all shape adult attitudes as the family shaped the attitudes of the child.

Religion

One basic human trait that binds nearly all people together is religion, the belief in a supernatural, universal power. Religion is a vital force. Both believers and nonbelievers are affected by it, and no effort to change public opinion can omit or deny its strong influence. The church is more influential in the formation of opinions than a mere survey of members might indicate. Religion is so important and pervasive that many Americans feel compelled to go through its forms even though they may not subscribe to the substance; and on the other hand, many religious people have no formal church connection.

Religion has been a major factor in Western civilization. Who can doubt, for example, the Calvinist influence in shaping the ideals of industry, sobriety, frugality, and thrift that stem from America's frontier? R.H. Tawney held that the Protestant Revolution was one of the most decisive factors in the development of the capitalist ideology: "Capitalism was a social counterpart of Calvinist theology."

Today, the effects of religion are being extended as the church increasingly turns to social issues in applied Christianity. Clergymen, as leaders of thought, are active on many fronts in striving to generate and guide public opinion on social issues. The churches are concerned with teen-age gangs and delinquent parents, with peace, slum clearance, civil rights, drug addiction, and racism. The important role religion plays in shaping attitudes on public questions was clearly demonstrated in the 1960 presidential election. Theodore White concluded, "There is no doubt that millions of Americans, Protestant and Catholic, voted in 1960 primordially out of instinct, kinship and past." And religion was again a factor in the 1976 presidential election. The intensity of religious views is plainly evident in the campaign for a Constitutional amendment banning abortion on demand. Similarly, religious views quickly surface in every referendum on fluoridating a city's water supply.

Yet current social trends suggest some slippage in the potency of religion, compared with past eras. About 75 percent of the American people think religion is losing its influence. For example, studies show that only 50 percent of Roman Catholics and 37 percent of Protestants attend church regularly. As another indication, the birthrate among Catholics is rapidly declining and will soon approach the birthrate for Protestants and Jews. Church authority is being challenged on many fronts; America is becoming increasingly a secular society.[23] Yet who can doubt religion's influence in the conflicts in Northern Ireland or the Middle East? Or the latter's fallout in U.S. politics?

Schools

The influence and importance of the school in the public opinion process is powerful in a state that regards an educated, enlightened electorate indispensable to a free society. Whereas there seems to have been some lessening of the influence of the family and church in recent decades, it appears that the schools have gained influence. More children than ever before are going to school; they are starting at an earlier age and attending for longer periods of time; and they are benefiting from expanded and improved teaching methods.

Because of their key role in shaping tomorrow's citizens, the schools are getting increased attention from the practitioner. The philosophy or cause he or she represents strives for a greater share in the education of young people. This is reflected in diverse, greatly increased pressures on schools—with respect to what shall be taught, who shall teach, and what textbooks and films they shall use.

Yet the schools' influence is not independent of that of home and family—a fact our nation has learned since the spotlight has been turned on the problem of providing adequate education for blacks. Sociologist William Sewell thinks, "Schools bring little influence to bear on a child's achievement that is independent of his background and general social context; and . . . this very lack of an independent effect means that the inequalities imposed on children by their home, neighborhood, and peer environment are carried along to become the inequalities with which they confront adult life at the end of school. For equality of educational opportunity through the schools must imply a strong effect of schools that is independent of the child's immediate social environment, and that strong independent effect is not present in American schools."[24] Sewell's views were affirmed in a study, "On Equality of Educational Opportunity," by Prof. Frederick Mosteller and Daniel P. Moynihan, which found that academic achievement depends far more on family background than on what happens in the classroom. This analysis of data on 570,000 pupils in 4,000 schools also found that the social class of a child's fellow students had more impact on individual achievement than any other factor within the school. These studies illustrate the *interaction of forces that shape knowledge, beliefs, and attitudes.*

Economic class

Sometimes overlooked in exploring the roots of attitudes are *economic associations and status,* the individual's stake in the economy. Although the "economic man" concept has been demolished, none would deny that economic motivation and influence are strong with most people. A person's status as an unskilled laborer or as a management executive determines, in large measure, the way his attitudes are bent and shaped. Attitudes of the different income groups toward the role of government are proof of this.

The economic status determines, to a large degree, the particular social orbit in which a person moves. The pictures in his head will be shaped, too, by the nature of his affiliations—whether he is a member of the National Association of Manufacturers or the AFL-CIO, a white-collar or a blue-collar worker. One's place of work, pay, and security are vital factors in life. Their influence is strong.

Hennessey points out, "Attempts to show the relationships between economic factors and patterns of opinion distribution often reveal the effects of differences in levels of knowledge. . . . Those of lower economic status usually have no knowledge or no opinion . . . and therefore fail to appreciate where their economic advantage lies."[25] On the other hand, Alford found that the political importance of economic status is probably a function of how voters compare the personal consequences of social-welfare measures with other influencing factors in their voting. He also found that war and personalities of candidates tend to soften the strength of social-welfare consideration by low-income voters.[26]

An example of the effect of economics on public opinion can be seen in the industrialization of the South and its effect on politics. A popular Tennessee senator explained his defeat as being caused in part by a shift in the union vote. David Halberstam elaborated, ascribing the defeat to the failure of the Democratic party "over the past twenty years to do anything about changing the tax burden placed on the working class and the middle class." Another example of economic impact can be seen in the political behavior of the "new affluents," who are due to rise to 61 percent of the population by 1980. Pollster Louis Harris finds that these "new affluents" are strongest for tough regulation against pollution, impatient about the lack of progress in race relations, and "growingly independent in their voting habits."

Here again we see environmental factors interweaving, overlapping in shaping attitudes.

Social class

Somewhat related to the influence of economic class is that of *social status.* Certainly one's position as a member of the yacht-club set will determine his outlook, sources of information, and opinions. Those who belong to art circles and travel widely see events differently from those without these advantages. But it is important not to confuse income with social status. High income may indeed mean high social status, but it may not. Determining factors are family background, education, occupation, home, and neighborhood. *Status influences every phase of one's life.*

David Riesman, in *The Lonely Crowd,* theorizes that there are three basic types in the American character structure: the "tradition-directed," the "inner-directed," and the "other-directed." The *tradition-directed* person is one whose conformity to the social order is assured by rigid adherence to the accustomed way of doing things. He "does what is proper." The *inner-directed* is one whose conformity is assured by early implantation—through parents, elders, and teachers—of goals and values that last throughout life. The *other-directed* person derives his character from the outside—from his contemporaries, peer groups, associates, friends, and the mass media. The other-directed character type is coming to the fore in America.

This theory has important implications for those who would influence opinion. The inner-directed person has clearly formulated personal goals and relies relatively little on the approbation of others in reaching his decisions. The other-directed person who strives to "keep up with the Joneses" is more easily persuaded. For example, an affluent couple calls a landscaper who has just completed beautifying the lawn of their next-door neighbor. They say, "We want the same thing—only make ours nicer." Riesman's theory would appear to hold despite the seeming contradiction posed by "nonconformist" rebels, for these people enforce a certain conformity in their own membership, in regard to beards, dress, or rhetoric. So it remains important to know who the Joneses are.

Every aspect of American thought and action is powerfully influenced by social class—whether it is the elite living in Scarsdale, Shaker Heights, or Winnetka, the new middle class or managers and technicians living in less affluent suburbs, the lower middle class living in the gray fringe areas of the central city, or the poor living in the slums. To think realistically and act effectively, the practitioner must know the status system.

Race

Another factor increasingly important in shaping our mental set in these days of schism and segregation, of black power and white backlash, is one's race. The misunderstandings and hatreds between the white and black communities of America bend and shape opinions on most public issues. In the sober view of the Kerner Commission, "Discrimination and segregation have long permeated much of American life; now they threaten the future of every American." This issue will gnaw at the vitals of America until the 25 million blacks get their share of the American good life: decent jobs, decent schools, decent homes, nothing less than full equality across the board. As Brink and Harris predict, "With dark undercurrents of distrust and tragedy still running strong on both sides of the color line, the inescapable conclusion is that race will remain an overriding issue in America for decades to come."[27] The difficulty white men and black men have in understanding each other is pointed up in this passage by black novelist Julian Mayfield:

> The wellspring of experience that drove one man was unknown to the other. Every second of every minute that had marched past since the black man was born in the slums of Gainesboro, every moment of self-hatred and frustration, of self-pity and pride and rejection, every night lain awake scheming and plotting after status and identity—all these had combined to make the black man a complete stranger to the white, and the total absence of this experience had made the white man a dangerous and unknown quantity to the black. . . . Thus each of the men had been chiseled by distinct realities, and they were conditioned to see different images when they looked at the same object.
>
> American Indians, Puerto Ricans, and Chicanos have the same problems as the blacks and hold similar attitudes toward whites.[28]

Sources of motivation

Different people respond differently to the same social pressures and persuasions, because of their different degrees of *motivational predisposition* to respond. So the practitioner must take into account these sources of motivation, which stem from the underlying social and cultural values developed in and expressed through the institutions of society.

Personal motivation: What motivates individuals? Casper Weinberger, when secretary of health, education and welfare, said: "Unless we can do a better job of motivating people to protect their health, we will continue to pay a fearful toll in sickness and premature death." For example, it is estimated that there are 22 million people in the nation who have high blood pressure and don't know it. How do you get such people to see a doctor or to go to high-blood-pressure mass screenings? A psychologist suggests that to motivate a person, one must "emphasize the benefits and satisfaction he will gain, not the benefits to . . . your organization," and that "people behave to satisfy their real motives, not the motives they should have."

All reactions of the members of a group, a public, occur within the individual. To understand the opinion process, we must study the individual's emotional and physiological drives. All people have certain basic drives in common—among them, *self-preservation, hunger, security,* and *sex.* Our basic emotional needs include those for *affection,* for *emotional security* or trust, and for *personal significance.*

The forces that motivate people were best discerned and described by Dr. Abraham Maslow, who studied human motivation for thirty years. His research showed three significant points about a person's physical and emotional needs: (1) Some of the needs are stronger than others and thus more difficult to fill or gratify; (2) the filling of these needs has a definite order or sequence—that is, some needs must be dealt with before others can be fulfilled; and (3) as each need in the sequence becomes filled, a person automatically seeks out gratification of the next highest level, until the final level has been attained.[29] Thus, to motivate a person, you help him or her advance up the Maslow Hierarchy of Needs, illustrated in Figure 6–2.

FIGURE 6–2

MASLOW'S HIERARCHY OF NEEDS

The needs grouped on the first level have the greatest intensity and must be filled before you can step up to next level.

Group motivation: People usually act within a social context that they take into account when making decisions on things they do. The variables that influence human behavior—*organizational membership, work roles, reference groups, cultural norms,* and *primary group norms*—find their expression within one's group. Thus, communicators have found it increasingly necessary to consider the group to which people belong. People, with rare exceptions, do not live in isolation but in constant association with others. As DeFleur points out, "Group-derived definitions of situations specify modes of orientation toward a wide variety of objects and events toward which responses must be habitually made."[30] We find in others the social validation of our beliefs and in that context test our beliefs for social reality.

There are essentially two kinds of groups, *statistical* and *functional.* It is helpful to enumerate the target audience both ways. To classify an audience by age, sex, income level, educational level, occupation, and so forth, is useful because members of the same *statistical* group tend to respond in the same general way to the same communications. Such classifications help to identify common bonds of interest that may be used in building a bridge between communicator and audience.

But the *functional* group plays the more vital role. Functional groups are composed of people who come together for some common purpose—a construction crew, a political club, or the congregation at a church service. People desire to belong to groups to find a sense of social security. In an "other-directed" society, we take our cues from our group associates. The group's influence appears to be on the rise; or it may be that, through research, we are merely learning more about the group role in opinion formation. *To belong to a group, we pay a price. We conform to its standards, its consensus.* There is evidence accumulating in social-science research of common attitudes among those who belong to the same group.

Our individual attitudes, and thus our opinions, are maintained in association with small numbers of others. We influence them, they influence us. A person's relatedness to others has an important bearing on efforts to persuade him this way or that. For example, to "belong" can be as strong an incentive as money;[31] employers have found that workers will forego the increased pay possible under wage-incentive plans rather than be ostracized by their work groups as "rate busters." Thus, whether you change a person's opinions or not will depend to some degree on the resistance or support the person encounters in his group. We are learning more and more that these interpersonal relationships intervene in the mass-communication process.[32]

A group develops standards for its members' behavior. These standards are shared. They represent the behavior and attitudes that members expect of one another. "There are some things you just don't do in *this* group." To the degree that a person is dependent upon his group, he is *motivated* to conform. Also, there are found in groups "situational cues" that operate to arouse the motives related to conformity. The study of group dynamics and the group structure of our society is essential for the practitioner. The results of research can be summarized:

1. People's opinions and attitudes are strongly influenced by the groups to which they belong and want to belong.
2. Each person is rewarded for conforming to the standards of the group and is punished for deviating from them.
3. People who are most attached to a group are probably the least influenced by communications that conflict with group norms.[33]

DeFleur and Ball-Rokeach suggest that the model of persuasion looks something like Figure 6–3.

The distinction between the public opinion process and the group-consensus process is important, but it is not easily made. In the public arena, opinions form around a particular issue or a number of related issues, whereas the range of subjects on which the group demands conformity is broad indeed. A second difference is that the group interaction takes place among those who know each other well and are in frequent contact, whereas the public opinion process involves those who may be in contact only one time, on one campaign. Davison

FIGURE 6–3 From Melvin L. DeFleur and Sandra Ball-Rokeach, *Theories of Mass Communication,* 3rd ed. (New York: David McKay, 1975), p. 249.

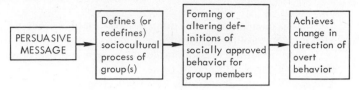

rightly concludes, "The *group opinion process* is an extremely important component of the public opinion process but the distinction between the two must be maintained if public opinion phenomena are to be explained adequately."[34]

A nation of many publics

It is a common mistake to think of "the public" as one massive, monolithic assemblage. No money-spending, vote-casting, goods-buying unit of more than 230 million Americans waits as one vast audience to be molded into "public opinion." "We the People" comprise many publics, many kindred interest groups as well as unorganized groups with like and unlike preferences in fashions, music, fiction, and so forth. The "mass-mind concept" is our time's special bit of nonsense. Fortunately, this country is too large and too diverse for any single group, class, or ideological view to prevail.

The risk in fashioning national campaigns for national audiences can be seen in the fact that a product may have great appeal in New England and yet be ignored in California. Many public relations failures in the past, and the waste of many millions of dollars, resulted from the assumption that public opinion could be molded from New York City down. Our efforts to communicate persuasively with "the general public" are, on the whole, inefficient and often ineffective. *The total public is complex, heterogeneous.* But within this great mass are smaller publics that can be defined and thus influenced.

For example, the university public relations director is primarily concerned with these publics: trustees, administrators, faculty, nonteaching staff, students, parents of students, prospective students, alumni, donors, community leaders, and legislators. To these groups he beams most of his communication. *The publics in public relations are those groups whose common interests are affected by the acts and policies of an institution or whose acts and opinions affect the institution.*

An individual can and does belong to a long list of publics simultaneously. It is dangerous to classify rigidly as "employees" or "customers" people who, in fact, play many roles. We are *whole* individuals. A person's overlapping memberships in many publics lend stability to this mercurial force, public opinion. Citizens are continually forming into, disbanding, and re-forming into publics holding specific views toward specific issues.

Americans are great joiners and intensively organize themselves, from Cub Scouts to Old Age Clubs. This makes it easier to focus on and communicate with individuals joined in groups. *To communicate with individuals in groups, appeals must be significant and relevant to a particular group interest in a particular situation.* Schramm says, "The kind of roles we play and the values and attitudes we build around

129

them are largely determined by the groups we belong to." A person's group relationships provide the setting for most of the communication he receives and transmits.

Today's citizen has many interests. He can be a voter, a taxpayer, a Baptist, a Mason, a Republican, a Rotarian, a war veteran, a merchant, a member of the Chamber of Commerce, an employer, a parent, a fisherman, and a consumer—all in the same day. Each of these "memberships" involves a special allegiance. The issue at stake determines which allegiance prevails in a given situation. All have their impact on a person's underlying attitudes. One minute a man may be a pedestrian crossing the street and mumbling about "those crazy drivers." A few moments later, he may be driving home from work and angrily honking his horn at "fool pedestrians who never watch where they're going." Both roles will have a bearing on shaping this man's opinions on a new traffic law. Quite often, too, a person's allegiances collide. When new taxes are proposed to build schools, will the individual respond as a taxpayer or as a teacher? Or picture, for example, the dilemma of a white Boston policeman opposed to school busing but directed to enforce it upon his neighbors.

Individuals also react in unorganized groups. Some describe these as "crowds"; others refer to "the mass." People simply sharing an attentiveness to the same thing at the same time may be said to belong to an *unorganized public*. Certainly, under the conditions of today's society, mass behavior has increasing magnitude and importance. The squeals of teen-agers excited about the latest recording idol are to be heard from Portland, Maine, to Portland, Oregon. Mass advertising of mass-produced goods appeals to mass behavior. It makes people wear the same style in clothes, drive the same kind of sports car, buy 25 million snowmobiles within a decade, become CB broadcasters, and idolize the same TV stars. The strength of mass behavior is a matter of spirited debate in scholarly circles. Certainly it is an important influence on opinions, mores, and values.

Governors of opinion change

As pointed out earlier, the factors of *culture, family, religion, schools, social group, economic class, and race* interact with the active, direct effects of what people see, hear, or read—their *experience. Our environment and our experience fuse.* These primary factors of opinion formation and change lead to the intense competition for public attention.

Because what people see, hear, or read is recognized as a primary force influencing their opinions, there is an inevitable struggle as to what the public shall or shall not see, read, or hear. This competition for men's minds becomes a battle of communication and censorship, waged with slogans, symbols, and stereotypes in all media of communication, in our schools, plants, stores, and offices. Communication and censorship, or the lack of them, tend to regulate one's opinions and the rate of change.

Communication

Social life is possible only through the ability to communicate, to transfer meaning between individuals. Group activity would be impossible without some means of sharing experiences and attitudes. Communication includes all the symbols of the mind, the means of conveying them, and the means of preserving them. To reach, to understand, and to influence another, a person must communicate. This is *the nub of public relations.*

Today's public opinion marketplace is loud with the voices of people, events, and issues clamoring for attention and consent. Every group faces strong, strident competition. The primary factors of our experience—the factors that *activate* our opinions—are selected out of a welter of things to see, read, or hear. Newspapers, books, and magazines in an endless torrent, radio programs from sunrise to bedtime, television and movies, bowling and baseball—all compete for our attention. Each person has less and less time, attention, and energy to give to more and more things thrust upon him. His time goes to those that seize his attention and seem to merit his support.

The importance of communication is underscored by the fact that *a person acts on the basis of what he knows or thinks he knows.* The world is a big and casual place; to the individual, it frequently appears confused and chaotic. Each person can have accurate, firsthand knowledge of only a tiny fragment of the world's affairs, yet he must have opinions and pass judgment. For this reason, one's judgments are rarely based on research and logical deduction. They are, for the most part, borrowed impressions accepted on the authority of others—a "talker" in the neighborhood, a union leader, the local paper, advertising, the boss, a TV commentator, a faraway "expert," or a favorite uncle.

Censorship

Censorship represents an effort to influence opinions by *suppression* of what people might otherwise see, read, or hear. A person's *opinions can be affected by what he does not know as much as by what he does know.* Opinions based on no facts, on part of the facts, and on all the facts are likely to be quite different. Thus, the tool of censorship is used to create or obliterate opinions. Dictators know this well. So do "managers of the news."

There are two kinds of censorship. *Artificial censorship* is deliberately invoked at the source or along the lines of communication. *Natural censorship* is effected by barriers of physical, psychological, and semantic distance and difference. These barriers are derived spontaneously from the environment of organized society and intervene at many points in the communication process. Not the least of them is the individual's self-imposed *censorship of attention.*

People see what they wish to see, hear what they wish to hear, believe what they wish to believe. Research indicates that, despite overwhelming barrages of information, changes in opinion over short time spans are small. Opinions are highly influential in determining one's exposure to information. But, as indicated earlier, research suggests that a person doesn't necessarily avoid adverse information when he is in the process of opinion *formulation.* Cantril holds that "the way we look at things and the attitudes and opinions we form are grounded on assumptions we have learned from our experience in life. . . . Once assumptions are formed and prove more or less effective, they serve both to focus attention and screen out what is apparently irrelevant and, as reinforcing agents, to intensify other aspects of the environment which seem to have a direct bearing on our purposes."[35] Cantril usefully suggests that a person's "assumptive world" is the only world he knows. Research also indicates that people easily and unconsciously remember those facts that enhance their views—thus, *selective retention* of impressions and information follows the *selective exposure.*

It is easy, especially in the mass media, for people to avoid exposure to information. It takes only a flick of the dial or a flip of the page. Breaking through the individual's wall of insulation of fixed attitudes and limited scope of interest is not easy. Sales managers know this. Psychologists generally hold that emotional experiences far outweigh information in shaping opinions. So if information is to have influence on attitudes and behavior, it must be related to people's values, since value judgments are essentially tied to the emotional processes.

The values each person gives a situation determine what he perceives. This brings us to a key point. *Nearly every problem in public relations has its roots in difference of perception—two or more people viewing the same situation in different ways.* Each person views the passing parade of public issues from a different place along the route. An individual's values stem from his heritage, his previous experiences, his sentiments, his likes and dislikes, his sense of obligation to others, his ideals, his goals, and his definition of self-interest—in short, his *mental set.* For each one of us, reality is whatever our values permit us to recognize as reality. We constantly seek to reinforce our beliefs and our values by selecting from a situation those facts that are consistent with what we believe, and ignoring those that conflict with our beliefs. The business executive reads *Business Week;* the UAW member reads *Solidarity.* The factors of *awareness* and *evaluation* guide each person in what communications he accepts and in what he censors. This underscores a basic point for practitioners as enunciated by Gerhard Wiebe: "The persuasiveness of a public relations message is not inherent in the message, nor is it inherent in the rational quality of the organization's self-interest. The persuasiveness of a message is a function of compatibility of the message with the dynamic equilibria into which it is injected."[36] Communication and censorship govern the flow of opinion change.

Generators of opinion change

A host of forces and groups are constantly at work promoting changes in old opinions and creating new ones. These *generators* of opinion keep the opinion process in a state of ferment and flux, and we must keep in mind their continuing interaction:

1. Programs of industry, labor, agriculture, government, education, social welfare agencies, and so forth.
2. Political parties.
3. Pressure, professional, and interest groups.
4. Propagandists for partisan causes.
5. Press, including all mass media.
6. Churches.

Attitudes shape opinion. Expressed opinions, in turn, reformulate attitudes. The family influences the child, who, in turn, influences the family. The group norms guide the behavior of the group's members, yet the members determine the norms. The press, through its content and emphasis, builds and changes opinions; yet the content and emphasis in the mass media are selected in response to the opinions of the audience. Men create and direct organizations; yet, as

Chester I. Barnard once noted, when the efforts of five men become coordinated in an organization, there is created something new that is wholly apart and different from the sum of the five individuals. The organization shapes their opinions as they guide it.

It is this host of variables interacting upon one another with varying effects that makes this mercurial substance, public opinion, so difficult to grasp. "At all times, it is difficult to determine whether public opinion is leading or being led, followed or manipulated." The answer is, both. *Public relations programs guide and are guided by public opinion.* The process will remain more of an art than a science until we build up what is now the imperfect knowledge and science of the mind.

Some "laws" of public opinion

Hadley Cantril some years ago worked out some "laws of public opinion" on the basis of intensive study of trends over a decade. Cantril believes that the trends, as recorded by the polls, support these generalizations:

1. Opinion is highly sensitive to important events.
2. Events of unusual magnitude are likely to swing public opinion temporarily from one extreme to another. Opinion does not become stabilized until the implications of events are seen with some perspective.
3. Opinion is generally determined more by events than by words—unless those words are themselves interpreted as "events."
4. Verbal statements and outlines of course of action have maximum importance when opinion is unstructured, when people are suggestible and seek some interpretation from a reliable source.
5. By and large, public opinion does not anticipate emergencies; it only reacts to them.
6. Psychologically, opinion is basically determined by self-interest. Events, words, or any other stimuli affect opinion only in so far as their relationship to self-interest is apparent.
7. Opinion does not remain aroused for any long period of time unless people feel their self-interest is acutely involved or unless opinion—aroused by words—is sustained by events.
8. Once self-interest is involved, opinions are not easily changed.
9. When self-interest is involved, public opinion in a democracy is likely to be ahead of official policy.
10. When an opinion is held by a slight majority or when opinion is not solidly structured, an accomplished fact tends to shift opinion in the direction of acceptance.
11. At critical times, people become more sensitive to the adequacy of their leadership—if they have confidence in it, they are willing to assign more than usual responsibility to it; if they lack confidence in it, they are less tolerant than usual.
12. People are less reluctant to have critical decisions made by their leaders if they feel that somehow they, the people, are taking some part in the decision.
13. People have more opinions and are able to form opinions more easily with respect to goals than with respect to methods necessary to reach those goals.
14. Public opinion, like individual opinion, is colored by desire. And when opinion is based chiefly on desire rather than on information, it is likely to show especially sharp shifts with events.
15. By and large, if people in a democracy are provided educational opportunities and ready access to information, public opinion reveals a hard-headed common sense.

The more enlightened people are to the implications of events and proposals for their own self-interest, the more likely they are to agree with the more objective opinions of realistic experts.[37]

Principles of persuasion

Research in the social sciences has brought, in recent years, some tentative principles of persuasion based on experimental research:

1. To accomplish attitude change, a suggestion for change must first be received and accepted. "Acceptance of the message" is a critical factor in persuasive communication.
2. The suggestion is more likely to be accepted if it meets existing personality needs and drives.
3. The suggestion is more likely to be accepted if it is in harmony with group norms and loyalties.
4. The suggestion is more likely to be accepted if the source is perceived as trustworthy or expert.
5. A suggestion in the mass media, coupled with face-to-face reinforcement, is more likely to be accepted than a suggestion carried by either alone, other things being equal.
6. Change in attitude is more likely to occur if the suggestion is accompanied by other factors underlying belief and attitude. This refers to a changed environment, which makes acceptance easier.
7. There will probably be more opinion change in the desired direction if conclusions are explicitly stated than if the audience is left to draw its own conclusions.
8. When the audience is friendly, or when only one position will be presented, or when immediate but temporary opinion change is wanted, it is more effective to give only one side of the argument.
9. When the audience disagrees, or when it is probable that it will hear the other side from another source, it is more effective to present both sides of the argument.
10. When equally attractive opposing views are presented one after another, the one presented last will probably be more effective.
11. Sometimes emotional appeals are more influential; sometimes factual ones are. It depends on the kind of message and kind of audience.
12. A strong threat is generally less effective than a mild threat in inducing desired opinion change.
13. The desired opinion change may be more measurable some time after exposure to the communication than right after exposure.
14. The people you want most in your audience are least likely to be there. This goes back to the censorship of attention that the individual invokes.
15. There is a "sleeper effect" in communications received from sources that the listener regards as having low credibility. In some tests, time has tended to wash out the distrusted source and leave information behind.[38]

Most of the foregoing can be compressed into four guiding principles:

1. *Identification Principle.* Most people will ignore an idea, an opinion, or a point of view unless they see clearly that it affects their personal fears or desires, hopes or aspirations. *Your message must be stated in terms of the interest of your audience.*

2. *Action Principle.* People seldom buy ideas separated from action—either action taken or about to be taken by the sponsor of the idea, or action that the people themselves can conveniently take to prove the merit of the idea. *Unless a means of action is provided, people tend to shrug off appeals to do things.*

3. *Principle of Familiarity and Trust.* We buy ideas only from those we trust; we are influenced by, or adopt, only those opinions or points of view put forward by individuals or corporations or institutions that we regard as credible. *Unless the listener has confidence in the speaker, he is not likely to listen or to believe.*

4. *Clarity Principle.* The situation must be clear to us, not confusing. The thing we observe, read, see, or hear, the thing that produces our impressions, must be *clear,* not subject to several interpretations. People tend to see things as black or white. *To communicate, you must employ words, symbols, or stereotypes that the receiver comprehends and responds to.* This will be discussed in Chapter 9.

ADDITIONAL READINGS

"Attitude Change," special issue of *Public Opinion Quarterly,* Vol. 24 (Summer 1960), DANIEL KATZ, ed. Also available in book form.

BERNARD BERELSON and MORRIS JANOWITZ, *Reader in Public Opinion and Communication,* 2nd ed. New York: Free Press, 1966.

REO M. CHRISTENSON and ROBERT O. MCWILLIAMS, *Voice of the People: Readings in Public Opinion and Propaganda,* 2nd ed. New York: McGraw-Hill, 1967.

G. WILLIAM DOMHOFF, *Who Rules America?* Englewood Cliffs, N.J.: Prentice-Hall, 1968.

LLOYD A. FREE and HADLEY CANTRIL, *The Political Beliefs of Americans: A Study of Public Opinion.* New Brunswick, N.J.: Rutgers University Press, 1967.

ROBERT T. GOLEMBIEWSKI, *The Small Group: An Analysis of Research Concepts and Operations.* Chicago: University of Chicago Press, 1962. Useful introduction to research centered on the group.

JOSEPH A. KAHL, *The American Class Structure.* New York: Holt, Rinehart & Winston, 1957.

ROBERT E. LANE and DAVID O. SEARS, *Public Opinion.* Englewood Cliffs, N.J.: Prentice-Hall, 1964.

OTTO LERBINGER, *Designs for Persuasive Communication.* Englewood Cliffs, N.J.: Prentice-Hall, 1972. Comprehensive enumeration of the theories of persuasion.

ALAN D. MONROE, *Public Opinion in America.* New York: Dodd, Mead, 1975.

NORMAN NIE, SIDNEY VERBA, and JOHN R. PETROCIK, *The Changing American Voter.* Cambridge, Mass.: Harvard University Press, 1976. A Twentieth Century Fund study.

JAMES N. ROSENAU, *National Leadership and Foreign Policy: A Case Study in the Mobilization of Public Support.* Princeton, N.J.: Princeton University Press, 1963.

RALPH L. ROSNOW and GARY ALAN FINE, *Rumor and Gossip: The Social Psychology of Hearsay.* New York: Elsevier North-Holland, Inc., 1976.

HERBERT W. SIMONS, *Persuasion: Understanding, Practice, and Analysis.* Reading, Mass.: Addison-Wesley, 1976.

HANS TOCH, *The Social Psychology of Social Movements.* Indianapolis: Bobbs-Merrill, 1965.

JACK E. WELLER, *Yesterday's People, Life in Contemporary Appalachia.* Lexington: University of Kentucky Press, 1966. A case study.

FOOTNOTES

1. Melvin L. DeFleur and Sandra Ball-Rokeach, *Theories of Mass Communication,* 3rd ed. (New York: David McKay, 1975), p. 250.

2. A classic discussion of public opinion, still of value, is James Bryce, *Modern Democracies* (New York: Macmillan, 1921).

3. The late C. Wright Mills's theory was expressed in *The Power Elite* (London: Oxford University Press, 1959), while Hunter's can be found in his study at Atlanta, Ga., *Community Power Structure* (Chapel Hill: University of North Carolina Press, 1953). Also see Hunter, *Top Leadership U.S.A.* (Chapel Hill: University of North Carolina Press, 1959). The Atlanta study is out of date.

4. Arnold M. Rose, *The Power Structure, Political Process in American Society* (New York: Oxford University Press, 1967), p. 3.

5. Robert A. Dahl, "Critique of the Ruling Elite

Model," *American Political Science Review,* Vol. 52 (June 1958), 463–69.

6. For a discussion of independent components of community power, see William H. Form and Delbert C. Miller, *Industry, Labor, and Community* (New York: Harper & Row, 1960), pp. 437–38.

7. Everett Rogers and F. Floyd Shoemaker, in Tom W. Carroll, "Diffusion Research, Application to National Surveys in Developing Countries," Working Paper No. 20, Department of Communication, Michigan State University, February 1968. Also see Rogers and Shoemaker, *Communication of Innovations, A Cross Cultural Approach,* 2nd ed. (New York: Free Press, 1971).

8. Bernard C. Hennessy, *Public Opinion,* (Belmont, Calif.: Wadsworth, 1965).

9. For elaboration, see Milton Rokeach, "Attitude Change and Behavioral Change," *Public Opinion Quarterly,* Vol. 30 (Winter 1966–67), 529–50. Most scholars agree that this is an excellent definition.

10. Gerhart Wiebe, "Some Implications of Separating Opinions from Attitudes," *Public Opinion Quarterly,* Vol. 17 (Fall 1953), 328–53.

11. Daniel Katz, "The Functional Approach to the Study of Attitudes," *Public Opinion Quarterly,* Vol. 24 (Summer 1960), 170.

12. Leon Festinger, "The Theory of Cognitive Dissonance," in *The Science of Human Communication,* ed. Wilbur Schramm (New York: Basic Books, 1963), pp. 17–27. For a fuller discussion, see Festinger, *A Theory of Cognitive Dissonance* (New York: Harper & Row, 1957).

13. See Jack W. Brehm and Arthur R. Cohen, *Explorations in Cognitive Dissonance* (New York: Wiley, 1962); and Leon Festinger et al., *Conflict, Decision and Dissonance* (Stanford, Calif.: Stanford University Press, 1964), for revisions.

14. For this point of view, see Joseph T. Klapper, *The Effects of Mass Communication* (New York: Free Press, 1960); and Bernard Berelson and Gary A. Steiner, *Human Behavior* (New York: Harcourt Brace Jovanovich, 1964).

15. David O. Sears and Jonathan L. Freedman, "Selective Exposure to Propaganda," *Public Opinion Quarterly,* Vol. 31 (Summer 1967), 212.

16. Wilbur Schramm, *Men, Messages, and Media: A Look at Human Communication* (New York: Harper & Row, 1973), p. 217.

17. For elaboration, see Steven J. Gross and C. Michael Niman, "Attitude-Behavior Consistency: A Review," *Public Opinion Quarterly,* Vol. 39 (1975), 358–68.

18. The concept of the stereotype was introduced by the late Walter Lippmann in his classic book, *Public Opinion* (New York: Harcourt Brace Jovanovich, 1922). This book still offers helpful insights into the nature of public opinion.

19. Harwood Childs, *An Introduction to Public Opinion* (New York: Wiley, 1940). See the chapter, "Formation of Opinion."

20. Robert A. Dahl, *Who Governs? Democracy and Power in an American City* (New Haven, Conn.: Yale University Press, 1961), p. 316, quoting from James A. Prothro and Charles M. Grigg, "Fundamental Principles of Democracy."

21. David Butler and Donald Stokes, *Political Change in Britain* (London: Macmillan, 1969), p. 47.

22. Harwood Childs, *Public Opinion, Nature, Formation, and Role* (New York: Van Nostrand Reinhold, 1965), p. 141. This book has a chapter on the role of public relations and advertising in molding public opinion.

23. Leo Rosten, *The Religions of America: Faith and Ferment in a Time of Crisis,* Preface, as digested in *Saturday Review,* July 12, 1975.

24. William Sewell, in his review in *American Sociological Review,* Vol. 32 (June 1967) of the report by James S. Coleman et al., *Equality of Opportunity* (Washington, D.C.: Government Printing Office, 1966).

25. Hennessy, *Public Opinion.*

26. Robert Alford, "The Role of Social Class in American Voting Behavior," *Western Political Quarterly,* Vol. 13 (1963), 180–93.

27. William Brink and Louis Harris, *Black and White* (New York: Simon & Schuster, 1967), p. 183.

28. Julian Mayfield, *The Grand Parade* (New York: Vanguard, 1961).

29. Abraham Maslow, *Motivation and Personality* (New York: Harper & Row, 1970). Pyramid chart reprinted with permission.

30. DeFleur and Ball-Rokeach, *Theories of Mass Communication,* p. 249.

31. See William Foote Whyte, *Money and Motivation* (New York: Harper & Row, 1955).

32. See Elihu Katz and Paul F. Lazarsfeld, *Personal Influence: The Part Played by People in the Flow of Mass Communications* (New York: Free Press, 1955). This book introduced the two-step flow theory of mass communication and is essential reading for the public relations student. It will be referred to at several points in this book. Its findings have been challenged in recent years.

33. Condensed by Herbert I. Abelson for Opinion Research Corp. in *Some Principles of Persuasion* (Princeton, N.J.: ORC, 1956), and based on the research of Katz and Lazarsfeld, S.E. Asch, H. Guetzkow and Leon Festinger, et al.

34. W. Phillips Davison, "The Public Opinion Process," *Public Opinion Quarterly,* Vol. 22 (Summer

1958), 91–106. Also reprinted in Reo M. Christenson and Robert O. McWilliams, *Voice of the People* (New York: McGraw-Hill, 1962), pp. 6–20.

35. Hadley Cantril, *The Human Dimension, Experiences in Policy Research* (New Brunswick, N.J.: Rutgers University Press, 1967), pp. 16–17.

36. Gerhart Wiebe, "The Gyroscopic Phenomenon," in Raymond Simon, ed., *Perspectives in Public Relations* (Norman: University of Oklahoma Press, 1966), pp. 138–46.

37. Hadley Cantril, *Gauging Public Opinion* (Princeton, N.J.: Princeton University Press, 1947), "The Use of Trends," pp. 220–30. For sharp criticism of these "laws," see the chapter, "The Behavior of Public Opinion," in Leonard Doob, *Public Opinion and Propaganda* (New York: Holt, Rinehart & Winston, 1948). Doob says it is premature to hazard a set of laws, and then proceeds to fashion some of his own.

38. These are condensed from a number of sources, including Abelson, *Some Principles of Persuasion;* Wilbur Schramm and Donald Roberts, eds., *Process and Effects of Mass Communications* (Urbana: University of Illinois Press, 1972); Katz and Lazarfeld, *Personal Influence;* and Carl I. Hovland, Irving L. Janis, and Harold M. Kelley, *Communication and Persuasion* (New Haven, Conn.: Yale University Press, 1953). All these sources are the research of many people in arriving at these "principles." These books cite, too, the original research upon which they are based. For an update on research supporting these principles, see Marvin Karlins and Herbert I. Abelson, *Persuasion,* 2nd ed. (New York: Springer Publishing Co., 1970).

Good public relations does not consist so much in telling the public as in listening to it. It provides a feedback that is otherwise lacking in the organizational structure.

—SIDNEY J. HARRIS

The Process: fact-finding and feedback— the first step

The four-step process

The organized practice of public relations is the continuing effort to bring about a harmonious adjustment between an institution and its publics. This adjustment requires, among other things, an exchange of opinions and information. But this does not automatically happen in today's society; it must be *planned* and *provided for*. This is the practitioner's job. He or she serves, in turn, in the role of *listener, counselor, communicator,* and *evaluator* in this process, because public relations is essentially a *problem-solving process* of four basic steps:

1. **Research–listening** This involves probing the opinions, attitudes, and reactions of those concerned with the acts and policies of an organization, then evaluating the inflow. This task also requires determining facts regarding the organization: *"What's our problem?"*
2. **Planning–decision making** This involves bringing these attitudes, opinions, ideas, and reactions to bear on the policies and programs of the organization. It will enable the organization to chart a course in the interests of all concerned: *"Here's what we can do."*
3. **Communication–action** This involves explaining and dramatizing the chosen course to all those who may be affected and whose support is essential: *"Here's what we did and why."*
4. **Evaluation** This involves evaluating the results of the program and the effectiveness of techniques used: *"How did we do?"*

Each one of these steps is as important as the others. Each one is vital to an effective program. Emphasis on fact-finding and planning is what distinguishes public relations from publicity. This process of mustering information and applying it in decision making must be geared to the goals and policies of the organization; otherwise, the four steps add up to meaningless wheel-spinning.

The way in which the public relations wheels turn are shown in Figure 7–1. The program moves steadily forward in one integrated, continuing process whose fluidity does not permit neat compartmentalization. The analysis, synthesis, communication, and interpretation are continuous, spiraling, and overlapping.

FIGURE 7-1

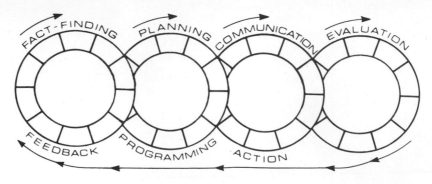

One morning the practitioner will find himself or herself called into the president's office and asked to ascertain, quickly, what the community's reactions will be if the university does not bow to demands to eliminate prayers from all its public functions. This requires *fact-finding*. Next, the practitioner may go into a conference with the admissions committee to devise plans for recruiting Merit Scholars. This requires *counseling* and *planning*. Next, he or she breaks away from this long meeting to keep a luncheon date with a newspaper reporter to discuss a research discovery in the College of Agriculture. Here, he or she serves as *communicator* and *interpreter*. In late afternoon, there is another meeting—this time with Personnel, to evaluate the usefulness of the house publication. This is *evaluation*. So goes the day. Between such tasks, the practitioner may be answering a query from a magazine, arranging for a series of on-the-job safety pictures, cleaning up last-minute details for a United Way drive, digging out material for a speech, or checking proofs on the forthcoming annual report.

In order to understand the process, it is helpful to break it apart and examine each phase. That is the purpose of this chapter, which deals with the first step, and the three chapters that follow. *The unity, overlapping, and continuity of the whole process should be kept in mind as parts are taken out of the running machine for examination.* The way the hard-driven PR wheel turns is shown in Figure 7-1.

The four-step process is illustrated in this problem, which confronted American Oil's public relations staff some years ago: American Oil decided to close its Mankato, Minnesota, sales division as part of a companywide reorganization to gain more efficiency. This meant that 600 employees would have to move or find new jobs, the Mankato community would suffer a loss in income, Minnesota customers would be concerned about getting equally good service under the new setup, and the public would be curious about the meaning of this move.

The first task was to marshal all the facts through research, so the decision could be explained and justified to those concerned. The next step was to plan announcement of the decision. Timing was an important factor. The news had to be broken swiftly, before rumors started, released simultaneously to all those affected, and communicated in such a way as to explain satisfactorily the necessity and wisdom of the change.

Materials included a procedure memorandum to guide the staff, a presentation script for meetings, letters to several different groups of employees, letters to all dealers, a news release, a statement on banking arrangements for Mankato banks, a general office letter, and plans for meetings. The news was released in meetings, via letters to all the different groups involved, and through the news media. Finally, the department *evaluated* its handling of this problem, with an eye to improving its procedures when the next move out of a community had to be communicated. The lessons learned were put to good use a few years later when the company closed a plant in Neodesha, Kansas.

Importance of feedback

As organizations grow in size, their executives become insulated. The busy executive has little time to read, watch television, or meet people outside his or her narrow circle. Administrators are zealously guarded by protective assistants. Most prefer to operate behind a wall of privacy and resent public constraints on their decisions. Few are as frank about it as is a Wisconsin Electric Power Co. executive, who advocates eliminating public participation in power-development decisions. This official, like many others, fails to understand that the price a living system may pay if it fails to take into account its environment can be death or serious injury. *Organizations, just like biological organisms, must carry out surveillance of the environment if they wish to survive in the face of outside hazards.*[1]

The isolation of today's executive from public opinion is epitomized in the president of the United States. A former White House press secretary has observed, "From the president's standpoint, the greatest staff problem is that of maintaining his contact with the world's reality that lies outside the White House. Very few have succeeded in doing so . . . it is only a matter of time until the White House assistants close in like a Praetorian guard."[2] The problem is seen in a lesser dimension when faculty members and students grouse about their "invisible" university president.

Failure to monitor public opinion has resulted in the ambushing of many organizations by crises. Several major public relations blunders of recent years have made clear the cost of such failure.[3] An organization insulated from the nerve ends of society becomes autocratic and paralyzed. Successful organizations have a dynamism that enables them to adjust to societal changes, with built-in provisions for self-criticism as a safeguard against organizational dry rot and public blunders. *Bureaucracies are mechanisms that encourage evasion of responsibility and guilt.*

Prof. James Grunig's studies to develop an organizational theory of public relations have led him to classify organizations into two categories: (1) open, problem-solving organizations, and (2) closed, fatalistic organizations. Interested in problem recognition, problem solving, and constraints on decisions, Grunig examined "fatalistic" organizations that close themselves off from outside forces. These behave mechanistically when constrained by an unchanging technology, a stagnant level of knowledge, and a declining demand for their products or services. He contrasts these organizations with "problem-solving" organizations, which tend to be more decentralized, less stratified, and flexible enough to define the public relations function in such a way that their staffs can devote extensive time to research, strive more for understanding than for persuasion, and spend more time outside the organization gaining the perspective of the public.[4]

Grunig concluded from one study that the role of public relations has been institutionalized in most organizations as an information-giving rather than an information-seeking role. But the role of practitioner is now gradually shifting to emphasis on information-seeking, as it must if the function is to remain useful to administrators.[5] This shift is reflected in the statement of General Telephone Electronics' policy manual shown in Exhibit 7–1.

SUBJECT: POLICY AND PRACTICE—PUBLIC OPINION SURVEYS

TO: Officers and Key Personnel of Parent Company and Subsidiaries

1. STATEMENT OF POLICY

It is a basic policy of General Telephone & Electronics Corporation to assure that opinions, viewpoints, and other information are obtained on a formalized and periodic basis from the general public and such major segments as customers, community leaders, key businessmen, financial analysts, share-owners, and other important groups, to assure an accurate appraisal of attitudes prevailing toward the operations of the over-all GTE organization, the Parent Company, and the individual Subsidiaries. Such surveys are conducted in sufficient depth and with reasonable frequency to assure that a basis is provided for measurement comparisons, so that trends can be determined.

2. RESPONSIBILITY AND SCOPE

The Public Affairs Department of the Parent Company is directly responsible for surveys to determine attitudes of the general public and specific groups toward General Telephone & Electronics Corporation and the over-all organization, and for establishing standards and procedures for surveys conducted by the Subsidiaries.

The Public Affairs Departments of the Subsidiaries have responsibility for developing and conducting surveys to determine the opinions and attitudes of customers, community groups, and the general public toward the specific Subsidiary. In the case of the Telephone Operating Companies, information is obtained on an exchange, district, or division basis, to provide adequate measurement comparisons. In the case of Manufacturing and Research Companies, community attitude surveys are conducted in localities in which plant or laboratory facilities are located. In addition, surveys of customer attitudes toward existing or proposed products are conducted in appropriate market areas by the Manufacturing Subsidiaries, and, in the case of communications products, by GTE Service Corporation, in close cooperation with the Manufacturing Subsidiaries.

In addition to accomplishing the primary objective of informing management of current public attitudes and trends so that appropriate action can be taken to maintain, enhance, or change these attitudes and trends, opinion surveys provide two important side-benefits:

A. The act of conducting the survey has public affairs value, since the normal reaction to those persons contacted in connection with the survey reflects favorably upon the company. Participants tend to respect the company for its efforts in determining the views and opinions of customers and other public groups as a reflection of the company's desire to provide high-quality service and products, and to discharge its responsibility as a corporate citizen.

B. Surveys provide information which can be used for comparative purposes with other available information, such as operating measurements and indices.

As executives climb the organizational pyramid, the barriers that cut them off from contact with reality multiply. The consequence is that when a crisis comes, as it does sooner or later to every organization, the administrator finds himself out in the storm but ill-prepared to cope with it. Thus, he must have aides to supply political, social, and ideological intelligence and to mediate organizational relationships with the outside world. It is part of the practitioner's charter to understand what's going on in society.

The trend is clear—*if organizations are to survive in a rapidly changing society, they must develop adequate radar systems to monitor and decipher these changes.* Those planning on a career in public relations must develop the capacity to provide this service to administrators. And public relations must bring more precision to its informational input, even though the kit of tools for doing so may not be fully adequate. Two practitioners counsel, "However lean the body of knowledge is in understanding people's reactions, attitudes, and opinions, public relations has the obligation to use the best of it and to apply it."[6] Public relations will come to use the knowledge of the behavioral sciences in much the same way the art of medicine uses knowledge of the life sciences.

Public relations serves as the link between an organization and its publics so that the organization may be responsive to those publics. Monitoring the public environment is not only the first step in public relations—it is the most important and most difficult one.

The research attitude

Like an iceberg, only a small part of public relations practice is seen above the surface. The part that does show—publicity—is too often taken for the whole thing; but the unseen mass—research, planning, evaluation—is more important in the long run. The stakes are high in business and institutions today, and management cannot afford to be taken by surprise by unforeseen difficulties. Modern technology, for example, requires heavy investment, and the time lag between the decision to produce and the emergence of the salable product makes accurate prediction imperative. So staff officers must provide facts upon which sound administrative decisions can be made.

An organization's human relations problems are just as specific and researchable as other problems. Wilensky sees an increase in "information consciousness" among executives. David Ogilvy has observed "an increasing tendency on the part of clients to welcome candor, particularly when it is based on the results of consumer research." Counselor David Finn, in his book, *The Corporate Oligarch*, takes a more pessimistic view; he says the business leader is deaf to constructive criticism. Nonetheless, the demand for hard data is growing, paralleling the maturing fields of public opinion measurement, market research, and public relations. *Methodical, systematic research is the foundation of effective public relations.*

A great researcher who helped build the automotive industry, C.F. Kettering, once described this desired attitude in these words:

> Research is a high-hat word that scares a lot of people. It needn't. It is rather simple. Essentially, it is nothing but a state of mind—a friendly, welcoming attitude toward change. Going out to look for change, instead of waiting for it to come.

Research, for practical men, is an effort to do things better and not be caught asleep at the switch. The research state of mind can apply to anything. Personal affairs or any kind of business, big or little. It is the problem-solving mind as contrasted with the let-well-enough-alone mind. It is the composer mind, instead of the fiddler mind; it is the "tomorrow" mind instead of the "yesterday" mind.[7]

The listening phase of public relations

One of the vitiating weaknesses of today's practice is a misplaced emphasis on publicity. Communication starts with listening, which requires humility and systematic effort. Too often, what purports to be communication is simply opposing ideas passing each other in psychological space—for example, in a management-versus-labor bargaining situation, in which each side is merely waiting to score points, not listening to the other's views. As Wilbur Schramm explains, "Feedback is a powerful tool. When it doesn't exist or is delayed or feeble . . . then the situation engenders doubt and concern in the communicator, and frustration and sometimes hostility in the audience."[8] Schramm sees feedback as "merely the reversal of the flow" of communication.

Listening is not an easy task. Channels from the worker out in the plant or the alumnus in Seattle must be provided and kept open. *Failure to listen leads to useless "communicating" on issues that do not exist to publics that are not there.* Research can be used to find the bridge of interest capable of carrying a communications payload.

Before there can be rapport through communication, there must be empathy. Empathy is achieved by open-minded listening. As Thoreau put it, "It takes two to speak the truth—one to speak, and another to hear." Public relations is a *two-way street.* Both lines of traffic must be given equal right-of-way. Unless you know the values, viewpoints, and language of your audience, you are not likely to get through. These values and viewpoints can be learned only through *systematic* and *sympathetic* listening.

An able practitioner of another generation, Abraham Lincoln, knew the importance of listening. Twice each week, Lincoln set aside a period of his valuable time for conversations with ordinary folk—the housewives, farmers, merchants, and pension-seekers. Lincoln listened patiently to what they had to say, no matter how humble their circumstances or how trivial their business. A military officer once protested to the president that he was wasting valuable time on these unimportant people. Lincoln rebuked him, saying, "I tell you, Major . . . that I call these receptions my public opinion baths . . . the effect, as a whole, is renovating and invigorating."[9]

Prudence dictates the systematic listening to an organization's publics through scientific research. Yet many organizations still fail to fully utilize this tool. Why? Because:

1. Sound opinion research is expensive.
2. A time lag exists between the formulation of an opinion study and the time when the results are needed.
3. Management does not want to listen to the views of their publics.
4. There is a lack of knowledge about these research tools on the part of publicity-minded practitioners.
5. There is a lack of confidence in the precision of the research tools now available.

Typical is this comment: "Two-way communication is slim in some school systems because superintendents are afraid of it. They see it as organized back talk and a potential threat rather than an essential tool of modern management. But in most systems, the two-way flow is a trickle because it takes a lot of effort and skill to obtain reliable feedback."

The objective look

Robert Burns wrote:

> Oh wad some power the giftie gie us
> To see oursels as ithers see us!
> It wad frae monie a blunder free us,
>   An' foolish notion.

More wrong decisions are made today on mistaken hunches about what the public thinks than on willful disregard of public opinion. Public relations can be the "giftie"—the mirror that reflects the public's image of the organization to its executives and the image of the organization to the public.

The practitioner relays the views and desires of an organization's publics to its policy makers. To do this accurately, he must be able to adopt the public's viewpoint. That is, he must do *objective* research, for this can provide an effective stimulus to self-correction. Subjective assumptions of "what the public thinks" are too risky in today's world.

Counseling and programming support

Executives are a fact-minded lot; they want figures, not hunches. When the public relations aspect of organizational problems must be brought home to them, the research-based approach can be most effective. Clarence J. Hicks, industrial relations pioneer, said, "It is characteristic of a profession that recommendations are of value in proportion as they are intelligently based upon a thorough diagnosis of the individual case or problem." This truism has been doubled in spades in the era of the computer.

Public relations research cannot replace intuition and experience—but it can greatly enrich them, clarify them, and make them more general. The function of research is to deepen and extend the policy maker's capacity for judgment. *The need is for research-supported diagnoses, not new medicines.*

Uncovering trouble spots

Too often, problems are allowed to define themselves in the form of a crisis. Too much effort goes into "fire-fighting" rather than "fire prevention." This is dramatized when deteriorating labor relations present the problem of a teacher strike or a lockout or a student sit-in. Such situations usually have long histories, and sometimes neither party even knows what caused the blowup. Heading off blowups is part of the public relations task. The earlier a complaint is caught, the easier it is to handle. Continuous fact-finding will uncover many problems while they are still small enough to permit quiet handling without a critical public looking on. The same attentive listening will permit the catching and scotching of rumors before they become widespread.

An example: A defective 20-cent part in the toilet of a mobile home manufactured by a subsidiary of the Bendix Corporation brought Bendix before the Federal Trade Commission, after it had repeatedly spurned the angry complaints of a determined Georgia owner who had suffered some $9,000 in damages because of the defect. Bendix got widespread unfavorable publicity and had to pay legal and damage costs. Corporate officers claimed that they had had no knowledge of the problem until the FTC hearing. A Bendix official apologized and said, "We have taken steps to correct the management insensitivity that was displayed in this incident." An effective organizational radar will prevent such damaging incidents.

Improving outbound communication

Failure to provide feedback from various publics inevitably results in communications breakdowns and wasted efforts. A pioneer practitioner, Sir Stephen Tallents, saw the problem clearly: "We must begin by studying the minds—the greatly differing minds—of those to whom our projection is addressed. . . . We must bring to our task a sensitive insight and a keen sympathy. And we must support them by the most carefully acquired knowledge of the different ways and tastes and needs of other peoples."[10]

For the maximum effect in communication and persuasion, each public must have special study and special treatment. This emphasis on the need to pinpoint the specific publics is one of the most useful contributions public relations has received from the social scientists. Much of today's publicity effort is characterized by wasteful misses. Research enables the practitioner to pinpoint his publics, discover their leaders, and learn their values, viewpoints, and language. *A public relations effort increases in effectiveness in proportion to the specificity with which it is directed to a group.*

Useful intelligence from research

Increasingly, administrators rely on the public relations department as a central source of information on the organization, the public's image of it, the industry or field, and the social, economic, and political trends. Such demands are to be encouraged, since this service enhances the effectiveness of the total program.

To provide such intelligence requires the stockpiling of facts and information analysis. Research has two basic purposes: *First,* the collection and collation of facts used in planning a course of action and in determining channels and content of the informational program; and *second,* exploration of basic attitudes, opinions expressed, and information held by members of an organization's publics—generally used more for long-range planning.

Measurement and analysis of opinions range from the highly informal and impressionistic to the methodical and near-scientific. Progress in any specialized field is marked by its advance from impressionistic observation to objective testing, with accurate measurement techniques.

Information center

When the boss or the client wants some information, he usually wants it *now!* Demands like this come frequently and often unexpectedly. In order to provide management with the intelligence it needs, as well as to provide content for the communications program, public relations must maintain an information center where data can be located, arranged, and analyzed. Useful information is to be found in government and trade publications, libraries, newspapers, industry reports, and a multitude of other sources. Keeping a current organizational "almanac" is a useful idea. Daily requests will tell what is needed.

In most organizations where there is no librarian or historian, the department becomes the central information bureau, handling queries that cannot be answered by other departments. Newspaper, magazine, radio, and TV journalists have come to expect quick answers. Such demands should be met promptly and media people thus encouraged to rely on the office for authentic information. Such practice has many valuable consequences—for instance, a reporter's query often gives the department a running start on a crisis in the making.

From fact files come ideas and information for speeches, pamphlets, special reports, institutional advertising, exhibits, special events, and background information for special projects. The department is responsible for assembling the factual content of its communications program. Often these items have to be whipped up in a hurry. For example, a department of a bank had to get out in two weeks a brief history booklet to help mark the occasion of the millionth depositor.

Practitioners are now making increased use of computerized information-retrieval systems to save time, energy, money, and file space. Many organizations maintain their own retrieval systems; others utilize systems in nearby libraries, or subscribe to a commercial service, such as the *New York Times* Information Bank. Prof. Albert Walker observes, "Computerized information retrieval systems take time from the search for knowledge and add to it time for putting the knowledge to use or creating new knowledge from it."

The research process

Opinion, market, and academic researchers have developed a pattern of research that involves nine basic steps:

1. Statement of the problem.
2. Selection of a manageable portion of the problem.
3. Definition of concepts and terms.
4. Literature search.
5. Development of a hypothesis.
6. Determination of a study design.
7. Gathering of the data.
8. Analysis of the data.
9. Recording of the implications, generalizations, conclusions.

Research for analysis of a specific problem should include these elements: (1) a broad overview of what has gone before that influences the present situation; (2) changes expected in the environment in the next year or so that could affect the organization; (3) social, political, and economic trends foreseeable in the next five to ten years that could affect the organization; and (4) what the organization can do to influence the public to accelerate favorable trends and slow down unfavorable ones.

Defining the problem and the publics

The starting point is to *define the problem.* Much waste in public relations practice is caused by attacking problems that don't exist and aiming messages at audiences that don't exist. Failure to accurately define the problem by ascertaining audience opinions leads to pillow-punching—devoting time, money, and creative energy to promoting a theme that simply is not perceived as relevant by the target audience.

Next, *the publics and their interrelationships must be defined,* and this also involves determining the effective channels of communication with each. Precise definition of a client's publics—their composition and their prevailing attitudes—goes beyond simple classifications, such as trustees, faculty, students, alumni. Members of a given public are constantly shifting. In public relations you communicate with a passing parade, not a standing army.

To illustrate: The post–World War II baby boom that lasted until the early 1960s slowly but inexorably rearranged the nation, as it rolled from overcrowded nurseries to overcrowded schools and colleges to the employment market. This generation, from ages 16 to 31, shows up in double-digit unemployment, in the housing crunch, in debate over a later retirement age, and as customers with a different life-style. It will manifest itself in the future in unpredictable ways.

There is a constant "to-ing and fro-ing" in age groupings, economic interests, political interests, and geographic residence—the last particularly, in mobile America. New publics are always coming into being, old ones fading away. Significant changes in society's values in opinion leadership, and in the composition of the public have taken place over the past two decades. These changes can be seen in the influence today's young adults exert on our life-style, politics, mores, and commerce. Today, half the nation's eligible voters are under 30. The more than 7 million college students exert themselves as a powerful force, outnumbering farmers by three to one, coal miners by fifty to one, railway workers by ten to one. Understanding and communicating with young people will be a prime task in the years ahead.[11]

The marketing and public relations problems caused by these population shifts can be illustrated in the relationship between newspapers and young readers, a matter that concerns publishers. Readership among the young is declining, for reasons that, despite considerable research, are not clear. Some see TV as creating the decline; others believe changing youth life-styles are a major factor; still other publishers blame current educational methods and the decline in reading ability. This problem underlines the observation of Jack McLeod and Garrett O'Keefe: "The points at which persons move from one part of the life cycle to another are likely to be periods of considerable reorganization of communications and other behavior."

Typical of new publics coming into being are those with an interest in foreign-made cars, or CB radios. Introduction of a new product may create a new buying public. Establishment of a new branch plant brings a new community public to be studied and understood. No two are exactly alike. Normally, regroupings take place gradually, almost imperceptibly, such as with changes in family living brought on by television. At other times, the shift comes with lightning swiftness—for instance, when a whole nation is plunged into war or economic depression.

It is imperative to keep current an accurate analysis of publics and their sentiments. For example, the bank credit card, which may in time completely replace currency, is defining new publics and involves a host of problems in gaining acceptance of change. New attitudes and behavioral patterns must be encouraged by the sponsor. One study categorized bank-card users as (1) convenience users, (2) early-acquisition users, (3) total users, and (4) non-users. Another bank study, focusing on attitudes of the student population, concluded, "In sum, banks may be seen as scoring moderate to high on task leadership, moderately well on communication behaviors, low to moderate on personality factors, and extremely low on social leadership."

Such analysis will reveal the group leaders or influentials in each of an organization's several publics. The importance of determining the *actual* as against the *presumed* opinion leaders was underscored in Chapter Six. Too often in public relations there is a tendency to short-cut this task in an effort to "economize"—by tagging lawyers, doctors, clergymen, and bankers as the sum total of leadership, or by assuming that a union leader is a leader in political or social affairs as well as in union matters. A person may be influential in his group and yet not prominent in the community. *Each social stratum generates its own opinion leaders.* Also, people look to different group leaders for guidance in different facets of their daily lives. Spotting the true group leaders requires laborious fact-finding; there is no shortcut. The political graveyard is filled with aspirants for office who ignored, or sought to circumvent, opinion leaders.

In conducting this "publics" research, learn and recognize the interrelatedness of all these groups. The practitioner needs to know which of them "listen in" on which others and gauge their reactions. Furthermore, what is said to one group may be heard by another. This presents a dilemma; the more that practitioners appeal to different groups in terms of their self-interest, as they must, the greater is the danger of offending other groups. Often, organizations have to choose which groups they want on their side.

Systematic definition of an organization's publics is needed also to determine an order of priority. Priorities must be assigned to an institution's almost infinite number of publics. Rarely does a practitioner have the staff and money to do all the things he or she thinks need to be done, a perpetual priority problem.

Reaching the audience

Once the publics have been identified, research is used also to ascertain the best ways of reaching them. This requires determination of channels of influence and communication. Pinpointing is essential if the message is to be designed in such a way as to gain the intended audience's attention.

It is not easy to attract the public's attention or to hold its interest. Careless or casual determination of group and geographic boundaries is too common. The more carefully the various publics are defined, the more ways will be found to reach and influence them. Research will best define the commonality of interests that will serve as a bridge to carry an organization's persuasive communications across to a public.

The manner in which research is used to define or redefine an audience is illustrated in Table 7–1, an analysis of the changing newspaper audience prepared for Harte-Hanks newspapers by a major research firm.

TABLE 7–1   A hypothetical map of the old versus the new marketplace

The Traditional Newspaper Audience	The New Audience
The American Family	*The American Family*
Permanent commitment	Commitment—not necessarily permanent
Explicit sex roles	Blurred sex roles
Children-oriented	Childlessness accepted
Family over individual	Focus on self
Togetherness a plus	Individualism
Rituals a plus	Rejection of ritual
The Community	*The Community*
Based on age, religion, ethnicity	Natural interests
Bounded by neighborhood	Bounded by values
Obligation	Voluntary
	Transitional
Role of Women	*Role of Women*
Goal: marriage and children—most outside interests discouraged	May include careerism
	Housewife now a profession
Education: oriented toward wife and motherhood	Non-domestic success goals
Work: from necessity	Self-fulfillment, few prohibitions
Family role excluded: basic earning power, major financial decisions	Equal financial responsibility
Religion	*Religion*
Organized religion an important personal value	Organized religion a declining personal value
	Interest in the occult, the mystical as part of learning about self
Criteria	*Criteria*
Technology	The natural
Bigness	Personalization
Popularity	Simplification
Complexity	Meaningfulness to the individual
Functionalism	
Communication	*Communication*
Verbal	Nonverbal as well as verbal
Formal	Informal
Mass	One to one

TABLE 7-1 A hypothetical map of the old versus the new marketplace (continued)

The Traditional Newspaper Audience	The New Audience
The Need to Know	*The Need to Know*
Obligation	Part of self-understanding
Nonselective	Selectivity
Goal-oriented	Self-oriented
Leisure Time	*Leisure Time*
Social	Solitude or social
Competitive	Noncompetitive
Useful	Self-fulfilling
Structured	Unstructured
Pleasing others	Doing what you want
Values	*Values*
All "new values" people are alike	Acceptance/modification/ rejection/innovation

Source: "Young People and Newspapers: An Exploratory Study," prepared for Harte-Hanks Newspapers, May 1976. Reproduced with permission. The research was conducted by Yankelovich, Skelly, and White, Inc.

The research tools

Informal methods

Pioneers in public relations lacked the precision tools available today to gauge opinion accurately. They were forced to fall back on whatever rough-and-ready means could be devised. Today, despite the development of the more accurate measuring sticks, reliance on informal methods still predominates. Because of lack of funds and the necessity of making quick, on-the-spot evaluations, it is not realistic to make formal research a part and parcel of the daily routine in a department or counseling firm. This is particularly true for thinly staffed one- or two-person departments or agencies.

These informal methods can be helpful if practitioners recognize their weaknesses. Inherently, such methods lack *representativeness* and *objectivity,* keys to sound opinion research. Still these ways can provide vital and significant clues to opinion trends and reveal sources of things people like or do not like.

Personal contacts: Lord Bryce said, "The best way in which the tendencies at work in any community can be best discovered and estimated is by moving freely about among all sorts and conditions of men." Skill in sizing up people's attitudes has long been and always will be one of the prime qualifications of a counselor. By probing, talking, listening, and analyzing while moving about, the practitioner can learn a great deal. The politician has been doing this for a long time. There is great value in wide acquaintanceships with representative leaders from all walks of life. Many practitioners consult regularly with such influentials as editors, reporters, ministers, labor leaders, bartenders, civic leaders, bankers, and cause leaders.

Imaginative practitioners find many ways to "move freely about among all sorts and conditions of men." A corporate practitioner, confronted with a management request to begin an employee communications campaign against drug abuse, realized he knew little of drugs, their use, and their effects. He got himself admitted as a patient in a drug-treatment center and spent three days acquiring firsthand knowledge of drug users and their problems. Faced with growing demands to modify government buildings for the convenience of the handicapped, the General Services Administration put its top officials in wheelchairs so they could find out what it would be like to go for a coffee break or to the restroom if they couldn't walk. Concerned about the changing newspaper audience, Don Carter, when he was publisher of the Lexington, Kentucky, *Herald-Leader,* went with his newsroom executives on a door-to-door subscription-selling campaign. They sold subscriptions, but more important, they got closer to the concerns of the ordinarily "faceless" reader.

Feedback from periodic personal visits can be encouraged, extended, and amplified in many ways. For example, Mayor Thomas Bradley of Los Angeles, after taking office, opened his door to local citizens one day a month. They were given a chance to talk to the mayor about poor sewer facilities, increases in school vandalism, and other citizen concerns. Those waiting their turn were provided coffee and reading material. The mayor of Utica, New York, went a step further: To encourage people to drop in and air their complaints, he took his door off its hinges and put up a sign over his couch, "The Town's Living Room."

A more structured use of the personal contact is exemplified in the Bell System's visits with 50,000 shareholders each year. Annually, Bell System managers visit shareholders, usually after business hours in investors' homes, to talk about the way the business is being managed. Some 8,000 management men and women from AT&T, local operating companies, Western Electric, and Bell Laboratories take part in these informal surveys. In the first twenty years of this program, more than a million shareowners were visited.

The National Environmental Policy Act of 1969 required, among other things, that the public be afforded an opportunity to have a say in highway planning. As one way of getting this feedback, the Utah State Department of Highways has used a travel trailer as a mobile information center to collect citizens' opinions on proposed federal highway routes. According to the department, "The Center provides a candid atmosphere and a 'one-on-one' relationship with highway personnel." The van gives people who are too timid to speak out in a public meeting an opportunity to air their views in relative privacy, and it can also be used to disseminate information. Many organizations have used mobile information vans in this way.

Idea juries, panels: It is only a short step from asking friends and associates for their reactions to organizing idea juries or opinion panels. These range from ad hoc to very formal arrangements, and the degree of continuity in these sounding boards also varies. The jury panel is one of the most economical "polls." Careful selection of such a group can provide a rough working idea of opinion within it; bringing the members together for a lunch or dinner once a month can pay good dividends.

A Wisconsin dairy cooperative developed a fruitful variation of the opinion panel when it held a series of "Neighborhood Huddles" for its membership. An influential member was asked to invite the members in his neighborhood to a "Neighborhood Huddle." Current information on the dairy situation was presented and comments were invited. At the end, each member was asked to fill out a form to evaluate the cooperative's program. Comments made during the meeting, as well as these open-end evaluation forms, were later collated and analyzed to draw a profile of member attitudes as feedback.

The panel technique can also be used to establish communication with minority groups. The aspirations, needs, and demands of Chicago's black community were voiced when the Chicago Welfare Council staged a "listen-in," "to hear and understand from black leaders the needs and feelings of the black community." Another variation of this technique, used with increasing frequency, is to arrange for a panel of customers or clients to "tell it like it is" to an industry or profession at the annual meeting.

Advisory committees: A variation of the idea jury is the advisory committee, which can be helpful in preventing many a misstep. Advisory committees, representing public groups, also serve on occasion as heat shields to absorb public criticism. Nonprofit organizations can tap the aid of skilled public relations people in this way. Formation of such a committee for a college or civil-rights group can serve to win the interest and participation of influential people in the community. Once members are interested and informed, they are likely to return to their own circle and carry the ball for the program.

But there is a price to be paid in using such committees. Their advice must be given earnest consideration, or else the gesture will backfire. No one likes to serve as a show-window mannequin. There are dangers in pseudo-participation. Influential persons quickly sense when they are being "used."

Government at all levels has found advisory committees of value in providing a sensitizing response from the public for increasingly large bureaucracies. By the late 1970s, the federal government had more than 1,200 advisory committees serving its countless agencies and bureaus, although many of these were inactive. Nearly one-fourth of these committees served the Department of Health, Education and Welfare. This trend was accelerated by the passage of the Environmental Policy Act, which required that the public be consulted before the government could build dams or undertake other projects that would affect people and the environment—*another indication of the growing force of public opinion.*

Government agencies have developed many ways of getting citizen feedback beyond formal public hearings such as those required by the EPA. For example, the U.S. Forest Service developed the charrette, or planning session. At these charrettes, usually held in a national-forest camp, some 200 people of different age groups and interests spend two full days and parts of two nights listening, questioning, arguing, and expressing their opinions on what the Service should do with a particular forest during the next decade. The participants are divided into teams of ten members each, with the teams balanced as evenly as possible between conservationists and nonconservationists, and each team is assigned to a small cabin where it talks things out.

Other organizations, profit and nonprofit alike, use advisory committees. For example, in response to the growing force of consumerism in the 1970s, the Scandinavian insurance industry created advisory committees and complaint bureaus to facilitate policyholder feedback. The president of the University of Georgia set up an advisory council composed of public relations practitioners and media representatives to advise him on public relations. The Chicago-based accounting giant, Arthur Andersen & Co., set up a public review board to "provide the firm with an outside perspective on its own operations." Only one member of the five-member board is an accountant. The Topeka, Kansas, board of education set up a 24-member Community Advisory Committee on Education to give it a better sense of community attitudes and needs. Membership on this committee ranges from housewives to lawyers. The New York Stock Exchange created an advisory committee of fifteen senior corporate officers "to facilitate communications between listed corporations and the Exchange Board of Directors." The American Frozen Food Institute formed an advisory council on frozen goods made up of food editors and home-economics instructors.

Several agencies and corporations have taken this device one step further by appointing representatives of the public to policy-making boards. Several years ago, General Motors named an outstanding black minister to its board to provide minority representation. The presence of women on corporate boards is now becoming commonplace. Gulf Oil, when caught up in public controversy, put a Roman Catholic nun, a college president, on its board to represent both these concerns. Many school boards now include one or two high school seniors as ex-officio members with the right to fully participate in board discussions. Students also serve on some college governing boards.

The ombudsman: Growing dissatisfaction resulting from ever-longer lines of communication to ever-less-responsive bureaucracies has brought about the widespread adoption of the ombudsman idea, to facilitate an inflow of complaints and criticism. The ombudsman position was first established in the Swedish government in 1713. In more recent times, the concept has gained popularity as a means of bringing bureaucracy under control and improving communications. Hawaii, in 1969, became the first state to establish an ombudsman post, to hear complaints from citizens who feel that they can't get the action they want, or that they have been dealt with unfairly.[12]

In countless nongovernment institutions, the ombudsman concept has proved useful in providing feedback and a means of solving problems while they are still manageable. Universities, newspapers, corporations, food chains, school boards, labor unions, and other organizations have created such offices. For instance, the Rockford, Illinois, *Star and Register* has an official it calls "Mr. Go-Between." Dow Chemical Company established an "ombudswoman" to promote the advancement of women in its company. Prof. Donald C. Rowat of Carleton College, who has studied the proliferation of this function over the past decade, categorizes two kinds of ombudsmen: (1) one that, true to the roots of the original, investigates and solves problems, and (2) an office that at best parries problems and is maintained to enhance the bureaucratic image. The former type has independent authority to take action on complaints; the latter is a facilitator of communications who recommends action to others.

The range of the function and scope of its authority varies widely. The ombudsmen of Hawaii, Nebraska, and Iowa derive their authority from their legislatures, and thus are independent of the political structure. Those of North Carolina and Oregon are appointed by the governor. Cornell University's ombudsman (the first appointee was a woman) is authorized to hear "complaints from anyone in the University . . . about anyone in authority in the University or about the operation of the University." At Bronx Community College, the ombudsman, appointed by the president, acts as a conduit for student complaints but has no authority to make full-scale investigations. At the University of Nebraska–Lincoln, the ombudsman sees his job as "reporting to nobody and responsible to everyone." In the U.S. Navy, the post was created in 1971 by

Admiral Elmo Zumwalt and is officially titled Pers P; a complaint goes first to the complainant's command and, if not solved there, then to Pers P.

Pan American World Airways set up in 1971 an Office of Consumer Action, which handled 7,000 complaints in its first year and a half. Utility companies have found this feedback channel of help in meeting a rising tide of criticism. Wisconsin Electric Power Company's consumer representative mainly investigates complaints and claims of customers whose service has been or is about to be shut off. He has independent authority to revoke cutoffs. The Social Security Administration initiated a program of ombudsmen in 1976 "to see if Social Security Service can be improved by a troubleshooter."

The Louisville, Kentucky, area schools, when wracked by a school busing controversy, installed an ombudsman's office. When Superintendent Frank Simpson opened the office, he assured citizens that "the buck will stop here." The Louisville newspapers pioneered in the use of an ombudsman to hear reader complaints and ensure the correction of errors in published stories. Readers are encouraged to call the ombudsman at any time, night or day. Many hospitals have set up an ombudsman position. A large New York hospital employs a "Patient Representative" to serve as an advocate on behalf of patients "to help them and their families find satisfactory solutions to problems."

Utilization of the ombudsman concept, if sincerely used and competently staffed, can be an important means of feedback.

The call-in telephone line: Reduced rates for leased telephone lines and the need for more channels of feedback have led to increased use of the call-in telephone line, sometimes called a "hot line," a "query line," an information center, or, in one instance, a "cool line." This call-in service provides the public with a quick means of getting needed information or registering complaints. These lines may be staffed by trained personnel adept at fielding complaints and providing information, or they may be hooked to recorders on which messages may be transcribed, to be routed to the proper office. This feedback channel is used in many ways. Some organizations use it internally, to provide quick answers to employees; hospitals use it to provide information to patients and their families; and government agencies use it to help citizens find their way through the bureaucratic maze.

Travelers Insurance Companies, troubled by the public's negative attitudes toward the insurance industry, set up an Office of Consumer Information with toll-free lines and then used advertising to encourage the public to call the office on any insurance-related question. A Travelers executive says "the idea took off and flew." Yet General Motors tested a "GM Open Line" in Chicago and found it not worthwhile. The company used a heavy advertising campaign to tell GM owners in the Chicago area of this service, which would relay their complaints to the right person, but got only 6,800 calls over a three month period—not enough to justify the cost, in GM's opinion.

The Whirlpool Corporation, which initiated its "Cool Line" service in the late 1960s in response to growing consumer dissatisfaction, had the opposite experience. This toll-free telephone service permits Whirlpool appliance owners anywhere in the continental United States to call highly skilled service consultants if they have trouble with their appliances and either are unable to get help locally or don't know how. The Cool Line program, located at company headquarters in Benton Harbor, Michigan, employs nine full-time consultants, plus six part-timers to fill in on vacations or at certain times of the year when the call-in load gets heavy. These are experienced professionals with many years in the field as district and regional service managers. The Cool Line operates 24 hours a day, 52 weeks a year, and averages 150,000 calls a year. The company has found through sales, opinion surveys, and customer letters, as well as other ways, that this investment is a sound one.

"Hot lines" are usually established in times of an emergency or a conflict. For example, striking school teachers may set up a hot line to answer an irritated public's complaints or questions. When the energy crisis broke in the United States in 1974, the Insurance Information Institute set up a toll-free telephone line to handle inquiries from the news media on the crisis as it related to insurance. It advertised in *Editor & Publisher* and *Broadcasting* a "New Hot Number" that newspeople could call free to get information. Those manning these lines were provided looseleaf manuals so that they could give prompt replies to most questions. Most states now have consumer-protection agencies with hot lines as a means of expediting consumer complaints. The first one was installed in Georgia in 1969, and many states followed suit. Georgia's office gets 50,000 calls a year.

The largest call-in system to answer queries and field complaints is the U.S. government's Federal Information Centers, which were started in the Johnson administration as a way of making government more responsive to people's needs. The first one was opened in Atlanta in July 1966; a decade later, there were centers in 36 major metropolitan areas, which, in turn, served another 36 centers by means of a toll-free tieline service. These centers also provide a walk-in service in their effort to answer questions or refer citizens to the agency that can.

To be effective, the call-in telephone service, like any other channel, must be used with sincerity. The U.S. Bureau of Mines, acting in the wake of several major mine disasters, announced with great fanfare that it was installing "hot-line" telephones at the face of every coal mine so that miners could alert the bureau if they found unsafe conditions in the mine, and it promised "instant action" on such complaints. A few months later, a *Wall Street Journal* reporter found that the bureau had failed to monitor the line, attached to a recording device, from November until late December when the check was made. The newspaper reported that bureau employees "had forgotten about the machine."

Mail analysis: Another economical way of gauging opinions—one frequently overlooked—is a periodic analysis of an organization's incoming mail. The correspondence will reveal areas of favor, disfavor, and lack of information.

It should be kept in mind that letter writers tend to be critical rather than commendatory. Letters often will hoist warning flags on sources of ill will or service breakdown, and will reveal the boomerang effects of a program. At the same time, *letters may indicate opinion, but they do not measure it.* For example, published letters to newspapers and magazines are more likely to reflect the editors' views than those of the audience. The larger cross-section of letters is not seen by the public.[13]

President John F. Kennedy borrowed a leaf from Franklin D. Roosevelt's book on keeping in touch with the public. Kennedy directed that every fiftieth letter coming to the White House be brought to him. Periodic mail samples helped both these leaders to bridge the moat surrounding the White House. And studies made of mail coming to the USIA's Voice of America have been helpful in indicating audience interest and belief in the VOA's output.

The Ford Motor Company's "We Listen Better" campaign, which at its peak brought in 18,000 letters a week from owners, is a dramatic example of the use of letters to get feedback. These letters are answered individually, not by form letter, and thus require a large investment of money and manpower. Says a Ford executive, "These letters help us to keep up with changing needs in the market and to make innovations in the way we do business. These letters are carefully coded, and a running tally of the comments, suggestions, and criticisms is programmed into a computer for our use. They are used by our product planners, our engineers, and our general counsel. It is an informal, unstructured, and nondisciplined source of information—but a very good source."

Specific mail responses can be significant, too. A large western company became concerned about the number of inactive accounts among credit-card holders. The manager sat down and wrote a personal, friendly letter to be sent to them. Thirty-four hundred letters were mailed and 1,100 responses came back, although no incentives or premiums were provided. Analysis of the letters revealed many implications for that company's program.

Field reports: Most organizations have district representatives, field agents, or recruiters who travel the organization's territory. These agents should be trained to listen and should be given an easy, regular means of reporting opinions they encounter. In this way, they can serve as the "eyes and ears" of the organization. Systematic reporting of opinions, complaints, and commendations should be part of their jobs.

However, it should be noted that reports of such representatives tend to gild the lily and get purified on their way to the top. For example, in an effort to measure the impact of a certain "Progress Week," an industry's sales representatives in Bangor, Maine, were asked for an evaluation. Forty percent would venture no opinion. About half of those responding thought that the week's promotion had produced more favorable attitudes toward the industry. Actually, a cross-section survey found that only 11 percent of the Bangor population was inclined to be more favorable toward this industry. In this case, only twelve of the 42 "grass-roots" observers were able to gauge opinions correctly. So all impressional measurements must be studied with caution. Field reports can be helpful if the built-in bias is kept in mind.

Media reports: Press clippings and broadcast monitor reports, all available from commercial services, have long been used as yardsticks. However, these services should be used only to detect what is being disseminated about your organization or about a competitor. They will indicate only what is printed or broadcast; they cannot report whether the message was read or heard and, if so, whether it was believed and understood. Newspaper clippings are useful in measuring the acceptability of releases sent to the press, but they cannot measure impact. Also, 100 percent coverage on newsclips is difficult to achieve; returns from a particular service will vary.

The press, when used with extreme caution, can be a fairly reliable guide to current opinions, particularly those of protest and criticism. Still, the wide disparity between the voting opinions of the people and the editorial opinions of newspapers, as demonstrated in elections, should warn against uncritical acceptance of newspaper editorial opinion. The same is true of radio and TV news commentators; interpretive reporting may or may not reflect public opinion. Mass media can be used as indicators, not as yardsticks.

More reliable methods

The surest way to learn someone's opinion and underlying attitudes would be to sit down and talk things over face to face. This is not often possible. Instead, social scientists and market researchers have developed the technique of talking to a small but representative group in each public. This is the sample survey. Sampling is a great money saver and is accurate when the sample is representative and the survey methods objective. Remember those two key words: *representative* and *objective*. Survey research is built on the laws of mathematical probability.

By the asking of precise, understandable questions of a truly accurate microcosm of a whole, public opinion can be measured with a high degree of accuracy. Just as the practitioner depends largely on the established channels to talk to the public, he surveys to listen to the public. Through such devices, representatives of the public are encouraged to tell their story to the institution. These survey tools offer an effective means of facilitating an inflow of information and opinion.

Cross-section surveys: A carefully prepared set of questions is asked of a cross-section sample of a given public. The interviews build a bridge between an organization and the public. There are three ways to draw the sample to be interviewed: (1) the *probability sample,* in which people to be interviewed are chosen at random by some mechanical formula, such as every *n*th name on the list; (2) the *area sample,* a form of the probability sample in which geographical areas are listed—cities, for example—then units to be surveyed are chosen at random; and (3) the *quota sample,* wherein the population in question is analyzed by known characteristics—sex, age, residence, occupation, income level—then interviews are assigned by quota in the same proportions as these characteristics exist in the whole population.

All these methods involve a degree of sampling error, which can usually be kept within tolerable limits. *The results obtained through cross-section surveys are more quantitative than qualitative in nature;* they often fail to reflect the depth and intensity of opinions expressed by respondents.

Survey panels: Under this method, a panel of people is selected and is interviewed several times over a period of time. The selection of participants is determined on a cross-section basis. Panels are used to learn what happens to people under varying conditions over a span of time. It is an effective device for controlled experiments.[14] A panel could be used, for example, to measure the impact of a series of projects in community relations, or to follow people's buying habits in a grocery store. Panels are difficult to administer, and it is hard to keep all members interested over a long stretch. Also, panel members tend in time to become atypical rather than typical.

Depth interview: This is a qualitative instrument to probe the attitudes underlying expressed opinions. It is an informal kind of interview, and the respondent is encouraged to talk fully and freely. This method requires highly trained interviewers and skilled analysts. Because of its informal nature and the fact that the most productive depth interviews are those that give respondents the widest latitude for responding, one major problem in its use is how to evaluate it. The really qualified depth interviewer is rare. The depth interview is one of the techniques used in motivational research.

Content analysis: This is a method of systematically coding and classifying the content of one or all of the mass media. It can tell an organization what is being said and published about it, and in what context. Media content can be measured as to how much is descriptive, how much favorable, how much critical. Content analysis will show the pattern of mentions of an organization and can provide helpful clues to the kinds of information its publics are being exposed to, but not necessarily what they consume and believe. It is also possible to couple content analysis with a sampling procedure and obtain, from a sample of some fifty daily papers, an accurate picture of nationwide dissemination of a given subject. Content analysis also can be useful in periodically assessing the content of informational output against its stated objectives.[15]

Mail questionnaires: The use of mail instead of face-to-face questionnaires is economical, and so it is tempting to the penny-pinched practitioner. But it gives no assurance that the respondents will be *representative* of the whole population. In putting questions by mail, you lose the flexibility and the interpretations possible in personal interviews. Besides, it is usually difficult to get an adequate response, particularly since so many people have been polled in this fashion that there is some resentment.

But this economical device can be useful when used with due caution and when space is left at the end for open-ended comment. It is most effective in soliciting opinions of homogeneous groups where the cleavage of opinion is decisive—such as of a group of employees on the question of overtime or night shift—and can also be helpful in uncovering sources of criticism and praise.

Semantic differential: This technique of measurement is easy and economical to use, and therefore of great utility for the practitioner who invariably faces a research-budget problem.

The semantic differential, developed to assess variations in the connotative meanings of objects and words, is based on the premise that such meaning constitutes one of the most significant variables motivating human behavior. The procedure is to have the subject rate one or more objects of judgment (or concepts) on a scale defined by a pair of adjectival opposites, with seven steps between them. For example, a person could be asked for his rating of Jimmy Carter on a number of bipolar scales such as strong-weak, active-passive, valuable-worthless, heavy-light, pleasant-unpleasant, and so forth, with the seven steps between the pairs of opposites allowing the subject to express both the direction of his association and its intensity. Thus, confronted with a scale such as "safe/ _____/ _____/ _____/ _____/ _____/ _____/ _____/ dangerous," the subject can indicate whether he regards the particular person, thing, or concept to be very safe or very dangerous, quite safe or quite dangerous, or slightly safe or slightly dangerous, with the middle point reserved for the feeling of neither safe nor dangerous.

With such sets of scales, measures of the connotations of various concepts can be obtained from specially selected individuals or groups, representative samples of the public. There is no basic restriction on the kinds of concepts that may be judged—individual personalities, corporation images, and so forth. The generality of the technique is attested to by the wide range of uses it has had in its relatively short existence—in attitude measurement, linguistics, psychotherapy, advertising, and image profiles in public relations.[16] Readers are cautioned that the semantic differential is a *rough measuring instrument,* not as reliable as a straight attitude-measurement device.

Case problem

Let's assume that you are serving as a speech writer in the public relations department of your college or university. The president has accepted an invitation to give the main talk at the annual alumni banquet during commencement week. He asks you to prepare a 30-minute speech (approximately ten typewritten pages) on "The Crisis Facing Higher Education Today." To carry out this assignment, you must:

1. Define your audience.
2. Determine themes to implement present and long-range objectives.
3. Assemble factual content through research.
4. Outline the suggested speech preparatory to a conference with the president on theme, tone, content, and so forth.
5. Write the speech.

ADDITIONAL READINGS

EARL R. BABBIE, *The Practice of Social Research.* Belmont, Calif.: Wadsworth, 1975.

WILLIAM P. EHLING, "Public Relations Research: A Few Fundamentals," *College and University Journal,* Vol. 1 (Fall 1962).

CHARLES Y. GLOCK, ed., *Survey Research in the Social Sciences.* New York: The Russell Sage Foundation, 1967.

HERBERT KAUFMAN, *Administrative Feedback.* Washington, D.C.: The Brookings Institution, 1973. A look at the problem of feedback channels in government.

OTTO LERBINGER AND MAX L. MARSHALL, "PR Research in the Corporation," *Public Relations Journal,* Vol. 27 (March 1971).

RALPH O. NAFZIGER AND DAVID M. WHITE, eds., *Introduction to Mass Communications Research,* rev. ed. Baton Rouge: Louisiana State University Press,

1963. The chapter on "Field Methods in Communication Research" is especially helpful.

EDWARD J. ROBINSON, *Public Relations and Survey Research.* New York: Appleton-Century-Crofts, 1969. Useful guide, with examples; subsidized by the Foundation for Public Relations Research and Education.

CHARLES W. ROLL, JR., and ALBERT H. CANTRIL, *Polls: Their Use and Misuse in Politics.* New York: Basic Books, 1972.

WILBUR SCHRAMM, ed., *The Science of Human Communication.* New York: Basic Books, 1963.

CLAIRE SELLTIZ, MARIE JAHODA, et al., *Research Methods in Social Relations.* New York: Holt, Rinehart & Winston, 1962.

DANIEL YANKELOVICH, *The New Morality: A Profile of American Youth in the 70's.* New York: McGraw-Hill, 1974.

FOOTNOTES

1. The tragic cost of lack of adequate feedback and of misleading feedback was etched deeply in the nation's involvement in Vietnam. David Halberstam's *The Best and the Brightest* (New York: Random House, 1972) suggests that a major cause of prolonged U.S. involvement in Vietnam was the continued failure of the U.S. government to base its policies upon a rational analysis of accurate, continuous intelligence.

2. George E. Reedy, *The Twilight of the Presidency* (New York and Cleveland: World Publishing Co., 1970), p. 95. Reedy cuts away many of the myths surrounding the presidency. His book foretold the tragedy of Nixon's "Imperial Presidency."

3. For a few examples, see Roy Hoopes, *The Steel Crisis* (New York: John Day, 1963); Grant McConnell, *Steel and the Presidency—1962* (New York: Norton, 1963); Dan Cordtz, "The Face in the

Mirror at General Motors," *Fortune,* Vol. 74 (August 1966); The Cox Commission Report, *Crisis at Columbia* (New York: Random House, Vintage, 1968); and Bob Woodward and Carl Bernstein, *The Final Days* (New York: Simon & Schuster, 1976).

4. James E. Grunig, "Organization and Public Relations: Testing a Communication Theory," *Journalism Monographs* (Association for Education in Journalism), No. 46, November 1976. A landmark study.

5. *Ibid.*

6. John F. Budd, Jr., and Robert G. Strayton, "Can Public Relations Be Measured?" *Public Relations Quarterly,* Vol. 13 (Winter 1969), 19.

7. "More Music Please, Composers," *Saturday Evening Post,* Vol. 211, No. 32 (1938).

8. Wilbur Schramm, *Men, Messages, and Media: A Look at Human Communication* (New York: Harper & Row, 1973), p. 51.

9. Carl Sandburg, *Abraham Lincoln: The War Years,* Vol. II (New York: Harcourt Brace Jovanovich, 1939).

10. Stephen Tallents, *The Projection of England* (London: The Olen Press for Film Centre, Ltd., 1955), p. 36.

11. The way one practitioner came to understand young war protesters is told in Louis Lundborg, *Future Without Shock* (New York: Norton, 1974).

Lundborg, who rose to the chairmanship of the nation's largest bank, has much to teach today's oncoming generations, because he was willing to learn from them.

12. For an account of the origins and uses of the ombudsman concept, see Donald C. Rowat, ed., *The Ombudsman: Citizen's Defender,* 2nd ed. (London: George Allen and Unwin, Ltd., 1968).

13. David L. Grey and Trevor R. Brown, "Letters to the Editor: Hazy Reflections of Public Opinion," *Journalism Quarterly,* Vol. 47 (Autumn 1970). Newspaper editorials are equally unreliable as a gauge of public opinion, as has been proved in presidential elections from Franklin Roosevelt to Jimmy Carter. Only 12 percent of the nation's dailies endorsed Carter in 1976.

14. For an illustration of the use of this technique, see Thomas E. Patterson and Robert D. McClure, *The Unseeing Eye* (New York: Putnam, 1976). A study of the impact of TV in the 1972 presidential election.

15. For a brief introduction to this tool, see Richard W. Budd and Robert K. Thorp, *An Introduction to Content Analysis* (Iowa City: University of Iowa School of Journalism, 1963).

16. For elaboration, see Charles Osgood, George Suci, and Percy Tannenbaum, *The Measurement of Meaning* (Urbana: University of Illinois Press, 1957).

8

It is not enough to be busy. The question is what we are busy with.

THOREAU

The Process: planning and programming— the second step

After a communications problem or opportunity is defined and the involved publics are identified, strategic decisions can be made concerning plans of action, in the form of projects or programs. The effectiveness of programming rests heavily on the validity of the planning. Lack of strategic thinking and thorough planning can lead into communications projects or programs that reinforce controversy rather than resolve it, or add confusion rather than clarity where there is misunderstanding. Harried, hasty planning is makeshift at its best and counterproductive at its worst.

Prudent long-range planning, anticipating conceivable developments, is more likely to result in:

1. An integrated program in which the total effort results in definite accomplishments toward specific goals.
2. Increased management participation and support.
3. A program emphasis that is positive rather than defensive.
4. Unhurried deliberation on choice of themes, timing, and tactics.

Even though the values of planned programming are evident and acknowledged, there is too little emphasis on this second step in the process. These appear to be the main obstacles:

1. Failure of employers to include the practitioner in deliberations that lead to policies and programs.
2. Lack of clearly agreed-upon objectives for implementing the public relations program.
3. Lack of time, because of the pressures of meeting daily problems.
4. The frustrations and delays that practitioners encounter in the endless task of internal clearance and coordination with other departments.

Where planning makes the difference

The failure or lack of effective planning is quite often seen in the marketplace. As one example, consider chlorophyll. In the 1950s and 1960s, chlorophyll was offered and promoted in toothpaste, chewing gum, mouthwash, soap, underwear, toilet tissue, suppositories, and even hair restorers. "A national hysteria," the *New Republic* dubbed it. "The era of good smelling," Life Magazine gushed.

Today, even though the properties of chlorophyll as a deodorizer have never been disproved or seriously disputed by authoritative sources, many of the products once tied to chlorophyll have been untied, or have disappeared. At the same time, there has been no lessening of public desire for pleasant breath. Obviously, something went wrong. One possibility is that chlorophyll suffered communications overkill, or overpromise to a point of public resistance or boredom. That happens. Millions of people may have started to think of it as just another passing fad, an advertising gimmick.

From a chemical standpoint, chlorophyll continues to be helpful embodied in a deodorizing product. Its exploitability as a marketing term, however, is jaded. Effective long-term planning and promotional restraint could have prevented this.

For every glaring example of planning fault or failure, there is a shining example of success. The value of systematic planning was brilliantly demonstrated when the United States put men on the moon in less than a decade's time and put a space lab on Mars a few years later. This same comprehensive systems approach can be applied to the nation's social problems or to an organization's problems. George Hammond, a veteran counselor and chairman of the board of Carl Byoir and Associates, Inc., isolated and identified the synergical elements of the space program that he thinks can be imaginatively applied to all planning. He provided the animated means of portraying them shown in Figure 8–1.

The purposes of planning

Planning can be for the purpose of *making something happen or preventing it,* for the purpose of *exploiting a situation or remedying one.* The practice of public relations is engaged more often in trying to create a viewpoint or a happening than to prevent one, and to take advantage of an opportunity more often than to remedy an undesired situation. There remain, however, too many situations and occasions when remedial public relations measures are required because preventive measures were not taken. A saving grace is that many situations calling for remedy provide the spark to ignite preventive planning for the future. Seismic surveys for oil off California created shock waves that jolted houses and killed fish. The sponsors researched and developed a slower-burning powder to replace the dynamite. When they were ready, a public-information program was launched.

Crises often give birth to public relations planning and add to the significance of communications. The appearance of a small number of swine-flu cases suggested the threat of an epidemic in the United States. Immediate plans required public relations assistance in the difficult task of persuading the elderly to submit to inoculation.

FIGURE 8-1 Substance excerpted from Jeffrey D. Bogart, "The Communicator's Role in Long Range Planning," *Public Relations Journal,* Vol. 32, No. 9 (September 1976). Graphic treatment, courtesy Carl Byoir & Associates, Inc.

1 Exhaustive study of every aspect of the problem in which all factors which led to situation under review are determined.

2 Determination of available resources to meet the need and of the source and amount of additional resources.

3 Acceptance of the magnitude of the task and commitment of the expense and time required for it.

4 An adequate organization fully staffed by specialists.

5 Determination to avoid short cuts or unrealistic schedules.

6 Passion for perfection by every participant.

7 Protection for human life at all costs.

8 Ability to learn from mistakes and rebound from failure.

Consumerism is a classic chronic-crisis situation. Product recalls and ombudsmen are remedial reactions. Consumerism led to the complete revamping of the Better Business Bureau's organization through the creation of a "Public Affairs Council." The desire for environmental protection has been another cause of crisis situations, leading to the banning of certain pesticides, more severe penalties for killing endangered species, and controversy over the Alaskan oil pipeline.

Strategy in public relations calls for long-term planning and programming in many areas such as public policy and social problems. In other cases, such as catastrophes, bonanzas, and other sudden, unexpected occurrences, short-term, immediate actions are taken. *Preventive public relations is tied most often to long-term planning. Remedial public relations actions tend to be of short duration and minimal planning.* The immediate need, quite often, is to pick up the pieces of a negative situation, or to exploit a positive one. After the initial purpose is achieved, remedial measures can be converted into long-range plans and programs designed to effect change. We see this, for example, in matters of image or obsolescence. With the discovery of the Salk vaccine, the March of Dimes became obsolete in its original concept and appeal. The images of the handicapped polio victim, and the iron lung were destined, in time, to fade away. Adaptation of the charitable program to help those with birth defects refreshed the concept of helping in many serious health problems. Similarly, private organizations serving youth—the YMCA, the Scouts—have had to reshape their strategic planning and programs to the new realities of adult–child relationships, life-styles, and value standards.

Although remedial, short-term programs can be effective in neutralizing the impact of problems looming in the future, the value of long-view, wide-angle planning cannot be overstated in dealing with public opinion. One of the Defense Department's most impressive peacetime projects was its efficient handling of the funeral and interment of President Kennedy after tragedy had struck. Despite the enormous amount of detail, events proceeded with clockwork precision and with grace and dignity. The eyes of the world were on the United States during those days, and the nation came off superbly. The reason was that there had been preplanning leading to preparedness for such an emergency.

An innovative, contemporary approach to preplanning preparedness in the corporate sphere has been devised by Howard Chase.[1] He describes it as an "Issue Management," by "Issue Management Task Forces." The way it works is that an organization first identifies those issues—public, local, internal, or external—that can affect its destiny. For each identified issue, a task force is formed consisting of the people who can be helpful in representing the organization. In meetings as needed, changing conditions are reviewed, and strategy is adjusted accordingly.

At the American Can Company, where Mr. Chase served as a consultant, the following issues were identified for task-force management: "ban-the-can movement, litter, OSHA, EEOC, ozone depletion, clear cutting [of timber], the Monongahela decision, community relations, stockholder understanding, product safety, lead, mercury, PCBs, land, air and water pollution, recycling, energy conservation, energy development, and consumerism."[2] The same approach could be applied in the preparedness planning of a municipal government, a county medical society, a state highway commission, or a federal energy commission.

The high value of preparedness planning applies also to small organizations.

Someone handling promotion, advertising, and publicity for a resort, for example, might pep up the newsletter before readership lags seriously, suggest new uniforms for the waitresses to stimulate morale, and arrange a surprise welcome party for the early arrivals of the next season—all *preplanned* activities.

A procedure for planning

Public relations planning starts with the stated objectives of the organizations served, as discussed in Chapter 3. It proceeds from the specific implementation assigned to it in the form of public relations objectives. It engages in whatever fact-finding is indicated and authorized, as discussed in the preceding chapter. The orderly investigative process involves the following four fundamentals.

A searching look backward

There is no organization, no problem, no opportunity without a history. Learning that history is the first step. In a newly created entity, who founded it? For what purpose? Is it time for an anniversary event, an institutional museum, a biography of the founder? Can public relations help? Background information is essential also if public relations is brought into a going entity to deal with a pressing problem. What's the background of the problem? What has happened that has caused public relations to be involved in a new or different way? Public relations problems, too, have a history.

A wide look around

Where there has been no continuing monitoring of public opinion toward the organization, that's the next step. How do employees feel about the conditions of their employment? their leadership? How do the neighbors feel about the presence and conduct of the organization? Is there a breakdown in understanding between the organization and any of its constituent publics? Is there a resentment simmering somewhere? In a crunch, on whom could the organization depend? In that crunch, what groups would delight in the troubles or embarrassment of the organization?

A deep look inside

Every organization has a character and a personality. Both tend to be reflections of those who control the organization by their ownership, management, votes, membership, tenure, or some other way. Character can be discovered by examination of the policies set down, and by whether day-to-day actions square with the words. Personality is evident in the "style" of administration—centralized authority or generous delegation, openness and candor or secretiveness and suspicion. It is portrayed by contemporary or traditional decor and equipment, open or closed doors on executive offices, symbols of stature, approachability of officials, and whether communication is formalized, as by memo, or casual, as by phone. The practitioner needs to know what makes the organization tick, and whether it ticks with convictions, values, and standards that the practitioner can share and honestly promote.

A long, long look ahead

Is the mission of the organization realistically attainable? Can public relations planning and programming fit in? Can they make a practical contribution? Will this organization be around in ten years? Will it be larger and more solidly entrenched, or will it be engaged in a slow retreat toward oblivion? What are the pros and cons? Are the game and the outcome worth getting involved?

Strategic thinking

Thinking in terms of a strategy is at the heart of public relations planning. In the pure sense, *a strategy is a plan* to use selected means in predetermined ways to attain a desired result. Strategic thinking links the fact-finding phase to the planning and programming. This is shown in Figure 8–2, which should be studied closely for precise understanding.

FIGURE 8–2   The four-step public relations process.

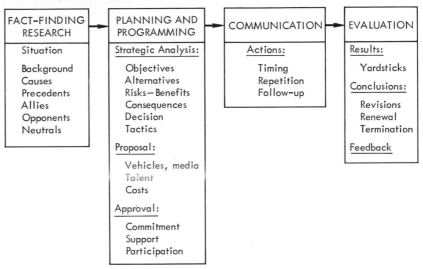

There are at least nine questions to be answered:

First: What are the *objectives* in influencing public opinion?
Second: What are the *alternative avenues* of action for attaining them?
Third: What are the *risks* in taking each avenue?
Fourth: What are the *potential benefits* in each?
Fifth: What are the *potential consequences* beyond each?
Sixth: Which avenue do we choose to take?
Seventh: What should be the *structure of a proposal* to proceed on the course chosen embodying the projects and programs we want to carry out?

Eighth: In what form do we present our proposal to best advantage for approval? To whom?

Ninth: What is the minimum commitment in support and participation acceptable from administration if the plan is to go forward and succeed?

The first six questions can usually be answered readily, although the matter of alternate courses, number 2, can be a stumbling block. An overriding consideration generally prevails. Something has to be done in a hurry. The vote has to be gotten out. Funds must be raised to meet expenses. New members have to be attracted or the present administration will be ousted.[3] For any of these, the avenue offering the fastest immediate return on communications would be taken. However, if the problem had to do with a controversial issue—neighborhood racial integration, election of a female president of the United States, or changing an old, private girl's school to a coeducational basis—the strategy would probably favor an avenue offering gradual but lasting change.[4]

Returning to the nine questions above, the last three are the most difficult in practice. Why? Because the views of others than public relations experts are entering the decision process. The plan and its implementation have to be "sold." Some questions seek hard facts:

- What will the proposed plan, its *programs, and projects cost?* at the outset? for the period being budgeted? for the proposed duration of the plan?
- How do these costs split up as to being irreversible (as with new employees) or being cancelable in midstream (as with a publication)? At what *rate of funding* will the total be needed and expended to meet the plan's timetable? What *methods of accounting* for expenditures will be used?
- What *involvement and support* is required of other departments? Who pays for that?
- What are the *specific media and audience* or circulation?

Assuming that all goes well in moving from planning to action, a commitment of support and participation should be forthcoming from management. There is the need for two clear understandings. Implementation of a project or program requires agreement on (1) the methods to be used in reporting progress, and to whom the reports are to be made; and (2) the standards that will be applied by public relations in tallying or measuring results. It must be recognized, for instance, that clipping services generally round up no more than 20 percent of the news printings, and that different kinds of results may be impressive or unimpressive to senior officials (circulation, letters of inquiry, new members, increased enrollment, and so on).

In the completion of the process, one of three decisions will be made by management:

1. Undertake or continue with the planned program as is.
2. Undertake or continue the planned program with some changes.
3. Terminate the plan on the basis that the program is not needed, or has succeeded, failed, or run its course, cannot be afforded, or places demands on participants that they cannot accommodate.

Strategic planning applied to the solving of a public relations problem can be envisioned as the second in a series of loops that make the four steps in the

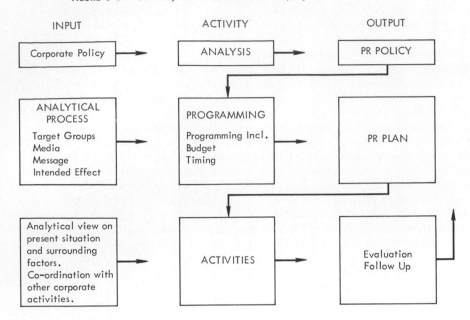

FIGURE 8-3 Courtesy Skandia Insurance Company Ltd.

INPUT   ACTIVITY   OUTPUT

| Corporate Policy | → | ANALYSIS | → | PR POLICY |

ANALYTICAL PROCESS

Target Groups
Media
Message
Intended Effect

PROGRAMMING

Programming Incl.
Budget
Timing

PR PLAN

Analytical view on present situation and surrounding factors. Co-ordination with other corporate activities.

ACTIVITIES

Evaluation
Follow Up

ANALYTICAL MATRIX FOR SKANDIA PUBLIC RELATIONS PROGRAMMING

TARGET GROUP	INFORMATION INTEREST (most receptive to ...)	INTENDED EFFECT (reaction or relation effect)	MESSAGE (policy and image values)	MEDIA (established and possible)	PRIORITY (long range or short term, permanent or temporary)	ACTIVITIES (rough outline)

process flow naturally from one to the next. The way planning and programming flow through an organization's work is illustrated in Figure 8–3, the program of the Skandia Group of insurance companies, headquartered in Stockholm. Figures 8–4 and 8–5 demonstrate the programs of other successful organizations.

Here is a specific plan devised in proposal form by public relations consultants to deal with a finite problem—swine-flu immunization in Colorado.

Objective:

To immunize 2.3 million Coloradoans above age 3 between Aug. 15 and Nov. 20 to avert a potentially dangerous epidemic of A/Swine New Jersey 1976 influenza.

The problem:

To gain the cooperation of the medical community, local health departments and county nurses in conducting the campaign and urging citizen participation.

To counter negative attitudes and apathy fostered by a difference of opinion in the medical-scientific community about the necessity for the vaccine.

To allay the fears of the public about reactions to the vaccine.

The plan:

Meet with the appropriate representatives of the Colorado Medical Society, the University of Colorado Medical Center and the Colorado Health and Environmental Council to explain the problem and the plan.

Form an advisory group representative of the special publics to be involved: medicine, osteopathy, nursing, nursing homes, hospitals, education, Governor Lamm's office, the elderly and the media.

Call together for a comprehensive briefing and a solicitation of cooperation the presidents of the Colorado Press and Colorado Broadcasting Associations, a representative of the television public service directors' organization, and representative Colorado newspaper and television editors from Denver and out-state.

Develop a fact sheet for use immediately by physicians and health workers in answering queries from the public and for use later by the news media.

The communications program:

Inform physicians through the *Communicable Disease Bulletin.*

Inform public health workers and community leaders through a comprehensive story in the May-June issue of *Colorado's Health.*

Write special articles for the state's medical, nursing home, nursing, hospital, education and state employee publications.

Appear before the Colorado Chapter of the Public Relations Society of America and the Colorado Association of Business Communicators to solicit their support and coverage.

Develop press kit for distribution by July 1 to all Colorado newspapers.

Develop radio and television spots for distribution by July 1 to all Colorado electronic media.

Develop posters with a blank space for date, location and time for distribution in heavy traffic areas by the schools, local health departments, county nurses, and medical, osteopathic, dental and pharmacy groups.

Arrange for appearances by state health officials, Medical Center physicians and Medical Society representatives on radio and television talk shows.

Ask the University of Colorado to devote a *"Medical Line"* television program to the immunization campaign.

Kick off media campaign in mid-July with mass inoculation of the Denver Bronco football team.

EXHIBIT 8-1 (CONT.)

Three weeks prior to the start of immunizations in local areas, blitz the local media with localized stories and spots, including time and place of clinics. Talk personally with editors. Solicit favorable editorials. Provide a glossy print of immunization form to newspapers so that parents can clip it, fill it out and take it to clinics.

Follow up in each community with stories on the number given protection against swine influenza.

Keep a running statewide tally in metropolitan dailies and on television of the number immunized, the number still to go.

Evaluation:

Success of the program can be determined by the actual number immunized.

FIGURE 8-4   Detailed planning produced this continuing program by the National Coffee Association. It was a major stimulus to the "coffee break." Courtesy Harshe, Rotman & Druck, Inc., public relations counsel.

N.C.A. PUBLIC RELATIONS PROGRAM

THE COFFEE STORY

Taste
- New Ways To Enjoy
- Coffee as A Flavor
- Enhances Other Flavors
- Variety of Flavors
- For Every Taste
- Brewing Methods
- Hearty Breakfasts
- Go-With Snacks
- Outdoor Beverage

Health
- Facts
- Nature's Pick-Me-Up
- Economical Energizer
- Tranquilizer
- Be Good To Yourself
- Flavor Without Calories
- Take A Break Often

Social
- Makes Living Easier
- Enjoy Any Time, Any Place
- Reward
- Friendship Beverage
- Coffee Dates For Youth
- Right For Every Occasion

Business Psychology
- Promotes Better Performance
- Eases Job Boredom
- Promotes Industrial Safety
- Humanizes Management

MEDIA

PERSONAL
- Speeches
- Visits and personal calls
- Tours
- Exhibits
- Conferences and conventions
- Meetings
- Educational courses
- Training programs
- Community projects
- Special events

MASS MEDIA – produced by others
- Newspapers
- Magazines
- Radio
- Television
- Motion pictures
- Newsletters
- Company publications

MASS MEDIA – self-produced
- Newsletters
- Bulletins
- Booklets and pamphlets
- Reports
- Bulletin Board posters
- Visuals -- slides, filmstrips, movies, etc.

INFLUENTIALS
- Peer Groups
- Parents
- Teachers & Home Economists
- Celebrities
  - DJ's
  - Movie
  - Sports
  - TV Stars
- Youth Leaders
- Doctors
- Nutritionists & County Agents
- Editors, Writers, Broadcasters
- Allied Interests
- Trade Press

TARGET PUBLICS

16-25 AGE GROUP
30,000,000

1. 16-18 High School
2. 17-22 College
3. Service
4. Young Married
5. Single Non-Students

OVER 25
- Families
- Workers
- Institutions

172

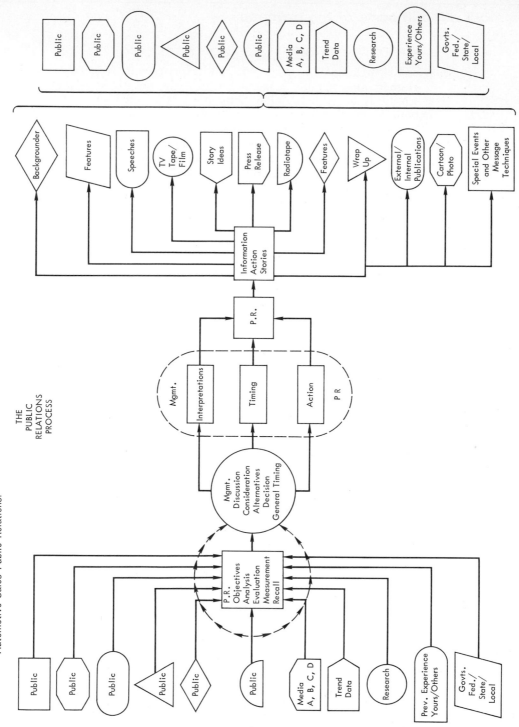

FIGURE 8-5 Chrysler Corporation's Frank Wylie visualized the step-by-step public relations process in this form. Courtesy Frank W. Wylie, Director U.S. Automotive Sales Public Relations.

The most difficult parts of the process

Writing the program

Research, analysis, precedents, and experience must be converted into program forms acceptable to non–public relations executives. Some are not tuned in sensitively to public opinion. Some are cost-oriented, or publicly gun-shy, or both. Some do not commit comfortably to speculative expenditures with no guarantee of return. Some are nervous about issuing information to news media. And abstract goals, like goodwill, are ephemeral to many.

Writing the program proposal is a worthy challenge. As one counselor put it, "A written public relations program aimed at specific objectives, with projects designed to achieve those goals, helps the administration make sure that the PR effort is consistent with the institution's goals."[5] When the program meshes with organizational goals, the employer knows that public relations understands what management is trying to do.

Presenting the program proposal puts the practitioner's persuasive and technical communication skills to the test. He must be effective on paper, on his or her feet, around a conference table, using slide films or other projectors, working with a blackboard or flip charts.

The task of writing an overall program or proposal would rarely fall on an intern or new member of a staff. It is important, however, that all members understand how proposals and presentations evolve. Seeing how all the parts come together, each member is better able to perform his or her segment or specialty when programs are implemented.

Jack R. Nowling, a counselor, calls program writing a "distillation of common sense." His distillation includes having the objectives up front and avoiding confusion between strategy and tactics. (Being a good outfit to work for is strategic; getting the media to say so is tactical.) He believes in being very specific about projects and activities listed for execution. Dates, times, places, and all details, he feels, show a thorough grasp of the mission. (If a conference is needed, describe it. If officials need to be trained as spokesmen, say how this will be done. If a new publication is needed, provide a format. If correspondence is tactless or clumsy, give examples of graceful letters.) Finally, he sees the writing of programs as a one-person job, with others on the staff chipping in with their inputs.[6]

Some of these thoughts have been applied to the political arena by firms specializing in that area:

1. Careful delineation of the strategy which will be followed and of the steps which will be taken in the development of that strategy, so that the action moves with precision and reaches its peak of impact in the closing days before election.
2. Thorough appraisal and development of all the principal issues of the campaign and agreement on the relative importance to be given each issue. This keeps the focus of public interest on the objectives and issues which have the most widespread appeal.
3. A complete outline of all the organizational aspects of the campaign—the foundation and framework for the vast volunteer organization which will man the battle lines and carry the crusade personally to the voters.
4. Detailed plans for the use of all media—campaign pamphlets, newspaper and magazine advertising, direct mail, radio and television, billboards, moving pictures, newsreels, "literature" of all types.[7]

A few words of caution are indicated. Plans and programs are generally infused with enthusiasm. That helps get approval by employers. But overenthusiasm carries with it the serious danger of *overpromising.* "This antipollution program has everything necessary to land on the cover of *Time* magazine." Those are dangerous words. Suppose the program falls short, landing only on the cover of *National Wildlife* magazine? Ordinarily, appearance in the latter outlet might be considered an acceptable performance. But evaluated against the lavish earlier statement, it might be downgraded to "pretty good" or "inadequate for the costs of the program."

Budgeting

There is as much art or artistry in public relations budgeting as there is science. The literature available on the subject is sparse. At professional seminars, the most frequently mentioned guideline seems to be, "Always ask for more than you need." Of course, the deliberate, habitual padding of budget requests is not peculiar to public relations. It has become part of "the system," defended much the same as the giving of bribes as a cost of doing business in foreign countries: "Everybody does it."

Everyone in public relations will be drawn into budgeting sometime. For examples of different approaches see Figures 8–6, 8–7, and 8–8.

In ongoing operations of established departments, budgets generally relate to one of four control factors. One is the total income or funds available to the enterprise. One is the "competitive necessity." The third is the overall task or objective set for the organization. And the fourth is the profit or surplus over expenses set as a bogey.

When total income or funds available is the criterion, as in marketing or fund-raising activities, public relations is generally allocated a percentage. The percentage relates to sales, to funds raised, or to funds allocated from taxes. When competitive necessity is the criterion, the amount spent by a similar charity or a competing product is matched or exceeded. This method is very risky. The "task to be done" or "objective to be attained" method usually provides for public relations to have a share of the funding for a combination of activities such as advertising, promotion, and public relations. All three might come under the allocation for the task of "development." The final approach usually sets a fluctuating figure that can go up or down depending on "the point at which we break even," or, in a nonprofit operation, "the point at which we cover all expenses."[8]

Budgeting is rarely a one-person job. Each specialist is called on to itemize and estimate expenses he or she will incur. The department head, or someone designated, will blend all the estimates. The next executive up the line screens those departments for which he or she is responsible. Eventually, the paperwork gets to the top official for approval, and that's where the buck stops.

Two guidelines may be helpful:

Know the cost of what you propose to buy: A news writer, for example, should know the cost of a typewriter, a duplicating service, rental of a copier, mailing lists, postal rates, photograph copies, the elements in a routine press kit, and everything else necessary to the job.

Remember that cost is but one basis for determining value: The ultimate value of a purchase is rarely evident in the price alone. Suppose it costs $1,000 to

FIGURE 8-6   A detailed budget approach that breaks out public relations and relates it to fund raising. Both can be seen as elements in a total operating budget and against the total source of revenue. Courtesy Girl Scouts of the United States.

GIRL SCOUTS, _____,COUNCIL - P.R. BUDGET

Both the Executive Staff and the Board Committees (Public Relations, Financial Services or specific Task Groups, etc.) submit yearly plans in the MBO style. Price tag is attached by staff advisor to specific group. (Approved by Board of Directors and Executive Director).

Agency information: Income generated fiscal year: $775,000
                     Operating Budget: $550,412

Budget for Development/Communications Department

	FUND RAISING & P.R.	P.R. ONLY
Staff Salaries:		
Full Time & Part Time Prof.	$17,000	$ 9,000
Clerical Salaries (est. shared services)	10,000	2,000
Office Supplies		
Media Kits	5,310	840
Fund Raising Materials		
Outside Printing		
Calendar	15,052	6,937
Membership Development		
Annual Report		
Bi-monthly Newsletter		
Program Folders (Summer/Camp)		
Recruitment Folders		
Purchase of Posters from National Org.	150	150
Tokens		
Volunteer & Youth Recognition		
Donor Acknowledgement	6,610	136
Photography	795	550
Postage	1,407	907
Community Cultivation	401	380
Special Events	225	225
Annual Meeting		
Displays Exhibits	290	260
Contingency	500	200
Memberships: P.R. Club/PRSA	155	155
Travel/Mileage/Conferences	1,115	915
TOTAL	$59,050	$22,655

FIGURE 8-7 An approach to budgeting based on costs of authorized projects, excluding salaries and office overhead. Courtesy University of Utah Medical Center.

University of Utah Medical Center Development and Community Relations

PUBLIC RELATIONS PROGRAM

University of Utah Medical Center

Objectives:

1. Publicize services and educational programs inside and outside.

   a. Clarify role of a teaching hospital

   b. Explain function of medical referral and research

2. Gain university, government and public support of $62.5 million expansion...$34.5 million via bonding, $10 million private fund campaign.

3. Assess attitudes of hospital patients and implement corrective programs.

4. Reactivate college of medicine alumni association support.

5. Develop preventive medicine program.

Projects and Costs:

Tape/slide presentation telling Center's story	$ 3,835
Center Annual Report	4,000
Report, a bi-monthly publication	4,700
Tours	150
Media relations get-togethers	300
National Hospital Week - tours for employees	140
Dean's Newsletter	330
Medical Staff Semi-annual meeting	2,510
Grassroots - Utah visits with editors statewide	500
Feasibility Study, for Capital Fund Campaign	7,500
College of Medicine Executive Committee	195
30th Anniversary of College of Medicine	4,451
Referral Directory	1,000
Display, State Medical Convention	190
Patient Questionnaires	750
Patient Survey	2,415
Travel, out-of-pocket and miscellaneous	5,790
Total budget, excluding salaries	$38,763

50 NORTH MEDICAL DRIVE   SALT LAKE CITY, UTAH 84132   (801) 581-7387

send a recruiter of basketball players for a high-scholastic university to several high schools. Then suppose it costs $500 to reach 500 young basketball players with packets of literature and invitations to apply if they are good students. Let's say the personalized recruiter approach brings in five recruits, and the literature brings only one. Obviously, the personal approach has been more effective, and

FIGURE 8–8   Caterpillar Tractor bases its public-affairs objectives (see Chapter 3) and its departmental budgets on its management by objectives (MBO). Courtesy Caterpillar Tractor Company.

 CATERPILLAR TRACTOR CO.

Peoria, Illinois 61629

1. The process of management by objectives begins with an analysis of problems and needs by the chief executive officer. In the fall, Caterpillar's president defines <u>areas</u> of objectives. Such areas as: factory efficiency, sales, employment stabilization, return on investment, personnel development, safety, equal employment opportunity, scrap, etc.

2. Against this background, Caterpillar plants and departments around the world set objectives for the year ahead, with these criteria:

   (a) They should be profit or improvement-oriented.
   (b) They should be clearly defined and specific.
   (c) They should be practical and attainable.
   (d) They should be measurable.

3. The public relations function (at Caterpillar termed "public affairs") is no exception to this process. Public affairs objectives are, therefore, expected to be <u>responsive</u> to the corporate needs...and <u>integrated</u> into future plans.

4. When public affairs objectives have been completed and discussed with the appropriate officers, a departmental budget is constructed.

5. The budget is then subjected to scrutiny by the president's office-- which includes the president and the two executive vice presidents. Out of this process, one or more of the following can result:

   (a) The objectives and budget may be accepted as is.
   (b) Flaws may be discovered in the objectives and/or in the projected costs.
   (c) Even if objectives and projected costs are not flawed, the over-all program--though excellent--must be adjusted downward to suit business conditions and prospects.

6. The budget is adjusted as necessary. There is no attempt to build a continuing ratio or relationship between the public affairs budget and sales figures. If budget adjustments have been substantial, some adjustment may also have to be made in objectives.

7. The technique of "flexible budgeting" is used. As time passes, the department head may seek a variance, increase or decrease, in order to do the best possible job of managing the public relations function in the light of current events.

8. The last step is the follow-up. The Public Affairs Department is required to submit a brief monthly report on the attainment or non-attainment of objectives, and the resultant effect on costs.

seemingly a better "buy." However, suppose that during the freshman year, two of the recruited six drop out when they fail to make first string, and two more flunk out. Then, the one who had come of his own choice, after seeing the literature, makes first string, rates Dean's First Honors, and is offered a Carnegie nonathletic scholarship for the remaining three years. Now, with this chain of events, the mail would actually prove to have been the better value for those concerned. This example is a straw house that can't withstand a strong assault, but it does point up that in budgeting, costs, prices, and values can be quite different.

Indoctrination: a continuing process

When a program has been approved at the policy level, it becomes necessary to indoctrinate colleagues in what is to follow. Otherwise, these important collaborators may wind up uninformed, like an outside counselor who is not allowed to participate in the planning. They would not be able to do their part. They would not be in a position to solicit support from the people under their supervision.

The mechanical process of indoctrination is a test of personal skill in persuasion and coordination. Some generally accepted tenets merit noting.

The basic problems should be explained in terms of the harm that can be done if they are left unattended. Then, the immediate remedial measures should be explained in relation to the long-term plans. The use of similar case examples or precedents is helpful. Surveys should be relied on to substantiate the plans. Personal opinion should be eliminated except as it applies to special knowledge already possessed. The program should be related to the climate in which the organization operates and that it hopes to enjoy in the future. It should be

FIGURE 8-9 In the large and heavily structured Department of the Army, policy matters pass through many offices for formal clearance.

SUMMARY SHEET (DA Memo 340-15)					
TO			**FOR**	**FROM**	
DCSLOG	COA	CLL	APPROVAL	AGENCY	TELEPHONE
DCSOPS	ACSI	CHIEF OF STAFF	SIGNATURE		
DCSPER	ACSRC	_____ S OF A _____	COORDINATOR	GRADE & NAME OF CONTACT OFFICER	
CRD	TAG	SECRETARY OF THE ARMY			
FILE REFERENCE			SUBJECT		DATE

IMPLICATIONS (The implications checked below are involved in this action, are discussed below or in a separate inclosure, and have been considered in the final recommendation.)

☐ CONTROL PROGRAM ☐ MANPOWER ☐ BUDGET ☐ LEGAL
☐ CONGRESSIONAL ☑ PUBLIC RELATIONS ☐ MORALE ☐ SECURITY ☐ NONE

stressed that the activities will have a desirable ultimate effect on public opinion. Explanations should be short and to the point. The practitioner should be decisive, a quality highly respected by managers and administrators.

After colleagues, the next group whose support must be enlisted is the one whose help with news preparation and the like is necessary. This is best handled through informal sessions in which people can air their views and talk things out. Quite often, meetings are arranged in which the practitioner presents the programming, then throws the meeting open to discussion. Where this is done, a summary should be supplied afterward to all participants in the discussion. It can take the form of meeting minutes, a program timetable, a roster of projects, or a brochure explaining the plans. It is important for the future relationship that the programming agreed upon be a matter of record. Getting it down on paper tends to put the details in the right places.

For an example of the process, assume that the ABC Manufacturing Company, makers of parachutes, has decided to convert from the use of nylon to a new type of material called Chemthin, claimed to be better and known to be lighter in weight and bulk. The raw materials for it are in free supply.

Assume, too, that the conversion idea originated years earlier. At that time, the organization learned that the weight and bulk of standard parachutes was a source of concern to military officialdom and flight personnel alike. Consequently, a specific research program was activated. Chemthin was created and engineered by the ABC Company as a private undertaking. The prospect of introducing the new material posed problems in the relationships between the company and the military, the suppliers, the parents of flight personnel, and others. Therefore, long before the fabric was ready, the public relations people presented a carefully planned program of information and events designed to gain a sympathetic understanding from certain publics and the enthusiastic support of others. The program was approved.

Indoctrination of the organization followed. The plans were explained down the line from executives through supervisors to employees in the offices and shops. Auxiliary channels of information were used. A letter went from the president to each employee's home. Everybody in the organization, by being fully informed, became a front-line participant in the conversion.

Next, the practitioner opened the communications gate a bit wider. The plan was not a rapid succession of events and news releases, but a slow fanning out, first to the community, then to the national level. In the dissemination of information externally, there were three basic components: (1) news, (2) media to carry the messages, and (3) funds and staff adequate to get the job done. It was agreed that the informative phase should tell a story of research, product refinement, quality, durability, and safety. It was to emphasize that the company's action was in the public interest because it contributed to the national defense effort. The arrangements for external communication might have looked on paper like Table 8–1.

Note that the specific target publics were those most keenly affected by what ABC was doing: soldiers and parents concerned about safety, stockholders who bore the financial risk of the change, hometown residents whose livelihoods were linked with the ebb and flow of ABC's business, new suppliers whose materials would now be needed by ABC, military officials, and the general public that shouldered the expense of the national-defense effort.

TABLE 8-1

Communications Vehicle	Immediate Purpose
First, a statement to the hometown press	To relieve any anxiety about the community's economic security in the changeover
Second, a statement to the national press	To confirm publicly that the move served the national interest as well as private interests
Third, a special letter to the shareholders of ABC Company	To reaffirm the confidence of investors in the stability of the company
Fourth, special magazine articles telling about the development of Chemthin	To impress on segments of the general public the safety and quality features of the product; to establish leadership
Fifth, an ABC hardship committee	To deal with employee hardship cases due to temporary layoffs during conversion
Sixth, a plant visit by military officials	To point up the progress of conversion and to identify activities with the defense effort
Seventh, a booklet on Chemthin	To reassure soldiers and other parachutists, parents, educators, scientists, students, and others who might inquire
Eighth, an open house on completion of conversion	To demonstrate the benefits to the community and to reaffirm the interdependence of company and community
Ninth, public demonstrations of the finished product	To prove the safety, quality, and value aspects of Chemthin

Timing as a key element

The chronology of the preceding program was deliberate, not accidental. One reason is that people rebel against any sudden, drastic change without some kind of reassurance that everything is going to be all right. Mental digestion leading to acceptance of change is normally a gradual process. A second reason is that communication, to obtain a desired reaction, should move out in waves from its original source. It should preserve, insofar as possible, its original form and integrity. It should be accurate. The normal path of information is from those most intimately involved to those who are only incidentally interested. A third reason is that news or advertising naturally follows the logical sequence of happenings.

The several elements of a program such as Chemthin's must be spaced and timed to produce the desired effect when wanted. In political campaigns, the strategists and practitioners strive to bring enthusiasm and support for their candidates and their cause to a peak the day before the voting. Similar timing is sought in fund-raising campaigns. However, such plans cannot be made in a vacuum. They must be related to the total situation.

The calendar offers many opportunities for positive timing. For example, the public relations director of Atlanta's schools wanted to get the public's attention focused on the serious school-dropout problem. She prepared a documentary entitled, "The Ghost Story—School Dropouts," and it was broadcast on Halloween night. Shrewd timing is also used to smother a story rather than have it spotlighted, or to smother an opponent's story.

Here are some examples of unfortunate timing: a leading manufacturer of home appliances took advantage of the news lull on Christmas Day to announce a sharp price cut effective January 1. Many a husband, eyeing a shiny appliance by the Christmas tree and thinking of the higher price he had paid, was resentful. Many said so. A leading steel firm announced that it was boosting the price of steel because of increased labor costs. Forty-eight hours later, it released its annual report, boasting of record profits. The coincidence of these two announcements brought public criticism that should have been expected. The time of the annual report was fixed; the price boost could have been delayed for a better psychological time. A few years ago, the du Pont Company announced grants of nearly $1 million to more than 100 universities and colleges. This laudable act of corporate citizenship should have brought du Pont much favorable publicity. But the news was smothered. It was released the same day that the Ford Foundation announced a $500 million grant to educational institutions and hospitals. The public plaudits went to the Ford Foundation.

On the other hand, a major corporation announced to the Securities and Exchange Commission, the day after the Presidential election, that it had made bribes to foreign government officials, knowing full well that its story would be buried in the avalanche of election news. This was excellent timing—from the company's viewpoint.

Planning for disasters

It is usually possible to time an open house not to conflict with other local events. It is usually possible to announce a decision of national significance when it will not be crowded off the front pages and the airwaves. But one type of event cannot be forecast—a catastrophe. *However, it can be planned for.*

Any institution or industry can be struck by a disaster and should plan accordingly. When it happens, time is a key element in the handling of communications. Plans made far in advance for calamity procedure must go into action. The on-the-spot planning, which would normally be given weeks, must be crammed into a few minutes, or a few hours at most.

When an earthquake struck Los Angeles some years ago, a disaster plan conceived years before went into action. As just one aspect, the Hospital Council had created a shortwave radio network—HEAR, for Hospital Emergency Administration Radio. Normal telephone communications were overloaded in some cases and knocked out in others, but the radio linkup of 118 hospitals picked up the slack. Blood, ambulances, first aid, medicine, and food went where it was needed. Trained communicators using modern technology made the difference. The existence of a plan brought it all together.

Standard Oil of Indiana experienced disaster at its Whiting, Indiana, refinery years ago, when a hydroformer unit exploded. Fragments of steel killed a boy, injured his brother, and smashed into nearby houses. In the refinery, steel fragments tore into storage tanks. Crude oil was soon ablaze in a ten-acre area. The fires lasted for eight days. Smooth, skilled handling of the events that followed the explosion and fires brought public understanding to the company and praise and awards to its PR staff. The underlying policies called for *consideration* for those affected and for complete *cooperation* with news media. The PR staff had *planned* for just such an emergency and thus was prepared to act swiftly.[9]

Despite the value of such plans, organizations continue to get caught flat-footed when disaster strikes. Such lack of foresight was demonstrated when three astronauts were burned to death while testing a space capsule. A critic of NASA's handling of this tragedy wrote:

> There were no reporters or correspondents from any media on hand at Cape Kennedy when the fire broke out . . . . The question of informing the public . . . was thus left entirely to the institutional machinations of NASA. The agency reacted predictably. It not only shut down all lines of communication, but, by either accident or design, issued statements that proved to be erroneous.
>
> Although NASA knew within five minutes after the accident that all three astronauts were dead, the information was not released until two hours later. It was nearly midnight before UPI and AP received a NASA picture of two of the astronauts entering the capsule for the last time . . . .
>
> NASA claimed that the withholding of facts and its issuance of misleading and

FIGURE 8-10 Organization structure of the Federal Disaster Assistance Agency.

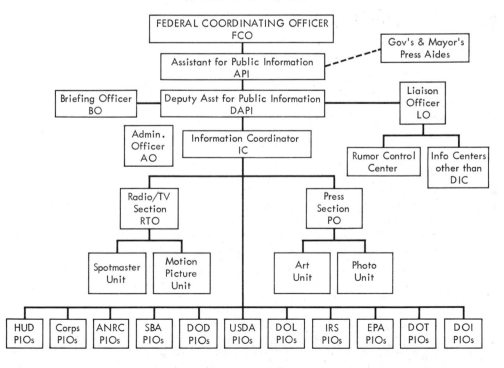

PUBLIC INFORMATION ORGANIZATION
FOR VERY LARGE DISASTER

wrong statements resulted from the lack of a plan for handling information in emergencies. As hard to believe as this may be, coming as it does from an agency with a public information staff of 300, there is undoubtedly some validity to the claim.

NASA's information office has since maintained that an emergency plan was in effect and followed at the time of the Apollo 204 fire. NASA states that it has contingency plans for each mission.[10]

As one of many responses to the need for disaster planning, the Federal Disaster Assistance Administration was created. It is a staff arm of the Department of Housing and Urban Development. The organization chart of its public-information wing is depicted in Figure 8–10. Of particular significance are the way its functions dovetail with other federal agencies and the fact that the structure works responsively to local problems.

The need for a public fact center

Many institutions and industries have discovered the dangers of rumors and the need to provide authentic information. When a crisis arises, it suddenly becomes apparent that some seemingly unimportant facets of an institution's operation have been overlooked and must be given hurried attention. Inevitably, one such area of weakness is the availability of information. A knee-jerk response usually results in a jerry-rigged rumor center that operates through the crisis period, then fades away without serious thought until the next crisis comes.

There are three major points to remember in planning for a rumor or fact center. *First,* the center must be recognized for what it is—a place where information moves from the institution to the general public. It is not a press operation. To saddle an organization's press office with an added responsibility to the general public reduces the effectiveness of both functions. Press and information centers must be closely coordinated, but, where it can be afforded, they must be entities, each directed toward its own specific goal.

Second, the center should be in two parts. Rumor centers are almost exclusively a telephone operation. Of course, there must be an answering service, or information center. So one group deals directly with the public, taking their questions and providing answers. If they don't have the information, they promise to have it within a certain period of time. The second group, however, is a coordinating agency, the point of contact between the information center and the institution staff and agencies. The coordinating agency goes to the institution staff for information. It checks material with the highest level of the administration for accuracy, coordinates it with the press office, and relays it to the center for use. Hence, all information—whether query or answer—flows through the coordinating agency, where it can be accounted for and logged. In addition to raw information—the factual material used to answer direct and simple questions—the coordinating agency should have qualified people available to speak on policy or conduct philosophical discussions of current issues. As the sole source of material for the information center, it controls the center and what is being said to the general public. Although not an official spokesman, it does provide for "one-voice" response to the institution's problems.

Third, and perhaps most important, any such center must establish credibility; it must be the accepted source of accurate information. This cannot be accomplished during the period of crisis alone. The flow of credible information must be established during routine times. The function must become an accepted part of the institution on a full-time, continuing basis, identical in crisis or routine situations. It must, over an extended period, encourage both internal and external publics to use it with faith and confidence. This amounts to more than establishing a reputation for truth; it involves education. Internally, all agencies of the institution must be made aware that such a system exists and must be encouraged to use it to make available information for which they are responsible.

Such a program, operating normally over a long period of time, sets the pattern within an institution for quickly and efficiently moving information. If the institution is tuned to such an operation in routine times, the transition in troubled times is far less shattering.

The outlook

Long-range planning *per se* is an immature science. It is gaining adherents in government departments, the armed services, and basic industries as an absolute necessity, spurred by the potential catastrophes inherent in energy shortage, environmental pollution, and nuclear holocaust.

The alliance between public relations and long-range planning is logical. One aspect is that successful long-range planning depends on the inflow of useful information. Public relations practitioners are qualified to gather, sift, collate, and interpret relevant information, and to report it in understandable and readable forms. A second aspect is that the alliance helps keep practitioners alert to what an organization is thinking about the future. Thus armed, public relations can be a support function in preparing employers for problems and opportunities.

To illustrate how this might work in practice, suppose a university needs to acquire some land, adjoining its campus, now occupied by some old oil storage tanks. The oil company headquarters is located elsewhere. The university would use the acquired land for a new physical science building. Knowing this, and being sensitive to the risks in "going public" too early, public relations could quietly reconnoiter. Information useful to the university officials would be the zoning situation, the history of the oil company's actions in helping universities, its capital gifts, its attitude toward the local community officials, and the importance to the company of this particular regional storage facility. From these and other inputs, the university's planning group would be well armed to decide how best to approach the acquisition. Should it be a personalized appeal for donation of the site? Or would a community petition for rezoning be best? Or an effort to condemn? Or is the prospect of acquisition so hopeless that no money or effort should be expended?

Some of the most respected public relations practitioners earned their reputations by being prepared. They painstakingly built idea, fact, and friend files. They accumulated a bank of precedents for every conceivable situation that might come up. Their files contained preapproved public responses to touchy situations just in case the need suddenly surfaced in a phone call from a reporter. They engaged in systematic polling, informal or formal, of the views held by their employers' publics. They were continuously abreast of the mood of the organization's constituents and opponents. They were thought of in their orga- nizations as the one person to check with on matters involving public opinion. Then, one day, circumstances handed them an opportunity. They were ready.

Obstacles persist, but the trend is toward awareness in management circles of the four steps to be taken in solving problems of relationships, and the impor- tance of planning as one of them. This awareness is documented by the place- ment, in a number of large institutions, of public relations in a team position alongside the long-range-planning function.

Effective planning, as one practitioner put it, "is the shortest route for public relations up the organizational totem pole."

Case problem in forced planning

You are a new Jill-of-all-jobs in the Red Cross local unit for a middle-sized eastern community heavily populated by elderly people. You and one other person make up the PR department. Frankly, you find the organization kind of passive, waiting for a flood or famine to show up. Word has come down that the unit is being allocated $25,000 of federal funds to teach 50,000 people cardio- pulmonary resuscitation. The head of the unit comes to you and says she has heard rumors that you don't think the place is as lively as it should be. She puts you on the spot to come up with a plan and program to do the cardiac teaching job. What is your plan, including the kind of campaign, timing, and communi- cations vehicles? Include a budget breakdown.

ADDITIONAL READINGS

DONALD C. BURNHAM, "Corporate Planning and So- cial Problems," in Herman Kahn, ed., *The Future of the Corporation.* New York: Mason and Lipscomb, 1974.

"Disaster Proves Value of Hospital Radio Network," *American Hospital Association,* Vol. XX, No. 3 (March 1971).

PETER DRUCKER, *Management Tasks, Responsibilities, Practices.* New York: Harper & Row, 1974. See "Strategic Planning," p. 121.

PHILIP LESLY, *The People Factor,* Chap. VI, "Plan- ning," p. 199. Homewood, Ill.: Dow Jones–Irwin, 1974.

RON LEVY, "Public Policy Publicity," *PR Tips and Tactics,* Vol. 13, No. 36 (November 17, 1975).

"Planning an Event," *Monthly Letter,* The Royal Bank of Canada, Vol. 56, No. 8 (August 1975).

ALFRED LLOYD ROBERTS, "Development of a Model Communications and Community Relations Pro- gram for the Dallas Independent School District," Ph.D. dissertation, Texas A & M University, 1973.

E. KIRBY WARREN, *Long Range Planning.* Englewood Cliffs, N.J.: Prentice-Hall, 1966.

For case studies in crisis public relations:

MAJ. RICHARD F. ABEL, "Bad News and How to Survive It," *Public Relations Journal,* July 1968.

BARBARA W. HUNTER, "Crisis Public Relations," *Pub- lic Relations Journal,* June 1974.

FOOTNOTES

1. Howard Chase Enterprises, "Corporate Public Issues and Their Management," *CPI,* Vol. 1, No.1 (undated).

2. "Issue Management as a President Sees It," *CPI,* Vol. 1, No. 2 (April 30, 1976).

3. Alfred M. Gertler and Robert E. Bouzek, "Chi-

cago's RTA: A Short Course in Getting Out the Vote," *Public Relations Journal,* Vol. 31, No. 6 (June 1975). Good case in point.

4. Gerald Zaltman, "Strategies For Planned Change," *Public Relations Journal,* Vol. 32, No. 2 (February 1976). Some additional inputs.

5. David Finn, "In Search of a Public: A Perspective on Public Relations for Cultural, Educational, Social, and Medical Institutions," *Public Relations Quarterly,* Vol. 21, No. 1 (Spring 1976), 16.

6. Jack R. Nowling, "How To Write the PR Program," *Public Relations Journal,* Vol. 32, No. 7 (July 1976).

7. For detailed examples of planning in political public relations, see Harold Lavine, ed., *Smoke Filled Rooms: The Confidential Papers of Robert Humphreys* (Englewood Cliffs, N.J.: Prentice-Hall, 1970). This book contains the Republicans' 1952 campaign plans. Also see American Institute for Political Communication, *A Study of Political Strategy and Tactics* (Washington, D.C.: The Institute, 1967).

8. Victor Waldeman, "How to Set Your Advertising Budget," *Public Relations Quarterly,* Vol. 20, No. 4 (Winter 1975).

9. John Canning, "The Whiting Fire, A Case History in Disaster PR," *Proceedings, Fourth Annual Minnesota Public Relations Forum* (Minneapolis: Minnesota Chapter PRSA, 1955). Also see John T. Hall, "A Fire Made Them Famous," *Public Relations Journal,* Vol. 11 (July 1955).

10. James Skardon, "The Apollo Story: What the Watchdogs Missed," *Columbia Journalism Review,* Vol. 6, (Fall 1967), 13–14. Also see his second article, "The Apollo Story: The Concealed Patterns," *Columbia Journalism Review,* Vol. 6 (Winter 1967–68).

9

The most precarious enterprise in the world is effective communication. It is the ultimate art.

NORMAN COUSINS

The Process: action and communication— the third step

In the third step of the ongoing process, the public relations function moves onstage from the wings of fact-finding and counseling. Once a problem has been defined and a program to solve it worked out, the next step is *action*. This action requires supportive communication to gain cooperation and to gain credit.

To illustrate: a nationwide retailer began to get complaints on a baseboard heater. Research found a fault in the heaters that made them potentially dangerous. It was decided to recall these heaters from the stores and customers. For this purpose, the action required was a communications effort to reach all purchasers of the defective heater. The marketer bought advertising space in the nation's daily newspapers and saturated the news media with warnings to purchasers. Danger was averted and the giant retailer got credit for candor and prompt action.

Another example: The Ford Motor Company wanted to protest what it considered excessive government regulation of auto making. A group of national editors was invited to Detroit for a special showing of four Pintos. One represented the car as it was first built; a second, as it was built the second year; a third, the way the federal government wanted it built; and the fourth Pinto represented the way Ford thought the car *ought to be produced*. Among those present was the publisher of the *New York Times,* and the next day, the *Times* carried a front-page story on the presentation. A broadcaster who was present asked for a videotape to air over his station. This is communication!

Communication and action make up the main thrust in a program. Public relations communication should be viewed as a catalytic agent, with little force of its own except as it can trigger action on the part of the person who receives it. *The other steps in the process are necessary to make this one effective.*

The nature of communication

The dictionary describes communication as "intercourse by words, letters, or messages; interchange of thoughts or opinions." It would be difficult to think of anything that takes place, that makes a sound or a gesture, that does not in some way communicate. Our social life abounds with communication, some of it overt, much of it unverbalized. The average American spends about 70 percent of his waking hours communicating verbally—listening, speaking, reading, and writing. Truly, Americans live under a waterfall of words. Inescapably, communications is the cement that holds society together.

The newborn infant's first cry says, "I am alive." From then on through life, a wink, a raised eyebrow, a smile, a cupped ear, a shaken finger communicate. Notice that these simple human gestures are not in the form of actual words. Still, they inform eloquently. The same is true of sounds from which the audience forms words or ideas. There's no doubt what's going on when one hears a church bell, the snap of a mousetrap, or thunder.

Building from sights, sounds, and sensations, one finds the means to express himself, to be understood, and to understand. In the process, words and actions are the main carriers. Using words or taking meaningful action, whether in the form of a news release or a protest march, constitutes the first common denominator.

Words are symbols. There are words that serve as symbols for real objects— *table, chair—thing words.* There are words that are symbols of abstract ideas, such as *freedom, love—nothing words.* Children are taught, for example, that a furry little animal with long ears and a short, fuzzy tail is a "rabbit." Once the word and the little animal are associated, the word will always evoke the image of that creature. Word symbols for real objects are readily understood and agreed upon. Not so with symbols for abstractions. Abstractions like "free enterprise" or "military morale" have no simple or universally agreed-on referents in the real world of objects. It is difficult for people to agree on an image of free enterprise when they cannot see, touch, hear, taste, or smell it. This difficulty goes right to the heart of the communications problem. *To communicate effectively, the sender's words and symbols must mean the same thing to the receiver that they do to the sender.* The word *communication* is derived from the Latin *communis,* meaning "common." *The purpose of communication is to establish a commonness.* There are three basic elements in communication: the source or *sender, the message,* and the destination or *receiver.* A breakdown can involve one or more of these three elements. Effective communication requires efficiency on the part of all three. The communicator must have *adequate information.* He or she must have *credibility* in the eyes of the receiver. The communicator must be able to transmit information in codes the receiver can *comprehend.* The communicator must use a *channel* that will carry the message to the receiver. The message must be within the *receiver's capacity to comprehend.* To reach its target, the message must (1) be *salient* to the receiver— that is, possess a "psychological closeness"; and (2) be *pertinent*—that is, relate to the discrimination a person makes when he is evaluating alternatives.[1] Finally, the message must *motivate the receiver's self-interest* and cause him or her to respond. Communicators must always bear in mind that communication is no substitute for policy and action.

A sender can *encode* a message and a receiver *decode* it only in terms of their own experience and knowledge. When there has been no common experience, then communication becomes virtually impossible. This explains a layman's inability to understand an Einstein; it explains why, despite the tremendous flow of words to and from Russia, Americans and Russians still have little understanding of each other.[2] Common knowledge and experience provide the connecting links. The greater the overlap in common interest and common experience, the easier it is to communicate. There are many barriers to achieving this *overlap of commonness.*

Commonness in communication is essential to link people and purpose together in any cooperative system.

Students should recognize that Figure 9–1 is a vast oversimplification of the communication process; space does not permit the book-length treatment this process requires. A prime difficulty in understanding the complex communication process is its deceptive simplicity. It would be helpful if we used the term "communication process" rather than "communications" to remind ourselves that communication is a complicated undertaking with many parts and stages.

FIGURE 9–1   The communication process.

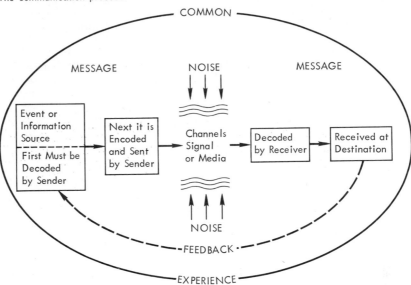

This is especially true of *mass communication,* an ambiguous term in itself. John McNelly sees mass communication as neither a *simple injection* into an entire population nor a neat *two-step flow* from mass media to opinion leader to the general public, but rather as the *complex, multistage, multidirectional process that it is.*[3] There is great need in communications research to identify and differentiate the many different processes that may simultaneously impinge on a variable outcome. The acts of *encoding, interpreting,* and *decoding* must be seen as one inseparable whole. Too many practitioners, by engaging in message sending only, put themselves in the position of a basketball player shooting at a hidden basket, unable to see the results of his shooting and, thus, unable to make necessary adjustments to ensure accuracy.[4] As Duke Ellington said, "There's no point in making noises if no one is listening."

The fundamentals

Many fundamental factors in the process must be taken into full account by anyone who would communicate effectively. These will underline the complexity of this process, a process that requires a minimum of two people coming together in an information-sharing relationship, using a set of common informational signs. A few of these fundamentals are shown in Figure 9-2.

Communicator: The credibility of the communicator is determined by his *expertness* and his *trustworthiness,* as these qualities are perceived by the intended audience. High credibility increases the probability of favorable attitude change, and low credibility lessens it. The more a communicator is known and liked by his audience, the more inclined the audience is to change its beliefs in the direction the communicator advocates. This is particularly true of trivial matters.

Many studies show that the audience's knowledge of the communicator's persuasive intent and bias do not necessarily impair effectiveness. Research also shows that a communicator's effectiveness is increased if he argues a position apparently opposed to his own self-interest. Also, personalized communications exert a stronger influence than do impersonal sources; Sargent found that communications identified by commentators' names are stronger than communications identified by the name of a newspaper, magazine, or network.

Message: Persuasive communications must be supported by events; facts alone do not persuade. Klapper concluded, "Facts may be successfully communicated without producing opinion changes that they are intended or expected to produce." Nonetheless, facts and information may perform a significant role in eliciting, triggering, or rationalizing behavior. Davison thinks the communication of information, although limited in changing attitudes, has a great potential in promoting action and behavior. Several studies have shown that communications are more effective when they include *an explicit statement of the communicator's position;* when the need for the information has already been aroused; and, in cases where both agreeable and disagreeable materials are to be presented, when the desirable material is presented first. McGuire suggests that repetition of messages does increase acceptance of the theme, but that only a small number of repetitions are necessary to produce maximum acceptance.

Audience: The more interested people are in an issue, the more likely they are to hold consistent positions on that issue. The more a person is emotionally involved in his beliefs, the harder it is to change them by information or argument. Once a person commits himself to a position, the commitment becomes a barrier to change. People less interested in an issue hold weaker opinions and beliefs and thus are more likely to change their minds, but the less interested take longer to make up their minds. The more pressured a person is, the less stable his opinions are during persuasion campaigns. A pressured person tends to change toward the prevailing attitude of his most favored group. An individual's behavior is influenced by many different groups; at any given moment, the group with the strongest influence will be the one that is most salient.

People tend to see and hear communications that are favorable or congenial to their predispositions. Berelson and Steiner asserted that "the more interested they are in the subject, the more likely is such selective attention." The basic fact is that a message is perceived by the audience in accordance with its predispositions, desires, wishes, attitudes, needs, and expectations. DeFleur and Larsen suggest, "When contact is achieved and symbols are brought to the attention of a receiver, the content passes through a filter of selective perception by means of which ideas irrelevant or destructive to existing attitudes are suppressed or modified." (As noted in Chapter 6, Sears and Freedman question this selective-exposure hypothesis.) *These processes are self-protective.*

One of the clearest conclusions of a now-substantial body of knowledge is that what the listener or reader brings to the communications situation is a much more important determinant of communications impact than is message content. Grunig found, for example, that the style of a science story was less important than whether the content was relevant to the perceived situation of the reader.[5] *Today's receiver is neither passive nor helpless in the face of persuasive communication. A message's acceptance is within the receiver's control.*

Another point worth noting: A person can and will accept a communication as authoritative only when four conditions simultaneously obtain: (1) He or she can and does understand the communication; (2) at the time of his or her decision, the receiver believes that it is not inconsistent with the purposes of the organization; (3) at the time of his or her decision, the person believes it to be compatible with his or her personal interest as a whole; and (4) the person is able mentally and physically to comply with it.

The two-step flow theory

In this seemingly simple process, there are a number of intervening variables. Research dating roughly from the 1920s has successively isolated and identified them as (1) *exposure, access, and attention given the communicator's message;* (2) *the differential character of the media of communication;* (3) *the content of the message*—its form, presentation, and appeals; (4) *the receiver's predispositions* that cause acceptance, modification, or rejection of the message; and (5) *interpersonal relationships* of individuals as members of groups. *Each one of these variables must be taken into account.*

The most recent variable found to be influential is that of the receiver's interpersonal relationships. This has led to formulation of the *two-step flow of mass communication* theory.[6] Recognizing the spectacular performances of the Creel Committee in World War I in mobilizing patriotism at home and support for war aims abroad, of the American Red Cross in raising unprecedented sums for welfare, and of the Liberty Bond drives in getting millions to buy bonds, communicators in the 1920s developed a mass-communications model that is now outmoded. This Model T vehicle was built on the assumptions that (1) the people are an atomistic mass of millions of isolated readers, listeners, and viewers eager and ready to receive The Message; (2) every message has a direct and powerful stimulus that will get an immediate response; and (3) there is a direct relationship between information and attitudes.

In short, the growing mass media were looked upon as a new kind of unifying force, reaching out to every eye and ear in a society characterized by an amorphous social organization and a loss of interpersonal relationships. This vertical theory of communications presumed that The Message from the mass media is beamed down in a direct line to newly urbanized, isolated, and lost individuals—"the image of the audience as a mass of disconnected individuals hooked up to the media but not to each other."[7]

The naive notion underlying this obsolete theory is seen in this advice given to professional publicists after World War I: "Although clearness and logical arrangement toward a climax are necessary in presenting arguments, the chief thing is to emphasize a supreme point by which . . . a prospect is 'swept off his feet.' " Research and pragmatic experience have shown this image of the direct effect of the mass media to be a great oversimplification. As Lazarsfeld says, "Paradoxical as it may seem, the closer one observes the working of the mass media, the more it turns out that their effects depend on a complex network of specialized personal and social influences."[8] Research has taught us that communications models almost invariably distort or oversimplify the process. Most models tend to be topic-bound. In Tony Schwartz's view, "The vocabulary of communication theory consistently fails as a tool for analyzing the mass media process."

Contemporary practice prefers a communications model that takes into account the *relay* and *reinforcement* roles played by individuals. This means less reliance on mass publicity and more on reaching thought leaders. Communications is a multifaceted *vertical* and *horizontal* process. This was first noted in Lazarsfeld, Berelson, and Gaudet's study of the 1940 presidential election, when "it became clear that certain people in every stratum of a community serve relay roles in the mass communication of election information and influence."[9] To communicate effectively, more attention must be paid to the group, its grapevine, and particularly its leaders. These leaders tend to specialize in issue areas, although not always. For example:

> Opinion leadership in family planning is usually informal, that is, the advice-giver provides information when she is asked for it in a nonofficial context of an informal exchange of conversation. Because the family planning opinion leader is not a specialized opinion leader, and may act as one in other areas, opinion leadership in this area is usually polymorphic.[10]

A more recent testing of this two-step flow theory generally supports the hypothesis but suggests a reinterpretation of the group process as more opinion-sharing than opinion-giving by the leader. Arndt found:

> The two-step flow . . . hypothesis was tested in a field experiment involving diffusion of a new brand of a familiar food product. . . . The opinion leaders seemed to be more influenced by the impersonal source [the direct-mail letter] than were the non-leaders. . . . The data supported the notion of a first-step flow of influence. In regard to the second step, the leaders were found to be more active communicators, both as transmitters and receivers of word-of-mouth communicators. An unexpected finding was the relatively large amount of word-of-mouth flowing from nonleaders to leaders. This finding was explained in terms of the opinion-sharing nature of the communication situation. The word-of-mouth transmitters did not simply pass on the messages received from impersonal sources, but shaded the messages with their own evaluations.[11]

Although the Katz-Lazarsfeld two-step theory has utility for mass communicators, users must consider its weaknesses. This simplistic theory doesn't adequately explain what happens in a *multistep, multidirectional* process. For example, the healing properties of a new drug are made known in a communications chain that moves from the laboratory to manufacture to marketing, to the medical journals and "detail men," to physicians and pharmacists, and finally to the patient. And it overlooks the fact that a great amount of information flows directly from the media to the consumers of the media. The Deutschmann-Danielson hypothesis states, ". . . initial mass media information on important news events goes directly to the people and is not relayed to any great extent."[12] McLeod and Blumler hold that the "limited effects" model errs because "it exaggerated (a) in general the homogeneity of the world of political influences, communication and extracommunication that play on the typical citizen and (b) more specifically, the amount of selective exposure in which most people engage in order to reinforce their previous leanings."[13]

Schramm sums up what we know:

> Perhaps the best way to say it, in the present state of knowledge, is that there is a continuing flow of information and ideas through society. The mass media greatly influence—directly or indirectly—what flows through these channels. Certain individuals also influence it, either by sharing their special knowledge, expertise, or conviction on a certain topic by being articulate and talkative. . . . Some influence it more than others. But there are not two classes, the leaders and the led, nor is there in most cases a two-step flow from media to leader to follower.[14]

The concentric-circle theory

Gaining acceptance of an idea or an innovation, then, is more than simply beaming it to an audience through a mass medium or internal publication. *To illuminate, communication must be aimed with the precision of a laser beam, not cast in all directions in the manner of a light bulb.* There is still not sufficient evidence to be positive about how ideas are disseminated among people; but Elmo Roper, after nearly 30 years of opinion research, formulated a hypothesis that has some value as a guide. In his "concentric-circle theory," Roper assumed that ideas penetrate to the whole public very slowly. This was shown when, at the time of the presidential election in November 1972, only 48 percent of the voters had heard of the Watergate crime that had taken place in June of that year.

Roper thought that ideas penetrate the whole public by a process similar to osmosis. They move out in concentric circles from Great Thinkers to Great Disciples to Great Disseminators to Lesser Disseminators to the Politically Active to the Politically Inert—as charted in Figure 9–2. This hypothesis assumes that American society can be stratified as indicated and emphasizes the importance of using opinion leaders in the public relations process. The theory generally squares with the findings of Lazarsfeld, Katz, and others. It deserves further testing.

But like other communications models, Roper's concentric-circle theory doesn't fully explain what happens. The *rate of flow* in the transmission and acceptance of ideas, for instance, is governed by many factors. These include Lippmann's "Barriers to Communication" and the "Regulators of Absorption Rate" named by George Gallup on the basis of three decades of opinion research, both listed on the chart.

FIGURE 9-2

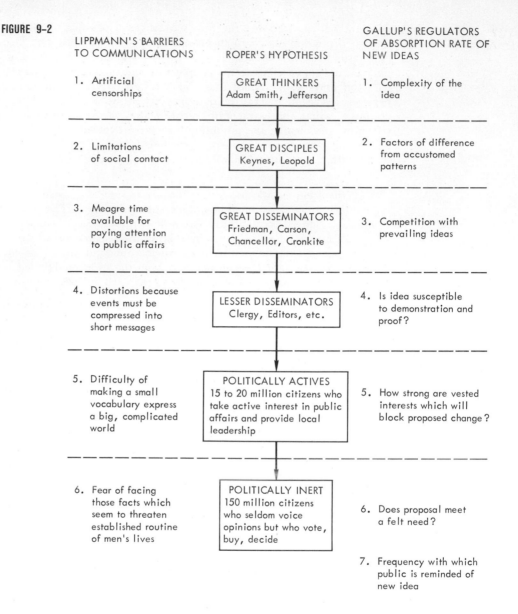

LIPPMANN'S BARRIERS TO COMMUNICATIONS	ROPER'S HYPOTHESIS	GALLUP'S REGULATORS OF ABSORPTION RATE OF NEW IDEAS
1. Artificial censorships	GREAT THINKERS Adam Smith, Jefferson	1. Complexity of the idea
2. Limitations of social contact	GREAT DISCIPLES Keynes, Leopold	2. Factors of difference from accustomed patterns
3. Meagre time available for paying attention to public affairs	GREAT DISSEMINATORS Friedman, Carson, Chancellor, Cronkite	3. Competition with prevailing ideas
4. Distortions because events must be compressed into short messages	LESSER DISSEMINATORS Clergy, Editors, etc.	4. Is idea susceptible to demonstration and proof?
5. Difficulty of making a small vocabulary express a big, complicated world	POLITICALLY ACTIVES 15 to 20 million citizens who take active interest in public affairs and provide local leadership	5. How strong are vested interests which will block proposed change?
6. Fear of facing those facts which seem to threaten established routine of men's lives	POLITICALLY INERT 150 million citizens who seldom voice opinions but who vote, buy, decide	6. Does proposal meet a felt need? 7. Frequency with which public is reminded of new idea

---

The diffusion process

The communications step in the public relations process requires influencing opinions and actions among sizable and distant groups. The accelerating rate at which innovations are being invented, developed, and spread makes it vital that communicators be able to transfer information to those who need it. Examples are gaining public acceptance of seat belts and air bags for motorists' safety, and getting the public to take swine-flu shots for its protection. *Diffusion* is the term given the process by which new ideas are spread to members of a social system.

The U.S. Department of Agriculture has been working at this task longer than most. It has learned that getting new ideas accepted involves more than simply discovering a new grain and publicizing it. It took 13 years to gain widespread adoption of hybrid seed corn on America's farms, for example. Out of their long experience and *evaluation,* agricultural sociologists have concluded that acceptance goes through five stages:

1. *Awareness.* The person learns of the existence of the idea or practice but has little knowledge of it.
2. *Interest.* The person develops interest in the idea. He seeks more information and considers its general merits.
3. *Evaluation.* The person makes mental application of the idea and weighs its merits for his own situation. He obtains more information and decides to try it.
4. *Trial.* The person actually applies the idea or practice—usually on a small scale. He is interested in the practice, techniques, and conditions for application.
5. *Adoption.* If the idea proves acceptable, it is adopted.[15]

As shown in Table 9–1, researchers have concluded that information about new farm and home practices are communicated by these agencies in this order: (1) mass media—radio, TV, newspapers, magazines; (2) friends and neighbors—mostly other farmers; (3) agricultural agencies—extension agents, vo-ag instructors, and so forth; (4) dealers and salesmen—purveyors of commercial products and equipment.

These media or agencies have a varying impact at each stage of the process. The mass media have their greatest impact and usefulness in creating *awareness.* For farmers and farmwives, at least, the mass media become less and less influential as the acceptance process advances toward adoption. In the *interest* stage, mass media still play an important part. But to learn more, the farmer turns to agricultural agencies and friends. In the *evaluation* stage, friends and neighbors play the dominant role. In the *trial* stage, agricultural agencies, friends, and neighbors are all important. Dealers and salesmen are influential in this stage when commercial products are involved. *The time span in each stage varies.*

This diffusion model, developed through extensive research among rural families, was confirmed in a comparable study of how doctors in four communities responded to the availability of a new "miracle drug." Despite the differences between a new seed and a new drug, and between farmers and doctors, the results are comparable. One of the investigators, Elihu Katz, warns, "Whether these generalizations apply equally to the diffusion of other innovations remains to be seen."

Chaffee suggests that there are several reasons for this pattern of diffusion:

The media are comparatively rich in news content, whereas personal associates are likely to have relevant "consumer" experience. Further, since consumption is partly a matter of defining one's social self, other persons would be able to offer normative social guides to appropriate consumption patterns that the media cannot. Finally, some matters may not be dealt with by the media in sufficient depth or detail to satisfy personal information needs.[16]

TABLE 9-1 Stages in the adoption process

AWARENESS Learns about a new idea or practice	INTEREST Gets more information about it	EVALUATION Tries it out mentally	TRIAL Uses or tries a little	ADOPTION Accepts it for full-scale and continued use
1. Mass media—radio, TV, newspapers, magazines 2. Friends and neighbors, mostly other farmers 3. Agricultural agencies, extension, vo-ag, etc. 4. Dealers and salesmen	1. Mass media 2. Friends and neighbors 3. Agricultural agencies 4. Dealers and salesmen	1. Friends and neighbors 2. Agricultural agencies 3. Dealers and salesmen 4. Mass media	1. Friends and neighbors 2. Agricultural agencies 3. Dealers and salesmen 4. Mass media	Personal experience is the most important factor in continued use of an idea 1. Friends and neighbors 2. Agricultural agencies 3. Mass media 4. Dealers and salesmen

Source: Herbert F. Lionberger, *Adoption of New Ideas and Practices* (Ames: Iowa State University Press, 1960), p. 32.

A common model of the communications process is that of SOURCE—MESSAGE—CHANNEL—RECEIVER—EFFECTS. In Figure 9–3, Rogers charts the way in which elements in the diffusion process and the S-M-C-R-E model are similar.

The research conclusions demonstrate that communicating a new idea or practice is a long, tedious task. Different media are effective at different points and in different ways. The influence of the innovator or influential leader is great in every community. It is important for the communicator to know what media and techniques to use at different stages and how to mobilize these influences effectively. Taken together, these theories provide a much surer approach. *Effective communication is expensive in time, in understanding, and in emotional control. The cost is higher than is commonly supposed.*

FIGURE 9-3 From Everett M. Rogers and W. Floyd Shoemaker, *Communication of Innovations* (New York: Free Press, 1971), p. 20.

Elements in the diffusion of innovations
and the S-M-C-R-E communication model are similar.

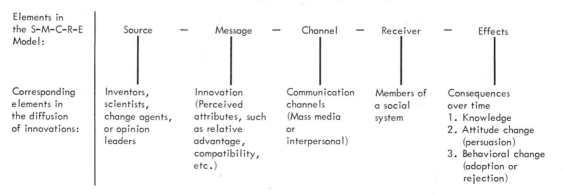

198

Barriers and distortion

Barriers to understanding and to clarity of message exist in the communicator and the audience alike. *Each person lives in the protective shelter of a cocoon of his own spinning.* This cocoon insulates him from the communications babble that beats in upon him all day long, a babble steadily increasing in intensity. There are social barriers, age barriers, language or vocabulary barriers, political and economic barriers. There is also the race barrier; the barriers and distortions that block communication are seen starkly in the gulf between American blacks and whites. There is peer pressure exerted within a person's groups, where "reality" is shared and interpreted—a factor discussed in Chapter 6. There is also the often overlooked barrier of the audience's ability to absorb the message. Discussing the widely prevalent notion that lack of information or ignorance can be remedied by more information, Gabriel A. Almond has observed that the problem runs much deeper: "A discriminating analysis of the evidence suggests that a large sector of the lower-income, poorly educated majority of the population is incapable of assimilating the materials of informational campaigns." J. Richard Udrey, in *The Media and Family Planning,* echoes this: "Our results suggest that no one should undertake mass media campaigns for family planning in the United States under the assumption important effects will result." Udrey's generalization, based upon a campaign that was not well planned, has been challenged by other specialists in family-planning communication. Finally, there is the constant roar of competition for people's attention in the noisy public arena.

The difficulty of public-information campaigns can be clearly seen in the battle to save us from polluted air, polluted water, and chemically dangerous foods. America's pioneer ecologist, Aldo Leopold, thought in his early years that "if the public were told how much harm ensues from unwise land-use, it would mend its ways." In his twilight years, he knew that this conclusion was based on three mistaken assumptions: (1) that the public is listening or can be made to listen; (2) that the public responds, or can be made to respond, to fear of harm; (3) that ways can be mended without any important change in the public itself.[17]

A case in point: The cereal manufacturer, Kellogg, put on an intensive week-long campaign costing $200,000 to get schoolchildren in the District of Columbia to eat a proper breakfast. The drive was capped with a free breakfast for every grade-school youngster in the city schools—72,000 in all. A before-campaign survey found that 18,892 pupils participated in the school breakfast program; during the campaign, the number rose to 22,244, but by the following June, it dropped to 17,498, fewer than before the campaign.

In a much-quoted article that has stood the test of time, Hyman and Sheatsley codified the major reasons why many information campaigns fail.

1. Repeated social surveys have revealed a hard core of chronic know-nothings.
2. There are large groups in the population who admit that they have little or no interest in public issues.
3. People tend to expose themselves to material that is compatible with their prior attitudes and to avoid exposure to that which is not compatible.
4. Selective perception and interpretation of content follows exposure: Persons perceive, absorb, and remember content differently.
5. Changes in views or behavior following exposure to a message may be differentially affected by the individual's initial predispositions and attitudes.[18]

More recently, another researcher, Harold Mendelsohn, has countered the Hyman-Sheatsley point of view with an analysis of why information campaigns can succeed. He writes:

> What little empirical experience we have accumulated from the past suggests that public information campaigns have relatively high success potentials:
>
> 1. If they are planned around the assumption that most of the publics to which they will be addressed will be either only mildly interested or not at all interested in what is communicated.
> 2. If middle-range goals which can be reasonably achieved as a consequence of exposure are set as specific objectives. Frequently it is equally important either to set up or to utilize environmental support systems to help sheer information-giving become effective in influencing behavior.
> 3. If, after middle-range objectives are set, careful consideration is given to delineating specific targets in terms of their demographic and psychological attributes, their life-styles, value and belief systems, and mass media habits. Here, it is important not only to determine the scope of prior indifference, but to uncover its roots as well.[19]

That public-information campaigns can succeed was demonstrated by Dorothy Douglas, who conducted one to increase public understanding of mental retardation and thus gain support for rehabilitation programs. Her campaign in a Wisconsin county brought an increase in the public's information and raised the level of favorable attitudes significantly when these were measured against a control group in a comparable county.[20] Chaffee says that such successes "hinge to a considerable extent on holding to information-transmission as one's main goal." The Sauk County experiment also suggests that chances of success are greater when there is no countercampaign.

The act of communicating

It would be disappointing, if not futile, to establish any single set of surefire rules for swaying public opinion. Such rules might appear perfect in principle, yet be rendered ineffectual by an *unseen characteristic of the audience*—for example, a religious belief that bans certain foods. *The timing could be bad.* Merchants know they can't sell snow shovels in July. A carefully timed announcement of a new stock offering by an oil company was smothered in the news by revelations that it had used corporate funds for political campaigns in the United States and bribes abroad. *The audience could harbor an unspoken prejudice,* such as confronts a Democrat campaigning in a Republican precinct. The wording of the message could be such that it does not square with the images in the heads of the audience. Or perhaps the audience is not in a listening mood. Regardless of the specific barrier, results from standardization of programming are generally frustrating and futile.

Effective communication must be designed for the situation, time, place, and audience. It means careful selection of media and technique. Example: The annual Spring migration of 200,000 college students to Florida's beaches poses health problems for that state—among them the spread of venereal diseases. One year, the Florida Health Department gave frisbees carrying messages on how to recognize and prevent VD to these students as they swarmed the Florida beaches. *This is targeted communication.*

Advances in technology are opening up a wealth of possibilities for serving the needs of special audiences. Practitioners would be well advised to think in terms of smaller and more circumscribed patterns of communication as they seek to modify or mobilize opinions. No communication or action, simply because it worked once before in a given situation, can be carted about like a trunk full of clothes and fitted to a new situation. With rare exception, the clothes will not fit the second wearer. If nothing else, they'll be out of style.

All public relations problems, however, do have people as a common denominator and require some communicating to bring the people and their viewpoints closer together. This applies whether the programming calls for news releases, institutional advertising, meetings, or any other tool of contact.

Continuity is required in communicating. So are repetition of a consistent message in simple form, careful selection of time, place, and method, and a variety of media that converge on the audience from several avenues.

Public relations, with its powerful and varied means of disseminating information, suffers from an overcapacity. Simon and Garfunkel sang to us, in "The Sounds of Silence," that our problem is people talking without speaking, people hearing without listening. As repeatedly suggested in this book, there is an urgent need to target *specific messages* to *specific audiences* to achieve *specific results.*

The practitioner must define his audiences with great precision, and he must use different strategies and techniques to accomplish different goals. Eugene F. Lane says, "The communicator must vary his communications strategy in accordance with the intensity of concern with an issue felt by his audience." He suggests, for example, these techniques to reduce the discrepancy between the communicator's position and the audience's attitudes:

1. Using media most closely identified with the audience's position.
2. Using a communications source that enjoys high credibility for the audience *on this issue.*
3. Playing down the differences between the communication and the audience's attitudes.
4. Seeking identification in vocabulary and anecdote with the audience in an area *removed from the issue.*
5. Establishing the communicator's position as being the majority opinion—defining the majority from the audience itself.
6. Bringing the audience's group identifications into play—when those identifications will help the development of a positive response. The converse is also true.
7. Modifying the message to fit the organization's needs—since you can't modify organizational objectives.[21]

A few fundamentals

There are four fundamental facts that the communicator must keep in mind: (1) The audience consists of people. These people live, work, worship, and play in the framework of social institutions in cities, in suburbs, and in villages. Consequently, each person is subject to many influences, of which the communicator's message is only one. (2) People tend to read, watch, or listen to communications that present points of view with which they are sympathetic or in which they have a deep personal stake. (3) The mass media create their separate communities. For example, those who read newspapers constitute a community separate from those who depend on TV for their news. (4) The mass media *do have a wide variety of effects* on individual behavior, not all of which are measurable.

Stereotypes

People have impressions about everything that touches the consciousness. Lippmann has bracketed these impressions into four groups: the person's approach to the world, his stereotypes, his personal interests, and his image of the world. *Everyone lives in a world of his or her own symbols.* Public figures, for example, during their lifetimes and afterward, are known partly through a personality created by images fixed in the public imagination. Astronauts and sports heroes are good examples. Their families and associates know them as people entirely different from their public personalities. People who live on one side of town tend to know people on the other side of town, as well as those in remote cities, in a half-fictional, half-imagined way. The only feeling that anyone can have about an event he does not experience or a person he does not know is by his own mental image of the event or person, developed from fragmentary, secondary sources.[22]

In communicating, nothing raises more problems than the fact that the audience has limited access to the facts. Access, as Lippmann has made clear, is limited by the six main factors listed in Figure 9–2. With limited access, and with some information tending to confuse as much as it clarifies, people rely heavily on *stereotypes.* Specific and significant impressions become generalities. Most stereotypes carry negative overtones.

The person looking at the cover of a magazine, for example, with a picture entitled "Criminal," may pick out two or three sharply defined features. Perhaps he selects a low forehead, a squinting eye, a scarred face, or a mouth that curls at the corner. From then on, the impression may be so deeply rooted that he feels sure he knows the "criminal type" whenever he sees it. He can classify everyone, including his friends, as to whether or not they are criminal types. Indeed, he has classifications into which he can fit almost everyone he sees or hears about. Distorted stereotypes pose public relations problems. For example, the stereotype of the old-maid schoolteacher persists despite the fact that 75 out of every 100 teachers are or have been married. The farmer in blue overalls and a straw hat little resembles today's agribusinessman. The long-haired student, absent-minded professor, strident "feminist" are other stereotypes.

Lippmann emphasizes the sacrosanct regard that people have for stereotypes as "the core of our personal tradition, the defense of our position in society." Stereotypes tend, as a defense mechanism, to express the hopes of the audience. They form a moral code from which personal standards are derived. The specialist learns to recognize the influence and the presence of symbols and stereotypes in the seeming contradictions and contrariness of public opinion. *Stereotypes are used to counter stereotypes.*

Another system of barriers encompasses the superstitions, prejudices, and vanities to which we all cling. Considering superstitions alone, one man may laugh at another for his refusal to open an umbrella in the house. But the man who laughed might himself walk two blocks out of his way to avoid letting a black cat cross his path. *We believe what we want to believe.* That is perhaps the best way to explain, in oversimplified terms, the grip that superstitions, prejudices, and vanities have on us.

Semantics

Semantics is the science of what words really mean. There is constant change in our language: Some words emerge from the dictionary into popular usage; others wither away from neglect or are banished by abuse; and the meanings of words frequently change. In this text, the science of semantics can only be kissed lightly; space denies a full courtship. Don't be misled, however—the subject really deserves and gets a great deal of attention from men and women in public relations. For in communicating and interpreting, practitioners live by words—and make their living by them. Practitioners seek mastery of word meanings both as users and as understanders. For communicators, there is no escape from what T.S. Eliot described as "the intolerable wrestle with words and meanings."[23]

The basic importance of semantics must never be lost. In communicating, a person is constantly making decisions on word meanings. When you decide whether the refusal of men to work should be called a strike, a work stoppage, or a damnable crime against the people, you are making a decision in semantics.

There is no one-to-one ratio between a word and its meaning; more likely, the ratio is one-to-fifty. In selecting words to use as weapons, the practitioner must remember that the same signs and word symbols have different meanings for different people. Not only that; they have two different *kinds* of meaning—*denotative* and *connotative*. *Denotative* meaning is the common dictionary meaning, generally accepted by most people with the same language and culture. *Connotative* meaning is the emotional or evaluative meaning we read into words because of our experience and background. For example, all people will agree that "dog" *denotes* a four-legged, furry, canine animal. For most people, the word "dog" *connotes* a friendly, faithful pet and usually awakens nostalgic memories. To some, however, the word *connotes* a dangerous animal to be feared. Another example is the word "bullfight." North and South Americans fully agree on what the term denotes, but its connotative meaning differs sharply north and south of the Rio Grande.

Words can be dynamite. There is evidence that a mistake in translating a message sent by the Japanese government near the end of World War II may have triggered the bombing of Hiroshima and thus ushered in atomic warfare. The word *mokusatsu,* used by Japan in response to the U.S. surrender ultimatum, was translated by Domei as "ignore" instead of its correct meaning, "withhold comment until a decision has been made." And some years ago, a crisis between the United States and Panama was caused by semantic difficulties between the English verb *negotiate* and the Spanish verb *negociar.* Panamanians interpreted *negotiate* as a commitment to negotiate a new treaty, whereas our State Department intended it simply in its noncommittal sense of "to discuss."

Words often become "code words" to convey an unspoken but unmistakable meaning—for instance, "law and order," "reverse discrimination," "ethnic purity of neighborhoods." Nor can the meaning of commonplace words be taken for granted. David Ogilvy used the word *obsolete* in an ad, only to find that 43 percent of the women in the United States had no idea what it meant. A refrigerator maker had the same experience with "trouble-free service." A *New York Times* story described a presidential speech as *masterful,* ("imperious, domineering"), when it meant *masterly* ("skillful, powerful"). Poet Anne Sexton cautions care in choice of words: "Words, like eggs, must be handled with care; once broken, they are beyond repair."

The practitioner as "answer man"

In the midst of the "wrestle with words" is the public relations practitioner. Studying the words that leap out of people's mouths, stare up from newspapers, and smile out from a television tube, he's expected to react and then to be able to tell what those words mean—*not what they say, but what they really mean.* Then, he's expected to combine words and actions that will correct misunderstandings, educate where there is a lack of knowledge, and, in general, clear up confusion.

A cardinal premise is that *you cannot tell anyone something he cannot understand. And you can rarely tell anyone something you cannot understand. You have to understand it first, and then you have to make it understandable to the other person.* Whether you are dealing with one person or with a crowd, the same premises apply.

Public relations people must be tuned in to the various meanings of words used by all self-interested groups. The term *peanut farmer* when used by a peanut farmer is a compliment. It's not always a compliment when spoken by a political opponent. A "heel" tacked onto a shoe is a different matter when the term is attached to a man. There are several kinds of "Yankee"; ask a baseball fan, a Southerner, and a Vermont farmer.

Public relations people must be able to select and to transmit for various audiences words that will be received as kinfolk. Think of the harm that has been done, the confusion created, by legal language. A book could be written on that subject alone. A single illustration will be enough.

Periodically, labor officials and management officials spend weeks talking out a new agreement on working conditions. When the negotiation sessions are all done, the union has a new contract, all properly drawn to stand up in court. *But not more than one out of every hundred employees bound by that contract could understand all of it if they read it.* So, generally, they don't read it. They are told what it's all about in words they can understand. They're usually told in a manner that compliments the source, whether labor official or management spokesman. In one case, it's, "Here's what we got for you"; in the other, it's, "Here's what we are giving you." The chances are that the employee is no nearer a real appreciation of the issues and solutions than he is when he gets through filling out an income tax form or reading an insurance policy, a financial statement, or instructions for claiming unemployment compensation.

For example, here is an actual excerpt from the minutes of a labor–management bargaining–committee meeting:

It is agreed, in response to the request by the Bargaining Committee, to change past practice and policy so that in the future when an employee is absent from work on one paid holiday qualifying day on a leave of absence that includes that day, one of the excused absences as provided in the labor agreement may be used to cover such absence to qualify for pay for the holiday subject to the contractual paid holiday provisions, with the understanding that this agreement is in no way to be interpreted to mean that past practice and policy is changed to provide that an employee absent from work on a leave of absence on both qualifying days is to receive pay for the holiday regardless of remaining excused absence credit.

That may have made sense to the members of the bargaining group. They had been talking about it for several meetings. But it can't be transplanted, as is, for any other audience; to another audience, it's just so much gobbledygook.

The same is true for the language of doctors, educators, the military, and government. *Each has a special jargon not readily understandable to others—legalese, Pentagonese, educationese, and militarese.* For example, when Secretary of State Henry Kissinger appointed a consumer affairs coordinator to improve State's public relationships, her job was to be to "review existing mechanisms of consumer input, throughput, and output and seek ways of improving these linkages via the consumer communication channel." And besides jargons, there are slangs, dialects, slogans, and exaggerations. The practitioner must work with his cousins in the press, radio, and television, and on the platform to help straighten things out for the public.

How do we go about it?

There are, within every generation, wonderful examples of word mastery—people such as Franklin Roosevelt, Winston Churchill, and John F. Kennedy. In specialized fields of word usage, Stuart Chase has made sense of complex economic matters. Paul de Kruif did the same with medical science. Some popular magazines do a marvelous job with fiction and features.

Of the communicators mentioned, Franklin Roosevelt had no equal. He always found the right word in a tight situation. He was particularly skilled in his radio projection, but radio appeal was not all of it. He knew words. For example, the Social Security Act was first drafted as an "Economic Security" bill, but FDR knew "Social Security" would be more acceptable. Another example of FDR's adroitness with words was shown when he termed the nation's military draft law of 1940 a "muster," thus evoking memories of the rugged farmers of Lexington and Concord, and softening the introduction of conscription.

In a later day, President Kennedy's polished prose aroused emotions around the world. His memorable inaugural address appeal, "And so, my fellow Americans, ask not what your country can do for you; ask what you can do for your country," will go ringing down the corridors of time. Kennedy's sensitive feel for the right word, the stirring phrase, was reflected in the construction of that address. His collaborator, Theodore Sorensen, has recounted the way each paragraph was reworded, reworked, and reduced.[24]

The tricks that can be played with words were shown by Richard Nixon, who paid close attention to such matters. He changed the name of a much-criticized antiballistic missile system from Sentinel to Safeguard, introduced a controversial annual-income proposal as a "work incentive plan," and, when he ordered the invasion of Cambodia, termed it an "incursion." Our involvement in the Vietnam War brought a bitter legacy of word corruption: Soldiers were "advisors," bombings were "interdictions," and defeat was "a failure to achieve our objectives."

Tagging your proposals with warm, favorable terms and the other fellow's with unfavorable ones is an important part of communications. What one group calls a "program," an opposing group brands a "scheme." The proponent for paying farmers not to grow crops calls it a "soil bank," coupling two warm, respected words; opponents call it a "subsidy." There's a difference in the impact of "sliding price supports" and "flexible price supports," yet both describe the same plan. Industries seeking tax postponements on new plants talk of "accelerated tax amortization." Critics of this law call it "fast tax write-off." Labor leaders plead the case for "union security," while industrialists plead for "the right to work."

The governor of New York pledges not to ask for higher taxes; he recommends an increase in "state fees" instead. The governor of Wisconsin vows never to sign a sales tax bill; he signs an "excise tax" bill instead. The campaign for national prohibition made "saloon" a dirty word, so today, those who drink do so in "taverns" and "cocktail lounges." Incidentally, the Drys were too wise to campaign for "prohibition," a harsh word; they advocated "temperance." A great coup in semantics was scored in coining the term "life insurance" to describe what could be called, more properly, "death insurance"—but the latter would be harder to sell. Another ten-strike in semantics has been the successful effort of bowling promoters to change "bowling alleys" to "bowling lanes." Milwaukee's garbagemen got their title changed to "combustible truck loaders," a title with more dignity. Another successful semantic coup was changing "educational television" to "public television," which has a more popular ring to it. Semantic manipulation is an old art. In World War I, Britain's propaganda boss, Lord Northcliffe, decreed that field hospitals be described as "evacuation stations," a less alarming term to kin of the injured. In the 1920s, AT&T started asking for "rate revisions," not "rate increases."

Getting your public relations word accepted by the public isn't easy. HEW public-affairs officers have made several attempts to come up with a more favorable word than *welfare*. They have tried "Fedcare," "Fedicare," "Americaid," and "Amerishare," all to no avail. In the end they admitted, "We didn't find any other word that helped the problem of communication."

Words change from one generation to another, from one context to another. In the eighteenth century, *awful* meant "full of awe," and *officious* meant "graciously extending a person's offices." Today these words have quite different meanings. Once, *bussing* was an affectionate pastime; now it is an angry word in racial conflicts. The way words are bent, like trees, by prevailing winds is illustrated in the word *dissent*. Long ago it meant speeches expressing unorthodox opinions or challenging ideas. In the 1970s, it came to embrace a wide variety of physical acts, including violence. *Progressive* and *education* when used separately are warm, solid American words. Put them together and you get the sneer term, "progressive education." Inept choice of a word can have unhappy consequences. Some years ago, in a call-up of reserves, the army referred to the casuals called to bring divisions to full strength as "fillers." This the troops resented. Today is is not good international public relations to describe any nation as "backward." Such nations are "emerging" or "developing."

A flair for the picturesque, memorable term and a feeling for words are important requisites for the practitioner.

Communication involves more than semantics; in large measure, it uses *symbols and stereotypes*. The symbol offers a dramatic and direct means of persuasive communication with large numbers of people over long lines of communication. Symbols have been used since the dawn of history to compress and convey complex messages to the multitudes. The Star of David and the Cross of Christ remind us of this. Most people need the shorthand of symbols to deal with whatever is abstract, diffuse, or difficult.

In David Berlo's view, this is the age of symbol manipulation. "In our grandfather's day, most people earned their living by manipulating *things,* not by manipulating *symbols.*" The need met by symbols was explained by Lippmann years ago: "This problem of the acquisition of meaning by things or of forming habits of simple apprehension is the problem of introducing (1) definiteness and distinction and (2) consistency or stability of meaning into what otherwise is vague and wavering. . . . We tend to perceive that which we have picked out in the form stereotyped for us by our culture. . . ." A current example of Lippmann's point: Black power is a powerful symbol because it condenses an enormous amount of information and experience into a little bit—there or not there, for me or against me, right or wrong.

The value and use of a venerated symbol is seen in the British monarchy. The British Commonwealth of Nations today is a free association of independent nations shakily held together, not by legal ties, but by the symbol of the Queen of England. She symbolizes the traditional loyalties, the common interests, the traditional institutional forms held more or less in common, the family tie. The American flag, our cherished symbol, movingly and dramatically symbolizes all this nation stands for and means to us every time we see it. Think of the symbolic use we make, in our patriotic and persuasive communications, of George Washington, Abraham Lincoln, the Minutemen at Lexington and Concord, and the Statue of Liberty.

Symbols play an important role in the public relations and fund-raising programs of health and welfare agencies. Probably the best-known symbol of its kind is the Red Cross, from which that agency takes its name. The Red Cross originated in Switzerland and created its symbol by reversing the white cross and red background of the Swiss flag. The upright sword of the American Cancer Society, chosen in a nationwide poster contest, was created to portray its crusading spirit. Another crusade, that of the National Tuberculosis Association, is symbolized by the Cross of Lorraine that dates back to the Crusades. Another popular symbol is that of the Red Feather, used by Community Chests and United Funds. Created by a local Community Chest in 1928, it was modified in 1955 to incorporate a large U, symbolizing the merging of Community Chests with United Funds. Another example is the symbol of those protesting war, which quickly swept around the world—the dove of peace.

One of the most effective symbols ever created is that of Smokey Bear, used by the U.S. Forest Service, the Association of State Foresters, and the Advertising Council to promote forest-fire prevention. The idea originated with a group of foresters and advertising people concerned about the need to protect our forests. After experimenting with drawings of deers, squirrels, and other small animals to carry fire-prevention messages, they hit on the idea of using a bear. A bear—with its humanlike posture, its way of handling itself, its universal appeal to young and old—seemed ideal to build into a persuasive symbol. Smokey's personality, as determined by artists, has been changed over the years as various interpretations were fused into this one symbol. Although a created symbol, Smokey has had wide impact, especially among the young people of the nation. A half-dozen girls are kept busy answering his mail, taking care of his Junior Forest Ranger program, and sending out his fire-prevention campaign material—not only in the United States but all over the world. In a typical year, some 23 million printed items bearing his imprint are distributed by the Forest Service, State Foresters, and other agencies (see Figure 9–4). Smokey had become such a useful symbol that in 1975, when at age 25 he "retired" with due ceremony, the Forest Service had collected $1.3 million dollars in royalties on this symbol. A 4-year-old Smokey, orphaned like his predecessor in the New Mexico mountains, was brought to the Washington Zoo to serve in his stead.

The Forest Service gave Smokey a pop-eyed partner, Woodsy Owl, (see Figure 9–5) in the 1970s as a symbol for the "save-our-environment" campaign. The chubby cartoon owl is dressed in green pants and a Robin Hood-style hat. Woodsy's admonition, "Give a hoot, don't pollute," is now seen widely on posters and on TV public-service announcements.

Increasingly, profit and nonprofit institutions alike are emphasizing their symbols in an effort to create a sharper, more contemporary public image. For example, corporate identity is a phase of industrial public relations growth. Even so, many business firms are wasting millions in advertising and public relations dollars by using corporate marks that do not truly or effectively represent their

FIGURE 9–4 Smokey

FIGURE 9–5   Woodsy Owl

companies. An industrial designer advises that a corporate symbol should be selected on the basis of (1) memorability, (2) recognition, (3) appropriateness, and (4) uniqueness. Surely the symbol should be distinct, different, and in character for the institution using it.

The 7 C's of communication

1. Credibility

Communication starts with a climate of belief. This climate is built by performance on the part of the institution, reflecting an earnest desire to serve the receiver. The receiver must have confidence in the sender. He must have a high regard for the source's competence on the subject.

2. Context

A communications program must square with the realities of its environment. Mechanical media are only supplementary to the word and deed that take place in daily living. The context must provide for participation and playback. It must confirm, not contradict, the message.

3. Content

The message must have meaning for the receiver, and it must be compatible with his value system. It must have relevance for him. In general, people select those items of information that promise them the greatest rewards. The content determines the audience.

4. Clarity

The message must be put in simple terms. Words must mean the same to the receiver as to the sender. Complex issues must be compressed into themes, slogans, or stereotypes that have simplicity and clarity. The farther a message has to travel, the simpler it must be. An institution must speak with one voice, not many voices.

5. Continuity and consistency

Communication is an unending process. It requires repetition to achieve penetration. Repetition—with variation—contributes to both factual and attitude learning. The story must be consistent.

6. Channels

Established channels of communication should be used—channels that the receiver uses and respects. Creating new ones is difficult. Different channels have different effects and serve effectively in different stages of the diffusion process.

7. Capability of audience

Communication must take into account the capability of the audience. Communications are most effective when they require the least effort on the part of the recipient. This involves factors of availability, habit, reading ability, and receiver's knowledge.

Case problem

You are public relations director in an industrial firm that manufactures outboard and other small motors. Normally, your firm employs 2,200 workers. Now, cancellation of a military order requires that the firm lay off 450 workers at the end of the month.

The personnel director works out plans for the layoff, including a three-week notice to the men as a matter of fairness to them. Personnel also makes arrangements to try to find other jobs for them in the community and to provide them with a list of available jobs.

As public relations director, you are asked to work out a plan of communicating this information to company officials, foremen, union officials, the men, and the community. Your plan should include:

1. A timetable designed to squelch rumors and prevent confusion.
2. Themes and tone of the announcement.
3. Wording of the announcement to employees and to the local press.
4. A letter from the president to opinion leaders.

ADDITIONAL READINGS

ELLIOT ARONSON, *The Social Animal*. San Francisco: W.H. Freeman, 1972. The chapter on "Mass Communication, Propaganda, and Persuasion" is helpful.

BERNARD BERELSON AND GARY STEINER, *Human Behavior: An Inventory of Scientific Findings*. New York: Harcourt Brace Jovanovich, 1964.

DAVID K. BERLO, *The Process of Communication*. New York: Holt, Rinehart & Winston, 1960.

ERWIN P. BETTINGHAUS, *Persuasive Communication*. New York: Holt, Rinehart & Winston, 1968.

REED H. BLAKE AND EDWIN O. HAROLDSEN, *A Taxonomy of Concepts in Communication*. New York: Hastings House, 1975.

JAY G. BLUMLER AND ELIHU KATZ, eds., *The Uses of Mass Communications*. Berkeley, Calif.: Sage Publications, 1974. Volume 3 of Sage's annual review of communications research, this one focuses on gratifications research.

STUART CHASE, *Power of Words*. New York: Harcourt Brace Jovanovich, 1954.

JOHN C. CONDON, Jr., *Semantics and Communication*. London: Collier-Macmillan, 1966.

EDWARD T. HALL, *The Silent Language*. Garden City, N.Y.: Doubleday, 1959.

S.I. HAYAKAWA, *Language in Thought and Action*, rev. ed. New York: Harcourt Brace Jovanovich, 1949.

MARSHALL McLUHAN, *Understanding Media: The Extensions of Man*. New York: McGraw-Hill, 1964. Paperback.

CHARLOTTE S. READ, "General Semantics," *ETC.*, Vol. 32 (September 1975), 243–53. An introduction to the subject.

EVERETT M. ROGERS, ed., *Communication and Development*. Beverly Hills, Calif.: Sage Publications, 1976. Originally published in *Communication Research*, April 1976.

CHARLES R. WRIGHT, *Mass Communication—A Sociological Perspective*. New York: Random House, 1975.

FOOTNOTES

1. Richard F. Carter, "Communication and Affective Relations," *Journalism Quarterly,* Vol. 42 (Summer 1965), 203.
2. For another example of the failure of much communication to bring mutual understanding, see John Hohenberg, *Between Two Worlds* (New York: Praeger, 1967); a study of the two-way news flow between the United States and Southeast Asia in the 1960s.
3. John McNelly, "Mass Communication in the Development Process," in Heinz-Dietrich Fischer and John C. Merrill, eds., *International Communication: Media, Channels, Functions* (New York: Hastings House, 1970).
4. For elaboration, see Edward Robinson, *Communication and Public Relations* (Columbus, O.: Charles E. Merrill, 1966). Robinson holds, as do we, that "the public relations practitioner is an applied social and behavioral scientist."
5. James E. Grunig, "Three Stopping Experiments on the Communication of Science," *Journalism Quarterly,* Vol. 51 (Autumn 1974), 399.
6. For full discussion of this significant theory, see Elihu Katz and Paul Lazarsfeld, *Personal Influence: The Part Played by People in the Flow of Mass Communications* (New York: Free Press, 1955), pp. 15–42. For later evaluation of this theory, see Elihu Katz, "The Two-Step Flow of Communication: An Up-to-Date Report on an Hypothesis," *Public Opinion Quarterly,* Vol. 21 (Spring 1957).
7. See A.W. Van Den Ban, "A Revision of the Two-Step Flow of Communications Hypothesis," *The Gazette,* Vol. 10 (1964), 237–49.
8. Paul Lazarsfeld and Herbert Menzel, "Mass Media and Personal Influence," in *Science of Human Communication,* Wilbur Schramm, ed. (New York: Basic Books, 1963), p. 95.
9. Paul Lazarsfeld, Bernard Berelson, and Hazel Gaudet, *The People's Choice* (New York: Columbia University Press, 1948).
10. Florangel Z. Rosario, "The Leader in Family Planning and the Two-Step Flow Model," *Journalism Quarterly,* Vol. 48 (Summer 1971), 303.
11. Johan Arndt, "A Test of the Two-Step Flow in Diffusion of a New Product," *Journalism Quarterly,* Vol. 45 (Autumn 1968), 457–65.
12. Paul Deutschmann and Wayne Danielson, "Dif-

fusion of Knowledge of the Major News Story," *Journalism Quarterly,* Vol. 37 (Summer 1960).

13. Jay Blumler and Jack M. McLeod, "Communication and Voter Turnout in Britain," paper presented to Association for Education in Journalism, Ft. Collins, Colo., August 1973.

14. Wilbur Schramm, *Men, Messages, and Media* (New York: Harper & Row, 1973), p. 124.

15. This theory of the diffusion process has emerged as the result of research by many people over a number of years. It is summarized in Herbert F. Lionberger, *Adoption of New Ideas and Practices* (Ames: Iowa State University Press, 1960); and in E.A. Wilkening, "The Communication of Ideas on Innovation in Agriculture," in *Studies of Innovation and of Communication to the Public* (Stanford, Calif.: Institute for Communication Research, 1962).

16. Steven H. Chaffee, "The Interpersonal Context of Communication," in *Current Perspectives in Mass Communication Research,* eds. F. Gerald Kline and Phillip J. Tichenor (Beverly Hills, Calif.: Sage Publications, 1972), p. 103.

17. For the Leopold story, see Susan Flader, *Thinking Like a Mountain* (Columbia: University of Missouri Press, 1974).

18. Herbert H. Hyman and Paul B. Sheatsley, "Some Reasons Why Information Campaigns Fail," *Public Opinion Quarterly,* Vol. 11 (Fall 1947). Also in Daniel Katz et al., *Public Opinion and Propaganda* (New York: Holt, Rinehart & Winston, 1954).

19. Harold Mendelsohn, "Why Information Campaigns Can Succeed," *Public Opinion Quarterly,* Vol. 37 (Spring 1973).

20. Dorothy Douglas et al., "An Information Campaign That Changed Community Attitudes," *Journalism Quarterly,* Vol. 47 (Autumn 1970), 479–87.

21. Eugene F. Lane, "Applied Behaviorial Science," *Public Relations Journal,* Vol. 23 (July 1967), 6.

22. For political examples, see Dan D. Nimmo, *Popular Images of Politics* (Englewood Cliffs, N.J.: Prentice-Hall, 1974).

23. Musts for the practitioner's working library are Edwin Newman's books on the deterioration of our American English language, *Strictly Speaking* (1974) and *A Civil Tongue* (1976), both published by Bobbs-Merrill.

24. Symbols, design, and printing all play a part in projecting an institution's image. For elaboration, see Russell R. Jalbert, "How to Create a Graphic Identity—and Save Money," *Public Relations Journal,* Vol. 18 (April 1962); Thomas C. Hassey, "How Sherwin-Williams Changed Its Image," *Public Relations Journal,* Vol. 31 (July 1975); and T.S. O'Connor and B. Render, "The Image and the Logo," *Public Relations Journal,* Vol. 32 (June 1976).

10

Systematic inquiry moderates the grip of yesterday's practices upon today's assumptions about tomorrow.

LASSWELL

The Process: evaluation– the fourth step

The final step in the process is to seek, through research, answers to the questions, *How did we do? Would we have been better off if we had tried something else? What did we learn?* Evaluation leads logically back into fact-finding and feedback—the first step. In a continuing program, the two aspects of research are hard to separate. They are treated separately here to emphasize the importance of evaluation and to facilitate classroom discussion. This may be a bit confusing, because pretesting logically comes *before* the communication–action step. It is discussed here because the tools for pretesting and posttesting are the same.

To hold costs in line, managers periodically reexamine the worth of each function. The day of "seat-of-the-pants" evaluation of a bagful of publicity clips is passing. Increasingly, practitioners are being asked to *document* that programs produce measurable results and that the return is commensurate with the cost. Public relations, like all other staff–line functions, is being measured by the degree to which it contributes to advancement of the organization's mission. Administrators, particularly controllers, have a nasty way of asking, "What did we get for all the money your department spent last year?"

Extensive feedback is essential to an effective communications program. The obstacles are, obviously, limitations of time, money, tools, and knowledge in the ways of research. One of the weaknesses of contemporary practice has been the lack of evaluation to measure overall success or failure of a program. As practitioners invest more time and money in evaluation, they will improve their precision and, therefore, their standing with management. Methodical research is the means of liberating practitioners and their bosses from what Harvey Jacobson terms "the perceptual traps of tradition." Harold Mendelsohn claims that past evaluation research suggests that practitioners are guided mostly by subjectively derived principles of communications, and that information campaigns so based are frequently ineffective. With rare exceptions, mass communications researchers have been documenting and redocumenting the obvious fact that when communicators fail to take into account fundamental principles derived from research, their efforts will be relatively unsuccessful.[1] *Evaluation is the common sense of learning from experience.*

This fourth step must be viewed as more than surveys or postaudits. *Evaluation is an ongoing process that enables executives to make the corrective adjustments required to guide an organization safely through the tides and winds of turbulent seas of opinion.* Evaluation must be accepted as a management tool to be used *on a consistent, continuing basis* upon which an operational base of information can be built. Evaluation studies serve administrators, those who participate in particular programs, governing boards, advisory committees, and the public. Program evaluation has emerged as a research specialty in recent years. The process, according to Suchman, includes goal setting (*objectives*), goal measuring (*criteria*), and identifying goal activity (*program operation*).[2] Only through such a rigorous, systematic process can programs be improved and resources allocated more effectively. The process is shown in Figure 10–1.

Evaluation techniques must be used to find out things, not "prove" things. Too often, evaluation is designed to "prove" or "do things," not to learn and thus advance the effectiveness of the program. For example, one organization set up a communications audit for the sole purpose of getting rid of its senior communications officer. What Stewart A. Smith terms "pseudo-research" is often used for these wrong reasons: (1) *organizational politics*—research used solely to gain power, justify decisions, or serve as a scapegoat; (2) *service promotion*—pseudo-research undertaken to impress on clients or prospects that the sponsor is sophisticated, modern, or sincere; (3) *personal satisfaction*—ego-bolstering attempts to keep up with fads, assuage anxiety, or make use of acquired skills.[3] Such spurious efforts are self-defeating.

The evaluation process generally embodies the same basic steps regardless of the size of the institution. Jacobson suggests that systematic evaluation should involve these steps:

1. *Select the rationale.* What is the guiding philosophy or model? Is the evaluation to be conducted by internal or external evaluators? Who is the major client?
2. *Specify objectives.* Define and state objectives of evaluation, objectives of overall institutional mission, objectives of specific elements of public relations program.
3. *Develop measures.* For example, measures of resources, finances, beneficiary groups, target groups, activities and outcomes.
4. *Administer the measures and collect the data.* Data can be collected in many ways—by observation, questionnaire, monthly reports, interview and other techniques.
5. *Analyze the data.* Allot sufficient time to assure summarization, synthesis and interpretation.
6. *Report the results.* Findings should be translated into recommendations and shared with others.
7. *Apply the results to decisions.* Recommendations must be expressed in operational statements to assure follow-through.[4]

Measurement by objectives

As computer technology advances, managers will become insistent upon definitive answers to their questions. Lack of meaningful evaluation of programs causes executives to look at public relations claims with doubt. A study of the rise and fall of a program in an organization found, "One major reason for the ambient attitude toward public relations by Blank's management is the absence of any yardstick for performance criteria." This finding echoed results of a Grey Public Relations survey of 500 organizations: "The need for better PR evaluation was

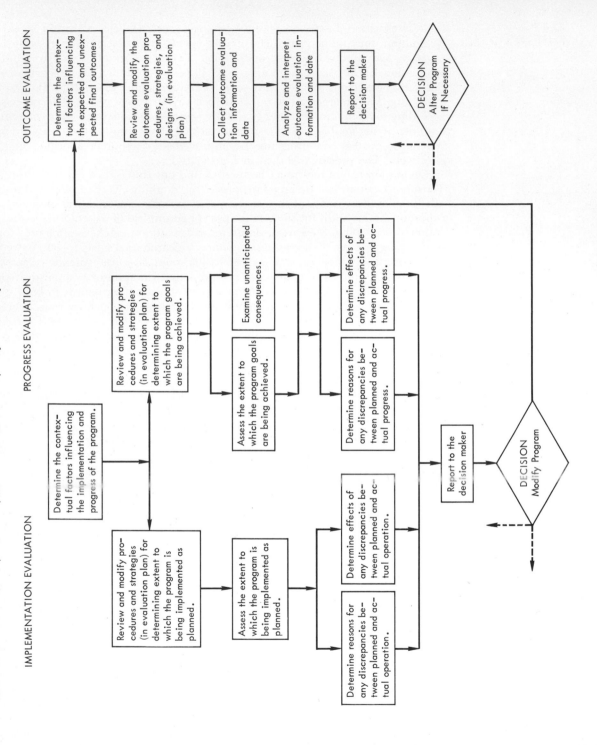

FIGURE 10-1 The evaluation process. Adapted from the model developed by UCLA Study of Evaluation.

voiced by nearly two-thirds of the respondents. First and foremost, the marketing executives surveyed said research was the key to improvement." As Professor Otto Lerbinger says, "Evaluation of results is becoming more crucial because of development in the management field of *the concept of management by objectives.*" The computer is being used by management to effect comparisons of results with objectives. Unless public relations can be subjected to such analysis, the function will suffer. Today's administrator is making increased use of such management tools as linear programming, PERT, critical path method, and simulation techniques.

Cunningham suggests the following list of questions in evaluating the results of specific programs:

1. Was the program adequately planned?
2. Did those concerned understand the job you wanted done?
3. Did all affected departments and executives cooperate?
4. How could you have made the results more effective?
5. Did you reach all pertinent audiences?
6. Did you receive desired publicity before, during, and after the completion of the program?
7. Could you have made better provisions for unforeseen circumstances?
8. Did the program stay within the budget? If not, why?
9. What provisions did you make in advance for measuring results? Were they adequate?
10. What steps were taken to improve future programs of the same type on the basis of this measurement?[5]

Before and after

Evaluation takes one of two forms: *pretesting* or *posttesting. Pretesting* is used to try out communications developed for a particular audience on a pilot group before making the full investment in a booklet, motion picture, or whatever. *Posttesting* is measuring the effectiveness of the communication–action program once it is completed. Not all the evaluation instruments are precise in measurements, but those available can provide helpful guides before and after. *Practitioners, limited by access, time, and budget, must make every item in the program count.* Testing before and after will serve this end.

Pretesting before launching an expensive, crucial informational campaign will prove economical in the long run. For example, OSHA (the Occupational Safety Health Administration) would have been spared much embarrassment had it pretested its 16-page booklet, "Safety with Beef Cattle." A pretest would have eliminated such nonsense as, "Be careful not to step into the manure pits"; "If your ladder is broken, do not climb it . . ."; "Beams that are too low can hurt you."

Posttesting will uncover mistakes that need not be repeated and point the way to improved techniques. It is delusive to rely on clippings returned on a press release or the postcards received in response to a TV promo, and other equally rough indicators of impact. For example, the USDA Office of information sends mail surveys to users of agricultural publications to discover ease of understanding, educational level of the user, and source of user's learning of the publication.

Despite the improvements in methods of evaluating content and impact, professionals have been slow to adapt them to their needs. This is nakedly revealed when the top public relations official of Mobil, a strong user of public relations advertising, asked whether Mobil's campaign was paying off, admitted, "I have no idea. Probably there's a wider recognition of Mobil." Such is the "evaluation" of a campaign on which millions of dollars have been spent.

One survey of large users of public relations advertising revealed that only a few sponsors had made a serious effort to gauge the impact of the expenditure of tens of thousands of dollars. Moore's Columbus, Ohio, study found that only 42 percent of the practitioners studied made systematic efforts to determine the effectiveness of their work.[6] This weakness is worldwide. The Swedish government distributed a brochure, "Your Right to Security," to all Swedish households to make its citizens aware of their social benefits. This program cost 1 million kroner, but not one was spent on evaluating its effectiveness. Yet a similar booklet was prepared and distributed three years later, at a cost of 1.4 million kroner, without the guidance that could have been gained from evaluating the first one. All too typical is this "evaluation" found in the AHA *Public Relations Newsletter:* "Judging by the avalanche of material and clippings received at AHA headquarters, the National Hospital Week was one of the most successful in terms of increased recognition of the importance of the role of hospitals in our society." Equally typical is the situation found in a public relations audit of Milwaukee's city government. A researcher found that most departments had imprecise methods of measuring reaction to their programs: Clippings, informal comments, degree of cooperation, number of complaints, and the like were the "yardsticks" used.

Many practitioners take refuge in such cliches as, "Public relations is an art," "We are dealing in intangibles," or, "Our problems are indistinct." In more stilted language, one says, "When you're talking about the broad marketing of a product, either consumer or industrial, you get involved in a number of factors which make it difficult to separate out the specific inputs and results of public relations activities, because you're involved in the whole pattern of marketing—the advertising, the salesmanship, the point-of-sale, the deals that are made, the pricing, the economics, the previous relationships of the company, and many other things."

The need for a merciless personal audit of the finished project has long been recognized. Pioneer Evart G. Routzahn told the 1920 National Conference of Social Work, "After the returns are all in—when the last meeting has been held, the final distribution of printed matter made, and all activities of the immediate effort have been recorded as history—is the time to put yourself and your methods through the third degree . . . with prayerful solicitude that you will be able to untangle the lessons to be applied to the next project." His counsel has yet to be fully accepted, nearly 60 years later, even though its merit is obvious.

The public relations audit

Unread leaflets, unheard broadcasts, unviewed films—however skillfully produced—cannot influence an audience that is not there. Nor does volume of output guarantee that an audience is reached. *Evaluation research will forcefully remind the communicator that dissemination does not equal communication.* Research may be conducted by practitioners themselves or obtained through commercial research services: Opinion Research Corporation, Roper Research Associates, Psychological Corporation, Yankelovich, Skelly and White, Inc., Daniel Starch and Staff, Gallup's Public Relations Index, Louis Harris, and others. Outside counselors can help through critical public relations audits. In addition to research firms and counseling firms, university research centers and independent consultants provide public relations audits. These outside experts have specialized knowledge, objectivity, experience in other organizations, and the prestige to gain management's ear. Such an audit permits an organization to have its program evaluated *objectively,* without any pressure to enter an ongoing relationship with the evaluator.

Joyce F. Jones suggests that the audit begins inside the organization and involves four steps:

1. *Finding out what "we" think:* This means talking to key persons in top and middle management to:
   a. Assess the organization's strengths and weaknesses
   b. Identify its key publics
   c. Determine what areas the external phase of the audit should cover—audiences, topics, etc.
2. *Finding out what "they" think:* Talking to important publics to find out how closely their view of the organization matches its executives' perceptions in key areas.
3. *Evaluating the disparity between the two points of view*—if any exists—to arrive at a public relations balance sheet.
4. *Recommendations* aimed at closing the gap.[7]

Counselor Gerald Wollan says, "Unlike the financial audit with its prescribed form and procedure, the communications audit has no specific structure. . . . There are as many ways to distill and present information as there are people. We know of no 'best' way." *The important thing is that programs be audited periodically.*

Understandably, practitioners are reluctant to recommend an external audit of their work. An audit can find a department or an outside agency failing to measure up. For example, the two top public relations officials of Princeton University were dismissed after an examination of Princeton's public relations that had been demanded by "the Concerned Alumni of Princeton."[8] More often, audits are sought by managers who are concerned about the effectiveness of their staffs or of outside counsel.

Pretesting

A careful precheck of material to be used in a project will pay off in detecting possible backlash effects. It will also help in sharpening the understandability of the information for its intended audience. Sometimes an appeal or technique can boomerang with unanticipated, unfavorable results. David Ogilvy, a successful communicator, asserts, "The most important word in the advertising vocabulary is TEST. If you pretest your product with consumers and pretest your advertising, you will do well in the marketplace. Twenty-four out of twenty-five new products never get out of test markets. Manufacturers who don't test-market their new products incur the colossal cost (and disgrace) of having their products fail on a national scale. . . . Test your premise. Test your media. Test your headlines and your illustrations. . . . Never stop testing, and your advertising will never stop improving."[9] The same holds true for all communications work.

Backlash effects can be avoided by conducting a response analysis. This means using a sample audience to observe immediate reaction to specific communication content. As an example, a large insurance company published a series of articles in its employee publication on representative employees—a salesman, a stenographer, an accountant, and so forth. The article on "The Management Man" boomeranged badly. It brought a heavy barrage of criticism, with these typical comments: "If this is the kind of a man _____ wants, I don't want _____ "; I didn't know you had to be an egomaniac to be a manager"; "Mrs. _____ is a snob"; and so forth. A cautious tryout can head off unhappy consequences.

Also, there is a need to pretest the understandability of messages. The symbolism chosen for a public relations document may represent perfect clarity to its creator but be both uninteresting and unintelligible to the reader. Or the symbol may be inappropriate, as when the U.S. Information Service put on an exhibit in India. The first panel featured a painting of Christ delivering the Sermon on the Mount, and the caption expressed the exhibit's theme, "Man Shall Not Live by Bread Alone." India's hungry Hindus and Muslims did not respond favorably. A few years ago, an experimental program of health education was undertaken in an isolated Peruvian community high in the Andes. As part of the program, a film on the transmission of typhus by lice, featuring graphic closeup shots, was prepared and shown to the villagers. It became apparent that the message wasn't getting through. A survey of the people who had seen the film revealed that although they had many lice in their homes, they had never been bothered by the "giant" kind shown on the screen. *To get results, appeals and symbols must be appropriate and understood.*

The value of pretesting, which is relatively inexpensive, before making a heavy investment in a communications project is shown in this example: The Equitable Life Assurance Society, like most life insurance companies, finds it profitable to promote health education. The company decided to issue a new booklet on communicable diseases for national distribution. The idea for such a pamphlet was stimulated by a U.S. Public Health Service report that more than 50 percent of preschool children were inadequately immunized against the common communicable diseases. Equitable probed more deeply. It found that the problem of inadequate protection against these diseases lay chiefly among the "lower socioeconomic" groups in the population, groups difficult to communicate with. It needed a brief, lively illustrated booklet that would reach this audience.

All available data on these diseases were brought together. A professional free-lance writer was hired. The writer first submitted draft manuscripts to health authorities and to Equitable's medical department to ensure technical accuracy. After these reviews, a pretest manuscript was prepared. The principal objective of the pretest was to determine whether the manuscript was "right" for its intended audience. One hundred and forty-two typed manuscripts were distributed to a sample of the intended audience in a "geographic scatter"—Westchester County, New York; Stamford, Connecticut; Atlanta, Georgia; Seattle and Tacoma, Washington; and Los Angeles. To save time and expense, these manuscripts carried no artwork or sketches. The results of this pretest were used to shorten the manuscript from 5,000 to 3,000 words and to make it more readable and persuasive, resulting in a highly successful pamphlet.

A cautionary note on the value of pretesting must be inserted here. The stream of public opinion rushes along swiftly. *An idea that worked well on a pretest might possibly prove a fiasco upon widespread use because of the intervening time lag.* Seasons change, and with them change people's buying patterns, recreational pursuits, interests, and so forth. The context of the public opinion marketplace can change markedly overnight with an unexpected news event. In using pretest results as a guide to a communications program, the practitioner ought to be as certain as possible that present conditions are akin to those that existed during the pretest.

Posttesting

Posttesting is valuable not only in determining aftereffects of a specific program but in advancing professional knowledge. Through such research, the roughhewn principles now relied upon can be proved true or false.

There are a number of maxims that are taken for granted in daily practice, but whose validity research tends to cast some doubt upon. One is, "What people know about a subject depends roughly upon the amount said or published about it." An experiment designed primarily to find ways and means of extending support for the United Nations was carried out in Cincinnati, Ohio. A survey was taken to determine attitudes and level of information about the UN; then an all-out saturation information campaign was carried out over a six-month period. A postcampaign survey indicated no fundamental changes in the degree of support for the UN in Cincinnati, although the information level had been raised somewhat.[10] Such findings clearly indicate that increasing the flow of information does not necessarily spread information effectively. Another maxim is, "If people know you better, they will like you more." Yet studies of attitudes toward big business and of foreign attitudes toward the United States have indicated the opposite. Still another is, "The more employees know about their company, the better they will like it." Research has thrown doubt on this premise.[11] There hasn't been enough research to make flat generalizations about these maxims one way or the other. *There is equal need to measure results of specific appeals, media, and methods.*

A standard element in most programs is speeches—the making of them and the mailing of them to "thought leaders." Through research in a comparatively rigorous test situation, U.S. Steel found that its wide distribution of speech reprints did "have a definite impact upon their intended audience—that they were remembered, regarded favorably, and comparatively speaking, were better than the usual run of speeches sent these individuals."[12] Data from this study were used in determining content and audiences for future speeches and mailings.

Another standard component of public relations is the staged event—one that calls for a comprehensive, detailed plan. Such events should be reviewed through a "merciless audit" when completed. A typical example: In May 1975, the U.S. Navy ships USS *Leahy* and USS *Tattnall* made an official visit to the Soviet Union port of Leningrad. This precedent-breaking event called for a no-hitches public-affairs plan. Afterwards, the Navy public-affairs officers prepared a "Lessons

Learned" report for their superiors. These officers concluded that "the Public Affairs Plan was comprehensive and sufficiently flexible to provide adequate guidance and authority to the on-scene commander." The report recommended that "a similar Public Affairs Plan should be adopted for any future visits."

A warning flag must be raised on the research mast. Research results must be used with discretion, tempered by value judgments. Discussing the value of readership research, Theodore Weber, Jr., vice-president for corporate communications for McGraw-Hill, cautions, "While it can be interesting and useful to find out what employees want to see in a house organ and what pleases them most, the real job is not to give employees what they want always, but to get employees to like and read some of the useful and important information the company wants to communicate to them. The company paper cannot shape its sentiments to the pleasures of the public." Research must be *ruled*.

Measuring impact

A specific program's effectiveness can be evaluated by measuring in terms of four dimensions. They are *audience coverage, audience response, communications impact,* and *process of influence.* Wright points up the importance of each of these measurements this way:

1. *Audience Coverage:* To produce results you must first reach the audience. How large an audience is reached? What are they like? What proportion of the desired audience do they represent?
2. *Audience Response:* How do members of the audience respond? Does the content of the message strike them favorably or unfavorably? Does it arouse their interest? Does it bore them? Do they understand it?
3. *Communications Impact:* After an appraisal of these immediate reactions, you must consider the impact which a message has on its audience. What are the lasting, discernible effects upon people exposed to a message?
4. *Process of Influence:* What is the process by which a communication operates to influence its target audience? Through what channels of influence and mechanisms of persuasion does the message finally affect the individual? How effective is the program in setting into motion the social processes necessary to influence the opinions and behavior of its target audience?[13]

Evaluation tools

For too long, measurement of the impact of public relations output has relied on a count of news clippings, air mentions, and film showings. These tell little beyond the degree of media acceptance of publicity output. In recent years, efforts to analyze publicity results have advanced beyond mere counting. A commercial firm, PR Data, Inc., took the first small step. An organization determines the objectives of its program, and these are then fed into the computer to provide a yardstick against which results can be measured. This comparison serves to keep a program on the track. Then each release is coded for punched-card use, indicating the story number, the messages loaded in, the date, and the publication. The computer readout report, based on newsclips and monitor reports, covers several points: number of messages per story printed, total inches of news space obtained, and the cumulative circulation. Management then gets a report such as this one: "During the past three months, we had exposure in 2,779 news stories carrying a total of 8,032 corporate messages—or an average of three each. Eighty-two percent of the circulation was in our primary market area. The return on our investment, expressed as cost per thousand readers, was 15.5 cents."

This small advance in using computers still does not measure the story's *impact* on the reader or viewer. Budd and Strayton put it in perspective: "For all its space-age showmanship, the system at this juncture merely substitutes electronic muscle for human labor to analyze clippings, to add volume, tally circulation, 'readout' geographic coverage and aid in working out an array of percentages that gives an impression of scientific communications planning. . . [It] could not be regarded as a major step toward a definitive *measurement of results.*"[14]

In business, the impact of product publicity can be gauged more accurately than it usually is. Counselor Carl Ruff demonstrated this in analyzing inquiries about a furniture company's new office system. He compared inquiries stimulated by advertising and those stimulated by publicity. He found that publicity outpulled advertising by a ratio of seven to one, and that a qualitative analysis of public relations effectiveness by inquiry count revealed that for a moderate fee, the client had obtained $1.4 million worth of query-pulling, product-selling, and attitude-reinforcing exposure over a period of 15 months. Ruff's effort to develop a method of analyzing results not only provided management with definitive data but further demonstrated the value of evaluation: "The breakdown on inquiries by publications proved that some of these magazines which the client—and we—had considered to be prime targets were actually of little importance in producing queries. And magazines which one management group had not considered important turned out to be among those productive." *Organizations can profit from such a systematic analysis.*

In addition to these approaches and to the fact-finding, formal and informal, described in Chapter 7, the practitioner has several evaluation tools. Each one is based on the principle of making a survey of a *representative sample* of the target audience in a systematic way.

Reader-interest studies: What people read in newspapers, magazines, employee publications, and so forth, can be measured through reader-interest surveys. *This tool is more a quantitative than a qualitative measuring device.* A reader-interest survey is made by taking fresh, unmarked copies of a publication to a representative sample of the total potential reading audience. After the interviewer makes the necessary introduction and qualifying statements, he goes through the publication with the respondent, page by page. The respondent shows the interviewer items he has seen or read. These are recorded on an interview form by code number. At no time does the interviewer point out items to the respondent. The key question is, "Did you *happen* to see or read anything on this page?" Checks on this method have proved that readers are honest in saying what they have read.

Published reader-interest studies offer valuable insights into what potential readers actually consume. In using the results of such studies, it is well to keep in mind this advice of a veteran magazine editor: "A magazine cannot be edited by arithmetic alone." Reader-interest results are guides, not mandates, for the responsible communicator. The research ought to be followed up, after a given interval, to determine the comprehension and retention of the material by readers. Both methods will provide healthy reminders that *readership doesn't equal circulation and readership doesn't equal comprehension and retention.*

Surveys can also gauge readership and impact of a particular publication. For example, Minneapolis's Model City program surveyed readers of *The Paper,* created to inform residents of what the urban rehabilitation program offered them. Two hundred thirty-five households were selected in a random sample and, of this number, 140 questionnaires were completed in a telephone survey. The survey found that 66 percent of the respondents read *The Paper,* women made up two-thirds of the readership, and two-thirds of those finding issue-type news important were also women.[15] Such information enables an editor to zero in on the target audience with greater precision. The questionnaire can also be used to determine readership and reader wants. For example, a West Coast manufacturer surveyed a sample of its more than 3,000 employees to gauge their evaluation of the company newspaper and the way it handled company topics. This study found that employees favor in-depth coverage of "bad" news but don't expect to find it in the employee paper.[16]

Audience-survey research must be viewed critically, bought carefully. Comparable methods sometimes produce different results. The need for care in evaluating such audience research was underscored when Time, Inc., brought a breach-of-contract suit against W.R. Simmons & Associates Research, one of several firms providing magazine audience research. *Time* filed its suit in New York State Supreme Court in January 1975, after a Simmons report showed *Newsweek's* audience the same as *Time's* even though *Time* had the larger circulation. Simmons, Target Group Index, and Starch's Message Report Service specialize in print audience and advertising research. Caution is required in using this kind of research, because its findings are consistent only in the broadest terms.

Readability tests: Yardsticks for the reading ease of printed materials have now been developed. It is possible to grade a given message as to how easy it is to read at any given educational level, be it seventh grade or college senior. A knowledge of this yardstick enables the communicator to write his message in such a way that it fits the reading ability of his intended audience. This should not be interpreted as "writing down" to people, nor should a person's reading ability be equated with his intelligence. It is simply that making copy more readable usually increases readership. It also improves comprehension.

These yardsticks should be used as guides rather than as commands to write inside a fixed formula. It should be clearly understood that readability is only one aspect of getting readership. Equally important are *content, format, organization,* and *writing style.* These factors, coupled with the fundamental understanding that the writer brings to his writing and the reader brings to his reading, all shape the reception and impact of the printed word. If used in this perspective, readability tests are helpful.

There are four commonly used methods for measuring readability:

1. *The Flesch Formula.* Dr. Rudolf Flesch's method is divided into two parts: Reading Ease Score is determined by the difficulty of words used, as measured by the number of syllables in words and by sentence length. Human Interest Score is measured by

the number of personal words per 100 words and the number of personal sentences per 100 sentences.[17]

2. *The Gunning Formula.* Robert Gunning's formula measures reading ease by the average sentence length, number of simple sentences used, verb force, proportion of familiar words, proportion of abstract words, percentage of personal references, and percentage of long words.[18] This is, perhaps, the least accurate of these formulas.

3. *Dale-Chall Formula.* This one, developed at Ohio State, measures reading ease by analysis of average sentence length and the proportion of words outside the Dale List of 3,000 Words Most Commonly Used.[19]

4. *Cloze Procedure.* This test was developed by Prof. Wilson Taylor of the University of Illinois and is somewhat different from the first three. It measures help provided the reader by the context of the total message. It can be applied to auditory as well as visual communication. This method tests readability by giving samples of the material to subjects with every *n*th word omitted. Success of subjects in filling in missing words on the basis of other parts of the message measures the item's readability. The Cloze Procedure is aimed at measuring readers' comprehension of material as well as its readability.[20]

Now researchers have available Cloze-based readability formulas that can help them predict the *comprehension difficulty* of American English prose. These are the Bormuth (Passage Level) Machine Computation and the Coleman No. 4 readability formulas. The Bormuth and Coleman formulas differ from the traditional formulas such as Flesch and Dale-Chall in that they were derived from tests that required readers to respond to Cloze *deletions in* a passage instead of to multiple-choice *questions about* that passage.[21]

A relatively new formula is that developed by Professor Edward B. Fry of Rutgers University. Like the Gunning formula, it is easy to use. In addition, it is very accurate, correlating with the complicated Dale-Chall and Flesch formulas at the 98 percent and 96 percent levels respectively. The Fry formula is illustrated in Figure 10–2.

In a review of these formulas, Prof. Blaine McKee found that of those listed, the three major methods usually give results that are close, and that Dale-Chall should be the most accurate but is the slowest of the three. He thinks these formulas are particularly helpful for people who need to improve their writing, but that practitioners should not continue to use them indefinitely.[22] Readability tests, when used in conjunction with reader-interest studies, offer practitioners useful guides.

Radio and TV audience research: There are seven basic methods for obtaining measurements of a program audience's size in the broadcast media, and three that combine methods:

1. *The Diary.* This requires that some member (or members) of the household keep a written record or log of program exposure.

2. *The Recorder.* This method electronically or mechanically records automatically individual set tuning, including frequency or channel.

3. *The Personal Coincidental.* Personal interviews are made throughout the duration of a given program or time period. Respondents are queried regarding program exposure at moment of call.

4. *The Personal Roster Recall.* Respondents are shown a list of programs and stations.

FIGURE 10-2 The Fry formula.

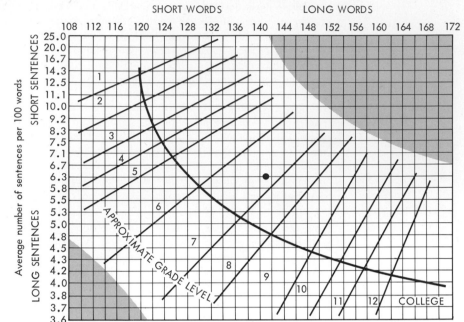

Average number of syllables per 100 words

DIRECTIONS: Randomly select 3 one hundred word passages from a book or an article. Plot average number of syllables and average number of sentences per 100 words on graph to determine the grade level of the material. Choose more passages per book if great variability is observed and conclude that the book has uneven readability. Few books will fall in gray area but when they do grade level scores are invalid.

EXAMPLE:

	SYLLABLES	SENTENCES
1st Hundred Words	124	6.6
2nd Hundred Words	141	5.5
3rd Hundred Words	158	6.8
AVERAGE	141	6.3

READABILITY 7th GRADE (see dot plotted on graph)

They are asked to indicate which they were exposed to during the measured time span.

5. *Personal Unaided Recall.* Personal interviews are made during which respondents are asked about program exposure for a preceding time span. Unlike the roster, the personal unaided recall uses no list of programs or stations. It depends entirely upon the respondent's unaided memory for exposure information.

6. *The Telephone Coincidental.* This method employs the same principles as the personal coincidental method except that interviews are made by telephone.

7. *The Telephone Recall.* This method employs the same principles as the personal unaided recall except that the interviews are made by telephone.

8. *Combination Telephone Coincidental and Diary.* This method combines broadcast exposure

information obtained by the coincidental telephone method in one sample of homes with information obtained by the diary method in another sample of homes.

9. *The Combination Telephone Coincidental and Telephone Recall.*
10. *The Combination Telephone Coincidental and Personal Roster Recall.*[23]

Among the leading commercial research organizations that use one or more of these methods in measuring audience size for clients are the A.C. Nielsen Company, American Research Bureau, Pulse, Inc., Trendex, Sindlinger & Co., and Arbitron. The Nielsen Company dominates radio-TV audience measurement, and its ratings shape far more than they should the content of broadcast programming.

Public confidence in the validity and honesty of commercial audience research in radio and television gets a jolt every now and then. For example, in the 1960s, the Federal Trade Commission obtained consent decrees from Pulse, Nielsen, TvQ, and the American Research Bureau that these firms would cease claiming that their findings are 100 percent accurate. In the same period, a congressional committee found evidence that radio and TV ratings were often based on faulty or dishonest research.[24] The same thing cropped up in the late 1970s, when Arbitron Radio discovered that a Memphis post office employee had taken diaries from the April/May market report and used them to artificially inflate the ratings of a Memphis radio station. Arbitron said this was the first situation of this type to occur in some 10,000 surveys.[25] Nonetheless, the problem of faulty samples and result-rigging is always present in surveys.

Another complaint often voiced against these rating services is that they do not properly measure the viewing of lower socioeconomic groups and ethnic minorities and thus fail to meet the commercial criteria that would encourage stations to present more programming of special interest to these groups. An example: Greenwood, Mississippi, is 58 percent white and 42 percent black, yet the American Research Bureau rating sample in Greenwood is 83 percent white, 17 percent black. The same lack of representativeness crops up in telephone surveys. For example, 38 percent of the San Francisco–Oakland population do not have telephones and are thus excluded from the sample in such surveys.

With each of these rating techniques, you gain some things, give up some things. For example, the Nielsen recorder technique is high in accuracy but cannot truly indicate whether or not anyone *watched* the show the set was tuned to. On the other hand, the diary method, one widely used, indicates who watched the show but is highly susceptible to inaccurate entries, as respondents tend to forget to write them in on a regular basis.

A practical, immediate way of getting audience reaction is to build a call-in into the program. One of the toughest of public relations problems is that of building public understanding of mental health and support for programs dealing with mental illness. Two creative women, Pat Powell and Kathy Tinker, produced a series of TV health programs for Boise, Idaho. They built in feedback and evaluation by providing for a phone-in while the programs were in progress. The producers listed four benefits of this: (1) The audience can share in the information being given, thus reinforcing and clarifying information in the TV program; (2) more people are encouraged to call in questions as they have time to mull over what they have seen and heard; (3) the question period will stimulate interest in the entire series; and (4) people with criticisms or suggestions have a built-in method of making these known.

Powell and Tinker did not rely on the random call-ins alone to evaluate their programs. They organized 15 viewing groups of from three to ten people to watch and discuss the program together. The members of these groups were given before-and-after tests to determine how much their information had been increased by watching the series and discussing its content with one another. Also, tests were given at the end of the series and again six months later to measure retention of the information. By all tests, the series was successful.

Program analyzer tests: These are mechanical devices for recording people's reactions to a program while they are being exposed to it. Reactions are recorded in terms of Like, Dislike, or Indifference. The member of the audience indicates his preferences by pressing one of two buttons. These reactions are recorded on tape as the program progresses. Time lines on the tape serve to identify parts of the program to which the member is reacting; thus, audience response to specific items of program content can be determined.[26] This device can also be used to pretest public relations presentations.

Measurement of results

The real test of a communications program is its results. Did it pay off at the box office? the sales counter? the voting booth? Did the program bring about the desired reaction and action? Did your message result in the desired modification of a group's attitudes? Actual results offer a sure test. They deserve to be studied and analyzed. In addition to observation of results *apparently* obtained, there are other ways of getting at the impact:

1. *The focused interview.* This involves interviewing recipients of communications and getting them to relate their experiences to various parts of a program.
2. *Impact analysis.* This involves studies to determine short-term and long-term effects of a given program. It includes determining the effects on individuals and on groups and subgroups. There are differences in impact to be studied in terms of time span and in terms of individual and group reactions.
3. *Experimental studies.* The ideal way to measure the impact of a program is by comparing two groups that are exactly alike except for the fact that one group has been exposed to a program whereas the other has not. The critical feature is in matching the two groups. In such experiments, it is essential to control extraneous influences. Results are obtained by surveys and by panel studies.

Overall review of program

The research tools described above are helpful, but they measure only the bits and pieces, not the overall program. The total effort must be kept in view. An important step is to periodically review the total program and measure its results against the assigned objectives. Several "report cards" have been designed for this purpose. One practitioner offers these check points as a guide in periodically evaluating a going public relations program:

1. *Objectives*—Are they clearly stated and understood throughout the company? Are there areas in which agreement on goals is needed?

2. *Organization*—Are related public relations functions organized as a single unit, or scattered throughout various departments? Does the public relations director have adequate management backing to see that public relations responsibilities are considered throughout the company? . . . Is size and training of staff adequate to achieve desired public relations objectives?

3. *Content*—Do your programs and activities give adequate consideration to all segments of the public—customers, employees, stockholders, and the financial community, government groups, civic, educational, and community organizations, the press, and suppliers? . . .

4. *Measurement of Results*—Do you have adequate staff, budget and management backing to gauge results of your work? How do these activities compare with those of others in your industry and in other industries? Have you considered an outside specialist to review your public relations program?

5. *Control*—What steps have you taken to improve future public relations activities in the light of audit findings? What steps need to be taken during coming years?[27]

Case problem

1. Measure the readability of an employee magazine, handbook, annual report, or university brochure by measuring samples of content, using:
   a. Flesch, Gunning, Dale-Chall, or Fry method
   b. The "Cloze Procedure"
2. Compare results obtained by the respective methods used.
3. How does the reading level of the material square with the probable reading level of the intended audience?

ADDITIONAL READINGS

RICHARD W. BUDD, ROBERT K. THORP, AND LEWIS DONOHEW, *Content Analysis of Communications.* New York: Macmillan, 1967.

W. HOWARD CHASE, "New Standards for Measuring Public Relations—A Program for Reorganization," *Public Relations Journal,* Vol. 31 (February 1975).

KEITH DAVIS, "A Method of Studying Communication Patterns in Organizations," *Personnel Psychology,* Vol. 6 (Autumn 1953).

REX F. HARLOW, "Management, Public Relations and the Social Sciences," *Public Relations Review,* Vol. 1 (Summer 1975).

JACK B. HASKINS, *How to Evaluate Mass Communication: The Controlled Experiment Field.* New York: Advertising Research Foundation, 1968. An ARF monograph.

FRANK E. HEWENS, "How to Audit Your Public Relations," *Public Relations Quarterly,* Vol. 16, No. 3 (Spring 1974). Reprinted from Vol. 8 (Winter 1964), issue.

HERBERT H. HYMAN, CHARLES R. WRIGHT, and TERENCE K. HOPKINS, *Applications of Methods of Evaluation.* Berkeley: University of California Press, 1962.

DONALD W. JUGENHEIMER, "How to Evaluate Corporate Advertising," *Public Relations Journal,* Vol. 31 (November 1975).

HARRY W. O'NEILL, "Survey Research as a Public Relations Tool," *Public Relations Review,* Vol. 3 (Fall 1977), 17–35. Valuable guidance.

H.R. ROWLAND, "The Evaluation Dilemma: Measuring Effectiveness in College Relations," *CASE Currents,* Vol. 2 (January 1976).

RAYMOND SIMON, "Two Decades of Scholarly Research about Public Relations," *Public Relations Journal,* Vol. 27 (December 1971).

FOOTNOTES

1. Harold Mendelsohn, "Why Information Campaigns Can Succeed," *Public Opinion Quarterly,* Vol. 37 (Spring 1973), 51. This article is also helpful in the communications step.
2. Edward A. Suchman, *Evaluative Research* (New York: Russell Sage Foundation, 1967).
3. "Research and Pseudo-Research in Marketing," *Harvard Business Review,* Vol. 52 (March–April 1974), 73–76.
4. Harvey K. Jacobson, "The Role of Evaluation and Research in Management," in A. Westley Rowland, ed., *Handbook for Institutional Advancement: Programs for the Understanding and Support of Higher Education* (San Francisco: Jossey-Bass, 1977).
5. John T. Cunningham, "Measuring Public Relations Results," American Management Association Management Bulletin, *Measuring and Evaluating Public Relations Activities* (New York, 1968), 4–5.
6. William Carter Moore, "A Critical Analysis of Public Relations Practitioners in a Midwestern Metropolitan Area," unpublished master's thesis, Ohio State University, 28.
7. "Audit: A New Tool for Public Relations," *Public Relations Journal,* Vol. 31 (July 1975).
8. Richard K. Rein, "The Nassau Hall Approach to Public Relations," *Prospect* (publication of Concerned Alumni of Princeton), Vol. 3 (September 15, 1974).
9. David Ogilvy, *Confessions of an Advertising Man* (New York: Atheneum, 1964), 86.
10. A summary of this landmark experiment can be found in Shirley Star and Helen M. Hughes, "Report on an Educational Campaign," *American Journal of Sociology,* Vol. 55 (1950), 389–400.
11. Dallis Perry and Thomas A. Mahoney, "In-plant Communications and Employee Morale," *Personnel Psychology,* Vol. 8 (Autumn 1955).
12. See Case 2 in E.J. Robinson, *Public Relations and Survey Research* (New York: Appleton-Century-Crofts, 1969).
13. Charles R. Wright, "Evaluation of Mass Media Effectiveness," *UNESCO International Social Science Bulletin,* Vol. VII, No. 3.
14. John F. Budd, Jr., and Robert G. Strayton, "Can Public Relations Be Measured?" *Public Relations Quarterly,* Vol. 13 (Winter 1969), 24.
15. Cecilie Gaziano, "Readership Study of Paper Subsidized by Government," *Journalism Quarterly,* Vol. 51 (Summer 1974), 323–26.
16. Stuart H. Surlin and Barry Walker, "Employee Evaluations of Handling News by a Corporate Newspaper," *Journalism Quarterly,* Vol. 52 (Spring 1975), 99–105.
17. Rudolf Flesch, *How to Test Readability* (New York: Harper & Row, 1951).
18. Robert Gunning, *The Technique of Clear Writing,* rev. ed. (New York: McGraw-Hill, 1968).
19. Edgar Dale and Jeanne Chall, "A Formula for Predicting Readability," *Educational Research Bulletin,* Ohio State University, Vol. 27 (January and February 1948).
20. Wilson L. Taylor, "Cloze Procedure: A New Tool for Measuring Readability," *Journalism Quarterly,* Vol. 30 (Fall 1953), 415–33; and "Recent Developments in the Use of 'Cloze Procedure,'" *Journalism Quarterly,* Vol. 33 (Winter 1956), 42–48ff.
21. Lawrence R. Miller, "Predictive Powers of the Flesch and Bormuth Readability Formulas," *Journalism Quarterly,* Vol. 51 (Autumn 1974), 508–11.
22. For discussion of these formulas, see Carolyn Clark Reiley, "Can They Read What We Write?" *Seminar,* No. 33 (September 1974).
23. Advertising Research Foundation, *Recommended Standards for Radio and Television Program Audience Size Measurements,* p. 15. Copyright by the Advertising Research Foundation, Inc. Reprinted by special permission.
24. "Is Pulse Running a Con Game? Rep. Harris Asks That Question, Then Puts Nielsen on Hot Seat," *Broadcasting,* Vol. 64 (March 25, 1963), 34–50. For details on hearing, see "Hearings, Subcommittee of the Committee on Interstate and Foreign Commerce, House of Representatives," *Broadcast Ratings,* Part I and Part II (Washington, D.C.: The Committee, Government Printing Office, 1963).
25. "Memphis Ratings," *Broadcasting,* Vol. 91 (Nov. 8, 1976). Also, David M. Rubin, "Tuning in Trouble at Arbitron," *MORE,* December 1977, 32–35.
26. Tore Hollonquist and Edward A. Suchman, "Listening to the Listener," *Radio Research, 1942–43* (New York: Duell, Sloan and Pearce, 1944).
27. John T. Cunningham, "Evaluating Public Relations' Effectiveness," *Public Relations Journal,* Vol. 19 (January 1962), 21–23.

II

Mechanical means of communication have their important places; but they are only adjuncts. None can take the place of personal contact.

W.M.G. WERNER

The Tools of Communication

In his work, the practitioner utilizes the printed word, the spoken word, and the image. He uses three avenues—*personal contact, controlled media,* and *public media.* The importance of personal contacts has already been emphasized. The news media pose special problems, which will be discussed in Chapter 17.

In this chapter we shall examine briefly the media that can be controlled by the communicator at the point of origin; their impact depends on the communicator's skill. These tools will be discussed in terms of what they are. Later on, in appropriate chapters, they will be discussed as to how and where they are used in specific situations.

The printed word

House publications

In a news item, the *Wall Street Journal* expressed the opinion that house publications had become "workhorses, instead of just management megaphones of intangible value." On another occasion, the same publication described the house organ as "a familiar element of corporate propaganda." Both statements are partially right and applicable in many instances. Neither is totally right as a flat generalization.

The house publication is versatile. It can be narrowly edited to massage the ego of its sponsor. It can be broadly edited to shed light on human objectives or public issues only remotely associated with its sponsor. Or it can mix the two, in a format as simple as a memorandum or as lavish in appearance as a popular newsstand magazine. See Figure 11–1.

All house publications have a few characteristics in common: They satisfy the desire of an organization to go on record for its own purposes. They permit the organization to select its audience. They let the organization express itself on paper, in its own words, in its own way, without interruption.[1]

The size of the house-publication activity is awesome. The International Association of Business Communicators (IABC) surveyed its 3,000 U.S. and

Canadian members in 1975. From the 1,250 replies, the IABC projected a total circulation for business publications of 300 million. This compares with a circulation of 68 million for the daily newspapers in the two countries.[2] *Gebbie's House Magazine Directory* estimates that there are more than 50,000 house publications. Obviously, with a census of 75,000 people employed in public relations pursuits, the house publication is a main factor.

Responsibility for editing house publications is not always vested with public relations. The IABC survey showed that the percentage of internal business communicators reporting to public relations was on a downward trend. Of the respondents, only 44 percent were in public relations departments.

From its findings, the IABC constructed a composite "typical" business communicator. He's male (54 percent versus 46 percent female), 35 years old, has a bachelor's degree in journalism, and is titled "Editor." He earns $18,000 (she earns $12,710) and has been in communications work seven years. His major publication is an $8\frac{1}{2}''$ monthly magazine of 14 pages, printed offset and in one color. He devotes half his time to it. The balance is spent on photography, advertising, employee relations, marketing, and public relations. He reports to a vice-president, the director of public relations, or a general manager. His office is near the top official.

Apart from what is "typical," there are many variations. For example, there is little uniformity in format and approach. House publications take the format of daily newspapers, newsletters, and magazines. Some are published as paid-for pages in local newspapers. There are slick-paper and newsprint publications; letterpress, offset, and multilith productions. A few sell advertising space. A few, such as *Woman's Day* and *Arizona Highways,* have paid circulations. In Great Britain, some one-quarter of the industrial firms publishing house magazines sell them rather than give them away. "The pro-sell group in Britain maintains that, psychologically, employees tend to place more value on a publication if it has a monetary worth. Even a nominal charge, they feel, establishes the publication as something too worthwhile to be given away."[3]

There is sophistication and specialization in house media. Objectives reach out from the profit sector to influence government and education. Conversely, publications from government agencies and educational bodies seek to influence the profit sector and other sources of funds.

The content of house publications varies as much as the format. Two basic editorial schools of thought predominate. One is that content should be what readers will enjoy: news about themselves, for example. The other is that content should be what the publisher wants readers to know: for example, news about the organization and its objectives. Some industrial editors argue strongly for presentation of management's views on controversial public issues. Others argue as vehemently that house organs should avoid the controversial. Some publications of organizations with collective-bargaining agreements include union news; most do not.[4]

As surveys have indicated, many publications lack the guidelines of definite policies and clearly stated objectives. This leads inescapably to much waste of money and manpower. The late counselor Fred Wittner distilled these principles out of more than a quarter-century of experience:

1. The publication should fill the needs of both the company and its employees.
2. It should provide useful, meaningful information, not small talk.

3. If distributed externally, it should go to the group leaders of the community, as well as to customers and prospects.
4. It requires the joint interest and effort of management and its appointed editor or counsel.

Most editors strive for a workable compromise between what the organization wants its publics to know and what those publics want to read. Properly viewed, the house publication is a direct channel to specific publics, not a vaguely conceived "morale booster." To justify the expense and effort required, a publication must accomplish something useful for the sponsor. A house paper has no intrinsic value; its only value is that put into it by the editor, guided by definite objectives. Intelligent editors do not confuse reader bait with the purpose and substance of the publication. The content of a publication determines its character and impact; its substance and tone provide the basis for talk in the coffee shop, cafeteria, and working area.

There is a trend toward making the publication two-way—inviting questions and making surveys of attitudes, then reporting them in print. It has been a tough job to sell management on the idea, and an even tougher job to get readers to submit questions. Nonetheless, house publications provide an excellent mechanism for feedback.

In the average budget setup, an effective use of the house publication can be attained without straining for special effects. Four-color covers are not essential. The prime needs are for candor, intelligent selection of subject matter that combines the objectives of the sponsor with interests of the readers, simple format, and the constant purpose of helping readers learn as much about matters of common interest as they desire.

Pamphlets, booklets, manuals, books

There are three general types of booklets and pamphlets:

1. *Indoctrination booklets* welcome the new soldier, employee, association member, student, supplier, or visitor. (Literature for the customer or product owner usually emanates from the sales or advertising department.) The beginner's booklet helps him to get off on the right foot. It tells him the rules of the game and the benefits of playing according to the rules. It seeks to instill a team spirit—the feeling that he has joined a winning combination.
2. *Reference guides* are a second type of handbook, one useful to all members. They concern themselves with the group insurance plan, pension plan, suggestion system, hospitalization, profit sharing, housekeeping and safety, library content, recreation program and facilities, contest rules, campus geography, and the like. Handbooks enable members to look up specific information easily. They tend to be definitive and instructive. They save time and encourage appreciation of the values of membership. They quickly provide information actually sought by the reader.
3. *Institutional booklets, books, and brochures* have subject matter devoted to an idea or a philosophy, a total concept or entity. Typical are messages related to the free-enterprise system, national security, educational benefits, or charitable aims. In another category are reports of dedications, celebrations, awards, history, success, expansion, and developments in science or the arts.
    Prime among these publications is the presentation booklet, which provides an

overall picture of the organization to visitors, prospective executives or students, prospective donors or customers, and other specialized audiences. Most institutions need booklets to tell their story quickly and effectively to interested publics.[5]

Another type of booklet sometimes used is the comic or cartoon book. It has readability, versatility, and economy to recommend it. Insurance companies have used comics to simplify complex insurance and health information, and to teach safety. Utilities have used cartoons with success to communicate safety information to non-English-speaking customers. Comics, long a popular, effective means of communication, are the easiest of all printed forms to understand. The usual criticisms of this general medium—poor writing, poor artwork, and bad grammar—are not inherent in the comic book.

There is no single "most effective" method of distribution for handbooks. Many organizations maintain libraries. Handbooks are seen in cafeterias, reception lobbies, club rooms, and in wall racks throughout an institution. This distribution is usually secondary, though, since copies have been mailed or handed to prime audiences. Employees and members get their handbooks variously at work or in the mail at home. Dealers receive theirs by hand from salesmen or in the mail. The government catalogues literature and makes it available at nominal cost from the Superintendent of Documents. Large corporations mail literature to the homes of interested people in their plant cities. Trade associations issue literature at conventions and by mail to members and thought leaders.

The important thing to remember about these tools is that they are supplementary, not primary. A handbook for the new employee is no substitute for the personal handshake, a thorough orientation, and a personally conducted tour. Many organizations profitably use the "buddy" system for newcomers.

A related medium being utilized more and more is the book or lengthy booklet tracing the history of an institution, or the biography of a founder. These are usually subsidized by the sponsor and published by a commercial publisher. The sponsor sees to it that copies are placed in libraries and freely distributed to influentials among his constituency. These sponsored books are high in initial cost but pay a long-term dividend if they are accurate, well written, and widely distributed. In libraries, such histories become source material for writers and historians.

Basic questions must be considered: (1) *Does the type of book under consideration fit the needs?* (2) *Will the nature and purpose of the book attract a capable outside writer?* (3) *Is the book to be sold commercially or given away?* (4) *Should it have a prestige hard cover or be a paperback?* (5) *What are possible tie-ins to promote it?* (6) *Does it further the organization's basic public relations objectives?*[6]

Letters and bulletins

Individually written and addressed letters have long constituted the backbone of interorganizational communication. Offset letters are being used in increasing volume to establish a direct, speedy line of communication with specific publics. Letters are used on a regular or spot-news basis to reach employees, dealers, alumni, or workers in a fund-raising or legislative campaign.

The letter to employees or members has been developed as a supplement to the slower, less frequently published house magazine. It offers an opportunity for the chief executive to talk to the employee and his family in a "you and I," conversational, newsy manner. Among its advantages are economy, direct and personalized approach, impressive appearance, and speed. Letters support line communication, by ensuring the accuracy of line transmission, pointing up what is important and newsworthy in the organization's affairs, and adding importance to line communication by proving that the line is well informed. This is increasingly essential in diversified, multinational organizations.

Other letters go from organization officials to community opinion leaders, to members of selected professions such as medicine or education, to congressmen, suppliers, retailers, or newspaper editors. Common methods of reproducing letters include typewriter, multigraph, mimeograph, copier, and printing.

More letters are mailed to the home than to business addresses. The home provides wider readership and a good climate for persuasion. There is a reluctance in some quarters, however, to send letters into employees' homes, particularly where there is a tense employee–employer relationship. This reflects a concern that union officials may interpret the technique as a measure to weaken their organization.

Even more important than these printed letters issued periodically is an organization's daily correspondence. The normal flow of letters and memos constitutes an important and influential means of communication. The importance of effective letters that evoke a pleased reaction, not irritation or confusion, is obvious. Yet many organizations continue in the rut of cold, stilted, hackneyed letters that do more to confuse or obscure than to clarify.

Newsletters

The commercial field has long made good use of newsletters; estimates of their number range from 3,000 to 5,000. One of the oldest and most familiar is the *Kiplinger Washington Letter.* The newsletter has a bright future. As Howard Penn Hudson, editor of the *Newsletter on Newsletters,* says, "Newsletters seem to fit the times. People have fragmented interests. There are certain things they want to know a lot about and other things they don't want to hear anything about. Newsletters have the advantage of speed. They are quick to read."[7]

The circulation of individual newsletters is usually small, under 1,000, going to a selected audience. Costs can be under $500, including addressing and mailing. It is interesting to note that a number of newsletters started as house publications and converted into commercial ventures.

The public relations use of newsletters is spreading rapidly into nonprofit fields. Associations and professional societies particularly find the format effective. Its use in politics and lobbying is burgeoning. With this format, users can reach constituents quickly on matters having both urgency and importance. The person-to-person nature invites reading. See examples in Figure 11–3.

Inserts and enclosures

Anyone who has received bills from utilities or oil companies knows about inserts. Content goes from news vignettes to offers of merchandise at bargain prices. The insert has been coming into public relations usage as a means of appealing to a natural constituency for support. We see this in mailings of quarterly reports to shareholders, accompanied by a statement of the organization's posture on a public policy or a social problem affecting it. A chemical

Legislative Analysis for Members of The Wilderness Society by The Wilderness Society Staff

Issue in Congress: Alaska Pipeline

Is America on the brink of a legislative public lands in ord...

...subject of the sessions, numerous potential witnesses qualified to present expert criticism of the pipeline plan stayed home. ...ut as it turned out the committee heard strong testimony on ...e pipeline's behalf from Alaska's Governor William A. Egan; ...eputy Under Secretary of the Interior Jared G. Carter; ...ward L. Patton, president of Alyeska Pipeline Service Co., ...consortium formed to build and operate the pipeline; Thorn-...F. Bradshaw, president of Atlantic Richfield, one of Alyes-...owners, and others. There wasn't much time left for the ...right-of-way questions.

...March 26 the Public Lands Subcommittee of the House ...r Committee announced the scheduling of its own hear-...April 11, 18 and 19, on oil and gas pipeline right-of-way ...troduced since February as well as the broader adminis-...and Jackson bills. (An additional hearing day, May 1, ...sequently announced.) The Jackson bill is sponsored ...ouse by Representative Lloyd Meeds (D-Wash).

...ril 2 the Supreme Court announced that it had denied ...of the administration, Alaska and the pipeline spon-...eview of the appellate court decision. Following the ...ment, the Senate Interior Committee was alerted for ...meeting to mark up a right-of-way bill, a preliminary ...g a bill to the Senate for floor action. No new ...ent was made concerning hearings on the bypassed ...vel and Mondale bills and the specifics of the ...ne issue, leading conservationists to fear that such ...t come too late to be more than a pro forma ges-...because conceivably as early as May both the

COME JOIN US

PRSA NATIONAL NEWSLETTER

Vol.4 No.2

ROCKEY CALLS ON PUBLIC RELATIONS
TO LEAD WAY TO BUSINESS CREDIBILITY

PRSA President Jay Rock...
ter members...
mont...

...to excellence and to leadership. We must
...ve in the potential and the power of
...c relations."

...L PRSA INSTITUTE IN APRIL
...TURE PETER DRUCKER

...rucker, noted writer and educator,
...one of the featured speakers at
...Annual PRSA Institute, April 9-
...e University of Southern Cali-
...s Angeles. Under the theme
...ppening to the American Dream?",
...ions will cover: Pluralistic So-
...t Still a Reality? Image and
...Is There Still a Difference?
...emma--Situational Ethics and
...ality? Increasing Needs vs.
...esources--Delusions of Ade-
...lt on Economic Illiteracy--
...l Weapons Cope? 1976--Is it

CONGRESSMAN CLAIR W...

THREE FEDERAL ED...
"Whatever...

A valiant band of tuna fishermen a...
of Congress and the Courts to plea fo...
frustration that the San Diego County ...
colleagues that present Federal and C...

1. Not save <u>one</u> porpoise if the...

ONE-TO-ONE

Edited by Hazel Casler
Published by Arts, Graphics and Educational Services

Texas Department of Mental Health and Mental Retardation
P.O. Box 12668, Capitol Station, Austin, Texas 78711

For Information Directors
TDMHMR Facilities
Community MHMR Centers

company, for instance, explains its position on the ozone question, or reports its program of pollution control.

One of the obvious advantages of the insert is that the message goes to a favorably disposed audience. Readership and receptivity should be high. Common bonds should be strengthened. Another advantage is economy. A small, lightweight printed insert need not add to the postage or change the classification of the mail. In the past, the main use of inserts or add-ons in mailings has been promotional. Looking ahead, this will shift more to public-affairs purposes and topics.

Position papers and printed speeches

Printed papers and packets containing an organization's public posture on controversial matters have had a sharp rise. The simple explanation is that more and more organizations have found their traditional policies or their methods under investigation and attack, and they are responding formally. The contents of such papers or packets frequently have their genesis in public speeches or statements by top officials. Reprinting them in their entirety provides a rebuttal if public media have extracted and reported only the "bad" part, or the "controversial and provocative" part.

But the rebuttal is the smaller part of the distribution. The larger intent is to reassure those who would naturally agree, and to stimulate redress elsewhere. Thus, these materials are sent selectively to employees, members of a legislature or municipal government, financial analysts, politicians, sympathetic pressure groups, and the like. This medium is often used for classroom presentations—for example, the Standard Oil of Indiana Divestiture Case Problem Kit. On occasion, positions taken in controversy and made a matter of public record come back to haunt sponsors. They may have changed their position, but the booklet or white paper stays where it was sent.

The bulletin board, posters, billboards

The use of bulletin boards is widespread and is here to stay. If there were no other reason, laws requiring the posting of an ever-increasing number of notices would preserve it. See Figure 11–4.

The bulletin board offers a good place to corroborate information with brief messages. It provides quick access for spiking rumors and for making desirable information stick. The dynamic board gets regular attention; it needs to be serviced often. There's a petty annoyance in seeing the same notice again and again after it has become history. Effective boards are placed at eye-level height where traffic is heavy and the reading light is good.

In somewhat the same category are the posters and placards placed on walls or columns of working areas. The theme of such posters is usually safety, housekeeping, economics, or security. They can be quite imaginative.

Information racks

The information rack is used primarily for morale and employee education, with the emphasis on economic education. The device was started in 1948 by General Motors as "an idea cafeteria for offering mental and spiritual nourishment to employees." Firms specializing in this service provide companies with

FIGURE 11-4   Bulletin board, posters—the megaphone in printed form.

PROTECT EAGLES

Golden Eagle

What Can You Do?

The magnificent eagle is in danger. Today there are fewer than half as many of these great birds in North America as there were 20 years ago. To blame: loss of nesting sites, disturbance by civilization, possible chemical-caused infertility and, worst of all, illegal shooting.

What does the eagle need to survive? To nest and feed protected from the expanding world. To fly freely without being shot. It's what we *don't* do to the eagle that will help him most.

It is a Federal Crime to Shoot an Eagle

A 1962 amendment to the Federal Bald Eagle Act made it a federal crime to indiscriminately kill golden eagles as well as bald eagles. In 1972 Congress increased penalties for taking bald and golden eagles — $5,000 and one year in jail ($10,000 and two years in jail for the second offense). Half of the fine, up to $2,500, may be paid to persons giving information leading to

Keep Virginia Clean.

Clean As They Found It

booklets and reprints of magazine articles in wholesale lots. These are distributed free to employees from these racks on a "take what you want" basis. The racks are usually placed in reception rooms and near plant and office exits, so employees may pick up a few items on their way home.

One supplier for these information racks suggests these values for the reading rack: (1) *The broad range of reading materials thus put in hands of employees tends to broaden the range of their reading and, consequently, their knowledge; (2) the voluntary pick-up has value for the employee, who has much communication forced upon him; (3) home readership of these pamphlets and reprints gets the message to the wives and children; (4) use of the rack enables the sponsors to disseminate information on subjects they would hesitate to take up in ordinary communication channels; (5) the booklets serve to repeat and reinforce messages directed through other channels; (6) it is a handy distribution medium that enables employers to get materials to employees quickly if need be.*

Institutional advertising

The one certain way to get publicity printed or broadcast is to buy space or time for it—to use advertising. The $25-billion advertising business was developed initially to sell goods and services. Increasingly, paid advertising has proved useful as a public relations tool. It is variously termed "institutional advertising," "public service advertising," "public relations advertising," "identity advertising," or "advocacy advertising." Advertising to disseminate information or promote opinion change was first used in the early 1900s and then on a small, spasmodic basis until World War II. Ivy Lee bought full-page ads in the Colorado newspapers in 1914 to tell the Rockefeller side of the story in the bitter Colorado Fuel and Iron strike.[8]

Advertising enables the sponsor to tell his story when he chooses and to the audience he selects. The artwork, headline, and message are exactly the way the advertiser wants them to appear, in print or on the air. On the minus side, the audience recognizes this as paid pleading, so resistance may be raised to some degree. News does not carry this handicap.

Advertising in public media is expensive. (A 60-second message on a nighttime TV network costs in the range of $40,000–$75,000.) Yet it is increasingly used in programs of public education by nonprofit agencies. A dramatic demonstration of its effectiveness was the anticigarette "commercials" of the American Cancer Society and American Heart Association on television. Advertising by the U.S. government is largely confined to the armed forces, which spend millions on recruiting. National nonprofit causes can sometimes get firms to finance advertising for a worthy cause, in which case, the advertisement does double duty. This kind of advertising has been found rewarding by many sponsors. The advertising industry's contribution to promotion of worthwhile causes through the Advertising Council has been especially noteworthy. Campaigns have promoted religion in American life, better schools, forest-fire prevention, civil rights, antipollution, health, and safety. The nation's communications media have contributed billions of dollars worth of services and facilities to such campaigns. See Figure 11–5 for 1978 campaign.

The major changes taking place are those of emphasis. There is great increase in the use of corporate advertising techniques for advocacy purposes, and a decrease in their use for institutional "identity" purposes. The largest corporations and industries have been beleaguered by defections of certain constituents, by criticism from public media, and by attacks of adversaries. More and more, these corporations and their associations have taken to the offensive. Financially able to do so, they have gone into mass media with advertising in which they could control the message. A classic case for study is Mobil Corporation.

Another part of the response is in the form of public-service advertising and program sponsorship. Some exciting ventures have led the way in this area.

DO YOUR KIDS HAVE A HIGHER E.Q. THAN YOU?

(Economics Quotient)

They might. Take this quick quiz and rate yourself.

True False

☐ ☐ **(1.)** One cause of inflation is when consumers, business and government spend too heavily on available goods and services.

☐ ☐ **(2.)** Since 1960, the U.S. has had the highest productivity growth rate in manufacturing of leading free world industrial nations.

☐ ☐ **(3.)** The value of all U.S. goods and services produced in one year is called the Gross National Product (GNP).

☐ ☐ **(4.)** If you have a savings account, own stock, bonds or life insurance, or are in a pension fund, you are an investor in the U.S. economy.

Did our little E.Q. quiz stump you? Your kids probably would have breezed through it. But don't feel too bad. Most people don't know even basic facts and figures about our American Economic System. In short, a lot of Economics Quotients, E.Qs., could stand improvement.

It's important. Not just because we all face some important decisions about our economic system. But because the more you know about our system, the more you'll be able to make it work for you.

A special booklet has been prepared to help you learn more about what makes our American Economic System tick. It's fact-filled, easy reading and free. It's also an easy way to raise your E.Q..

For your copy, write: "Economics," Pueblo, Colorado 81009.

ANSWERS:
1.T 2.F (U.S. ranked last) 3.T 4.T

The American Economic System.

We should all learn more about it.

  A public service message of This Newspaper & The Advertising Council & U.S. Department of Commerce.

FIGURE 11-6 Rules for effective public relations advertising. Hill & Knowlton has formulated these guides for preparing effective copy. Courtesy Hill & Knowlton, Inc.

1.
Be frank, fair, and honest.

2.
Tell your story directly to an individual in his own language.

3.
Don't talk up or down to anyone.

4.
Use simple, unvarnished words and facts so that everyone in the community will both understand and believe what you have to say.

5.
Tell one story at a time—don't overload your copy.

6.
Use figures sparingly — and only when illustrated by simple, everyday examples.

EXHIBIT 11–1

> *Advertising is a Versatile Tool*
>
> Some uses of advertising have been catalogued by George Hammond, chairman of the Carl Byoir firm: (1) community relations—plant openings, expansions, open houses, anniversaries, annual statements, promotion of community activities such as cleanup weeks, safety, Community Chest campaigns, and so forth; (2) employee relations, including the employer's side in labor disputes; (3) recruitment; (4) promotion of art contests, essay contests, scholarship awards, and so forth; (5) statements of policy; (6) proxy fights for control; (7) consolidation of competitive position; (8) records of accomplishment; (9) public misunderstandings that must be cleared up immediately; (10) position on pending legislation; (11) consolidation of editorial opinion; (12) supplier or member relations; (13) celebration of local institutions, such as the press during National Newspaper Week; (14) presentation of employer's points of view on matters of public concern. As Hammond says, "These 14 suggestions only scratch the surface of possible uses."

Among them have been such TV series as "Masterpiece Theater" and "Sesame Street" on public broadcast networks, and commercial network programs dealing with social and environmental problems and their resolution.

The big question remains, *How effective is it all?* The answer defies generalization. There are claims of incredible success. There are instances that imply a waste of money, because "nobody was listening or looking." Too little significant research has been done, but evidence to date indicates that *specific campaigns aimed at specific objectives by reputable sponsors are the most effective.* Ads with a "news" approach, personal involvement, and human-interest pictures draw the biggest audience.

Many are using advertising to talk directly to the media gatekeepers by placing ads in the trade journals of press, magazines, and radio. Many have done this to place their public relations policies on record for journalists.

Legal considerations involving advertising are covered in Chapter 12.

The spoken word

Meetings

Meetings bring people together, *face to face,* providing both an opportunity to communicate to a selected audience and *an opportunity to listen*—two-way communication. As more has been learned about effective person-to-person vehicles, this tool has come to the fore. There has been a shift of emphasis in employee and member communication from printed and visual media to work-group and study-group meetings. One of the newer approaches makes use of an ombudsman who hears complaints. Industries have found, too, that the surest way to reach educators is to invite them in for conferences or fellowships. Face-to-face get-togethers are expensive but economical in the long run. See Figure 11–7.

The most impressive form of get-together is the mass meeting where officials give a progress report to employees, where the commanding officer explains to all troops why they are shipping out, where the college president tells the student

FIGURE 11-7 Meetings, face-to-face remain the best vehicle, one-on-one or a full stadium. Courtesy Pitney-Bowes and General Motors public relations departments.

body of the decision to drop football, where the office manager announces plans for the move to another city. And then the official listens to reactions, with empathy. The mass meeting has been most effectively used in middle-sized groups of employees or members.

Meetings, to be effective, require purpose, careful planning and staging, and skillful direction. In meetings, exchange of viewpoints is open, but controlled so that the meeting doesn't drag, and so that discussion sticks to the important features. Otherwise, the discussion roams into other pastures or explodes in gripes or clashes of personalities. Effectiveness depends, too, on the moderator's being a leader and articulate.

Other meetings take the form of discussion groups, with a roundtable or conference of from ten to 35 people. Among supervisory personnel, charity volunteers, and civic committees, these meetings are well attended even outside of working hours. For the hourly employee, the soldier, or the student—the person on the bottom rung of the ladder—meetings are usually scheduled as a part of the work program. To avoid the inference of a "captive audience," attendance is usually voluntary.

Staging such meetings is often the task of the public relations staff. There are several checkpoints:

1. Comfortable facilities.
2. "Breaks" in the middle of long sessions.
3. Exhibits, displays, charts, graphs, and films, or other visual support wherever suitable to the subject matter.
4. Refreshments if participants give up their spare time.
5. An opportunity for everyone to get into the act, even if it's only through a note pad and a pen.
6. Press notice of the occasion if newsworthy, with credit to the departmental people who were responsible for it.

Meetings have long used public-address systems to good advantage. Two other tools are coming into play more and more. One is multiple-screen-and-image, automatically controlled rear-slide films, with voice on tape or live on PA; the other is closed-circuit TV.[9]

The speakers' bureau

There are few organizations of any size without some officials who can get on their feet and talk interestingly for a few minutes. There are, however, some commonly practiced alternatives. One is to engage outside public-speaking specialists and pay their fees. Another alternative is for the organization to call on its friendly associates—a public relations or public affairs counsel, management or legal counsel, or a nonresident director. In all cases, the kind of talent available determines its use. Practitioners are frequently called on to research a speech, prepare an outline, or write a complete manuscript. In other cases, the public relations department collects appropriate material and functions as a speakers' library.

The speakers' bureau is a *planned* means for providing speakers on request. Subject matter has both latitude and variety. The speakers' pool is a valuable medium for any kind of organization with something interesting to say.

Here are four points worth remembering:

First, select and coach the lineup of speakers with some care.

Second, select topics of broad interest that serve the needs of the potential audience and carry the organization's story.

Third, provide speakers with helpful visual aids—flip charts, flannel boards, slide films, etc.

Fourth, promote and publicize the availability of the speakers, to get maximum mileage.

Akin to a speakers' bureau is the use of qualified employees—scientists, scholars, artists—as authors of magazine and newspaper articles. The employee gets visibility and recognition. The employer gets credit for having such talent aboard. Both are credited for the breakthrough, program, or success described by the author. Many companies encourage this with financial awards to employees. Along this same line, qualified employees can tell the employer's side on radio and television programs by interview.

Several counseling firms and advertising agencies provide training for executives and others called on as spokesmen. The impetus for this training came from the ineptitude and poor showing of industry spokesmen on TV camera at congressional committee hearings. The trend in this direction was indicated in the C-C Survey, where practitioners cited "training of employers in public relations and public affairs" as one of their most important responsibilities.

Telephone newslines and public address

Telephone newslines and public-address systems are utilized to link the front office with many others. Establishment of a telephone newsline from which people can get late, authentic information simply by dialing has proved especially helpful in organizations caught up in conflict. Many universities have set up rumor centers that public and students alike can call to get accurate information from recordings in times of crisis. Illinois Bell Telephone found that management personnel made greater use of Telephone Communicator than nonmanagement personnel did. Up-to-the-minute recorded messages over tele-

Telephone newsline. Courtesy University of Wisconsin Center for Health Sciences.

phone newslines provide a fast, flexible means of communication in an organization scattered over a large geographical area.[10]

The public-address system, often used in conjunction with a recorded music service, deserves more experimentation. Its effectiveness in promotional work and in stirring protests has stimulated more interest in its advantages and limitations. The system can be made mobile. The messages can be relayed. It can be tied in with closed-circuit TV. This kind of use requires a working knowledge of tape recorders, the turntable, and telephone relays.

The grapevine

The grapevine is not a formal tool or avenue. But word-of-mouth gets around. Keith Davis, Indiana University, reported in the *Harvard Business Review* the example of an official's wife who had a baby at 11 P.M. By 2 P.M. the next day, 46 percent of the executive group knew about it. The grapevine is a potent line of transmission. It carries information much more exciting than simple facts or truth. Sometimes it is actually harmful, or threatens to be. Rumors of layoff, of friction among officials, of trouble, or of bad blood between factions can hurt. The word travels far beyond the local group, becoming more and more distorted as it goes. The hints of trouble tend to breed trouble wherever there happens to be a chip on anybody's shoulder.

The public relations staff usually stays tuned in on the grapevine. When the gossiping and rumoring are harmless, nothing is done. When real trouble brews, the gossip is squelched by the release of full facts on the topic. Once in a while, a counterrumor or an exposé of the facts among the natural leaders of an organization is sponsored to offset a harmful rumor. A more positive use of the grapevine was made by the Indian government in its difficult task of disseminating birth-control information. First it used the traditional channels—radio, movies, lectures—to educate Indian women. When these proved inadequate, India's Health Minister turned to introducing birth-control devices to a few women in each village, relying on them to spread the word along the grapevine. He termed this "indoctrination by gossip."

The image

Motion pictures, news film clips, and films

Sponsored films are those conceived within and commissioned by an organization for a sales, training, or public relations purpose. They are paid for by the sponsor. The intent is not to reap direct, immediate monetary return but rather to develop favorable ideas, motivations, attitudes, or reactions in the viewing audience.

Television has provided the greatest impetus. It has preconditioned two generations to the forming of impressions and opinions from audiovisual media. The Reverend John Culkin of Fordham University has estimated that by the time students have graduated from high school today, they have watched more than 15,000 hours of television and seen 500 movies, while spending a total of only 10,800 hours in school.

The basic factors that gave television its great potential are used in the motion picture to transmit ideas, stimulate imagination, and produce action. With TV and pictorial journalism, a tremendous audience awaits the timely, skillful film presentation of a sponsor's story. This is an effective means of reaching selected groups with real impact. TV has helped create an amazing growth in the use of films for public relations purposes.

In the United States, the sponsored slide, film, and videotape activity amounts to well over a billion-dollar business annually. Of 14,000 nontheatrical films produced in 1977, some 7,750 were of an in-plant nature, and 4,600 were sponsored. The slide film format remains the mainstay. Hope Reports cites $583 million spent by industry to produce 113 million slides in 1976. Another major user of AV media is government. Altogether, federal agencies spend an estimated $160 million annually, mainly for training and recruiting purposes.

There have been several significant changes in the nontheatrical film business. A major one is that the number of producers has doubled in the 1970s. This means, among other things, that there have been jobs for an increasing number of specialists trained by universities.[11]

Although the initial costs of production and distribution of AV materials are high, the proper yardstick to use is the cost per viewer. Studies have shown this cost to be as low as 4.6 cents. When a sponsored film is also shown on TV, the cost per viewer drops to about 1.6 cents. One organization that has used films since 1938 figures its total audience at 300 million, at a unit cost of $.0005.

The expansion in sponsored films has been matched in growth by audience potential. It is a rare club, business, or educational group that doesn't use

Filming a documentary. Courtesy of the Foundation for Public Relations Research and Education.

carousel or 16mm sound projectors occasionally in its program season. Libraries, schools, resort hotels and motels, and even private offices and boardrooms use audiovisual equipment with increasing regularity. The American Family Film Library has had 6,500 bookings in a year, with 655,000 viewers. U.S. Steel has estimated that, on the average, one of their films is shown every seven minutes of every working day to an audience of about 60 people. The film "A Question of Hunting" by the Remington Arms Company has been seen by more than 30 million viewers. All of this creates the need for new films—films that educate, inform, and entertain.

The communications strengths of the motion picture are readily apparent:

1. It combines the impact of sight, sound, drama and movement, color, and music with group enthusiasm.
2. It can present certain ideas involving motion that cannot effectively be described by print or audio means.
3. It attracts sustained, exclusive attention to a message for the length of the showing.
4. It clarifies the time factor in any operation or series of events.
5. It provides a reproduced record of events.
6. It can present processes that cannot ordinarily be seen by the human eye.
7. It can bring the past and the distant to the viewer.
8. It can enlarge or reduce objects and can use cartoons to dramatize abstractions.
9. Above all, it lets the viewer see with his own eyes and enforces the conviction that "seeing is believing."

There are more than a million 16mm motion-film projectors, and another million slide projectors owned by organized groups meeting regularly—schools, colleges, churches, clubs, fraternal organizations, and labor, veterans', farm, and women's groups. Eighty-five percent of all films shown in schools are sponsored. These outlets, together with the use of sponsored films on TV stations, cable TV channels, commercial theaters, airport theaters, and resorts, provide a tremendous potential. Among other advantages, they can bring understanding to people of limited reading ability.

To get the best public relations value, films must get maximum exposure. Therefore, the distribution of a film is extremely important. Films may be distributed through certain film producers, through the educational film libraries, by the sponsor, or through firms specializing in this service. There are hundreds of titles available for immediate and free-loan showings.

A major reason for the growth of this medium is the willingness of TV stations to use commercially sponsored films at no cost. Films on social problems, safety, pollution, human rehabilitation, health care, and other timely subjects with mass appeal are particularly acceptable. The Morton Salt Company, for example, produced "Water," exploring the wise use and reuse of this natural resource.

Local TV stations, which are on limited budgets, cannot afford to produce documentary films. Consequently, TV program managers welcome films of the proper length—23 to 28 minutes, or 14 minutes—for program time slots, as long as they are not blatantly commercial. Phillips Petroleum made five films, "American Enterprise," examining the five strongest influences on the nation's economy. The only mention of the sponsor was in the credit line at the end of each film.

The growing use of public relations films in theaters and drive-ins parallels the drop in Hollywood's output of cartoons and short subjects. Hard-pressed by TV competition, movie houses are more and more receptive to free program material.

Sponsored films are also used for more specific public relations communications purposes. The public relations calling has its own 37-minute sponsored film, "Opinion of the Publics," composed of mini-cases, produced at a cost of $50,000 by the Public Relations Foundation. One company put its annual report on film. A newly merged company produced a film on the combined entity for showings to employees throughout the world. A navy unit filmed an exercise at sea. The community-affairs function finds sponsored films to be a helpful ally.

Because of the expense and effort involved in a good film, all aspects must be weighed carefully:

1. Why is the film being made?
2. What special audiences do we want to reach with it?
3. How long should it be, to have the best possible chance of use?
4. What budget should we figure for production and distribution?
5. How much commercialism may the film include, if any?
6. Which producer is best qualified for this task?
7. Are we sure it will successfully compete with TV shows and feature movies so as to gain exposure on these vitally important media?[12]

Another film technique is the TV newsclip. The content is controlled by the sponsor. It is constructed to fit a time segment of seconds or minutes, according to its sponsor's judgment of its news value. The use of the clip is predicated on the program or news director's assessment of its news value, and whether its quality matches the station's or network's standards. Newsclips are relatively expensive, and their use and acceptance are debatable. As a practical matter, costs and results are difficult to justify. Employers are accustomed to seeing clippings and hearing circulation counts relating to news items in which they participated. Television, to most, is an unreal world as far as news is concerned. Time, and many more TV newsclip success stories, will change this.[13]

The advent of relatively inexpensive videotape makes it possible to film speeches, interviews, panel discussions, instructional lectures, or sales demonstrations in the offices of the sponsor or a lecture hall, and reuse these tapes hundreds of times for selected audiences. Some large organizations use this equipment in a studio setting to record executive speeches for rehearsal playback. Coca-Cola turned to videocassette programming as a medium for explaining temporary dislocations and major moves of people and functions when shifting into the company's new Atlanta headquarters.

Competition is spirited among manufacturers of videotape recording and playback equipment for personal as well as organizational use. The time approaches when a person will be able to load a home TV set with modestly priced videotapes of his choice, as today he loads a phonograph with records. He will, the experts say, be able to play discs that reproduce in television images. (The principal originators in this field are RCA and MCA.) Experts predict that the 1980s will see a billion-dollar personalized communications industry. These reproduction methods and computer storage of information will bring with them complex problems in the protection of copyrights.

The rapid growth of film as a tool, plus the refinement in audio-visual hardware, makes it desirable for large institutions to develop libraries of films. The outright sale and rental of prints to other film libraries is common and helps recover part of the cost.

Closed-circuit and cable TV

This tool, developed as a by-product of commercial TV, offers great potentialities. This type of TV is not transmitted to stations for broadcasting to home viewers. By means of a closed circuit, leased through a telephone company, it pipes live pictures and sound from an originating point to one or more receiving locations across the country. It is simpler and less expensive than broadcast TV, and as private as a telephone conversation. Yet it combines the power of TV with programs designed for specific, invited audiences.

The cost of staging a program or conference through closed-circuit TV continues to be relatively high. It can, however, be more economical than assembling a conference or convention in one city. "Telelectures" are being used widely in education and business. Dentistry and medicine are being taught through this medium. Firms use it to make reports or to hold sales meetings. Political parties use it for fund-raising dinners and rallies. More and more universities and colleges are using it to reach students across campus and across the state. Charities have used this medium to kick off fund drives, assembling volunteers in groups across the nation. Where no TV outlets are available, kinescopes of the program can be shown.

Closed-circuit television was first used on a worldwide basis June 26, 1969, when more than 1,000 people at functions in New York City, London, Tokyo, Perth, Sydney, and Melbourne participated in the official opening ceremonies of the Mt. Newman Iron Ore project in western Australia. This worldwide circuit was made possible by the communications satellite system. Although expensive, it was cheaper than flying 300 key writers and officials to the mine site. Total cost of the event, including the satellite transmission, was under $200,000. The high costs and the difficulties caused by differences in time are the major obstacles to the use of the tool on a nationwide and frequent basis.

Cable television has emerged as another important outlet for sponsored films and newsclips. There are more than 3,000 operating cable systems in the United States, serving nearly 6,000 communities, and thousands more have been approved. The number of subscribers approaches 11 million households. The fee averages about $6.50 per month.[14]

A small converter, installed in the viewer's home, improves TV reception in areas where distance or conditions pose problems. This enables the set owner to view channels that are closed-circuit cable only. Most metropolitan areas are covered by cable TV. There are channels programming weather, time, and news reports, and others showing sports events, cultural programs, and movies. Stations use individual films and combinations, including videocassette, with host introductions and closing.

Displays and exhibits

In almost every factory, there is a reception room, a showroom, a museum, or an employees' lunch area. In every college, there is the equivalent of an "Old Main," a Students' Union, a museum, or a visitors' room. Every branch of military service has its sites to perpetuate its memories, receive its guests, and

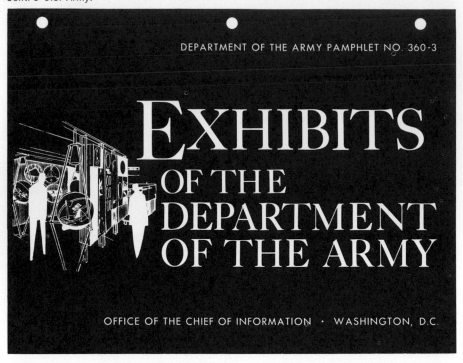

show its progress. These places are natural areas for displays and exhibits. For
anyone who has ever taken a plant tour or visited a world's fair, the content of
such exhibits needs no explanation. The point is that preparation and servicing
of such displays usually fall to the public relations staff.

In addition to the stationary or permanent displays, there are temporary
exhibits in communities marking special events. There are national industrial
shows, state and county fairs, and traveling displays. Some business houses have
exhibits of materials, processes, or products that they lend their customers and
their suppliers. The National Guard has equipment it can put on display or
wheel out for parades and local events. Occasionally a university takes a dramatic
show to other cities. Welfare agencies are usually happy to take part in exhibits
where the nature of their work can be dramatized.

Exhibitors know that the objective is to entice the footsore visitor to stop in
front of the display, remain long enough to look at the material, and be stimulated to immediate or future action. Lynn Poole of Johns Hopkins University
says that to accomplish this, an exhibit must be something different that creates
an action and promotes good humor while stimulating participation.

Staged events

Almost every city has some kind of annual occasion all its own. Perhaps it's
Milkman's Day, Pickle Harvest Festival, Sidewalk Sale, Fashion Parade,
Founder's Day, Help Your Neighbor, Junior Government Day, Community
Auction, or All-Sports Parade.

These events are wonderful. They are crowd days. People shed their routines and some of their inhibitions. They turn clown, auctioneer, beauty-contest judge, auxiliary cop, hog caller, past-champion pie eater, trombonist, or flag bearer for a few hours. On these occasions, the people who make most of the money the other 364 days of the year spend some of it freely.

Handling visitors is another direct-contact vehicle. Its most prevalent use is in open-house events and in the day-by-day handling of plant tours. The idea behind the careful reception of visitors is to merchandise an organization's facilities and its practices. Open-house events attract the community. Plant tours catch outside friends and relatives, vacationers, schoolchildren, foreigners, financial analysts, alumni, customers, and retirees.

Tours constitute an important medium for government in hosting visitors. This form of hospitality is favorably received by foreign guests. Tours help convince voters that their taxes are being well spent. A tour of facilities also works well for tax-supported universities and service academies. Private hospitals and charitable agencies use tours to reassure patients and donors. Most people are good hosts in their own houses, because they work at it.

The use of tours is increasing. There have been a growing number of circumstances urging their usage. New plants and installations have opened. Old facilities have been renovated. New technology has been abundant. Organizations have merged. In short, there has been much to show off and much to talk about. If you were a foreign manufacturer opening a U.S. plant, you'd have reason to reassure the community.

Techniques have become quite elaborate. Clever invitations, special transportation, greeters, souvenirs, motion pictures, and refreshments figure among the enticements. Then, too, the events regularly make news locally and sometimes nationally. Within the community, an open house is a news story of civic

The staged event—supporting common interest with participation.
Courtesy The Parker Pen Company.

spirit that the local press welcomes. When notable visitors drop in from afar, their own hometown papers are glad to get word. If they are public officials of some community, a photograph may be in order.

Art as a public relations tool

Although it does not fit neatly in a kit of communications, sponsorship of art and cultural pursuits is being used increasingly as a public relations tool. The use is in keeping with efforts of institutions to show that their interests go beyond their immediate activity. The public goodwill furthers the identity of an organization, and the cultural support makes an employer's community more attractive. Richard Eells sees an "irreversible trend toward corporate involvement in the arts." Other institutions, likewise, find art helpful in advancing their objectives. Through painting collections, traveling collections, landscaping, sculpture, concerts, and lectures, organizations support the arts and link themselves in the public's mind with the finer things of life.[15]

Historically, sponsorship of the arts has been largely the province of the profit sector. In the mid-1970s, expenditures were estimated at above $150 million, with the main recipients museums and symphony orchestras. Others are now joining in this activity. Federal government departments, particularly Defense and State, have built collections of art. Some segments are available on loan; others repose

Art is a growing, promising avenue for public relations expression.
Courtesy Continental Illinois Bank, Chicago.

in government facilities of historical significance. Universities, in their libraries and guest facilities, are using art for education and decoration.

Taken altogether, what we have seen is no more than the beginning of art, music, theater, and photography sponsorship as public relations vehicles. Such sponsorship is a way of identifying with lasting, esthetic, cultural values. The identification is noteworthy and newsworthy. It can reverse some of the negative impressions that the public holds of large institutions; a display of paintings, or a benefit symphony concert, can speak of its sponsor more loudly than his or her own words.

At least one senior official believes that business sponsorship of the arts has benefits in employee relations: "If business is to attract good people and keep them, and motivate them to do their best, the arts must become an important part of the business environment." Certainly this applies equally to nonprofit entities.

ADDITIONAL READINGS

SCOTT M. CUTLIP, "The Challenge Ahead," *College and University Journal,* Vol. 12, No. 5. Insight into implication of new technology—optical scanning, information monitoring, two-way cable TV.

RALPH C. DARROW, *House Journal Editing.* Danville, Ill: Interstate Printers and Publishers, Inc., 1974.

KEITH DAVIS, "Let's study the Grapevine," *Journal of Organization Communication,* Vol. 3, No. 1 (Fall 1973).

RICHARD EELLS, *The Corporation and The Arts.* New York: MacMillan, 1967.

"Exhibits of the Department of the Army," Office of the U.S. Chief of Information, Washington, D.C.

DAVID FINN, "How the Media Have Changed," *Public Relations Journal,* Vol. 31, No. 10 (October 1975).

FRED W. FRIENDLY, "Asleep at the Switch of the Wired City," *Saturday Review,* Vol. LIII (October 10, 1970). Also see E. BRYAN CARNE, "Telecommunications: Its Impact on Business," *Harvard Business Review,* July–August 1972. Glimpses of changes coming in the 1980s.

MAURICE I. MANDEL, *Advertising.* Englewood Cliffs, N.J.: Prentice-Hall, 1974.

BEN R. PARKER and DR. PATRICIA J. DRABIK, *Creative Intention: About Audio-Visual Communications.* New York: Law-Arts Publishers, Inc., 1974.

STANLEY PETERFREUD, "Employee Publications: Deadly but Not Dead Yet," *Public Relations Journal,* Vol. 30, No. 1 (January 1974).

ALVIN H. REISS, *Culture & Company.* New York: Twayne Publishers Inc., 1972.

TONY SCHWARTZ, *The Responsive Chord.* New York: Anchor Press/Doubleday, 1973.

FRED STUART, "Guidelines to a Successful Motion Picture," *PR Tips and Tactics,* Vol. 13, No. 38 (December 1975). A practical guide in planning step by step.

RICHARD WEINER, *Professional's Guide to Public Relations Services* New York, Richard Weiner Inc. A valuable compendium.

JAMES J. WELSH, *The Speech Writing Guide.* New York: Wiley, 1968.

REX WILSON, "An Editor Speaks," *Direction,* March 1974. The editor of *Hoist,* navy newspaper, offers advice.

FOOTNOTES

1. Stuart H. Surlin and Barry Walker, "Employee Evaluations of Handling of News by a Corporate Newspaper," *Journalism Quarterly,* Vol. 52, No. 1 (Spring 1975). This article points out that employees feel management gives the "good" news, is reluctant about the "bad" news. Also see Lawrence W. Nolte, *Fundamentals of Public Relations* (Elmsford, N.Y.: Pergamon Press, 1974), pp. 371–75, which describes 17 objectives of industrial house publications.

2. From *Profile,* Syracuse University and The International Association of Business Communicators. A valuable document, measuring the size and nature of the communications function among a cross section of businesses. Available from IABC, 870 Market Street, San Francisco, 1975.

3. Jack J. Honomichi, "In Britain They Sell Their House Organs," *Public Relations Quarterly,* Vol. 10 (Spring 1965). A summary of the survey appeared in *PR Reporter.* Meriden New Hampshire, Vol. 18, No. 27, July 7, 1975.

4. See J.W. Click, "Employee Magazines in the Public Relations Program," *Public Relations Quarterly,* Vol. 12 (Summer 1967). A scholarly analysis of content in ten prize-winning publications. Worth repeating to discern changes.

5. For planning and production details, see William H. Gilbert, ed., *Public Relations in Local Government* (Washington, D.C.: International City Management Assn., 1975), Chap. 11, "Publications Planning, Development and Production," pp. 185–210.

6. For more on this, see Richard Weiner, "Books Are Effective Public Relations Tools," *Public Relations Journal,* May 1969.

7. Howard Penn Hudson, "What Every Public Relations Practitioner Must Know about Newsletters," *The Newsletter on Newsletters,* June 1973.

8. "AT&T's Quest for Public Understanding: 1908 Origins of the Nation's Oldest Continuous Institutional Advertising Program," *Journal of Advertising,* Winter 1976. A definitive study.

9. Eugene Marlow, "Ten Rules for Corporate TV Employee News," *Public Relations Journal,* September 1976, p. 4. Also see Marilyn Benber, "When the Boss Goes on Television," *New York Times,* April 29, 1973. Information on multiple-screen projection can be obtained from Eastman Kodak, Rochester, N.Y.

10. A variation in the use of the telephone for inquiries is gaining many adherents. Libraries provide a number children can call and hear a story (Dial-a-Story). Hospital patients may dial a number and request a taped message on any of hundreds of topics (Dial Access Health Line). Government agencies provide a service for news (Dial-a-News Item). The surface has barely been scratched.

11. See Hope Reports, Inc., Hope Reports Education and Media, Hope Reports Perspective. Also, a wealth of information in an advertisement in *Wall Street Journal,* September 12, 1977.

12. Marlene Weber McGarry, "The PR Film Handout: Effective Tool or a Waste of Time?" *Public Relations Journal,* Vol. 31, No. 8 (August 1975). Challenges the assumption that usage of public relations films is broad or general.

13. Hilliard A. Schendorf, "The How-to of TV Newsclips," *PR Tips and Tactics,* April 2, 9, and 16, 1973. A three-part series, worthy of study.

14. Carl H. Lenz, "Cable TV and Public Relations," *Public Relations Journal,* Vol. 32, No. 2 (February 1976). Also see "A Short Course in Cable, 1974," *Broadcasting,* April 22, 1974.

15. Egon E. Weck, "Photography's (not so) Latent Image," *Public Relations Journal,* Vol. 31, No. 3 (March 1975). Speaks for photographic art as art.

12

It is the purpose of the First Amendment to preserve an uninhibited marketplace of ideas in which truth will ultimately prevail.

JUSTICE BYRON WHITE

Public Relations and the Law

In the past decade or so, there has been a plethora of laws, regulations, and court decisions that affect and regulate public relations practice. One authority on communications law estimates that 35 percent of all legal statutes make reference to communications practices. This is equally true of government regulations that have the force of law. Beyond those statutes and court decisions governing public relations practice, there also has been an explosion in regulatory law in fair employment, consumerism, and the environment that requires legal knowledge on the part of the practitioner. The growing reach and complexity of government regulation is reflected in the fact that within one decade, the number of federal regulatory agencies doubled and the number of employees involved in regulation increased from 58,455 to 105,000. In 1974 alone, Congress passed 404 laws and the federal bureaus issued 7,496 new or amended regulations. A host of these either regulate the practice or create public relations problems for clients and organizations. The fact that we live in a litigious society in which everyone is taking everyone else to court compounds the problem.

Morton Simon, an authority on public relations law, thinks today's public climate is such that "increasingly dangerous public relations legal exposures" lie ahead. Thus, it is important that practitioners and students become versed in all aspects of the law that govern or relate to this practice. This chapter enumerates in broad, outline form the major areas of public relations law, but space doesn't permit exhaustive discussion or full coverage of legal requirements being imposed on practitioners in increasing number and complexity.[1]

Public relations and the first amendment

Public relations campaigns waged in the economic or political interest of one group against another are protected by the Constitution even though such campaigns may exceed ethical bounds or cause economic damage. Freedom to engage in "no-holds-barred" campaigns to influence government or the marketplace is generally ensured under the protection of the First Amendment, which provides that Congress shall make no law abridging freedom of speech or the right "to petition the Government for a redress of grievances." The right of free speech and the right of petition, although not identical, are inseparable. Both are protected against state action by the Fourteenth Amendment. However, these rights are not absolute and must be exercised in the public interest. In *American Communications Association* v. *Douds,* 339 U.S. 382, 399 (1949), the Supreme Court said:

> When particular conduct is regulated in the interest of public order, and the regulation results in an indirect, conditional, partial abridgement of speech, the duty of the courts is to determine which of these two conflicting interests demands the greater protection under the particular circumstances.

A bitter public relations battle between the trucking industry and the railroads culminated in a lengthy legal battle, which established the practitioner's right to plead a client's case in the court of public opinion, however unethical such pleading might be. In what *Fortune* termed "The Railroad–Truckers Brawl,"[2] both parties used dubious and dishonest means to sway public opinion. The railroads had hired Carl Byoir & Associates in August 1949. The truckers' association engaged Allied Public Relations Associates, another New York agency, to present the truckers' case. The battle was on.

The legal conflict opened in 1953, when 41 interstate long-haul trucking firms and their trade association, the Pennsylvania Motor Truck Association, brought suit against 35 eastern railroads, the Eastern Railroad Presidents Conference, and Carl Byoir & Associates. The truckers charged the defendants with conspiring by means of a publicity-lobbying campaign to prevent the Pennsylvania legislature and governor from adopting legislation favorable to the truckers. The truckers also alleged that efforts were made to damage their relations with the truckers' customers. The plaintiffs argued that these acts had violated the Sherman Anti-Trust Act. The suit had been triggered when a disgruntled Byoir secretary took the railroad account files to the truckers; these files laid bare a series of unethical "third-party" techniques.

The trial in the U.S. District Court for Eastern Pennsylvania lasted a year. In October 1957, Judge Thomas J. Clary ruled in favor of the truckers. (*Noerr Motor Freight, Inc. et al.* v. *Eastern Railroad Presidents Conference et al.,* 155 F. Supp. 768–841 [E.D.Pa. 1957].[3] The Byoir firm and the railroads appealed to the U.S. Court of Appeals, which upheld Judge Clary's finding in a 2–1 decision in 1959. (273 F. 2d 218 [3d Cir. 1959]). Judge Wallace Biggs dissented.

Encouraged by Bigg's dissent, Byoir and the railroads carried their case to the U.S. Supreme Court. They contended that a campaign aimed at influencing public opinion—no matter how untruthful—could not constitute a violation of the Sherman Anti-Trust Act. Moreover, they held that Judge Clary's enjoinment of them from further public relations activity stood as an infringement of their right of free speech. The Supreme Court agreed and reversed the decision of the lower court in a unanimous opinion, handed down February 20, 1961 (365 U.S. 127 [1961]). Justice Hugo Black wrote the opinion, which said in part:

> In doing so, we have restored what appears to be the true nature of the case—a "no-holds-barred fight" between two industries, both of which are seeking control of

a profitable source of income. Inherent in such fights, which are commonplace in the halls of legislative bodies, is the possibility, and in many instances even the probability, that one group or the other will get hurt by the arguments that are made. In this particular instance, each group appears to have utilized all the political powers it could muster in an attempt to bring about the passage of laws that would help it or injure the other. But the contest itself appears to have been conducted along lines normally accepted in our political system, except to the extent that each group has deliberately deceived the public and public officials. And that deception, reprehensible as it is, can be of no consequence so far as the Sherman Act is concerned.

The Court's unanimous opinion "was a rather resounding affirmation of a legal right which has almost never been involved in litigation, the right of petition." A noted authority on constitutional law further notes "that the right of people to associate together in order to make their activities effective" was closely allied in this case.[4]

The legal right of a public relations practitioner to plead a cause was thus determined, but, like all rights under the Constitution, it is not absolute. In the *Noerr–Railroads* decision, the Supreme Court warned (365 U.S. 127, 144 [1961]):

> There may be situations in which a publicity campaign, ostensibly directed toward influencing governmental action, is a mere sham to cover what is actually nothing more than an attempt to interfere directly with the business relationships of a competitor and the application of the Sherman Act would be justified.

Therefore, even though an organization has the *right* to petition and to publicize, this does not mean organizations are protected from the application of antitrust laws if, in fact, the First Amendment guarantees are used to obtain an illegal monopoly. A weighing and balancing of these interests will depend on an evaluation of the damaging activities and an interpretation of their intent. The contrary decisions of the district court and the Supreme Court in the truckers–railroads case, the continuing debate on interpretations of the First Amendment and the antitrust laws, and the availability of compensatory damages for persons injured through private antitrust litigations suggest that there may be future tests of the *Noerr* doctrine.[5]

Advertising also protected

Reversing a Federal court decision dating back to 1942, *Valentine* v. *Chrestensen* (122 F.2d 511 [2nd Cir., 1941]), the Supreme Court in 1975 and 1976 decisions brought paid advertising under the protection of the First Amendment to a qualified degree. In *Valentine,* the Court had upheld an ordinance forbidding distribution of advertising handbills. In 1975, in *Bigelow* v. *Virginia* (421 U.S. 809 [1975]), the notion of unprotected "commercial speech" all but passed from the scene. The high court reversed a conviction for violation of a Virginia statute that made circulation of any publication to encourage or promote the processing of an abortion in Virginia a misdemeanor. In *Bigelow,* the court rejected the contention that the publication was unprotected because it was "commercial."

This doctrine was expanded a year later in *Virginia State Board of Pharmacy et al., Appellants,* v. *Virginia Citizens Consumer Council, Inc., et al.* (425 U.S. 748 [1976]), when the Supreme Cout ruled that a Virginia law prohibiting pharmacies from advertising prescription drug prices was unconstitutional. Justice Harry Blackmun, in the majority opinion, held that a state cannot completely suppress the dissemination of concededly truthful information about entirely lawful activity even though it may be "fearful of that information's effect upon its disseminators and its recipients." In concluding that commercial speech, like other varieties, was protected, the Court did hold that paid advertising could be regulated in other ways. Justice Blackmun wrote:

> We have often approved restrictions of that kind provided they are justified without reference to the content of the regulated speech, that they serve a significant governmental purpose, and that in so doing they leave open ample alternative channels for communication of the information.

He made clear that the First Amendment "does not prohibit the State from insuring that the stream of commercial information flows cleanly as well as freely." Justice Potter Stewart, in a concurring opinion, added that there are many cases holding that the First Amendment does not provide absolute protection for false statements that cause private injury. This decision ended the never-never land created when a federal district court ruled in *Valentine* v. *Chrestensen* that "purely commercial advertising" was not protected by the First Amendment.

Even though advertising is now protected, the courts won't compel publication. For example, in *Chicago Joint Board, Amalgamated Clothing Workers of America, AFL-CIO* v. *Chicago Tribune Co.,* 307 F. Supp. 422 (N.D. Ill. [1969]), the plaintiffs sued to compel the four Chicago daily newspapers to publish advertisements giving the unions' objection to the sale of imported clothing by the Marshall Field department store. Federal Judge Abraham Marovitz granted the newspapers' motion for a summary judgment. The judge implied that if the right of access were to be recognized, it should be done legislatively, not judicially.

The U.S. Supreme Court in May 1977 issued two rulings in support of First Amendment protection of commercial speech. In an 8–0 decision, the Court struck down a New Jersey ordinance forbidding the display of "for sale" signs. The signs had been outlawed in an attempt to prevent "white flight" from the New Jersey suburb. The court ruled that the ban violated the right of the people to receive information about houses for sale, overriding other interests in promoting integrated neighborhoods.

The Supreme Court also let stand an appeals-court decision in the case of *FTC* v. *Beneficial Corp.* The FTC tried to stop Beneficial from using the sales line "instant tax refund" in promoting their tax-preparation service. The appeals court ruled that the FTC can impose prior restraint on protected commercial speech only to the extent necessary to avoid violations of valid laws.

Writing in the July/August 1977 *Columbia Journalism Review,* Prof. Richard A. Schwarzlose says:

> In *Virginia* the Court appears to be handing a weapon to those who wish to pry more out of the media. The decision says implicitly that if the sender is unwilling to produce the communication that the public wants or needs, the consumer or receiver has a right to demand that information. If citizens' groups and others take this possibility seriously, the news media may abruptly find themselves folding the old "right to know" umbrella.

Lobbying: the right of petition

Many practitioners engage in representation of clients or employers before federal and state legislative bodies or regulatory agencies—an activity commonly described as lobbying. This right "to petition the government" is protected by the First Amendment. When he was a U.S. senator, John F. Kennedy defined lobbying as "efforts by which various groups of individuals attempt to secure the passage or defeat of legislation."[6] Despite the impreciseness of the term, lobbying can be defined as efforts to influence government legislation or rule-making; it implies the presence of an intermediary between citizens and government decision makers. Lobbying relies on persuasive communication, which calls for the skills of a lawyer or a practitioner, or both. Coca-Cola's campaign against the government ban on saccharin, which it needs for its diet soft drinks, would be an example.

The U.S. government and most state governments have laws regulating this activity, including the requirement to register and to report lobbying expenditures. Lobbying in the federal government is currently regulated by provisions of Title III of the Legislative Reorganization Act of 1946, known as the Federal Regulation of Lobbying Act, Chap. 8A, 2 U.S. Code, sec. 261–270 (1970 ed.). Passage of this act represented the federal government's first official recognition of the lobbying function as an essential element in modern government. This law, which requires registration and quarterly reports of expenditures by lobbyists, has not been strictly enforced. In these reports, the lobbyist is supposed to list the amount and source of all income of $500 or more, and all expenditures of $10 or more. The law applies only to those whose "principal purpose" is lobbying, which leaves a large loophole through which many escape registration.

Three categories of people are exempt:

First, a person who merely appears before a committee of Congress in support of or in opposition to legislation.

Second, a public official acting in his official capacity.

Third, a newspaper or any regularly published periodical or a reporter employed by newspapers or periodicals.[7]

The laxness of this 1946 law was reflected 30 years later when the *Washington Post* estimated that of the 10,000 lobbyists roaming the corridors of power along the Potomac, fewer than 2,000 were likely to be registered. With such a weak law, the public and members of Congress are unable to learn the full dimensions of lobbying and find out who has invested how much money in various campaigns to affect the public policy.

Efforts to tighten controls on lobbying and to require disclosure of more information on lobbying activities and expenditures failed in Congress in 1976. A "Public Disclosure of Lobbying Act," passed by both the House and Senate, died in conference committee in the waning hours of the Congress—killed by the lobbying of lobbyists, including public relations practitioners. This legislation would have required organizations to register and report as lobbyists if they (1) spend $1,250 in any quarterly period to retain outside persons or firms to make oral or written lobbying communications on their behalf, or (2) employ one person who spends 20 percent of his time engaged in lobbying.

Self-government is based on the philosophy of open, robust debate in a free marketplace of ideas. This concept was first enunciated in 1644, by John Milton in *Areopagitica:* "Let her [Truth] and Falsehood grapple; who ever knew Truth put to the worse, in a free and open encounter?" A contemporary statement of this democratic faith is found in Justice William O. Douglas's dissent in *Dennis* v. *United States,* 341 U.S. 494, 584 (1951): "When ideas compete in the market for acceptance, full and free discussion exposes the false and they gain few adherents. Full and free discussion keeps a society from becoming stagnant and unprepared for the stresses and strains that work to tear all civilization apart." The practitioner plays an important if unseen role in public debate. He or she has the responsibility of making certain that the ideas, information, or cause of every individual, industry, or institution are heard in the public arena. In a day of mass communication, this requires access to the nation's news media.

The print media

Our traditional constitutional protection of freedom of the press has served thus far to block a definition of a legal right of access to the print media for any cause, idea, or spokesman. An advocate of laws requiring newspapers and magazines to grant access to all points of view, Prof. Jerome Barron, writes, "There is inequality in the power to communicate ideas just as there is inequality in economic bargaining power. . . . The 'marketplace of ideas' has rested on the assumption that protecting the right of expression is equivalent to providing for it. But changes in the communication industry have destroyed the equilibrium in that marketplace. . . . A realistic view of the First Amendment requires recognition that a right of expression is somewhat thin if it can be exercised only at the suffrance of the managers of mass communications."[8] As the law stands, print-media gatekeepers are free to reject news, letters, or advertising as they see fit. The thrust of court decisions has been that a newspaper or magazine is not a public utility and thus has full freedom to reject what it chooses. Only one case, *Uhlman* v. *Sherman* (22 Ohio N.P. [n.s.] 225, [C.P. 1919]), has recognized the right of access. In this case, an Ohio lower court held that the dependence and interest of the public in the community's only newspaper imposed the reasonable demand that the purchase of advertising be open to members of the public on an equal basis. Other actions to compel newspapers to accept advertising offered to them have repeatedly failed.[9]

The right-to-advertise forces have won considerable support in recent years, although not specifically against privately owned publications. In the past few years, courts, departing from a long tradition of depriving advertising of First Amendment protection, have upheld the right of political candidates to advertise in such public places as buses, subway platforms, and the like; struck down state bans on the advertising of abortion referral services and lawyers' services; ruled that public high schools and college newspapers cannot reject advertising for causes they dislike; and recognized that the public has a right to receive the often valuable information and views that ads contain.

In 1913, Florida enacted a statute that gave the right of reply to any candidate for public office whose personal character was assailed by a publication. This law went untested until 1972, when the *Miami Herald* published an editorial calling a candidate for the state legislature a "czar" and a lawbreaker. The candidate, who had led a teachers' strike in Miami in 1968, sought to reply. The *Herald* refused his reply, and he filed suit. The Dade County Circuit Court held the right-to-reply statute unconstitutional, but the Florida Supreme Court, in a 6–1 decision, reversed the lower court. The *Herald,* with wide newspaper support, appealed the decision to the U.S. Supreme Court, which held in 1974 that the Florida law was unconstitutional and an abridgement of freedom of the press. In a unanimous opinion, written by Chief Justice Burger, the Court rejected as a right public access to newspapers. The supremacy of the editor's authority to edit was affirmed. Chief Justice Burger wrote (*Miami Herald Publishing Co.* v. *Tornillo*), "A responsible press is an undoubtedly desirable goal, but press responsibility is not mandated by the Constitution, and like many other virtues, cannot be legislated" (418 U.S. 241, 256 [1974]).

The broadcast media

The fairness doctrine: The right of public access to the broadcast media has stronger legal support than that to the print media. From its inception some 60 years ago, broadcasting has required government regulation to ensure the clarity of each broadcast channel over the nation's airwaves. Over the years, the fairness concept in broadcasting and the idea that radio and TV stations use a publicly owned resource evolved into a collection of decisions and policies first announced by the Federal Communications Commission in 1949 as the "Fairness Doctrine." Since then, this doctrine has been expanded and further defined, and has become an increasingly important consideration for broadcasters and those seeking access to these media. The doctrine as it stands says that broadcasters, unlike the print media, have an affirmative obligation to afford reasonable opportunity for presentation of contrasting viewpoints on any controversial issue covered, including advertising. Although broadcasters are encouraged to do so, they are not required to editorialize or permit use of their facilities for presentation of views on controversial topics. But if they do, the doctrine requires that contrasting views be presented. The "Fairness Doctrine" has importance for the practitioner.

First enunciated in the FCC's *Report to the Commission in the Matter of Editorializing by Broadcast Licensees,* 13 FCC 1246 (1949), the doctrine was codified into law in 1959 with an amendment to Section 315 of the Communication Act of 1934, which requires broadcast stations "to operate in the public interest and to afford reasonable opportunity for the discussion of conflicting views on issues of public importance." This new policy, imposed by Congress as "a restatement of the basic policy of the 'standard of fairness,'" reversed the FCC's stand against broadcast editorials announced in the *Mayflower* case (8 F.C.C. 333 [1941]), when the regulatory body, in a license hearing, held that "the broadcaster cannot be an advocate" and that a licensee has "the obligation of presenting all sides of important public questions fairly, objectively, and without bias." The *Mayflower* ruling was reversed in 1949, and in 1959 a new provision was added to Section 315 that upheld the right of broadcasters to editorialize, provided that they gave time to opposing views.

The "Fairness Doctrine" got its first constitutional test in the mid-1960s, when author Fred J. Cook brought action against the Red Lion Broadcasting Company, Red Lion, Pennsylvania, after the station refused Cook the opportunity to reply to a personal attack on him by the Reverend Billy James Hargis. When the FCC ruled against the broadcaster, Cook took the issue to the Supreme Court in

1969 with the charge that the law was vague, imprecise, and unconstitutional. The Supreme Court upheld the FCC and ruled against the broadcaster (395 U.S. 367, 390 [1969]). Justice Byron White, in the majority opinion, wrote, "It is the purpose of the First Amendment to preserve an uninhibited marketplace of ideas in which truth will ultimately prevail."

Counteradvertising: In 1967, the FCC ruled that cigarette advertising must be countered with antismoking advertising because smoking, with its inherent dangers to health, was an issue of public importance. In December 1966, John W. Banzhaf III, an attorney, had asked WCBS-TV in New York for time to reply to cigarette commercials. WCBS-TV rejected the proposal, and he took his case to the FCC, which ruled that the licensee's obligation to operate in the public interest includes "the duty to make a fair presentation of opposing viewpoints on the controversial issue . . . posed by cigarette advertising" (WCBS-TV, 8 FCC 2d 381 [1967]). The U.S. Court of Appeals ultimately sustained the FCC's decision ordering reply time to cigarette commercials, in *Banzhaf* v. *FCC* (405 F.2d 1082 [D.C. Cir. 1968]). This resulted in the first countercommercials, the American Cancer Society spots against smoking. In April 1970, Congress went a step further and banned all cigarette advertising over the broadcast media after January 1, 1971, a step viewed with concern by civil libertarians (15 U.S.C.A. 1335).

The *Banzhaf* case set loose a series of challenges from interest groups engaged in public opinion battles. In the *WREO* case, *Retail Store Employees Union, Local 880 Retail Clerks International Ass'n, AFL-CIO* v. *Federal Communications Commission* (436 F.2d 248 [D.C. Cir. 1970]), the U.S. Court of Appeals held that a radio station could not carry the ads of one side of a labor dispute while refusing to sell ads to the other which would enable it to explain its side of the controversy.

Although the FCC had made clear that it considered the cigarette decision "unique," the exception in time became the rule. In March 1970, Friends of the Earth (FOE), an environmental group, asked the FCC to rule that auto and oil company ads implicitly presented one side of a controversial issue—pollution. The FCC rejected FOE's arguement, and concluded that it was not in the public interest to restrict such advertising. But the District of Columbia Court of Appeals found that *Banzhaf* and *FOE* were indistinguishable (449 F. 2d 1164 [D.C. Cir. 1971]). Next, the FCC rejected a demand for counteradvertising to ads promoting a new gasoline additive, but then a few months later (30 F.C.C. 2d 643 [1971]), sustained a fairness complaint concerning Esso advertising, which asserted that the Alaska pipeline would not damage Alaska's ecology. The commission said the advertising inherently raised the controversial issue of the effects of oil exploration on the ecology; however, the FCC took no action because the NBC TV network was providing opportunity for opposing viewpoints to be heard.

Another example: The Texaco Company, seeking to reach the influential Washington, D.C. audience, took to WTOP-TV, the capital's top-rated station, a proposed series of institutional ads opposing divestiture. WTOP required some revision in the storyboards, then aired the Texaco commercials. Quickly the Energy Action Committee, a consumer-interest group, protested the antidivestiture ads, claiming that they dealt with a "controversial issue of public importance." The committee filed a complaint with the FCC, which ruled that the Fairness Doctrine required WTOP-TV to allow time for presentations that favor divestiture of oil-company holdings.

These challenges have led broadcast stations to closely monitor advertising that may involve "controversial opinions." In 1974, in the midst of the Arab oil embargo, the Mobil Oil Company found it couldn't "get on the air with what it wanted to say" when the three TV networks refused to air several Mobil prime-time commercials. ABC turned down the commercials because they dealt with "controversial opinions." The CBS Broadcast Group upheld the oil companies' right to air time if their messages were "capable of substantiation and not the subject of specific public controversy."[10] Mobil even agreed to buy time for opponents to express their opposing viewpoints, an offer that was rejected by broadcasters. In this same period, the three networks had rejected a Phillips Petroleum Company commercial extolling the free-enterprise system because it was "controversial."

In May 1976, the FCC issued what amounted to a 42-page primer on the Fairness Doctrine and its application to commercials that editorialize on one side of controversial issues of public importance. Responding to charges of environmental groups that Pacific Gas & Electric spots promoting the building of nuclear power plants required presentation of the opposite point of view, the FCC directed eight radio stations to report in ten days on how they intended to meet their fairness obligation. In this decision, the commission held that "an imbalance in the presentation of contrasting views would be reflected in the total amount of time afforded each side, the frequency with which each side is presented, and the size of the listening audience, or a combination of these factors."[11]

The right of broadcasters to voluntarily control program content was thrown into legal doubt that same year when U.S. Federal Judge Warren J. Ferguson ruled that an agreement to limit program content to that suitable for families between the hours of 7 and 9 P.M. violated the right of free speech. The action had been brought by guilds representing writers, producers, directors, and actors, which had filed two suits to block the family-viewing plan. Judge Ferguson said, "The plaintiffs have exposed a joint agreement on the part of three major networks, the FCC, and the National Association of Broadcasters to permit one group—the NAB television code review board—to act as a national board of censors for American television."[12]

Although the FCC has expanded its application of the Fairness Doctrine to advertising, it has generally held the line in restricting the doctrine's application to news coverage, with some disturbing exceptions. Many such demands have been brought to the FCC in recent years, but in most cases the commission upheld the broadcasters. In 1976, the FCC ruled that a Clarksburg, West Virginia, station must carry news on the issue of coal strip-mining or risk loss of its license. This decree clearly raised the issue of freedom for broadcast journalism in contrast with the freedom granted print journalism. Another exception was when a Seattle TV station was denounced for devoting more coverage to one side of school-levy issue than to the other (23 F.C.C. 2d 41 [1970]). In a highly controversial case, the FCC upheld in December 1973 a staff ruling that an NBC TV documentary about pensions gave views advocating one side of a controversial issue. The commission ordered NBC to submit a statement on how it intended to meet its fairness obligations arising out of the documentary. NBC went to court, and the U.S. Court of Appeals in Washington overturned the FCC ruling, 2–1, in September 1974. Subsequently, the FCC vacated its ruling, and then the court vacated its ruling. Accuracy in Media, which brought the suit, and NBC both objected to the case's being declared moot.[13]

The courts' contradictory rulings in the *Retail Clerks* case and in *Chicago Joint Board* v. *Chicago Tribune Co.,* in which issues were virtually identical, suggests the uneven treatment accorded the print and broadcast media. Justice Douglas, in an opinion in the case of *CBS* v. *Democratic National Committee,* pointed this out: "I fail to see how constitutionally we can treat TV and the radio differently than we do newspapers. . . . The Fairness Doctrine has no place in our First Amendment regime." In that suit (412 U.S. 94 [1973]), the Democratic National Committee sought unsuccessfully to make CBS sell it time for fund-raising appeals.

Broadcaster decisons, court rulings, and FCC decisions involving the Fairness Doctrine are increasing in number each year, suggesting that the requirement to carry countermessages may one day encompass virtually all issues in public debate. The doctrine itself is under increasing attack. Sen. William Proxmire has proposed legislation to repeal it to "extend First Amendment protection to broadcasters equal to their print counterparts." The Fairness Doctrine poses opportunities—and problems—for the practitioner.

Access to government information

The Freedom of Information Act, first enacted in the mid-1960s as an amendment to the Administrative Procedure Act of 1946 and greatly strengthened in the mid-1970s, is intended to open access to information held in the files of the federal government. This act is of importance to government and corporate practitioners and has far-ranging consequences for citizens and institutions alike.

Responding to persistent demands of the news media, Congress in 1966 amended Section 3 of the Administrative Procedure Act of 1946, 5 U.S.C.A. 1002, to include the Freedom of Information Act, 5 U.S.C.A. 552. The bill, signed into law July 4, 1966, became effective one year later. The 1946 measure had required that federal agencies must publish in the *Federal Register* or make available for public inspection material such as opinions, orders, or policy statements. The fatal weakness of that law was that it gave bureaucrats the power to withhold material requiring secrecy in the public interest, a very elastic loophole. The act of 1966 worked only moderately well in opening public access to information sought by the public. Many loopholes in its enforcement were developed by bureaucrats and by the courts.

Because of the time delays bureaucrats could impose, the news media made relatively little use of the law. Most of the actions brought under the 1966 law were brought by corporations, interest groups, or private citizens. In the view of a *Wall Street Journal* reporter, "The nature of the business does not ordinarily allow the reporter . . . to wait around for weeks or months for a court which may, or may not, require an agency to hand over its files. . . ." For example, in *Consumers Union* v. *Veterans Administration* (301 F. Supp. 796 [1969]), the VA's tests and ratings of hearing aids produced by several manufacturers were sought, and a long legal battle ensued. The case was ultimately dismissed as moot when the VA revised its procedures to permit disclosure of this information. Despite the provision in the Freedom of Information Act that confidential business data collected by the government will not be made public, courts can order federal agencies to produce some secret reports. This was done in *Consolidated Box Co.* v. *U.S. Court of Claims* in 1974. In this case, the judge let a government contractor see the sales, costs, and profit figures filed by two competitors. The contractor was engaged in a dispute with the Federal Renegotiation Board.

Commissioner Alexander M. Schmidt of the Food and Drug Aministration estimated in 1976 that about 90 percent of the requests for disclosure of documents support "industrial espionage—companies seeking information about their competitors—and not the public's right to know." Defenders of the act say businessmen are as entitled to use its provisions as any other citizen, corporate or individual. Business's use of the act, particularly in the Food and Drug Administration, has led to the development of small firms that monitor such requests. For example, Freedom of Information Services, Inc., Rockville, Maryland, monitors such requests at the FDA and offers a weekly index listing of requests.

The weakness of the 1966 act was revealed in *Environmental Protection Agency* v. *Mink* (410 U.S. 73, 74 [1973]), when the U.S. Supreme Court ruled that the government could claim exemption from provisions of the law "for matter specifically required by Executive order to be kept secret in the interest of the national defense or foreign policy."

Stung by the implications of the *Mink* decision and general dissatisfaction with the law on the part of journalists and consumer groups, Congress in 1974 enacted, over a presidential veto, 17 amendments designed to strengthen the act and to compel federal agencies to disclose information promptly without charging excessive costs for the service. For example, Section 552(a)(4)(B) guarantees the right of a citizen to seek judicial review of the propriety of classification that has been cited by the agency as the basis for denial of access to records. The wording is cautious and is no absolute guarantee that an independent judge will actually examine documents *in camera* "to determine whether such records or any part thereof shall be withheld." The amendments were designed to make it easier, quicker, and less costly to get government information; for example, one amendment set a strict timetable for the government's response to such a request. All in all, the 1974 act fairly balances the people's right to know and the government's obligation to protect defense and commercial secrets and criminal prosecution. The revised act became effective February 19, 1975.[14]

How to use the act

The act states that any "person" may make a request under the act without offering any reason or explanation for the request. The person or corporation seeking information must be able to "reasonably describe" the information sought but is not required to know a specific document or docket number. (A typical form request letter is shown in Exhibit 12–1, and an appeal letter in Exhibit 12–2.) Government information officers are usually involved in these requests, and a punitive provision declares that an "arbitrary" or "capricious" denial of information sought under the FoI Act can subject the government employee to administrative penalites, including the loss of salary for 60 days, by the Civil Service Commission.

The new act sets reasonable search fees, and agencies are required to establish search-fee schedules. The same applies to charges for reproducing documents. If a person or institution's request is denied by the secretary or the head of the agency, commission, or department, or if it is not answered within 20 working days, the requestor can file a Freedom of Information lawsuit in the most convenient U.S. district court. The FoI Act provides that such suits must be given "expedited" treatment.

EXHIBIT 12–1   Form request letter.

Agency name   Return Address
Address   Date

Dear

   I hereby request personal access to (a copy of—describe the document,
report, or information sought as specifically as you can)—under 5 U.S.C. 552 et
seq., The Freedom of Information Act.
   If you agree to this request in whole or in part, please inform me of the search
fees and the reproduction fees in advance of fulfilling the request (or please
supply me with the information if the search and copy fees do not exceed a total
of $).
   If any part of this request is denied, please inform me of your appeal
procedures. I will consider my request denied if I have no communication from
you within 10 working days of receipt of this letter.
   Please be put on notice that I consider this information clearly releasable
under the Freedom of Information Act and that I consider your refusal to release
the information to be arbitrary and capricious as defined in the Act.
   Thanking you for your kind attention, I remain,

                                                                         (signature)

EXHIBIT 12–2   Form appeal letter.

Head of Government department,   Return address
commission or agency   Date

My dear Mr. Secretary:

   On (date), I sent a letter requesting access to (use the same description of
the information sought as in your request letter) under 5 U.S.C. 552, The
Freedom of Information Act.
   On (date), I received a letter from (name, title, address) denying my request.
   I hereby appeal that denial and if I do not hear from you within 20 working
days, I will consider my appeal denied.
   I consider the information requested clearly releasable under the Freedom of
Information Act and I hereby inform you that I would consider your denial to be
clearly arbitrary and capricious as defined by the Act.
   Enclosed please find a copy of my original request and the response, and I
remain,

                                                                         Sincerely,

                                                                         (signature)

Employee communications

Communicators who work for union employers must be mindful of the Taft-Hartley Act's provisions relating to communications directed to employees. The basic law that may apply to employee communications related to collective bargaining is Section 8(c) of the Labor Management Relations (Taft-Hartley) Act:

> The expressing of any view, argument, or opinion or the dissemination thereof, whether in written, printed graphic or visual form, shall not constitute or be evidence of an unfair labor practice under any of the provisions of this Act, if such expression contains no threat of reprisal or force or promise of benefit.

The last clause is the key one—"no threat" or "promise of benefit." Although the law in this area is far from definitive, administrative rulings and judicial decisions have made it clear that for employee communications to constitute an unfair labor practice, these communications must be judged in the "totality of conduct" of the employer toward his employees. The determination of permissible boundaries of employer antiunion expression poses a vexing legal question. The trend since the enactment of the National Labor Relations Act of 1935 (the Wagner Act) had been in the direction of enlarging the area within which the employer was legally free to express himself against the union, until the *General Electric* case, which was finally adjudicated in 1970.

The Wagner Act prohibited an employer from making antiunion statements and required strict neutrality in communications to employees that involved organization of employees or collective bargaining. In 1941, the U.S. Supreme Court struck down this ban in *NLRB* v. *Virginia Electric* (314 U.S. 469, 477 [1941]), by holding that neither "the [Wagner] Act nor the Board's order enjoins the employer from expressing its view on labor policies. . . . The sanctions of the Act are imposed not in punishment of the employer but for the protection of the employees. . . . The employer in this case is as free as ever to take any side it may choose on this conroversial issue."

Nonetheless, Justice Murphy's opinion warned employers, "If the total activities of an employer restrain or coerce employees in their free choice, then those employees are entitled to the protection of the Act." The Supreme Court was saying, in effect, that pressure exerted through employee communications, coupled with pressure exerted by intentional circumvention of traditional bargaining, might combine to erase the freedom allowed in the earlier part of the opinion.

This Supreme Court decision was, in effect, codified into law with the passage of the Taft-Hartley Act of 1947, including the "totality of circumstances" hedge on employer expression.[15] The conference committee on this legislation stated that the purpose of Section 8(c) was "to protect the right of free speech when what the employer says or writes is not of a threatening nature or does not promise a prohibited favorable discrimination."[16]

The landmark case for employee communicators is the *GE* case, which is instructive if not definitive. On the heels of an ineffective three-week strike against the General Electric Company in October 1960, the International Union of Electrical, Radio and Machine Workers (IUE) filed charges of unfair labor practices against GE with the National Labor Relations Board. The IUE had filed similar charges of unfair bargaining against General Electric in 1951, 1954, and 1958 negotiations, but the NLRB had rejected them as being without merit. A long legal battle was set in motion in February 1961, when the general counsel for the NLRB issued a complaint based on the 1960 charges and the issue went to a hearing. The final decision came a decade later. This is the background:

From 1947 on, for some 20 years, General Electric had followed a firm policy *vis-à-vis* its unions, backing up this hard-line policy with an intensive program of employee communications. The program was formulated largely by Lemuel R. Boulware after he took charge of GE's employee and community relations in 1947. He later brought public relations into his domain at GE and restructured his department as Relations Services. Union critics labeled his hard-bargaining, intensive-communications program "Boulwarism." ("Boulwarism" may have passed into labor and public relations history in 1973 when, in the bargaining of that year with GE, the unions did not raise the "Boulwarism" charge for the first time since the late 1940s.)[17]

Boulware's stated purposes for his hard-hitting employee relations/communications program were to (1) integrate and motivate the management team, (2) develop supervisors as leaders of their people, and (3) build employee confidence in management. An industrial relations writer identified "Boulwarism" by these characteristics:

1. Management has a tendency to bypass the union and communicate directly with its employees on day-to-day problems.
2. Management attempts to win its employees' allegiance in competition with the union by convincing them that it is sincerely interested in their welfare and is doing its best to promote it.
3. Management follows a policy of firmness in negotiating with the union; for example, giving out a statement of its best and final offer with a deadline for acceptance and a warning that there will be no retroactivity for any later settlement.
4. Management communicates its offers directly to its workers and the public, independently of the union.[18]

It was the fourth practice that brought a citation for unfair labor practices from Trial Examiner Arthur Leff, who based his ruling on what lawyers call the "totality of conduct" doctrine. Leff found, in part:

> Note has . . . been made of the great mass of employee communications to which GE employees were subjected during the period following the IUE convention, as well as of the apparent purpose of the communications to impair employee faith and confidence in the motives of the IUE top leadership, to induce a form of vote more to the Company's liking, and to impress upon employees the finality of the Company's position and the futility of strike action. . . .
>
> During the same period, the Company in its communications continued to plug hard on the merits of the company offer. The communications did not always confine themselves to arguments that had been presented to union negotiators. In some instances the Company elaborated its arguments far more fully to employees than it had at the bargaining table. In some others, the Company presented arguments to employees that it had not presented at all to the union negotiators. . . .[19]

The NLRB ruled on December 16, 1964, that GE had "failed to bargain in good faith" with its union. In a 4-1 vote, the board "cited both major facets of the company's 1960 bargaining technique—an intensive communications campaign among the employees before and during negotiations to disparage and discredit the IUE as bargaining representative, and adamant insistence at the bargaining table on GE's 'fair and firm' contract proposal."[20] General Electric appealed the decision to the U.S. Court of Appeals for the Second Circuit, where the case was heard June 3, 1969, and decided October 28, 1969. The court, in a 2-1 decision, upheld the NLRB's findings.

In the majority opinion, Judge Kaufman held (418 F 2d 736 [2nd Cir. 1969]), "that an employer may not so combine 'take-it-or-leave-it' bargaining methods with a widely publicized stance of unbending firmness that he is himself unable to alter a position once taken. It is this specific conduct that GE must avoid in order to comply with the Board's order."

In a concurring opinion, Judge Waterman elaborated, "What makes these practices unfair is GE's 'widely publicized stance of unbending firmness,' that is, GE's communications to its employees that firmness was one of the company's independent policies. Two distinct evils derive from such publicity. First, publicity regarding firmness tends to make the company seal itself into its original position in such a way that, even if it wished to change that position at a later date, its pride and reputation for truthfulness are so at stake that it cannot do so. Second, publicity regarding firmness fixes in the minds of employees the idea that the company has set itself up as their representative and therefore that the union is superfluous."

In January 1970, GE appealed the decision to the U.S. Supreme Court, which in April 1970 in effect upheld the court of appeals decision by denying GE certiorari to the case (396 U.S. 1005, [1970]). In closing the book on this case, the Supreme Court let stand judicial endorsement of the 1964 NLRB decision that restricts to some undetermined degree the employer's freedom of communication. In the eyes of a GE public relations official, the Supreme Court's ruling put "the right of a business to communicate to its employee" in "serious jeopardy." Herbert Northrup asserts, in the *Harvard Business Review:*

> In a very real sense, therefore, what is at stake in the GE case is not only the right of a company to communicate, it is also the right of employees to evaluate the views of both management and union officials before making decisions which affect not only their livelihoods but also those of many others in the community.[21]

This complaint was also made by Judge Friendly of the Second Circuit in his dissenting opinion (418 F. 2d 773 [1969]): "In view of the general obscurity of what GE is and is not permitted to do, the Company could take little comfort from the majority's assurance that it will be given a full opportunity to show it has made a good faith effort at compliance before it is held in contempt." Despite its duration of ten years and some 13,000 pages of testimony, the GE case fell short of providing a clear mandate for employer communications practices. Although the case dealt with collective bargaining, its relevance for industrial communicators is underscored by such judicial comments as that GE's bargaining approach "would be utterly inexplicable without the background of its publicity program. . . ."

There are a few other cases that provide guidance. One is the *Procter & Gamble* case, which involved a long stalemate between P&G and its union. P&G, a pioneer in employee communications and employee benefits, relied heavily on its communications to employees in this bargaining standoff of 28 months. The significance of the difference in bargaining tactics was made apparent in the NLRB's direct comparison, after its review, of the GE and P&G cases *vis-à-vis* use of employee communications:

> In the recent GE case . . . we were confronted with a communication campaign which, coupled with the employer's fixed position at the bargaining table, effectively excluded the Union from meaningful bargaining, and represented a patent attempt to bypass and undermine the Union as bargaining agent. The instant case is clearly distinguishable. . . . Respondent entered negotiations with a "sincere desire to resolve differences. . . ." [22]

In the *Stark Ceramics* case (155 NLRB Dec. 12, 58 [1965]), concerning a failure to bargain in good faith, the NLRB trial examiner made a quantitative distinction on employee communications, comparing Stark's distribution of six letters to employees with GE's "virtual avalanche" (418 F. 2d 736, 740).[23]

Another key case, one that went to the U.S. Supreme Court, centered on the thin line between employer prophecy and employer threat in the midst of a representation election. The Court upheld a bargaining order reversing a 7-6 election setback for the Teamsters union, and in a majority opinion written by Chief Justice Warren, a stalwart defender of freedom in communications, held in *Sinclair* v. *NLRB* (395 U.S. 575, 618 [1969]):

> Thus, an employer is free to communicate to his employees any of his general views about unionism or any of his specific views about a particular union, so long as the communications do not contain a "threat of reprisal or force or promise of benefit." He may even make a prediction as to the precise effects he believes unionization will have on his company. In such case, however, the prediction must be carefully phrased on the basis of objective fact. . . .

There has been some indication that the NLRB, influenced by court decisions and a change in political climate, has eased the position it took in the GE case. For example, the NLRB held in 1974 that an employer's showing of the film, *And Women Must Weep,* was neither a violation of the Taft-Hartley Act nor a sufficient basis for setting aside a representation election, even though the showing may have occurred in the context of other acts of unlawful interference (*Litho Press of San Antonio 2 11 NLRB,* Dec. 1014 [1974]). This overruled prior decisions to the contrary. The NLRB was undoubtedly influenced by a court of appeals disagreement with its ruling in *Southwire Co.* v. *NLRB,* 164 NLRB Dec. 1018 (1967).

These NLRB and court decisions provide working if not definitive guidelines for the communicator. The thrust of Section 8(c) is to protect the employer's freedom of communication and expression of views, argument, or opinion. Statements constitute an unfair labor practice if they contain the threat of reprisal or force, or promises of benefit. What constitutes such threat or promise will never be an easy question to resolve. Prof. Jack Barbash has said, "It is the configuration of factors—the interweaving of the words themselves, the form in which communicated, the quality of the union–management relationship, the character of the community—which determines whether there is promise of reward and threat of reprisal or not." Barbash holds that "the circumstances more than the words deserve the weight of consideration" in answering this thorny question.[24]

The whole issue raises many questions. One commentator notes, "One key issue is whether a company can take its case to its employees directly. If it cannot, then the whole structure of employee communication changes, for central to this problem is the question of a company's right to tell its workers where it stands on all issues affecting operations: working conditions, pay, profits, job security, management's position on a union's proposal."[25]

This legal pitfall in employee communications may trap the unwary public relations staff. That it continues to be a matter for caution was emphasized when the International Association of Machinists brought before the NLRB an unfair labor charge against the Lockheed Company in late 1977 for "circumventing union negotiators, failing to bargain in good faith and inducing members to cross picket lines and quit the union." Basis for the charge was Lockheed's mailing copies of a 108-page rejected contract offer directly to 8,500 strikers at the Lockheed-California division.

Beyond the law, communicators must remember one basic fact: Neither administration nor unions can sell a bad case with good communication. General Electric was quite correct in asserting that "the public increasingly and properly expects more maturity and responsibility on the part of both management and union representatives in collective bargaining."[26]

Financial reporting

Practice in the financial area is subject to legal regulations flowing from the Securities Act of 1933, the Securities Exchange Act of 1934, and the Investment Company Act of 1940. Rules set down by the Securities and Exchange Commission (SEC) to implement these acts have the force of law.

The Securities Act of 1933 stemmed from the stock-market crash in 1929. In essence, it required that a company publish a revealing prospectus about itself when it chooses to sell securities to the public. The Exchange Act of 1934 dealt with an aspect of the "conflict of interest" for a corporate official between his duty to fellow stockholders and his personal gain in benefitting through investment by personal possession of information not known to the public.

The SEC and the courts are taking increasing cognizance of the important role public relations plays in the financial market. In 1963, the SEC published a *Special Study of the Securities Market,* which took due note of the importance of corporate publicity:

> Informal corporate publicity is an important supplement to disclosures required by the securities acts. In order to keep shareholders, the investment community, and the general public continuously informed of corporate developments, it is desirable for issuers to disseminate publicity through the channels of news distribution as well as by other means. This fact has been recognized by the Commission, which has encouraged publicly held corporations to employ publicity and public relations for this purpose.[27]

The practitioner serving the publicly owned corporation must understand the laws and regulations that govern his work, because a legal misstep is easy—and costly. The PRSA Code requires that members engaged in financial relations "understand the rules and regulations of the SEC and the laws which it administers as well as the other laws, rules and regulations affecting financial public relations—and to act in accordance with their letter and spirit." [28] This applies to any practitioner.

The trend of SEC regulations is making corporate reporting requirements more complex and placing a heavier responsibility on the practitioner to make certain of the accuracy of information he disseminates. The SEC in recent years has been working toward a policy of "continuous disclosure." "This program has entailed both the development of new requirements for inclusions in registration statements for public offerings . . . and the periodic filings under the Exchange Act." [29] The basic guide is the SEC's Rule 10B-5, which specifically prohibits fraudulent and deceptive practices in connection with the purchase or sale of securities.

The SEC's suit against the management of the bankrupt Penn Central Railroad, filed in 1974, sought to extend responsibility for corporate misdeeds to anyone who was in a position to know what was going on and to do something about it, and didn't. In the *Penn Central* action, the SEC brought suit not only against the corporate officers, but against three outside directors, the company's auditors—Peat, Marwick, Mitchell & Co.—and a broker who had marketed Penn Central's commercial paper. In the *Pig 'n Whistle* case, the SEC held the public relations counsel liable for putting out incorrect information.

Securities offerings

The Securities Act restricts the use of publicity either before or in conjunction with a new securities offering. Issuance of publicity about or related to a new offering is governed by the filing and effective date of registration. Section 5 of the Securities Act was enacted to put an end to efforts to go beyond the carefully defined "offer" by the use of publicity or sales literature. The key case in understanding the restrictions on prefiling publicity is *SEC* v. *Arvida Corp.,* 169 F. Supp. 211 (1958). The organization of Arvida as a private corporation to sell land in Florida was announced in a news release on July 8, 1958. That September, another release was issued, announcing that certain brokerage firms had agreed to underwrite an Arvida common-stock issue. Wide publicity as to the company's plans and projects brought in more than $500,000 in "expressions of interest" to non-underwriter brokers. An SEC commissioner said:

> The release read like a letter distributor might send to a prospective customer to persuade him to invest in the enterprise. . . . [Furthermore] the information contained in this release and its manner of presentation were not recognizably consistent in many respects with the contents of the registration statement and prospectus subsequently filed with the Commission. [30]

The SEC brought proceedings against the two broker-dealers, and also sought an injunction against them, the company, and individual defendants. The district court denied the injunction, but the SEC appealed. While the appeal was pending but after the effective date of registration, a permanent injunction was entered by consent. Later, the SEC suspended the First Maine Corporation from the National Association of Securities Dealers for 20 days for distributing publicity before the filing and during the waiting period (*First Main Corp.,* SEC Sec. Ex. Act Rel. No. 5898 [1959]).

The *Texas Gulf Sulphur* case

Hard questions concerning public relations practice were raised under the provisions of Rule 10B-5, when Texas Gulf Sulphur et al. were charged with violation by the SEC in April 1965. In this litigation, the SEC charged that certain "insiders" traded on inside information concerning a promising ore discovery, and that persons privy to this information passed tips on to their friends.[31] *At the same time, the company itself issued a false and misleading press release relative to this ore discovery.*[32]

A U.S. district court ruled in the main favorably for the defendants. The SEC appealed. On August 13, 1968, the U.S. Court of Appeals for the Second Circuit found the defendants guilty of violating the disclosure laws, in *SEC* v. *Texas Gulf Sulphur Co.,* 401 F. 2d 833 (2d Cir. 1968), in a divided opinion. Four judges signed the majority statement, four partly to wholly concurred, and two dissented. On April 21, 1969, the U.S. Supreme Court let the ruling stand (394 U.S. 976 [1969]). Subsequently, another federal court ordered Texas Gulf Sulphur to reimburse some stockholders who had sold out after the firm had issued the press release minimizing the Canadian mineral find. In the latter case, the U.S. Supreme Court, on December 20, 1971, also denied without comment the company and the nine individual defendants a hearing.

Within a few days, Texas Gulf announced that it had agreed to settle the bulk of the private damage litigation brought by former stockholders, including a pending class action brought on behalf of those claiming they had sold TGS stock in reliance upon the April 12, 1964, press release. These damage suits were filed in a U.S. district court in Utah before Judge Willis W. Ritter in 1969, and in October of that year, the judge found against TGS in three of the four actions. These verdicts were upheld on appeal to the Tenth Circuit of the U.S. Court of Appeals (Fed. Sec. Law Reports No. 367 [1971]).

The same circuit, in a later case, decided that the decision in *SEC* v. *Texas Gulf Sulphur* (404 U.S. 1005 [1971]) had suggested that liability may be imposed upon a corporation that fails to make timely disclosure of material corporate information. In *Financial Industrial Fund, Inc.* v. *McDonnell Douglas Corporation* (474 F. 2d 514 [10th Cir. 1973]), the corporation was alleged to have failed to make timely disclosure of a decrease in earnings. The Tenth Circuit court held that liability could be imposed if the corporation "failed to issue the special earnings statement when sufficient information was available for an accurate release."

The key points in the *TGS* case were improper use of inside information and dissemination of an inaccurate news release. Both are of concern to the practitioner.

Inside information

In a book-length discussion of the *TGS* case, practitioner Kenneth G. Patrick wrote, "One of the subjects thrust into the spotlight by the Texas Gulf Sulphur case is 'insider trading' in securities—broadly, the use of information by those who have it against those who do not have it, presumably for financial gain."[33] In August 1968, the SEC brought action against Merrill Lynch, Pierce, Fenner and Smith, charging that the brokerage firm had used inside information to help some customers, but not others. Although denying the charges, Merrill Lynch settled with the SEC that November. This settlement involved censures and suspensions without pay for the employees who had been involved.[34] The settlement broke new legal ground regarding the obligations of insiders not to capitalize on privileged information in the stock market.

The same issue was raised when the SEC filed charges in June 1973 against Daniel E. Provost III, corporate director of communications for Liggett & Myers, Inc., asserting that he had given several securities analysts and financial institutions "nonpublic inside information" about a decline in the company's earnings before the figures were made public. On November 4, 1973, a federal court enjoined Liggett & Myers and Provost from disclosing inside information about the company in the future (S.D.N.Y. Oct. 24, 1973). In addition, Liggett & Myers agreed to adopt and enforce a written corporate policy designed to prevent the future disclosure of nonpublic corporate information by its employees.[35]

The SEC has put practitioners on notice that those handling news releases are considered "insiders." An insider is anyone who is deemed to have information not available to the general public.

Accuracy of information

In June 1966, on the heels of the *TGS* case, the SEC brought charges against Great American Industries, some of its officers, and others. The commission charged GAI with creating exaggerated impressions about the company's program to acquire mining claims in Arizona, California, and Colorado. In a federal court, Judge Sylvester Ryan denied the SEC's motion, holding that the news releases were not false (*SEC* v. *Great American Industries, Inc., et al.,* 259 F. Supp. 99 [D.C.S.N.Y. 1966]). The SEC appealed, and in December 1968, the Second Circuit of the Court of Appeals reversed the lower court and granted an injunction against GAI, although stating that the record was incomplete and disorganized (407 F. 2d 453 [1968]). In May 1969, the U.S. Supreme Court declined to rule on the legality of the SEC's rule forbidding issuance of news releases that may mislead the public. The high court, in effect, upheld the appeals court's ruling that the company's reports to the SEC said one thing, its news releases another.

In its effort to make all those involved responsible for continuous disclosure of accurate information that may affect public stock trading, the SEC reached the public relations counsel in 1971 when it charged violations of securities laws in the purchase and sale of stock in the Pig 'n Whistle Corporation of Chicago. In addition to the firm's principals, the suit also named as a defendant Pig 'n Whistle's former public relations counsel, the Financial Relations Board. In an affidavit filed as part of the action, the SEC alleged that the public relations firm had issued press releases and other materials that "contained false and misleading statements and omitted to state material fact."[36]

In the U.S. District Court for Northern Illinois, Eastern Division, the Financial Relations Board signed a consent decree on February 14, 1972, which included this provision:

> It is further ordered, adjudged and decreed that the defendant Financial Relations Board, Inc., shall within 30 days . . . establish procedures, reasonable in the circumstances, for selecting and accepting new clients, which . . . shall be designed (i) to prevent said defendant from accepting clients which would require said defendant to violate the federal securities laws in the performance of its services and (ii) to provide

said defendant, with respect to any client which is accepted, such information as will aid in preventing violations of the federal securities laws . . . in the performance of services for such client.[37]

Veteran practitioners see in the *Pig 'n Whistle* case the SEC's extension of the same standards it had long applied to lawyers, underwriters, and auditors working for corporate clients. This decree, which stands as governing law on this matter, requires that public relations counselors must take prudent caution to ascertain the accuracy of information given them for release by either a client or an employer. As a result of this case, an agency must disclose in its news releases that it is acting on behalf of an issuer. Richard S. Seltzer, former SEC special counsel, in writing about this case, observed, "The SEC apparently believes that fraudulent schemes initiated by corporate insiders may be facilitated by the action—or deliberate inaction—of outside professionals: the accountant who 'stretches' generally accepted accounting principles; the lawyer who is willing to 'overlook' material disclosures; and even the public relations practitioner who seeks to portray a convincing, but inaccurate, picture of corporate events."[38]

Many counselors, to protect themselves from damages arising out of issuance of false or misleading information on behalf of a client, have inserted protective provisions in their contracts with clients. This one is typical:

> You agree to indemnify and hold harmless from and against any and all losses, claims, damages, expenses or liabilities which Padilla and Speer, Inc. may incur based upon information, representations, reports or data furnished by you to the extent such material is furnished or prepared by or approved by you for use by Padilla and Speer, Inc.

Timely disclosure

The basis of federal securities regulations is disclosure of information. Dissemination of pertinent information must be *timely*—that is, must get information that could affect the price of stocks to all publics simultaneously and promptly.

Concurrent with the final stages of the *Texas Gulf Sulphur* case, the New York Stock Exchange expanded its policy concerning the adequate and timely disclosure of corporate information.[39] This policy defines corporate information as "that which might reasonably be expected to materially affect the market for securities." It stipulates that a corporation should "act promptly to dispel unfounded rumors which result in unusual market activity or price variations." It states that a company "should not give information to one inquirer that it would not give to another or willingly give to the press for publication." News on matters of corporate significance should be given national distribution by "one or more of the national news wire services." In case they do not carry the news, supplementary distribution is indicated. This has led to increased use of the paid publicity wires and the Dow Jones broad tape wire.

There are two basic areas of uncertainty confronting practitioners on this matter of disclosure: (1) definition of what is a material fact, and (2) the timing of stock transactions by insiders. Critics of the SEC claim that it has been shifting its definition of the standards to be applied in both these areas. Spokesmen for the SEC assert that the lack of specificity in the rules should be of no concern to the ethical practitioner. In any event, the practitioner must be fully alert to the need for timely disclosure and the financial reporting requirements as these are set down by the SEC and the various stock exchanges.[40]

Public relations advertising

The use of paid advertising in public relations has been somewhat circumscribed by the regulation of the U.S. Internal Revenue Service providing that costs of advertising designed to promote or defeat legislation or to influence public opinion on pending legislation are not tax-deductible business expenses. This holds even if the proposed legislation directly affects the advertiser's business, industry, or occupation. The IRS regulation permits no deduction from gross income for tax purposes of the cost of advertising designed to (1) influence members of a legislative body directly or indirectly, by urging or encouraging the public to contact such members for the purpose of proposing, supporting, or opposing legislation; or (2) influence the public to approve or reject a measure in a referendum, initiative, vote on a constitutional amendment, or similar procedure. The IRS regulation was upheld by the Supreme Court despite strong protests by the advertising media, advertising associations, and the Public Relations Society of America.[41]

In a ruling, the Federal Power Commission disallowed expenditures for institutional advertising by a private utility as a factor in fixing the rates of that company. Neither the IRS nor the Federal Power Commission, however, disallows deductions for goodwill advertising.

The issue of what constitutes tax-deductible advertising was momentarily blurred in Administrative Law Judge David I. Kraushaar's lengthy opinion reversing the Federal Communications Commission decision to break up the Bell System. In a 535-page opinion, Judge Kraushaar ruled that there is no reason to break up AT&T and its Bell System subsidiaries just because of its size. In the same opinion, Kraushaar did order that charitable contributions and certain advertising expenses be paid for out of earnings rather than as operating costs (*FCC* v. *AT&T*, Docket No. 19129, August 2, 1976).[42] But this point was overruled by the Federal Communications Commission on February 23, 1977, when a majority of four commissioners sided with AT&T. The chairman, Richard Wiley, dissented, and another commissioner wrote a separate opinion, concurring in part, dissenting in part. Commissioner Abbott Washburn, a former practitioner, wrote the majority opinion:

> We find no evidence on the record of this case to suggest that AT&T's expenditures for advertising during the 1972 test year were anything other than normal operating expenses related to the provision of interstate telephone service. Accordingly, we see no reason here to disturb our present treatment of these expenses for ratemaking purposes. As we view it, the appropriate test here is that announced in *West Ohio Gas Corp.* v. *Public Utilities Commission of Ohio,* 294 U.S. 64, 72 [1935], that "[w]ithin the limits of reason, advertising or development expenses to foster normal growth are legitimate charges upon income for rate purposes as for others." . . . [T]here is nothing in the record which suggests that the amount AT&T expended for advertising in 1972, representing 0.35 percent of total interstate expenses that year, could reasonably be described as excessive. . . .[43]

Thus the FCC reaffirmed the right of a regulated utility to charge against customers reasonable advertising expenses for both sales and institutional advertisements. The FCC said, in effect, that (at least, in the view of four out of seven commissioners) AT&T had the right to communicate with customers in an effort to build goodwill and for other persuasive reasons besides simply increasing revenue. The FCC could reverse itself in the future, of course.

Utility expenditures for public relations advertising and philanthropic gifts have also come under attack in several state regulatory commissions in this era of consumerism. An example is the order of the New York Public Service Commission, passed in 1973 in the wake of the oil crisis, prohibiting the use of bill inserts to promote the company's position on controversial issues and barring any communication with customers to encourage the use of electric heat. Utility companies challenged this regulation in the courts, and the matter was still under litigation in 1977.

Public relations and libel

The laws of libel (written defamation) and slander (oral defamation), which protect a person or an institution's right to a good name and reputation, make up a complex field of law that is important to public relations practitioners. For example, Robert A. Maheu, a former Howard Hughes employee, successfully pressed a libel suit against the Hughes Tool Company and its public relations agency, Carl Byoir & Associates, because the account executive, Richard Hannah, had provided newsmen with a transcript of a telephone interview between Howard Hughes and newsmen.[44] Maheu claimed that he had been libeled and slandered by Hughes during this telephone interview set up by the Byoir agency.

In 1976, a $29 million libel suit was filed in Austin, Texas, against AT&T because of allegations the company had made public against two former officials. The company subsequently lost the suit.

In 1975, Michael Harrington, a journalist, filed a $550,000 libel suit against officials of the U.S. Navy, alleging that these officials had "fabricated" letters critical of Mr. Harrington and sent them to former naval personnel, with the suggestion that they sign these letters and mail them to local newspaper editors to indicate that Harrington's views were "held in disrepute" by the community.

Libel or slander is a perplexing legal concept, because what is libelous in one time or place or context might not be adjudged libelous in another set of circumstances. Courts over the years have made it increasingly difficult for people in public life or an institution to recover damages for libelous material printed or circulated about them. However, the wide latitude granted the press in *New York Times* v. *Sullivan* (376 U.S. 254 [1964]) in 1964 has been narrowed in recent years. In that landmark case, the Supreme Court decided that in the interest of a vigorous social dialogue, public officials would have to live with "vehement, caustic, and sometimes unpleasantly sharp" verbal assaults, and that actual malice must be proven. In 1971, this "fair-game" doctrine was extended to private persons embroiled in public issues, in *Rosenbloom* v. *Metromedia, Inc.*, 415 F. 2d 892 (3rd Cir. 1969). The Supreme Court affirmed the court of appeals decision that the fact that Rosenbloom, a magazine distributor, was not a public figure "cannot be accorded decisive importance if the recognized important guarantees of the First Amendment are to be adequately implemented" (403 U.S. 29, [1971]). The decision of the Court's plurality in *Rosenbloom* was superseded by new standards regarding defamation when the Supreme Court issued its *Gertz* v. *Robert Welch, Inc.* decision, 418 U.S. 323 (1974). In *Gertz,* the Court narrowed its public-figure doctrine, and refuted the "public or general interest" requirement for application of the *New York Times* standard in defamation cases involving private citizens.

Application of the "Gertz Doctrine" was broadly upheld by *Firestone* v. *Time, Inc.,* 424 U.S. 448 (1976). In this case, a wealthy divorcee who had been much in the news was held not to be a public figure. In 1977, a libel award against the *New York Times* and an official of the Audubon Society was thrown out by a U.S. court of appeals in a decision that stressed the press's right to fairly report serious charges involving public figures. The Audubon Society had made such charges against three scientists, but the *Times* was exonerated because it had made an effort to get both sides of the story. The plaintiffs appealed the decision of the Second Circuit of the U.S. Court of Appeals to the Supreme Court. The high court, in a decision December 12, 1977, let the appeals court decision stand, holding that "disinterested reporting" of serious charges against a public figure by a prominent organization is constitutionally protected.[45]

The law of libel is a bit muddled and must be treated on a case-by-case basis. Prof. George Christie, Duke University, asserts, "The law in the area of injury to reputation is on the verge of chaos." There are three essential elements that must be present to constitute an actionable libel: (1) *identification*—the person or institution must be clearly identified; (2) *defamation*—the words, picture, drawing or other material must defame; and (3) *publication*—the libelous material must have been published or circulated. In this regard, issuance of a news release has been adjudged to constitute publication. Libel, a tort in civil law, is defined by Prosser as "an invasion of the interest in reputation and good name." Practitioners dealing with news releases, speeches, or other communications material that attacks or possibly defames another person, group, or institution are advised to consult counsel.

Copyright and public relations

Public relations communicators make extensive use of the works of others in news releases, photographs, speeches, booklets, and the like. Thus, practitioners must be sensitive to the property rights of journalists, photographers, playrights, and song writers. The Copyright Act of 1909, because photocopying, videotaping, and cable television put great strains on it, was extensively revised by Congress in 1976 (P.L. 94 553). It provides that the copyright owner "shall have exclusive right" to use of such protected material, but does permit a "fair use" to protect the public interest in a free flow of ideas. "Fair use" is rather liberally interpreted by the courts; determination of what constitutes it generally hinges on these factors: (1) the purpose and character of the use, (2) the nature of the copyrighted work, (3) the amount and substantiality of the material used in relation to copyrighted work as a whole, and (4) the effect of the use on the copyright owner's potential market.[46]

Practitioners and institutions using photographs of others must be cognizant of the requirement to get a signed release from the persons or persons in the photograph. If a person is a minor, permission of the parents is required. Use of a person's name or photograph in an advertisement or in any other commercial manner is an actionable invasion of privacy.

Even the revised act cannot cope with the new technologies. What are the restrictions on cable TV in regard to airing feature films? Are the rights of filmmakers and TV stations being compromised by home videotape recorders? The use of visuals from publications and many other situations are also matters for copyright considerations.

Most problems in this area can be averted by remembering that Congress, in passing copyright, patent, and trademark laws, intended to create a limited monopoly, in the holder of the right, to obtain maximum benefits from his property.

Foreign-agents registration

Counselors who serve foreign governments must register annually with the U.S. Department of Justice as foreign agents, according to Public Law 89–486, last amended in 1966. This Foreign Agents Act was first passed by Congress in 1938 in an effort to deal with Nazi and Fascist propaganda in the United States and to identify foreign agents working here. In making the conference report to the House of Representatives, Cong. Emanuel Celler said, "We believe that the spotlight of pitiless publicity will serve as a deterrent to the spread of pernicious propaganda. We feel that our people are entitled to know the sources of any such efforts, and the person or persons or agencies carrying on such work in the United States."[47]

As the result of 1963 hearings before the Senate Foreign Relations Committee under the chairmanship of Senator J. William Fulbright,[48] Congress in 1966 amended the act and moved its administration from the Department of State to the Department of Justice. The amendments served to remove the act from the so-called subversive area and to place, in Attorney General Ramsey Clark's words, "primary emphasis on the protection of the integrity of the decision-making process." As of January 1976, there were 555 foreign agents registered.

Under the provisions of the Foreign Agents Act, as amended, persons or organizations must register if they function on behalf of a foreign entity for at least one of the following: (1) political activities, (2) public relations, (3) information or as a political consultant, (4) collection or disbursement of money or loans, or (5) other activities of value or as a representative before government agencies or officials. Accredited diplomats, lawyers performing legal activities, and newsmen are exempt from registration.

The amended act, signed into law by President Johnson on July 4, 1966, also provides for:

1. Greater and more explicit disclosure by agents who are engaged in political activities.
2. Civil injunctive procedure for the Attorney General in dealing with a violation (avoiding the necessity of filing criminal charges).

3. A procedure for notifying a registrant he has filed an incomplete statement instead of filing an indictment against him (legalizing past practice).
4. A requirement that a registrant maintain separate books and records for inspection.[49]

Failure to register promptly under this act can bring difficulty—as it did to the Daniel J. Edelman agency in 1975 (Civil Action No. 75-2041). Daniel J. Edelman, Inc., and Edelman International were retained by Aereospatiale, manufacturer of the supersonic Concorde airplane, to assist in winning public support for landing rights for the controversial airplane. Aereospatiale also retained DGA, a Washington-based marketing company, to help in the campaign to get permission for the Concorde to make regularly scheduled flights to New York and Washington. Indirectly, these firms were representing the British and French governments, sponsors of the supersonic air carrier, and Air France and British Airways, which were seeking permission to land at Kennedy and Dulles international airports. Understandably, there was strong public opposition to granting such permission, particularly from residents in the vicinity of the two airports. Public opinion had, some years earlier, blocked U.S. construction of an SST plane.

DGA and International Public Relations, an agency representing Aereospatiale in New York City, were sued by the Justice Department for having in their contracts a contingency provision calling for a substantial bonus in addition to their regular fee if the Concorde was approved for regular flights to the United States. The bonus feature, a provision contrary to the PRSA Code of Ethics, was not a part of the Edelman contract, but the Justice Department sued the two Edelman firms for (1) failure to register as foreign agents, and (2) not marking lobbying materials as having come from a foreign agent. John Meek, general manager of Edelman's Washington office, was also named as a defendant in the civil action. He had not registered the firms within the required 30 days after taking the account, and his office had sent to members of Congress documents, under a cover letter from him, carrying no notation that Edelman was registered. The agencies subsequently registered as foreign agents.

Even though attorneys representing DGA, IPR, and the Edelman entities agreed to all that the Justice Department asked them to do to remedy the situation, nonetheless the Justice Department brought civil suits against them. On December 29, 1975, the U.S. district court in Washington entered a consent decree, agreed to by the attorneys for Edelman and the Justice Department, which terminated the litigation without admission by any party that the law had been violated. This action confirmed a stipulated order, approved by the court December 19 that year, requiring the Edelman firms to advise government officials of their relationship to the Concorde program. The issue was settled without "evidentiary hearing or adjudication of any issue in fact or law . . . without . . . any evidence or admission that the Foreign Agents Registration Act . . . has been violated in any way."[50] A joint statement by the defendants was released that day, stating that "the alleged technical violations have been resolved for all companies and we thought the suit was unnecessary."

The Concorde case also illustrates the stakes involved in decisions made in the public arena. All told, it is estimated that French interests spent some $3 million over a three-year period in hiring consultants, transportation specialists, lawyers, lobbyists, and public relations counselors in an effort to get permanent landing rights for the supersonic jet.[51]

A cautionary note

The maze of legal pitfalls into which the untutored practitioner can fall, sketched in this chapter, suggests the need for counselors and communicators to become knowledgeable about laws applicable to their work. This is especially true in this era of increased use of litigation in pressing causes or claims. The complexities of laws affecting public relations further suggest a close, cordial working relationship with the organization's inside or outside legal counsel.[52] Because the law moves and changes, sometimes swiftly, a constant updating by the practitioner is also dictated.

ADDITIONAL READINGS

ACLU FOUNDATION, *Litigation under the Amended Federal Freedom of Information Act,* manual prepared (1977) by the foundation's Project on National Security and Civil Liberties. 122 Maryland Ave. N.E., Washington, D.C. 20002.

JAMES DEAKIN, *The Lobbyists.* Washington, D.C.: Public Affairs Press, 1966.

LEWIS A. DEXTER, *How Organizations Are Represented in Washington.* New York: Bobbs-Merrill, 1969.

FREEDOM OF INFORMATION CENTER, Report No. 342, *The Privacy Act of 1974.* Columbia: University of Missouri School of Journalism, September 1975.

RAY GARRETT, JR., "The Role of Financial Public Relations," *Public Relations Journal,* Vol. 30 (October 1974). By a former chairman of the SEC.

RUSSELL WARREN HOWE and SARAH HAYS TROTT, *The Power Peddlers.* Garden City, N.Y.: Doubleday, 1977. Deals with the work of foreign agents.

EARL W. KINTNER, *A Primer on the Law of Deceptive Practices, A Guide for the Businessman.* New York: Macmillan, 1971.

GAIL J. KOFF, "Right of Privacy vs. Society's Need to Know," *Public Relations Journal,* Vol. 31 (October 1975).

DAVID S. RUDER, "Current Problems in Corporate Disclosure," *The Business Lawyer,* Vol. 30 (July 1975).

DAVID SHERIDAN, "The 'Lobbyist' Out of the Shadows," *Saturday Review,* April 8, 1972.

U.S. ATTORNEY GENERAL, *Report of the Attorney General to the Congress on the Administration of the Foreign Agents Registration Act of 1938 as Amended.* An annual report.

HARVEY ZUCKMAN and MARTIN J. GAYNES, *Mass Communication Law in a Nutshell.* St. Paul, Minn.: West Publishing Co., 1977.

FOOTNOTES

1. There are three basic references dealing with communications law that are useful in understanding legal problems arising in public relations:
   a. Morton J. Simon, *Public Relations Law* (New York: Appleton-Century-Crofts, 1969). This comprehensive work by a Philadelphia lawyer was underwritten by the Public Relations Foundation for Education and Research. Many of the developments described in this chapter have occurred since Simon's book was prepared.
   b. Harold L. Nelson and Dwight L. Teeter, Jr., *Law of Mass Communications,* 2nd ed. (Mineola, N.Y.: Foundation Press, 1974). A comprehensive text dealing with "freedom and control of print and broadcast media."
   c. Donald M. Gillmor and Jerome A. Barron, *Mass Communication Law,* 2nd ed. (St. Paul, Minn.: West Publishing Co., 1974). Also a comprehensive text.
2. *Fortune,* Vol. 47 (June 1953). Also see Robert Bendiner, "The 'Engineering of Consent'—A Case Study," *The Reporter,* Vol. 13 (August 11, 1955).
3. For a thoughtful discussion of this case, see Andrew Hacker, "Pressure Politics in Pennsylvania: The Truckers vs. The Railroads," in Alan F. Westin, ed., *The Uses of Power* (New York: Harcourt Brace Jovanovich, 1962).

4. David Fellman, *The Constitutional Right of Association* (Chicago: University of Chicago Press, 1963), pp. 10–12.

5. See also *First National Bank v. Belloti*, 435 U.S. 765 (1978).

6. "Congressional Lobbies: A Chronic Problem Re-examined," *Georgetown Law Journal,* Vol. 45 (1957), 535.

7. Simon, *Public Relations Law,* p. 808.

8. Jerome Barron, "Access to the Press—A New First Amendment Right," *Harvard Law Review,* Vol. 80 (1967), 1641. For other cases in which courts held that there is a right of access, see Barron's *Freedom of the Press for Whom?* (Bloomington: Indiana University Press, 1973). Also see Benno C. Schmidt, Jr., *Freedom of the Press vs. Public Access* (New York: Praeger, 1976).

9. See *Bloss* v. *Federated Publications*, 5 Mich. Appl. 74, 157 N.W. 2d 241 (1968); *Associates & Aldrich Company, Inc.* v. *Times Mirror Company*, 440 F 2d 133 (9th Cir. 1971); *Chicago Joint Board, Amalgamated Clothing Workers of America AFL-CIO* v. *Chicago Tribune Company*, 435 F. 2d 470 (7th Cir. 1970).

10. "Mobil Learns to Expect No for an Answer from the Networks," *Broadcasting,* April 1, 1974, pp. 26–27. For an overview of subject, see Freedom of Information Center Report No. 368, "Government Regulation of Broadcasting" (Columbia: University of Missouri, March 1977).

11. "Fairness Case Goes Against Eight California Radio Stations," *Broadcasting,* May 24, 1976.

12. For a digest of this decision, see *Broadcasting,* November 15, 1976, pp. 40–53.

13. "Major Victory for Broadcast Journalism: NBC Judgment on 'Pensions' Upheld by Court," *Broadcasting,* September 30, 1974, p. 6.

14. For details, see Freedom of Information Center Report No. 343, "Implementing the Amended FoI Act," (Columbia: University of Missouri School of Journalism, September 1975). For an evaluation of the new act, see Harold C. Relyea, "The Freedom of Information Act: Its Evolution and Operational Status," *Journalism Quarterly,* Vol. 54 (Autumn 1977), 538–544.

15. U.S. National Labor Relations Board, *Legislative History of the Labor Management Act, 1947,* Vol. 1 (Washington, D.C.: Government Printing Office, 1948).

16. *Ibid.,* p. 549.

17. For this view, see Lindley H. Clark, Jr., "End of an Era?" *Wall Street Journal,* June 21, 1973, p. 14.

18. Robert N. McMurry, "War and Peace in Labor Relations," *Harvard Business Review,* Vol. 33 (November 1955), 48. For a full examination, con and pro, of this approach to labor relations, see Herbert R. Northrup, *Boulwarism* (Ann Arbor: Graduate School of Business, University of Michigan, 1964); and L.R. Boulware, *The Truth about Boulwarism* (Washington, D.C.: Bureau of National Affairs, 1969).

19. National Labor Relations Board, *"General Electric Company and International Union of Electrical, Radio and Machine Workers, AFL-CIO, Case No. 2-CA-7851,"* issued by the NLRB April 2, 1963, p. 47.

20. NLRB news release, December 16, 1964, R-992.

21. "The Case for Boulwarism," *Harvard Business Review,* September–October, 1963, pp. 86–97.

22. *Procter & Gamble,* 160 NLRB 334 (1966), p. 340.

23. NLRB Examiner Leff had used such phrases as "employees were flooded" and "flood proportions" to describe GE's employee communications.

24. Jack Barbash, "Employer 'Free Speech' and Employee Rights," *Labor Law Journal,* April 1963, pp. 317–18.

25. L.L.L. Golden, "What Can You Tell Employees?" *Saturday Review,* Vol. 46 (August 10, 1963), 50.

26. In General Electric's *Relations News Letter* for September 21, 1961. Also see Freedom of Information Center Bulletin No. 131, "Freedom in Company Communications," (Columbia: University of Missouri School of Journalism, October 1964).

27. Securities and Exchange Commission, *Special Study of the Securities Market* (Washington, D.C.: Government Printing Office, 1963).

28. An "interpretation" of the PRSA Code as it applies to financial relations, adopted in 1963 and amended in 1972.

29. Chairman Ray Garrett, in John G. Gillis, "Securities Law and Corporate Disclosure," *Public Relations Journal,* Vol. 32 (April 1976), 18–20ff.

30. Byron D. Woodside, speech, quoted in Simon, *Public Relations Law,* p. 778.

31. For the complete text of the opinion, see *U.S. Court of Appeals for the Second Circuit, No. 296, September Term, 1966* (Chicago: LaSalle Street Press, 325 West Ohio Street, Chicago 60610). See also John Brooks, "Annals of Finance," *The New Yorker,* November 9, 1968, a complete, day-to-day account of circumstances leading to and through the SEC-TGS litigation. The case was Civil No. 65-1182 in Southern District New York Federal Court.

32. For details, see Henry Rockwell, "A Press Release Goes to Court," *Public Relations Journal,* Vol. 24 (October 1968), which includes a copy of the disputed release. The author points out that the

judges were divided 3-3-2-1 on the news release. One judge devoted 7,000 words to the release in his opinion.

33. Kenneth G. Patrick, *Perpetual Jeopardy: The Texas Gulf Sulphur Affair* (New York: Macmillan, 1972). The full story told from the TGS point of view.

34. *Ibid.,* p. 202.

35. "Liggett & Myers, Officer Enjoined from Disclosing Firm's Inside Information," *Wall Street Journal,* November 5, 1973.

36. G. Christian Hill, "Financial Public Relations Men Are Warned They're Liable for Their Clients' Puffery," *Wall Street Journal,* March 16, 1972, p. 30.

37. *Securities and Exchange Commission* v. *Pig 'n Whistle Corp., et al.,* C.A. No. 71 C 545 (N.D. Illinois) February 14, 1972.

38. Richard S. Seltzer, "The SEC Strikes Again," *Public Relations Journal,* Vol. 28 (April 1972), 22. Michael Porter, a principal of a New York agency, who signed a consent decree with the SEC in 1976, was the fifth practitioner to do so. He was charged in connection with his work for Giant Stores Corp.

39. See New York Stock Exchange, *Company Manual,* August 1, 1977, Section A-2, Part I, "Timely Disclosure," and Part II, "Procedure for Public Release of Information."

40. *Public Relations Journal,* Vol. 33 (April 1977), 21–30.

41. "Political Action Ads Ruled Non-Deductible," *Editor & Publisher,* Vol. 93 (January 2, 1960), 10.

42. See Stephen M. Aug, "FCC Judge Says No to Bell System Breakup," *Washington Star,* August 2, 1976; and Associated Press, "Long-Lines Rates of AT&T Upheld," *New York Times,* August 3, 1976.

43. Federal Communications Commission Decision on Docket 19129, February 23, 1977.

44. *Maheu* v. *Hughes Tool Co.,* 384 F. Supp. 166 (D.C.Cal. 1974). The court awarded compensatory damages but held that Maheu, a public figure, was not entitled under California law to recover punitive damages. The U.S. Court of Appeals for the ninth circuit reversed this judgement late in 1977. Hannah, longtime Byoir vice-president who was assigned to the highly unorthodox Hughes account, died January 15, 1976. His mysterious client's death came the same year. Byoir held the account for 30 years.

45. For the basis of current judicial interpretation, see *New York Times* v. *Sullivan,* 376 U.S. 254 (1964) and its modifying decisions *Gertz* v. *Robert Welch, Inc.* 418 U.S. (1974), and *Time, Inc.* v. *Firestone,* 424 U.S. 448 (1976). In the latter case, the high court held that the mere fact that a person is a celebrity, or well known in "high society," is not sufficient in itself to make that person a public figure under libel law. Also see Harry W. Stonecipher and Robert Trager, "The Impact of *Gertz* on the Law of Libel," *Journalism Quarterly,* Vol. 53 (Winter 1976), 609–618.

46. Gillmor and Barron, *Mass Communication Law,* p. 739.

47. *Congressional Record,* 75th Cong., 3rd sess., p. 8022.

48. *Activities of Non-Diplomatic Representatives of Foreign Principals in the United States,* Hearings before the U.S. Senate Committee on Foreign Relations, 88th Cong., 1963, Parts 1 through 13. (Washington, D.C.: Government Printing Office, 1963).

49. Harry Kennedy, Jr., "What You Should Know about the Foreign Agents Registration Act," *Public Relations Quarterly,* Fall 1966, pp. 17–18.

50. Memorandum from John Meek, dated December 30, 1975, to top officers of the Edelman firms, provided by Mr. Meek.

51. For background on the Concorde controversy, see Peter Gillman, "Supersonic Bust: The Story of the Concorde," *The Atlantic,* Vol. 239 (January 1977).

52. This need is spelled out by David H. Simon, "Lawyers and Public Relations Counselors: Teamwork or Turmoil?" *American Bar Association Journal,* Vol. 63 (August 1977).

13

Effective leadership depends primarily on mediating between the individual and the organization in such a way that both can obtain maximum satisfaction.

WARREN G. BENNIS

The Employee Public

The term *internal public* or *employee public,* as used here, means the people working in an organization—both the governors and the governed, the managers and the employees. Employee relations is the shortcut term used to describe this internal relationship. Employee relations is a prime concern of management in every field.

The working relationship

"The primary function of any organization, religious, political or industrial, should be to implement the needs of [participants] to enjoy a meaningful existence. For the first time in history we have the opportunity to satisfy man's inherent wants."[1] This is at the heart of working relationships.

Reaching the internal public is not difficult. The working relationship itself brings daily communication; and in addition, there are the auxiliary tools discussed in Chapter 11. But the effectiveness of communication depends on a satisfactory relationship. Before there can be effective employee communication, there must be a climate of trust.

Communications must be viewed as a tool of leadership. The chief executive must establish the right climate. The communications program should be underwritten by policy. For example, one organization's policy manual includes this statement: "It is the direct responsibility of every member of management, at every level, to communicate effectively with employees under his or her supervision and to find out [their] thinking and reactions. . . . It is also a responsibility to maintain open communications with line superiors and fellow supervisors." This need is as urgent in an employee body of 300 as in one of 30,000. Yet the barriers to free-flowing internal communication in organizations are many.

The most pressing need is for more adequate upward communication. Feedback channels are important. Research on feedback invariably shows that members of an organization want more information than they usually get. It also shows, repeatedly, a disparity in the views of management and staff. For example, one survey revealed that supervisors and department heads thought good wages were what employees wanted most, whereas employees said it was full appreciation for work done. Another survey, in which top executives rated themselves and their subordinate managers rated them, found that the executives saw themselves as better bosses than they were considered to be by their subordinates. Top-management respondents were unanimous in stating that they encouraged subordinates to suggest ideas; but of 420 subordinate managers, only one in four said his superior encouraged suggestions. Administrators tend to seek self-assurance instead of communication.

Internal surveys of an organization's communications system reveal its strengths and weaknesses. Illinois Bell operates a comprehensive, intensive program to reach its more than 37,000 employees. It includes heavy emphasis on face-to-face communicating, a sophisticated closed-circuit television operation, and a telephone "newsline"—brief reports of up-to-the-minute developments at least twice a day. In addition, an information bulletin goes to supervisors on the job and a semimonthly news magazine to the homes of all employees. Five departmental papers, distributed on the job, are scheduled alternately with the magazine. The overall program is directed by experienced communicators aided by systematic research. Yet despite this concentrated effort, only 66.7 percent of management and 52 percent of nonmanagement responded favorably in a survey when asked about "the job the company is doing to inform you about your work and the things that directly affect your job." When asked about "the job the company is doing to keep you informed about what's going on in the telephone business, beyond your own work assignment," 75.8 percent of management and only 44.3 percent of nonmanagement responded favorably.

The study reaffirmed that the supervisor is the most important source of job-related information. It identified higher management and the established internal media as preferred sources of information on general company policy and developments.

Isidore Silver has written, ". . . one of the great problems, and a cause of frequent grievance, is not the unfairness of management actions, but the inexplicability. It is ironic that in our over-communicative society, communications breakdowns frequently occur. Even in corporations—where internal communications networks are the lifeblood of their activity—decisions are sometimes made without adequate explanation. Often such decisions appear to be arbitrary when in fact they are not. Equally often, worker discontent is caused by lack of understanding as to the reasons for such apparently unfavorable decisions. . . . The failure is by no means one-way."[2] What Silver says of the corporation applies with equal force to universities, government agencies, labor unions, and other entities. All managers need to keep in mind that an employee's ego is under assault from the time he or she enters the door until he leaves—the time clock, the badge or ID card, and like regimentation bruise one's ego. Further, employees come to work freighted with the attitudes of family, associates, and the community. Managers may mistakenly choose to manage on the basis of the traditional closed system, but employees live much of their lives outside that system.

Each organization is, within itself, a productive or service unit with production or service responsibilities. But it is a social unit, with social responsibilities

FIGURE 13-1 Courtesy of Communications and Management Magazine.

Consequently, in any approach to the internal public, the social needs as well as the economic needs must be acknowledged and satisfied. A paycheck falls short of being the only thing an employee wants.

Howard Wilson lists the social or psychological needs of humans as:

1. *Need to belong,* to be part of a group.
2. *Need for accomplishment* toward worthy goals.

3. *Need for self-esteem.*
4. *Need for acceptance by peers.*
5. *Need for security.*
6. *Need for self-expression* in creative forms.[3]

These needs are expressed in a different form, as Maslow's Hierarchy of Needs, in Chapter 6.

The nature of tasks to be performed in an automated society makes personal satisfaction an ever-greater problem. For many, boredom is a daily companion.[4] Eric Fromm asks, "Is man, during the next hundred years, to continue to spend most of his energy on meaningless work, waiting for the time when work will require no expenditure of energy? What will become of him in the meantime? . . . Is not work such a fundamental part of man's existence that it cannot and should never be reduced to almost complete insignificance?"[5]

Ideals and actualities

Ideally, the working relationship would be characterized by at least seven conditions:

1. Confidence and trust between employer and employees.
2. Candid information flowing freely up, down, sideways.
3. A satisfying status and function for each person.
4. Continuity of work without strife.
5. Healthy surroundings.
6. Success for the enterprise.
7. An optimistic outlook for the future.

The facts of socioeconomic life, however, are such that these possibilities are tempered by forces at work in the competitive system and in the democratic process. At times these forces make the ideal and the reality seem incompatible or unattainable.

Consider satisfaction for the employee and success for the employer. Whether the employer is a business or a private charity, success depends on making the best possible use of the funds available. That means trying to maximize the spread between the money coming in and the money paid out, including the money paid out for work and the place of work. An accountant would call this a cost-efficiency effort.

For the employee, satisfaction embraces status and function. But it also means getting the highest possible reward in money and recognition that personal skill, time, and effort justify. At the same time, the employee wants these without loss of dignity, individuality, or independence of thought and action. Adjusting the needs for satisfaction agreeably is but one aspect of the continuous reconciliation process that goes on in this nation's employer–employee relationship.

The impact of other factors

Many of the traditions and assumptions in the employee–employer relationship have come under assault by sweeping changes, societal forces that were discussed in Chapter 5. Among the resulting changes is the ratio of blue-collar to white-collar employees. White collars now outnumber blue collars by 40 percent. As one aspect, more than half the work force is salaried, not on hourly wages. There is also the factor of minority employment; equal opportunity has the force of law. The women's-rights movement has focused on the job market. The level of education and sophistication among the internal public has risen. Benefit programs once considered "extras" or beneficences are taken for granted. Young people coming into the internal public expect their diplomas or training to mean jobs. They expect early recognition, and advancement on merit, not seniority.[6] Unemployment, despite a growing total work force, has held stubbornly to levels intolerable for millions who want to work. Finally, automation and computerization proliferate, adding efficiency and speed at the expense of personal identity and self-expression.

The special problem of labor–management relations

A heavy factor in the industrial sector is labor–management relations. This is usually thought of as a "blue-collar" matter. However, more and more groups—office workers, teachers, police, nurses—have turned to union organization in order to negotiate with a single voice. They have shown a willingness to strike, if the need arises.

Where unions and bargaining agreements are part of the relationship, a dual leadership is present, spurring divided loyalties. The employer, by nature, tends to resent the intrusion and the loss of his right to deal directly with the internal public. His right to communicate freely with employees is inhibited, since such communication, at certain times, under certain conditions, and in certain ways, comes under the Taft-Hartley Act, as was discussed in Chapter 12. Thus, the basics for misunderstanding and an adversarial relationship are established.

In organizations with collective-bargaining agreements, mutual accommodation by labor and management involves the following fundamentals:

1. Full acceptance by management of collective-bargaining principles.
2. Full acceptance by unions of private ownership and operation of industry for a profit, and of efficient productivity in nonprofit organizations.
3. Strong unions that are democratically and responsibly run.
4. No management interference in union affairs.
5. Mutual trust in all dealings.
6. No legalistic approach by either party in negotiations, which should be problem-centered, not issue- or personality-centered.
7. Full sharing of information and widespread consultation on matters of mutual interest.
8. Prompt settlement of grievances as these arise.

Many employers do not have to deal with unions. Nonetheless, they must gain acceptability. They must share information, consult on matters of mutual interest, and promptly settle grievances. In many cases, management has taken some of the thrust out of organized labor's efforts to unionize all employees by providing voluntarily what the unions might reasonably obtain through collective bargaining. Nonprofit agencies have had to write a comparable set of fundamentals, given the recent growth of unions in the public sector.

Establishing effective leadership

Educators and researchers differ over the kinship of morale, motivation, and productivity. There is no quarrel over desirability; questions are those of degree and variation. As one management consultant put it, "When an organization, through its leadership, can create an environment that has a strengthening effect on its members, it leads to the belief that, collectively, through the organization, they can determine or change the course of events. This, in turn, generates *organizational excitement.*"[7] The generation of "organizational excitement" starts with the acceptability of leadership.

The components of leadership acceptability

The process of earning leadership acceptability for the manager or administrator is not complex. There are three components.

Interest: The first component is *a demonstrated interest in the employees' or members' affairs.* The interest must be genuine, not simulated. It must be humane. It must be attentive to the employees' expressed desires and anxieties. It must be studious. It must recognize that, in Heilbroner's phrase, "armies and corporations alike have ways of sweetening the news as it ascends the hierarchy of command."

Expression of interest starts with listening and learning. The format may employ periodic questionnaires. One widely used, which was developed by Rensis Likert, deals with working conditions, job satisfaction, security, supervision, performance standards, communication with associates and supervisors, recreation, and benefit programs. With this effort at insight repeated at intervals, personnel policies can be reexamined and updated.

Another survey technique involves the use of cards. Respondents "play cards" by selecting those containing statements with which they agree or disagree to varying degrees. This format has substantial appeal and preserves anonymity.[8]

A time-worn but effective listenership is provided by the suggestion system. Its main purpose is to stimulate the upward flow of ideas. Along with suggestions flow complaints and ideas for improving personnel policies.

A growing number of organizations make use of employee counselors for personal redress. Pioneer exploratory work in this field was done at the Hawthorne (Chicago) Western Electric plant. The employee counselor was an outgrowth of Elton Mayo's historic Hawthorne studies, which have had a profound effect on human relations. Many organizations without a full-scale employee-counseling program retain the services of consultants in psychiatry or psychology. In the armed forces, the work performed by the classification sections, the Inspector General's office, and chaplains is a counterpart. In education, there are faculty advisors and student counselors. In social work, the caseworker counsels on a personal basis.

An alternative to the private consultation is the group session. A technique developed by a Chicago consultant, A.A. Imberman, has been widely followed. The technique calls for six to eight people with common problems discussing them for about a half-hour, with a trained counselor sitting in.[9]

A readily available tool for listenership is the telephone "hot line." Another is the house publication. Best of all is the knowledge that an employee can carry his or her grievance step by step up through the structure, without recrimination, until satisfaction is obtained. The chief executive officer's door is open.

One of the more unusual vehicles for handling inquiries, complaints, and responses has been the "Speak Up" or "Speak Out" program. See Figure 13–2. At IBM, letters from employees, with the individual's identity protected, are answered openly in an employee publication, *IBM News.* A novel technique by a small German consulting firm, Metaplan, revolved around a company "fair" for interchange of views. Each booth offered a place for discussion of a specific issue or problem.

A prime necessity in the handling of employee complaints and expressions of dissatisfaction is empathy. The employer must give the employee credit for sincerity and the right to differ. This is not always easy. Some actions that have sprung from employee dissatisfaction have put empathy to a severe test. The worst, other than deliberate property damage, is "whistle-blowing"—an action in which the employee turns the employer in for a faulty product or service, a public deception, an illegal act, or questionable conduct.[10] Genuine interest and empathy require that the employer approach instances of whistle-blowing as acts of conscience or reform. As follow-through, conclusions reached after investigation of such instances should be disclosed openly and candidly. They should not be shielded or left to the grapevine.

Response: The second component of leadership acceptability consists of *the actions taken to respond to information coming up from employees.* This starts with policies that are in tune with the times—and no actions that are foolhardy or that consist of giving away something for nothing. It means, specifically, a regular review and appropriate overhaul of personnel policies. This adds positive action to the employer's genuine interest, with deeds supporting good intent. An interest in employee health is backed up by actions providing for sanitation, safety, and medical services. An interest in the employee's dignity is sustained by elimination of any unnecessary condition found demeaning, whether it's the time clock, poor lighting, invasions of privacy, or racial discrimination.

Participation: From policy implementation, the response proceeds to the third component, *mutual participation activities. Face-to-face participation is the key. An ounce of meaningful participation can be worth a ton of pamphlets.*

As organizations learn this, there is a consequent shift to group discussions. An affiliate in the Bell System made a study of its presentation of a rate-increase request to employees. It was found that participation-type meetings were the most effective in getting this complex story across. Researchers found that "belief and knowledge were best in situations where employees said they had a 'whole lot' of discussion." Straight presentations with little or no discussion were much less effective.

This controlled study followed extensive research on employee attitudes in the parent Bell System by an outside research team. From it, the company learned that (1) when people get a lot of satisfaction out of their work, they reflect their feelings to outsiders, and they are more effective on the job; (2) often, important information fails to reach an employee because of employees' lack of interest or lack of involvement; and (3) employees want an opportunity to ask questions and express their ideas in small meetings. Out of these findings came a program of regular work-group meetings.

Situations in which employees fully participate can (1) provide two-way communication, including feedback of employee questions, mistaken notions, and so forth; (2) give people a means of self-expression and tap the creative ideas

FIGURE 13-2 A typical form for upward-flowing information, with the format providing the employer's self-addressed, stamped return envelope. One employer's experience was that 6 percent of employees used the form each year, 25 percent with gripes, 50 percent with inquiries, and 25 containing usable ideas.

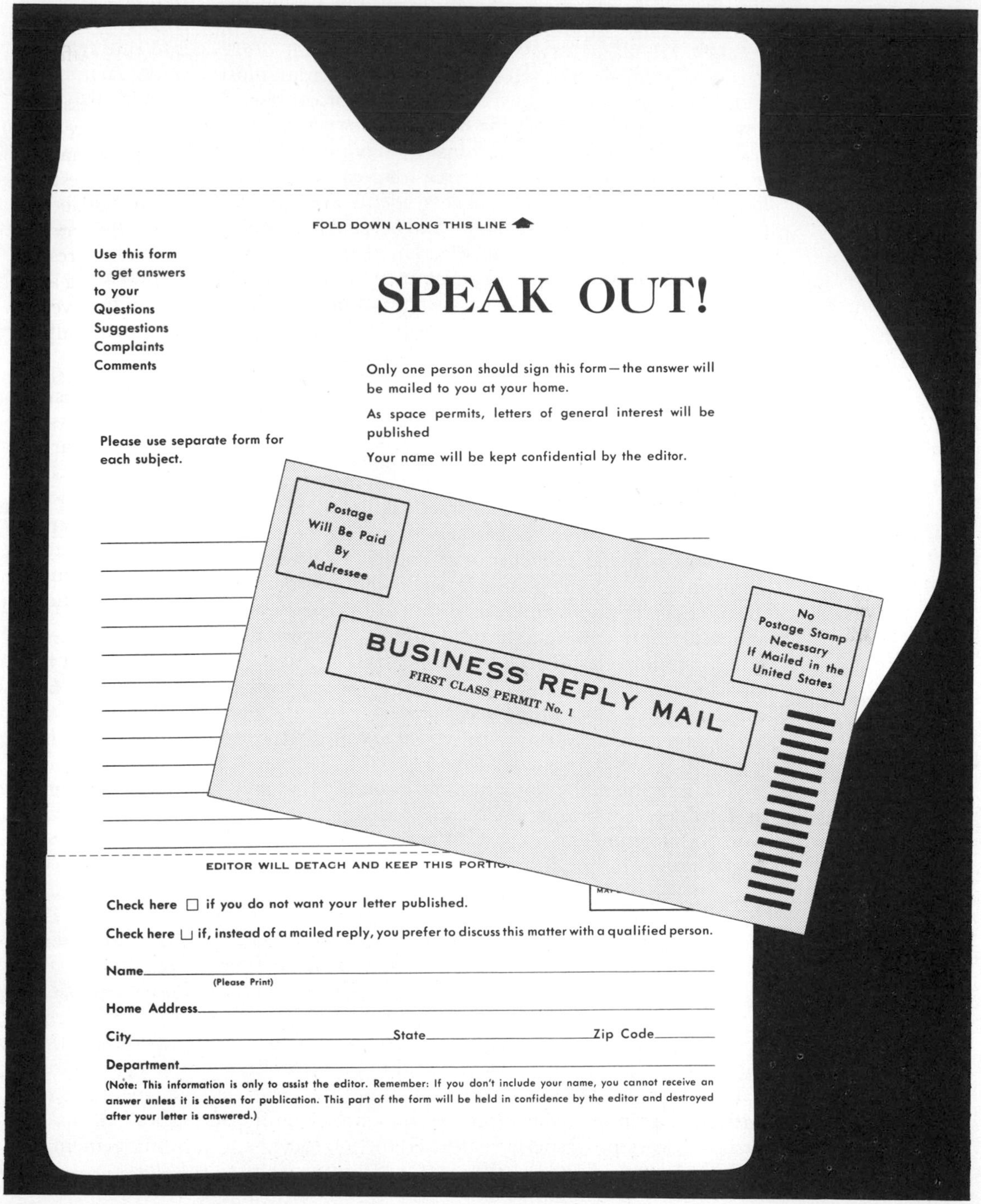

FOLD DOWN ALONG THIS LINE ⬆

Use this form
to get answers
to your
Questions
Suggestions
Complaints
Comments

SPEAK OUT!

Only one person should sign this form — the answer will be mailed to you at your home.

As space permits, letters of general interest will be published

Your name will be kept confidential by the editor.

Please use separate form for each subject.

Postage
Will Be Paid
By
Addressee

BUSINESS REPLY MAIL
FIRST CLASS PERMIT No. 1

No
Postage Stamp
Necessary
If Mailed in the
United States

EDITOR WILL DETACH AND KEEP THIS PORTION

Check here ☐ if you do not want your letter published.

Check here ☐ if, instead of a mailed reply, you prefer to discuss this matter with a qualified person.

Name_____
     (Please Print)

Home Address_____

City_____State_____Zip Code_____

Department_____

(Note: This information is only to assist the editor. Remember: If you don't include your name, you cannot receive an answer unless it is chosen for publication. This part of the form will be held in confidence by the editor and destroyed after your letter is answered.)

latent in any group; (3) uncover opposition and obstacles to plans before they are effected; and (4) encourage a sense of responsibility for the decisions made, and thus pave the way for change.

There is a price to be paid for these returns. Employee views must be heard and given due weight. Participation cannot be merely a sounding-board operation.

There are many ways of strengthening the line organization through group participation, including self-administered activities: music groups, parties, sports teams, outings, hobby clubs, credit unions, or contests. Selection of such activities, weighing one against the other, is of secondary importance.

Participation of internal groups by having a voice in the actual conduct of management-level affairs is an area long considered sacrosanct. But it is being invaded more and more. College students are demanding a voice in making policies, in determining curricula, and in selecting faculty. Public-school teachers are demanding a voice in the selection of their principals. Union members are increasingly insistent upon a voice in management of their affairs. This self-assertion of the right to have a say in matters affecting one's livelihood or role will spread. Meaningful channels of consultation and communication must be the response. Participation must be sincere, not manipulative.

The pace of and example for participation start with the chief executive officer. He *does* take part in the overall employee program. The part he takes has to be consistent with the nature of the organization. For instance, there would be differences of participation dictated by distances in a nationwide magazine subscription operation and in a local, home-owned department store.

It would be beneficial, if impractical, for the chief executive officers of large, dispersed organizations to get into things in the same way as the late Harvey Swados, a writer and teacher, and Patricia Cayo Sexton, another teacher. They went to work in auto plants. Later, Swados wrote that it came as a shock to discover that among employees different from each other in ethnic background, education, and ambition, the one unifying force was hatred of their work—a fact that his middle-class friends had difficulty accepting. Sexton, after three years in a plant, found that the "worker's world—as one lives it—is very different." She concluded that such phrases as "powerful unions" and "enlightened management" conveyed very little of the essence of life on the assembly line.[11] See Figure 13–3.

The attitude of the worker on the assembly line came into focus dramatically at Lordstown, Ohio, in 1972. The occasion was a strike of several thousand workers, most under 27, against the speedup and the monotony of "the world's fastest assembly line," producing 100 GM Vegas per hour.

> In the words of Gary Bryner, then 29, president of the local union: "I don't give a shit what anyone says, it was boring monotonous work. . . . A guy could go there eight hours and there was some other body doing the same job over and over all day long, all week long, all year long. . . . If you thought about it you'd go stir. . ."[12]

In the wake of Lordstown there were many experiments and innovations to make factory work more creative and interesting. Among many, the efforts by Volvo of Sweden were noteworthy. Two new factories were designed, at a cost of $40 million, to get away from the moving assembly line. Elsewhere in Volvo facilities, work programs were pitched to "job rotation," "job enlargement," and "job enrichment."

FIGURE 13–3 Courtesy *U.S. News & World Report,* December 1, 1975.

THE 10 MOST BORING JOBS —ONE EXPERT'S LIST

Which day-to-day tasks involve the most drudgery, the least payoff in satisfaction? Manpower consultant Roy Walters, head of a New Jersey management firm, provides this list of 10. Jobs are given at random, not necessarily in order of boredom:

ASSEMBLY-LINE WORKER

ELEVATOR OPERATOR IN PUSH-BUTTON ELEVATOR

TYPIST IN OFFICE TYPING POOL

BANK GUARD

COPYING-MACHINE OPERATOR

KEYPUNCH OPERATOR

HIGHWAY TOLL COLLECTOR

CAR WATCHER IN TUNNEL

FILE CLERK

HOUSEWIFE

THE "BOREDOM FACTOR" IN 23 TYPICAL JOBS

Based on interviews with 2,010 workers performing 23 different jobs, the Institute for Social Research at the University of Michigan drew up "boredom factors" for each occupation — with 100 the average and the higher the rating, the more boring the job:

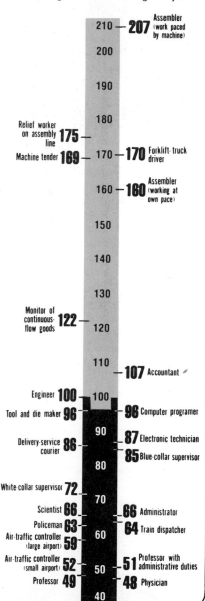

207	Assembler (work paced by machine)
175	Relief worker on assembly line
170	Forklift-truck driver
169	Machine tender
160	Assembler (working at own pace)
122	Monitor of continuous-flow goods
107	Accountant
100	Engineer
96	Tool and die maker
96	Computer programer
87	Electronic technician
86	Delivery-service courier
85	Blue-collar supervisor
72	White-collar supervisor
66	Scientist
66	Administrator
63	Policeman
64	Train dispatcher
59	Air-traffic controller (large airport)
52	Air-traffic controller (small airport)
51	Professor with administrative duties
49	Professor
48	Physician

Few industrial chief executive officers, except those who have founded enterprises or started at the bottom, will ever have the benefit of working on an assembly line, or the advantage of personal contacts enjoyed by the head of a large airline who flies 200,000 miles per year to hold meetings with his 50,000 employees at airport offices. Most CEOs have to do the best they can with vicarious experience.

The more normal situation is the organization with the size and scope of a resort, a local unit of a government agency, a subsidiary industrial operation, or a private hospital. And in most localized organizations of less than 500 employees, the administrative head *can* get around the premises frequently. He *can,* if so inclined, drop in on meetings taking place at the mid-management level. He *can* assemble and talk to the entire employee body if circumstances call for it. He *can* go personally to see a newly installed piece of equipment. There is no reason acceptable to employees for the boss's itinerary to be confined to a private parking place, private office, executive dining area, and top-staff meetings. There is no reason acceptable to employees for his or her internal communications to be confined to memos and bulletins.

The chief executive officer is expected to clearly identify his alternatives in various situations. He delegates authority down the line, and he specifies the pecking order, to preclude political infighting. The CEO's attitudes in dealings with the internal public are interpreted in working groups by the supervisors of those groups.

The qualifications of supervisors are extremely important. These are the people whose counterparts are the top sergeant or chief petty officer, the branch office manager or regional sales manager, the ward captain in a charity drive, the police lieutenant. It falls to the supervisor to assign work face-to-face, speak for management policies, and absorb the brunt of pressures from above and below. At one and the same time, he or she is the parent figure, the boss, and the understanding friend. In the supervisor–employee relationship, emotions are always near the surface.

With the trends to conglomeration, dispersal of facilities, and internationalizing of many activities, the mid-range management function is critical to success. This is being reflected in several ways. One is in training programs in economics, labor law, international law, and human and public relations. Another is a marked upward salary trend. Supervisors enjoy full membership on management teams. They take part in meetings where organizational objectives are set, strategy is devised, and timetables are established. Supervisors are included in both executive social events and all-employee events. Their numbers are increasing, and they retain their own identity through clubs and associations that bolster their craft.

Recent innovations in leadership

Employees as owners

One of the trends of participation in the corporate sphere has been that of making employees part of ownership. At the managerial level, the usual mechanism is the stock option or stock gift in lieu of a bonus. For the employee body, the main vehicles are the stock-ownership trust, and the profit-sharing and pension plans.

The stock-ownership trust involves borrowing funds from a bank to buy a block of the company's stock. The company guarantees the loan and makes contributions to the trust to cover interest payments on the loan. Shares are held in trust until an employee leaves the company. Such trusts confer tax benefits on the company.[13]

The other vehicle, profit-sharing trusts or pension funds, has been called "pension fund socialism" by Peter Drucker. These funds have attained massive size. Sometimes the largest single investment in the portfolio is the stock of the employing company. Consequently, pension funds are sometimes the largest single shareholder of a company. Drucker has estimated that corporate employee funds, plus industrywide funds for unions, teachers, and so on, own enough stock to control almost every one of the 1,000 largest industrial corporations in America. This reaches down into corporations with less than $100 million sales. The actual equity owned is about 35 percent of the total, according to Drucker.[14] The ultimate consequences of this trend in ownership have implications far beyond employee relations. It is a subject worthy of study in depth.

Other innovations

In the name of participation and concerned leadership, the 1970s produced many innovative projects and productivity experiments. Among them were these:

- Production employees were taken to visit customers.
- Special facilities and work for handicapped people only were established.
- Employees were lent out for extended periods to perform humanitarian tasks for government and private agencies.
- Employers sponsored family garden plots.
- Employers sponsored commuter vans and buses to relieve parking-lot congestion.
- Day-care centers near employing facilities were established for working mothers.
- Auto-firm suppliers granted rebates to employees purchasing customers' cars.
- Employers extended employment policies to provide special programs to rehabilitate and retrain addicts and parolees.
- Productivity plans permitted employees to build a complete product instead of a part or subassembly.
- Productivity plans set up work modules enabling employees to fulfill a quota or complete a normal day's work in less time, and leave.[15]

Employee communications

Effective communications—the tone, the methods, and the tools—is importantly involved in all four phases of employment:

The start, in which advertising, pamphlets, and interviews are used to attract and indoctrinate recruits.

The work, during which many internal media provide instruction, news, and job-oriented information.

The rewards and recognitions, involving announcements, publicity, and special events concerning compensation, promotions, benefit programs, recreation events, and the awards and winners.

The termination or work interruption, whether caused by layoff, strike, sit-in, breakdown of equipment, disaster, termination of jobs, or dismissal of individuals.

As a mirror of the relationship desired, effective communications would meet at least five basic needs:

1. To create among all hands an awareness of the oganization's goals.
2. To keep all hands informed on significant developments that affect the organization and the employee.
3. To increase effectiveness of all hands as ambassadors on and off the job.
4. To encourage favorable attitudes in staff and to increase its productivity.
5. To satisfy desires of employees to be kept informed about what's going on in their organization.

Fulfillment of these needs requires a free and candid flow of information between management and employee. The flow uses the line organization and auxiliary tools.

The high cost of breakdowns

Despite good intentions, reasonable goals, and planned communications, maladjustments, misunderstandings, and breakdowns do occur. In large organizations, the lack of social integration leaves many workers asking, "Where do I fit?" "What does my boss think of me?" "How can I be a success?" Communication that answers such questions helps reduce anxieties, create security, and bring job satisfaction. But such meaningful, two-way communication becomes ever more difficult—from university president to student, from general to troops, from department head to field agent.

In unionized organizations, there is the matter of dual leadership and divided loyalties. In all organizations, there is the confusion and glut of information coming from management sources, from the grapevine, and from the "other" world where the communicators are people on television and in the news. If that weren't enough, there are societal pressures and forces linked to politics and to public and social issues.

In this environment, credibility of leaders is in delicate balance. From seeds of gossip or an isolated incident can grow the suspicion or mistrust of an entire internal public. If the process is not detected early and treated or eradicated, if the working conditions are bad or boring, or if the results of the work have no social significance, a process of actual alienation is set in motion. The manner in which this process moves is illustrated in Figure 13–4.

Alienations and communications in perspective

Unfortunately, alienation has been demonstrated repeatedly in the employer-employee-union triangular relationship. Historically, since World War II,

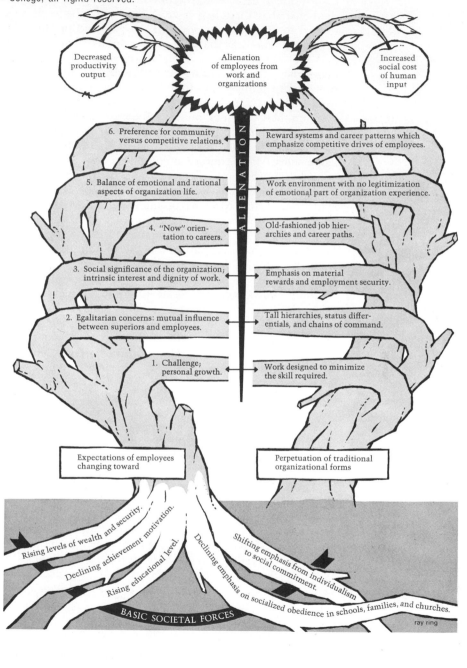

303

employers with bargaining agreements have felt that employees needed to be better educated, or "reeducated," in the U.S. economic system. The premise, oversimplified, has been that employee grievances and demands indicate an inadequate understanding of, or a hostility to, that system. Along with this went the belief that there was a vital correlation between an employee's attitudes toward the employer, morale on the job, and productivity.

A third tenet was that if employees understood the values of the system and had the "facts," they or their representatives would be more reasonable in demands at the bargaining table. Finally, it was believed that the more information an employee had from and about the employer, the better the rapport would be.

From these premises, downward communications grew and grew in amount, variety, and budget. Minor miracles were promised and expected. Some communicators presented their wares as a panacea to cure all the ills, frictions, and aggressions. Many concerned employers created special departments and periodically launched intensive, hurry-up campaigns. Communications specialists multiplied. Nonprofit organizations and tax-supported employers followed the lead of industry. Millions of man-hours and billions of dollars have been involved in the decades since 1946, a lot of it sheer waste.

The validity of the original premises and the approaches taken remains open to doubt. Much of the political-social-economic education effort of employers has been shrugged off by employees as irrelevant or irritating propaganda. The massive indoctrination effort by industry, specifically, had something of a numbing effect. In Peter Drucker's opinion, most of the campaigns failed because of these mistaken assumptions: (1) that employees consider the same things to be important and relevant that management considers relevant and important; (2) that employees are hostile to the free-enterprise system.

Two researchers who tested the assumption that "good communications bring about high morale" concluded, "There is no significant relationship between employees' attitudes toward their company and their knowledge about the company."[16] Likewise, as mentioned earlier, any direct, measurable relationship between worker morale and productivity requires a great deal more evaluation. Two psychologists, after reviewing research testing this premise over a period of 20 years, concluded, "It is time to question the strategic and ethical merits of selling to industrial concerns an assumed relationship between employee attitudes and employee performance."[17]

The reader should not draw the conclusion that all employee-communications programs are wasteful or ineffective. To the contrary, there is solid evidence that effective employee communications contribute to the successful operation of all kinds of enterprises. Shadows of doubt are cast here to bring the matter into reasonable perspective. For the efforts that have failed, there are several questions: *Did they fail by dealing with the anxieties of employers rather than of employees? Did they fail by promising too much, or by saying one thing and doing another? Did they fail in expecting too much of mechanical media? Did they fail in use of the media?* The answer to all these questions is probably yes, in varying degrees.

The role of public relations

In practice, public relations supports the chief executive officer and the personnel or industrial relations functionaries in the communications aspects of their roles. Seldom do the public relations and personnel functions combine into one. The exception is in the small organization that cannot afford separate functions. The prevalent arrangement (Texaco is a notable exception) is for the two functions to be separate. Public relations is not normally involved in labor negotiations, or in general employee hiring, classifying, training, counseling, or promotion.

As a support function, the public relations role makes a major contribution. It includes (1) correctly interpreting management and personnel policies, (2) helping to shape the attitudes employees reflect in their relationships outside the place of work, (3) creating an environment favorable to the work of the personnel or industrial relations function, and (4) providing vehicles and stimulating two-way communications as part of the working condition.

Actual support starts with agreement on the goals of communications, the vehicles, the reporting relationships, and the timetable. The goals are tied to the objectives of the organization as a whole, and to the established human relations policies. Clarifying the who-does-what in reporting relationships avoids frictions later. The timetable jibes with the specific programs and the needs of the human relations department or office.

The planned effort fits the organization

One internal-communications task of increasing concern to management today is that of sustaining appreciation of employee benefits, commonly termed "fringe benefits." These benefits are designed to get employees to stay with the organization and to motivate them to work with maximum efficiency. Many employers complain that employees take the growing range of benefits for granted, but a survey showed that 85 percent of employees interviewed wanted more information about their benefits. Many of them, for instance, were unaware that their employer matched their personal contributions to Social Security. Others were puzzled about provisions of the retirement plan.

Explaining benefit programs is not an easy assignment, especially if lawyers insist upon legal language. The task calls for imagination and ingenuity. So, one year, the Minneapolis Civic Council issued a stock certificate with 24 dividend coupons to its 4,842 "stockholders"—the coupons detailed the council's accomplishments for the year, including employee benefits. Con Edison, the New York City utility, one year issued a four-color, spiral-bound calendar that used a few words of text and an appropriate cartoon to publicize a different benefit to employees for each month of the year. Several organizations have used the checkbook idea—giving employees a checkbook with entries showing the amount of money the organization had spent on employee benefits the previous year. The check stubs carry explanations of the benefits and show the payments accumulating from check to check.

The planned communications efforts must be tailor-made to each organization. A good plan in one place may be ineffective elsewhere. There are many considerations. It makes a difference if the organization is widely dispersed in small units like Holiday Inns, Inc., or localized like the Greenbriar, at White Sulphur Springs. It matters whether ownership or management is resident with the internal public, or lives elsewhere. It matters whether the source of funds is sales and profits, subscriptions or donations, or allocation from taxes. It matters whether the spokesmanship and personality are colorful as with a Joe Namath, cautious or reserved as with an Arthur Burns when chairman of the Federal Reserve, provocative as with a William Buckley or Ralph Nader, controversial as with a Henry Kissinger, articulate as with a Billy Graham, or stereotyped like a Colonel Sanders.

The tailor-making should start with analysis of what the internal public thinks about its employment. If inadequate information is at hand, a survey is indicated. This must not be a one-time thing. Many organizations, like S.C. Johnson, periodically recheck employee attitudes scientifically. Tools such as the suggestion box, "Why I Like My Job" contests, and Q-and-A sections in the house publication are informal vehicles.

The ongoing program of communications may entail the use of any tools mentioned in Chapter 11. The question is, What fits this organization? Among the most frequently used are house publications, letters and newsletters, bulletins, and small group meetings. And as important as the selection of media is a flexibility that permits running changes when checks of reaction and response indicate they are needed. Changes needed may be as drastic as the termination of a program or vehicle because "nobody is reading or listening." Changes may be as simple as softening a message that is abrasive. They may involve strategic revamping of a message to make it square with "what's happening upstairs in the ivory tower."

Even employee news publications, long a bread-and-butter public relations function, are subject to evaluation and change. Traditional assumptions are not inviolate. As Prof. Noel Griese of Georgia found in his studies, "The brevity of an article, employee perceived interest, and utility are more important determinants of readership than readability."

One industrial relations writer, George S. Odiorne, sees these benefits in utilizing public relations skills in employee communications: (1) Public relations people have a facility with verbalizing and writings; (2) they add color, vigor, style, and impact to their messages; (3) the department is staffed with people who have creativity and imagination, and these qualities show themselves in the ingenuity and élan that go into communicating information; (4) few personnel people are specialists in communications.

Odiorne also warns against these pitfalls that ensnare some practitioners when they move into employee relations: (1) failure to develop a clear image of who is "the employee"; (2) undermining credibility by being too strongly antiunion; (3) failure to know the substance of employee relations; and (4) tendency to indulge in "class" forms of communication and to see administration as a class of people rather than an activity necessary for the success of everyone in the organization. In short, the employee relations benefits are lost if the communications expertise is "rooted in inexperience and unrealism."[18]

The most common fault or failing in employee communications is that it is too busy "selling" a management view *downward*. It neglects to stimulate an equivalent *upward* flow of employee viewpoints. As a consequence, it doesn't tell employees what they want to know, or reassure them that management knows what's bothering them. Public relations, even more than human relations, is positioned to inform management *objectively* of employee concerns. It is positioned to help human relations provide adequate listening devices for management.

One of the traps into which practitioners fall is that of overstating the story to employees and overpromising results to management. Both expect too much. Both are disappointed. An otherwise sound communications program ends up being considered inadequate, or a failure. If there is a secret, it is to underpromise and overdeliver.

EXHIBIT 13-1

A Case Study in Internal Communications

The internal communications systems required at the University of Michigan start with listening. Drawing on its Survey Research Center, the university has taken periodic surveys to provide upward channels for the faculty, the non-instructional staff, and students. For example, a survey of student opinion some years ago found, among other things: Nearly 67 percent of the students thought the administration provided enough information to explain its actions. Nearly 28 percent thought not. Some 40 percent regarded the University of Michigan as "cool and/or impersonal," and 90 percent thought students ought to be consulted on allocation of university funds.

Not long after the survey, the university's internal budget-setting mechanism was redesigned to incorporate a formal channel for student as well as staff participation. It was planned to devote a portion of the monthly meetings of the governing board of regents to comments from the university community and to more discussion of issues of interest to faculty, staff, and students.

A survey of faculty found that the greatest weakness in internal communication was lateral communication among departments. The most satisfactory exchange of information was between the professor and his department chairman or chairwoman. A similar survey among noninstructional staff members revealed that employees received most of their information about the university through its internal publications (as opposed to word of mouth, bulletin boards, or their supervisor, for example). Further, they preferred that order. At the same time, employees indicated the desire for more opportunities for upward communication.

The University of Michigan's administrators strive to meet faculty, staff, and students on an informal basis to facilitate dialogue. Sharing service on departmentwide and universitywide committees is one method.

Vice-President Michael Radock describes the university's program:

> Our internal communication effort is built around a number of distinct audiences within the University family and their particular information needs. Although interest in any given issue, policy or program overlaps different constituencies, the information we present is packaged for different groups. We consider specific information needs and perspectives, which vary from teaching faculty to unionized secretarial and service staffs to the non-teaching professional administrator.
>
> The core of our print program is the *University Record,* with a circulation of 23,000. It is a six-page weekly newspaper distributed early Monday morning via newsstands at major campus traffic areas. Though its primary focus is on the needs of the faculty, it serves the entire campus community, including students. Contents provide a forum and clearing house. Included are research proposal deadlines, job postings, a calendar of meetings, lectures and conferences.
>
> The *Record* is supplemented by the *UM News,* a semi-monthly magazine for non-instructional staff members and their families. It was launched in 1968 to fill an apparent gap between the University as an employer and its non-instructional staff and their families. The four-page tabloid, in a professionally crafted format, provides job-related information. It is mailed to employees' homes.
>
> Additional internal publications are used for ad-hoc collective bargaining status reports; interpretive, policy-oriented articles for supervisors of unionized employees; and for "crisis" communications, when immediate production and maximum distribution are required.
>
> In addition, University Relations is responsible for the educational radio station, WUOM, a member of the National Public Radio network. WUOM programs several hours of news and community affairs daily.

EXHIBIT 13-1 (CONT.)

Another medium is the 24-hour "news brief" telephone service. Recorded and regularly updated information on coming events, news happenings and University features are available around the clock. The phone number is promoted by bus cards, stickers and references in assorted publications. Since both individuals and radio stations use the service, a mix of actualities (voices of news makers) and events information is provided. Normally about 150 calls a day are made. In times of labor disputes or campus disturbance, as many as 4,000 calls a day swarm in.

The Office of Student Services maintains a phone-in/walk-in student counseling service which provides general information and functions as a crisis referral center. The 76-GUIDE (named for its telephone number) staff members offer personalized counseling and information.

At the Table is a flexible, easily produced newsletter to inform interested constituencies about collective bargaining negotiations. The University has been bargaining with seven labor unions. Most of those talks occur in a reporting vacuum, with the contract substance reported only after the agreement is signed. Negotiations with one campus union—representing some 2,000 graduate teaching and research assistants—have been conducted in public, however. *At the Table* has covered those talks and helped to solicit reaction from the most interested community—the faculty.

There is occasional need to reach staff and students "immediately" when the *Record* is not scheduled. For crisis communications overnight, a *Report to the University Community* most often is the answer. Generally one to four pages (8½" by 11") in length, the report provides updated information during critical periods of labor negotiations. *Report to the University Community* may be attributed to the president or another university official.

The Office of Information Services provides feedback, distributing clippings and analysis of media coverage to internal audiences of the University.

ADDITIONAL READINGS

ERNEST G. BORMANN, WILLIAM S. HOWELL, et al., *Interpersonal Communication in the Modern Organization*. Englewood Cliffs, N.J.: Prentice-Hall, 1969.

RICHARD W. DARROW, "Employee Communications—Neglected Need," *New York Times*, December 28, 1975.

C.J. DOVER, "The Three Eras of Management Communication," *The Journal of Communication*, Vol. 9 (December 1959).

PETER F. DRUCKER, *Management: Tasks, Responsibilities, Practices*. New York: Harper & Row, 1974. See Chapter 21, "The Responsible Worker."

ROBERT DUBIN, *Human Relations in Administration*, Englewood Cliffs, N.J.: Prentice-Hall, 1974.

MITCHELL FEIN, "The Real Needs and Goals of Blue Collar Workers," *The Conference Board Record*, New York, 1973.

ALAN L. HANLINE, "Motivating: So Easy For Some," *Public Relations Journal*, Vol. 31, No. 10 (October 1975), 10–13.

W. BENTON HARRISON, "Improving Managerial Communication," *ETC., A Review of General Semantics*, Vol. XXXII, No. 4 (December 1975).

HARRY LEVINSON, *The Great Jackass Fallacy*. Boston: Harvard Business School, 1973.

DOUGLAS MCGREGOR, *The Human Side of Enterprise*. New York: McGraw-Hill, 1960. A landmark book.

RICHARD NEMEC, "Internal Communications—A Scary Science," *Public Relations Journal*, Vol. 29, No. 12 (December 1973).

JUDY PICKENS et al., *Without Bias: A Guidebook for Non-Discriminatory Communication*. San Francisco: International Association of Business Communicators, 1977.

RICHARD J. SCHOENBERGER, "Taylorism Up-To-Date—The Inevitability of Worker Boredom," *Business and Society*, Spring 1974.

ROBERT C. SEDWICK, *Interaction—Interpersonal Relationships in Organizations*. Englewood Cliffs, N.J.: Prentice-Hall, 1974.

A.W. WILLSMORE, *Managing Modern Man*. New York: Pitman, 1973.

For industrial case studies, see *Case Studies in Organizational Communication*, a joint project of Towers, Perrin, Forster & Crosby, consulting firm, and the Industrial Communication Council. New York: ICC, 1975.

FOOTNOTES

1. Agis Salpukas, "Reform of Work: Move for Creative Jobs Stirs Debate," *New York Times,* Nov. 13, 1974, quoting Dr. Frederick Herzberg, Western Reserve University.

2. "The Corporate Ombudsman," *Harvard Business Review,* Vol. 45 (May–June, 1967), 77–87.

3. Howard Wilson, "Psychological Needs of Man," *PR,* Vol. I (October 1955).

4. Interesting input: "Those 'Boring Jobs'—Not All That Dull," *U.S. News & World Report,* Dec. 1, 1975.

5. Eric Fromm, *The Sane Society* (New York: Holt, Rinehart & Winston, 1955).

6. See "Survey Finds Young U.S. Workers Increasingly Dissatisfied and Frustrated," *New York Times,* May 22, 1974, Sec. M, p. 37.

7. David E. Berlow, "Leadership and Organizational Excitement," *California Management Review,* Vol. XVII, No. 2 (Winter 1974).

8. For details, see "Playing Cards: A New Employee Survey Technique," *PR Tips and Tactics,* Vol. 13, No. 34 (October 13, 1975).

9. "It Pays to Listen to the Workers' Complaints," *Business Week,* October 6, 1975.

10. For case studies, see "Journalism Teacher Fires Up Students—and Ends Up Fired," *New York Times,* Jan. 21, 1975; "The Aircraft Brake Scandal," *Harper's Magazine,* April 1972; and Robert Heilbroner *et al., In the Name of Profit* (New York: Doubleday, 1972).

11. Harvey Swados, "Work as a Public Issue," *Saturday Review,* Vol. 42 (Dec. 12, 1959), 13–15 and 45; and Patricia Cayo Sexton, "The Auto Assembly Line: An Inside View," *Harper's Magazine,* Vol. 224 (June 1962), 52–57.

12. Studs Terkel, *Working* (New York: Pantheon, 1974), p. 258.

13. "Every Employee an Owner? Old Idea Gets a New Boost," *U.S. News & World Report,* June 9, 1975, 68–70. Explains the procedure.

14. "The Revolution No One Noticed," *Chicago Tribune,* Perspective Section, July 18, 1976. Describes his "pension fund socialism" concept. This is also treated by Howard Chase, "The Issue: Employee Ownership of the Industrial System through Their Own Pension Plans," *Corporate Public Issues,* Vol. I, No. 11 (September 15, 1976). For later developments on stock-ownership plans, see "Stocks for Workers—Spreading, but Raising Questions, Too," *U.S. News & World Report,* August 16, 1976.

15. Robert L. Kahn, "The Work Module—A Tonic for Lunchpail Lassitude," *Psychology Today,* February 1973.

16. Dallis Perry and Thomas A. Mahoney, "In-plant Communications and Employee Morale," *Personnel Psychology,* Vol. 8 (Autumn 1955), 339.

17. Arthur H. Brayfield and Walter H. Crockett, "Employee Attitudes and Employee Performance," *Psychological Bulletin,* Vol. 52 (September 1955), 421. Still worth reading.

18. George S. Odiorne, "Public Relations and Industrial Relations," *Personnel Journal,* Vol. 38, No. 3 (March 1960), 366–69.

14

What people say behind your back is your standing in the community in which you live.

H.W. LONGFELLOW

The Community Public

The community, as a public, is changing. The changes relate to the societal trends in the human environment. Of particular significance is the urbanization of America. As Irving Kristol put it, "In terms of quality of life, the United States is now one vast metropolis." As a result, the functional specialties within public relations that are called community relations or local public affairs are becoming much more demanding and sophisticated.

The community—by definition

When defining a community in a contemporary context, an authoritative source on public relations in local government emphasizes sociological overtones. It is "a place of interacting social institutions which produce in the residents an attitude and practice of interdependence, cooperation, collaboration, and unification."[1]

This author points out that while large urban conglomerations *do not* exhibit the characteristics in the definition, smaller and remote communities *do*. Public relations researchers are advised to "center their primary interest on how people live together and meet their functional needs through community social institutions. The community might best be seen as a web of social structures all closely interrelated."[2] This is good advice for researchers. The best hope of harmonizing the "web of social structures" for future generations is by coupling research knowledge with long-range public-interest planning.

Community change

Meantime, "attitudes and practices of interdependence, cooperation, collaboration, and unification" are not automatic. They need to be stimulated. Conditions in the metropolitan areas, and in many smaller cities, are not in themselves conducive to cooperation and collaboration. Some of the conditions strike many residents as being a far cry from what has been promoted and proclaimed as "advances in living standards."

311

Neighborhoods, villages, and cities cannot always anticipate events that change their physical condition and their destiny; and even if they could, they might be helpless to stem the tide. Nothing illustrates this helplessness with more clarity than the once-booming and now derelict mining towns that dot the nation's countryside. The depletion of mining resources in certain localities is but one example of how economic health affects a community. The destiny of Neodasha, Kansas, first changed when American Oil opened a refinery there in 1897; it changed again when Amoco pulled out in 1970. Saltville, Virginia, existed as a small community from 1892 because Olin Corporation had a soda-ash operation there. Saltville almost died economically in 1972, when Olin shut down because it was less expensive to move than to meet new state pollution standards.

Economics and change are not restricted to natural resources or product manufacture. It was Milwaukee's gain in 1953 when the baseball Braves moved in. The whole community was proud when they won the World Series in 1957. Fans and bystanders could not prevail, however, when the Braves were sold and moved to Atlanta in 1964. On a national scale, hundreds of communities have sprung to new life when new interstate highways were constructed nearby. Others, on the old side roads, have fallen on hard times. The downtown shopping areas of cities have become quiet, as shopping malls have sprouted in the suburbs. Hundreds of small villages serving and depending on a cluster of family farms have suffered because contract farming took over huge tracts for distant food processors.

Community relationships hinge on social as well as economic change. The Boston community experienced a change and a great cleavage when leaders undertook to force busing for school integration. Mother Nature, too, sometimes deals a community a low blow. In Wilkes-Barre, Pennsylvania, 75,000 people were driven from their homes when a devastating hurricane struck.

It is the anticipation, actuality, and aftermath of realities such as these that occupy community relations practitioners in organizations being benefitted or hurt by change. As a practical matter, the focus of community relations activity shifts with the needs. In one instance, the communications task may be wrapped up mainly in the movement to or from a *geographical location*. For example, Johns-Manville moved its world headquarters from the East Coast to Colorado. An entire new community relationship had to be created. See Figure 14–1. In another instance, the focus of activity may be on the concept of a community as a desirable *hometown*, or a *place to be educated*, or a *place to visit*. In another, the focus may be on a *promotional* aspect, like the Rose Bowl Festival in Pasadena. Or the community may represent an available *bloc of public opinion* needed in the form of votes, members, or customers.

As a working perspective, perhaps the best advice for a practitioner is to be ready for the unexpected, and to count on change.

The makeup of community opinion

A community is a miniature of the national public. This is where national opinions are born. Judgments expressed as the voice of the community predict the views and interests of the national spectator and voter.

Community life moves in and around interest groupings. Community spirit is

FIGURE 14-1 A whole new relationship had to be established when Johns-Manville changed its main location from the urbanized East Coast to a 10,000-acre ranch southwest of Denver. New neighbors included ranchers and wildlife. Courtesy Johns-Manville.

the ability to compromise interests and act together for the common good. The interests may be in lower taxes, a new sports arena, attraction of industry, or rejecting a land-development proposal. Alliances form around the interests. They come and go, overlap, and shift.

Each community has special characteristics that are important to residents, and often inviolate in their minds. Philadelphia has its Liberty Bell. Greenbay, Wisconsin, has its Packers. Deming, New Mexico, calls itself the "rock capital of the world." Salem, Illinois, was Lincoln's boyhood home, and Plains, Georgia, now has its own distinction. Programs exploiting these special features provide catalysts that bring residents together in common bonds of interest and joint activities. They provide a "claim to fame" that can be projected out to the rest of the world.

The power structure

Each stratum and each major issue in a community develops its own leaders. The mayor or village manager may not be the political leader. He or she may be a puppet placed in a referee position by the real leaders, so that decisions fall in favor of the business, agriculture, or recreation faction. It is necessary in community relations work to know who's *really* who on the political, economic, and social scene.

The opinion leaders

Opinion leadership is not static. It moves with issues. In modern times, you cannot rely on the traditional biases—rich versus poor, conservative versus liberal, generation versus generation, and so on. Issue by issue, the one consistent factor is that those who stand to gain and to lose oppose each other. Each issue or proposal attracts leadership to push for and against. A prominent banker and a prominent farmland owner, both with large families, might join in leadership of a bond issue for a new high school. The same two might oppose each other over a new interstate-highway route that would rip through prime farmland to pass alongside the town. And they might both sidestep leadership for or against a neighborhood integration plan.

The multistep flow discussed in Chapter 9 applies in community opinion formation. Identification of the influentials in the community, and of their views on relevant issues, is fundamental. The conventional power structure in large cities lends itself to the shape of a pyramid. At the top is that handful of people responsible for providing the city's economic underpinnings. Alongside are those few top officials responsible for allocating the city's available funds.[3]

The prime movers

The impact of the influentials, as depicted in Figure 14–2, is often quiet and behind the scenes. Of equal importance to the practitioner are the vocalized groupings and alliances that make up the prime movers, issue by issue. It is their support and activities that form the climate of opinion, the goodwill or the

FIGURE 14–2 The power pyramid.

disapproval accorded an organization and its people. Millard Faught suggests the following groupings as basic prime movers:

1. Employees' or members' families.
2. The press, radio, and TV, their editors and commentators.
3. Thought leaders, including clergy, teachers, city officials, prominent retailers and professional men, union officials, bankers, civil workers, and industrialists.
4. Organizations, including city planning commission, welfare agencies, youth groups, veterans, fraternal, and service groups, cultural and political-action bodies.[4]
5. Crusaders, such as protest groups, petitioners, voice-of-the-people, special events, and the rumor factories.

The practicalities of achieving persuasion through the prime movers should not be sloughed off. Caterpillar Tractor's open house for barbers suggests that special audiences have a good-sized hand in formulating community opinions. Barbers and hair stylists have the attention of male and female residents for a half hour or more every two weeks or so. Bartenders have a nightly audience. Then there are the local librarian, the auctioneers, the mailmen, the milkmen, and the hotel desk clerk. All these people are in a position to influence others. All of them talk with the audience that organizations need to win.

The independents

Within any community there is a scattering of residents whose views cannot be dependably identified with those held by any leader or prime-mover group. Some people just don't care. Some take pride in being independent or aloof. Some affect passive or neutral inclinations toward matters that excite others. Many simply haven't the incentive for "getting involved." This group might include seasonal visitors, military and other temporary residents, and those whose jobs call for tact, caution, and neutrality—for instance, hired staffs of associations and societies whose members' convictions are divided. The same occasionally applies to political aspirants and public officials, depending on the particular community issue or project.

Taken as a group, those who deliberately stand aside neutrally or passively often have the potential to influence the outcome in controversies. They can furnish this leverage if persuaded out of their neutrality, or perhaps when persuaded to remain silent, passive, and uncommitted. How to deal with them, situation by situation, is one of the ingredients in the civic and public-affairs functional role.

The dissidents

The final important segment of residents in the community power structure is made up of the vocal and active dissidents and resisters. Seldom can these clusters be won over by any persuasion less than opposition to the views or people they oppose. Their strength derives from being at odds, unconvertible, and uncontrollable. The two mainstays in this segment are opposites in nature: There are those who will stoutly *resist* change of almost any kind. Then there are those who will aggressively *seek* drastic and sudden change of almost any kind.

In dealing with dissidents and resisters, the principles of persuasion in Chapter 6 apply. Their application does not, however, promise surefire resolutions for all community issues and crises. There are exceptions and variables. In one situation—say, votes for 18-year-olds—efforts to silence or discredit resisters might backfire, by giving exposure and encouragement to what otherwise might be an unpopular resistance. In another situation—say, a school bond issue—failure to meet resistance promptly and openly might raise questions about the merit of the proposition and the sincerity of its proponents. The principles remain valid. They need to be pretested, situation by situation.

In making use of the community power structure, the neutrals, the uncommitted, and the dissidents and resisters cannot be ignored. Strategy must be on a case-by-case, move-by-move basis. It is a chess game in public opinion.

The basic approach

Interdependence

A platform for continuing effective relationships is based on an admission of interdependence among all who share in the well-being of the community. All sectors bear a share of the responsibility. A business cannot prosper without good employees, municipal services, and freedom from needless local regulations. A municipal government cannot provide proper services without valuable real estate and a humming economy to tap for funds. Residents need good employment and places to shop. They need the schools, hospitals, and recreational facilities that taxes pay for.

There was a time when many institutions in the private sector felt they had choices of whether, and to what extent, to become involved in community affairs. This was particularly true of employing institutions. In the 1950s, we wrote of two schools of thought on community relations for industry. One was the "community-centered" or "personal-service" school, in which company presidents and their administrative staffs assumed great personal responsibility for the development of the city and its institutions. The other was the "company-centered" school. This concept concentrated on educating citizens in "basic economics" and on the use of persuasion by professionals to develop attitudes favorable to the profitable operation of business. In those days, each school of thought held vague reservations about the other.

A third school of thought surfaced visibly in good economic times. This one held that community relations was simply an extension of employee relations. Whatever relationship was attained among employees would echo out in the surrounding community. Employee satisfaction would produce a waiting line at the employment office, would result in cooperative attitudes by local officials. No more than soft suggestions or slight nudges would be needed to produce no-parking zones, larger sewers, condemnation of land, or whatever else was needed in the name of growth and progress.

Vestiges of all these schools of thought exist today. With increasing interdependency, there is no longer an either-or, all-or-none choice. Leader organizations mix in, or else.

Analysis

Beyond acceptance of a philosophy of interdependence, the next step is to make the kind of analysis that can lead to efficient, profitable implementation. A good starting point is analysis of the community's overriding needs. All will fit somewhere among twelve goals:

1. Commercial prosperity.
2. Support of religion.
3. Work for everyone.
4. Adequate educational facilities.
5. Law, order, and safety.
6. Population growth.
7. Proper housing and utilities.
8. Varied recreational and cultural pursuits.
9. Attention to public welfare.
10. Progressive measures for good health.
11. Competent municipal government.
12. A good reputation.

From the analysis, priorities can hopefully be set in a master plan. Decisions must be made. Should relief of unemployment, improvement of utility services, or law-enforcement cleanup come first?

Among six small towns that staged comebacks through the 1970s, Leavenworth, Washington, decided to put the development of tourist traffic first. Hillsboro, Ohio, set out to bring in industry. Albion, Louisiana, interested utilities in providing major redevelopment help. Toccoa, Georgia, turned to the federal government for funds, and then to professional management help. Sawmills, Maine, concentrated on its recreational facilities to attract some of the traffic racing through town. Cooper, Texas, started by rebuilding an old bandstand in the center of town as a focal point for social events.

Among the efforts of middle-sized cities to rejuvenate themselves, Atlanta built its Peachtree Center and Omni complex. Houston activated its Pennzoil Place. San Antonio retrieved the beauty and utility of its riverfront. Kansas City emphasized its new Crown Center. Denver restored the Larimer Street district.[5]

Through the 1980s, the rebuilding of places from old ones will flourish.

Policies

When the homework is done and priorities are set, the time is right for leadership organizations to put themselves on record. They should go public with pride, enthusiasm, and specific plans. This need not be an immediate shouting from the hilltop or the ivory tower. The revelation or revamping of organizational policies constitutes a positive expression. The word gets around. On this point, employees do help.

Policies can address themselves in general to the twelve needs or goals of the community mentioned earlier. Or policies can deal directly with the anxieties of the community. Or they can commit the organization to exemplary citizenship. A simple policy statement that no one in the organization may accept a gift from a supplier or offer a gift to a public official says a lot about how the organization feels toward all unethical hanky-panky. A statement that no help will be hired or supplies purchased elsewhere if they are available at fair prices locally says a lot. A policy statement that charitable contributions will be concentrated in areas where employees live, and in activities that improve the quality of life for the community, says something neighbors want to hear. A statement that conservation of energy and reduction of pollution are constant aims puts others on notice that the same is expected of them. A policy encouraging employees to pursue their personal interests and convictions in civic affairs has significance. A promotion and recognition policy that favors those who live in the community where they work would be welcome to local merchants and officials.

Participation

Policies require implementation as the final step. Until something actually happens, the community judges by the participation it sees and feels. Policies are just words on paper. As we explained in the preceding chapter, participation starts with the executives. What they do sets an example for the organization. It alerts the whole community to what can be expected. The officials reflect in policies and actions their decisions and *the personality of the organization.*

Participation requires a costly investment of executive time. A study of community relations activities in one eastern city disclosed that ten to fourteen hours a week, more than half of it spent at luncheons and evening sessions, was about par for the most active executives; six to ten hours a week was fairly common. As pressures mount on organizational executives to give more time and energy to pressing community problems, the need increases to deputize subordinates—often the public relations man—for these emotion-wearing chores.

A public relations practitioner, James J. Bowe of Minneapolis, quit that city's Urban Coalition because the top businessman, active at the outset, withdrew and delegated the job to lower executives. Bowe said, "The top executive himself must participate. He too often just sends a messenger. That's what we've done with all our middle-class social agencies for years. His opposite number across the table knows damn well that this subordinate hasn't got the authority . . . and he's tired of fooling with these subordinates. Businessmen must change and that can come only through personal experience."[6] This is equally applicable to the college president, the government bureaucrat, and the superintendent of schools.

The principle in Mr. Bowe's action was sound. In a time of massive organizations, however, top management has to be a shared responsibility; otherwise the organization flounders. A floundering organization is of no help to any of its publics, including its communities. To be specific, the diversity of social problems in a large city like Minneapolis would render personal participation in all of them impossible for the top official at 3M, Pillsbury, the University of Minnesota, or the Vikings. It is important that those to whom the participation responsibility is delegated be qualified by function and nature for each problem at hand. They must have the authority to speak for and to commit their organizations.[7]

All too often, titled regional and local authorities of billion-dollar enterprises lack the authority of their titles. They can't pledge manpower, equipment, or financial aid for a joint community project without approval from above. The approval source may be across the country. The decision may be made by people without understanding of the local mood, or by those who simply don't care about it. If the decision is wrong by local standards, more harm than good is done, and the stature of the local manager is undermined. Local people come to regard him for what he is—a stand-in, a messenger with a smiling face. It is in these situations that Bowe's point goes to the heart of community relations.

Community leaders, including business chief executives, have many choices of activities in which to participate. The selection is a highly personal matter. The important thing is that leaders make their choices and give more than lip service to them. There are *angelic activities:* the Community Fund, Red Cross, YMCA. There are *controversial projects:* slum clearance, gun control, crime and addiction, integration, nuclear development. There are *educational and cultural activities:* new schools, parks, the arts. There are *public-policy activities:* transportation, airports, smog. There are *promotional activities:* sports, recreation, entertainment. See Exhibit 14–1.

EXHIBIT 14-1   Illustration courtesy California Bankers Association.

Banking. . . . No Place To Hide

Of all leader entities in a community, none has greater civic tenacity than banking, and with sound reasons. Most people who can't find jobs in town can go elsewhere; retailers, salesmen, schoolteachers and even manufacturers can transplant themselves. Bankers, however, have everything riding on the health and continuity of their community. Available funds are lent out all over the area. Depositors keep coming and going. Lockboxes hold residents' valuables. Loans are tied up with rental properties, farms, and new construction. Just about the only "escape" for a banker is by selling out, going to jail, or dying.

COMMUNITY PERFORMANCE UPDATE

AN ACTION REPORT OF CALIFORNIA BANKERS

EXHIBIT 14-1 (CONT.)

The California Bankers Association compiled an inventory of its members' community endeavors.[8] The booklet (its cover is illustrated above) listed 208 one-paragraph vignettes. They fell into twelve categories as follows:

Youth and education	72	For senior citizens	16
Affirmative action	17	Cultural enrichment	33
Job assistance	11	Special projects	13
Low-income housing	12	Minority & small-business	
Environment	10	assistance	12
Bond financing (a summary)		Area development	5
Counseling	7		

Here are a few examples of the innovative thinking. These projects were listed in the "Special Projects" category:

- Several banks made available Braille account programs for the visually handicapped, at no extra cost to the customer.
- United California Bank, as a result of a CORO Foundation study, revamped its charitable contributions program, creating a committee, specific criteria, a more thorough evaluation process, and the setting of priorities.
- Security National Bank allocated space at its Walnut Creek office on weekends for a local Farmers' Market. The bank coordinated the market and underwrote all maintenance and publicity costs.
- Security National Bank had monthly hypertension and glaucoma screening tests at branches.
- Sixteen members of the board and top management of Wells Fargo Bank participated in a program with representatives of the Center of Ethics and Social Policy of the Graduate Theological Union in Berkeley. The challenges confronting corporations today and new criteria for decision making were explored. As an outgrowth, a monograph was published by the Graduate Theological Union entitled, "Ethics and the Corporate Policy Process," and was distributed to business, government, and community leaders throughout the country.
- Wells Fargo Bank's Corporate Responsibility Committee examined and made recommendations on all aspects of the bank's activities. The committee's twelve members included a lending officer, data-processing officer, vice-presidents from the retail division and public relations, the head of personnel, and an executive vice-president. Two members were women, one was black, and one was a Mexican-American. Among committee recommendations adopted were a policy of not scheduling official bank functions at any facility that discriminates against women and minorities, and the payment of interest on real estate impound accounts.
- Through media that include posters and the employee magazine, Security Pacific National Bank encouraged its staff members to engage in volunteer work for the benefit of their communities.
- First State Bank of Northern California, San Leandro, published a monthly newsletter in which local nonpolitical groups could mention their meetings, events, drives, and sales.
- Several banks had community rooms that they made available to charitable, nonprofit, and civic groups. A northern California bank opened a room Monday mornings for churches to count their offerings.
- Bank of Marin assisted local charities in preparing applications to foundations for grants. The bank's lobbies and phones were used for various telephone auctions, telethons, and fund drives.
- Bank of Marin staffed temporary banks for various community fairs such as the Grape Festival, Marin County Fair, and Greek Festival.

Communications is not a sometime thing

Civic-minded policies, acts of participation, and a well-run organization are building blocks. Continuous communication about policies, participation, and the affairs of the organization cements them together. The affairs of an organization that mix with the affairs of a community are properly public domain. Silence on internal matters that affect the community is eyed by the hometown people with great suspicion, as if the person or organization had something to hide. Holding back bad news is self-defeating. One du Pont official has observed, "Bad news doesn't necessarily have a bad effect. You gain the sympathy and understanding of the community. And getting the facts out quickly avoids incorrect stories and damaging rumors." Officials of a chemical plant in Memphis, Tennessee, learned this the hard way. Many people became ill when deadly chlorine gas escaped from a ruptured pipeline. The victims were hospitalized, but the company made no public explanation. The story became "news" when the state board of health closed the plant. A company official subsequently admitted to the community, "Chlorine brought the wrath of God down on our heads. Perhaps we were lax explaining what we were doing here, and we realize things that are unknown can create fear and suspicion about our activities." Enlightened management anticipates community questions with information.

A community looks around its own confines first for its news and opinions on grand-scale matters. Thoughtful analyses of national happenings come right into the home through the radio and television; but the hometown newspaper and prominent local spokesmen carry more day-by-day weight than the most highly paid outside sources. This emphasizes the extreme importance of the hometown audience to public-affairs programs. So businessmen, state officials, military leaders, and social-agency heads have come around more and more to the idea of communications programs individually tailored within the community rather than modeled after a single pattern cut in Washington or New York. There is much more work to the local tailoring, but the result is vastly more satisfactory.

If each institution seeks and gains acceptability and popular support of its views locally, public opinion for that type of institution will follow suit on the national level. The efficiency of federal government is judged by the way its programs are administered locally. Utilities in general are judged by the behavior of the hometown power and light company. Manufacturers as a group are judged by what the local machine-tool company does or fails to do. Consumer protection is judged by actions of hometown stores. The armed forces are judged by impressions of the nearest installation. And so it goes. The local branch delivers to the national institution a bloc of favorable opinions in much the same manner that the county political-party chairman delivers a bloc of votes. People judge the whole by the parts they know.

Community relations at work

There is an immense variety of ways in which the auxiliary public relations tools can be put to work. We will touch on seven of them regularly employed: (1) the open house and tour of facilities, (2) the special event, (3) extended house-publication circulation or special newsletter, (4) volunteer activities, (5) local advertising, (6) contributions of funds, and (7) media news services.

EXHIBIT 14–2

Case Study in Pollution Control

Problems can be turned into public relations opportunities. There are many stories of community frictions that concerned organizations turned into opportunities to demonstrate citizenship.

One of them involved International Harvester. IH built a new plant outside Memphis in open country. As happens with many manufacturing plants, government ordnance facilities, airports, and nuclear sites, the surrounding fields were soon covered with homes and people living in them. IH recognized that its smoke and soot would become a problem. It could not solve it by telling people, "We were here first, you had no business to move so close." The company took these steps:

1. Company representatives rang all the doorbells in the affected neighborhood to talk over the problem with the housewives.
2. Samples of the offending dirt were taken from lawns and clotheslines. Then letters were written to the homeowners telling them that Harvester's powerhouse smoke was responsible.
3. The women were promised that Harvester would search for a solution. No promises of fast relief were given.
4. Harvester went to work on a solution and kept these women informed each step of the way. It put gas burners in the foundry cupolas, sprayed its coal with oil, put a warning bell in its smokestack, planted a parklike buffer zone of trees and grass. These measures cost $70,000 and helped to alleviate the problem. Still, IH kept up its search for a solution and, after three years, found a type of air-control equipment that would solve it. This was put in at a cost of $71,900.
5. When the solution had been found, the company called in its plant's neighbors and the community leaders. It explained the new equipment and thanked them for their patience and understanding.

In the end, the company came out a good neighbor.

The open house

The open house has the advantage of bringing large numbers onto the premises of the organization. Its weakness is that such large numbers do not have the opportunity for much personal discussion about interests they share.

The size of attendance suggests keeping arrangements for refreshments and personal services to a minimum. Hosts should go all out for devices that will facilitate pleasure and ease for the guests: exhibits that can be seen quickly, ample guides or signposts leading to appointed areas, seats for the overflow crowd, and a carefully supervised method of regulating traffic. Of great advantage is the participation of employees. Many guests are relatives and friends of the rank and file. Participation as hosts gives employees a renewed pride in their working group.

The most important part of the tour of facilities is the planning that precedes it. It can be conducted as a special event, such as Homecoming, or as a routine system to handle daily visitors. Planning must include these factors:

1. An itinerary that is logical in telling the story.
2. A duration that accommodates the comfort of the tourist. Many tours are too long

and arduous. If the tour requires a lot of walking or exertion, there should be a break somewhere along the way with seating facilities.

3. Competent guides who not only understand the various phases of the operations but can put them into words that laymen can understand.

4. A running story that shows the interlocking of the organization's interests with those of the community.

5. Some sort of simple gesture at the end of the tour to make the occasion memorable. It can be a pause for refreshment, a handshake with the president, a product sample, an opportunity to operate a unique machine or device, or a pamphlet about the organization.

6. Above all, enthusiasm in the treatment of visitors.

Special events

The special event or project has a limitless range: for instance, ground-breaking for a new structure; sidewalk-engineer arrangements for one under construction; dedication of the completed structure; a time capsule in the cornerstone for posterity. Open house, tour, or reception can be hitched up with any of

FIGURE 14–3   A special panel truck checks exhaust emission for motorists. Courtesy Atlantic Richfield.

these nonrecurring events. Programming can span a year or two, and longer for projects like a nuclear-energy facility, an Alaskan pipeline, or a new aircraft carrier.

There are many projects sponsored on behalf of those who need help: a turkey farm, with the produce given to the Salvation Army for Thanksgiving; a contest of homemade dolls for orphans; a school for parolees and the handicapped locally; a seminar on safe driving or conserving energy in the home; free X-rays or blood-pressure tests; employment offices in ghetto areas; high-risk loans to minority businessmen; scholarships.

More and more programs turn up related to the environment and quality of life as in Figure 14–3. There are collections of recyclable refuse, antilitter campaigns, hikes for hunger, gardens for children, and unsightly earth blemishes redeemed for public use.

To attempt a complete list here would boggle the imagination. Practitioners and students can turn to the periodicals serving the calling, and to the annual Silver Anvil Awards of the Public Relations Society of America, for up-to-this-month ideas and innovations. The nation's bicentennial spawned hundreds oriented to communities.

Extended house-publication circulation

Little additional news matter is needed to make the employee publication of interest throughout the community. This is a worthwhile project. Among the readers close at hand are the people waiting in the laundromat, the doctor's office, the barbershop, and the airport. Employees' activities are followed keenly by the clergy. Organizational activities are a matter of concern to merchants and to city officials.

Actually, there is no area of the community in which the house publication is not welcome. Features such as burglarproofing hints from the chief of police, comments on citywide events, articles dealing with area legend and lore, and perhaps a calendar of future special events can be added. A real service is performed without conflict with local daily or weekly newspapers. A few organizations have special publications recognizing employees who have made contributions in their communities. The publication goes to all civic, education, and welfare officials in the community.

The prime movers can also be reached by occasional *letters from officials* of an organization. These are quite helpful, especially in anticipating rumors and quieting harmful talk. Topics in such letters are generally maintained at a high level of discussion. There is no overt intent to force thought leaders to serve the interests of the organization. Rather, the intent is to place them in a better-informed position to serve the interests of their constituents.

Volunteer activities

Volunteering for community activities was mentioned earlier, in the context of participation. As an auxiliary tool, volunteerism can be stimulated within a sizable organization. The right person can be found for the public-service job needing help. The right person is the one qualified by skill or knowledge, *and* desirous of rendering service. A mechanism for stimulating volunteerism is shown in Figure 14–4, a questionnaire by which employees indicate their areas of enthusiasm and interest. By canvassing employees, an organization serves notice that it approves. Having the information leads to a logical follow-through: The

FIGURE 14-4   Courtesy Motorola, Inc.

ACTIVITY	(1) Check this column if you are an active member.	(2) Describe location or chapter of organization you refer to in Column (1), e.g. Phoenix Kiwanis, Roosevelt Troop #89, etc.	(3) Indicate office or committee assignment you hold now or have held in the past. Describe past by suffix "P".	(4) Check this column if not active but would like to become active.
E. LOCAL OR STATE GOVT.				
Committee				
Board				
Commission				
Precinct Worker				
Other				
F. CIVIC ACTIVITIES				
Civil Air Patrol				
Civil Defense				
Chamber of Commerce				
Jr. Chamber of Commerce				
Community Council				
Other				
G. MILITARY & VETERAN				
American Legion				
Vets of Foreign Wars				
National Guard				
Army, Navy, Marine or A.F. Res. (circle one)				
Other				
H. PROFESSIONAL & TECH. (such as IRE, ASME, AIEE)				

GENERAL COMMENTS

Make sure you have printed this survey promptly to:

MOTOROLA INC. Semiconductor Products Division

PHOENIX, ARIZONA

COMMUNITY ACTIVITIES SURVEY

PLEASE PRINT

LAST NAME, FIRST NAME, MIDDLE INITIAL	TITLE	PHONE

DATE	HOME PHONE	HOME ADDRESS	CITY

ACTIVITY	(1) Check this column if you are an active member.	(2) Describe location or chapter of organization you refer to in Column (1), e.g. Phoenix Kiwanis, Roosevelt Troop #89, etc.	(3) Indicate office or committee assignment you hold now or have held in the past. Describe past by suffix "P".	(4) Check this column if not active but would like to become active.
A. SERVICE CLUBS				
Exchange				
Kiwanis				
Lions				
Optimists				
Rotary				
Toastmasters				
Other				
B. YOUTH ACTIVITIES				
Amer. Jr. Red Cross				
Boys Club				
Boy Scouting				
Camp Fire Girls				
Cub Scouting				
Girls Club				
Girl Scouting				
Jr. Achievement				
Sports (such as Little Leag.)				
YMCA				
YWCA				
4-H, FFA				
Other				
C. EDUC. & CULTURAL				
School Board				
PTA				
Advisory Committee				
Dramatic Groups				
Music & Art Organ.				
Museums & Hist. Soc.				
Other				
D. SOC. HEALTH & WELFARE				
United Fund				
Red Cross				
Hospital Bds. & Other				
Crippled Children				
Goodwill Industries				
Mental Health				
Jewish Comm. Center				
Retarded Children				
Family Service Agency				
Salvation Army				
Cerebral Palsy				
Day Nursery				
Other				

---

organization can recognize in its house publication employees who give of themselves. Some organizations have gone even further, granting leaves of absence for public service or to conduct personal campaigns for local public office.

This is a fertile field for experimentation. There are, however, some risks.

Employees given encouragement to follow their convictions into community affairs may join enterprises or crusades that work against their employers' interests. Freedom of conviction and expression rub in several directions. For example, Ashland, Wisconsin, businessmen joined ranks with Northland College students in the community to march in protest against a du Pont plant's pollution of a stream dubbed "Bloody Mary Creek."[9] Enlightened management, taking a more aggressive posture itself in public and community issues, tends to take the perennial critic or one-issue dissension in stride. Criticisms and accusations provide opportunity for dialogue, with the proper audience tuned in.

Local advertising

Hometown advertising is becoming more popular. Its subject matter often leans toward social or economic issues. Advertising is a partial answer to the problem of absentee ownership. It is a method of completely controlling the message. It serves a helpful purpose with employees who after working hours are swallowed by the remote sections of the city and have little contact with each other.

The stigmas of impersonalization and propaganda often attach themselves to paid advertising space. The reaction is that the organization did not have to air its views or fight its battles in that manner—it could have come directly to the people. Organized labor is inclined to interpret such advertising, when it touches on industrial relations, as an act of bad faith, especially if it is used in time of crisis or strikes. Reactions depend on the use, not the medium.[10]

To praise or discourage the use of the tool would be an unsafe generalization. Much is heard of its successes, as judged by sponsors. The failures are screened in silence, or claims are made that they "were satisfactory" or "did what we wanted." One reported success was a series by the Armco Steel Corporation, Middletown, Ohio, in a house publication with spillover readership through the community. The headlines indicate the contexts (parenthetical notes by the authors):

- This Slot-Machine Always Pays Off—in Cash (picture of time clock).
- A Boy Who Needs $10,000 (amount invested in business per employee).
- The Spade That Dug a Fortune (used to break ground for expansion).
- Baby, You've Got a Future at Armco (planning for future).
- Armco's $1,000,000-a-year Fishing License (retirement plan).
- The Man Who Brings Us Paydays (plug for salesmen).
- Henry, How Is Armco Doing? (family's stake in company).
- A Million Dollars from a Cornfield (monthly payroll at plant).
- No Future in the Buggy Business (moving ahead for the future).
- Bought Any Steel Mills Lately? (rising costs).
- If Every Hen Laid Two Eggs a Day (plug for productivity).
- A Sure Way to Get a New Pair (shoes pictured, plug for building surplus).

Contributions of funds

Financial contributions for community causes and events come largely from profit-making organizations, independent professionals, associations and unions, the personal funds of the wealthy, and high-salaried public officials. The usual and obvious recipients are the private health, welfare, and educational agencies that get no government funding. Contributions to these agencies are deductible for income tax purposes, the same as business-related expenses.

Suppose a doctor, after deducting all his expenses, has a taxable net income of $50,000, as many do. The federal income tax rate is 35 percent. So if he contributes $100 to his favorite private hospital, the cost to him would be only $65, because the other $35 would be taxed away anyway. This is why you hear talk that it costs a billion-dollar corporation only 50 cents to give away a dollar. The corporation is in the maximum 50 percent tax bracket. But there is more to it. A corporation may donate only a small percentage of its net proceeds tax-free. Most corporations do not donate up to that limit; shareholders and insiders have a say in that.

Nonfinancial contributions to the community can be in lent equipment; computer, cartage, or other services; manpower; and use of facilities.

Media news services

Media services to hometown news outlets is a large muscle in the local program. It cannot be said accurately that the public relations man exercises a control over this tool. He doesn't. But the local press, TV, and radio want news; they don't have to be sold on the idea. Local news builds circulation and listening audiences. The doings of any organization significant in the life of the community are news. Organizational news is a service to the newspapers, radio, and TV.

Quite apart from the desire and need to cover the news, the local press takes pride in the community and is dedicated to its growth, prosperity, and good reputation. What helps the community helps the news media and the organization. What helps the news media and the organization helps the community. The interrelation is a well-rooted and close one.

The local press, radio, and TV should have access to all information that the townspeople want. Exceptions, of course, are pieces of information that could at times be damaging for competitive, legal, or security reasons. As a good reporter, the organization is expected to supply information to its own employees and principals first, to its community second, and to the outside public third. Members of a "family" are hurt when they learn "family" news secondhand. The good reporter makes a point of knowing what the local press considers news. The main thing is to pursue a policy of candor and at the same time keep a check on community reactions.

Media relations is the subject of Chapter 17.

The community relations audit

To this point we have stressed communications needs related to the conditions existing through the 1970s—to urbanization, and to the social stresses of the times. Thus, the most vivid colors in the picture have been those of controversy, crisis, dissension, and emergency. We have suggested strongly that even more interdependence is the wave of the future.

It is not likely that the trend will be reversed in the 1980s.[11] Cities and their occupants will continue to have to make adjustments as best they can to changing patterns and ways of living. For public relations, this necessitates periodic audits of community opinion. Indications of national views and moods are available in a general way from polls by Harris, Gallup, and Roper. These are useful, but they do not pinpoint local feelings on matters of local significance, nor do they test the amount of headway being made by present programs to improve relationships in the community. As a basis for decisions to terminate, continue, or revise organizational community relations programs, audits have to be homegrown.

The usual formats are the poll for a specific question, and a questionnaire or interview when several areas of information are desired. The style of questioning, direct or oblique, is not as important as knowing what it is you are trying to find out. It is also important to know beforehand that the audit, as constituted, will be accepted and acted upon by those for whom it is done. If it will be ignored or shot down by its sponsors because the results are unwelcome, don't undertake it. Finally, the taking of an audit must imply an assurance to those audited that their views have value and will be heeded.

Case problem in local community

In a large metropolitan area, an automobile dealership comes up for sale. The owner wants to retire. The sales area has had predominantly white residents, but it is now surrounded by areas of black population. A black man has shown an interest in buying the dealership. Opposition develops from a citizens' Area Planning Association (APA), set up by whites to regulate the pace and nature of racial integration in the area. The APA contacts the auto manufacturer's regional manager about the rumored ownership change. The auto-company executive explains that the transaction does not directly involve the auto maker, except in ensuring that the buyer is qualified as a financially responsible businessman. He is. The buyer's race is not a factor to the auto maker.

The APA feels that the sale of the dealership to a black would be premature based on retention of a balanced integration. After this meeting, the auto maker is contacted by the APA urban specialist, who warns, in great detail, that ugly rumors have indeed been circulating. Tensions are mounting. They could erupt. If the sale goes through, a restaurant will close, a florist will move out, the dealership will be boycotted, real estate values will be threatened. There may be firebombs from white gangs. The police would not bother these gangs, and the fire department would be late answering any calls. The churchwomen will jam the dealership phone, as they have done to put certain real estate firms out of business.

As the staff public relations director for the auto manufacturer, would your instincts tell you that the company could and should remain aloof on the basis that it was not party to the transaction? If so, how would you have your employer handle the tensions, adverse publicity, and possible protest or legal actions that might derive from black groups?

If your instincts tell you that some kind of involvement is implicit, could you do your investigative homework without feeding the rumors? Presumably, you need to know more about the people spearheading the APA, the outside urban specialist, and what the residents might do if the deal went through or was called off.

Because the auto company is one of the "Big Three"—a major corporation—actions must be fair, legal, in the company's interests, and not contrary to the public interest. What would be the best strategy?

Case problem in trade-off

Following severe floods in early summer last year, the health department of a medium-sized city initiated a crash program to control mosquitoes. This was the first really intensive control program in this particular community, and it included both larviciding (spraying the surface of stagnant pools of water with insecticide) and fogging (spraying the air with a heavy mixture of insecticide, which resembles a heavy fog).

The program aroused severe criticism from certain groups in the community, which claimed that the program had resulted in a great loss in the city's bird population. Most of the criticism was in letters to the local newspapers.

The city is the site of the state university, and the population is of above-average education. In the past, letters to the papers have produced public concern and agitation, and, owing to the high number of citizens holding advanced college degrees, public issues have produced conflicting views argued at a high educational level.

Your counseling firm has been retained by the city council to aid the health department in preparing a program to gain public acceptance of the pest-control program for this year. You find that a neighboring city has been using the same type of program for several years with no adverse results. You also learn that the extension division of the state university has been conducting research into the development of an effective educational program concerning the use of agricultural chemicals.

What would you want your firm to recommend to the city council?

ADDITIONAL READINGS

RICHARD L. COLE, *Citizen Participation in the Urban Policy Process*. Lexington, Mass.: D.C. Heath & Co., 1974.

MARCIA PELLY EFFRAT, *The Community: Approaches and Applications*. New York: Free Press, 1974.

VIRGINIA HART and MARGARET JONES, *The Union and the Community*. Honolulu: University of Hawaii, Industrial Relations Center, 1968.

WILLIS D. HAWLEY and FREDERICK M. WIRT, *The Search for Community Power*. Englewood Cliffs, N.J.: Prentice-Hall, 1974.

LOUIS B. LUNGBORG, *Public Relations in the Local Community*. New York: Harper & Row, 1950. Continues to be definitive text.

WILBUR J. PEAK, "Community Relations," in Philip Lesly, ed., *Public Relations Handbook*. Englewood Cliffs, N.J.: Prentice-Hall, 1978.

S. PRAKASH SETHI, *Up Against the Corporate Wall*. Englewood Cliffs, N.J.: Prentice-Hall, 1977. See chapter on "Corporate Decisions and Their Effects on Urban Communities."

U.S. CIVIL SERVICE COMMISSION, *Community Relations: A Guide for Federal Agencies*. Washington, D.C.: The Commission, 1958. Management Series No. 12.

ROLAND L. WARREN, *Perspectives on the American Community*. Chicago: Rand McNally, 1973.

"What a Big City Faces When Federal Aid Is Revamped," *U.S. News & World Report*, May 21, 1973.

FOOTNOTES

1. William H. Gilbert, *Public Relations in Local Government,* (Washington, D.C.: International Management Association, 1975), Chap. 7, "Community Group Relations," p. 103.
2. Ibid.
3. For insight on power structure in a small town, see Vidich and Bensman, *Small Town in Mass Society* (Princeton, N.J.: Princeton University Press, 1958).
4. Gilbert, *Public Relations,* pp. 104–5. Cites national totals for members and local units of associations, fraternal societies, and others. Worth studying for affairs at community level.
5. For small-town case-study material, start with "Comeback from Hard Times—How 6 Towns Did It," *U.S. News & World Report,* July 16, 1973. For larger cities, "Cities on the Comeback Trail," *Saturday Review,* August 21, 1976.
6. *Jack O'Dwyer's Newsletter,* Vol. 2 (October 1969).
7. See S. Prakash Sethi, "Conflict with a Minority Group—FIGHT," *Up Against the Corporate Wall* (Englewood Cliffs, N.J.: Prentice-Hall, 1977), a classic case of delegating responsibility without equivalent authority.
8. "Community Performance Update 1976," a booklet edited by John D. Horall, California Bankers Association, San Francisco.
9. For cooperation between polluter and community, see "Keeping a Promise; How a Town and a Paper Company Reconciled," *Wall Street Journal,* June 23, 1973—the story of Mead Corporation's efforts to eliminate offensive odors from its Escanaba, Michigan, paper mill. The availability of considerable information in the local media and from Mead make this case worthy of study in depth. A classic example of trade-offs.
10. For a specific case, see Allen H. Center, *Public Relations Practices* (Englewood Cliffs, N.J.: Prentice-Hall, 1975), Case #3, "A Work Stoppage—What GM Said Before, During, and After."
11. For a viewpoint, see Alvin Toffler, *Future Shock* (New York: Random House, 1970), Chap. 2, "The Accelerative Thrust," and Chap. 3, "The Pace of Life."

15

Any time more than two Americans meet on the street, one of them is sure to begin looking around for a gavel to call the meeting to order.

WILL ROGERS

Special Publics

The American public is growing: Each ten seconds, a baby is born, which adds up to a daily total of 8,657, equivalent to the population of a town. At the other end of life, Americans are living longer: In 1978, there were more than 23 million people over the age of 65; and by 2030, there will be twice as many. Americans are restless, on the move: Annually, an average of 18 million change residence. The American mood keeps shifting; the main constants are discontent and determination to change things for the better.

These conditions have profound significance for the practice of public relations. Communicating with 215 million Americans, seeking to persuade them, would be well nigh impossible except for one thing. Americans have an unmatched penchant for organizing into common-interest groups.

There are men's groups, women's groups, children's groups, parents' groups, racial and ethnic groups, labor unions, trade associations, professional societies, religious denominations, service clubs, media groups, safety clubs, transportation groups, fraternities and sororities, newcomers' and oldtimers' clubs, ad infinitum.

The American urge to organize into groups is old and indestructible. De Tocqueville observed more than a century ago, "The Americans of all ages, conditions, and all dispositions constantly form associations." The impact of TV and other distractions notwithstanding, the number of camps, clubs, conclaves, clans, circles, groves, hives, aeries, and nests of common interest grow and spread.

In religion alone, there are 330,000 local churches, with more than 131 million members. There are 13,000 national associations and fraternal and social organizations, with more than a million local units. The rosters range in size from the multimillion Masons down to a handful in the Liberty Boys of '76. Some groups, like labor unions, have billion-dollar budgets; others are penny-ante. Most of the national organizations have formalized public relations departments or agency arrangements. Most have conventions, committees, meetings, publications, and spokesmen who take public positions.

Organizations with something to sell—a product, service, or idea—must find ways of identifying those special-interest publics that might be available as buyers or constituents. They must find ways of appealing for the goodwill or support of those groups on the basis of common interests and purposes.

Increasingly, practitioners target their messages to special publics. Here is a typical delineation of special publics by the Sixth United States Army, headquartered in San Francisco: (1) civil organizations, (2) trade and industrial associations, (3) veterans' organizations (army alumni), (4) youth groups, (5) women's clubs, (6) clergy, (7) educators, and (8) communities. Army commanders and information officers are advised, "The most efficient system by which the Army can retain and increase support of its publics is by working through the leaders of those publics."

Space here permits description of only a few of the hundreds of special-interest groups. To dramatize their importance, we have selected four so powerful that their votes can decide a national election, their purchases or boycott can make or break an industry. These publics are women, youths, blacks, and senior citizens. Each public is catalyzed by the natural and inseparable bond of sex, race, or age.

Women

Historians may well conclude that the most significant psychological readjustment in twentieth-century America was the emergence and acceptance of women as having equality of rights in the performance of political, social, and economic roles. Liberation from many concepts of "a woman's place" as long memorialized in literature, song, and customs is part of the readjustment, for male and female alike.

"The hand that rocked the cradle" has become the hand that more and more often "mans" the tiller. It is the hand clasped warmly by those with goods to sell, stocks to promote, and votes to win. The most recent statistical abstract of the census showed 109 million females and 103 males, a 6-million voting advantage for women.

Women make up 40 percent of the nation's work force and possess 47 percent of the nation's wealth. It is often claimed that women do 85 percent of the nation's buying. More women than men vote in elections, local, state, or national. Secretary of Commerce Juanita Kreps predicts that the last quarter of this century will find workers "more often female, more often not married, and more often with college degrees."

There are many straws in the wind indicating that, whether the Equal Rights Amendment is ratified or not, current trends of change will continue. To name a few:

- Women now attend the military service academies.
- From September 1974 to July 1975, some 300 court cases had an impact on women's rights, compared with a total of 500 suits in the preceding 100 years.
- No longer can you be sure of a feminine voice when you dial "Operator."
- Women's share of arrests was up to 35 percent in 1976.
- Sixty colleges offer athletic scholarships for women.
- Women married to public officials have been challenged on conflict of interest.
- Boys' Republic has a woman counselor.
- Women make up 45 percent of registered drivers.
- Burns Security Services is using more women guards because they are more adept in getting people to open briefcases, lunchboxes, and purses or wallets.

The fields of law and politics have had major appeal to women. Female enrollment in law schools has moved up to 20 percent of the total, and the distance from law to politics is short. After the last national elections, there were 18 congresswomen, and nearly 600 female state legislators, two governors, a national party chairman, and two cabinet members.

Richard M. Scammon, director of the Election Research Center, offers one insight into the success of women in politics: "It is a little difficult to think of a lady leaning over a green baize covered table playing poker with the boys and selling jobs."[1]

Women in public relations

As a chosen function, public relations did very well during the first twelve years after President Kennedy's order to end sex bias in hiring and promoting federal employees. In fact, public relations showed the largest percentage of gain among all professional fields, going from 19 percent in 1964 to 29 percent in 1974—a female total exceeding that for designers, accountants, pharmacists, physicians, lawyers, and judges.[2]

Major problems remain

As with any major movement, not everything has been peaches and cream behind the scenery. Going into the 1980s, women, job for job, still earned less than men. Among young women, enthusiasm for the movement was high for those with a college education, but much lower for noncollege women. There had been evidence of disarray and dissension within the National Organization of Women. There were questions of common cause with racial minorities, the poor, and lesbians. Viewpoints on the various means and ends of liberation ranged from aggressive radicalism to conservative feminism.

Opposition to the Equal Rights Amendment has been formalized. One leader, Phyllis Schlafly, chairman of "Stop ERA," contended that the amendment would take away rather than increase rights. Among those "taken away" would be the right to be exempt from the draft and combat duty, the right to be supported by a husband or have minor children supported by their father, the right to attend a single-sex college, and the right to join a sorority or other women's organization.[3]

This last factor is not a minor one. Women's clubs represent a membership of 40 million, mostly middle- or upper-middle-level women. Included are the League of Women Voters, the D.A.R., NOW, the National Federation of Business and Professional Women, the American Association of University Women, and Altrusa International. These are influentials.

The increased inclusion of men in traditionally female organizations and the converse are phenomena of significance to public relations. No doubt, when a woman was accepted as a member of the all-male Kiwanis Club of Elk Grove Village, Illinois, that was something of a public relations problem at the Headquarters of Kiwanis International. The dimension of the problem increased when the club changed her membership to "honorary." She quit over the discrimination, and talked to a female reporter on the *Chicago Tribune*. At that point, the situation became "public domain."

EXHIBIT 15–1   The female public relations executive

A survey of 104 female heads of public relations departments provided this aggregate profile: She was "42 years old, had a bachelor of arts degree, 11 years experience, earned $17,000 annually, administered a budget of $89,000, supervised two other employees, and reported to the chief executive officer."[4] Based on a random sampling, the same survey showed the female head of a counseling firm or advertising agency department to be "39, a college graduate, in the field 12 years, earning $29,000 and supervising three other employees."[5]

A seasoned practitioner has offered this advice to any young woman entering the calling:

1. Get a thorough grounding in some kind of media to know the people, the jargon, the procedures and the attitudes toward public relations people.
2. Do not be ashamed to admit you're going into public relations because the money is better.
3. Don't sell out. Do the best you can for your employer. If you feel ill at ease, get out. If you stay do not forget who is paying you.
4. On the other hand, do not let your employer make you betray your sense of right and wrong.
5. Fight for responsibility.
6. Learn how to be angry without weeping.
7. Don't take yourself or your job too seriously.
8. If you really want to succeed, be ambitious for yourself in the same sense that men are. Being ambitious in no way lessens one's "womanness" or sexuality.
9. Do not forget the rest of your life.[6]

The youth public

Youth, or the "younger generation," is defined statistically by the U.S. census as ages 14 to 25. This embraces 44 million young people. At the lower-age end are those completing elementary school and entering high school. They are starting to think about employment, getting a driver's license, making independent decisions, and in general pushing off from childhood. At the higher-age end are most of those who have finished with educational commitments or plans. They're altering their life-styles toward steady work, a home neighborhood, and family formation, and otherwise seeking fulfillment in the adult mainstream.

The youth public, categorized as above, totals one-fifth of the nation's population. It is a powerful force whose impact will mount through the 1980s.[7] As a factor in the economy, during school years the youth public spends an estimated $20 billion annually, largely on food, clothes, entertainment, and recreation. This is in the main unearned money from parents and represents little capital formation by youth. As youths leave school and take employment, they begin to account for a share of the estimated $250 billion that shoppers between 18 and 35 spend annually.

The social and political characteristics of the youth mood change with the prospects of attaining the ideals and dreams of childhood. Thus, for youth of the 1960s and early 1970s, Vietnam loomed like a large cage set for their entrapment. Resentment, protest, and rebellion resulted. Effective communication between draft-age youth and established adult authority depended on whether it was acceptable within the context of rebellion, or in spite of that. A classic case for study is the experience of Dow Chemical Company, manufacturer of napalm, in seeking to recruit college students. See Figure 15–1.

FIGURE 15–1   A classic case—the student protests when Dow sought to recruit on campuses. Courtesy Dow Chemical Co.

With the wind-down of Vietnam, the natural fires of youth idealism and antiestablishmentism were refueled by the Watergate episode and a series of exposures of bribery, kickbacks, and other wrongdoings in business and public offices. However, the recession and the diminishing availability of jobs in the late 1970s rendered in rather somber colors the prospects for a meaningful and rewarding livelihood. Naturally, the mood and stance of youth became more favorable and receptive toward business and other potential employers.

The changing needs, moods, and life-styles of the youth audience have critical meaning to all sectors, public and private. To the cosmetic industry alone, underneath those casual clothes, youth is a $1 billion customer. To education administrators and teachers, youth is a $61 billion annual investment in the future of the nation and the educational system. For employers, youth make up a notable percentage of the work force. For law-enforcement and social agencies, youth represents a substantial share of the arrests, detentions, and rehabilitations to which their work is committed by law and humanitarianism. For the nation,

EXHIBIT 15-2

Life-style of Postmodern Youth

A nation's culture is reflected in what has come to be termed "life-style," one's approach to living and values. *Business Week* singled out four major features of the life-style of young people in the 1970s:

1. *Present-minded.* Students believe that how one lives today is more important than how one lives tomorrow. They are not goal-oriented and chide business for having goals. They are truly a "now generation."
2. *Personalism.* They seek open, honest relationships and fight what they term nonreciprocal personal ties. They flout convention to identify their individuality.
3. *Hedonism.* They live for pleasure, and the most common expression of this is their desire for sexual freedom. They believe in "if not happiness, at least pleasure," a view that prompted one wag to comment, "To an activist student, chaste is waste." The Puritan culture is rejected by postmodern youth as well as the work ethic that is fundamental to it.

    (While the article does not point this out, my own observations prompt me to stress again that it is not work itself that is rejected, but the glorifying of work as a great moral imperative—the so-called work ethic. Vast numbers of the young are tremendously hard-working, but they are more likely to be working for a purpose than just because someone has preached to them about the virtues of hard work.

    It seems paradoxical that the young should reject so many elements of the Puritan ethic, including its views on work, and then embrace so many teachings of the Buddhists who revere work. But perhaps it is not as much of a paradox as it at first appears; because the Buddhists esteem work for its humanizing values—not just its economic values alone. The Buddhist view would seem, to many of today's young, much more valid than the Puritan as a reason for working.)

4. *Involvement.* Postmodern youth believes that a decision is illegitimate unless the people affected by it participate in its making.[8]

the large and growing number of unemployed youth in the 1980s loomed as a most serious and challenging problem demanding resolution.

The stakes are so large that studies in depth are made regularly to analyze this audience, its sensitivities, and its complex reactions and responses.[9] Based on the results of detailed investigations, new products and services are created—LP records, modular stereo equipment, tape players, dune buggies, motorcycles, necklaces for men, exotic-looking shoes, high-style scarves—school buildings are constructed, curricula changed, scholarship and fellowship grants extended or withdrawn. And the content of news media is altered to strengthen its appeal to youth.

Narrowing the focus to communications, it is the mood and interest of the youth audience that creates the underground press, helps *Playboy* flourish, popularizes a *Peanuts* comic strip, and makes after-midnight old movies valuable television property. It is the reading of the mood that dictates the selection of media, third-party endorsement, copy language, and artwork and headline for advertising, brochures, promotion, and publicity.

Obviously, the size and influence of the youth public cannot be ignored in any public relations programming with marketing, social, educational, or political objectives.

Traditional approaches

Almost a permanent part of life in this country and in many others are such organized groups as the Boy Scouts, Girl Scouts, Sea Scouts, Camp Fire Girls, 4-H Clubs, Future Farmers of America, Boys Clubs of America, YMCAs, and YWCAs. The organized activities of such groups provide many public relations opportunities for sponsorship, contests, granting of awards, presentation of programs, tours, displays, and books. Support of these activities demonstrates social responsibility and bids for future customers or supporters.

FIGURE 15–2   A Reynolds Metals official, David P. Reynolds, poses with a group of Scouts to show recycling in connection with a one-day national cleanup. Courtesy Reynolds Metals Co.

Special efforts by business

The once-deep gulf between the worlds of education and business is steadily being bridged. Vehicles include corporate support of education, business-sponsored educator conferences, provision of specialists as part-time teachers, visits by teachers to industry, visits by businessmen to schools, and similar projects. Better rapport and closer collaboration on matters of *common interest* are the happy result.

Industry assistance to schools and colleges takes varied forms. The most direct approach to youth is *Junior Achievement*. Founded decades ago by Horace A. Moses and Theodore N. Vail, it has been carried on by thousands of business leaders to show young men and women, by actual participation, just how the competitive-enterprise system ticks. The Junior Achievement program calls for adult businessmen to function as advisors to companies formed by teen-agers. In these junior corporations, boys and girls 15 to 21 sign up for jobs, sell stock, and operate a corporate business. The jobs are rotated, and everybody gets paid if the enterprise clicks. There are directors' meetings, stockholders' meetings, and all the problems and procedures of a corporate enterprise. The activity has exceeded 190,000 enrollees running 7,400 companies.[10]

Another vehicle that has proved mutually beneficial is *B-E* (Business–Education) *Day*. This brings teachers and pupils to industrial plants and business firms for a close look and for conferences. (The National Association of Manufacturers calls it Business-Industry-Education Day.) The idea started in 1946, when a Michigan State University professor took a group of school administrators on a flying tour of Michigan industries. The idea spread rapidly. The Chamber of Commerce of the United States, the NAM, and other trade groups have vigorously promoted it. Astute school administrators have turned the idea around to bring business leaders into the schools on Business-Education Days. It can work both ways.

Career Day has been a standard event in many high schools, offering another means of reaching tomorrow's citizens and employees. Community leaders are anxious to keep youthful talent in the home community. Industrialists, editors, bankers, and others seek to attract young people into their callings. In these programs, businessmen and professionals describe the many careers open to students. The Miami Beach Chamber of Commerce added an extra twist. It sponsored a "Boss for a Day" program for high school seniors, to provide them with a close look at work in stores, professional offices, and business establishments.

The Evansville, Indiana, Manufacturers' and Employers' Association stressed career guidance in its educational relations program. This association published a 192-page book, *Your Career Opportunities in Evansville Industry,* which included a "Dictionary of Job Opportunities in Evansville Industry." This was a collaborative effort of a technical committee, representing industry, and an editorial board of five educators. Plenty of copies were made available through the high school libraries, and the book served as a text in a ten-week freshman course. This association has also sponsored a contest among high schoolers for the best career-planning notebooks.

Conferences That bring schoolteachers and university professors into a business for joint conferences are growing in number. Du Pont and International Harvester were among the pioneers. The chemical industry of Delaware collaborated to get the opportunities in science across to hgh school students. Several firms sponsored a "New Frontiers Day" at the University of Delaware. Every secondary school in the state, public and parochial, was represented by at least one teacher, and most sent two. Executives and scientists told of the opportunities and demands for young men and women in the chemical industry. *To permit the teachers to attend, the companies provided chemists, engineers, and physicists as substitute teachers for them. This provided a two-way impact.*

One of the oldest successful industry-educator conferences was started by du Pont in 1950 for university professors. The original guidelines called for no fewer than 40 and no more than 44 educators to be invited from institutions of various sizes and from all sections of the nation. The letter of invitation was sent to the president of the college or university, and he selected those to attend. The groups were small enough for two-way discussion; top management of company participated, including members of the du Pont executive committee; and there was no ducking of the educators' probing questions.

Summer jobs/internships for teachers and students are a needed bridge between teaching, learning, and doing. An increasing number of organizations, private and public, are providing temporary employment for teachers and university students. This has great potential for development of rapport. It provides the teacher with a realistic view to impart, and those outside the academic world with an opportunity to learn the educator viewpoint. Government agencies, hospitals, newspapers, advertising and public relations agencies, and business firms are providing an increased number of summer jobs and senior-year internships. Some firms lend executives to colleges as visiting professors.

A field for innovation

The youth market offers opportunity for imaginative public relations programming. One company among those that pay special attention is Greyhound; youth groups are major sources of chartered fares. Greyhound has distributed a cartoon booklet, "Driving Like a Pro"; sent safe-driving posters to schools; and staged appearances of its "Lady Greyhound," a live dog that supposedly symbolizes the bus line's "dependability and well-coordinated speed." One approach tried by Greyhound that did not work too well was a prose and poetry contest.

Typical college examples include the Ford College Roundtable, in which up to ten company executives meet with 100 representatives of faculty and students. A typical subject is "The Expectation and Realities of a Business Career." In a ten-year period, there were 77 round tables. TRW sponsored at 40 colleges an English play, *By George,* based on the life of George Bernard Shaw. Oneida Silversmiths presents "Community Service Awards" to coed organizations.

The black public

As America's black population has discovered its voice and marshalled its power, it has become of great importance to the practitioner. It is a public that requires careful study and deep understanding. It is not easy to generalize about, because it is not a monolithic public. Still, its members have in common a burning pride and a soul-deep determination to attain equality of citizenship.

Four phases of contemporary progress

In the advancement of the black population as a powerful force in public opinion, there have been several discernible long strides. The initial emergence was launched when Mrs. Rosa Parks was arrested in Montogomery, Alabama in December 1955 for refusing to give her seat on a bus to a white passenger. News media fastened the nation's attention on the 381-day boycott that followed.[11]

A second long step came after the enactment of the Civil Rights Act of 1964, with the singular leadership of Dr. Martin Luther King in a series of nonviolent protests. Perhaps the most notable was the Selma march. Not only did the nation's news media cover that in depth, but thousands of whites crossed the country to Selma to join in. This phase gave evidence that the black power bloc could make gains *within the system.* But progress was slow, and there was a white backlash.

Consequently, militant protests sprang from the impatience and the leadership ambitions of a few less qualified than Dr. King. There were riots in 1967 in several major cities. In the wake of the riots, the Kerner Commission found that the chief cause for black violence was white racism.

Since then, a continuing succession of barriers has been broken down. Realistic advances have characterized the movement. Not only blacks but other ethnic groups have gained access to several pockets of inequity long considered restricted by those in control. The gains have been mainly in employment opportunity, fair housing, integrated education, and election or appointment to public office.

In the continuing pursuit of equality in all aspects of life, there has been some splintering among blacks. At the core have been questions of method and leadership. A classic for study is the rise and disappearance of the Student Nonviolent Coordinating Committee (SNCC).[12]

The past progress is prologue. If there were no other reason, Black America has shown that it can be decisive at the polls. No one seriously questions that the 1976 presidential election went to Jimmy Carter because of his support by labor and blacks. Almost as an echo, two eminent blacks were named to President Carter's transition task force, and a black woman was named to a cabinet post. A close advisor, Andrew Young, was appointed chief U.S. delegate to the UN with cabinet status. This is the same man who joined Dr. Martin Luther King to lead a huge antiwar demonstration in front of the UN in 1957.

The dimensions and location of the audience

The 24 million American blacks constitute 88 percent of the nonwhite population, and 11 percent of the U.S. total. Some 14 million are concentrated in central-city living quarters. This translates into a majority of the population in Washington, D.C., Atlanta, and Newark, and more than 40 percent in 14 very large cities, such as Detroit. It means that as whites and industry flee to the suburbs, dominance of central-city life-style and local laws shifts to blacks. Urbanization, city taxes, low-cost housing complexes, and industrial expansion in the suburbs and abroad do not automatically come on strong as "progress" to city-locked blacks. Their concerns relate poignantly to the 6 million households, averaging more than four people each, crowded into space too small for the best of health, employment, and recreation.

Employment and purchasing power

Of the U.S. work force of 85 million, 11 percent are black. Functionally, this breaks down into 42 percent blue-collar, 29 percent white-collar, 26 percent services, and 3 percent farming. Obviously, whatever goes on in the factories, the offices, and the councils of local government affects this audience.

The purchasing power of the U.S. black has been estimated to be $54 billion. The median family income approaches $9,000, compared with $13,000 for white families. But despite this disparity, 40 percent of black families manage to own homes, 80 percent autos, 80 percent televisions, and 48 percent air conditioners.

John H. Johnson, publisher of *Ebony* and other periodicals, characterizes the black consumer market this way: "It is not a special market within the white consumer market. It is a general market, defined precisely by its exclusion from the white market. . . . Psychologically, geographically, socially, and culturally, the black consumer market is a distinct reality with a definite character of its own."[13]

The black consumer market is larger in dollar volume than the total of U.S. export sales abroad. The concentration of the market in metropolitan centers is illustrated by New York. The million and a half blacks there make up a market larger than all of Boston or San Francisco. Black families, Johnson points out, outspend whites at the same income levels for housing, clothing, tobacco, and certain beverages.

Communicating effectively

Whether seeking to persuade the black public to purchase, join, give, or vote, communicators must deal with a dichotomy. One branch of the dichotomy is black solidarity, which fosters varying degrees of separatism. Many blacks are aligned with the absolute concept of nationalism espoused by the Black Muslims. This hampers persuasion efforts seeking to bring whites and blacks together in philosophical and practical commonality. Other blacks subscribe to a less rigid perception of "nation within a nation" separatism. Walter Morris defines this concept of nationalism as embodying "all those expressions and activities by Black Americans that emphasize their common origins, experiences, and aspirations, and that seek to dignify the race."[14]

On the other branch of the dichotomy, black voters, shoppers, students, and public officials have not sought to set themselves apart. Rather, as a bloc, the thrust of the movement has been to share and to participate fully in the ways of life that whites have long pursued and enjoyed.

How long will separatism be a factor? At the marketplace, John Johnson says, "It will last until all external barriers to the free movement of people and the access to goods and services are torn down."[15]

Meantime, all those of whatever color or ethnic origin seeking public office, selling products, or rendering services will have to deal with the realities of a dual white and nonwhite society. This poses an enormous challenge to public relations, a calling that has been white-dominated from its inception. To this day, many practitioners find it difficult to talk with blacks or to communicate persuasively with black audiences. The hard fact is that many practitioners are uncomfortable, aware of their inadequacies, in trying to do so. Because of this, more and more large departments and counseling firms have added blacks to the payroll in decisive roles.

Selection of channels and media

The most effective channels to this audience are political leaders, religious leaders, businessmen, and educators *chosen by the black audience.*[16] The most persuasive media are national television, local radio, and *those newspapers and magazines edited and published by blacks.* A veteran counselor, the late Frank M. Seymour, explained, "Black-oriented media afford direct, acceptable and effective communication with the Black market. General or white market media still ignore too many facets of the so-called 'Black Experience' in America. It is no longer enough for media to incorporate black faces in the crowd, black voices, and black tokens into the system without paying homage to different value systems, and respecting the standards of others. As long as omissions occur, use of Black media, particularly for advertising, will be necessary to effectively reach

EXHIBIT 15-3 Excerpt from a letter to the authors from Frank M. Seymour.

A Historical Vignette

Until recently, any discussion about Blacks and the media would undoubtedly be based on the black press in America, which now numbers about 200 publications. Starting in 1827, with the publishing of *Freedom's Journal* by John Russwurm and Samuel Cornish, the first black newspaper was strictly aimed to promote advocacy and abolitionism. Among other editors in the period was Frederick Douglass, who founded *The North Star:*

> The object of the *North Star* will be to attack slavery in all its forms and aspects, advocate Universal Emancipation, exact the standard of public morality, promote the moral and intellectual improvement of the colored people, and to hasten the day of freedom to our three million enslaved countrymen.

The emergence of Blacks as purveyors of public opinion in America can be traced to black leaders Booker T. Washington and William Edward Burghardt DuBois—both of whom relied on the printed media as well as superb elocution to harness power throughout the black and white communities.

Washington effectively utilized coercion, journalistic control and even spies to combat opposing forces (like DuBois). T. Thomas Fortune's *New York Age* was an organ closely tied to Washington that enjoyed readership by Theodore Roosevelt. The *Philadelphia Tribune,* the *Independent* of Atlanta, the *Planet* of Richmond, the *Freeman* of Indianapolis, and the *Afro-American Ledger* of Baltimore were other papers which Washington either subsidized or controlled.

W.E.B. DuBois was himself a journalist of the finest order, and served as editor of the NAACP *Crisis* magazine for decades. Among the papers which he influenced were: The *Washington Bee,* the *Cleveland Gazette,* the *Conservation* of Chicago, and the *Advance* of St. Louis.

---

the Black American."[17] Another veteran counselor, D. Parke Gibson, puts it this way: "White-oriented media continue to ignore vital dimensions in the lives of nonwhite Americans, and almost without exception these media talk *about* Negroes and not *to* them."

Blacks pay particular attention to television. One survey in Pittsburgh found that inner-city residents depended almost entirely on the evening television newscast for news of the world outside the neighborhood. Television in its programming and commercials has been responsive to the black public. Its visual nature enables it to put its equal employment opportunity on display in its programs, commercials, and newscasts. But Churchill Roberts calls television and the other media "the fantasy world" in which minority groups are portrayed as "full-fledged members of society." Roberts found that during a studied one-week period, "blacks were presented in approximately half the entertainment programs, most often in professional roles that sometimes reflected 'superhuman' traits. Blacks also appeared in about 10 percent of the commercial advertisements . . . in generally 'glamorous' settings."

The popularity and influence of television do not cancel out other media. The large auto ownership by blacks and the large number of blacks driving trucks, for example, indicate a massive audience for car radios. Radio stations in areas with large black populations cater to this audience. Newspapers also vie for it. *Bacon's Directory* in 1976 listed 239 daily and weekly newspapers directed at the minority-group audience. *Ayer's Directory* lists 163.

There are many widely distributed magazines, of popular and of scholarly nature, for the black public. The variety ranges from *Ebony* (1,273,839) and *Jet* (640,623) to *Black World* (50,000), *Crisis* (100,000), and *Journal of the National Medical Association* (4,750). The number of books in public and university libraries concerning and catering to blacks has grown substantially in the past decade.

Senior citizens

At the turn of the century, those over 65 made up only 3 percent of the U.S. population.[18] With the average life expectancy 47 years at that time, those living beyond 65 were exceptional. Most of them resided with their children in those days. Some were in "old people's homes," or on local "poor farms." Few enjoyed pensions of any kind. There was no Medicare, Medicaid, or Social Security.

The change in this public since then has obviously been dramatic, with longevity the main factor. A baby born now has an average life expectancy of over 71 years. A 65-year-old today has a life expectancy of approximately 15 more years. The over-65 group totals nearly 23 million, exceeding 10 percent of the population. By the year 2000, the group will number 35 million or more.

Another aspect of the drastic change is inherent in the trend to earlier retirement from steady employment. More and more industries are allowing employees to choose retirement as early as 55. Statistically, there are 42 million Americans over 55, and 32 million who are 60 or over.

How to use the extra time?

The manner in which senior citizens, free from traditional responsibilities, use their time is a major force in American social and economic life. One widespread assumption is that they sit and stare at television, and wait for the end. Of course, some do—but that's not what the vast majority do. They are a far from sedentary or passive group. Only 5 percent live in nursing homes. Most live independently. Some 70 percent of those living as couples own and care for a home. As a group, seniors are generally healthy, financially comfortable, and politically active.

Seniors like each other. In a Louis Harris survey of public attitudes about aging, people 65 and over rated "socializing with friends" as the activity that absorbed most of their time (47 percent). This was followed by raising plants and gardening (39 percent), sitting and thinking (31 percent), caring for younger and older family members (27 percent), participating in hobbies and recreation (26 percent), walking (25 percent), sleeping (16 percent), just doing nothing (15 percent), and participating in sports (3 percent).[19]

It is significant that respondents did not rank "watching television" as their prime activity. Statistics do show that those over 65 spend an average of $3\frac{1}{2}$ hours daily watching television. But apparently, the watching is not entirely by preference.

An available voting bloc

Senior citizens can be a powerful force politically. Although those over 65 make up only 10 percent of the total population, they account for 17 percent of the voting population. And they use their votes. In the 1974 congressional elections, 63 million people voted. Twenty-two million were 55 and older. Of those between 55 and 64, 58 percent voted; among those over 65, some 70 percent voted.

Voting patterns follow the lines of natural self-interests. Of major concern are Social Security, health and welfare programs, and any taxation programs or regulations that stimulate price rises in staple foodstuffs or that reduce return on investments. Interestingly, the lines of natural interests often create an alliance between senior citizens and labor.

Many elected and appointed public officials owe their positions to the support of senior citizens. Seniors have had many prominent congressional allies—among them, Senators Church, Kennedy, Muskie, Percy, and Javits, and Representatives Randall, Pepper, and Prior.

To this writing, "senior power" has not constituted an organized bloc. There are volunteer spokesmen and organizations, however, offering leadership rallying points. The most aggressive person on the scene has been Maggie Kuhn, who launched the Grey Panthers. She claims 6,000 followers. The stated aims are to lift mandatory retirement laws; enlist the help of older people in monitoring nursing homes, public agencies, and the courts; improve Medicare coverage; and set up communal housing projects for the elderly to replace dependence on nursing homes. The Grey Panthers have a monthly newsletter and a speakers' bureau. They bid regularly for TV and radio appearances.

Three other groups bear mention. The combined American Association of Retired Persons (AARP) and National Retired Teachers Association (NRTA) are made up of about 7 million members nationwide and 2,500 local units. The NRTA was organized in 1946 to provide a nationwide health-insurance program for retired teachers. The AARP was added in 1958 as a separate arm to offer similar coverage to all those aged 55 and older. Since then, the group has extended its package benefits to include discounts on drugs and travel. It has engaged legislative representatives who monitor political actions and promote the interests of the group's largely Republican, middle-class membership. The main communication vehicle is *Modern Maturity,* a monthly newsmagazine with 4 million circulation.

The National Council of Senior Citizens (NCSC) is regarded as one of the most effective lobbies on Capitol Hill. The NCSC was formed by participants in the first White House Conference on Aging, to represent "the views of older persons on major issues confronting the nation." Supported heavily by labor and strongly Democratic, the NCSC has 3 million members who belong to 3,500 affiliated clubs across the United States. Rather than hiring lobbyists, the group monitors the House and Senate by notifying members of important issues and encouraging local groups to keep track of their congressmen's voting record and take appropriate action. Members are kept informed through the *Senior Citizens News,* a monthly newspaper. The NCSC also offers discount drugs, travel, and Medicare-supplemental insurance.

The National Council on Aging (NCOA) is made up of 1,500 public and private agencies. Their interests run the gamut of better jobs, housing, health care, education, and leisure activities. They have focused on changing negative images through a "National Media Resource Center on Aging." Some of the center's activities include (1) a weekly column, "Going Strong," carried by more than 300 newspapers; (2) a nationwide study of public attitudes by Louis Harris and Associates; (3) a popular pamphlet, "Facts and Myths about Aging," available free to the public; and (4) a $20 million Advertising Council campaign, launched in 1976. Using TV and radio commercials, newspaper and magazine ads, transit cards and posters, the campaign challenges Americans to "Get off Your Rocker for Grey Liberation," and urges older people to be active in community affairs.

An available market

Senior citizens, as a market, represent much more than has been indicated by the communications efforts of businesses to capture their dollars. The annual spendable income of the 65-plus group is estimated at $60 billion.[20] This is a much larger figure than that of the sought-after youth market.

The median income for a single is $4,900, and $7,200 for a couple. With Social Security accounting for and guaranteeing roughly half, there is an income dependability and a uniformity that is appealing to mass marketers. Additionally appealing to producers of value-priced lines is the fact that seniors have the time and inclination to be discriminating shoppers. They have the time to read the advertisements, clip the coupons, comparison shop, and take advantage of specials and bargains. There is a growing trend to senior-citizen discounts, courtesies, and special privileges. Response to civic and commercial gestures of this nature has been excellent.

Again, contrary to stereotyped notions, the purchases of the elderly are not confined to bifocals, hearing aids, nonprescription medicines, and soft foods. They do spend three times as much on health care as those under 55. But they also travel. They eat out regularly. They paint, weave, garden, repair, redecorate, read, smoke, drink, dance, write letters, and mail packages. They are a market for anything that helps keep them busy, comfortable, and enjoying life.

Special publics as areas of opportunity

The four large special-interest publics discussed in this chapter head a long list. There are 14,900,000 government employees at the federal, state, and local levels who have a strong thread of common experience. There are 29,400,000 U.S. armed-forces veterans who see eye to eye on matters affecting their national service and its benefits. There are 2,600,000 teachers, and 2,000,000 people actively engaged in the armed forces.[21]

When developing communications programs, practitioners identify those special groupings whose support or opposition can be vital to the objectives of the employer or client. A descriptive analysis of each is worked up in greater detail than we have done here. The analysis contains pertinent information about size, location, leadership, and predispositions. It includes an appraisal of the media available. It offers educated speculations as to strategy, and the nature of messages calculated to help gain the support desired, to assure neutrality, or to offset opposition, as the case may be.

A case problem in propriety

Burger King Corporation is a fast-food chain with heavy marketing in urban centers. The organization wanted to identify with the goals and objectives of a national black community movement. Operation PUSH (People United to Save Humanity), headed by the Reverend Jesse L. Jackson and based in Chicago, was selected.

The first step was for Burger King public relations and urban-development personnel to meet with Burger King's black franchisees from key market cities. A month later, a meeting that included the Reverend Mr. Jackson, took place at Burger King corporate headquarters. Out of that meeting came commitments for Burger King to support Operation PUSH in specific ways:

1. Underwrite a Businessmen's Breakfast opening the 7th Annual PUSH Expo in Chicago. Cost, $4,000.
2. Establish, jointly with black franchisees, a minority-student college scholarship in the name of Mr. Jackson. Cost jointly, $6,000.
3. Organize national Burger King/PUSH Day, with 10 percent of sales revenue that day from cooperating Burger King restaurants going to PUSH. Some $19,000 was raised.[22]

In the course of the program, public relations counsel sought to tie Burger King, PUSH, Burger King management spokesmen, and the Reverend Mr. Jackson closely together in the news wherever possible (see Figure 15–3). PUSH letterheads were used sometimes for news releases. Parallel efforts succeeded in drawing a public official, Mayor Richard Hatcher of Gary, Indiana, to a Burger

FIGURE 15–3 A Burger King official and the Reverend Jesse L. Jackson share a press conference concerning Burger King/PUSH Day. Courtesy Public Communications Inc., Chicago.

King restaurant, with press coverage. All parties in the program were reported in trade media to be pleased with the overall success.

In any program tying a public figure to a commercial venture, there are questions of ethics or propriety. The public figure may lose some of his or her image as "public servant," "untouchable," "not for hire." Certainly this vulnerability was present in the situation above. What advance precautions had to be taken by representatives of Mr. Jackson, Burger King, and Mayor Hatcher to prevent the accusation of commercialism? If none, why was this situation different from that of a U.S. president endorsing a commercial product, even for a noncommercial purpose? How and where would you draw the lines of propriety?

ADDITIONAL READINGS

MORTON J. ADLER, gen. ed., *The Negro in American History, 1928–1968.* Chicago: Encyclopedia Britannica Educational Corporation, 1969.

MARY JO BANE, *Here to Stay.* New York: Basic Books, 1970. Treatise on what is happening to the American family.

SIMONE DE BEAUVOIR and BETTY FREEDAN, "Sex, Society and the Female Dilemma," *Saturday Review,* June 14, 1975. A dialogue.

JOSHUA D. BOWEN, *The Struggle within Race Relations in the United States.* New York: Norton, 1965.

M. BARBARA BOYLE, "Equal Opportunity for Women is Smart Business," *Harvard Business Review,* May–June 1973.

ROBERT BUTLER, *Why Survive? Being Old in America.* New York: Harper & Row, 1976.

HOPE CHAMBERLAIN, *A Minority of Members.* New York: Praeger, 1973. All about women in Congress.

ROBERT E. FOREMAN, *Black Ghettos, White Ghettos, and Slums.* Englewood Cliffs, N.J.: Prentice-Hall, 1971.

JOHN J. GREEN, "Frank Seymour, a New and Necessary Kind of Businessman," *Detroit News Magazine,* October 22, 1967. Profile of a leading black counselor.

ROYAL LITTLE, "Don't Let Your Brain Go Down The Drain," *Fortune,* November 1971.

WILLIAM C. MATNEY, ed., *Who's Who among Black Americans.* Northfield, Ill.: Who's Who Among Black Americans, 1976.

KATE MILLETT, *Sexual Politics.* New York: Doubleday, 1970. Insight into the drives behind the women's movement.

HERBERT C. NORTHCOTT, JOHN F. SEGGAR, and JAMES L. HINTON, "Trends in TV Portrayal of Blacks and Women," *Journalism Quarterly,* Vol. 52, No. 4 (Winter 1975).

"Old Peoples' Revolt: At 65 Work Becomes a Four-Letter Word," *Psychology Today,* March 1974.

HENRY J. PRATT, "The Gray Lobby. Chicago: University of Chicago Press, 1977. Treats growing clout of senior citizens.

RICHARD SCAMMON and BEN J. WATTENBERG, *The Real Majority.* New York: Coward-McCann, 1970. Insight into the American electorate.

BERT SEIDMAN, "Pensions: The Public-Private Interplay," *AFL-CIO American Federationist,* Vol. 83, No. 7 (July 1976).

RUDOLPH M. WITTENBERG, *The Troubled Generation.* New York: Association Press, 1967.

"Women in Office: Foretaste of the Future," *Nation's Business,* April 1975.

"Women Preachers—The Fight Rages On," *U.S. News & World Report,* June 16, 1975.

NATHAN WRIGHT, JR., *What Black Politicians Are Saying.* New York: Hawthorn, 1972.

DANIEL YANKELOVICH, *The New Morality: A Profile of American Youth in the 70's.* New York: McGraw-Hill, 1974.

———, "Youth and the Establishment," report on research, for John D. Rockefeller 3rd Task Force on Youth, 1971.

For insight into the news media and black audiences, see *Journalism Quarterly,* Vol. 49, No. 1 (Spring 1972).

FOOTNOTES

1. "Women in Office: Foretaste of the Future," *Nation's Business,* April 1975.
2. "The American Woman on the Move—But Where?" *U.S. News & World Report,* December 8, 1975).
3. "Is Equal Rights Amendment Dead?" *U.S. News*

& World Report, December 1, 1975, p. 39.

4. "Typical Female PR Department Head Earns $17,000, Has $89,000 Budget," *PR Reporter,* Vol. 18, No. 24 (June 16, 1975).

5. *Ibid.*

6. Judith Anderson, "Thoughts on Being a Woman in Public Relations," *Public Relations Journal,* June 1975.

7. For details, see "Rising Power of the Young," *U.S. News & World Report,* August 25, 1975, pp. 62–63.

8. Louis B. Lundborg, *Future Without Shock* (New York: Norton, 1974).

9. See Daniel Yankelovich, "Changing Youth Values in the 70's, a study of America Youth," booklet by JDR 3rd Fund and others, 1974.

10. For update on Junior Achievement programming, see *Public Relations News,* Case Study #1488. One of a collection in 1975.

11. Vernon Jarrett, "Montgomery 20 Years Later: Peaceful Coexistence," *Chicago Tribune,* December 5, 1975.

12. For a case study, see James Forman, *Sammy Younge Jr.* (New York: Grove Press, 1968), a biography of the first black college student to die in the liberation movement. It weaves in the story of the SNCC.

13. John H. Johnson, "The Greening of the Black Consumer Market," *The Crisis,* Vol. 83, No. 3 (March 1976).

14. Milton D. Morris, *Politics of Black America* (New York: Harper & Row, 1975).

15. Johnson, "The Greening." For income information, see Barbara Becnel, "Profiling the Black Worker, 1976." *AFL-CIO American Federationist,* Vol. 83, No. 7 (July 1976).

16. Leadership groups encompass the NAACP, with 500,000 members, headed by former FCC Commissioner Benjamin Hooks; PUSH, headed by the Reverend Jesse Jackson; the Southern Christian Leadership (SCLC), headed by the Reverend Ralph Abernathy; and the Congressional Black Caucus of 16 House members, headed in 1977 by Rep. Parren Mitchell. There are many more.

17. Drawn from an extensive letter to the authors, February 21, 1977. Mr. Seymour died February 10, 1978 while this text was in production. Another excerpt from this letter is in Exhibit 15–3.

18. The facts and supporting data in this segment are drawn largely from an unpublished paper by Mary Wampler in a graduate degree program at San Diego State University, 1977. She is managing editor of *Senior World,* a monthly publication.

19. Survey conducted in 1974, funded by the National Council on Aging. Obviously, respondents were asked to name more than one activity.

20. See "The Power of the Aging in the Marketplace," *Business Week,* A special report.

21. Standard reference sources in public relations libraries include up-to-date copies of the *World Almanac; Statistical Abstract, U.S. Department of Commerce, Bureau of the Census;* and the *World Book Yearbook.*

22. For more detail James B. Strenski, "How to Communicate with Minority Publics," *Public Relations Journal,* Vol. 32, No. 7 (July 1976).

16

In thousands of impalpable but undeniable ways, the journalist shapes for the outside world images of men and events.
JOSEPH KRAFT

The Mass Audience

The economical, effective avenue of communication with the general public is through the mass media: newspapers, magazines, trade journals, radio, television, and cable or broadband communications. To handle this part of his or her job, the practitioner must understand the role of publicity, these media, and those who control access to them. This chapter will be divided into two parts, the first treating the role of publicity in public relations and the second discussing the media. Chapter 17 will outline principles for successful relationships with the men and women who work in these media.

The role of publicity

Publicity is an important—but not all-important—part of public relations. *Successful publicity, over the long pull, must be grounded in works that the public defines as good, motives that the public accepts as honest, and presentation that the public recognizes as credible.* As Cantril suggests, "opinion is generally determined more by events than by words." But there must be words and images, too—or else the good works are apt to be overlooked or misinterpreted by those with differing purposes or those separated by distance. There can be quite a difference in impact between an act that is carefully explained and one that is not. A utility can simply go ahead and tear up a city's streets to put in larger gas mains. Or it can manifest concern and consideration for the inconvenience and noise, and dramatize this work as proof of a desire to provide the community with better service. Publicity is not a cure-all, but effective communication can get results.

Publicity's role must be understood in the larger framework of the total communications process. It cannot be used for any length of time as a substitute for good works or for desirable corrective action. It can only serve as a spotlight to focus attention on good works and to clothe institutions with personality. The fallacy of using publicity as a substitute for performance was demonstrated early in the presidency of Gerald Ford. Soon after taking office, he was confronted with a deepening economic crisis born of inflation and high unemployment; his public relations staff came up with a "WIN" campaign—Whip Inflation Now. The whoop-it-up campaign, button and all, was a flop.

In publicity practice, the operator of the spotlight naturally tries to put highlights on the good and to soften the unfavorable with shadows. But always remember that there are other operators with spotlights to cast a revealing glare into the dark corners of any organization. Also, it must be recognized that there are times publicists can do little to counter the impact of a news story. For example, publicists serving Philadelphia's prestigious Bellevue-Stratford Hotel could not save it when the hotel became linked in the news with "Legionnaires' Disease," which killed 29 people.

The objective of publicity is to make something or somebody known. The desire to be known stems from competition and from the news media's partial failure, in terms of news coverage and values, to keep pace. The increased effort to make one's voice heard above those of others encourages an overemphasis on publicity.

Publicity is potent but not omnipotent. We live in an age of publicity. What we buy, what we do, what we think, and what others think about us are heavily influenced by publicity. Publicity tries to persuade you to buy Fords or Toyotas, to buy tickets to a ball game or a ballet, to vote the Democratic ticket, to feel patriotic or cause you to march in protest, to take a plane to Tahiti, or to spend your last dime. But it may not succeed. *Publicity will not, by itself, sell goods, raise funds for a charitable cause, or win elections.* These things require a good product, a good cause, and a hard-working organization. Publicity can, however, convey ideas and information and can shade the public's interpretation of what it sees, reads, or hears.

There are testimonials galore to the accomplishments of publicity. The Rose Bowl Parade and Miss America are examples. The "blood bank" is another. When it was publicized that a U.S. president was eating beef bacon for breakfast, beef bacon sales skyrocketed and pork bacon sales slumped. When C.W. McCall recorded "Convoy," CB sales zoomed. The *Reader's Digest* published an article about the Tracer Company of America, an organization that locates unclaimed bank accounts, legacies, and so forth; six months later, this firm had received 438,000 letters as a result. Perhaps most notably, "Jimmy Who?"—unknown nationally one year before—became President Jimmy Carter. These success stories can, of course, be matched by examples of efforts that misfired or, worse, backfired. For example, the surgeon general, federal and state health agencies, and volunteer agencies such as the American Cancer Society have saturated our media for two decades about the fact that cigarette smoking is hazardous to health. Yet Americans smoked 84 billion more cigarettes in 1976 than they did in 1970.

History is replete with examples of the "big buildup." The techniques are many and varied, and most of them are easily mastered. This open sesame to "easy success" has led practitioners, on occasion, into an exaggerated idea of the power of being "known." Richard Nixon got to be well known in his presidential years, but he didn't profit from the exposure. Neither did Spiro Agnew. That's another side of the publicity rectangle. Getting known by having frequent mentions in the press and on the air is a relatively simple and standardized procedure. "News" situations are fairly easy to contrive, and contrivance is a common practice.

Lavish testimonials to publicity break down, however, when one stops to consider that simple exposure of an institution to public gaze does not mean absorption of information, or support and understanding, by the public. There's a big gap between being heard and being appreciated. Contrast, for example, the public image of Azie Taylor Morton, whose name is publicized on every dollar bill, with that of David Rockefeller, who is selective in the publicity he seeks.[1] The public image of Rockefeller is proof of the power of good performance coupled with shrewd, dramatic publicizing of that performance.

Excessive publicity can backfire by, *first,* irritating the media, and *second,* creating false expectations or impressions. For example, when the federal government launched its "War on Poverty," press releases outran performance. Two Washington reporters criticized the agency's "merchandising" as outpacing its "capacity to deliver the goods." The classic example of the way skillful publicity over a period of years can ultimately backfire is the tragedy of J. Edgar Hoover, longtime head of the FBI. By means of *planned, controlled publicity,* Hoover built a myth that portrayed him as an intrepid fighter for justice. After his death, this myth was tarnished by truth.[2] Another example of publicity that misled the public, however unintentionally, was the annual fund appeal of Father Flanagan's Boys Town, which publicized its needs and its good works in providing a home for disadvantaged youths. Its publicity created the impression of a hand-to-mouth existence, but a newspaper ultimately exposed the fact that Boys Town had nearly $200 million in net worth. Gifts from the public declined sharply.[3]

Publicity items in the media soon become conversation pieces in offices, taverns, barbershops, and living rooms. Publicity provides a means of introducing your message into the word-of-mouth communications web. The publicity task should be approached with these thoughts in mind: (1) *Too much publicity* can be, in fact, poor public relations; (2) it is the *content* and the *absorption* of that content, not the amount of publicity, that eventually registers in public opinion; (3) *publicity disseminated is not equivalent to information received;* (4) publicity inevitably reflects the character of the institution it seeks to promote; (5) much publicity that an institution receives originates beyond its control; (6) not all public relations activities result in publicity, nor should everything be so designed. In fact, there are times when avoidance of publicity is wisest. For example, when a large insurance company opened a 3,000-unit biracial apartment project in central Chicago, a highly volatile area, it chose not to use publicity. The decision proved wise, as the move came to be accepted without a single incident.

Before publicity is created, the organization must focus on the *effects,* short-term and long-term, sought in a campaign. As emphasized in Chapter 8, publicity to be productive must be planned to achieve predetermined goals. A guide to such planning is provided in Doyle's Communications Chart, Table 16–1.

The mass media of publicity

A vast audience awaits—or does it?

The mass media reach into every home in the land, showering our citizens with more messages than they can absorb. These media represent a large sector of the economy; the creation, fabrication, and distribution of newspapers, magazines, radio, television, hi-fi, and film occupy a substantial segment of the nation's work force. These media also appear to represent an easily used means

TABLE 16-1 Doyle's communications chart

Group	Objective	Management Action	PR Action	Communication Channel	Type of Message
General public	Goodwill Respect Support	Conduct business in public interest Support community projects	Survey Plan Communicate Evaluate	Mass media Mail replies Plant-tour folders	Institutional ads News on basic information about company
Prospective customers, clients	Sales	Produce good product or service	" "	Mass media Trade journals Direct mail Films	Sales ads Product news Institutional ads
Customers, employees, management, ranks	Loyalty Goodwill Efficient production Good morale	Help employees find work satisfaction, self respect, fun	" "	Company publications Bulletin boards Mass media Direct mail Film	News and features about company and individual employees and employee groups Institutional ads
Stockholders, bankers, investment counsellors	Operating capital Confidence Goodwill	Good management	" "	Company publications Newsletter Mass media	Progress reports Future plans Financial reports Institutional ads
Government officials, civic leaders	Goodwill Support Favorable decisions	Conduct business in public interest Support community projects	" "	Personal contact Speeches Mass media Films	News about company progress and plans Editorials Institutional ads
Press, radio-TV	Respect Confidence in statements	"Open door" policy Truth	" "	Personal meetings Memos Press tours General news tips*	Shop talk Background on company news
Educators	Respect Support Goodwill	Host Plant visits Serve on PTA boards, etc.	" "	Personal contact Speeches Direct mail	Offers to help educators

Table prepared by Robert J. Doyle, University of Wisconsin System.

* The greatest favor you can do a reporter or editor is help him get a good story.

of bringing ideas and information to the public—but *this can be delusive.* Just because these media exist, have audiences, and convey messages does not necessarily mean that those messages are *received* or *accepted,* or *that action is taken* on them. For example, print messages have no effect on the 21 million Americans who cannot read. For another thing, these media have a relatively fixed capacity, and thus cannot accommodate all the messages fed into them. And the receivers have limited time and attention to give to the millions of messages hurled at them.

Nonetheless, power in America is largely exercised through control of the means and content of mass communications. "In a complex, institutionalized society, one thing is certain—the mass media vicariously provide access to the world. Local, national, and global reality are what is indrectly perceived through the media."[4] These media govern the way men and women deal with each other and with the distant world. A community fluoridates its water supply without public notice. Nothing happens. Then this fact becomes known, and a community row ensues.

The mass media constitute the nation's public-information system—a system in which public relations men and women play an important role. This public-information system embraces a nation's government, staffed by political leaders, bureaucrats, and information officers; its political parties, manned by agents, active workers, and public relations experts; the political pressure group, staffed by executives and public relations personnel; and the media, manned by reporters and gatekeepers. *Each of these elements performs an important, integral function in the democratic process of the public's being able to arrive at a consensus after issues are debated.* One element works in relation to other elements, so all may be lumped together under the rubric of "public-information system."

The struggle to shape and manage the news has escalated in intensity as the media's power and the political stakes have increased. The competition for access to these media is spirited and becoming more so each passing day. It is in this context that the publicist works to insert his messages into the "system."[5] Practitioners must adjust their work to the fact that these media are in a rapidly changing state, owing to a combination of the computer, innovations in transmission of signals, and new ways of feeding images into this system and of taking them out.[6]

There are three significant trends in the nation's media: The *first* is electronic transmission and computerized production of information. This requires adaptation of messages to new formats. *Second* is the almost exponential growth in the number of channels of public communication. For example, since 1950, the broadcast media have expanded sharply—AM radio has more than doubled, FM is up fourfold, and TV outlets have multiplied sevenfold. These outlets are amplified by cable TV, which today serves some 15 percent of the sets in the United States. In a decade, cable or broadband communication should reach 50 percent of all homes. In the print media, the number of newspapers has held steady, but magazines have greatly multiplied in variety and in number. *Third* is the narrowing of audience targets to specialized interests. Research indicates that growing segments of the population are able to choose the media they prefer for various kinds of information and entertainment. Message strategies calling for captive or semicaptive audiences won't work in a world of growing audience autonomy. *Superficial, repetitious messages are likely to be tuned out in favor of messages offering reward in terms of either useful information or entertainment.*

Today's communicator must cope with the fact that the news media have not adjusted their values to society's need for new information. Max Ways asserts, "Conditioned by its own past, journalism often acts as if its main task were still to report the exceptional and dramatically different against a background of what everybody knows. News today can concentrate with tremendous impact on a few great stories. . . . But, meanwhile, outside the spotlight, other great advances in science and technology, other international tensions, other causes of social unrest are in motion." Nonetheless, it must be acknowledged that the task of our news systems is difficult. Ben Bagdikian reminds us, "The total potential information from all places is incalculable. To observe everything everywhere is impossible. Even if possible, to transmit it all would be unimaginable. And even if all that somehow could be done, no individual could ever absorb the results."

Sound practice requires extensive knowledge and full understanding of the mass media; it requires a first-hand acquaintance with the men and women who staff them; it requires a keen insight into the potentialities and limitations of each medium. The practitioner must know which specific medium or media to use. He must know, too, the rules of the game. He must have a *planned* program for use on a coordinated basis, using one to reinforce and supplement the others. Walt Disney's program is a good example. The Disney firm uses its TV programs to promote its motion pictures and uses both media to promote the sale of books, records, Disneyland, Disney World, and other ventures. The Disney organization is also innovative in arranging tie-in promotions so that other organizations provide much of its publicity. Its radio contests, for example, bring an additional 150,000 visitors a year to Disney attractions. The seasoned practitioner knows that the pressure points of the system are (1) the news source, (2) the news gatherers and program writers, (3) the gatekeepers, and (4) the audiences. *Essentially, news coverage depends on the occasional and selective interest of the news gatherers and gatekeepers.*[7]

Public communication also requires a revision in contemporary practice, which relies too heavily on the print media for the dissemination of information. For five hundred years, the print media have dominated mass communication. Most of today's senior practitioners worked in print media, with the consequence that practice has lagged in a radically changed media situation. Only a tiny fraction of all communication takes place through print. Yet, as Tony Schwartz reminds us, "it remains an idealized form of communicating the most important information."

Today's busy citizen lives for the most part in an auditory-based communications environment. A typical person spends 47 percent of his media time with TV, 41 percent with radio, 8 percent with newspapers, and 4 percent with magazines. This translates into daily averages of 3 hours 48 minutes with TV, 3 hours 22 minutes with radio, 37 minutes with newspapers, and 20 minutes with magazines. Also, the national average for book purchases per year per person is .3. Such figures call for revision of many programs.

Newspapers

Although the number of daily and weekly newspapers has stabilized and newspaper reading has declined in recent years, the newspaper remains the workhorse of a public-information program. When people think of publicity, they almost instinctively think of the newspaper. American newspapers—daily, weekend, and Sunday, weekly and semiweekly, black, labor, religious, college and scholastic, and foreign-language—are read by most literate people. Publicity in newspapers, day in and day out, 52 weeks a year, forms the foundation of most informational programs. Reading the newspaper is as much a part of the influential American's daily habits as eating and sleeping. The influence of the press is still great. As an example, take this item from the wires of United Press International:

BERKELEY, CALIF. (UPI)—An elderly St. Paul (Minn.) man dying of cancer changed his will and left $21,000 to the University of California cancer research program *after reading newspaper articles about it,* the university disclosed Saturday. [The italics are ours.]

The newspaper is the moving force of current history. The late Justice Felix Frankfurter once said, "The unconscious, and therefore, uncritical absorption of print is much more powerful than any skeptical alertness which most readers bring to print. To an extent far beyond the public's own realization, public opinion is shaped by the kind, the volume, and the quality of the news columns." Edwin Emery gives the reason: "The power of the press is not in its persuasion by opinion, but in its dissemination of information and its arousal of interest in important issues hitherto submerged in public apathy." Nor should editorial endorsement be totally discounted. One study found that independent voters exposed to a newspaper endorsing George McGovern for president in 1972 were twice as likely to vote for him. Even when other factors are taken into account, voters' choices are related to endorsements by newspapers to which they are exposed.[8] *Although no longer the dominant medium, newspapers are still a powerful force in shaping the public agenda and in deciding the outcome of public debate.*

Dailies: From the early part of the century to 1940, the number of daily newspapers declined. This decline tapered off by 1950 and, by 1970, the number took a slight upturn with the growth of newspapers in metropolitan-area suburbs and in once-small towns now swelling through population growth. The number of daily newspapers stabilized in the mid-1970s. In 1970 there were 1,758 daily papers in the U.S.; in 1977 there were four more, 1,762 dailies, the great majority of which were monopoly newspapers.

However, newspaper circulation and newspaper reading have declined slightly in this period. A recent survey of newspaper editors found that one in four thought declining circulation was the industry's major problem. Newspaper circulation has failed to keep pace with the increase in population and in number of households. The decline has been marked in the metropolitan newspapers. Over a 15-year period, major dailies disappeared from New York, Chicago, Los Angeles, Boston, San Francisco, Detroit, Houston, and Cleveland. Total daily circulation in 1976 was 60,977,011, compared with the record high of 63,147,280 reached in 1973; thus, the circulation slide also appears to have stabilized. Total weekday circulation of daily newspapers gained two-tenths of a percent from 1975 to 1976. There were gains in the morning and Sunday papers, but evening newspaper circulation showed a continuing erosion in every circulation category above 50,000.

Users of this media must note the continuing decline in newspaper reading. According to a study by W.R. Simmons, average weekday penetration for all adults, 18 years or over, declined from 76 percent in 1967 to 72.3 percent in 1974, or a net decline of less than 4 percent. Among young people, the decline was 10 percent during this same period. (See Figure 16–1.)

Newspaper space allocated to news has also shrunk, at least relative to the increased amount of newsworthy information being fed into newsrooms. A 1976 survey found that the typical daily uses slightly less than 45 percent of its space for nonadvertising content on the average day, about the same as reported in a 1957 study. There is, however, wide variation. Some papers devote as little as 25 percent of their space to news. Most editors say local news makes up the largest proportion of editorial content—about 75 percent of all news published. Financial, state, and international news receive the least amount of space. These figures reflect the increasing reliance upon network TV for national and international news.[9] These figures suggest to the publicist that the quickest way into a daily or weekly newspaper is to provide *news with a local angle;* they also suggest the dimension of the competition the communicator faces.

Despite these trends, *the strengths of the newspaper are many.* Newspapers are produced in local communities and are indigenous to those communities. They have a firsthand intimacy with their local publics. The local YMCA can reach its community public through its local newspaper. The state Department of Health can reach its publics through the daily and weekly newspapers of its state. A commercial concern with regional distribution can reach its publics by a regional selection of newspapers. Similarly, a national organization, such as the NEA, can reach that national audience through all newspapers. American newspapers—from the mass-circulation giants down to small dailies of 3,000 or so circulation—vary a great deal in content, character, and audience. Yet all have a fairly standardized definition of news. The number, locale, and variety of newspapers enable the publicist to pinpoint the geography of his publicity, as

FIGURE 16–1   Daily-newspaper readers (average issue, weekday only). From W. R. Simmons's annual "Study of Selected Markets and the Media Reaching Them." Reproduced with permission from Yankelovich, Skelly and White's study, for Harte-Hanks, "Young People and Newspapers," 1976.

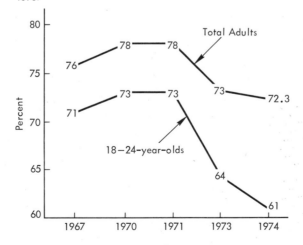

well as its audience, with precision. This capability has been enhanced by the development of city, state, regional and national paid publicity wires.

There are other advantages. A person buys his newspaper as something he wants, not as something thrust upon him. Newspapers constitute a medium of sustained interest and information. Readers are generally the interested, influential people. Because they reach most of their readers daily, newspapers are the most acceptable medium for a cumulative publicity buildup and thus are especially valuable in promotional campaigns. Newspapers are read at the reader's leisure and convenience, in sharp contrast with the broadcast media, where a program missed is gone forever.

The value of utilizing newspapers to build audiences for radio and TV shows can be seen in these facts. In a typical television season, some 400 companies will sponsor, with varying degrees of participation, several hundred network TV shows. These shows require multimillion-dollar investments. The network publicity staffs provide routine promotion for them, but they cannot do an effective, intensive job for each and every sponsor. For a corporation investing such sums (up to $75,000 for 30 seconds) in an entertainment medium, it is only sound business practice to spend the thousands additional that are needed to assure the maximum audience. The smart sponsor uses newspaper publicity to push his message beyond the confines of the TV page and beyond the major marketing areas.

The newspaper also has its *limitations.* An important one is that the average reader reads only a portion of his daily newspaper; the typical readers spends 20 to 30 minutes reading one-fifth to one-fourth of the editorial content. Thus, it is a mistake to assume that publicity printed is publicity received. Basic though newspapers are, they cannot carry the information task alone. The press must be used in coordination with other channels of communication. Another limitation is imposed by the press's fetish for speed and the resulting haste with which newspapers are put together. *This pressure leads to many inaccuracies and fragmented, superficial coverage—a fact of life that the practitioner must cope with.*

In contacts with the daily newspaper, the publicist quickly learns the importance of dealing with the specialist in the newspaper office. If it is a sports event that you seek to promote, you work directly with the sports department. If it is a straight news story of local interest, you deal with either the city editor or the reporter on the specific assignment. If the publicity program is aimed at the feminine reader, then material is channeled through the women's editor. Caution: No two newspaper organizations are exactly alike, and the same titles often mean different things on different newspapers.

Sunday papers: The publicist should be especially alert to the publicity possibilities of the Sunday newspaper, which, in many ways, is much different. The Sunday paper generally gets a longer, more intensive reading on a full day of leisure. It tends to emphasize feature material—copy without a time element—more than the daily paper does. Special features and pictures without a time peg are supplied early in the week. Because of the five-day workweek, news is relatively scarce on Sundays and Mondays. Thus, newspapers are more receptive to material on these publication days. The publicist must also know and use the national Sunday supplement magazines, such as *Parade* and *Family Weekly,* and the local weekend magazine developed by large-city newspapers. In

1977, *Parade* was distributed by 113 newspapers with a circulation of 19,537,044; *Family Weekly* was distributed by 328 newspapers with a total circulation of 11,000,000. A newspaper supplement for blacks, *Tuesday Magazine,* is distributed by some 27 metropolitan newspapers published in cities with large numbers of blacks. The content of these national supplements and the local weekend magazines tends to be more magazine than newspaper. These supplements prefer to put their own writers or free-lancers on a story, rather than accept one from a practitioner, but they are eager for tips and story memos. Through these supplements, you can reach the nation's major market centers.

To keep current with newspaper practices and problems, the practitioner should read regularly *Editor & Publisher, Columbia Journalism Review, MORE, Nieman Reports, The Quill,* and *Journalism Quarterly.*

Weeklies: In 1977, there were 7,579 weekly and semiweekly community newspapers in the United States, with a total circulation of some 38 million copies and an estimated readership of 115 million. The average circulation of a community newspaper is 3,200. This segment of American journalism has a steady readership. The death of weeklies in small towns of 1,000 to 1,500 population has been offset by circulation growth in the fast-growing suburbs. Community newspapers led the way in converting to photocomposition and offset production. These newspapers offer an effective, direct, and intimate means of reaching the people of suburbs, small towns, and farms, who are often the source of grass-roots opinion. The weekly-newspaper reader is loyal and reads his paper through. Most experts agree that the weekly newspaper exerts a far greater impact on opinions in ratio to its circulation than does the average daily. And these opinions count. This group exerts great power in most state legislatures and has repeatedly demonstrated great power in Congress.

Most of these weeklies heavily emphasize news of local government, schools, public affairs, and personal news. A few militant ones have appeared in recent years.[10] The public relations practitioner, hedged in by the skyscrapers of the city, should not forget the people of small-town and suburban America or the newspapers that help shape their opinions.

Labor: Labor journalism has developed extensively and matured considerably over the past 25 years. The exact number of labor newspapers is difficult to determine. Just about every union has its own magazine or newsletter. Recent estimates place the total at about 200 labor papers and magazines circulated on a national basis, in addition to thousands of regional and local ones. Their total per-issue circulation is estimated at more than 30 million. It is safe to assume that every union member receives at least one labor newspaper. To get a story into a union member's newspaper increases its acceptability to him. Naturally, the information must be of special interest and must square with the policies of organized labor.

The following labor publications and press services offer important outlets for stories with a labor angle:

AFL-CIO News: A weekly paper published by the AFL-CIO, 815 16th Street, N.W., Washington, D.C. 20006.

AFL-CIO News and Mat Service: A mimeographed version of material prepared for the *AFL-CIO News.* It is sent to a list of official labor papers twice a week.

AFL-CIO American Federationist: A monthly magazine published by the AFL-CIO, 815 16th Street, N.W., Washington, D.C. 20006.

Labor: A labor paper published every third week by the Railway Brotherhoods, 400 First St., N.W., Washington, D.C. 20001.

Press Associates, Inc. (PAI): A labor news and mat service, 805 15th Street, N.W., Suite 314, Washington, D.C. 20005.

In addition, the International Labor Press Association, AFL-CIO/CLC, promotes three supplemental news and mat services reaching more than 2,000 union publications featuring union-made goods or services, public-employee union members, and professional employees who are union members. Its office is in the AFL-CIO Building, 815 16th Street, N.W., Washington, D.C. 20006.

Black: The increased importance of the black media in reaching this segment of the public was discussed in Chapter 15. Ayer's 1977 *Directory* listed some 210 black publications, mostly weeklies.

The wire services and news syndicates

For high reader-interest value and spot news of state, regional, or national significance, the wire services offer the most economical and effective outlet. Publicity with a "local angle" can be more properly directed to the individual newspaper where that interest exists. Getting a story on the wires ensures immediate and widespread coverage. It also increases the acceptability of the publicist's copy. Publicity that comes racing into the newspaper's computer or over fast-speed printers is no longer "publicity." It is "news." A well-written wire story can reach newspaper readers and radio and TV listeners across the nation at little cost. The wire services are influential beyond calculation.

Feeding material to the press via the wire services generally means that the story will be rewritten and compressed as it goes through the wire-service blender. Timothy Crouse wrote, in *The Boys on the Bus,* "Wire stories are usually bland, dry, and overly cautious." He thinks there is "an inverse proportion between the number of persons a reporter reaches and the amount he can say." Shrewd publicists understand the one-dimensional format of the wire service, which emphasizes the hard, punchy lead and has little room for qualifying details. Fat and puffery will be squeezed out on the wire copy desk. What starts out as an 850-word release in Washington, D.C., may wind up as a 50-word story in an Oregon newspaper. There is a steady compression and cutting of the tremendous bulk of material fed into the wires as news progresses from Moscow, Russia to Moscow, Idaho. This is shown in the flow chart in Figure 16–2, which was based on a five-day analysis of the content and flow of news in the Associated Press from trunk wire to state wire to daily newspaper. Electronic transmission has altered this pattern somewhat, but not substantially.

Each of the two major wire services operates with national trunk wires, regional wires, and state wires in the United States. Both have audio services for broadcast stations. Each has its general headquarters in New York with bureaus and clients around the world. The easiest approach to these networks that transmit millions of words daily is through the nearest bureau or "stringer" correspondent. With the advent of electronic transmission of news and photographs, the importance of using the AP and UPI has greatly increased. AP's

FIGURE 16-2

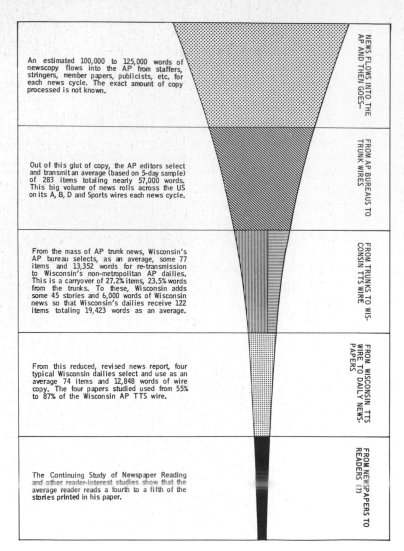

An estimated 100,000 to 125,000 words of newscopy flows into the AP from staffers, stringers, member papers, publicists, etc. for each news cycle. The exact amount of copy processed is not known.

NEWS FLOWS INTO THE AP AND THEN GOES—

Out of this glut of copy, the AP editors select and transmit an average (based on 5-day sample) of 283 items totaling nearly 57,000 words. This big volume of news rolls across the US on its A, B, D and Sports wires each news cycle.

FROM AP BUREAUS TO TRUNK WIRES

From the mass of AP trunk news, Wisconsin's AP bureau selects, as an average, some 77 items and 13,352 words for re-transmission to Wisconsin's non-metropolitan AP dailies. This is a carryover of 27.2% items, 23.5% words from the trunks. To these, Wisconsin adds some 45 stories and 6,000 words of Wisconsin news so that Wisconsin's dailies receive 122 items totaling 19,423 words as an average.

FROM TRUNKS TO WIS-CONSIN TTS WIRE

From this reduced, revised news report, four typical Wisconsin dailies select and use as an average 74 items and 12,848 words of wire copy. The four papers studied used from 55% to 87% of the Wisconsin AP TTS wire.

FROM WISCONSIN TTS WIRE TO DAILY NEWS-PAPERS

The Continuing Study of Newspaper Reading and other reader-interest studies show that the average reader reads a fourth to a fifth of the stories printed in his paper.

FROM NEWSPAPERS TO READERS (?)

DataStream and UPI's DataNews speed copy in breathtaking quantity to the nation's newspaper computers. The mailed release or picture is, by this changed circumstance, less and less effective. With the advent of Teletypesetter, which a few dailies still use, and computerized wire transmission, the wireheads have become the key to effective newspaper publicity. The accuracy and coverage of the two major services is roughly comparable.

Standing beside AP and UPI equipment at most of the nation's major news media are high-speed teleprinters of commercial "PR wires." These wires are used by practitioners to speed time-critical press releases simultaneously into newsrooms. The enlarged time-sensitive press relations responsibilities of practitioners are reflected in the dramatic growth of a domestic and international publicity wire network.

The "press release by private wire" concept was originated by PR Newswire

FIGURE 16-3 VDT editing terminal, used by publicity news wires in preparing
punched-paper tapes for transmission over teleprinter lines to news
media around the country. Courtesy PR Newswire.

in New York City in 1954. It has evolved into a worldwide news-release distribution system in which the sponsors of the messages, not the media, pay for the delivery. These wires are now relied upon to flash paid publicity and news material ranging from major new-product introductions and corporate earnings to yachting race results, obituaries, and press-conference announcements. These wires are especially useful in times of emergency—for instance, when a utility is suddenly confronted with an energy shortage and must get word quickly to the public via the media. Part of the process is shown in Figures 16–3 and 16–4.

Releases for transmission over these circuits may be submitted by messenger, phone, facsimile, TWX, Telex, or mail (if time permits) and will be processed and disseminated in a matter of minutes. The newswire does little editing.

Today, the pioneer company, PR Newswire, a subsidiary of Western Union Corporation, serves some 250 leading news media in about 75 U.S. cities over 10,000 miles of 50-word-per-minute teleprinter lines. PRN, headquartered in New York City, also has offices in Boston, Los Angeles, San Francisco, and Miami. In addition, several local "PR wires" have been established in Chicago, Detroit, Washington, D.C., Dallas-Houston, Minneapolis–St. Paul, Philadelphia, and Atlanta. These relay copy to each other when the source requests such additional local distribution. PR Newswire alone carries some 125 press releases daily into newspaper, wire-service, radio/TV, and trade- and business-paper

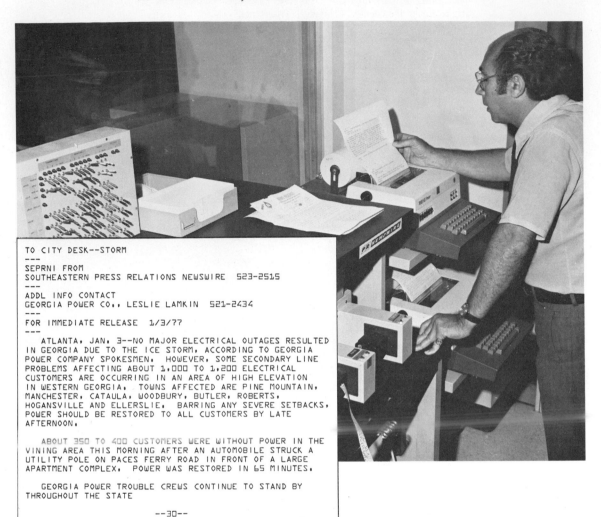

FIGURE 16-4 As copy is transmitted over the teleprinter, it is monitored by the wire chief. Courtesy PR Newswire.

```
TO CITY DESK--STORM
---
SEPRNI FROM
SOUTHEASTERN PRESS RELATIONS NEWSWIRE  523-2515
---
ADDL INFO CONTACT
GEORGIA POWER CO., LESLIE LAMKIN  521-2434
---
FOR IMMEDIATE RELEASE  1/3/77
---
    ATLANTA, JAN. 3--NO MAJOR ELECTRICAL OUTAGES RESULTED
IN GEORGIA DUE TO THE ICE STORM, ACCORDING TO GEORGIA
POWER COMPANY SPOKESMEN.  HOWEVER, SOME SECONDARY LINE
PROBLEMS AFFECTING ABOUT 1,000 TO 1,200 ELECTRICAL
CUSTOMERS ARE OCCURRING IN AN AREA OF HIGH ELEVATION
IN WESTERN GEORGIA.  TOWNS AFFECTED ARE PINE MOUNTAIN,
MANCHESTER, CATAULA, WOODBURY, BUTLER, ROBERTS,
HOGANSVILLE AND ELLERSLIE.  BARRING ANY SEVERE SETBACKS,
POWER SHOULD BE RESTORED TO ALL CUSTOMERS BY LATE
AFTERNOON.

    ABOUT 350 TO 400 CUSTOMERS WERE WITHOUT POWER IN THE
VINING AREA THIS MORNING AFTER AN AUTOMOBILE STRUCK A
UTILITY POLE ON PACES FERRY ROAD IN FRONT OF A LARGE
APARTMENT COMPLEX.  POWER WAS RESTORED IN 65 MINUTES.

    GEORGIA POWER TROUBLE CREWS CONTINUE TO STAND BY
THROUGHOUT THE STATE

                  --30--
```

editorial centers. Recently, PR Newswire introduced a Feature News Wire for low-cost, overnight delivery of feature releases on all its circuits.

Outside the United States, PRN has reciprocal copy-exchange agreements with similar PR wires that have been created in Canada, the United Kingdom, Germany, Austria, and Japan. Through the combined facilities of all these companies and their associates in other countries, same-day worldwide distribution is possible, including translation when appropriate. The largest overseas wire is Universal News Service of London, which operates a network reaching all major media in England, Ireland, Scotland, and Wales. Universal News Service also provides special audio services for British broadcasting stations.

Use of teleprinter transmission for publicity releases has been hastened by the ever-increasing need for speed; traffic congestion in cities; the dispersement of media offices; new demands on practitioners to communicate rapidly with media locally, nationally, and sometimes internationally; and requirements of the Securities and Exchange Commission, discussed in Chapter 12. In 1966, PR Newswire started feeding its clients' releases directly into stock exchanges and brokers' offices on a separate delayed (15 minutes) circuit. PR Newswire states that this service to the financial community "was expressly designed to aid publicly owned corporations in complying with stock exchange and Securities and Exchange Commission 'timely disclosure' requirements." Today, this PRN service, Investors Research Wire, also reaches major banks, mutual funds, and investment advisory and research organizations.

Another large portion of newspaper content is supplied by the feature, photo, and specialized news syndicates. Here, as in the case of the wire service, placement of a feature or a picture with a syndicate ensures wide, economical coverage and increases the acceptability of material.

For example, the feature news service, NEA—Newspaper Enterprise Association—serves some 750 daily newspapers in the United States and Canada and supplies ready-printed color comics sections to 150 Sunday and weekend papers. In addition, nearly 400 weekly papers use features distributed through the Suburban Features division of NEA. The world's largest feature news service, NEA provides news features, Washington columns, op-ed features, editorials, pictures, sports, and family-page and food features, astrology columns and crossword puzzles. Material can be channeled to the press through such syndicates as NEA, King Features Service, United Feature Syndicate, and many others. A story carefully targeted to the right syndicate will get a nationwide ride.

A complete list of feature and specialized syndicate outlets for publicity is published annually in the *Editor & Publisher International Yearbook*. The 1976 edition, for example, listed 341 general feature services. Many of these deal in a specialized type of news, such as *Auto News Syndicate, Religious News Service,* and *Fashion 'n' Figure.*

As in the case of paid publicity wires, there are also feature services that supply the press with client-sponsored material without charge to the newspaper or periodical. The client pays the bill. Typical is the Derus Media Service, Chicago, which mails out a clipsheet, *Editorial PACE,* to dailies and weeklies. It also distributes individual releases. Another such service is Associated Release Service, Inc., Chicago.

The magazine market

The number, variety, and circulations of magazines are almost limitless. Their broad array and variety, from the circulation giants of *Reader's Digest, Time, Cosmopolitan, McCall's, Family Circle, Playboy,* and *Penthouse,* to the more specialized audience magazines, such as *Ms, Rolling Stone,* and *Village Voice,* to trade journals like *Women's Wear Daily, Forbes,* and *Advertising Age,* to such recreational magazines as *Sports Illustrated* and *Ski Magazine,* provide an effective publicity medium. Magazines reflect the fact that the media create their separate communities. Thus, this medium enables the publicist to target a *specific message* to a *specific audience* more economically than most media do. Including the powerful news magazines, there are approximately 1,445 consumer magazines (those purchased by the general public). These range in appeal from *Woman's Day* to *The New Yorker*. Another 8,000 or so publications serve very specialized audiences, from children's-wear manufacturers to tree farmers. And the magazine market is characterized not only by *specialization,* but by *sub-specialization.* There are now magazines for *young* physicians, and for *new* lawyers.

The magazine field is always in the midst of great change. Each year, some publications die and new ones are born. As the popularity of the large-circulation, general-interest magazine has given way to the pervasiveness of television, a whole crop of specialized and regional magazines has come into being, finding and filling specific needs that broadcast journalism cannot provide for. Gone are the giants of old—*Collier's, Life,* and *Look.* The *Saturday Evening Post* has undergone metamorphosis to emerge as a class quarterly, radically different from the picture-filled weekly it was 20 years ago. In the stead of the old news-feature magazines has come a new breed: *Rolling Stone, New York, New West, New Times, People,* and *Village Voice* today reflect the interests of a new generation of Americans. *Rolling Stone,* for instance, began in the 1960s as a counterculture pop magazine. A decade later, its radical readership now in their thirties, it extended its coverage to politics and became one of the hottest properties in the magazine world. Clay Felker started *New York* when the *New York Herald-Tribune* folded in the 1960s, and made the slick weekly a powerful voice of the "new" journalism. He used the same formula for *New West,* started in Los Angeles in 1976. In 1977, Australian publisher Rupert Murdoch bought both publications and also the *Village Voice.* As new audiences create new interests, new magazines will appear. As old audiences die off, publications serving them will probably disappear.

Of the 4,477 magazines published in the United States, 1,445 are considered "magazines of general circulation," 522 are targeted for agriculture-oriented markets, 1,133 are college publications, 459 are foreign-language publications, and 918 cater to ethnic, religious, and fraternal groups.[11] Advances in offset printing and computerized production have stimulated circulation and advertising revenues in the magazine–periodical field. Regional advertising in such national magazines as *Time,* for example, allows advertisers to sell to a "market within a market."

There is a magazine or periodical catering to every known interest, vocation, and hobby in America. For the promoter of pet foods, for example, here are only a few of the possible outlets: *Audubon Magazine, Cats Magazine, Popular Dogs, Pet Age, Pet News, Cat Fancy, Dog Fancy, Dog Lovers' Digest,* and *American Cage.* To reach the larger, more lucrative market of women—consumers, voters, and shareholders—a strong group of women's publications provide outlets. *Seventeen* and *Teen Magazine* are two that cater to teen-aged girls, a group with much spending power; *Glamour* and *Mademoiselle* reach women in their twenties; *McCall's, Ladies' Home Journal,* and *Good Housekeeping* are a few homemaker-oriented magazines. The trend in magazines is from the general to the specialized publication. To reach today's college students—both men and women—the publicist can aim his shots at *Esquire, Playboy, Sports Illustrated,* and *Penthouse. Nutshell* and *The Graduate* are two annuals aimed at college seniors; many religious-oriented publications reach the 16–29-year-old market; and *Tiger Beat* is but one pop-music "fanzine" devoured by adolescents. The readers of all these magazines have distinct, non-interchangeable characteristics.[12]

The practitioner should not overlook the opportunities offered by a new breed of magazines—the slick city magazine, such as *Philadelphia, Atlanta,* and *Los Angeles.* Their approach to journalism has been described as a marriage between say, *Harper's* and *Ramparts.* Many, of course, are inoffensive slicks that provide publicity outlets to reach the affluent in a city. The better ones, however, are providing a stimulating challenge to urban dailies and to national publications.[13]

The advantages to the practitioner of using magazines can be shown in the following facts: Opinion leaders read many magazines. Magazines provide more durable information than newspapers do. The magazine reader has the opportunity to read, reread, discuss, and debate the information gleaned from this source. The trend in general magazines today is away from fiction and entertainment features toward more investigative and interpretative reporting of controversial issues. The vitality and force of magazines in shaping opinions, creating fashions, designing houses, setting standards for profession or business, and enlisting political support have been demonstrated since the first two American magazines were published, in January 1741.

Somewhat apart are the news magazines, which want information of a spot-news nature and which emphasize the time element, except for special features in "the back of the book."

From these, the practitioner builds a series of specialized mailing lists to reach his particular publics.

Publicity placement should be preceded by a careful analysis of the publication's readers, its editorial formula, its advertising content, and the market it serves. Clay Schoenfeld, both a magazine writer and a practitioner, counsels, "The best hint on how to communicate with a particular magazine audience is the magazine itself. If the editor weren't communicating well, he wouldn't be in business." The smart writer studies the magazine's topics, style, policies, trends, format and so forth, and then translates this knowledge by slanting his pieces for a particular publication.

Magazine publicity is supplementary to press publicity. In working with mass-circulation magazines of general interest and those dealing with broad groups in our population—women's magazines, men's magazines, youth magazines, and so forth—publicists generally do not submit prepared material. Rather, they work on a tip or query basis when they have something that would have reader appeal for these broad audiences. They submit story outlines or feature suggestions. If one is accepted, they work with the magazine's staff or free-lance writers in its development. The job here is one of selling an idea and then providing cooperation to writer and photographer, who build the idea into an article.

Magazine publicity placement is almost essential for organizations seeking to influence a national or specialized audience. Yet many publicists fail in their efforts to get such publicity because they don't understand the long lead time of national magazines, the length of time it takes to put a story idea into final, publishable form, and the stiff competition for space; and also because they don't make adequate market studies so that material is targeted for the particular audience. The competition comes from the editors and staff writers on the magazines, frequent contributors, and the 300 or so free-lance writers who write regularly for national magazines.

An avenue of approach often used but sometimes overlooked is that of dealing with a free-lancer. Free-lance writers who sell to the national magazines are interested in a real *account* of an institution, a man, or an event that possesses at least one of these three qualities: (1) national importance or significance; (2) elements of struggle, conflict, contest, or drama; (3) anecdotal enrichment and entertainment value. It is common practice to give a free-lancer a good story to develop. The free-lancer gets a check; the publicist, a publicity break in a magazine. The Society of Magazine Writers, 123 W. 43rd Street, New York City, operates a Dial-a-Writer Service for those seeking writers for special projects.

Business and professional publications

Several thousand publications serving the specialized needs of professional groups, trade associations, or business and industry offer countless opportunities to the alert practitioner. These publications will generally use prepared news releases, if the content serves their readers' economic or professional needs. The business press includes some 2,400 magazines, newspapers, and directories with an estimated circulation of more than 65 million. Of the total number of business publications, only 908 are regularly audited for circulation and readership. But, following the lead of their consumer counterparts, they are in the process of developing audits to validate readership and total-audience claims. New procedures are being developed to measure pass-along readership. Each of these publications caters to a carefully defined audience composed of highly motivated men and women.[14]

The growth of business and technical publications to accommodate exploding knowledge in all fields poses productive possibilities for the publicist who has ideas and pinpoints the target. There is increasing demand from the public for scientific and technological information in easy-to-understand language. This requires a staff of writers who can make complex technology understandable and provide accurate information. This publicity outlet will grow rapidly in the years ahead.

Radio

Radio broadcasting, once thought to be in danger of extinction because of the greater pull of TV, has by now adjusted to the newer medium and reasserted its right to a place in the mass-communications net. Radio offers to the publicist a wide range of possibilities. It is a mobile medium, well suited to a mobile nation. It reaches the breakfast table and living room, rides to and from work in the car, invades the bedroom, and goes along to the beach, to the woods, and even on fishing trips—a flexibility that TV finds hard to match.

Radio's versatility is indicated by these examples: One practitioner, Richard McDonald, and his wife, Paula, used daytime talk and nighttime call-in shows to sell more than a million copies of their book, *Loving Free*. Texaco's long-term sponsorship of the Saturday afternoon Metropolitan Opera broadcasts has brought it the loyalty and patronage of opera fans, most of whom are affluent and influential in their communities. During the season, individual broadcasts reach some 2 to 5 million music lovers in the United States and Canada over a special network of 295 American and 71 Canadian stations. The Texaco-Metropolitan Opera radio network includes both commercial and noncommercial stations—which illustrates how the latter can be used to supplement what is basically a commercial broadcast. However, Texaco views this program as a public relations vehicle and utilizes only a small percentage of the allotted commercial time for messages that identify the company but contain no "hard sell." As one writer observes, "The messages have a public relations impact that a hard pitch would destroy."

Radio's vitality and ubiquity are reflected in these figures: By 1977, there were more than 401 million working radios, including those in cars—an average of 5.5 per household. Radio reaches more than 98 percent of all homes. The sets can receive programs up to 24 hours a day (a small number of stations operate around the clock,) fed from 8,098 radio stations. Of these, 4,463 are AMs, 2,793 FMs, and 842 educational FMs. FM stations are gaining in popularity as listeners flee to them to escape the din of commercials on the AMs. Radio stations blanket the nation; today they are almost as common in small towns as in larger cities. Radio is ubiquitous. Although the popularity of the CBs has cut into radio's "drive time," 95 percent of Americans over the age of 12 listen to radio, and the average person spends 17 hours a week listening. Among women 18 years or older, 58 percent view no TV between 10 A.M. and 3 P.M., yet 21 million women listen to an average of $2\frac{1}{2}$ hours of radio during this period.

Even though it is a mass medium, radio possesses the qualities of a direct, personal touch, as it uses the spoken word, for the most part, to convey its message. Arthur Godfrey, who pioneered in radio, put his finger on this *intimate* quality in describing the turning point in his career: ". . . lying in that hospital listening to the radio, I realized for the first time how really intimate the medium is and how ridiculously ineffective most of the speakers were. . . . They were not *talking,* they were *reading,* and therefore convincing no one. . . . I decided I'd do things differently. . . . When I face a mike I have a mental image of only one person listening to me and I talk to that one person."

The practitioner should heed the fact that radio is a person-to-person medium, received in the home or in the car. As Tony Schwartz points out, "A singer who dazzles the studio audience on 'The Johnny Carson Show' may have a different effect on the home audience, listening to him at low volume on three-inch speakers."[15] Politicians, Jimmy Carter among them, have learned that loud, strident oratory on the political stump doesn't go over to a couple listening to the evening news in their living room.

Today's radio fare is largely built around music, weather, news, and sports, all heavily loaded with commercials. The disc jockey is a central figure in this program mix. Radio flourishes on conversation, debate, discussion, and talk. The increased emphasis on news and discussion-type programs opens up many possibilities for the publicist. Talk shows and telephone interviews focusing on controversial issues have become increasingly popular in recent years, expanding opportunities for those with a message. Although radio offers a blanketing medium, it can also be used to select specific audiences—ranging from those who like classical music on FM stereo to those who listen to the rock stations. More than 500 of the nation's AM radio outlets devote at least part of their time to materal directed toward blacks. Most of these are white-owned. The first black-owned station, WCHD, went on the air in Detroit in 1957. *Broadcasting Yearbook* and Standard Rate and Data Service provide information on stations serving the black market. Some 80 black-oriented stations are linked in the National Black Network, started in July 1973. Its major product is an hourly five-minute news segment, from 6 A.M. to midnight, on which it sells $1\frac{1}{2}$ minutes of time.

An illustration of radio's value: There was no advance newspaper publicity, no advertising, no posters printed, for four concerts to be given by the rock group "Who." The only announcement came at the end of a taped concert on 131 FM stations nationwide, plus a 60-second spot on seven key East Coast stations. These said only that the concerts were scheduled and that tickets could be obtained at Madison Square Garden. And yet, when the box-office windows went up at 12:32 P.M., a long line of people was there, and all four concerts were sold out within hours.

One researcher has pointed out that "although total program audience must always be of primary concern, a dissection of this audience is of tremendous value to many who would influence certain strata. Actually, the 'radio audience' is no more a homogeneous whole than is the population of the United States. It is composed of many 'cells' which can be stratified not only by economic group but also by geographic region, community size and character, family size and composition, etc." If you want to reach influentials, you sponsor classical music; if you want to reach a rural audience, you play country music. If you want to reach today's lively, knowledgeable teen-agers, you do it through their favorite disc jockey. If you want to reach the broad span of the general public via radio, your best bet is the frequent newscast.

Radio's use as a public relations tool must be approached within this context. The ways to reach the radio audience are (1) through news and informational programs, (2) with programs of entertainment that will successfully compete with other program fare, and (3) through the feature programs, such as advice for the housewife. Methods of using radio include furnishing news, arranging for broadcast of special events, obtaining free "public-service" time from the station for programs or from the sponsors of commercial programs, by the purchase of paid time for a message, or by utilizing call-in talk shows.

Those who would use the broadcast channels to reach the public must bear in mind that stations are business enterprises, operated to make a profit for their owners. Just as the newspaper has space to sell, the broadcaster has only one commodity to sell—*time*. Except for bona fide public-service announcements, the broadcaster ordinarily cannot afford to air free advertising. Thus, it is essential that the practitioner seeking to use these outlets send genuinely *newsworthy* releases—written in the special style and format preferred for *on-the-air delivery*—to the news directors of stations or networks. Broadcasters are complaining increasingly about the flood of pseudo-"news" releases and other efforts to get free air time.

Every listener survey shows newscasts at the top or near the top of the list of programs preferred by most listeners. By providing news for the radio newscast, the publicist can get a wide hearing for his story within the audience limits of a given station or set of stations. Radio newsrooms want news prepared for radio, not carbon copies or mimeographed copies of newspaper releases. They want news written for bulletin presentation. Radio news editors want all difficult names and words phoneticized for the announcer. Radio must cover the world in 13.5 minutes, or sometimes in only 3.5 minutes! The headline story on the newscast is 100 words long. Radio wants news written for the ear, not for the eye. Radio news must be informal, conversational, brief, to the point—and, above all, accurate! Once spoken, errors cannot be recalled and corrected; besides, one never gets exactly the same audience twice in radio. Radio journalists expect and deserve equal treatment with print journalists in the release of news and in the coverage of special events. Good results in radio news can be obtained by supplying tape-recorded interviews and news events.

Nonprofit organizations depend greatly on public-service programming.

Public-service time is seldom prime listening time, but it is not without value. In nonprime time, the competition with other stations is not so stiff, and one can still reach sizable audiences if the program fare attracts and holds listeners. In any event, radio requires a good bit of money in script and production costs as well as air time. These are the main possibilities in public-service programming:

1. Special programs based on interviews, group discussions, demonstrations, and so forth, either in a series or in a one-time-only presentation.
2. Similar but shorter presentations inserted as "participating" features of other programs.
3. Brief spot announcements made at various times during a broadcast day. With radio's local format, the opportunities for free spots are much greater than formerly.
4. Personality spots made by on-the-air personalities, such as disc jockeys, farm directors, or directors of women's shows.
5. News items sent directly to the station or fed in by way of the station's news service.
6. Editorials prepared by the station endorsing your program or campaign.

Many institutions now provide stations with a dial-access recorded newscast, which is kept updated as news develops. Copy for the newscasts is prepared in the public relations office, then recorded on tape. Stations serving the publicist's area are given an unlisted telephone number for these recorded newscasts. The playback system is automatic and does not require an attendant. Many institutions have found it profitable to equip their publicists with cassette tape recorders so they can record interviews for this newscast. This "hot-line" service is popular with radio stations in a day that emphasizes the "direct report." For example, one state university maintains a Code-A-Phone toll-free call-in service, 365 days a year, that enables state newspapers to get taped news reports and "actualities"—taped interviews. These messages vary from 40 seconds to 10 minutes in length. The state AP and UPI radio wires are used daily to "billboard" whatever reports are available to state broadcasters.

Monitored transcripts on what radio and television are saying about one's clients can be obtained from firms that provide "listening" service and will monitor specific stations or specific programs for a fee. The major one, Radio and TV Reports, operates in New York, Washington, Chicago, Los Angeles, Detroit, and San Francisco.

Television

The communications phenomenon of the century, television, has great force and scope as a publicity medium. Outstripping all other mass media, TV grew to full size in one decade—the 1950s. A medium that permits the use of the printed word, spoken word, pictures in motion, color, music, animation, and sound effects—all blended into one message—possesses immeasurable potency. It offers a vast range of possibilities for telling a story, from a terse, 60-second film clip on a TV newscast to a half-hour or one-hour documentary film. And with satellite transmission now commonplace, the powerful, pervasive impact of television is fast becoming worldwide.

Television has grown with incredible rapidity. Developed on an experimental basis prior to World War II, TV was held back by the war. A few stations were started in the late 1940s, then the FCC imposed a freeze on new stations until it could work out channel allocations. During the 1950s, the number of homes with TV went from 4 million (9 percent of all homes) to 46 million (88 percent of all homes), a swifter expansion than that of radio two decades before. By 1970, 95 percent of all American households had at least one TV set. However, use of these sets varies. As Bower notes, "Reliance on the medium for entertainment or for information may vary according to people's life circumstances—a necessary link to the outside world for the widower or a neglected piece of furniture for the popular single girl."[16]

By 1977, there were 958 television stations—513 commercial VHFs, 206 commercial UHFs, 91 noncommercial VHFs, and 148 noncommercial UHFs. Most commercial TV stations are affiliated with one of the three networks—ABC, CBS, or NBC. About 100 operate as independents. In 1976, TV's revenue totaled $5.2 billion, which earned the owners $1.25 billion in profits before taxes. There are 120 million TVs in the United States, more than half of which are color sets. Today, TV reaches 97 percent of all households.

Yet many practitioners do not fully capitalize on TV's power. In one person's opinion, "Of all the media presently at the disposal of the publicist, perhaps the least understood and most neglected are those of the electronic age—radio and television." These are truly cradle-to-the-grave media. Today's young people are bombarded by TV, for example, right from infancy. The average young person in the United States today has spent 20,000 hours in front of a TV set by the time he is graduated from high school, compared to only 14,000 hours in the classroom. The average American spends 28 percent of his or her leisure time watching TV. This is our most intimate mass medium, yet it can pack in 70 million people for a political debate or for a Super Bowl.

The overpowering fact of our times is the thrust of television. It has become a dominant force in the rearing of our young, the prime source of news and entertainment for most Americans, and a powerful soapbox from which citizens' protests can be communicated to the nation and the world. This medium has greatly altered presidential election campaigns and has diminished the role of the political parties. The national newswires and TV networks have created a truly national forum. Events made large by TV move and shape public opinion.

Television greatly heightens citizen awareness of the conduct of public institutions and emphasizes the impersonal, interdependent nature of his environment. It also creates a sense of frustration for the citizen, who is witness to much that he cannot control—be it a battle between police and protestors in Boston, the wretched life in ghettos, or developers' filling in San Francisco Bay. This frustration leads alternately to anger or apathy. TV is the most popular and credible source of news—a fact that many practitioners, most of whom once worked in print media, fail to reckon with. Television took the lead from newspapers in 1963 as the primary source of news.

An isolated but typical example of TV's impact: An art patron's viewing of "Sunrise Semester," the early-morning educational TV program sponsored by New York University, resulted in a gift of $1 million for a new art museum from Abby Weed Grey of St. Paul. Mrs. Grey, a Vassar graduate, had been collecting current art from the Middle East and Far East. One morning, viewing a lecture on the art of Iran, she was sufficiently excited by what she heard to call the lecturer, who suggested the idea of a museum to house her collection. The gift resulted.

Yet TV's impact can be overstated. For example, since 1952, when TV profoundly altered the nature of our presidential campaigns, it has been assumed that TV has played the decisive role in our elections. Two Syracuse University political scientists dispute this on the basis of a thorough study of the role of TV in the 1972 presidential campaign. They found, among other things, that:

> Political commercials, considered a devastating weapon since 1964, have almost no power to overcome a voter's preexisting view of a candidate and his party.
>
> These television spots, scorned by the intelligentsia as too short and gimmicky to provide an honest basis for political choice, actually furnish voters with a great deal of serious issue information.
>
> Television news coverage of the campaign, long touted for its impact, was no more influential than newspaper coverage in affecting the voters' views of the candidates.[17]

Nonetheless, the influence of TV is potent, pervasive. The TV set in the average American home is on for six hours and 56 minutes each day, according to A.C. Nielsen statistics. More than 65 percent of our citizens turn to TV as their primary source of news. Most viewers regard TV as the most credible of the news media, and have since 1961. By 1976, TV enjoyed a 2-to-1 advantage over newspapers in credibility, according to a Roper poll conducted under the auspices of the TV industry. Newspaper-sponsored polls cloud this wide margin with some doubt, but overall, TV ranks today as the most popular and credible news medium. This disturbs thoughtful observers who know that the limits of time and dominance of picture stories inevitably oversimplify and thus distort the news. For example, the evening network news shows, watched by more than 50 million people each night, must tell the story of the world in 4,000 words or less—the equivalent of four columns in a standard-sized newspaper.[18] Fifty-eight seconds is a major story! Av Westin, longtime network executive, admits, "Television news is an illustrated headline service which can function best when it is regarded by its viewers as an important yet fast adjunct to the newspapers." NBC's John Chancellor admits, "We can't tell the whole story." BBC's Robin Day is more blunt: "TV, by virtue of its dependence on the camera, is a tabloid medium which deals in crude, visual headlines."

The common frustration of the practitioner seeking to convey hard information to the public and of the viewer seeking hard information from a TV newscast can be clearly seen in this admission from Richard Kaplan, producer for the "CBS Evening News": "We just can't handle issues the way a newspaper can. A writer can go into all kinds of detail to explain things. We have to have something on that film. And you've got ninety seconds to tell it."

The compression involved in a TV news program, coupled with today's news values, brings a compound of fiction and fact in terse fragments to the viewer in his living room or bedroom. Karl E. Meyer, a former foreign correspondent and well-known author, describing his work in writing a TV documentary, wrote this: "Far more difficult than writing was the process of compression—it was like squeezing an orange so that only the pulp remained, while the juice is poured down the drain. Here the wasteful prodigality of television seemed at its melancholy worst."[19]

Television is essentially an entertainment, not an information medium. The average station allots about 10 percent of its broadcast day to news, the remainder to entertainment and advertising. The success or failure of the entertainment

FIGURE 16-5 Assignment sheet for TV reporters.

CHANNEL TWO NEWS INSIGHTS
Wednesday, April 14, 1976

PAGE ONE

FOR THE SIX

8:00a MILES & CREW investigate the strike of waiters, cooks, etc., at Grossinger's...the Catskills resort hotel...on the day the Passover holiday arrives. Management has said non-striking workers will be on duty in place of the strikers. GROSSINGER'S, (OUTLOOK)

8:00a CRAWFORD & CREW shoot the story of six-year-old TJ Kearns...a victim of hemophilia for whom some 40 Westchester Lions Clubs will be starting a blood drive tomorrow. The first interview will be with Dr. Margaret Hilgartner, medical dir of the Metropolitan Chapter of the Hemophilia Chapter of the Hemophilia Foundation ...then to Westchester to talk with the boy and the dentist who is chairman of the Lions Club Blood Bank, the man who conceived the idea of the drive. PEDIATRICS SECTION OF NY HOSPITAL, 2ND FLOOR, 68TH ST EAST OF YORK AVE, (OUTLOOK & NOTE IN FOLDER).

8:00a CORRESPONDENT TBD & CREW can take a look at the mock political nominating convention through today at the Wayne Hills HS in NJ...Gov Byrne will be speaking, Mrs Jimmy Carter will be representing her husband, and an audience of some 3,000 incl state senators and congressmen is expected. WAYNE HILLS HS, VERDON AVE, WAYNE, NJ, (OUTLOOK, NOTE & LETTER IN FOLDER).

(More)

10:30a BRADY & CREW film a business story on the fraudulant use of "Cents Off" coupons in supermarkets...It appears customers often give in coupons and receive money on products never purchased. This is not a loss for the supermarkets because they are reimbursed by the manufacturers. PATHMARK SUPERMARKET, 371 N CENTRAL AVE, HARTSDALE, & THE NY STATE FOOD MERCHANTS ASSOC, 280 N CENTRAL AVE, HARTSDALE, (OUTLOOK & NOTE IN FOLDER).

11:00a MONSEES & CREW profile Victoria Fyodorova Puoy...the young Russian woman who came to the US over a year ago to meet her American father, a naval officer who was expelled from the Soviet Union in 1945 for his international romance. Vicky has since married a pilot here and is now eight months pregnant. Her mother Zoya has just received a visa to come to the US for the birth. 36 FLYING CLOUD RD, STAMFORD, CONN, (OUTLOOK, COPY & CLIPS IN FOLDER).

11:15a SIEGEL & CREW can put together a piece on the early Passover Seders for elderly and infirm residents of the Jewish Home and Hospital for the Aged who tire too soon to wait for the conventional sundown observance. 120 W 106TH ST, MANHATTAN, (OUTLOOK, HANDOUT & INFORMATION SHEET IN FOLDER).

(More)

programs is determined not by their quality, but by their ratings and subsequent amount of advertising the programs can attract. These same criteria, all too often, are applied to television news programs. Consequently, in the view of three students of TV, "many news programs have slowly evolved a slick, showbusiness approach to news presentation in an effort to attract larger ratings and revenues."[20] These "happy-talk" news shows are a blend of gimmickry and information. TV's approach to news is partially shown in Figure 16–5. The *Chicago Journalism Review* made a study of Chicago's TV news programs and found that less than half of the 30-minute show was devoted to general news and comment. The results are shown in Figure 16–6.

An increasingly larger portion of TV time is being given to news broadcasts and to the news documentary, social issues, and action coverage. These programs offer many opportunities to the alert publicist. Local stations find news coverage costly and welcome an assist from the source who can provide TV newsworthy film or relevant situations.

An example: The growers of bananas seek to increase the sales of their fruit. They organize as a trade group, the Banana Bunch, and retain a New York public relations agency. The agency in turn hires Barbara Bertelli, a dietitian and nutritionist. The agency arranges for her appearance on one talk show after another to plug bananas. This promotion is typical of the public relations use being made of these radio and TV talk shows. Another: Author Anthony Scaduto appeared on 50 radio and TV shows in ten major cities during a nationwide 17-day tour to promote his latest book. The tour cost $3,000 in expenses; a full-page ad in the *New York Times Book Review* costs nearly $5,000.

A local-station TV executive offers these tips to practitioners seeking time on local TV stations: (1) Approach the right person in the station. (2) Have a definite plan to discuss. (3) Have an idea with audience appeal, so that the station won't lose its viewers while your program is on the air. (4) The program idea must be within the station's capabilities. (5) Don't forget to say "Thanks." For the local nonprofit agencies without money and manpower, TV news and hitchhiking public-service announcements offer the cheapest and easiest ways to reach the TV audience.

Thus far, TV has developed these formats for its programming: (1) studio productions—musicals, comedy, drama, vaudeville, puppet shows, audience-participation shows, and so forth; (2) remote broadcasts of sports events, public events, political conventions, congressional hearings, and so forth; (3) films—old or reissued Hollywood movies, special documentaries, docu-dramas, and films

FIGURE 16–6   Typical allocation of TV news time.

	WMAQ-TV (NBC)	WLS (ABC)	WBBM (CBS)	WGN (Trib.Co.)
minutes of news and comment	13:05	13:15	14:35	11:40
minutes of weather, sports and stocks	6:35	6:00	5:35	8:40
minutes of advertising	7:00	6:45	5:45	5:00
messing around	3:15	4:00	4:05	4:40
number of news stories	11	15	15	12
average length	1:00	0:45	0:58	0:58

prepared for other audiences. As it has developed its own pattern of programming, TV has borrowed heavily from radio, journalism, Hollywood, and the stage. Sig Mickelson, longtime CBS executive, once admitted, "This medium owes more of its heritage to show business than to journalism."

Selling story ideas to TV producers—such as getting an author's new book reviewed, getting personalities on the audience-participation shows (for example, NBC's "Today," "Tonight," or "Tomorrow," the syndicated "Phil Donahue Show," or WSB-TV's "Today in Georgia"), providing videos for news or documentary programs, or arranging for on-the-spot coverage of a staged event—is the most common way of getting a sponsor's message into this medium. Most TV stations are now equipped with Electronic News Gathering (ENG) units, which increase their mobility and thus their willingness to cover a story outside the studio. These ENGs, minicams coupled with microwave equipment, make live news coverage possible on a continuing basis even in the smallest cities, permitting TV news to compete with radio news in immediacy at a time when radio news is losing ground as a major news medium. Most TV stations now broadcast in color, and thus want color video, film, or slides. The TV newscaster wants news written for TV, not newspapers, and he wants supporting visuals.

The 30- or 60-minute news-magazine programs will use short features as well as spot-news film. The trend in many local newscasts is to expand to one hour and use a "consumer-oriented magazine format," with many soft features on consumerism, health, and how-to-do-it around the house. These programs offer an excellent opportunity to the publicist. The new format enables organizations to "sell" to TV producers and sponsors program ideas that will carry their message to large audiences that believe what they see on TV. One major obstacle to widespread use of TV as a publicity medium is the heavy cost of preparing and producing programs. Here, as in the case of films, the cost of per-person impact rather than initial outlay should be weighed.

Even though it may be costly to sponsors and stations, TV programming is within the capability of nonprofit institutions if their counselors use initiative and imagination. The University of California, San Diego, has demonstrated this in recent years. A comparatively new institution, UCSD suffered initially from constant TV coverage of its protesting students, which irritated the conservative San Diego community. UCSD hired a TV coordinator who showed that the university could make positive use of TV's power. She knew that TV needs and uses vast amounts of material; she saw that the problem was to make material available to the five local TV stations in such a way that it would be acceptable to both the program producers and the university community.

So this is what the coordinator did: She kept the stations informed on campus events; provided background material; helped them locate principals involved in news stories; arranged news conferences before the TV film-processing deadline; encouraged administrators to be available for short interviews; provided slides of newsmakers to be used with telephone statements; assisted assignment editors by finding professors who could be tied into national newsbreaks; looked for special stories with a high visual impact—for example, the glassblower who makes special equipment for scientific experiments; studied local shows and looked for university personnel who would fit into their pattern; and provided material and guests for the educational television station.

In one year, on a limited budget, UCSD provided over 300 segments of TV programming and balanced the news coverage of unfavorable news with news of positive accomplishments on the campus.

The key to use of the electronic media is knowledge of their news values, program needs, and changing technical requirements. For example, electronic video recording makes it easy and economical to provide cassettes to TV stations. Similarly, the Electronic News Gathering cameras, which weigh only twelve pounds or so, enable stations to cover your news on the spot if you have a good story and alert them in time. The minicams have completely altered TV news coverage since 1974.

Cable TV, once it moves beyond being a mere relay agent for network and regional programs, has considerable potential for the communicator. Cable TV's value as a community channel was greatly enhanced with the advent of two-way communication, introduced in Columbus, Ohio, in 1977.

Here is a list of publications that will enable the practitioner to keep abreast of the electronic media so that he or she can tailor publicity to their changing requirements:

AV Communication Review, published quarterly by the Dept. of Audio-Visual Instruction, National Education Association

Broadcasting, weekly trade journal

Educational Broadcasting Review, bimonthly, National Association of Educational Broadcasters, Washington, D.C.

Journal of Broadcasting, quarterly, University of Georgia, School of Journalism and Mass Communication, Athens, Georgia

Television–Radio Age, biweekly, Television Editorial Corp., New York City

TV Guide, weekly, designed for the listener

Case problem

You are the public relations officer for a state department of health. You know that few words in the English language have a more frightening connotation than "plague." The state health officer informs you that plague in rodents has been confirmed in 20 of the state's 63 counties, and that there has been one human case.

He directs you to prepare an information campaign that will candidly inform the state's population, but to minimize alarm by emphasizing that the risk of human infection is small.

Draft an information plan that will fully alert your state's citizens to this danger, a plan that will utilize the mass media of communication in a coordinated campaign. You may assume that new discoveries of infected rodents will be made as the campaign progresses.

Outline the steps to be followed as the plan unfolds, the media to be used, and the themes to be emphasized in your multimedia campaign.

ADDITIONAL READINGS

MICHAEL J. ARLEN, *The View From Highway 1.* New York: Farrar, Straus & Giroux, 1976. Insightful critique of TV.

EDWARD W. BARRETT, "Sex, Death and Other Trends in Magazines," *Columbia Journalism Review,* July/August 1974, pp. 24–26.

J.W. CLICK and RUSSELL N. BAIRD, *Magazine Editing and Production.* Dubuque, Ia.: Wm. C. Brown, 1974.

ROBERT DALEY, "We Deal with Emotional Facts," *New York Times Magazine,* December 15, 1974. A biting critique of TV news.

EDWIN DIAMOND, *The Tin Kazoo: Television, Politics, and the News.* Cambridge, Mass.: M.I.T. Press, 1975.

CLIFTON C. EDOM, *Photojournalism: Principles and Practice.* Dubuque, Ia.: William C. Brown, 1976.

JAMES F. EVANS and ROLDOLFO N. SALCEDO, *Communication in Agriculture: The American Farm Press.* Ames: Iowa State University Press, 1974.

IRVING E. FANG, *Television News,* 2nd ed. New York: Hastings House, 1972. A useful manual for TV users.

J. WILLIAM FULBRIGHT, "Fulbright on the Press," *Columbia Journalism Review,* November–December 1975. Calls press to task for its shortcomings.

ERNEST C. HYNDS, *American Newspapers in the 1970s.* New York: Hastings House, 1975.

BRUCE M. KENNEDY, *Community Journalism.* Ames: Iowa State University Press 1973.

DON R. PEMBER, *Mass Media in America.* Chicago: Science Research Associates, 1974. Focuses on issues affecting the public.

CARL RIBLET, JR., *The Solid Gold Copy Editor.* Tucson, Ariz.: Falcon Press, 1972. Useful in preparation of copy.

WILLIAM L. RIVERS, *Free-Lancer and Staff Writer: Writing Magazine Articles.* Belmont, Calif.: Wadsworth, 1972.

JOHN TEBBEL, *The Media in America.* New York: Thomas Y. Crowell, 1975.

ROLAND E. WOLSELEY, *The Changing Magazine: Trends in Readership and Management.* New York: Hastings House, 1973.

FOOTNOTES

1. For one version of the way David Rockefeller's "image" is handled, see Madeline Nelson, "Money Makes the Press Go Round," *MORE,* March 1974.

2. For discussion of the Hoover public relations myths and fact, see Paul Clancy, "The Press Barely Laid a Hand on Hoover," *The Quill,* February 1976; and Sanford J. Ungar, "This is Your FBI?" *MORE,* March 1976.

3. Paul N. Williams, "Boys Town: An Expose without Bad Guys," *Columbia Journalism Review,* January/February 1975, p. 30.

4. Frederick C. Whitney, *Mass Media and Mass Communications in Society* (Dubuque, Ia.: William C. Brown, 1975). A useful overview of the mass media.

5. For studies showing public relations' role in shaping the day's news, see David B. Sachsman, "Public Relations Influence on Coverage of Environment in San Francisco Area," *Journalism Quarterly,* Vol. 53 (Spring 1976); and John E. Ross and Marjorie Bean, "The Role of Technical Information in Decisions on Nuclear Power Plants," Report 19, Institute for Environmental Studies, University of Wisconsin–Madison, 1974.

6. For background, read Ben H. Bagdikian, *The Information Machines* (New York: Harper & Row, 1971).

7. For a closeup of the nation's news system and the role of public relations in this system, see Timothy Crouse, *The Boys on the Bus* (New York: Random House, 1973); and James M. Perry, *Us & Them* (New York: C.N. Potter, 1973); excellent studies of the press coverage of the 1972 presidential campaign.

8. John P. Robinson, "The Press as King-Maker: What Surveys from Last Five Campaigns Show," *Journalism Quarterly,* Vol. 51 (Winter 1974).

9. Dan Drew and G. Cleveland Wilhoit, "Newshole Allocation Policies of American Daily Newspapers," *Journalism Quarterly,* Vol. 53 (Autumn 1976).

10. "The Irrepressible Weeklies," *Columbia Journalism Review,* Vol. 7 (Summer 1968).

11. For one example, see: "The Emergence of a Specialized Newspaper: *The Chronicle of Higher Education,*" *Journalism Quarterly,* Vol. 52 (Summer 1975).

12. For an overview of magazines, see Theodore H. Peterson, *Magazines in the Twentieth Century* (Urbana: University of Illinois Press, 1964). Useful but a bit dated.

13. For more on these lively urban magazines, see Bob Abel, "The City Slickers," *Columbia Journalism Review,* Vol. 7 (Spring 1968); John Tebbel, "City Magazines: A Medium Reborn," *Saturday Review,* March 9, 1968; and A. Kent MacDougall, "Clay Felker's *New York,*" *Columbia Journalism Review,* Vol. XII March/April 1974.

14. When evaluating size and characteristics of magazine audiences, practitioners must take all circulation claims with some caution. See Chris Welles, "The Numbers Magazines Live By," *Columbia Journalism Review,* Vol. 14, (September–October 1975).

15. Tony Schwartz, *The Responsive Chord* (New York: Anchor, 1974), p. 32.

16. Robert T. Bower, *Television and the Public* (New York: Holt, Rinehart & Winston, 1973), p. 7. A useful reference for the practitioner who wishes to use TV.

17. Thomas E. Patterson and Robert D. McClure,

The Unseeing Eye, The Myth of Television Power in National Elections (New York: Putnam, 1976). Quotes are from Warren Weaver, Jr.'s foreword.

18. Martin Mayer, "How Television News Covers the World (in 4,000 Words or Less)," *Esquire,* January 1972, pp. 85ff.

19. "Candy Telegrams to Kiddyland," *MORE,* February 1975. Meyer is the perceptive TV critic for the *Saturday Review.* For insight on how network news is put together, see Edward Jay Epstein, *News from Nowhere* (New York: Random House, 1973).

20. Joseph R. Dominick, Alan Wurtzel, and Guy Lometti, "Television Journalism vs. Show Business," *Journalism Quarterly,* Vol. 52 (Summer 1975). For a full discussion of the unhappy trend of "happy talk" news, see Ron Powers, *The Newscasters* (New York: St. Martin's Press, 1977).

17

Good media relationships are earned through honest, helpful news service provided in an atmosphere of mutual respect and candor.

Working with the Media

Media relations represent an important part of the practitioner's daily work. Practitioners' standing with media gatekeepers and reporters shapes and limits their accomplishments. Journalists' confidence is one of a practitioner's most valuable assets. Employers and clients come and go, but the press and its gatekeepers are here forever. (*Press* is used here broadly, to include all news media.)

The person in the middle

To be effective in their *go-between role,* practitioners must have the full confidence of their organization and of the press. This is not easy. The interests of the organization and those of the media frequently clash. Organizations want news reported in a favorable manner that will promote their objectives and will not cause them trouble; the press wants news that will interest readers and viewers. Administrators complain, "Why does the press always sensationalize things?" "The papers never get things right." "They take things out of context." "You can't trust reporters." "I didn't say that at all." "Why do reporters enjoy stirring up trouble?" Newsmen countercomplain, "That organization will never come clean." "They won't give us the real news, only a lot of puffs." "They won't let you in to see the person with the news." "What are they trying to hide?"

The gulf that too often exists between organization and news media can be seen in these comments: The chairman of the University of Minnesota regents, criticizing the university's public relations staff, said, "I don't want our news service to be objective." An Associated Press science writer sees many practitioners as "*inhibitors* who do everything they can to interfere with the reporter who's trying to get a story." Both sides have a point. Practitioners in the middle must *patiently* bring each side around to understanding of the problems and viewpoint of the other.

Ever since public relations emerged early in this century, the practitioner and the journalist have functioned in a *mutually dependent relationship*, sometimes as *adversaries,* sometimes as *colleagues* cooperating in respective self-interest. Not as frequently, but sometimes, the news media become captives of the practitioner, who often has not only superior resources but also news control. Yet, equally often, practitioners are frustrated in getting useful information to the public by the inadequacies, incompetence, and frozen patterns of the media. From day to day and from situation to situation, the advantages and antagonisms in this relationship alternate. Consequently, the relationship is sometimes a difficult one, *a relationship requiring the skills of an arbitrator.* Unhappily, neither executives nor journalists comprehend the arbitrator role of the practitioner.

Press relations

It is important to keep in mind the underlying conflict of interest that hovers in the background of this somewhat adversary relationship. The basic difference between the publicist's advancing of a particular cause and the newsman's representation of the public point of view is a healthy thing. It should be so viewed by both parties. Although it is often emotionalized beyond all proportion, it does exist and is to be reckoned with.

The irritation of the press is understandable. It is all too often flooded with uninteresting, poorly written releases. The publicist may drown a few facts in a sea of words, in an effort to get more news space. Or a journalist may encounter a tightly drawn news-release curtain put up by an inept practitioner or by order of the boss. On the other hand, the media often fail to recognize the service provided by filling a void in comprehensive, constructive coverage. *Practitioners are an influential and integral part of the nation's news system.*

The basic conflict lies in the never-ending quest of the media for exciting news, in their efforts to keep the news stream uncontaminated, and in the need for money coming into their cash registers. On the other side are individuals, institutions, and industries that find it imperative to have their stories told to the public with accuracy and fairness. *Much of the public relations expertise goes into trying to put news about an institution into a total mosaic that lends perspective.* Too often, the news media are interested only in colorful fragments.

The media's definition of "news" is at the heart of this problem. To illustrate: An archbishop criticizes, with reason, the two major wire services when they base their nationally circulated story on seven lines of a 20-page document that was issued after prolonged deliberation by America's Roman Catholic bishops. The former chairman of the president's Council of Economic Advisers, Herbert Stein, echoes this common complaint: "Not only do the media concentrate on the short-term aspects of the economy, they also dramatize them in ways that further exaggerate their importance. Prices do not rise, they *soar.*"[1] Kerryn King, a veteran practitioner, suggests part of the problem: "The ideal of objective reporting has gone out of the window in far too many cases. If you are not on the same side of the fence as the editorial page, your chances of being heard are minimal in many of our largest cities. In many newspapers there is no attempt to balance the news. . . . Dramatic pictures, often less important than hard news, are given preference by television news shows."

King's complaint against the press is an old one. In 1892, when he was president of the University of Chicago, William Rainey Harper, who built the university with skilled use of public relations, wrote a friend, "I wish very much that there could be enacted a law in the State of Illinois inflicting the death penalty upon irresponsible reporters for the miserable way in which they misrepresent the truth."

Roots of the differing perspectives between news source and news media can be seen in this somewhat exaggerated view of journalists held by Gay Talese, former *New York Times* reporter:

> Most journalists are restless voyeurs who see warts on the world, the imperfections in people and places.
>
> The same scene that is much of life, the great portion of the planet unmarked by madness, does not lure them like riots and raids, crumbling countries and sinking ships, bankers banished to Rio, and burning Buddhist nuns—gloom is their game, the spectacle their passion, normality their nemesis.[2]

Nonetheless, most journalists are competent and fair-minded in reporting the day's news within the limitations imposed on them—limitations of space or time, pressures for speed, and demands for content that excites. The practitioner must learn to live with the fact that the wheel that drives the press drives it too hard, too fast. Robert J. McCloskey, reflecting on many years as public-affairs officer of the State Department, counsels, "Neither side has a corner on the market of infallibility or of being more sinned against than sinning. . . . What must be avoided at all costs are disputes which run the risk of putting the interests of the people last."

But the media's news values are not the only source of conflict. The media's lack of manpower, in numbers and in the expertise required to cover today's broad spectrum of complex news, is part of the problem.[3] Also, the limitations of time and news space, either print or electronic, result in a condensation that often distorts a complex story. Another important ingredient in this conflict is the frequent charge of denial of access to the news media altogether.

The wry view of the practitioner and his work held by some newsmen is reflected in the Associated Press Managing Editors' manual, *APME Guidelines:*

> A flack is a person who makes all or part of his income by obtaining space in newspapers without cost to himself or his clients. Usually a professional . . . they are known formally as public relations men. The flack is the modern equivalent of the cavalier highwayman of old. . . . A flack is a flack. His job is to say kind things about his client. He will not lie very often, but much of the time he tells less than the whole story. You do not owe the P.R. man anything. The owner of the newspaper, not the flack, pays your salary. Your job is to serve the readers, not the man who would raid your columns.[4]

It might be helpful to list the grievances on both sides of the fence.[5] The complaints most often heard from the media are about:

1. Attempts by practitioners to color and check the free flow of legitimate news.
2. Space-grabbing for "free advertising," with consequent loss of revenue to the media.
3. Attempted use of "influence" and pressure to get into news columns; indirect and sometimes direct bribery of reporters.
4. Gross ignorance of the media's editorial requirements; no conception of what news is or how it should be written.
5. Raiding of news staffs for experienced men with the lure of higher salaries.

Countercharges most frequently listed by the practitioner include:

1. Failure of the press to do its whole job; failure to increase its reportorial staff to keep pace with the expanding list of socially significant activities demanding news coverage (in the fields of industry, finance, education, medicine, and so forth).
2. The slowness of change in the press's definition of news, which puts emphasis on conflict and minimizes the socially constructive events—the press's sensationalism.
3. Failure to treat news as news regardless of the source; attacks on publicity only to rationalize a basic money motive.
4. Failure to discriminate between the honest, helpful practitioner and the incompetent.
5. Increasing dependence of the press on the function it so frequently condemns.

Rules for good press relations

Good relationships can best be achieved by the practice of a few basic principles: (1) *shoot squarely,* (2) *give service,* (3) *don't beg or carp,* (4) *don't ask for kills,* (5) *don't flood the media,* and (6) *keep updated lists.*

Shoot squarely: It is not just an academic nicety to counsel that "honesty is the best policy" in dealing with the press. It is plain common sense. Journalists can spot a phony or a shady practice a mile off—they see so many of both. It is their job to get the news, and they generally get it, one way or another. Anyone who tries to thwart or block them through trickery, evasion, and censorship will encounter tough opposition. A publicist may win the battle in such instances, but is likely to lose the war; the press fires the last shot. Unless a practitioner has the confidence and goodwill of the media gatekeepers, his value to an employer is minimal. This confidence is compounded of a record of *accuracy, integrity,* and *performance.*

Journalists know the hokum of circus publicity, but they play along with it. They recognize the inflated and artificial news pegs in the publicity output of a local charity or civic event; they understand and appreciate the position of the person charged with making the most favorable presentation of a cause that the facts will allow. The copy submitted may be rewritten or tossed aside. If the publicist is candid, he or she won't lose their confidence.

A couple of examples: (1) An Eastern plastics factory had a major explosion. Plant officials admitted newsmen to a plant meeting, but told them nothing. Reporters finally got the story from the hospitals, and in many cases, they were the first to notify families of injured workmen. (2) A call by a Midwest chemical plant for fire protection while plant workers repaired a break in a chlorine gas line accidentally became exaggerated into a major poison-gas threat. Radio broadcasters flashed warnings; schoolchildren were sent home. Plant officials, knowing the danger to be slight, could have eased this anxiety, but when the press called, they were not available.

Another fundamental principle is that *a publicist cannot favor one news outlet at the expense of others.* When he gets caught, he risks losing the confidence and goodwill of those others. The publicity tune has to be played straight across the keyboard. This is not easy in a cacophony of stiff competition. The safest rule is that spot news should go out as fast as possible, letting the media determine the cycle in which it breaks. News and feature material for which the time peg can be fixed should be alternated evenly among the competitors. As a corollary, the publicist must protect a journalist's initiative in going after a story. If a reporter gets a tip and asks for information, it belongs to him or her. The same information should not be given to other outlets unless they come after it. This is a policy with which no reporter can justly quarrel.

Give service: The quickest, surest way to gain the cooperation of media men and women is to provide them with *interesting, timely stories and pictures* that they want *when they want them* and *in the form in which they can readily use them.* Newsmen lean on and cooperate with the practitioner who willingly responds to a midnight call for a picture and biographical sketch of an executive who has just died. News, a highly perishable commodity, occurs around the clock; newspaper and newscast deadlines must be met around the clock. Therefore, *the practitioner must be on call around the clock.*

Don't beg or carp: Nothing irritates media men and women more than a publicist who begs or carps. If the material is not sufficiently newsworthy to earn space in print or time on the air, it is not likely to attract interest. Editorial people get and hold their jobs by knowing what interests people. Don't beg to have stories used. Don't complain about the treatment of a story if it is used. Don't ask editors to serve as clipping bureaus by asking for tear sheets.

Too many people who deal with the press try to be "editors" on the assumption that they know as much about defining or writing news as the editor or reporter does. Too many executives insist on having news releases put out just as they would like to have them appear in print or on the air. They refuse to accept the fact that news is the newsman's job.

The admonition, "Don't beg" also covers a warning against trying to pressure publicity into news columns and newscasts by using advertising as a wedge. *There is nothing a journalist resents more than to have the publicist work through the advertising department.* In most cases, it won't work and will bring only resentment. That's what happened in the case of a Utah editor when a bank public relations official came in and said, "Here's a list of stories I want you to run in connection with the opening of our new branch bank. We'll be a heavy advertiser, you know." Asked what irked him most about practitioners, a *Louisville Courier-Journal* editor said, "By far my biggest gripe is that they don't know anything about my business, which is their business. *And their general pushiness.* The idea that persistence pays off." Advertising belongs in the advertising department, and news—if it is news—will get in the news columns or newscasts.[6]

Don't ask for kills: A publicity man has no right to ask a newspaper, magazine, or radio station to suppress or kill a story. To any journalist, this is a crude insult. It is asking media men and women to betray their trust. It seldom works and brings only ill will as a reward. *The way to keep unfavorable stories out of the press is to keep situations that produce such stories from taking place.* There are occasions when it is perfectly legitimate to request a delay in publication or to explain to the press any part of a story that might be damaging to the public interest. If there are valid reasons, cards should be laid on the table, face up. The newspapers will cooperate 99 times out of 100. But if more than two people know a story, the chances of suppressing it are almost nil. General Creighton Abrams once said, "In all my Army experience, I have never known bad news to improve with age."

Don't flood the media: Study and experience teach the boundaries of news interest, and common sense dictates respect for them. If a financial editor repeatedly receives from the same source items appropriate for the fashion or sports editor, he loses respect for that source. A tendency of the inept and the opportunistic publicist is to flood all media with all releases in order, he thinks, to increase the potential circulation and exposure. This reasoning is fallacious. It identifies the publicist as being untrained or incompetent and his employer or client as being unreasonable, unknowledgeable, or unethical. *Forbes* editors complain, "We're constantly being plagued by PR men who come bounding into the office or who telephone bubbling over with 'a great story idea.' They're right; it's a great story idea—for them, but not for our readers, who are busy men." The editor of *Domestic Engineering* reported that he received 1,500 releases in one month, and of these only 126 were used in whole or in part—a 90 percent rejection rate.

In a survey covering 348 editors of U.S. and Canadian business publications, Paul Wichterman found:

> Fewer than 100 of those questioned received less than 100 news releases per month, while 19 publications get an average of more than 1,000 a month.
> Of the 346 editors, 99 said that 25 to 50 percent of the material they received was of at least some value.
> Many made the comment: "Too many public relations people use the 'shotgun' technique for sending out releases."
> The great competition for editorial space is reflected in the fact that 161 editors use 25 percent or less of the relevant releases received.

In the preparation of news material, the potentially interested audiences should be selected and catered to, and in the distribution, those media that normally and naturally serve that audience should be thoroughly covered, with special consideration where a special "angle" is involved.

Keep lists up to date: The transiency and mortality of press personnel and of media require that distribution lists be dynamic. This means continuous updating. The purchase of annual media directories by departments and agencies represents a productive economy.

Few things could be more annoying to an editor than to receive news addressed to the person he or she had replaced in the job two or three years earlier. The same reaction occurs when a publication or station outlet receives news material forwarded from or misaddressed to a location it vacated years before.

The sophisticated practitioner will use modern data processing to keep his mailing lists up to date and to target his releases to specific audiences with interest in their content. Today, progressive organizations are using the computer in the development of news releases, feature articles, and backgrounders, as well as the more standard roles of information storage and retrieval. Form stories, such as hometown releases on college students, can be computerized and thus save much repetitious labor.[7]

These principles or "rules of the game" can serve to establish profitable press relationships. One editor once told a group that what the press wants is *honesty, speed, brevity, confidence.* Another newspaperman advises, "Be frank, be as cooperative in giving bad news as the good, realize that what your organization does affects a good many people in the community and they have a right to honest reports about your activities." Good press relations flow from the unreserved acceptance of the fact that the public has a right to public **information.** *Good press relationships must be earned.*

EXHIBIT 17–1

Useful Publicity Directories

Ayer's Directory of Newspapers and Magazines. Annual. N.W. Ayer & Sons, 210 West Washington Square, Philadelphia, PA 19106. Lists more than 22,000 periodicals by city and state, including newspapers, magazines, newspaper feature syndicates, special interest publications. Helpful in pinpointing local media.

Bacon's Publicity Checker. Annual. R.H. Bacon Publishing Co., 14 E. Jackson Blvd., Chicago, IL 60604. Lists 4,000 special-interest publications by category, plus general-interest magazines and major newspapers in the U.S. Most useful in zeroing in on a specific industry or subject.

Broadcasting Yearbook. Annual. Broadcasting Publications, Inc., 1735 De Sales St. N.W., Washington, DC 20036. Lists AM and FM radio stations and TV stations in the U.S., Canada, and Latin America. Published by *Broadcasting Magazine.*

Editor & Publisher's Yearbook. Annual. Editor & Publisher Co., 850 Third Ave., New York, NY 10022. Lists comprehensive information about every daily newspaper in the U.S. and Canada, plus information on weekly newspapers in the U.S. Special sections devoted to college, industry, foreign-language, and special-interest daily newspapers; minority newspapers; news and picture syndicates; clubs and associations, books and awards related to the newspaper field.

Gebbie House Magazine Directory. Annual. National Research Bureau, 424 No. Third St., Burlington, IA 52601. Lists information on more than 4,200 magazines and newsletters published by U.S. and Canadian companies, clubs, and government agencies. Cross-referenced by city and state, organizational name, title, printer, industry, subject, and circulation.

Gebbie Press All-in-One Directory. Annual. Gebbie Press, Box 1000, New Paltz, NY 12561. Lists every daily and weekly newspaper and radio and television station; most consumer, business, trade, farm, and black publications.

National Radio Publicity Directory. Annual. Peter Glenn Publications, 17 E. 48th St., New York, NY 10017. Lists information on over 2,000 radio network, syndicated, and local talk shows in the U.S., including college stations. Lists address data, information on coverage area, format, names of programs, public service, news, business news, and sports directors.

News Bureaus in the U.S., Richard Weiner, ed. This media guidebook lists names of personnel, addresses, telephone numbers, etc., for 400 news bureaus. Richard Weiner, Inc., 888 Seventh Ave., New York City 10019.

Standard Periodical Directory. Biannual. Oxbridge Publishing Co., 150 E. 52nd St., New York, NY 10022. Probably the most comprehensive, it lists some 39,000 publications in the U.S. and Canada, including newsletters, house publications, and various special-interest publications. Primarily a library reference.

Standard Rate and Data Service. Publication varies by volume. Standard Rate and Data Service, Inc., 5201 Old Orchard Road, Skokie, IL 60076. The major source on rate information for advertisers; also contains valuable information for PR. Published in six volumes: Newspapers, Business Publications, Consumer and Farm Magazines, Network TV, Spot Radio, and Spot Television.

Television Factbook. Annual. Television Digest, Inc., 1836 Jefferson Pl., N.W., Washington, DC 20036. Considered the most detailed reference in the television field, this directory contains complete data (except specific programming) on every commercial and educational television station in the country. Includes maps of TV coverage not published elsewhere.

TV Publicity Outlets—Nationwide. Biannual. Public Relations Plus, Inc., Box 327, Washington Depot, CT 06794. Invaluable source for publicity on local TV shows. Lists all shows known to accept publicity materials (including guests, scripts with slides, and films), by station, by market, and by state. Includes information on whom to contact.

Working Press of the Nation. Annual. National Research Bureau, 424 No. Third St., Burlington, IA 52601. Most comprehensive. Lists detailed information on many media, except contact information for radio and TV shows. Published in five volumes: Newspapers (Vol. 1); Magazines (Vol. 2); Radio and TV (Vol. 3); Feature Writers & Syndicates (Vol. 4); House Organs (Vol. 5).

EXHIBIT 17-1 (CONT.)

REGIONAL

California Publicity Outlets. Annual. Unicorn Systems Company, 3807 Wilshire Blvd., Los
   Angeles, CA 90010. Lists major media outlets in Northern and Southern California.
Free Radio Air Time. Annual. Sam Smaltz, Publisher, 1906 Alpha Ave., South Pasadena, CA
   91030. Lists information on all interview shows and features on Los Angeles and Orange
   County radio shows, the topics covered, hosts, contacts, etc.
Hudson's Washington News Media Contacts Directory. Annual. w/3 revisions. 2814 Pennsylvania
   Ave. N.W., Washington, DC 20007. Most comprehensive compilation of the press corps of
   the nation's capital. Includes extensive data about 4,000 publications, bureaus, corre-
   spondents, editors, and free-lance writers.
Middle West Publicity Media Directory. Annual. Derus Media Service, 8 West Hubbard St.,
   Chicago, IL 60610. Handy reference for those concentrating publicity efforts in Chicago
   and the Midwest. Contains information on the full range of media in Illinois, Wisconsin,
   Minnesota, Iowa, Missouri, Indiana, Michigan, and Ohio.
New York Publicity Outlets. Annual. Public Relations Plus, Inc., Box 327, Washington Depot,
   CT 06794. Contains information on national and local media in Greater New York City.
Simon's Editorial Offices in the West. Biannual. Simon/Public Relations, 11661 San Vicente
   Blvd., Los Angeles, CA 90049. A comprehensive listing of editors and stringers on the West
   Coast.

Executives and the media

Increasingly, organizations are finding it advantageous to have their top
executives deal directly with the news media. This practice has the pluses of
providing an authoritative spokesman, of gaining public recognition for the
executive, and of exposing the executive to the blunt questions of a journalist,
who often voices questions on the public's mind. For example, public relations
officials of one organization have the philosophy that it is the public relations
function *"to facilitate communications between the organization and its publics,"* not just to
"handle the company's communications." Advantageous or not, executives,
especially at the regional-office, branch-campus, or branch-office level, must deal
with the media on a face-to-face basis. There is no local public relations official to
serve as the intermediary.

Facing the press is difficult for many top executives. One board chairman
admits he is "scared" to be interviewed by the press: "The power of the press
scares me, with its unsupervised access to tens of thousands of people." Former
Dean Harold M. Williams of UCLA, now a government official, believes that the
press is especially threatening to an executive who seeks to "control his environment."[8]

Thus it becomes a responsibility of the public relations department to ease
these fears and train top managers so that they can deal with the press with
confidence and with candor. Several standard training courses for this purpose
have been developed by public relations agencies and media consultants. "Typically, executives are put through a two-or-three-day seminar that uses videotape
techniques to teach public speaking, and television interviewing techniques.
Some courses include methods for disarming hostile inquisitors."[9]

Some specific guidelines

Practitioners and executives alike can profit from close study of these ten
guidelines developed by an experienced counselor, Chester Burger:

1. *Talk from the viewpoint of the public's interest, not the organization's.* The soft-drink bottler who launches a campaign to collect and recycle bottles can frankly admit that it does not want to irritate the public by having its product litter the landscape.
2. *Speak in personal terms whenever possible.* When many people have worked on developing a new product or adopting a new policy, it becomes difficult for the executive to say "I."
3. *If you do not want some statement quoted, do not make it.* Spokesmen should avoid talking "off the record," because such statements may well wind up published without the source.
4. *State the most important fact at the beginning.* The executive's format may first list the facts that led to the final conclusion, but such organization will fail when talking with the news media.
5. *Do not argue with the reporter or lose your cool.* Understand that the newsman seeks an interesting story and will use whatever techniques he needs to obtain it.
6. *If a question contains offensive language or simply words you do not like, do not repeat them even to deny them.* Reporters often use the gambit of putting words into the subject's mouth.
7. *If the reporter asks a direct question, he is entitled to an equally direct answer.* Not giving one is a common error executives are prone to make.
8. *If a spokesman does not know the answer to a question, he should simply say, "I don't know, but I'll find out for you."* With this, the spokesman assumes the responsibility of following through.
9. *Tell the truth, even if it hurts.* In this era of skepticism and hostility, the most difficult task is often simply telling the truth.
10. *Do not exaggerate the facts.* Crying wolf makes it harder to be heard next time out.[10]

These guidelines simply add up to the rule that profitable press relations require adherence to the "five Fs": dealing with journalists and program producers in a manner that is *fast, factual, frank, fair,* and *friendly.*

The news conference

The news conference is frequently used as the occasion for the release of news and as a vehicle to cultivate good media relations. There is no better way to give out a story simultaneously to all media, provided the subject is newsworthy. When is a news conference justified? The best practical answer is, "Seldom." Generally, important controversial matters such as labor–management disputes, political pronouncements, and major industrial policy changes suggest a conference, because a discussion, rather than a one-sided statement, is in order. In this era of science, *complex matters that require backgrounding,* such as a technological breakthrough, *often justify a conference.* Simple matters that constitute no public issue or are not complex in nature can usually be handled without one.

There are, of course, exceptions. A special event, like the annual introduction of new automobiles, lavish with showmanship or drama, may not contain a public issue or complexity. But the spectacle, the impact, broad public interest, and the opportunities for feature and photographic angles make it desirable that it be witnessed personally. The same applies to the exposure of celebrities on occasion.

Who should be invited to a news conference? As a rule of thumb, all news media representatives who will not go away disappointed. If you are in doubt about a particular medium, inquire in advance. For local events having national significance, the local press should always be given the same welcome and courtesy extended those from out of town. In modern news networks, most local press is linked up with a national or international association.

With the high degree of mobility and instant communications in society today, the location of a press conference is not as critical as it was in former times. Given a choice, a location handy for the newsmen involved should be a consideration. Their time is precious. Some organizations have equipped trailers as press rooms, so they can take them to the location of an event. This facility has proved popular with newsmen covering stories in remote locations.

As host for the conference, the organization should have an executive or official to function as spokesman. On hand also should be experts and specialists capable of explaining the particular news matter at hand. All members of the organization participating in the conference should be briefed in advance on the questions that will most probably be put by press members. That will facilitate the answers, provide complete accuracy, place the organization in a favorable light, and put everyone at ease. If the conference takes place at a mealtime, a meal should be served, and the conference should proceed during the meal. If light refreshments are indicated, serve them. Neither should delay the news beyond the appointed time.

How should guests be invited? Invitations should be oral whenever possible. If written, they should be informal and friendly. A mailgram or follow-up telephone call sometimes lends a touch of urgency to an invitation.

What equipment should be on hand? For a spot-news break, telephones should be handy, and representatives of the wireless service should be standing by. Typewriters, paper, and working space will most likely be needed. For discussion groups, when the news does not have the same urgency, comfort is a prime consideration. For crowds of over 50 people, public-address equipment should be used.

Kits containing information and photographs pertaining to the meetings should be passed out, preferably at the beginning when there is time to examine them, so that reporters can know what questions they want answered. If the story is complex, exhibits or demonstrations are very much in order. They tend to lighten heavy news substance and enable reporters to interpret in language that readers can understand.

The conflicting requirements and spirited competition between reporters from radio and television and those from the print media pose a difficult problem for the sponsor of a press conference. Space requirements and the distractions of TV cameras, lighting equipment, and so forth, make it difficult to accommodate both electronic- and print-media reporters in the same conference. Whirring TV cameras that muffle the interviewee's words and block reporters' views of him or her, and the eagerness of some reporters to be seen on TV, are common causes of complaint by reporters. Some practitioners have developed the practice of having two conferences, one for the electronic media, one for the print media. Members of the press invited but unable to attend should be sent the news material. Radio and TV gatekeepers wish to cover "news conferences," not "press conferences."

The exclusive interview

There are many occasions in large organizations that, in response to competition among the media, call for interviews between an official and a journalist. The principles cited earlier apply, with additional responsibilities on the part of whichever one solicited the interview.

When the journalist seeks the interview, the burden of guiding the discussion is on him or her. If asked to, the reporter may submit an advance outline of the information sought—say, the university president's views on athletic overemphasis, or the governor's views on the need for more taxes.

When the newsmaker initiates the occasion, in the hope that a profile of his organization or a white paper on his viewpoints will result, he and his public relations advisor assume the burden. The proposal or suggestion to the reporter should state the general subject matter they want covered and render an opinion of its news validity. If it is a union–management settlement, for instance, what is unusual about it that recommends an interview? Areas considered secret or privileged should be made clear ahead of time; the union leader who seeks an interview to air a favorable settlement but does not wish to reveal the vote count of union members should preclude the question. The interview itself must be characterized by a maximum of candor on the part of the newsmaker, to indicate that he has done his homework. "Off the record," "I'd rather not comment on that," and disclaimers must be used sparingly. Otherwise, the reporter will use the option of seeking and quoting other sources for the information withheld.

When the interview lends itself to photography, this should be anticipated with whatever props or arrangements are relevant. Tape recording of interviews is desirable for both parties.

Ground rules for interviews

Whenever a spokesman or executive agrees to an interview with a correspondent, it is best that both parties agree in advance to the rules under which the source of the information given will be identified. From the point of view of the correspondent, it is usually most desirable that the interview be *on the record*—that is, have everything said attributable directly to the person being interviewed. Obviously, this makes the interviewee phrase the answer to each question with the utmost care, particularly when a delicate subject is being discussed.

Of course, there are instances in which the interviewee does not want to be quoted directly or does not want his statements to be attributed to him in an identifiable way. The most frequently encountered ground rules for this kind of an information exchange are these:

1. *Indirect quote*—Remarks that may be used in substance (but *not verbatim*) and attributed to a specific source. There is seldom a reason to be interviewed on this basis.
2. *Background*—Information that can be used by a correspondent but attributed only to a nonspecific source, such as "a college authority," "a White House official," or "a knowledgeable authority." The form of attribution must be agreed upon in advance.

3. *Not for attribution*—Information that may be used by a correspondent but not attributed to any source. This is sometimes referred to as "deep background."

4. *Off the record*—Information that is to be held in confidence by the correspondent, not to be released in any form. This basis is used whenever it is deemed necessary to provide information that will permit a correspondent to grasp the full meaning of a complicated news event. This information is provided only to the most trusted reporters with the understanding that, if more than one reporter is involved, they will not even discuss it among themselves. *All reporters concerned must state in advance their agreement to take information on this basis.* Some will not.

Two final notes

The *news conference* should not be confused or mixed with the *press party* or *junket.* Newsmen and women prefer not to mix their work and their fun. There is a time and a place for each. In fact, many journalists share the view of a *Milwaukee Journal* editor: "I dislike the constant suggestion that the reporter and the person go to lunch to do the interview. I say no; you get neither a decent lunch nor a decent story."

Regarding souvenirs and gifts: To the extent that they are not expensive and are pertinent to the occasion, propriety and taste would approve. Items like imprinted plastic brief cases or note pads, key chains or holders with the organization's emblem, luggage tags or passport holders, food or confection samples, are safely free from criticism as being coercive. Extremely questionable, however, are irrelevant gifts such as boxes of candy on Valentine's Day, cases of whiskey at Christmas, overpaid travel allowances when travel is in order, interest-free loans, costly product gifts, and ridiculous discounts.

Practitioners must be highly sensitive to the changed attitudes on the part of journalists toward gifts—freebies and junkets. The *Milwaukee Journal*'s Code of Ethics suggests the trend. The *Journal* outlaws free tickets except for reporters covering the event or show; permits gifts of only insignificant value, such as a calendar or ballpoint pen; outlaws junkets by stating that free or subsidized travel may not be accepted by its reporters or editors; discourages "freeload affairs" that have little or nothing to do with news coverage; and requires that books and records received for review be turned over to libraries or deserving organizations. Prizes and awards provided by public relations sources for "outstanding journalistic performance" are also coming under increased criticism by working journalists.[11]

The difficulty of drawing the line of propriety in media relationships was illustrated in the furore that followed Xerox's sponsorship of an article written by Harrison E. Salisbury for *Esquire* magazine. Xerox, bold and innovative in its public relations programs, commissioned Salisbury, retired *New York Times* editor, to write a 23-page article, "Travels through America," giving him a free hand, and paid him a fee of $40,000 plus $15,000 for expenses. Xerox contracted for $115,000 worth of advertising in *Esquire* over a year's period in exchange for its publication of the Salisbury article. All this was made a matter of public record. Yet E.B. White, retired *New Yorker* essayist, publicly blasted this arrangement as "a disaster for freedom of the press." In the words of David J. Curtin, vice-president of communications for Xerox, "He stopped us dead in our tracks. . . .

We have enormous respect for Mr. White and if this was unsettling to him, it was just not worth continuing the program." Mr. White's blast is shown in Figure 17–1.

FIGURE 17–1   From the *Washington Post,* January 10, 1976.

E. B. White

The Esquire-Xerox Axis

I think it might be useful to stop viewing fences for a moment and take a close look at Esquire magazine's new way of doing business. In February, Esquire will publish a long article by Harrison E. Salisbury, for which Mr. Salisbury will receive no payment from Esquire but will receive forty thousand dollars from the Xerox Corporation—plus another fifteen thousand for expenses. This, it would

This article by author E.B. White appeared originally in the Ellsworth (Maine) American.

seem to me, is not only a new idea in publishing, it charts a clear course for the erosion of the free press in America. Mr. Salisbury is a former associate editor of the New York Times and should know better. Esquire is a reputable sheet and should know better. But here we go—the Xerox-Salisbury-Esquire axis in full cry!

A news story about this amazing event in the December 14th issue of the Times begins: "Officials of Esquire magazine and of the Xerox Corporation report no adverse reactions, so far, to the announcement that Esquire will publish a 23-page article (about travels through America) in February 'sponsored' by Xerox." Herewith I am happy to turn in my adverse reaction even if it's the first one across the line.

Esquire, according to the Times story, attempts to justify its new payment system (get the money from a sponsor) by assuring us that Mr. Salisbury will not be tampered with by Xerox; his hand and his pen will be free. If Xerox likes what he writes about America, Xerox will run a "low keyed full-page ad preceding the article" and another ad at the end of it. From this advertising, Esquire stands to pick up $115,000, and Mr. Salisbury has already picked up $40,000, traveling, all expenses paid, through this once happy land.

What splendid vistas the "sponsored writer" system opens up to out wondering eyes! I can hardly wait to have Craig Claiborne, food expert of the Times, commissioned by Gulden's Mustard to write a long article called "The Place of the Hot Dog in American Society." The Times won't owe Claiborne a cent—Gulden will take care of the whole package, including a full page low-keyed ad in the Times if Mr. Claiborne spreads the mustard thick enough. The writer's hands will be free: he need only open them and in will tumble fifty grand. How jolly!

Apparently Mr. Salisbury had a momentary qualm about taking on the Xerox job. The Times reports him as saying, "At first I thought, gee whiz, should I do this?" But he quickly conquered his annoying doubts and remembered that big corporations had in the past been known to sponsor "cultural enterprises," such as opera. The emergence of a magazine reporter as a cultural enterprise is as stunning a sight as the emergence of a butterfly from a cocoon. Mr. Salisbury must have felt great, escaping from his confinement.

Well, it doesn't take a giant intellect to detect in all this the shadow of disaster. If magazines decide to farm out their writers to advertisers and accept the advertiser's payment to the writer and to the magazine, then the periodicals of this country will be far down the drain and will become so fuzzy as to be indistinguishable from the controlled press in other parts of the world.

Preparation of news

In preparing news for the press, radio, or television, the questions Who? What? Where? When? Why? and How? should be answered. Preferably, they should be answered in the first sentence or the first paragraph, with details following.

Example: (*Who?*) John Jones (*What?*) died (*Where?*) in his home at 10 Main

FIGURE 17-2

Walter W. Seifert
School of Journalism
Ohio State University
242 West 18th Avenue
Columbus, Ohio 43210
    PHONE: 293-2683 (Area 614)

<u>Immediate Release</u>

COLUMBUS, Ohio -- Basic rules for preparing and placing effective news releases were suggested here today by Walter W. Seifert, professor, School of Journalism, Ohio State University.

Releases should be mimeographed cleanly on white 8 1/2" x 11" paper, Seifert said. They should be mailed first class to all logical mass media, including radio and television news directors, weekly papers, and trade magazines. Individually typed copies should be delivered personally to city editors of local dailies, he suggested.

Other rules are:

IDENTIFICATION: The name, address, and telephone number of the author should appear at upper left.

RELEASE DATE: Most releases should be "immediate." Only stipulate time when news obviously warrants holding until a certain hour.

MARGINS: Use wide margins, so editors can edit.

HEADLINES: Do not indicate a heading. (That's the editor's business.) Skip two inches between release line and body of copy so editor or rewrite desk can insert desired headline.

---more---

FIGURE 17-2 (CONT.)

Release Rules   2-2-2-2

LENGTH: Never make a release two pages if one will do. Edit your material tightly. Make sure it's accurate, timely, and not too pluggy. Dont' split a paragraph from first to second page. Put "more" at bottom of first page.

SLUGLINE: Put the traditional journalistic slugline at upper left of second page. Indicate pages as shown above.

AVOID: Fancy, tinted, printed news bureau stationery is in poor taste. It looks commercial and doesn't fit normal copy style. Don't shout NEWS. Editors decide that.

STYLE: Use summary lead (who, what, when, where, why) most of the time. Double-space. Prefer short, punchy sentences with active verbs. Make sure spelling and grammar are 100%.

CHECK: Never trust your typist. Proofread every stencil. Get client to initial a file copy of each release. Don't hesitate to check your copy with your sources.

PLACEMENT: Take general news to local city desks. Don't arrive near deadline. (2 P.M. is good for most AM'S and PM'S). Discuss special news with specialized writers. Send comprehensive factsheets on major developments that merit staff coverage. Query magazine editors on prospective articles to get their slant. Never place same story twice with same publication.

AT END: Put this

-30-

Or this

###

Street (*When?*) at six o'clock Wednesday evening (*Why?*) of a heart attack brought on by overwork. (*How?*) He had returned home in midafternoon complaining of a difficulty in breathing and was dead when the doctor arrived.

To ensure accuracy in transmission, news copy should be typewritten. Changes of text should be clearly indicated following the accepted rules of marking manuscript. Typewritten copy should be written on plain white paper of the standard $8\frac{1}{2}$-by-11 inch size. Text should be double-spaced for print media, triple-spaced for electronic media. *Only one side of the paper should be used.* If the text runs more than one sheet, the word *more* should be placed at the bottom of each sheet except the last one, and page numbers should be used. *The name, address, and telephone number of the person supplying the news should be written on the release so that it can be readily verified if desired.* A sample release is shown in Figure 17–2.

The release must be tailored for its medium. Write news stories for newspapers; articles for trade and business publications; terse, radio-style releases for radio; TV news scripts for TV. After many years of TV, practitioners continue to swamp that potent medium with newspaper releases, usually to no avail. And more than one unthinking practitioner has sent photographs along with releases to radio stations.

Experienced radio and TV news editors suggest these guidelines: (1) Send only one copy of a release and send it to the news director by name. (2) Write releases in broadcast conversational style and broadcast length. (3) Be timely—news that has appeared in the morning paper is no longer news. (4) *Call* the news department with spot news. (5) Know your audience—do not send in-depth news to rock stations. (6) Give ample advance notice of news conferences.

Photographs

In an increasing variety of news, a photograph is invaluable. Quite often, the photograph is, in itself, the news. If ever in doubt, include a photograph. The *matte-finish* still picture or one- to two-minute film clip is almost a must for television news. TV is primarily a visual medium, so TV releases call for pictures, pictographs, screen slides, and videotapes. The matte-finish photos for TV use should be horizontals in the ratio of 4 units of width to 3 units of height, since this is the shape in which TV information is transmitted. This age of pictorial journalism has put a new premium on the good publicity picture, and the same for the pictograph.

Photographs should be used for what they are—*an economical, effective means of reporting a story, and of getting your story told in the media.* Take, for example, the publicity photograph (Figure 17–3) set up by Hughes Aircraft, manufacturer of the first commercial synchronous satellite, Early Bird, when it was about to be launched from Cape Canaveral by NASA. Hughes' public relations agency, Carl Byoir, saw a way to dramatize the fact that the satellite contained 240 two-way channels of communication, thus deflecting media attention to the manufacturer. The cutlines read, "480 telephones were assembled for this picture; that's the number able to use—at the same time—the Early Bird communications satellite, which provides 240 two-way voice channels between Europe and North America." The girl in the picture was a professional model; General Telephone

Figure 17–3   Courtesy Carl Byoir and Associates.

Company provided the phones without charge, typical of the trade-offs in publicity work. The picture was a smash hit; it was distributed by AP, UPI, and NEA. All told, Byoir got back 885 photo clips.

Another example of imaginative use of photos to get publicity was that of a transit company that took a night photograph of all its buses, lighted and arranged in the form of a Christmas tree, as a way of saying "Merry Christmas" to its patrons through the local newspaper.

Photographs are especially effective in conveying the needs and values of welfare services. One such user is the Cincinnati Family Service Agency, whose photographer says, "Photographs 'spell out' a story more quickly, clearly, and powerfully than any other means of communication, perhaps because of their inherent capacity for conveying mood and evoking emotional response."[12]

Generally, the less descriptive matter needed to amplify or to explain the photograph, the better the acceptance. The best photographs of dramatic events are those that need no explanation beyond identification. An example would be a scene showing a wrecked car, photographed from such an angle that the reader could see the street marker at the corner, the clock on a nearby store, a body in the street, and the upset bicycle nearby. That tells almost the entire story except for the name of the victim.

Photographs of groups of more than six or eight people discourage publication because of the space required for identification. Activity implied in a photograph gives it greater interest and sometimes eliminates the need for identifying all the people.

People being photographed have great trouble with their hands and feet. If standing, they don't know what to do with their hands; if seated, their feet seem to get in the way. Objects held in the hand and objects placed in front of the feet tend to relieve the awkwardness.

Rarely will an experienced photographer provide for publication any type of reprints other than glossy ones. No other kind should be submitted for publication unless specifically requested. Many publicists use a standard-sized print, say 7″ × 9″ or 8″ × 10″, to effect savings.

A saying nearly as old as the press is that babies, animals, and pretty girls are surefire news pictures. A minority of projects are involved with the interests of these three subjects, but by clever arrangements it is quite often possible to tie in one of them with news subjects as seemingly remote as a new wastebasket or an institution's participation in an antipollution campaign.

Essentials of good copy

Essentials of good publicity copy are essentials of good news writing. A few reminders can serve as a checklist.

Content

Will the information or news really interest the intended audience?

Does the information answer every reasonable question that readers or listeners may ask?

Is the significance of the information explained in terms of audience?

Is the copy sufficiently newsworthy to survive stiff competition for public attention?

Will the information further the objectives of our institution? Is it useful?

Does the publicity accurately reflect the character and nature of the institution it represents?

Are the facts, names, and dates *accurate*? Are technical terms explained?

Style and structure

Will the lead catch and hold the busy reader's attention? Will it produce a bright, eye-catching headline? Is the lead terse, to the point?

Do the facts of the story support the lead in fact and spirit?

Is it readable copy, stripped of superlatives? Good news copy must be *curt, clear, concise.*

Has padding been stripped from the copy? (If you don't do this, the editor will.) Is the copy written so as to preclude the charge that it is an effort to get "free advertising"?

Is the information presented as dramatically as possible with this set of facts? Squeeze all the news value you can into your story, but don't exaggerate.

Mechanics

Is the copy legible, double-spaced, each page or ad correctly marked, end of the story indicated?

Is the source of the release fully, correctly given? Will it be easy for the editor to check back with the source if necessary?

If a fixed time is intended for the release of the story, is it plainly indicated on the outgoing release?

Is the top third of the first page blank, for editors who write heads directly on copy?

Is the copy of genuine interest to readers of each publication slated to receive the release? If not, don't send it.

Would the information be of genuine interest to an audience not provided for in the present list? If so, what other outlets should receive the copy?

Will the release reach the intended outlets while the information is still fresh, timely?

If you can answer these questions affirmatively, your copy should pass muster with the toughest-minded news editor. If you can't, you had better take another look at your story. *News is* anything *timely* that is *interesting* and *significant to readers* in respect to their personal affairs or their relation to society. The best news is that which possesses the greatest degree of this interest and significance for the greatest number.

Case problem

A nationally known chemical manufacturer opened a plant in the hills of a southeastern state. The location was chosen on the basis of labor supply, raw materials, tax rates, and humidity conditions. Shortly thereafter, in an interview with local editors and wire-service reporters, a top company executive said, "One of our major reasons for locating here—and thus one of our contributions to this community—was to help raise the standard of living of these hillbillies."

The story was widely reported. A storm broke. Nationally known natives of the state wrote burning letters to the newspapers. A syndicated columnist wrote a column, half in anger, half in fun. The governor, senators, and other politicians got into the act with duly indignant protests. People in the community expressed bitter resentment.

As public relations director, what do you recommend be done to remedy or repair this situation?

ADDITIONAL READINGS

GERALD ASTOR, "The Gospel According to Mobil," *MORE*, April 1976. Account of oil giant's head-on clash with WNBC-TV. For more on Mobil's PR, see Michael Gerrard, "This Man Was Made Possible by a Grant From Mobil Oil," *Esquire* Jan. 1978.

N.W. AYER & Co., *'77 Ayer Public Relations and Publicity Style Book,* 8th ed. Philadelphia: N.W. Ayer, 1977.

JAMES K. BUCKALEW, "The Radio News Gatekeeper and His Sources," *Journalism Quarterly,* Vol. 51 (Winter 1974). See also, in the same issue, Jerry R. Lynn, "Effects of Persuasive Appeals in Public Service Advertising."

HELEN HORWITZ BURDETT, "Professionalism and the Consumer Magazine Editor," *Public Relations Journal,* Vol. 30 (March 1974).

RICHARD M. DETWILER, "Press Officer's Terrible Secrets," *Public Relations Journal,* August 1976. Some guidelines.

NEWSOM and SCOTT, *This Is PR: The Realities of Public Relations.* Belmont, California: Wadsworth, 1976. Ch. 9, "Working with Media People," pp. 136–152.

TED KLEIN and FRED DANZIG, *How to Be Heard: Making the Media Work for You.* New York: Macmillan, 1974.

DAVID LINDT, ed., *The Publicity Process,* 2nd ed. Ames: Iowa State University Press, 1975. Best text on "how to" aspects of publicity.

MAXWELL E. MCCOMBS, *Mass Media in the Marketplace.* Minneapolis: Association for Education in Journalism, *Journalism Monographs,* No. 24, 1972.

DAVID RUBIN, "Anatomy of a Snow Job," *MORE,* March 1974. Close look at Chase Manhattan's press relations.

S. PRAKASH SETHI, "The Schism between Business and American News Media," *Journalism Quarterly,* Vol. 54 (Summer 1977).

ARTHUR D. STAMLER, "Public Service Time—An Opportunity for PR," *Public Relations Journal,* Vol. 25 (October 1969). Suggests radio and TV welcome well-packaged noncommercial material.

HARLAND W. WARNER, "Guidelines for Product Recall," *Public Relations Journal,* Vol. 33 (July 1977).

RICHARD WEINER, *Professional's Guide to Publicity.* New York: Richard Weiner, Inc., 1975. A manual for publicists.

FOOTNOTES

1. In "Media Distortions: A Former Official's View," *Columbia Journalism Review,* March–April 1975. Also see Lewis Donohew, "Newspaper Gatekeepers and Forces in the News Channel," *Public Opinion Quarterly,* Vol. 31 (Spring 1967), a case study in forces governing the play of news; and Max Ways, "What's Wrong With the News? It Isn't Enough," *Fortune,* October 1969, which questions the emphasis on outdated news practices.

2. Gay Talese, *The Kingdom and the Power* (New York: World Publishing Co., 1969), later published as a Bantam paperback. This "inside story" of the *New York Times* is helpful in understanding the media and its gatekeepers.

3. For elaboration, see Scott M. Cutlip, "Public Relations in Government," *Public Relations Review,* Summer 1976; Jules Witcover, "Washington: The Workhorse Wire Services," *Columbia Journalism Review,* Summer 1969; and Dwight Jensen, "The Loneliness of the Environmental Reporter," *Columbia Journalism Review,* January–February 1977.

4. *APME Guidelines,* a loose-leaf manual prepared by APME, p. 44. Available from the Associated Press, Rockefeller Center, New York City.

5. See Frank W. Wylie, "Attitudes toward the Media," *Public Relations Journal,* Vol. 31 (January 1975); Paul Poorman, "Public Relations—The Newsman's View," *Public Relations Journal,* Vol. 30 (March 1974); and Bernard E. Ury, "A Question for Editors: What are You Doing to PR?" *Editor & Publisher,* February 1, 1969.

6. For examples of efforts to influence news by use of the advertising club, see Freedom of Information Center Report No. 367, *Advertising Pressures on Media* (Columbia: University of Missouri School of Journalism, February 1977).

7. Stephen A. Kallis, Jr., "Computer Augmented Public Relations," *Public Relations Journal,* Vol. 31 (December 1975).

8. Thomas Griffith, "Must Business Fight the Press?" *Fortune,* June 1974, pp. 202–7ff.

9. "Grooming the Executive for the Spotlight," *Business Week,* October 5, 1974.

10. Chester Burger, "How to Meet the Press," *Harvard Business Review,* July–August 1975. Copyright © 1975 by the president and fellows of Harvard College; all rights reserved. Paraphrased.

11. Articles abound on the boiling issue of freebies and junkets: Typical are Lane Talburt, "Personal Favors and the Press," *Public Relations Journal,* Vol. 30 (February 1974); Norman Mark, "TV Junketeers," *Columbia Journalism Review,* July–August 1974; J. Anthony Lukas, "I Got the Queen in the Morning and the Prince at Night," *MORE,* November 1974 (the anatomy of a junket); David Zinman, "Should Newsmen Accept PR Prizes?" *Columbia Journalism Review,* Spring 1970; Frank W. Wylie, "Journalism Contests and Why," *APME Report on Professional Standards,* APME, October 1975, pp. 8–10; and Chris Welles, "The Bleak Wasteland of Financial Journalism," *Columbia Journalism Review,* July–August 1973.

12. Margaret R. Weiss, "Communicating a Community Service," *Saturday Review,* Vol. 46 (September 1963). For use of photography to crack TV, see Don Phelan, "TV Film Handouts Can Work," *Public Relations Journal,* Vol. 32 (January 1976). For the value of still photography, see Egon Weck, "Photography's (not so) Latent Image," *Public Relations Journal,* Vol. 31 (March 1975).

Part

II

THE PRACTICE AND THE PROFESSION

18

The challenge of the second half of the Twentieth Century is to
bridge the gap between promises and performances.
ADLAI STEVENSON

Public Relations
for Business:
an evolving role

The public relations function has had its most extensive development in business.[1] This sector is the largest employer of public relations professionals: Nearly half the 8,500 members of the Public Relations Society of America work for industrial or commercial employers. The clientele lists of counseling firms are dominated by corporations and the trade associations that serve business. Budgets for public relations run to millions of dollars in some of the giant multinational corporations. In some of these that include national advertising, the level of expenditure approaches those of major departments in the federal government.

Because of this dominance, the employment opportunities and the reputation of the calling both depend heavily on the business sector.

Some distinguishing features

Every institution has an employee public and a community public. Almost all have other special publics of importance: Hospitals have their patients and doctors; universities have their students, parents, and alumni. *Business has its owners or investors as a special public. And business also has its customers and prospects as a special public.* If owners withdraw their capital, the business ceases to exist. If customers are not satisfied and prospective ones won't buy the products or services, the business withers.

Thus, for public relations to survive in a business, it must do more than help satisfy the wants and needs of employees and neighbors. It must help the business create an environment in which owners or investors are satisfied with the return on their invested capital. It must help the business attract new customers and keep present customers satisfied with the products or services. *The function must relate helpfully to the profit motive of the business in a competitive environment.*

Not all practitioners have been able to adjust to this absolute relationship between public relations practices and profit motivation. Such a shortcoming comes into painful focus during dips in the national economy. At these recurring times, it may cost a business more to make products or render services than they can be sold for in the marketplace. What happens? Management looks at all the functions that make up the cost of its goods or services. It decides what can be cut out or cut back with the least damage to the ability of the goods or services to compete, and it reduces or eliminates those activities of marginal value. If public relations is not considered to be directly helpful in competing successfully, it is cut back or eliminated in periods of economic hardship.

This may appear to be stating the obvious. Yet the vulnerability of business public relations employment has been demonstrated repeatedly. And on each occasion, practitioners have expressed anguish that "at a time when better relations were most essential," their function was curtailed or eliminated. But there is a lesson to be learned from this. *Public relations in any organization that is dependent on profit must be regarded within the organization as being cost-effective and part of the formula for successful competition.* Thus, the competitive nature and the profit necessity of business make public relations work extremely demanding. Its productivity, along with that of marketing, finance, and manufacturing, is subject to continuing evaluation. The yardstick is progress toward the goals and timetables set by management.

The work is also demanding, and evaluations are made, in terms of organizational loyalty. *Practitioners are expected to have their first loyalty to the organization, not to a professional discipline.* They must be "on the team" and "in tune with the objectives" in their attitudes and efforts. In business, years of service or seniority in non-union positions provide little job protection. Unlike some public officials, practitioners are not elected to a term. There is no equivalent of the tenure found in educational institutions. There is no protective civil-service classification relating either to income level or to qualifications, as is found in certain government institutions.

When the business is going along successfully, unworried about criticisms from outside and feeling no need to change, internal dissent or criticism of communications policies and management decisions is generally tolerated. Sometimes it is solicited, as long as it is rendered privately, upward through channels, and beneficially to existing policies or programs. The receptive attitude alters, however, when the business falters, or is under attack or censure from outside. *At times of stress, management's concern for the public interest yields to concern for the survival of the business and its stewardship. Internal dissent or criticism of communications policies or actions tends to be regarded as an act of disloyalty.* The attitude is that when the business is threatened like a boat in a storm, everyone should row or bail harder, not blame or criticize one another.

Similar attitudes prevail in the nonprofit sectors, but with subtle differences. Those in charge of a community hospital, a Marine Corps station, or a state university do not see themselves as competing for survival every day against all other hospitals, Marine Corps stations, or state universities. But an auto maker perceives his firm as locked in competitive struggle every day against all other auto makers.

The competitive and private nature of the business system, and the demands placed on each function, make for variety in the role and stature of public relations. As pointed out in Chapter 1, the function varies widely. It performs whatever it is assigned to do. It has whatever place and stature in the organization is decreed by the top official of the enterprise. Officials have their own ideas.

For example, Thomas Watson, as head of IBM, reputedly did not care for the term "public relations." To him, it implied an admission of problems in the company's relationships. Practitioners at IBM were not given public relations titles. Instead, they had such titles as "Manager, Community Affairs," "Director, Communications Programs," "Information Representative, News Bureau." At ITT, the overall function is titled "Corporate Relations and Advertising," is highly placed, and is headed by a senior vice-president who reports directly to the top official. The function embraces a multimillion-dollar advertising program as part of ITT's extensive communications efforts. At du Pont, the function has had a long and illustrious history in the defining and pioneering of the calling. Its functions are regarded as important by top management and relate closely to it. Yet the head of public relations at du Pont has not been accorded a vice-presidency.

The variations cited above are not unusual. In some business departments, public relations is a subfunction under advertising or personnel. In some, it is confined to employee or financial communications. In thousands of small businesses, its responsibilities range across personnel, trade, consumer, and financial relations. These variables do not apply the same way in the other sectors. For example, in the armed forces, Pentagon orders tend to standardize the role and the positioning of public relations for all units.

Each industrial or commercial organization tailors its public communications to reflect the character and personality of its management, the kind of profile it desires, the competitive stance it chooses, and those standards of ethics and performance with which it is comfortable. The private nature of the free-enterprise system permits this latitude, although increasing public constraints are narrowing the boundaries.

Many practitioners in their early years find that the realities of practice differ from the standards, principles, and procedures advocated in the classroom. One young practitioner wrote us, "I've had four PR jobs, and not one of them has come close to the gospel of Cutlip and Center." *Understanding the reasons for the gap between concepts and practice helps practitioners to make personal adjustments and to lead their employers into more effective communications in an open society.*

Free enterprise and the public interest

Even before the turn of the twentieth century, government acting on behalf of the electorate found it desirable to impose controls on the private-enterprise system. The Sherman Act of 1887 was concerned with monopoly. In 1914, the Clayton Act dealt with local price discrimination. The creation of the Federal Trade Commission that same year was concerned with a broad range of unfair practices. The Securities Act of 1933 required publication of a business prospectus. The Securities Exchange Act of 1934 created a Commission (the SEC) to implement the 1933 law. In the employer–employee area, the Taft-Hartley Act in 1947 provided for negotiated settlement of industrial disputes.

As these and other restraining measures were taken, the business sector, with Big Business and trade and commerce associations doing the vocalizing, protested the measures as unnecessary and antibusiness. Over the years, the defensive posture became habitual, and less meaningful to bystanders. Meantime, more and more of the business sector's natural constituency—employees, shareholders, plant communities, customers—became uneasy and suspicious.

Major interruptions of the defensive posture and of public suspicion came in World War I, the depression of the 1930s, and World War II. In these periods, all sectors came together in shared hardship, tragedy, and national purpose. *These periods gave impetus and sophistication to the use of public relations techniques in attaining goals related to patriotism, propaganda, morale, and productivity.*

The era of business growth and public affluence

At the close of World War II, the vast industrial machine converted to peacetime pursuits. The public mood was that now, life could be enjoyed to the hilt. Instead of rationing, there would be plenty of everything for everybody. Technology born in wartime would spawn product and service miracles—a consumer cornucopia. And to this end, the industrial wheels began to spin. Out came automobiles with annual design changes, new gadgets, and prestigious names like "Ambassador," "Imperial," and "Royal." New homes, and whole new neighborhoods, sprang up. Into the homes went labor-saving devices, wall-to-wall carpeting, and oil-burning furnaces. In the factories and offices, some 45 million people were working.

Public relations people were put to work by business, beating the sales drums with publicity to aid marketing, cheering employees on to greater productivity, and issuing reports of business progress in ever more lavish terms. Many of these people were freshly out of public-information assignments in the military services. Many were from low-paying trade and daily-press reporting jobs. In public relations they saw a greener pasture financially.

The year 1946 had not passed before something was amiss. Employees, through their unions, were seeking a bigger share of the economic proceeds with which to buy more of the things that business was advertising as "new," "revolutionary," "necessary," and "irresistible." Because of this situation, coupled with a toughening of competition and some economic imbalances, business leaders decided that public goodwill had slipped. To reverse this, business, through the National Association of Manufacturers, embarked on a grand-scale advertising campaign with economic-education overtones. The rationale was that if employees, consumers, and others fully understood the free-enterprise system, they'd support it without reservation. The content of the campaign in national advertising, reinforced by publicity and by echoes in house publications, pointed out the cause-and-effect relationship between the business system and the high U.S. standard of living. Comparisons were drawn with living standards in other nations.

The multimillion-dollar effort (considered massive at that time) was not effective in any significant way. It did convince many in advertising and public relations that *an abstract idea could not be sold in the same way as a bar of soap.* Nor could a bar of soap be attached to an abstraction in the same way as a war bond could be allied with patriotism. *The campaign raised a question among many educators and professional communicators concerning the psychology of promoting high standards of living at a time when people's stomachs were already full, and the effectiveness of whetting people's appetites by comparing their full stomachs with empty ones in other lands.*

After analyzing some of the early efforts to resell free enterprise and reaffirm appreciation of the ultimate role of profits, *Fortune's* William Whyte came to an important conclusion: *Better understanding hinged on closer cooperation between each corporation and its publics on matters of common concern.*[2]

Most large businesses pulled away from the mission of reselling free enterprise as a concept, in favor of harder efforts to sell their wares. *The efforts of public relations practitioners were augmented with employee newspapers and magazines of local personal-interest content, proud and colorful reports of sales and financial progress, neighborly gestures in the home communities, and cultivation of a friendly, sympathetic relationship with news media.* The theme was, "Good deeds first, then words."

A friendly press

It is relevant to note here that in the postwar decade, news media in general were not adverse to industry. On the contrary, publishers and editors shared the public desire to put the war behind and get on with the promise of a better world. New products and improved services were hailed in the news media as harbingers. Matters of style or design were accorded almost as much news value as technical innovations. The working relationship of news and public relations people was that of journalistic cousins. Reporters were reluctant to take umbrage at a "no comment" given on grounds of competitive security. Going "off the record" was acceptable. As for practitioners, they rarely found it desirable to duck press inquiries or avoid candor. At a time when business was humming on Main Street and exposure of wrongdoing was rare, there was little reason for business leaders to crouch silently.

These were good years for the creative, adept, and personable practitioner specializing in publicity. His or her work was aided by the impact of pictorial news as in *Life* magazine, and business profiles as in *Time, Newsweek, Fortune,* or *Business Week.* Television offered a new medium. In the spirited competition among the media, practitioners benefited.

Meantime, in the 1950s, the business bid for popular approval shifted from efforts for "share of market" to "share of mind." Instead of, "How would you like to own this washing machine with all its features?" the message became, "American ingenuity has taken the drudgery out of washday." There was less concern with whetting the appetite for material possessions as ends in themselves and more with establishing a relationship between affluence and human progress.

A return to the fundamental of fact-finding

Many leaders in industry held the traditional narrow viewpoint that industry's destiny depended on keeping the consumer happy—and that, as long as business was good, the consumer was expressing satisfaction. But in the 1950s, influenced by their practitioners, they came to an overdue realization: They had very little useful and factual information about how their constituents really felt toward them. They didn't know specifically how people felt about their bigness, their power, their integrity, the wisdom or objectivity of their views on public issues, or how well they were currently performing their role. There was need for more sophisticated inbound communication from industry's publics.

So research into public attitudes began to increase. Some of the studies showed interesting and promising results. A typical study was that by Social Research, Inc., reported by Burleigh B. Gardner and Lee Rainwater.[3] Gardner and Rainwater studied the "middle majority" or mass market, totaling 65 percent of the population, as distinguished from the factory wage earner. This middle majority was found to have five definite favorable attitudes toward Big Business:

1. Big Business was seen as the pacesetter of the American economy.
2. Only Big Business could handle the job of production.
3. Big Business was good because the mass-production techniques provided goods of uniform quality at a low cost.
4. Big Business was good because it invested heavily in research and development.
5. Big Business provided many jobs and greater opportunity to work.

But even granting business these virtues, its constituents retained some anxieties. In the 1960s, the performance and the questionable ethical behavior of many businesses frequently disquieted their publics about their professed good intentions. Again and again, stories appearing in national news media showed a lack of self-discipline in matters of ethics and integrity. There were news stories of excessive profiteering on government contracts, false and misleading advertising, inadequate and improper labeling, meaningless warranties, defective products, exorbitant service charges, and poor service. In one classic case, 29 electrical companies admitted having rigged their prices in a collusion that spanned *seven years*.[4] Employer–employee-relations breakdowns and legal suits proliferated, stemming partly from the Civil Rights Act of 1964.

And through it all, there was an incredible vocal insistence by industry spokesmen that government intervention was counterproductive and unnecessary.

Viewed objectively from the standpoint of influencing public opinion, *the actions of many businesses simply did not match their promises.* The result was that blue-collar employees leaned more on organized labor to negotiate for them. Consumers, and in some instances investors, turned more to government legislators and agencies for protection. Business critics were repeatedly rearmed by events.

One piece of federal legislation in that decade was of major significance, in that it presaged the protection of consumers by law. This was the Kefauver-Harris Drug Amendments Act of 1962. Then, several others followed:

Fair Packaging and Labeling Act	1966	Fire Research and Safety Act	1968
National Traffic and Motor Vehicle Safety Act	1966	Truth in Lending	1968
		Natural Gas Pipeline Safety	1968
Child Protection Act (toys)	1966	National Commission on Product Safety	1969
Drug Abuse Amendment	1966		
Cigarette Labeling Act	1966	Public Health Smoking Act	1970
Wholesome Meat Act	1967	Product Safety Act	1972
Flammable Fabrics Act	1967	Warranty Act	1975
Clinical Laboratories Act	1967		

It was also in this period that Ralph Nader came on the scene as a champion of the consumer, challenging first the safety of the General Motors Corvair, and subsequently the company's actions in other areas.[5] Efforts by the Nader group and others widened a new arena of consumer and investor protection by private-citizen groups. Federal regulatory agencies, in turn, became much more active and aggressive. The president appointed a special assistant to head an Office of Consumer Affairs.

A defensive business response

Business's response to its critics and regulators was more defensive than corrective. Business public relations was kept busy fending off reporters, delaying responses to inquiries, and trying to change the subject. Practitioners were in the position of creating programs and projects *after* allegations, *after* misunderstandings, and in general, *after* it was too late to be positive or preventive. When an offshore oil operation along a stretch of California coast polluted the waters, the resulting dialogue was typically confusing, defensive, and inconclusive. Public debate was more concerned with the misquoting of a Union Oil official about the value of bird life than with measures taken and planned by the oil industry to prevent spills in particular and pollution in general.[6]

In 1967, five leading drug makers were convicted of fixing the price of a medicine so that for a long span of years, one capsule costing less than 2 cents sold for as much as 51 cents. The outcome of that was scarcely calculated to reassure consumers. The companies, insisting that no antitrust law had been violated, nonetheless offered to settle treble damage claims amounting to $120 million. When a nationally prominent businessman was convicted of conspiracy and perjury for falsifying financial reports, it spurred public uneasiness about the dependability and honesty of other prominent businessmen. From the actions of a few came labels put on all, and each incident was ammunition for business critics. *The parade of misbehavior made it tougher for public relations people to proclaim that the private enterprise of their employers, in truth, served the public interest. Public relations practitioners were presumed by the public to be cut of the same cloth as their employers or clients.*

One of the defensive arguments advanced by business and its public relations people was this: For every instance of transgression by a company or individual, there were hundreds of thousands of businesses and businesspeople that every day pursued their calling quietly and honorably. As a statistical fact, the point was well taken; but it didn't wash in the public forum. To critics, the argument omitted their contention that on any given day there were many companies and individuals breaking laws, or maneuvering around them, *but not getting caught.* To bystanders, the recurring unsavory incidents came as corroboration of whatever unsatisfactory experience they had experienced personally with the quality or price of a product, the return on an investment, or the conditions of their employment.

The resolution of social problems

During this period, business was confronted with more problems than those stemming from government regulations and from the embarrassment of exposed misconduct in high places. Business had handled its first responsibility well. It had created a sensation of affluence for the majority of people. It had generated the wealth on which everything else depended. And at the same time, it had been able to provide the materiel needed in sustaining the national commitment in Vietnam. But contentment had not come out of affluence, and public concern about the long Vietnam engagement alone could not be blamed for widespread discontent.

Some of the discontent related directly to the performance of the business system. This included shortages of trained manpower, pockets of unemployment, movement of industrial jobs away from the central cities, atmospheric pollution, foreign competition, conglomerations, labor strife, inflation, and more. *Each of these problems had its social implications and involvement.*

Consequently, business attention had to be diverted to expressions of public sentiment on these matters. And the public concerns were about equal employment opportunities, the unpopular war in Vietnam, the concentration of wealth in funds and trusts, the dangers of pollution, financial support of education, overpopulation and poverty, public school desegregation, prospective world starvation, and the inevitable U.S. shift into a service-based economy.

Meaningful dialogue toward early resolution of these problems *was thwarted, although the state of the skills and art in public relations would have been most helpful.* One hindrance lay in the divergent views among business leaders themselves. Another was the nature of approaches used by public pressure groups. Many represented revolts or noisy protests in which dialogue or compromise was unacceptable. Others were couched in editorials and intellectual questions about moral values and political systems.

The need for dialogue and practical approaches intensified as more and more of the public came to expect business to undertake the resolution of social problems by means other than those that spin off from economic success.

The great and continuing question

Traditionally, most business leaders have resisted and resented the notion that their businesses should seek to fulfill social responsibilities beyond providing jobs, earning a profit with which to pay investors and underwrite growth, paying taxes, and voluntarily supporting nonprofit health, education, and welfare activities. Broader concepts of social responsibility as a part of economic responsibility had been labeled variously as "phony," "lip service," or "outside our orbit." Noted economist Milton Friedman, at the University of Chicago, described the social responsibility notion as "a fundamentally subversive doctrine".[7] "If businessmen do have a social responsibility other than making a maximum profit for stockholders," he said, "how do they know what it is?"[8] Friedman warned that if businessmen behaved like civil servants, they would eventually become nothing more than civil servants, elected or appointed like all the others.

Nonetheless, in the 1960s and into the 1970s, the overlapping and interacting of business and government in all areas of public interest continued and magnified. Both controversy and collaboration intensified. Carlton Spitzer, a public relations counselor who served both government and business, emphasized the benefits of collaboration this way:

> It follows that each can serve best by serving together. Government can help business by reducing bureaucratic red tape, coordinating related and overlapping programs, and offering specific ideas. . . . Business can help government by offering realistic plans and proposals that respond to general needs as well as to company goals.[9]

The dilemma of public relations

The debate over business as a social institution did not originate in the 1960s. Philosophic in nature, its roots are deep. There are many shades of conservatism

FIGURE 18-1 How much pollution is acceptable in return for the products and services the public wants?—a matter of trade-off.

FIGURE 18-2 How much risk and how much blight are acceptable in return for the energy the public wants?—a matter of trade-off.

and moderation expressed among industrialists and commercial leaders. The debate will be resolved more by events than by viewpoints. See Figures 18–1, 18–2, and 18–3.

For the practice of business public relations, the need for employers or clients to speak up, put up, or shut up added another element to a mounting professional dilemma. Increased regulations, reporting requirements, monitoring, and investigations of business by government had been productive in news value for the public media. There were interesting instances of insider trading in securities, conflicts of interest among senior officials, bribery of public officials, kickbacks on contracts, collusion on prices, and illegal political contributions. The environment was ripe for investigative journalism, and the media were ready. It was as though the muckraking era of the "robber barons" was staging a revival, with the added attraction of television. Commenting on the rise of investigative reporting, James Reston, of the *New York Times,* traced its revival to a specter worse than business misdoings. He said, "The role of the press changed with the A-bomb and the ICBM. Man had too much power. The press had to watch the psyche and the nature of the man who could press the button."

Businesses exposed to allegations or litigation had no choice but to fight back. Among them were some members of *Fortune*'s Largest 100 Corporations. Legal defense was costly and time-consuming, and it was worrisome in terms of possible penalties in products, services, and money at the marketplace. Many businesses not exposed publicly to questions or allegations of improper conduct sought internally to make sure their houses were clean and their closets free of skeletons. In their external posture, the tendency was to maintain a low profile.

The public relations task became incredibly difficult—that of enhancing the reputation or success of a public entity that was reluctant to be seen in any robes but royal purple or heard on any subjects but happy, self-serving events.

Therefore, issuing good news or no news was all too often the public relations assignment through the 1960s and into the 1970s. Employers and clients, harassed by government agencies externally, by unions internally, by the need to grow as a survival factor, and by troubles with consumer and investor relations, needed no bad publicity. But it seemed that that was about the only kind of publicity available through their public relations people, or directly from the news media. Understandably, even casual inquiries from government or media people regarding financial, marketing, or employment practices were suspect—as though they had asked, "When did you stop doing wrong?"[10] Symptomatic of the growing problem, a survey by Opinion Research Corporation in 1972 showed that a clear-cut majority of 60 percent of the public held business in low esteem. Loss of esteem was to go even further.

In this situation, a prime public relations precept—"As long as people talk, they don't start fighting"—was being threatened. Business didn't want to talk with public media if only the contentious portions and none of the explanations were to be printed or broadcast. Media bias was one factor; lack of knowledgeable reporters and adequate coverage were others. Public relations concepts notwithstanding, "No comment" or "Unavailable for comment" was preferable to a partial statement taken out of context, misunderstood, or misquoted. The risk of appearing to have something to hide was preferable to answering slanted or unwanted questions. Having deductions drawn from silence or defiance was preferable to having one's private affairs aired or tried in public print. *The public relations practitioner, as interpreter for the employer and supplicant to the news media, was caught in the middle with no place to hide.*[11]

There were some other damaging blows dealt to the effectiveness of the practice in business. One stemmed from the incident and court case, discussed in Chapter 12, involving Texas Gulf Sulphur.[12] The legal liability of public relations in matters of materiality, disclosure, and fraud was a dubious distinction.[13] Some instances of questionable behavior by practitioners surfaced. The term "public relations" was used a few times negatively in matters of antitrust, unfair trade practices, and conflict of interest. The usage implied exaggeration, distortion, concealment, deliberate deception, or artificial façade in the presentation of "facts." Some of the adverse connotations were pinned on public relations by news-media writers and editors; some slipped off the tongues of White House officials during the Agnew and Watergate scandals.

It was obvious to many sophisticated heads of large businesses that the credibility and confidence they had lost could not be regained through traditional public relations "techniques" openly bidding for popular support. Public relations "experts" could not even control their own public image or credibility in media relations. Without a "good press," broad public support was, at least temporarily, unavailable.

Thus, imperceptibly in the late 1960s and obviously in the early 1970s, there was a shift of public relations tactics by many of the large, pacesetting, multinational corporations and commercial institutions. The shift was away from traditional dependence on public media to present the business story, and toward more use of controlled media. Booklets, advertising, speech reproductions, and statements of corporate missions and of social concern made their appearance. Selective, well-planned nonpublic efforts were made to influence legislation, legislators, and the implementation of government programs, social and economic. Associations serving industry and commerce followed suit on behalf of all businesses, large and small.

Public relations specialists and counseling firms experienced in government and government relations found their stars in the ascendant. Corporation legal counsels and firms specializing in corporate law were drawn more importantly into the management strategy and policy decision process. Their views and preferred tactics weighed heavily in communications policy positions. In the main, legal advice favored positions that were cautious and secretive, whether or not an obvious public interest was involved. "Privacy" rights, given legal protection by the Constitution, took precedence over the public's right to know anything affecting it, which was regarded by legalists as a moral obligation not reinforced by legal compulsion.

Management communications decisions in the 1970s much more frequently fell back on legal screens or other avenues for avoiding publicity. For example, since the courts frown on any efforts to "try a case in public," a corporation in litigation could, on occasion, invoke this as the compelling reason for its reluctance to comment on a potentially adverse newsworthy matter. Another convenient legal device was available when a corporate security was in registration; the SEC disapproves of anything said publicly that might be intended to influence the market value of the stock. To inquiries concerning announcements from government agencies of pending investigations or censure for improper acts, a legally inspired response was, "We cannot comment on the news report. We have not seen the full context of the announcement or ruling." The hope, of course, was that by missing a news deadline, the story would die or be incomplete, leaving time for a carefully considered evasion or favorable reply. Also, during this transitional period there was considerable shunting of news inquiries

FIGURE 18-3 Concern about social matters was expressed by some of the businesses whose products constituted part of the problem—like beverage containers. Courtesy The Coca-Cola Company.

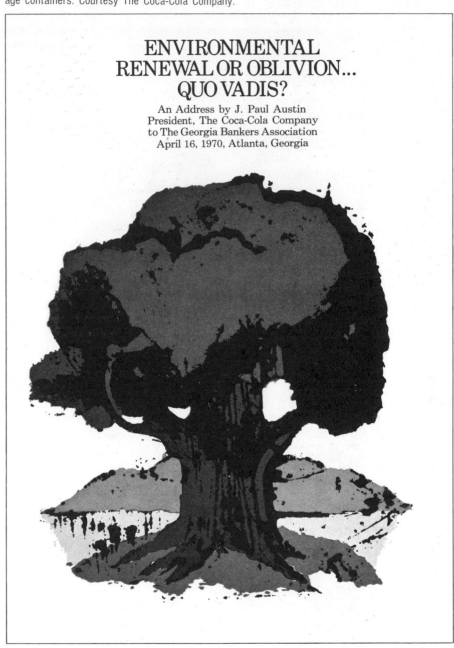

ENVIRONMENTAL RENEWAL OR OBLIVION... QUO VADIS?

An Address by J. Paul Austin
President, The Coca-Cola Company
to The Georgia Bankers Association
April 16, 1970, Atlanta, Georgia

FIGURE 18-4 One of the ideas advanced about social responsibility is that resolution of many problems lies with consumers themselves, as suggested in this Advertising Council campaign. Courtesy The Advertising Council.

FROM GARBAGE TO GARDEN BECAUSE ENOUGH PEOPLE CARED.

Over 2000 species of plants grow at South Coast Botanic Garden in Palos Verdes Peninsula, California. Over 3 million tons of trash and garbage lie just beneath the surface. A dump transformed into a paradise. Impossible? Not when enough people in a community get together and work.

The needs of every community are different. A park to be cleaned up...pollutors to be notified...trees to be planted...litter receptacles to be placed. All over America, community volunteers are making the land good again.

But all around us are reminders that we still have far to go. You can help by becoming a community volunteer. We'd like to send you the name of the Keep America Beautiful group nearest you. Find out what they're doing and how you can help. Write: Keep America Beautiful, Inc., 99 Park Avenue, New York, N.Y. 10016

 People start pollution. People can stop it.

 Ad Council — Keep America Beautiful, Inc.

and inquirers between corporate financial, legal, and public relations people, trade and commerce associations, and their public relations wings.[14]

No doubt such tactics of delay or avoidance spared some large businesses embarrassment and preserved the vanity of some business leaders. No doubt also, the costs or penalties were related directly to the adversary climate that developed between news media and business. Certainly the posture and tactics did nothing to decrease the strain on credibility or capability when such disturbing events as the energy crisis, sugar price rise, or coffee shortage came along.

The status quo: debits and credits

Through the 1970s, the business ledger of public opinion was heaviest on the side of debits. As one veteran public relations consultant added it up, "Business has a great many well-deserved problems." There were, however, some credits on the ledger.

Realities and realizations

· *The credits:*   Among the favorable indicators were these:
1. The economy had absorbed the recession of 1974–75 and had revived.
2. Consumers continued to buy the products and services that technology had spawned, despite an awareness that technological advances were depersonalizing their jobs.
3. The economy and the private-enterprise system had emerged intact after a number of bruising shocks, such as the collapse of Penn Central, the ITT antitrust case, the Equity Funding scandal, and the questionable gasoline and natural-gas shortages. In the process, the bad odors had been dissipated somewhat by open admissions of wrongdoing in political contributions, and of bribes of foreign officials, price fixing, and kickbacks. With these matters out in the open, their resolution became a government problem.
4. Business spokesmen, in talking to each other, agreed more frequently that survival of the system required weighing the social consequences of their actions against the profit potential as part of the decision process. Authority and credibility for business in the social areas would have to be earned, as it had been earned in mass production and marketing, automation, and the creation of capital for sustained growth.
5. There was a growing realization that instinctive opposition to government programs as encroachments was often fruitless and unprofitable. By the adoption of a more objective, cooperative posture, business gave notice that the public interest was not to become a territory reserved for politicians and dissidents.
6. Another realization was that the stance of a "loyal minority," backed by selective lobbying, too often faltered for lack of popular support that would stand up in elections.
7. Finally, a new determination was being articulated: that, by whatever measures necessary, public confidence and trust had to be regained to the extent necessary for the capitalistic system to function effectively.

The debits: The length of the hill that business had to climb to get back into public favor was indicated by opinion research barometers and qualified analysts. Louis Harris surveys recorded the drop of confidence in major companies: In 1966, 55 percent of the public had confidence; in 1972, 27 percent; in 1974, 21 percent; in 1975, 19 percent. Even worse from the standpoint of business

EXHIBIT 18-1

The Business of Regulating Business

Government has found that in responding to needs voiced by substantial segments of the nation, its role goes beyond that of a referee among various self-interests. More and more it finds itself, with assistance from academia, defining social needs and problems, and it turns to business, labor, and the professions for solutions and implementations.

Business, for its part, has been responsive where it could benefit by performing its natural functions. But the whole process has spurred the growth of government. A former chairman of the Chase Manhattan Bank put it bluntly: "I can think of nothing that would put brakes on big government faster than for business to identify critical problems and take the initiative in dealing with them before Washington felt the need to act."

The dimensions of government growth in the regulatory area can be seen in a few statistics of the mid-1970s:

There were 63,000 government personnel involved in regulatory activities.

Regulatory directives and decrees filled more than 45,000 pages of the *Federal Register.*

The Commerce Commission alone was adding 400,000 new tariff schedules annually for the transportation industry.

There were over 5,000 varieties of forms required of the public for one reason or another.

The U.S. Council on Environmental Quality estimated it would cost business at least $195 billion between 1974 and 1984 to meet EPA antipollution standards.

The federal government's costs annually simply for maintaining regulatory activities stood at about $4 billion.

communicators was the fact that 50 percent of the public thought that major companies were "mostly out of touch." Opinion Research Corporation studies in 1974 dealt with the problem of "bigness." Some 76 percent of those questioned felt that one or two companies dominated many industries; 75 percent felt there was too much power centered in a few companies; and 75 percent felt that as companies got bigger, they "usually got cold and impersonal in their relationships."[15]

It was, indeed, a deep pit to climb out of. And public relations techniques or words by themselves obviously represented only paper ladders. One trained observer phrased it thus:

As I see it, the problem is one of candor and credibility, not—repeat: not—of "public relations." Indeed, one of the reasons the large corporations find it so difficult to persuade the public of anything is that the public always suspects them of engaging in clever public relations, instead of simply telling the truth. And the reason the public is so suspicious is because our large corporations so habitually do engage in clever public relations instead of simply telling the truth.

For instance, what is one to make of a corporation which proudly announces that it has just completed the most profitable year in its history—and then simultaneously declares that its return on capital is pitifully inadequate, that it is suffering from a terrible cost-squeeze, etc., etc.? In 1973, most corporations were engaged in precisely this kind of double-talk. Is it any wonder they created so enormous a credibility gap?[16]

A majority of executives in 1976 held the dark view that the game had already been lost. They did not expect the free-market concept to prevail in America for another decade.[17] There appeared to be no practical way to resolve that portion of the problem dealing with morality and ethics. Surveys repeatedly showed the public felt that moral and ethical standards were not high enough. Yet no practical means had been devised to balance natural human greed and envy with human ideals.

FIGURE 18–5 An 80-page bibliography compiled by BankAmerica and updated annually, as "a roadmap to the maze of material dealing with corporate, government and other group responses to social problems." Its purpose: "to assist business and academic research in the subject." Courtesy BankAmerica Corporation.

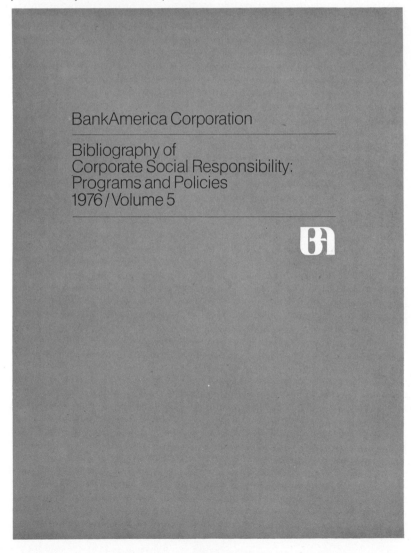

Meantime, "economic education," as it has been known, would not instill new confidence, no matter how it was magnified, intensified, or packaged. For one reason, there had been no demonstrable connection between the amount of economic education and the degree of sympathy for free enterprise. And there was an even more sobering fact: You can't educate when people don't believe what you say.

A return to fundamentals

In the practice of public relations, the experiences of the 1970s reemphasized some basic principles of effective communications. One was that to be believed, you must have authority as a source of information. Another was that to persuade, you must have a capacity for empathic listening. Competence in one area (the marketplace) can't be transplanted as is to another (politics): Looking ahead, practitioners and some enlightened business spokesmen were urging a return to these and other fundamentals instead of the harvest reaped by fascination with monetary gains and growth as ends in themselves.

One crying need, as expressed in 1975 by Michael Blumenthal, then president of the Bendix Corporation, was for "meaningful dialogue with critics as well as constituents." His recommendations called for a new moral approach in which businessmen and others would form an organization to devise and promote new "ethical behavior codes" to which all businesspeople would be expected to subscribe.[18]

Robert Tisch, president of Loew's Corporation, in 1976 advised his peers, "We need to spend less time thinking how we might alter what we say to the public and more time thinking through our attitudes toward the public. . . . If business leaders want people to believe in them, they are going to have to learn to believe in people. . . . We must seek new, higher standards of openness and accuracy."[19]

Public relations practitioners, responsive to the extent of their individual intellects and talents, have been making changes in techniques, areas of emphasis, and messages. These are discussed in the next chapter. The focus is on the growing significance of advocacy in public affairs, the blending of social responsibilities into the economic formula, and the trends in dealing with those special publics, consumers and investors.

A case problem in multinationalism

The headquarters and main plant of the Homelike Foods Company has long been located in Midway, Ohio, a city of 200,000. Homelike is an equal opportunity employer; company employment in Midway is 5,000, of which 20 percent is black, reflecting the black–white ratio in the city.

Homelike's business has grown. Last year it was decided to put a plant in Taiwan, to process certain products closer to where they are grown. Other advantages would be lower labor costs, favored taxation, and room for expansion.

When Homelike made this move, employees, townspeople, and union representatives were assured that there would be no adverse effects on Homelike employment. In fact, the expansion would enable the company to compete better and to grow faster, with benefits to all.

The Taiwan plant has now come on-stream. Concurrently, a dip in the economy occurred, so a cutback was required in the home plant. Some 500 employees are furloughed. The management, at the time, expressed the feeling that the layoff would be of short duration. Rumor has it however, that no layoff is occurring in Taiwan, although management has said nothing about that to employees, union, or townspeople.

Within the home plant and in Midway, rumbles of resentment, encouraged by union representatives, are reported. A friendly city-council member has privately told Homelike public relations people that minority-group organizations are concerned. The word is that the mayor will have to say something soon to the news media about the city's attitude toward the hardship cases. First, he will request a meeting with the Homelike president.

Yesterday, a meeting was held in the Homelike president's office, involving the heads of domestic and international operations, finance, legal, industrial relations, marketing, and public relations. Discussion ranged all the way from the possibility of reviving old rumors about transferring Homelike headquarters to another state, to adoption of a plan for reimbursing furloughed employees for lost pay when business returns to the level it enjoyed before the economic dip.

The decision was to ride out the storm, on the basis that the company cannot control the economy; to bring employees back as soon as feasible; to undertake special product-promotion plans to pep up sales; to avoid doing anything that would put union leadership in a negative light; and to neutralize community rumors in any way that seems best.

The industrial relations and public relations departments were assigned to implement and communicate the decision, within and outside the plant, respectively.

The public relations officer has summoned you, head of the news bureau and community relations sections, and asked you to draw up a plan.

What is your plan, the projects in it, the timetable, the expenses, the means of monitoring it, and the revisions in case it fails or backfires?

ADDITIONAL READINGS

JULES BACHMAN, *Social Responsibility and Accountability.* New York: New York. University Press, 1975.

"The Free Society and Planning," a conversation on the future of the mixed economy. New York: The Conference Board, 1975.

L.L.L. GOLDEN, *Only by Public Consent: American Corporations' Search for Favorable Opinion.* New York: Hawthorn, 1968.

C. JACKSON GRAYSON, "Let's Get Back to the Competitive Market System," *Harvard Business Review,* November–December 1973.

"The Great Banking Retreat," *Business Week,* April 21, 1975. A profile of banking; several articles.

MICHAEL HARRINGTON, *The Twilight of Capitalism.* New York: Simon & Schuster, 1976.

KENNETH HENRY, *Defenders and Shapers of the Corporate Image.* New Haven: College & University Press, 1972.

Hill & Knowlton executives, *Critical Issues in Public Relations.* Englewood Cliffs, N.J.: Prentice-Hall, 1975.

IRVING KRISTOL, "On Conservatism and Capitalism," *Wall Street Journal,* September 11, 1975, p. 12.

———, "On Corporate Capitalism and America," *The Public Interest,* No. 41 (Fall 1975). Copyright 1975 by National Affairs, Inc.

DONELLA H. MEADE, DENNIS L. MEADOWS, and others, *Limits to Growth.* New York: Associate-Universe Books, 1972.

"Public Relations for the Smaller Company," Research Institute of America, Dept. 111, Mt. Kisco, N.Y., 1974.

WILLIAM RUDER and R. NATHAN, *Businessman's Guide to Washington.* New York: Macmillan, 1975.

"Special Report on Major Business Problems: Executive Portfolio," issued annually by *Business Week Magazine.* Excellent resource and case-study material.

HARRY H. STEIN, "The Muckraking Book in America, 1946–1973," *Journalism Quarterly, Vol. 52, No. 2 (Summer 1975).*

ARTHUR A. THOMPSON, *Corporate Bigness—For Better or for Worse? Sloan Management Review* (Massachusetts Institute of Technology), Fall 1975.

MAX WAYS, "Business Needs a Different Political Stance," *Fortune,* September 1975, p. 97.

FOOTNOTES

1. For its beginnings in business in this century, see Alan R. Raucher, *Public Relations and Business, 1900–1929.*

2. William W. Whyte and the editors of *Fortune,* "Is Anybody Listening?" (New York: Simon & Schuster, 1950). A definitive work. Its thesis became the career entry card for many practitioners.

3. Burleigh B. Gardner and Lee Rainwater, "The Mass Image of Business," *Harvard Business Review,* Vol. 33 (November–December 1955).

4. The electrical price-fix story is recorded in two books, and in the periodical press of that period. See John G. Fuller, *The Gentlemen Conspirators* (New York: Grove Press, 1962); and John Herling, *The Great Conspiracy* (Washington, D.C.: R.B. Luce, 1962).

5. Ralph Nader, *Unsafe at Any Speed* (New York: Grossman, 1965). For case studies of Naderism, "What Makes Ralph Nader Run," *Reader's Digest,* June 1973, pp. 113–18,; David Ignatius, "Nader: Today GM, Tomorrow the System," *Los Angeles Times,* August 15, 1975; and Allen Center, *Public Relations Practices* (Englewood Cliffs, N.J.: Prentice-Hall, 1975), Case No. 11, "Campaign GM."

6. Major oil companies and the Petroleum Institute, 1801 K Street, N.W., Washington, D.C. 20006, provide pamphlets concerning oceanic oil spills, prevention, and correction. Excellent for case studies.

7. From "Business and Government: A New Balance of Power," *Business Week,* July 17, 1965. A special report.

8. *Ibid.*

9. In "Wanted: A Business-Government Partnership," *Public Relations Journal,* Vol. 24 (December 1968).

10. For critical views and cases, see S. Prakash Sethi, *Up Against the Corporate Wall* (Englewood Cliffs, N.J.: Prentice-Hall, 1971); and Robert L. Heilbroner, and others, *In The Name of Profit* (Garden City, N.Y.: Doubleday, 1972).

11. For one analysis of why the news media gave a "raw deal" to business in those years, see Chet Huntley, "Media Antipathy toward Business," *Wall Street Journal,* August 7, 1973.

12. To study the case in depth, see Kenneth G. Patrick, *Perpetual Jeopardy* (New York: Macmillan, 1972); and Center, *Public Relations Practices,* Case No. 10, "Timely and Adequate Disclosure."

13. See *Public Relations Quarterly,* Vol. 17, No. 4 (Spring 1973), an issue devoted to the vulnerability of public relations in the financial relations area.

14. See Morton J. Simon, "You Could Get into Legal Hot Water," two-part article in *Public Relations Journal,* Vol. 32, Nos. 5 and 6 (May and June 1976).

15. Extracted from the summary of an Opinion Research Corp. conference, August 21, 1974, published by Hill and Knowlton, Inc., New York.

16. Irving Kristol, "The Credibility of Corporations," *Wall Street Journal,* January 17, 1974. A thoughtful piece by the coeditor of *The Public Interest* and a member of the *Journal*'s board of contributors.

17. From a survey of business executives by the *Harvard Business Review,* in 1976.

18. From a talk given at the University of Detroit.

19. Robert Tisch, "A Way to Rebuild Public Confidence in Business," *Nation's Business,* April 1976.

19

Some fifty years ago, Calvin Coolidge could make his famous remark that "the business of America is business." Today, the business of business is America.

TED SORENSEN

Public Relations for Business: changing emphases, priorities, and programs

To the extent that public relations practices in the 1980s are engaged to correct the problems of the 1970s, the highest priority is the regaining of credibility and trust. This represents perhaps the greatest test of maturity and skill the calling has ever faced. Not the least of the hurdles is the mood within business itself. As analyzed by two qualified observers:

> The mood of business leadership is strikingly similar to that of other groups in one important respect: a feeling of impotence, a belief that the future is in the hands of outside forces. . . .
>
> Businessmen, like other groups . . . tend to react defensively when blamed for the nation's troubles or for the widespread loss of confidence in its institutions. Economic troubles are held to result from a crypto-socialism, or excessive government interference, that is undermining the free enterprise system. Environmental problems, they contend, are distorted by extremists. Business corruption is blown out of all proportion by the foes of business, and business wrongdoing is no worse than that of other elements in society, and probably not nearly so bad.[1]

The mood of impotence and self-defense are not seen as universal:

> Not all businessmen . . . take this complacent or defensive posture; some are deeply concerned about the viability of traditional economic-policy views, the values held by the business community as a whole, and the disclosures of unethical or illegal behavior. However, even these concerned individuals have been hesitant to criticize publicly those companies whose behavior has hurt business as a whole.[2]

Housecleaning within business is a first step in regaining credibility and trust. Bribery abroad and payoffs at home brought this into sharp focus. One of the voices heard on the subject is that of a former businessman, Senator Charles Percy: "An essential ingredient in any reform effort is for business to put its own house in order."

Business communications, having been a contributor to the loss of credibility and confidence, will be on trial in the reform process. Among the communication tendencies that helped foster incredibility and suspicion were these:

Exaggerating facts
Overpromising benefits or results
Disclaiming responsibility
Withholding valid information
Creating pseudo-news events

Deliberately deceiving media and public
Evading legitimate inquiries
Assisting questionable enterprises
Ignoring ultimate public interests

The correction or elimination of such tendencies can move no faster, and with no more force, than the efforts by business leaders to clean house and demonstrate that they have set upon a new course. *Communications can do no more than mirror an organization. It is not the essence.* The exceptions, of course, are the communications media.

Reformation of business communications is not a hopeless task, as some analysts have said. The goal is both attainable and urgent. "If business does a better job of cleaning up the messages, intended and unintended, that it sends, if it manages to explain more about what it does and how it works, society may trust business enough to let it have a highly significant share of leadership in tackling the huge tasks ahead. Otherwise, business, known mainly by its scandals and other samples of its pathology, will become less and less able to fulfill its mission." [3]

The rise and role of public affairs

The most visible change in the practice of public relations has been the emergence and maturing of "public affairs" in Big Business as part of, or alongside, public relations. One executive has termed public affairs "the growth discipline" in public relations.

An outgrowth of what had been called "government relations," public affairs has a breadth that goes beyond lobbying. According to an early definition, it was "a significant and substantial concern and involvement by individuals, business, labor, foundations, private institutions, and government with the social, economic and political forces that singly or through interaction shape the environment within which the free enterprise system exists."

This umbrella concept has been refined as practitioners have fastened their efforts onto a number of specific tasks as properly in their working domain:

1. Creating contacts and programs to improve communication with government personnel and agencies.
2. Monitoring the activities of legislators and regulatory agencies regarding statutes and prospective laws affecting business.
3. Facilitating business participation in carrying out social programs.
4. Advancing the awareness and understanding of natural constituents about matters affecting their interests.
5. Encouraging the participation of constituents in the political process at all levels of government.
6. Advocating the values of the capitalistic system at home, and where business is done abroad.

EXHIBIT 19-1

The Washington Game—Not for Penny-Ante Amateurs

Here are just a few of the Washington-based efforts to have an effective voice and presence in the nation's capital:

- The American Petroleum Institute, following a move in the Senate to break up the oil companies, mounted a million-dollar campaign to head off legislation.
- The American Bankers Association, with a war chest of $100,000 annually, courts members of the Congressional Banking Committee to oppose legislation that aids savings and loan associations in competing with banks.
- The natural-gas industry established a Natural Gas Supply Committee, budgeted at nearly $1 million, to plump for deregulation.
- The Business Roundtable, numbering more than 150 of the largest corporations, led an offensive against revision of the antitrust laws.
- Multinational corporations' staff and factory executives flooded their congressional representatives with calls opposing legislation intended to close a tax break received for exporting goods and services.

A Washington firm specializing in government communications offered the following services to a public relations firm it sought as a client:

First, an analysis of Washington for each of the public relations firm's clients

Second, a choice of these optional services:

A weekly newsletter to clients.
Speaking engagements for client executives.
A seminar on monitoring and issue analysis.
Press luncheons for client discussions.
Exhibits for Washington conventions or shows.
Client receptions for Washington officialdom.
Monitoring and reporting on agency activities of interest to clients.
Opening doors to government personnel for clients' executives.
Developing press coverage for client news.
Counseling on approaches to sensitive issues.

Lobbying: a specialty

Lobbyists for business fall within three general categories: the traditional lobbyist, who represents a corporation or association on a continuing basis; the "issue" lobbyist, who acts in connection with a specific proposed bill or action; and all others, who may be, by primary profession, lawyers, consultants, or public-affairs people. Lobbying is generally handled separately from the ongoing work of the public relations department or counseling firm. One reason is that industry associations and large corporations usually prefer to use registered-lobbyist specialists under the direction of the legal counsel. Another reason is that the relatively narrow definition of "lobbyist" is considered too restrictive a commitment for public-affairs or public relations executives.

Moving from stout defense to stout advocacy

The monitoring of government activities and the lobbying for a business or industry are generally carried out quietly and discreetly. Communications are routinely handled by letter, telephone, interview, or other one-to-one contacts. When this pattern gives way to public airing and debate, one of three conditions prevails: The direct, private approach has failed; the supplicant's position or petition has been questioned by news media or by groups affected by it; or the subject transcends private interests, as would be the case with a public policy matter. At these times, business interests are depicted by opponents as rich, powerful, self-righteous, or arrogant Goliaths. Frequently, public debates have tended to reaffirm the difference between opponents and to emphasis the "impossibility" of settlement without government intervention, locally or nationally.

Occasions requiring public airings have multiplied as more and more watch-dog groups have sprung up and have used the news media adeptly. As a result, applications for changes in utility rates, clearances for nuclear-plant sites, issuance of new drugs or electrical appliances, and zoning changes do not always proceed without challenge. Political considerations enter into what business people would prefer to have confined to questions of economics. The shift from defensive responses by business to initiatives that anticipate opposition and aggressively bid for public support has come to be regarded by corporate leaders as a necessary element in survival.

Change has been gradual: During the early period when "social responsibility vs. economic responsibility" was being argued, considerable effort was made to project the human side of business. "We care" became a communications theme: "We care" about employee fulfillment, job enrichment, and customer satisfaction. "We care" about the cleanliness of the air and water, and the conservation of natural resources. "We listen" to customers' complaints and new needs or wants. "We protect" the investor's stake. "We're involved" in better things for a better life.

There was considerable merit in the effort, and considerable sincerity in its sponsorship. But evaluated as a public relations strategy, there were serious shortcomings. The principal pronoun used was still "we," not "you." The media and the messages were both controlled by the sponsor. It was one-way communication. It lacked the authority or believability of impartial, third-party appraisal. And the messages encountered serious static generated by public hearings in which business conduct and performance did not seem to match the promises and assurances given. There were suggestions publicly that the gasoline shortage was contrived. There were admissions of bribes extended to foreign-oil-country officials, with a defense of such acts as a "necessary cost of doing business"; of bribes and payoffs involving officials in Japan and Korea, as a means of "gaining business contracts." Finally, there were admissions of illegal political contributions given in the hope that attitudes, and perhaps votes, would be favorably disposed toward corporate objectives.

If nothing tangible was gained by the admissions, a good share of the responsibility for dual standards of behavior at home and abroad was transferred onto the federal government's back. Meantime, public airings had cleared the deck for business to restate its case and rebuild credibility.

This proved a boon to the practice of public relations in the large, dominant corporations where the pace and style are set for all of business. The airings set the stage for a resurgence of advocacy of capitalism on a global basis. This has become a foremost workaday function for public relations.[4]

The several garbs of the new advocacy

The main media used for advocacy are statements of mission and integrity, speeches and reprints, advertising, and attitudes of candor and availability.

Statements of missions and integrity

These are usually couched in booklets or brochures and bear the signatures of top officials. The substance relates the goals and products or services of the organization to the expressed needs or wants of the public. (See Figures 19–1 and 19–2.) Often, a tie is shown between material and emotional wants or needs—the products and services are related to the improvement of the environment or human relationships. The language tends to be humanistic. The "heart" and the "character" of business are depicted. The quality of life and a high standard of living are woven together, if not synonymous.

External distribution of these booklets and papers encompasses present constituents and reaches out for new supporters. Mailings may go to educators in liberal arts as well as business administration; to investment funds and foundations as well as individual shareholders or analysts; to legislators and federal agency personnel; to members of trade associations and professional societies; to leaders of labor, ethnic, welfare, and charitable entities; to distributors, dealers, franchisees and suppliers.

Speeches and reprints

Platform appearances by executives are not new as public relations vehicles. The newness is in the breadth of the subject matter tackled, the variety of it, the diversity of audiences, and the professionalism of the presentations. Executives are speaking less into each others' ears and more to groups known to be critical or previously thought to be uninvolved, like educators or clergy.

Speakers are drawn from within business. Their speeches wrestle with subjects as far off the beaten "necessity-of-profit" trail as ozone depletion, zero population growth, or central-city renovation. Executives on the platform are displaying an uncommon open-mindedness, if not enthusiasm, toward dialogue and debate about the imperfections as well as the benefits of the free-enterprise system. And a great many have submitted to special training and preparation provided by advertising and public relations people. A particularly fertile field has been instruction in how to communicate effectively via the electronic media.[5]

Advertising

The use of advertising as a public relations tool for business advocacy has practical advantages. It fits the need to speak up and out to vast audiences beyond those that already support business. Advertising enables its sponsors to control the messages beamed into an environment of public opinion harboring various shades of approval, suspicion, hostility, and apathy. Businessmen feel

426

FIGURE 19–1   Courtesy Caterpillar Tractor Co.

A CODE OF WORLDWIDE BUSINESS CONDUCT

CATERPILLAR TRACTOR CO.

To Caterpillar Managers:

As you know, large business corporations everywhere in the world are being given increasing public scrutiny.

This is understandable. A sizable economic enterprise is a matter of justifiable public interest—sometimes concern—in the community and country in which it is located. And when substantial amounts of goods, services and capital flow across national boundaries, the public's interest is, logically, even greater.

Not surprisingly then, the growth of multinational corporations has led, among other things, to increasing public calls for standards, rules, and codes of conduct for such firms.

It seems unlikely the world will any time soon agree on a "code" or single set of rules pertaining to all facets of international business. But, nevertheless, we conclude it is timely for Caterpillar to set forth *its own beliefs,* based on ethical convictions and international business experiences that date back to the turn of the century.

This "Code of Worldwide Business Conduct" is therefore offered under the several headings that follow. Its purpose is to guide us, in a broad and ethical sense, in all aspects of our worldwide business activities.

Of course, this code is not an attempt to prescribe actions for every business encounter. It *is* an attempt to capture the basic, general principles to be observed by Caterpillar people everywhere.

To the extent our actions match these high standards, such can be a source of pride. To the extent they don't (and I'm by no means ready to claim perfection), these standards should be a challenge to each of us.

I can think of no document bearing my signature which I consider more important than this one. So I trust my successors will cause it to be updated as events may merit. And I also trust *you* will give these principles your strong support in the way you carry out your daily responsibilities as Caterpillar managers.

W H Franklin
Chairman of the Board

FIGURE 19–2   Courtesy Badger Meter, Inc.

Code Of Corporate Ethics

PREAMBLE

As a business corporation, Badger Meter, Inc. functions in an interdependent world where the actions of its officers, directors and employees can affect many other segments of society. Therefore, everyone associated with Badger Meter has an obligation to adhere to the highest ethical standards and to conform with laws that benefit society as a whole.

Most businessmen and businesswomen feel confident that their standards of conduct fulfill this obligation. However, the rapid changes in our society and in our laws make it advisable that we keep updating our knowledge about standards established by statute or by organizations such as IRS, SEC and the American Stock Exchange. A lack of knowledge, rather than a disregard for ethics, often is the reason for the illegal situations in which business managers and their companies find themselves.

This Code of Corporate Ethics was developed so the officers, directors and employees of Badger Meter, Inc. will have up-to-date guidelines about what is expected in modern business practice. Obviously, the guidelines cannot cover every conceivable situation, but must focus on matters of major concern.

A modern business organization is so complex that no one person can be knowledgeable about all the legal and ethical situations that require evaluation. Any activity which raises a question of doubt should be cleared with a supervisor, a member of the Management Executive Committee or the office of the President.

All concerned should keep in mind the high standards of business and personal conduct to which Badger Meter is committed.

Badger Meter, Inc.

4545 West Brown Deer Road
Milwaukee, Wisconsin 53223

JAMES O. WRIGHT
Chairman and Chief Executive Officer

EXHIBIT 19-2

The Project of One Early Advocate

Not all large corporations conducted their public relations from a crouch during the years when it seemed there was no hope for public empathy. One of the notable exceptions is the Eaton Corporation. It is notable not so much because it fought back against a tide of adverse public opinion, but because it undertook to do so with a program born of careful preplanning, not anger or indignation.

Eaton's "Business Speak Out" program was labeled "Comm/Pro '73" in its initial phase. The program called for Communispond, Inc., a subsidiary of J. Walter Thompson Agency, to train Eaton managers to "go out into their communities and not just read a written script of facts and figures, but to boldly tell the business story and *listen* . . . and be fully prepared to provide the needed answers that must be provided if person-to-person dialogue and environment is to be established."[6]

Some 105 Eaton executives were trained in 1972, and 20 more in 1973. Among their subjects were "Business, People, Community and Government," "The Multinational Corporation," "Business, Youth, and Future," and "Business, People, and Productivity." See Figure 19–3.

---

more comfortable with advertising than with publicity. In a climate of adversity, advocacy advertising can be justified as one of the business activities necessary to portray motives and performance accurately. And this in turn can be rationalized as a significant contribution in preserving the profit system.

Advocacy advertising cannot be distinguished in its essential purpose from the institutional, goodwill, and public-service advertising programs of an earlier era. All have sought to reassure constituents, and to disarm adversaries without attacking them. The same essential purposes applied to the "corporate identity" concept that characterized the period of mergers, when independent companies and familiar brand names were being absorbed into the maws of a Tenneco, Gulf & Western, ITT, Mobil, A-T-O, or Northwest Industries.[7]

The limitations of advertising: Advertising on a national scale, particularly for purposes of advocacy rather than marketing, is beyond the financial means of small or marginally profitable companies. Small businesses are dependent on the ripples from national expressions by their trade associations and large industrial and commercial service institutions. They can echo the messages in their home communities through local news media, house publications, bulletin boards, and public utterances. In fact, on critical public policy issues, like divestiture in the oil industry, large companies often provide kits of materials for educators and students, suppliers, and other known allies to use.[8]

One of the most notable advocacy (or public-issue) campaigns ever undertaken by a corporation is that started in 1973 by Mobil Oil, stimulated in part by the adverse spotlighting of the U.S. oil industry during the gasoline-shortage crisis. At that time, oil-industry executives had been insisting publicly, and seemingly in unison, that they needed higher prices and profits to explore for new oil sources to reduce dependence on foreign sources. Subsequently, prices and profits did go up.

429

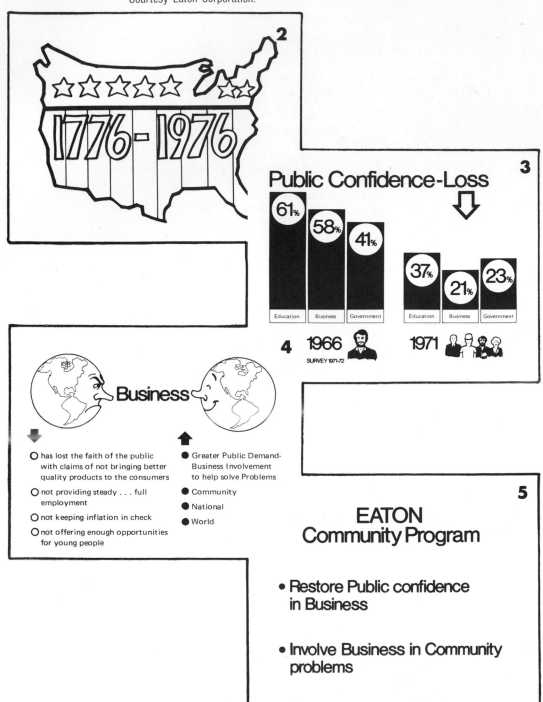

FIGURE 19-4 One of the more imaginative advertising responses to the loss of public confidence was that of Pennwalt. In this ad, the business dilemma was shared with Congress. In another, the fable of the Little Red Hen was linked with profit and productivity. Courtesy Pennwalt Corporation.

Mobil Oil, meanwhile, took an action that seemed to contradict the industry's case, and to imply a serious concern about the long-haul viability of the oil business. The action was a tender offer to acquire control of Marcor (Montgomery Ward and Container Corp.). This committed millions of oil dollars to businesses having no apparent connection with oil exploration. Doubtless, the action made sense to Mobil executives on behalf of Mobil stockholders; but it was greeted with dismay on Capitol Hill, and with consternation by much of the consuming public. From a public relations viewpoint, it was a gross error of timing, if nothing worse.

An editorial in *Business Week* magazine assessed the public relations damage this way: "If the oil industry is ever to win back public confidence—and head off regressive legislation—its executives have to learn they no longer can practice business as usual. Gone are the days when only financial business and economic matters need to be considered. To ignore the public reaction, as Mobil did, is to beg for government intervention."[9]

Coincidentally or not, Mobil's public relations program was enlarged in 1973 with "$10 million more a year to spend on good works and opinion molding." This enlargement was augmented further in 1974, following the "upsurge of hostile publicity generated by booming oil-company profits."

The advocacy-issue portion of the company's advertising sponsorship was embodied in opposite-editorial messages. (See Figure 19–5.) Although it was concentrated in five major metropolitan area newspapers, the op-ed series peaked at one point in 1974 to 103 papers around the country. This vehicle was supplemented by a column titled, "Observations," a breezy potpourri of short items on the industry, running as advertising in Sunday supplements and dailies with a combined circulation above 30 million, and supported by a $3 million annual budget.

In 1976, the Mobil public-affairs department (embracing public relations) was operating on a $21 million annual budget, with two-thirds being spent for public and commercial television and print media space.

There is much more to be studied in Mobil's varied and aggressive public relations programming. For example, what is likely to be its effectiveness in the longer term, in competitors' attitudes toward it, in its durability in the face of economic downturn, and in any emulation of its messages and media by other corporations and industries?[10]

Candor and availability

Having found a low profile to be both uncomfortable and unproductive in the 1970s, business spokesmen generally have become readily accessible to legitimate public inquiries, and more candid in their public statements.

"There is no prescription drug that is absolutely safe," says the head of a leading drug company, after a Senate hearing. A few years ago, this might have been considered naïve within corporate circles and a form of industrial heresy.

"Your editorial 'B-1 Politics' indicates a serious lack of understanding of the weapon system acquisition process of the United States government. . . . I find this distortion difficult to comprehend," writes the head of a defense contracting firm to the publisher of the *New York Times,* in an open letter.

"Work does not satisfy material needs alone, but in a very deep sense, gives a measure of sanity and the ability to define and respect one's self," says the head of a small corporation, speaking to university students at a commencement.

FIGURE 19-5   From the *New York Times,* August 9, 1973. Prepared by Doyle Dane Bernbach for Mobil Public Affairs. Courtesy of Mobil Oil Corp.

Capitalism: moving target

The list of things wrong with business in this country is almost endless. Nearly as long, in fact, as the list of what's right with it.

Perhaps the most frustrating thing about business, for those who keep trying to shoot it down, is this: Corporations are so tenacious that they will even do good in order to survive. This tenacity goes beyond the old maxim that man, in his greed for profit, often unavoidably serves the public interest. In times of crisis, business will even do good *consciously* and *deliberately.*

Nothing could be better calculated to confound business's critics than this underhanded tactic. The Marxist dialectic has it that capitalism must inevitably founder in its own inherent contradictions; that it contains the seeds of its own destruction. But business also contains the seeds of its own adaptation and survival.

Businessmen are pragmatists, and with their daily feedback from the marketplace, they readily abandon dogma whenever their survival instinct tells them to. It has become less and less a question of what they *want* to do or might *like* to do, but of what their common sense and survival instinct tell them they *have* to do.

Remember the Edsel? That was one of the fastest plebiscites in history. But it wasn't the American public that took the loss; it was the shareholders of Ford Motor Company. (Then, you'll recall, Ford changed course and bounced back with the Mustang, which quickly showed its tailpipe to the competition by breaking all sales records for a new make of car.)

Because it is keyed so closely to the marketplace and so responsive to it, private business is necessarily the most effective instrument of change. Some would call it revolutionary. Many of those who attack business fail to comprehend its constructive contributions to responsive change. And this sort of change is one of the basic reasons business manages to survive.

Not *all* businesses survive, of course. The record is replete with companies that expired because they didn't adapt rapidly enough to a new milieu.

While businessmen as a whole are not exactly social reformers, they do respond to criticism and to sustained social pressures. The alert businessman regards such pressures as a useful early warning system. The danger is that criticism can become a mindless reflex action that persists long after the basis for it has been dissipated.

Partly because of its ability to adapt—which is simply another word for responsive change—private business remains the most productive element in our society and on balance the best allocator of resources. If you decide to draw a bead on it, remember you're aiming at a moving target. Because, as we've said here before, business is bound to change.

433

"Business has allowed its enemies to define it, its critics to explain it, and its foes to report it. Well, today I'm here to holler, 'Now, just a damned minute,'" says the head of a large appliance-manufacturing firm.

"The raw truth is simply this: We are a people uneducated in economics," says the head of a pharmaceutical firm.

"Questions might well be asked about the more than 1,000 advisory groups to government, costing millions of dollars, advising on subjects such as tea tasting, rifle practice, antiperspirants, the dance, personality research, and sunburn treatment." This was in a position paper widely distributed by a major corporation.

"In this market system of ours is the salvation of the world's problems," says the head of a steel company, without reservations.

"The best advertising reeks of truth . . . truth and simplicity are the key," according to a senior official in one of the nation's ten largest ad agencies.

"We will not buy commercials on TV programs characterized by violence or antisocial behavior," a large national advertiser instructs its agency, and alerts the public.

Other pronouncements deal candidly with other harsh realities. They point out that consumers cannot have absolutely pure air and water without paying for it and sacrificing some comfort, convenience, or pleasure. Blunt questions are posed. How much ozone depletion is acceptable in order to enjoy aerosol sprays? How much increase in the price of automobiles is acceptable as a cost of emission control? How much inconvenience in parking, added personal expense, and risk of mugging is acceptable in return for the location of factories in central-city areas?

This is an era of trade-offs. Business is laying some of the choices out in the open. *This trend augurs well for the role of public relations in providing counsel to management on communications decisions and in interfacing with news media and public audiences.*

There are also signs of increased candor by public relations practitioners concerning media relations. As one executive put it, "Open communications is the best course of action. . . . We have to get over our fears of the press. It's time to say to ourselves: 'Let's get off the media's back and speak up for business.'"[11]

Advocacy, candor, and personal availability sound fine in speeches and are impressive on paper. *In practice they run the risk that, once more, the promises and reassurances of business may raise expectations far beyond the actualities.* If so, credibility and confidence could be washed even farther down the tube.

As a practical matter, integrity and self-discipline that are demonstrated rather than merely proclaimed stand to gain more than public trust. Among the spin-offs are less government intervention and lowered costs of doing business.

Philanthropy: aid to education, health, welfare, and the arts

The philosophic debate by economists as to whether business has social responsibilities beyond its obligations to its employees, shareholders, and neighbors—and if so, what they might be—occupies the center of the stage. Meantime, off to one side, corporate philanthropy continues to play its part in the business scenario. Management, as a group and as individuals, cheerfully participates financially and socially in the private causes preferred by its members and their spouses.

Every profitable corporation, whether ownership is spread widely or dominated by a single family, has its favorite causes and charitable organizations. The range of favorites goes from day-care centers to community chests, from college scholarships to fine-arts centers, from symphony orchestras to illiteracy in other nations.

The corporate rationale for philanthropy is not quite the same as that for the resolution of social problems related to unemployment, urban decay, or crime in the streets. To begin with, philanthropy is strictly up to top management as a matter of whim, vanity, or humanitarianism. Donations can be cut down or out in a recession. Contributions of money or executive time are not regarded as adversely affecting the corporation's ability to function effectively or efficiently. Actually, one survey showed executives devoting an average 6.8 hours per week to charitable and civic endeavors. Finally, in philanthropy, a big splash, like calling in a gift on a telethon, can be made with negligible impact on the bottom line of the operating statement.

The public relations function becomes involved in the philanthropic gestures of corporations, and of wealthy individuals associated with them, in several ways:

1. Staging appropriate events for making a decisive contribution, as in a welfare fund drive, or in the creation of a scholarship fund bearing the name of the donor.
2. Assisting in a charitable campaign or endeavor, with communications-strategy counsel, preparation of printed or audiovisual materials, news-writing skill, or placement of publicity.
3. Heading a project or campaign, or serving as the alternate for a corporate senior official who is nominally the head.
4. Auditing various causes in a community to determine where and how a corporation might best be of assistance.

Corporate giving: large in dollars, small in percent

The total dollar volume of corporate giving ($1.2 billion in 1975) is impressive, but its percentage is not. In 1975, total philanthropy in the United States was $26 billion. Of this, wealthy individuals gave 79.7 percent, bequests were 8.3 percent, foundations gave 7.5 percent, and corporations gave 4.5 percent.[12]

A Conference Board study of practices in 457 corporations pointed out that beyond outright giving to various causes, there is another form of contribution of equal size. This is the "business-expense" type, whose costs have been rising steadily. It includes such programs as special employment for ex-addicts and ex-convicts, public-service projects, loans of equipment, and the use of corporate facilities.

Current laws permit a corporation to donate up to 5 percent of its net pretax income. But before bumping into that legal ceiling, corporate giving has a long way to go. The average level has stubbornly persisted at about 1 percent of corporate income.

Corporate executives cite four main reasons for their involvement in philanthropy:

1. It demonstrates good corporate character and citizenship.
2. It preserves the intangible values inherent in private education, welfare, and the arts. This is seen as essential to the well-being of the private-enterprise system.

3. It sets a good example for those who would emulate corporate practices.

4. It advances the quality and enjoyment of life in a community.

A foremost beneficiary, education

A prime recipient of corporate philanthropy has always been higher education. Contributions for the improvement of education can usually be measured in dollar value, even though they assume a variety of forms other than cash. Among them are facilities and equipment, teaching aids, employees' time in training and teach-ins, scholarships, fellowships and internships, research grants, and matching of the gifts of employees. See Figure 19–6.

FIGURE 19–6   Allocation of corporate contributions in 1974, a period of recession, placed health and welfare ahead of education. Courtesy of The Conference Board.

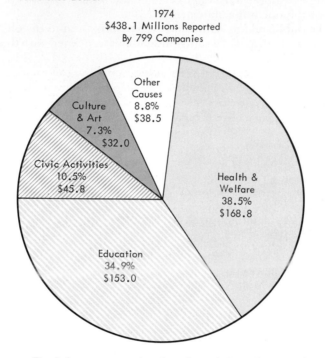

1974
$438.1 Millions Reported
By 799 Companies

Other Causes 8.8% $38.5

Culture & Art 7.3% $32.0

Civic Activities 10.5% $45.8

Health & Welfare 38.5% $168.8

Education 34.9% $153.0

Recipients are variously selected, but they tend to reflect plant-community relationships, the number of employees in each college or university city, the alma maters of employees or executives, the judgment of executives, the degree of alumni support mustered, or the simple whim of a top official.

In recent years, evaluations have questioned whether the interests of the corporation are ultimately served best by the concentrated allocation of funds and effort in plant communities that might be suburban and relatively free of blight or poverty. Some hold the view that the final gain to the business system would be greater if the funds were concentrated in areas of serious social problems and were clearly marked for education to improve the skills of the least qualified.

Projects run the kindergarten-to-adult education gamut and range from multimillion-dollar projects to mailing folders. "Reddy Reader," a preschool primer from Reddy Kilowatt, Inc., helps parents to teach reading. The New Detroit Committee gave $100,000 for the sixth-grade textbooks in poverty neighborhoods. Coca-Cola prepared a slide film, "Black Treasures," for distribution to schools, libraries, and youth organizations. Corn Products trained several hundred disadvantaged youths, and its educational subsidiary, MIND, upgraded reading and mathematics skills for thousands. Xerox sponsored a Latin-American version of "Sesame Street." Smith-Kline sponsored foreign fellowships for medical students.

Scholarships lend themselves to communications programs. Annually, General Motors grants several hundred scholarships in universities and colleges. Oscar Mayer provided scholarships for the sons and daughters of employees. Hundreds of companies have participated in a competitive National Merit Scholarship program.

Quite a record has been compiled by E. I. du Pont de Nemours. Its aid-to-education program, in existence more than 60 years, made grants in 1977 totaling $3.3 million to 164 colleges. A recent phase sought to stimulate interest among minority groups and women in science and engineering careers.

Health and welfare

Corporate philanthropy directed to the privately supported health and welfare agencies and institutions is long established and well known, as are the communications programs supporting fund campaigns and giving recognition to large contributions. Occasionally something exceptional pops up, such as the gift by Masonite Corporation of its $1.5 million Medical Center in Laurel, Mississippi, to the people of the county. Dow Chemical ran a sales contest in which distributors got 10 cents for charity for each $1 by which they exceeded quota. The 250 winners donated 350 gifts to community organizations, ranging from $50 radios to $6,000 tractors.

Culture and the arts

Not so highly developed or known are the expanding relationship between the corporation and the arts, and imaginative communication vehicles for dramatizing and expressing the relationship. In the period between 1967 and 1977, financial support of the arts by business increased tenfold, from $22 million to $221 million.[13]

The traditional pattern consists of regular monetary gifts for ongoing institutions such as opera companies and symphonies. In the renovation of many older urban areas, business has had a major part in new and reconstructed centers of the performing arts. Among many are the Chicago Auditorium Theater, the Atlanta Memorial Art Center, and Houston's Alley Theater. See Figure 19–7.

Occasionally, grants are for specific projects. American Export's Isbrandtsen Lines gave the New York Metropolitan Opera the cost of a new production of *Aida*. Eastern Air Lines granted $500,000 for a new production of Wagner's Ring Cycle. Both Johnson Wax and Container Corporation of America maintained traveling exhibits of contemporary art. Trane Company supported community theater in La Crosse, Wisconsin. Hallmark has sponsored art competitions and annually gives awards to encourage promising artists.

Thompson, Ramo, Woolridge (TRW) sponsored performances of a live

London–Broadway show, *By George,* based on the life of George Bernard Shaw, before some 50,000 students at 40 colleges in a ten-week span. Its stated objectives were to extend the company's dialogue with students, broaden appreciation of the arts, and show that the modern corporation is interested in the cultural side of society. A program initiated by Bamberger's department store in New Jersey, to bring the great artists appearing in nearby New York City to New Jersey audiences, won the respect and applause of audiences and performers alike. The first sponsored performances were of the Ballet Russe in Newark.

A few flies in the ointment

Corporate philanthropy has grown. Rarely have its benefits to private enterprise been challenged; its desirability has many eminent spokesmen. Consequently, one portion of the remarks by Henry Ford II on resigning as a trustee of

438

the Ford Foundation seemed to suggest that businessmen take a closer look:

> The foundation exists and thrives on the fruits of our economic system. The dividends of competitive enterprise make it all possible. . . . In effect, the foundation is a creature of capitalism—a statement that, I'm sure, would be shocking to many professional staff people in the field of philanthropy. It is hard to discern recognition of this fact in anything the foundation does. It is even more difficult to find an understanding of this in many of the institutions, particularly the universities, that are the beneficiaries of the foundation's grant programs.[14]

Rarely has there been a legal question about the use of corporate funds for charitable purposes. However, in 1973, the Illinois Supreme Court took the position that Illinois Bell Telephone, a major unit in the Bell System, could not include its charitable contributions as "costs of doing business" for rate-making purposes. This meant that the $1,125,000 Illinois Bell had donated to various charities in a year constituted an "involuntary assessment" on the utility's customers. By implication, contributions should come only from profits. This matter is covered in Chapter 12, concerning the Kraushaar decision.

As business moves off the defensive and speaks out more on sensitive matters, Mr. Ford's view presages further questions by corporate officials or wealthy individuals as to the usage of the fruits of free enterprise, or their unrestricted gifts, and whether donations need to be more selective or specifically restricted. As business critics and minority shareholders, investors or consumers find access to proxy proposals an easy and newsworthy route, the Illinois Bell experience brings up questions as to the propriety involved when publicly owned companies appear to extract sums for charity from shareholders, or from customers. It is but a small step from these questions to the validity of advertising, promotion, or publicity as factors in the price the customer pays.

Whether in the form of prevention or remedy, public relations thinking will have a significant role.

Corporate financial relations

There is one sobering fact of economic life that dominates all other considerations in the financial affairs of American business. *More than $4 trillion in investment capital must be raised between 1977 and 1987.* Current investors and potential new ones hold the key—both individuals with small holdings and institutions holding or administering large blocks of business securities. Without fulfilling this capital need, the economy cannot grow and the business sector cannot provide the jobs the public seeks.

Investors, by their purchases and holdings of business stocks, bonds, and notes, tend to express confidence in a corporation, an industry, or the private-enterprise system. Conversely, unwillingness to buy and hold these securities tends to express a lack of confidence, approval, or support. The mood of investors is of critical importance when a privately owned company converts to public ownership, when a corporation seeks to borrow money for its expansion, when a corporation competes poorly but rewards its executives handsomely, or when questions of corporate behavior or legality are raised.

Obviously, where both public mood and the need for investors are involved, public relations techniques of persuasion and reassurance have the capacity to be decisive.

Corporate ownership

Its makeup: There were 6,490,000 shareholders in U.S. corporations in 1952, 17,000,000 in 1962, 20,000,000 in 1965, 30,850,000 in 1970, and a peak of 32,000,000 in 1972.[15] The total turned down during the period of the recession and mounting scandals. Going into 1978, the total was moving back toward 30,000,000.

Ownership figures represent numerous crosscurrents. One is the increase in the number of individual small investors. Another, in an apparent opposite direction, is the increase in dominance of ownership by large institutions and investment funds. Still another is the increased significance of employee pension-fund investment in total corporate ownership. The New York Stock Exchange estimates that there are approximately 100 million direct or beneficial shareholders, an average of one per American family. Share ownership, however, is not to be confused with corporate management.

Lack of organized power: The voice and power of shareholders in corporate affairs has been described as more theoretical than actual. John Galbraith has labeled shareholder power a "myth." In *The Industrial State,* he points out, "A small portion of the stock is represented at a stockholder's meeting. . . . The rest is voted by proxy for the directors who have been selected by the management. The latter, though their ownership is normally negligible, are solidly in control of the enterprise."

Another factor is that corporate shareholders have not historically been organized into common-interest groups with collective voices, like employees in a union, or financial analysts in a professional society.

A third factor is that not all corporate managements have felt equally obligated toward their stockholders, or considered it vital to keep them well informed about the company's doings. However, bitter proxy fights, dissidence expressed by shareholders at annual meetings, successful tender offers, court actions by the SEC, and an expanded statement of disclosure policy by the New York Stock Exchange have sharply reduced the number of managers who would contend "We make a profit and pay our shareholders a good dividend. That's all they need to know."

A fourth factor is that small investors feel overawed by a huge corporation. They may own 50 or 100 shares, a big sum to them; but they read that investment funds often buy and sell in lots of 50,000 shares. Their only contact with management is through the printed mailings and the news media. Naturally, they feel remote and helpless. To management, they may appear apathetic.

Feelings of helplessness and concern have tended increasingly to be offset by challenges of corporate conduct. For many years, the only challenges came from a few persistent "hecklers," like the Gilbert Brothers and Mrs. Wilma Soss. To these voices have been added the Ralph Nader group, Mrs. Evelyn Davis, church leaders, and environmentalists. Challenges are no longer confined to questions of how to select and reward directors or management. There are social, ethical, and moral questions.

It follows logically from all this, and from readjustments in management attitudes, that *the role of financial public relations has attained more importance in corporate affairs. Specialists have grown in numbers, responsibility, and scope of work.*

The responsibility and the role

A corporation's policies concerning financial relations are strictly the province of top management. Guidance is by law, as described in Chapter 12, by SEC rules and regulations, by stock-exchange requirements, and by the attitude of management toward minimal, moderate, or generous disclosure.[16] The implementation of policies falls largely to financial officers and public relations staff or outside counsel. Legal counsel also has a significant role. In most publicly owned corporations, the financial relations wing of public relations will be found closely related to top management.

The usual assignments given to public relations in a shared responsibility fall into five categories:

1. Measures taken to monitor attitudes toward the company, the industry, or free enterprise on the part of shareholders, financial analysts, federal agencies, or legislative bodies.
2. Recommendations concerning communications strategy, and particularly changes in strategy relating to corporate goals.
3. Preparation, in part or in total, of financial literature such as letters welcoming new stockholders, interim and annual reports, dividend enclosures, and information for brokerage-firm research reports. (The annual proxy statement, or a prospectus, is normally prepared by financial or legal officials.)
4. Physical arrangements and informational materials for the financial meetings, tours of facilities, and presentations.
5. Financial news releases and the handling of inquiries from financial media.

Effective workaday programming

Letters: The first direct contact management can establish with a stockholder is at the time of the stock purchase. A *letter of welcome* can enclose the most recent financial report, or a booklet about the products and the history. The letter can offer to supply any information wanted personally, issue an invitation to visit the firm's offices or factories, pave the way for a sample product, submit a questionnaire, or merely reflect management's desire to justify the confidence expressed by the purchase. See Figure 19–8.

There is also intermittent correspondence from investors to be handled. Some submit suggestions or inquiries about products, sales, processes, or research. Others ask seemingly unnecessary questions about the current market price of the stock, the number of shares they own, or the total number owned by people whose first name is John or people over 50. Some are chronic gripers.

Letter exchanges with stockholders can function as a useful "listening" communications tool. Perhaps this is why so many corporation presidents handle responses personally.

Annual report: The keystone of any program is the annual report—this is the report card of business. This tool has been brought to a high degree of technical and graphic excellence, much of which is due to the public relations emphasis.

Pacific Northwest Bell

W. R. Bunn
President

Sixteen Hundred Bell Plaza
Seattle, Washington 98191
Phone (206) 345-3223

March 11, 1977

Allen H. Center
12039 Caminito Cadena
San Diego, California   92128

Dear Share Owner:

Welcome to our organization as a share owner.

As you probably know, PNB is a member of the Bell System, a
nationwide organization which includes American Telephone and
Telegraph, Western Electric and Bell Telephone Laboratories.

With the help of these Companies, our goal at PNB is to provide the best telecommunications service available to the 216
communities we serve in the Pacific Northwest. And while
we're doing that, we'll keep your investment working just as
profitably as we can for you.

Our dividends are paid, as declared, on the last business day
in March, June, September and December. Along with the dividends, we will send you a summary of earnings and important
Company news for that quarter. You will also receive a copy
of our Annual Report each spring.

Through these regular communications, we hope to keep you
fully informed about the progress of your Company. If you
ever have any questions, we'll be glad to answer them; and
your comments and suggestions are always welcome.

Sincerely,

W R Bunn

The trend is for reports to do more than reflect and compare a company's current financial results. Some reports show a company's international scope, or its impact on the economy of its plant cities. Some relate products and services to social problems such as air or water pollution, illiteracy, poverty, or urban renewal. Some convey the position of management on public issues. The emphasis is on the role of the modern corporation in society beyond its own immediate survival and growth.

An effective annual report ought to have most of these characteristics:

- A distinctive cover to attract interest and reflect corporate character.
- A table of contents, if the report is lengthy.
- A brief summary or table of highlights.
- Identification of officials, by function.
- A statement or letter from the chief executive officer summarizing the year's events and emphasizing developments that bear on the corporation's continuing ability to meet what its management sees as its obligations, private or public.
- Operating statement and balance sheet.
- Financial highlights compared over a ten-year span.
- An auditor's statement.

There are two main practical considerations with which financial public relations people must be involved:

1. *Readability.* This applies particularly to the corporation engaged in a complex technology, or structured financially in a complex manner. Technology (say, an integrated circuit) must be stated in terms of what it *does* (in a computer, or a TV set), not what it *is* scientifically. The same for depreciation, amortization, LIFO, the lower of cost or market, or sinking fund.
2. *Cost.* A mailing list of only 1,000 would make it uneconomical to put out a four-color, 32-page, slick paper booklet. Conversely, a homespun, two-sheet multilith, one-color report to 50,000 stockholders would be ill-advised. The large majority of reports cost between 50 cents and $1.50 per copy. If stockholders are also potential customers, it might go higher.

It is common practice for companies to print substantially more copies than are needed for registered stockholders. The extra copies are for employee recruiting, the financial press, analysts and funds customers, suppliers, libraries, trade associations, contract proposals to customers, students, and selected community and government officials.

A typical schedule for production of the annual report is shown in Figure 19–9.

The annual meeting of stockholders

The annual meeting is a corporate ritual whose value is hotly debated. Theoretically, the meetings have the virtues of face-to-face contact. True, but with the geographical spread of shareholders, it is usually only those living nearby or representing huge blocks of shareholders that can afford the time or money to attend. Again, in theory, the mail-out of pertinent facts and proposals

FIGURE 19–9   Courtesy of Chilton Book Company, *Marketing Problem Solver.*

Annual Report Schedule

OPERATION	RESPONSIBILITY	START DATE	FINISH DATE	WORKING DAYS ALLOWED	CUMULATIVE WORKING DAYS
Planning meeting to discuss budget, schedule, format & organization					
Develop general theme and content presentation					
Preliminary format in rough outline form					
Management review of preliminary outline					
Select printing paper — size, color, weight					
Specifications to printer for pricing					
Weigh blank dummy and envelope to establish estimated postage costs					
Expand outline, gather all photos and information, draft president's letter					
Select printer; enlist his aid; order paper					
Finalize photos, data, and all revised text material					
Select typeface					
Comprehensive layout					
Presentation of final copy & layout to management					
Final alteration of copy & layout and circulation for approvals					
Final copy and photos to artist for preparation					
Develop mailing list					
Proofread type prior to paste-up					
Final artwork from artist; stats of assembled book with photo indications in place					
Review and approval of final artwork and copy					
Last minute alterations made					
All artwork to printer					
Pre-address mailing envelopes					
Brownlines for approval					
Press proofs for approval					
Check job on press and in bindery					
Insert and mail					

weeks in advance, and the rounding up of votes (proxies) from absentees, represent corporate democracy in action. However, with a small number of trustees of massive investment and pension-fund holdings voting the shares of many thousands of small investors, the process can scarcely be said to express the will of all shareholders as individuals. Managements, aware of this, have turned to postmeeting reports to all shareholders.[17]

Questions most often raised at annual meetings fall into eight areas:

1. Executive salaries, bonuses, stock options, pensions, and special privileges.
2. Employee wage levels, programs for training and advancement, seniority rights, and benefits.
3. Working conditions, safety and health provisions.
4. Stock ownership by management, and possible conflicts of interest.
5. Cumulative voting.
6. Outside directors representing the public at large or a special-interest group; selection of directors, compensation of directors.

7. Size of dividends, use of retained earnings.
8. Products or services, as to defectives, discounts, warranties, prices, or nature of advertising.

In conjunction with annual meetings, the public relations department is called on to perform several tasks. Generally, these might involve the physical arrangements for speakers, visitor parking and comfort, refreshments if any, handouts of information, program if needed, tours or souvenirs where involved, accommodations for news media, and arrangements for interviews following the meetings when requested.

Financial analysts: a growing factor

Financial analysts, bankers, fund managers, and brokers in the professional financial community make up a major financial audience. Investors represented by this fraternity account for more than 50 percent of the trading volume in the stock market.

Visits with individual analysts, presentations to groups such as the Financial Analysts Society, and tours of facilities are regular events for large corporations. A survey of 94 firms by The Conference Board revealed that firms granted no less than 20, and as many as 100, personal interviews to analysts annually. Members of the financial community, and stockholders also, are frequently surveyed by corporations for their reactions to corporate decisions, actions, and communication with them.

William G. Maas, president of the Investment Analysts Society of Chicago, gave these do's and don'ts in presentations and other contacts:

Among the subjects to avoid:	Among the subjects to discuss:
Long corporate history	Current sales
Rehash of annual report	Interim statement
Enumeration of plants and properties	Sales breakdowns by divisions
Industry statistics	Types of operations and customer classifications
Flag-waving about free enterprise	New products and their potentialities
Sales talks	Plant expansion and modernization
	Management
	Existing problems
	Forecasts

Consumer relations: area of foment

Public relations has long been an essential element in the marketing formula, particularly in consumer product and services companies. There are seven main forms of assistance rendered to marketing:

1. News and events related to the launching of new or improved products or services.
2. Promotion of established products or services to the extent they are newsworthy.
3. Creating a favorable image of "the company behind the product."
4. Arranging for public appearances of marketing spokesmen.

5. Probing public opinion in market areas.
6. Focusing news-media attention on sales conferences and other marketing events.
7. *Assisting in programs concerning consumerism.*

For a great many counselors and staff practitioners, participation in the "marketing mix" is the bread-and-butter portion of the job. With government entering more into the regulation of marketing, there is no indication that this condition will diminish in the 1980s.

The resurgence of consumerism

Until about 1960, the first three functions listed above made up the bulk of public relations work in marketing. They were regarded as the "fun" part of the job in many companies (see Exhibit 19–3). This has now changed; the seventh service listed has come into dominance. Consumerism, according to a veteran counselor, "presents what might be the ultimate challenge to the public relations profession."[18]

The origins of consumerism can be traced with ease at least as far back as the term *caveat emptor*. Since the beginnings of mass production, the subject of consumerism—what to do about the buyer–seller relationship—has been bandied about in trade and business circles almost to the point of exhaustion.

Theoretically—say, as Plato's *Republic*—there should be no serious or unresolvable problem between buyer and seller. A combination of integrity, fairness, understanding, and good faith on both sides should take care of everything. In actuality, no sticky problem would exist if humans could produce only faultless products and services, of faultless materials, design, and performance, and sellers exchanged these products and services at prices and with assurances that were acceptable to all.

At the heart of dissatisfactions and controversy are variations in the standards of quality or performance, and in the use to which products are put. The main burden is on the seller. One notable business observer distributes the ultimate responsibility for standards among "costs, profit aims, competitive position, and the conscience of the seller."[19] That seems to cover it all.

As mentioned earlier in another context, self-discipline in standards and competitive practices by industrial marketers is fundamental to any relief in the stress between sellers and customers. Efforts have been made, but they have fallen short of long-range goals. As early as 1912, there were vigilance committees for truth in advertising. Eventually, these evolved into the Better Business Bureau (BBB). This organization was reconstituted as a council of 150 bureaus in 1970, handling more than 8 million contacts annually as a bridge between manufacturers and consumers.

Corporations have made individual efforts to create bridges. General Motors established an owner-relations department as early as 1937, forerunner to the ombudsman activity in vogue during the 1970s.

Private groups representing consumers are also not a new phenomenon. In 1936, Consumers Union was formed as a nonprofit adjunct of the labor movement. Its subscribers grew to exceed 2 million.

The greatest upsurge of consumerism came in the 1960s, with government intervention in the form of many consumer-protection laws. Then, in the early 1970s, the post of Assistant to the President for Consumer Affairs was created, with Virginia Knauer occupying it. A National Business Council for Consumer Affairs was created by the president to encourage self-regulation.

EXHIBIT 19-3

The Fun Part of the Job

Grist for the mill of product and service promotion has been limited only by the imagination of practitioners and the budget available. Examples are legion.

American Express boosted sales with a "Fly Free for Life" contest, and United Airlines did the same by sending 2,500 female executive secretaries a fresh rose—"Rose to a First Lady"—each Friday.

Alcoa had a newsworthy aircraft, a DC-7, outfitted as an exhibit of the company's products and capabilities.

The Men's Tie Foundation campaigned to identify ties with grooming and success. Among the vehicles were a $25,000 historical tie collection, a Presidential Tie Poll, a "Tie Tack" directory, and films, "Dressed Up" and "Good Grooming."

U.S. Steel sponsored "Operation Snowflake" to help sell home appliances for Christmas; Goodyear stimulated store traffic with a bargain album, "Great Songs of Christmas"; and Oneida Silversmiths honored organizations for "significant service to the academic, civic or international communities."

To glamorize work clothes, Work Wear Corporation staged a fashion show tracing the history of work clothes, evolving to such modern interpretations as airline personnel's costumes.

The Bicycle Institute plumped for safety paths by stressing the health and fun aspects of cycling. One stunt found the U.S. secretary of the interior leading a bike parade of congressmen on a ride to the Capitol.

The California avocado growers cashed in on the popularity of "natural" cosmetics with an avocado formula for facials and hair treatments.

By 1975, The Conference Board could report that more than 300 corporations had formed consumer-relations departments. A few, like Coca-Cola, were structured with an officer reporting directly to the chief executive officer. Of all 300 consumer-affairs departments, however, only 17 percent were headed by an officer. How well the other 83 percent were positioned to influence the policies of the companies was moot.

The sheer weight of numbers of concerned companies has not won over the private-citizens' groups organized for consumer protection. Carol Tucker, formerly executive director of the Consumer Federation of America, maintained that consumer-affairs departments are window dressing: "They are quite literally in an untenable position. I have never met a consumer-affairs person who gives me confidence that they can do anything." Peter Barasch, staff director of the House subcommittee on consumer affairs, perceives these departments as extensions of marketing departments, with little influence on actual policy. He says, "They can serve, however, as a focus for consumer complaints, cut corporate red tape, and, in this capacity, have some impact."[20]

The role of public relations in consumer affairs

New consumer relations departments notwithstanding, public relations has become significantly involved. In a study of 100 corporations drawn randomly from *Fortune*'s 500 Largest, naval public-affairs officer Stephen Becker found that 32 percent of the responding companies were each handling more than 10,000 consumer inquiries annually. In 43 percent of the companies, the responsibility was vested in the public relations department.[21]

There are four public groupings with which consumer-oriented practitioners concern themselves: the consumer, the government "referees," consumer activists, and consumer-oriented media. Of course, competitors and their activities cannot be ignored.

Some measure of the professional priority of consumerism is indicated by the involvement of the Public Relations Society of America. Its Consumer Task Force prepared a model speech with slides, compiled a consumerism bibliography, curriculum, case-history file, and appropriate news-media list. Its publication, *Public Relations Journal,* carries a monthly "Consumerism Update" section.

The outlook

Theorizing consumerism out of existence on moral or ethical grounds is simple. In practice, palliatives and token gestures by sellers are not difficult or uneconomic. Durable resolutions, however, are bound up in the whole matter of public confidence. Meantime, despite multiple choices in the marketplace, there has been a rising tide of hostility in the buyer–seller relationship, and stepped-up government regulation. The regulatory trend, according to the head of The Conference Board, "is not only well established but has become institutionalized. It's something that is going to be with us for a long time."[22]

Those words are well reinforced by events. Surveys and polls have shown that 80 percent of consumers favor more government regulation for product safety, and one person in five feels he or she has been cheated on purchases.

Predictably, in the 1980s *the practitioner will continue to help promote the sale of products and services, with novel and news-making projects but with more attention to truth and accuracy of claims. The functional emphasis will shift still more in external communications to communications projects and vehicles for product-problem alerts and recalls, consumer education in the care and use of products, and forms of easy redress for settlement of grievances by private arbitration.*

A case problem in crisis

It was reported in this morning's *Wall Street Journal* that eight officers of a regional utility with annual revenues of $400 million were involved in maintaining an illegal "slush fund" to help selected politicians of both parties who were standing for election. These executives are alleged to have collectively contributed about $50,000. There have been no indictments, but there will be "further investigation" as to whether it was company money or their own. The news story contained some inaccuracies and incompletions, but all eight people were identified by name and title, and the company's name appeared in the story several times.

The company's switchboard has been bombarded by the media, shareholders, financial analysts, and customers with requests for confirmation, denial, interview, or explanation. Only four of the eight accused are in, and they've been instructed by the CEO, Charley Dynamic, to take no calls. Of the four absentees, one is in Washington, and two are at a business convention and have their wives along. The fourth is vacationing.

Charley's information from his associates is confusing. They feel innocent. Some of the money was theirs. But some did come from political-science funds for employee education, although there's apparently no way the money can be traced to the company.

Early in the morning, the PR officer called the CEO's office for guidance. Everyone had been bouncing the outside calls to her office. The message from Charley's secretary was that he'd get back to her as soon as possible, and meanwhile she should stall.

Meantime, Charley was calling each of the company's board members to brief them and get their opinions. Their unanimous view was that the CEO should make a statement to the media, employees, shareholders, and customers as soon as possible.

At 11:45, Caspar Milquetoast, on the legal staff (and one of the executives named in the story), unsuccessfully attempted suicide, leaving a note saying that he was innocent of any wrongdoing, but could not bear the embarrassment and trouble that would be heaped on the company and himself by the critics and enemies of business.

Shortly after that, the CEO summoned his PR/PA department heads, Sarah Trueblue and Bill Stoutfellow. He told them that preliminary information was confusing, but that regardless of what might prove to be the whole story later on, there was no choice but to respond to the press now. Rumors would only make matters worse. He said he had told the *Wall Street Journal* he would have something to say by 2:00 P.M. The *Journal* was sending a man to his offices. The CEO expressed the opinion to Sarah and Bill that a press call should be put out to all interested media.

It is now 12:15. As a professional PR/PA practitioner, what would your first advice be to Charley Dynamic? If he disagreed, what would be your alternative advice? How do you support your advice, based on the principles you know as a professional, on the circumstances as you understand them, on the decision and action that Charley presented to you, and on what you have already done this morning between 9:00 and 12:15? Put it all down on paper, including any public statements involved.

ADDITIONAL READINGS

"Annual Reports," *Public Relations Journal,* September 1974 and September 1975.

"Capital Contacts in Consumerism," a booklet by Washington Communications Counselors, 1701 K Street N.W., Washington, D.C.

PETER DRUCKER, *Management: Tasks, Responsibilities, Practices.* New York: Harper & Row, 1974.

JOHN KENNETH GALBRAITH, *The Twilight of Capitalism.* New York: Simon & Schuster, 1976.

"The Great Banking Retreat," *Business Week,* April 21, 1975, pp. 46–102.

HERMAN KAHN, *The Future of the Corporation.* New York: Mason and Lipscomb, 1974.

FREDERICK C. KLEIN and JOHN A. PRESTBO, *News and the Market.* Chicago: Henry Regnery, 1974.

MORRIS M. LEE, JR., "Tender Offers: Strategies & Tactics," *The Journal of Corporate Ventures,* Vol. 10, No. 3 (Fall 1975).

RONALD N. LEVY, "Public Policy Publicity: How to Do It," *Public Relations Journal,* June 1975.

"Meadows: Curbing Growth," an interview, *Business Week,* May 12, 1975.

H. FRAZIER MOORE and BERTRAND R. CANFIELD, *Public Relations, Principles, Cases and Problems.* Homewood, Ill.: Richard D. Irwin, 1977. See Chaps. 14, "Shareholder Relations," 15, "Distributor Relations," and 16, "Supplier Relations."

JOSEPH NOLAN, "Protect Your Public Image," *Harvard Business Review,* March–April 1975, pp. 135–42.

"The SEC, the Stock Exchange and Your Financial Public Relations," a booklet by Hill and Knowlton, New York, 1972.

LEONARD SILK and DAVID VOGEL, *Ethics and Profits.* New York: Simon & Schuster, 1976.

HARRY H. STEIN, "The Muckraking Book in America, 1946–1973," *Journalism Quarterly,* Vol. 52, No. 2 (Summer 1975).

1. Leonard Silk and David Vogel, "Rx for a Tarnished Image," *Saturday Review,* July 10, 1976, pp. 8–12.
2. *Ibid.*
3. Max Ways, "Business Needs to Do a Better Job of Explaining Itself," *Fortune,* September 1972.
4. Sylvan M. Barnet, Jr., "A Global Look at Advocacy," *Public Relations Journal,* Vol. 31, No. 11 (November 1975), gives detailed insight.
5. The Cutlip-Center survey of the calling, 1976–77, showed "Training Management in PR/PA" to be rated "important" by 62 percent of the respondents. Methods used by large firms are worthy of internship study.
6. From an Eaton Corp. kit of information. Suitable case study: What has happened to Comm/Pro? What is its ultimate range of topic issues?
7. For authoritative appraisal, see J.W. Click, "Corporate Identity Relationships with Public Relations," *Public Relations Quarterly,* Winter 1973, pp. 10–12 and 25.
8. For case-study materials, see Standard Oil of Indiana Divestiture Kit. Available from public affairs department, 200 E. Randolph Dr., Chicago, Ill. 60680.
9. "A Public Relations Shocker," *Business Week,* June 29, 1974.
10. See Irwin Ross, "Public Relations Isn't Kid-Glove Stuff at Mobil," *Fortune,* September 1976; also *Jack O'Dwyer's Newsletter,* September 1976.
11. Charles H. Zeanah, Director, Corporate Public Relations, Ethyl Corp., in a talk given to several professional groups in 1976.
12. From "Giving USA, 1976 Annual Report," American Association of Fund-Raising Counsel, Inc.; and "Annual Survey of Corporate Contributions, 1974," The Conference Board.
13. From a report of the Business Committee for the Arts, a survey of 68,456 businesses in 1976.
14. Patrick J. Buchanan, "Foundation Undercuts Its Support," *San Diego Union,* January 24, 1977.
15. The terms *shareholder, shareowner,* and *stockholder* are used here interchangeably.
16. Changes in corporate reporting requirements have been recorded annually for several years, including 1977, in the April issues of *Public Relations Journal.*
17. Some corporations, including General Mills, General Electric, AT&T, Westinghouse, Gulf Oil, IBM, Woolworth, Xerox, and U.S. Steel, have held regional meetings in major population centers—a step worth studying for the pros and cons.
18. Edie Fraser, president of Fraser, Rudn and Fuin, in "Consumerism in the Role of Public Relations," a speech, University of Georgia, October 22, 1976.
19. Alexander Trowbridge, president, The Conference Board, in "The Rising Tide of Consumerism," *Association Management,* October 1976.
20. "Disgruntled Customers Finally Get a Hearing," *Business Week,* April 21, 1975.
21. From an unpublished thesis, "The Corporate Inquiry Process," American University, Washington, D.C., December 1975.
22. Trowbridge, "The Rising Tide."

The concept of a business or professional association is a highly civilized one. It calls for what people do least well, subordinating their self interests to the betterment of all. And when members of the group are competitors, it seems an unnatural alliance that won't work. Yet it does, as the proliferation of associations has demonstrated.

HOWARD P. HUDSON

The Practice: trade associations, professional societies, and labor unions

Trade associations, professional societies, and labor unions exist to advance the interests of their members. This is done in three ways: *They provide information. They promote high standards of self-discipline. They present the organization's case to the general public and to government bodies at various levels.*

We will look at associations and societies together. Their membership is mainly employers or entrepreneurs. Then we'll look at unions, whose membership is mainly employees.

Associations and societies

Differentiation

Public relations programming is essentially the same for associations and societies. It is nonetheless helpful to understand the subtleties of structure and operation that distinguish one from the other.

The trade association is generally oriented commercially, promoting a product, like milk, or a service, like air travel. Members are predominantly companies or large individual entrepreneurs. The professional society generally promotes a field of knowledge, like chemistry or theology, or a skill, like writing. Members are, for the most part, individuals.

Sometimes several associations or societies join forces in promoting the same product or service. Similarly, several separate professional societies may be tied loosely together as a *Council* on Education, an *Academy* of Sciences, or an Insurance Information *Institute*.

Although associations and societies both seek to foster self-discipline and raise the ethical and performance standards of members, societies tend to be more insistent. They are more aware of their public stature and their academic underpinnings. Their awareness and discipline show up in a number of ways. For example, certain kinds of advertising or other promotion that are open to the American Tobacco Institute would be regarded as improper for the American Medical Association.

An epoch of gains

Associations and societies have proliferated. Commerce Department studies estimate that there are 20,000 national or international in scope, 25,000 regional or statewide, and 400,000 of local or county scope.[1] In addition, there are more than 1,000 professional societies.[2]

Some associations have small but mighty memberships. The Aluminum Association has only 65 members, but each one is a corporation. Others have long membership rosters. The National Association of Home Builders boasts 75,000 individual and company members. The American Medical Association has more than 220,000 dues-paying physicians as members.

The 17,000 U.S.-based associations cover a wide range of special-interest groupings. Among them are these:[3]

Trade	22%
Cultural	9.8
Health or welfare	9.2
Educational	7.8
Scientific, engineering, and technical	7.5
Public affairs, social welfare, religion, agriculture, and other specialties	43.7

A profile drawn by the American Society of Association Executives shows the *average* association to have an income of $500,000 and a staff of 17; therefore many obviously have budgets high in the millions, and staffs in the hundreds. Among these is the American Bankers Association (ABA), with an annual budget exceeding $24 million and a headquarters staff of more than 300. On the staff are ten registered lobbyists and a public relations department of six members.[4] The ABA spends about $3 million for advertising, including network television spots. It receives about half its income from dues assessed its 14,000 members, and half from selling publications and operating conferences, workshops, and seminars. Another huge association is the American Dairy Association, which has budgeted as much as $15 million to promote dairy products. Of this sum, $12 million went for advertising and sales promotion; $265,000 for market research and economics; $620,000 for information and publicity; $775,000 for program support and field services; and $775,000 to collaborating trade associations.[5]

The problem of serving many masters

In contrast with corporate internal allegiances—which serve a solidarity of interests, policies, and problems peculiar to each corporation—the association or society serves membership interests that may differ widely, shaped by a regional influence, a particular phase of a craft, or varying political, ethnic, or proprietary predispositions.

The difficulties a corporation has in marshaling its employees or gaining the support of a few publics are multiplied in an association seeking to satisfy a diversity of members and public opinion groupings. The inability of the association to speak for members with authority was illustrated when the attorney general of Iowa invited the heads of GM, Ford, and Chrysler to testify at a public hearing on auto safety. They declined. A representative of the Automobile Manufacturers Association refused to answer any questions dealing with the three companies because he was "not authorized to speak for any company's policy." And the Insurance Information Institute was confronted with a dilemma when its members were found divided on the matter of no-fault insurance.

In the diversity of members lies an inherent weakness of the association when it is confronted with handling a controversial issue. The managers of a corporation can decide with comparative ease whether—and the degree to which—the corporation's interests are affected by high or low tariffs, a drought in a southwestern state, a strike in the copper industry, or a change of administration in Washington. Union leaders can also be decisive. But such decisions are much more complex for an association's executives or elected officials. The views of all members, and perhaps an evaluation of which ones count most, must somehow be synthesized, represented, and weighed in decisions. This can be a lengthy process.

This problem is reflected in a statement of policy of the National Council of Farmer Cooperatives:

> We recognize the wide divergence of political opinion among our employees, member cooperative personnel, and farmer-owners. It would be inappropriate for us to express a partisan viewpoint. Therefore, we will support non-partisan programs, as far as is practicable, and will encourage employee participation in partisan programs of their choosing.

Thus, the natural inclination of the association in its traditional programming is to be limited to areas of action in which there is an obvious, predetermined unanimity or a substantial majority.

An era of change and gain

Traditional inclinations and public postures have been changing. While normal, noncontroversial services to members continue, the element of public advocacy by association and society spokesmen is growing. The need became evident in the 1960s with the passage of many regulatory laws. Actual change was spurred through the 1970s by the wave of regulation enforcement and consumer activism.

Explanations given for the change in posture vary with the self-interest being expressed. From a member's viewpoint, a more aggressive stance might be termed necessary to counter government intervention in the natural forces of commerce and competition. An executive in a regulatory agency might hold that there has been too little self-discipline within the trades and professions. To a bystander, it might seem that there has been too little responsiveness by private entrepreneurs to the needs and standards of the consuming, voting public.

But whatever the rationale, the crunch of controversy seems to have left little choice. The mounting tide of social and environmental concerns, protests, boycotts, and litigation simply could not be treated as routine business, as exceptions, or as nuisances. Response would not wait for an association consensus to develop. Nor would the adversaries accept silence.

Making matters worse, some of the situations were unexpected. Some involved only a few members. Some had implications far beyond the scope of the association's franchise. Nonetheless, they stained the public image of the association or society. Situation by situation, they called for quick reaction and response, spontaneous or planned.

A typical situation among hundreds calling for public response by authoritative spokesmen was the revelation that three of the nation's largest dairy-farmer cooperatives had given political gifts of up to $10,000 to members of the House Judiciary Committee. This made a national front-page story, just when that committee was investigating charges that President Nixon had been influenced by donations from the same groups. The story pointed out that the three dairy cooperatives controlled about one-fourth of the nation's milk production. Their identification with the American Dairy Association was implicit. Obviously, the association could expect to be asked by its members for its stance on conduct of this nature.[6]

Disapproval is not necessarily a complete or acceptable response. For example, it has been "customary" for lawyers all over the country to take kickbacks from title-insurance companies. The homeowner may not be aware of it, but he or she pays for this. Apparently, lawyers had not expected this to be publicized or to create a furor. When it was reported publicly, the American Bar Association board adopted a resolution that kickbacks were "highly improper." But subsequent news reports indicated that no real effort was being made to follow through with all the state bar associations. This prompted *Business Week* to label the profession editorially as having "an ethical blind spot."[7]

One lesson taught by such experiences is that the reputation and effectiveness of the whole association or society depends to an extent on its individual members. A posture that is purely defensive, defiant, or protective serves neither the consuming public nor the ultimate goals of the membership. Consequently, associations and professional societies have been increasingly prone to flex their advocacy muscles and their vocal chords.

The revamping of the Better Business Bureau is symptomatic. It had become widely regarded as a tool to fend off complaining consumers. It was restructured—with a name change to the Council of Better Business Bureaus, and with an articulate president, a public-affairs committee drawn from member companies, and a female consumer representative of stature. It set up mechanisms to assure consumers that manufacturers were both sensitive and responsive to inquiries and complaints. One mechanism was the creation of local consumer councils. Another was the financing of the National Advertising Review Board as a self-regulating device. And the CBBB president went on record often and positively.

Other symptoms of change are the publicly announced product recalls and rebates when indicated, and the acknowledgment of bribery as a "cost of doing business" abroad, of improper financing of political candidates, and of kickbacks. Then, there have been the admission that such federal programs as Medicare and Medicaid are open to exploitation, the advocacy of arbitration between parties in dispute, and counterattacks on the efficiency of government administration. The trend is clear.

Not all efforts to take overt or drastic action have been public opinion successes. When cattle growers, in protest over their plight, killed calves to attract attention, the action backfired. The pictures on TV revolted the public.

One association executive who finds the more aggressive stance a boon is James P. Low, president of the American Society of Association Executives. He says that association members for many years "took associations for granted . . .

456
CHAPTER 20

they were social or charitable investments . . . a chance to meet the good old boys." All this was changed, he points out, by Ralph Nader, whom he calls "the patron saint of trade associations."[8] Mr. Low also credits price controls for stimulating new activities by the association movement.

Not all associations and societies have assumed an aggressive stance. The degree of advocacy and public response to criticism or protest usually reflects the example set by those members who dominate a given association. As a generalization, however, more and more industrial and professional leaders are speaking up in efforts to shape public opinion when their interests were at issue. And staff spokesmen for their associations and societies have been following suit.

Some variations in approach

Opposition to federal, social, or regulatory schemes is not automatic. There is often the desirable option of fitting into the schemes and benefitting from them. This is the case with urban renewal and the banks, Social Security and the medical profession, low-cost housing and the builders, and aid to developing nations and maritime interests.

Some associations prefer a low public profile to public debate. This does not mean they are unconcerned or passive. More likely, the leaders feel that members' interests are better served by other tactics. One of the other approaches is embodied in efforts to influence decisions made by legislators at the national, state, and county levels. This approach involves lobbying. Most large associations and professional societies find it necessary and desirable to engage in sophisticated lobbying, and also to be prepared for open advocacy or public response.

The trek to Washington is well documented statistically. Of the 17,000 or more trade and professional organizations with headquarters in the United States, 26 percent now have them in Washington. This is a considerable increase from 19 percent during a five-year period in the early 1970s. These 4,500 or more Washington-based organizations employ more than 40,000 people and pump at least $1 billion into the economy.[9]

The growing importance of public relations

With such heavy stakes riding on effective communications in a climate of public skepticism and opposing advocacies, public relations strategy and skill assume major importance.

The following objectives provide a framework:

1. To provide members with helpful information.
2. To expand the association itself; to recruit young people.
3. To harmonize member viewpoints; to activate positive positions.
4. To promote the industry or profession.
5. To influence government attitudes or actions.
6. To improve products and services.
7. To gain popular support and combat adverse publicity.
8. To train recruits and provide programs of continuing education for all members.
9. To equate with social progress; to sponsor public-service programs.

10. To promote acceptable public behavior among members that will gain public credit and stave off government regulation.

The nature of programming

Much of what associations and societies do in the name of public relations is fixed into the annual rhythm—seeking new members, making reports to them, holding conferences. The Public Relations Society of America lists twelve activities that come under the heading of "normal routine":

- The preparation and dissemination of technical and educational publications, motion pictures and audio-visual materials.
- The sponsoring of conventions and meetings, instructional seminars and exhibitions.
- The handling of government contacts and the interpretation to members of the legislative and administrative actions of government agencies.
- The compilation and publication of relevant statistics.
- The preparation and distribution of news and informational material to the press, radio and television.
- Public service activities.
- The promulgation of codes and ethics.
- The dissemination of governmental and other standards to members.
- Cooperative research: scientific, social and economic.
- Institutional and/or product advertising on behalf of an industry and its products or on behalf of a field of professional or business endeavor, or in furtherance of such matters as public health, safety or welfare.
- The furtherance of good employer-employee relations.
- The promotion of accident prevention within the industry and among the public.[10]

The relative importance of functions

In the execution of programs and campaigns, six normal departmental functions are rated "important" in the following descending order:[11]

Function	Rated "important" by
News releases, media relations	95%
Communication policy decisions	83
Counseling top management	72
Producing publications	72
Producing speeches, scripts	70
Contacts with public officials	70

The public audience of first importance is "members," with "public officials" second, the "voting public" third, and "consumers" or "customers" fourth. Had the survey been confined to trade associations, "consumers" would have ranked higher. Comments volunteered by survey respondents concerning trends most frequently cited the growing emphasis on public affairs, on advocacy communications, and on the use of newsletters to reach constituents.

EXHIBIT 20-1

A Few Straws in the Association Wind

The National Education Association, nearly 2 million strong, "went political," throwing its substantial weight behind a presidential candidate.

The Los Angeles Chamber of Commerce came up with a catalog of 114 public-interest areas. It offered to supply the latest information on each, and the phone number of an expert in each field.

The Grocery Manufacturers of America came out openly and vigorously with facts and figures showing the amounts that growers, shippers, wholesalers, and retailers received in the prices of food items. The purpose was to head off more, or new, investigations.

The Institute of Life Insurance developed a "Businessman in Residence" program in which senior officials of insurance companies spent several weeks on university campuses teaching subjects *other than insurance,* usually social responsibility.

The California Bankers Association has its own "most wanted robbers" program, complete with posters and pictures taken by surveillance cameras during robberies. Rewards are offered for tips.

The National Nursing League seeks to have an active public relations committee appointed in each of its constituent communities.

The Toy Manufacturers of America spent $250,000 one year to prove publicly that it was making safe toys. The idea was that the Product Safety Commission could rest easy when it next drafted a listing of banned toys.

Labor unions

Organized labor unions, with about 20 million members, represent less than 25 percent of the nation's wage and salaried employees. Yet organized labor symbolizes and speaks for the working men and women of America.[12] The power of labor's voice in shaping national opinions and policies goes far beyond what might be suggested by its modest numerical share of the popular electorate. One reason is that the movement's specific and deeply held convictions hold strong attraction for adherents. Another is that union leadership has been able to obtain gains for members and to deliver a majority of their votes as a bloc in national elections.

The power of the union movement weighs heavily in another way. In the attainment of stated goals, and in the actions taken to achieve them, unions and their leadership share in the burden of responsibility for the health of the economy. With serious problems besetting the economy for more than a decade, it follows that there has been a decline in public confidence in unions as well as in business, government, and most professional bodies.

Surveys in 1974, during a recession, showed the movement to be third from the bottom among major institutions in public confidence. In 1976, with the nation emerging from that recession, a study based on Gallup survey data placed unions at the very bottom of the list.[13] The authors of the study attributed the poor showing mainly to the public assumption that labor's demands had helped refuel inflation, and to strikes by members of public-employee unions, including teachers, police, and firemen.

459

The role of public relations

Understandably, public relations has taken on added emphasis as the movement's political, educational, and community involvements have increasingly supplemented its traditional role in labor–management relations. The skills of public-information specialists and others have been augmented and honed to meet the needs of expanded, more sophisticated programs. It is indicative of this trend that most unions have designated a "public relations director," rather than a "publications director" who simply responded sporadically to news-media inquiries.

Awareness of the need to be more responsive constitutes a major change for the labor movement from the time when AFL-CIO President George Meany reputedly received his first public relations advice more than 50 years ago after saying: "Kick the damn reporter down the stairs." At this writing, no group in American society has a more identifiable, outspoken, and unquestioned spokesman than labor's George Meany. See Figure 20–2.

FIGURE 20–2 Press conference when AFL-CIO President George Meany announced support of the longshoremen in their decision to hold up loading of grain bound for the Soviet Union. Courtesy AFL-CIO.

Tools and media

Labor's primary public relations orientation remains to print media, both within and outside the labor movement. For example, although the AFL-CIO produces a national weekly network-radio news conference on specific issues, as well as filmed documentaries and audio tapes, its budget, according to Albert Zack, director of public relations, is insufficient to permit broad-scale electronic productions. This doesn't seem to bother Zack, who says, "A movement of people cannot be sold like deodorant, even though Americans once got a president that way." At the AFL-CIO, public relations concentrates on press contacts, preparation and distribution of materials on specific subjects, and interviews and press conferences to get across labor's point of view. See Figure 20–3.

Of increasing importance are the estimated 5,000 publications of unions on the national and local level. Many of these have improved their format and

FIGURE 20-3 On occasion unions do turn to print advertising to tell their story. Courtesy Teamsters union.

Jenny Rodhe never realized that TEAMSTERS are. . .

TEST PILOTS, Interior Decorators, Opticians, Telephone Repairmen, News Directors, Social Workers, Flight Control Agents, Surveyors, Draftsmen, Lab Technicians, Lab Analysts, Technicians, Bacteriology Employees, Lab Technicians . . .

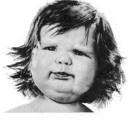

SCHOOL TEACHERS, Chemists, Chief Technicians, Lab Employees, X-Ray Helpers, Bacteriologists, Design Draftsmen, Technical Writers . . .

ANIMAL TRAINERS, Technical Radio Mechanics, Radio Operators, Cable Operators, Pharmacists, Audio & Video Engineers, Communication Technicians, Engineers . . .

NURSES, TV Technicians, Combo Technicians, Hotel & Reservation Clerks, Night Auditors, Dental Mechanics, Conductors, Railroad Trainmen, Funeral Directors, X-Ray Technicians . . .

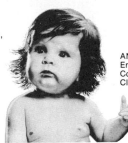

ANNOUNCERS, Embalmers, Case Aides, Cosmetic Employees, Clerical Employees, Head Regional Pharmacists, Animal Keepers, Surgical Technicians

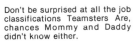

Don't be surprised at all the job classifications Teamsters Are, chances Mommy and Daddy didn't know either.
. . . Yes Jenny, Teamsters are truck drivers, too! . . .

TEAMSTERS
A part of the American Life

writing quality and toned down their rhetoric. They now receive special materials on issues affecting the movement from the International Labor Press Association. The largest publications receive a twice-weekly mimeographed national news service from the AFL-CIO, largest of all unions, with 16 million members.

The AFL-CIO program

The AFL-CIO publishes a monthly magazine, *The Federationist,* which features in-depth commentary on current issues, written by experts from both inside and outside the labor movement. A weekly tabloid newspaper, the *AFL-CIO News,* provides comprehensive coverage of national labor news.

In several cities, labor and management jointly sponsor trade and industry shows, the largest of which is staged by the AFL-CIO Union Label and Service Trades Department. Its annual "Union Industries Show" is held in a different city each year and emphasizes product promotion and public relations, stressing harmonious labor–management relations and the craftsmanship of American workers.

But in general, labor's main public relations thrust centers around legislative and political action. Public relations specialists make every effort to participate in the decision making, and thus maximize their "inside" role to better communicate labor's positions. Keeping union members infomed of collective bargaining and other union activities falls to labor's network of national, state, and local publications.

In an election year, labor endorses candidates whose records are favorable to its legislative goals. It uses its publications and direct mail to inform union members of the candidates it supports, and why. In addition, it seeks to register members and their families for voting, through direct contact—in person, by telephone, or by letter.

In summer schools run by individual unions, often on college campuses, and in its own George Meany Center for Labor Studies (founded in 1969 in Silver Spring, Maryland), the AFL-CIO seeks to develop public relations awareness and expertise among union officers. Schooling is also provided in a range of work-related subjects, such as collective bargaining, job evaluation and grievance procedures, basic economics, and labor law and history.

With rapid and broad expansion of the labor force in the professional, service, and government areas since the mid-1960s, the AFL-CIO has developed specialized councils and departments to serve the needs of these relatively new union members. Examples are the Public Employee Department, the Food and Beverage Trades Department, and the Council of AFL-CIO Unions of Professional Employees. Each of these bodies has developed specialized internal and external public relations programs.

The problem of strikes

Labor has had its problems in developing and sustaining a broad base of sympathetic support from the non-union lay public. This fact stems, of course, from the strategic use of work stoppages to gain concessions from employers. Stoppages sometimes have to be timed to be of maximum inconvenience generally and to exert the greatest pressure for settlement on the employer. The number of strikes annually comes to over 5,000. The number of employees who go out on strike, however, is less than 3 percent of total employment. Despite the inconveniences and the dollar costs to all involved, the strike weapon is considered essential to labor's success. It is visible, in contrast to management's policies or reactions and the bias of the news media, which are unseen. Palliatives for public inconvenience are part of the public relations functional participation.

Albert Zack points out that "any public relations man who thinks just of the general public—without any knowledge or concern for the needs of the workers involved—would advise unions not to go on strike. But unions have an obligation, first and foremost, to meet the needs of the people they represent. Heeding never-strike advice would mean putting the public's perception above the real needs of union members." *Strategic public relations often requires actions that will not be popular.* At the same time, Zack says, "A union has a concurrent obligation to let people know why it is striking and for what, and not 'kick the damn reporter down the stairs.' A union that lets management do all the talking to the press during negotiations faces an uninformed and unsympathetic, if not hostile, general public."

Thus, in the final analysis, it is labor's position that its success should be measured not on a barometer of public opinion of its "image," but on results. Similarly, labor public relations efforts should be measured by the quality and persuasiveness of information presented to union members and to the general public on important issues, rather than on any image-building advertising program that ignores a union's inescapable responsibility to its members.

A case study in conservation

The porpoise is not a food fish, but it is a lovable, trainable aquatic performer. The yellowfin tuna, a valuable species desirable for food, is friendly with the porpoise; in fact, they go around together. That simplifies finding tuna: Fishermen look for surfacing porpoise.

When the 1972 Marine Mammal Protection Act (MMPA) was passed to protect the porpoise, commercial tuna fishing became involved, because porpoise get caught in the purse-seining nets. Then they can't surface for needed oxygen, and they die. Dead porpoise have no market. They're throwaway waste.

Under the MMPA, a porpoise kill quota is set each year by the National Marine Fisheries Service (NMFS), for conservation reasons. The quota is based on how many have been killed in recent years, how many are estimated to be left, and the rate of reproduction.

The Fisheries Service set the 1977 kill quota at 29,920, compared with 134,000 killed in 1975 and an estimated kill of 78,000 in 1976. The tuna industry reacted as though *it* had suddenly become the endangered species. The industry opposed the quota and through the American Tunaboat Association, it said so.

Then, a bit later, in October 1976, the NMFS said, "That's enough porpoise killed; fishing must stop." The order was appealed to the Supreme Court, but it stuck. Fishing by U.S. boats stopped November 11. However, it did not necessarily stop also for tuna boats of foreign countries. They are not bound by U.S. laws or conservation policies, except where an international agreement exists.

Through December of that year, the fishing industry, joined by canners, appealed to the courts, sought relief from other government sources, and took its case to the consuming public.

News reports indicated that the industry had proposed a new quota system, that the industry was "weary of the fight," that individual owners and canners were negotiating to sell vessels to Mexico or to reregister them under foreign flags. Mutterings of mass violation were reported, despite threatened penalties of up to two years in prison, $25,000 fine, and confiscation of catch. Panama and Costa Rica were said to have issued invitations for reregistry. A UPI story said that a tuna boat monitored by researchers had experienced "marvelous success" in catching 1,050 tons of tuna and killing only 15 porpoise. The secret was in using a different mesh net. Adding to the incongruity, researchers said the results of the overall study would not be available until July 1977, halfway through the fishing season.

Early in 1977, about two dozen tuna vessels left San Diego to fish under surveillance of the Coast Guard. Some flew the American flag at half mast in protest.

The industry's appeal to the government for relief had been rejected in court. The court indicated to the association that it should be talking to Congress about the law protecting the porpoise. It was pointed out that the industry had had a four-year "period of grace" in which to make adjustments of fishing gear and techniques to reduce the kill gradually. *The industry had dragged its feet. Government had done little to meet the requirements of the law.*[14]

At this point, as a public relations consultant:

- What strikes you as the most effective way for the association to have responded to the court's "foot-dragging" conclusion? Keep in mind the court's suggestion that relief should be sought through Congress, and that that could be a lengthy process. If you favor another alternative, what is it?
- If the association had decided to seek a change in the 1972 MMPA, how would you have had it go about communicating with Congress? with the consuming public?
- Assuming an aggressive advocacy, how would you have had the association prepare to counter the appearance and the public posture of a "Society for the Preservation of the Porpoise"?
- Assuming a controversy, if not confrontation, what special public groupings might have been the natural allies of the tuna industry? What groups might have been the natural opponents? How might the association have been advised to exploit the potential alliance and neutralize or effectively oppose the potential opposition?

A case problem in compromise

You are in a public relations firm that has been called in by a state medical society caught up in a rash of malpractice suits leading to large monetary settlements. The society wants to persuade patients to sign agreements for arbitration of grievances rather than redress through the courts. This society has never had a professionally planned public relations program. You are assigned to develop a strategy (for oral delivery in class) that will detail your plans for research, action, communication, and evaluation during the next year. Be sure to include plans for actions intended to influence all publics involved, and for effective communications through all relevant media available.

ADDITIONAL READINGS

America's Working Women. New York: Vintage, 1976. A documentary history, 1600 to the present.

RAY AVERY, FRANK BIGGER, and RICHARD L. MOORE, "Search for Originality," *Public Relations Journal,* Vol. 32, No. 2 (February 1976). A case history, on the occasion of the 100th anniversary of the American Chemical Society.

A. LAWRENCE CHICKERING, ed., *Public Employee Unions.* San Francisco: Institute for Contemporary Studies, 1976.

JAMES DEAKEN, *The Lobbyists.* Washington, D.C.: The Public Affairs Press, 1966.

MARTEN S. ESTEY, *The Unions: Structure, Development, and Management.* New York: Harcourt Brace Jovanovich, 1976.

MARGARET FISH, ed., *Encyclopedia of Associations,* 7th ed., Vol. 1, "National Organizations." Detroit: Gale Research Co., 1972.

ROBERT D. HULME and RICHARD V. BEVAN, "The Blue-Collar Worker Goes on Salary," *Harvard Business Review,* March–April 1975.

LANE KIRKLAND, "Labor and the Press," an A.J. Liebling Memorial Lecture, San Francisco, September 29, 1975. Available from the AFL-CIO, Department of Public Relations.

JUANITA M. KREPS, *Contemporary Labor Economics: Issues, Analysis and Policies.* Belmont, Calif.: Wadsworth, 1974.

PHILIP LESLY, *Public Relations Handbook,* 4th ed. Englewood Cliffs, N.J.: Prentice-Hall, 1971. See Chapter 20, "Public Relations for Trade Associations," by J. Carroll Bateman.

A Look at Association Committees. Washington, D.C.: Chamber of Commerce of the United States.

HUGH MCCAHEY, *Association Public Relations Communications Guide.* Washington, D.C.: Chamber of Commerce of the United States, Association Department, 1968.

DANIEL QUINN MILLS, *Government, Labor and Inflation: Wage Stabilization in the United States.* Chicago: University of Chicago Press, 1975.

EDGAR PARSONS, *Audio-Visual Communications for Associations.* Washington, D.C.: Chamber of Commerce of the United States, Association Department.

J. ROLAND PENNOCK and JOHN W. CHAPMAN, *Voluntary Associations.* New York: Atherton Press, 1969.

Principles of Association Management. Washington, D.C.: American Society of Association Executives and Chamber of Commerce of the United States, 1975.

LEO TROY, "American Unions and Their Wealth," *Industrial Relations,* (Institute of Industrial Relations, University of California at Berkeley), Vol. 14, No. 2 (May 1975).

FOOTNOTES

1. William H. Jones, "Trade Associations Flourish," *Washington Post,* July 4, 1976, p. F-1.
2. Craig Colgate, Jr., ed., *Directory of Trade and Professional Associations of the U.S.* (Washington D.C.: Columbia Books, 1976).
3. Jones, "Trade Associations."
4. *Ibid.*
5. Information from the American Dairy Association.
6. "16 in Probe of Milk Fund Got Co-op Cash," *Chicago Tribune,* June 5, 1974, p. 1.
7. "The Bar's Ethical Blind Spot," *Business Week,* April 20, 1974, p. 124.
8. Jones, "Trade Associations."
9. "Washington Attracts More Trade Groups as Government Eyes Business Closely, *Wall Street Journal,* December 17, 1976, p. 1.
10. Business and Professional Section, Public Relations Society of America, *Association Public Relations.* Copies of this booklet are available on request from the society, at 845 Third Avenue, New York 10022.
11. From the survey of the calling by Cutlip and Center, 1976–77.
12. Much of the material in this segment, and all references to AFL-CIO programs and media, were supplied by Albert J. Zack, director, Public Relations Department, AFL-CIO.
13. James J. Kilpatrick, "Populace's Confidence on Upbeat," *San Diego Union,* January 5, 1977, p. B-6.
14. Benjamin Shore, "Tuna Industry's Appeal Rejected," *San Diego Union,* December 29, 1976, p. A-2.

21

The voluntary sector is a large and vital part of American society, more important today than ever. But the sector is undergoing economic strains.

GIVING IN AMERICA

The Practice: voluntary agencies, hospitals, and churches

The fields of social welfare, public health, hospitals, and churches are expanding. The growing number of nonprofit agencies—either tax- or gift-supported, or both—is almost staggering. The practice of public relations serves the full range of these institutions from charitable organizations to social-work agencies, health foundations, hospitals, libraries, religious bodies, and government agencies. And it furnishes them with as wide a range of services—from no formal programs at all, to simple promotional publicity, to full-scale departments.

Generally, the concepts and practice in the nonprofit field are enlarging. These agencies and their activities are supported, to a large extent, by public gifts and by taxation. Most are staffed by a small corps of paid professionals directing large groups of volunteer workers. Some use lay citizens as consultants and board members. One out of every ten service workers in the United States is employed by a nonprofit organization, as is one out of every six professionals.[1]

The primary public relations objectives are:

1. To raise funds to keep going and growing as needs enlarge.
2. To broaden and maintain volunteer participation.
3. To win public acceptance of new ideas and new concepts, many of which are highly controversial.
4. To effectively market programs and services.
5. To develop channels of communication with the disadvantaged who are cut off from society's mainstream.

It is estimated that, in addition to churches, colleges, and hospitals, there are 500,000 gift-supported agencies. Many of these are aided by United Way of America, the national association for local United Ways. There are 2,300 local United Way community-planning, allocating, and fund-raising organizations in the United States. In 1976, they raised and allocated $1,104,329,744 to support more than 36,000 programs and agencies involved in helping to meet human needs. About 84 percent went to organizations with programs for family and children's services, general dependency services, recreation, informal education,

467

and community planning. These figures represent an untold amount of promotion and participation in more than 2,000 campaigns. The United Way estimates that more than 37 million individuals, groups, and corporations took part in the 1976 fund drives. More than 8 million people serve as volunteers in United Way agencies year-round.

Philanthropic giving passed the $32 billion mark in 1977. In 1976, American citizens, corporations, and foundations gave $29.42 billion to charitable causes, an increase of 6.5 percent over the previous year. Of this sum, individuals contributed $21.4 billion—8.2 percent more than in 1974, roughly 2 percent of individuals' disposable income—80 percent of the grand total. The nation's corporations gave $1.35 billion, down from the year before owing to a sag in the economy. More than $2 billion was given by the nation's foundations, some 7.5 percent of all giving.[2] America's contributions to philanthropy have steadily increased in recent years, but there will have to be more if the needs of nonprofit agencies are to be met. *Much of this giving will come in response to planned, effective public relations programs.*

Also, these nonprofit agencies need more than funds. *They need public understanding and citizen participation to attain objectives* that are partly educational partly remedial, and partly palliative. From the viewpoint of the practitioner, this vast range of social-welfare activity has three important aspects.

First, there is the possibility of a career that offers deep satisfaction in the service of one's fellow man. It is one of broadening opportunities, especially for women. However, the financial rewards are comparatively lower than in other fields. *Second,* as the social-responsibility concept evolves for profit-making concerns, practitioners in business give an increasing amount of time and talent to these public causes. *Third,* as agencies multiply and competition for funds intensifies and state regulations become more difficult to comply with, the pressure on profit-making institutions likewise mounts. The decision as to which agencies to support and which requests to decline has become a tough problem for corporations and labor unions.

The importance of expert public relations practice is slowly but surely being recognized. Progress has been slower than in other fields, particularly at the state and community levels. The emphasis has been on publicity and promotion rather than on education. The cramp of funds has been a large factor in slowing full-scale programs. In the opinion of Don Bates, a leader in this field, there is need for more professionalism. "There are simply too many persons lacking in writing and editorial skills, as well as knowledge and background in the principles of the practice. Some of these problems are caused by the lack of funding, but that is only part of the difficulty."[3]

Other leaders in the nonprofit sector see a compelling need to overhaul the underlying principles of philanthropy to bring resources more in line with society's needs. For example, the Committee for Responsive Philanthropy argued:

> We view the issues of philanthropy and public needs in the context of a society in which power and resources are grossly misallocated. Ours is a society in which racial, ethnic, sexual and other forms of discrimination deny many the political, economic, and social advantages enjoyed by other Americans. . . .
>
> Given this general point of view, we view private philanthropy as a valuable tool to be used in meeting public needs. . . . We do not believe that philanthropy should have

as its primary purpose the support of private institutions performing essential public services that are being delivered by business or government.[4]

Welfare and health agencies

The perspective

To see this field in its full dimension, we must realize that, aside from those aided with food stamps, public housing, and Medicaid, there were 16.2 million public dependents and $17 billion being spent on public welfare in 1976 through government agencies. These welfare recipients represented half of all Americans living in poverty. Further, there were approximately 22 million people 17 years of age or older who were disabled to some extent by a chronic ailment at the start of this decade. In the late 1970s, 7 percent of the nation's work force was unemployed. Public and private agencies represent a still-imperfect response to society's needs and pose public relations problems of awesome complexity.

A Pennsylvania official sees the lack of adequate collaboration by these agencies as a prime problem. Norman V. Lourie, of the Pennsylvania Department of Public Welfare, asserted, "There is general consensus that, in relation to the complex and conflicting needs of our pluralistic society, the social services offered by the thousands of voluntary and governmental organizations . . . are not only inadequate in amount but also are generally poorly articulated and coordinated. . . . Oversimplistic, unplanned, uncoordinated solutions can lead to greater social fragmentation. . . . Responsible change is produced by cooperation of social forces." Solution to these complex problems must be accepted by a public now ambivalent in its attitudes toward welfare. A 1977 CBS–*New York Times* poll found that the public "is deeply antagonistic to the concept of public welfare yet strongly supports what welfare programs do." The term *welfare* has come to have a pejorative ring.

The work of welfare, health, and religious agencies is society's response to the consequences of its social disorganization. It is an outgrowth of the conflicts and maladjustments produced by America's high-speed, urbanized living and a shedding of the notion of "survival of the fittest." The desire to help others dates from ancient civilizations. The humanitarian urge to give aid and comfort to those needing them is deep within us. Caught up in the turmoil and tension of today's world, social work is in the midst of difficult problems and on the threshold of great opportunities.

A few older social-welfare leaders still insist upon the cloak of confidentiality that shielded welfare recipients in years past. But the concept has undergone profound change with the new militancy of those on welfare rolls. The press has long insisted on access to welfare records as an essential safeguard against waste, inefficiency, or other misuse of relief funds. Today, welfare clients and others are eager to identify themselves and explain their problems. However, identifying them can also mean exposing them to the harassment of extremists and taxpayers' groups. Still, welfare workers' overlong insistence on confidentiality may account for the nation's slowness in recognizing and dealing with its acute social problems.

The barriers are coming down in many areas. Television and other forces have increased the frequency of public appearances by adoptable children, the handicapped, and the mentally ill. For example, young patients at the Utah State Hospital for the Mentally Ill in Provo have taken the story of mental illness and the hospital's program to the community. These public appearances were found to be helpful therapy. In one year, adult patients provided guided tours through the hospital and participated in 126 panel presentations outside the hospital. But such novel ideas often meet resistance from the older generation of health and welfare executives.

Fund raising on a mass scale became big business after World War I. The writing of persuasive messages and mapping of campaigns became, more and more, a highly specialized task, bringing the professional publicist to philanthropy. Evart Routzahn launched his drive for recognition of this function when he read a paper, "Elements of a Social Publicity Program," at the National Conference of Social Work in 1920. Spontaneous response to his demand for "a new type worker in the social welfare field . . . trained in the technique of expressing social information in ways that will attract attention" led, ultimately, to formation of the National Publicity Council for Welfare Services in 1922. After several changes of title over the years, in 1975 this organization became the National Communications Council for Human Services, and in 1977 it was merged into the Public Relations Society of America. Nearly 1,000 practitioners joined the PRSA in this merger. Some of the council's services are being continued by the PRSA to serve those in the nonprofit field—including publication of the monthly newsletter, *Channels*.

Complete public understanding of social workers and their endeavors is yet to be achieved. Much of the criticism of welfare agencies stems from general misunderstandings, but workers in the field have to accept a great deal of responsibility for creating them. Arthur P. Miles, a professor of social work, lists these fountainheads of criticism: (1) intellectual confusion of the social sciences, (2) confusion over what should be held confidential in the public-welfare field, (3) gobbledygook of social workers, and (4) anti-intellectual trends in America.

Social agencies have yet to capitalize fully on thorough and frank accounting of their affairs to the public. Too many old-timers in this field have the attitude that "our noble motives and good works need no reporting to the donor citizen." There is need to distinguish between once-a-year mass publicity–promotion campaigns to raise funds and continuous and candid reporting, week in, week out.

Agencies are constantly working against deep prejudices, deep fears, and ignorance, which characteristically breed rumors and gossip. The American Red Cross has repeatedly proved its dedication to humanity, yet it is frequently the victim of malicious rumors. Many of the charges that were bandied about by Vietnam veterans were updated rumors common after the Spanish-American War. A child-welfare agency must be steeled against the day when a newspaper will make a sensational crusade of the agency's withdrawal, before the end of the probationary period, of a child put out for adoption. The answer to such unfounded, emotional attacks is to establish credibility through performance and to build enduring support based on education rather than emotion.

Nonprofit agencies must have appreciation and tolerance for the plight of today's citizen, hounded by the multiplying demands of this cause and that agency for funds, while his tax bill to pay for like services continues to rise. They must realize that each person can give only so much time to the doorbell-ringing chores he is asked to perform by a multitude of agencies. *More effective two-way communication will bring the desired rapport between agency and citizen.*

A convincing demonstration of this principle was provided by the program of the State Charities Aid Association in New York, outlined in Chapter 6, to bring the critics of public welfare face to face with the grim problems of poverty, illegitimacy, and illiteracy.

The program

A welfare agency starts out in an enviable position. Its sole reason for existence is to help people. The agency can gain ready entry to mass media and opinion leaders. It presumably has no selfish axe to grind. There are, however, organizations born to promote legal or social reform—Planned Parenthood, or Fight for Life, for example—that run head-on into solid blocs of opposition. Such controversial agencies and causes have a more difficult path. These days, the sale of Girl Scout cookies can stir up a protest, and the lack of security at a Girl Scout camp can become a serious public relations problem.

On the other hand, social agencies are "selling" intangibles. The United Way has widely proclaimed, "Everybody Benefits, Everybody Gives," but still, many people regard these agencies as existing for the "other fellow." Much of the service provided by social agencies is shunned because "it's charity." Many who could use these services simply do not know of their availability. There is difficulty in making concrete presentations of the tangible benefits derived by the individual citizen—and it is compounded for the charitable and family-service agencies because of the confidential relationship that must exist unless voluntarily given up by the client. Another problem for the United Funds is debate as to the relevance of long-standing Red Feather programs. And there are tough questions from both blacks and whites about priorities and leadership. "Is too much being funneled into middle-class institutions like the Boy Scouts rather than the ghetto?" "Must the organizations be dominated by the rich or wellborn or labor leaders, with minimum participation by the needy?"

Some social agencies have drifted into an undue reliance in their fund drives on the fear technique, exploiting the emotions. This approach may raise funds, but it doesn't serve well in the long run. The trend is in the direction of more positive appeals, but fear as a primary motive is being cast out too slowly by a few agencies. Use of emotional appeals has served to cloud the purpose of the agency in the public mind and to blunt its educational objectives. For example, people must be motivated to get periodic cancer checkups, not frightened into an attitude of hopelessness. As *Channels* observed, "Pitying words used in fund-raising messages sometimes hurt the cause for which the funds are sought. Describing persons who have a particular deformity or disease, for example, as 'helpless,' or 'hopeless' or 'incurable' tends to dehumanize them, deters the rehabilitation process, and generally reinforces the harmful stigma that already exists."

Concepts and programs for rehabilitation of society's unfortunates are constantly changing and are often a matter of emotional debate. The public's understanding and response to these problems suffers from time lag. For example: Some years ago, the media exposed the wretched conditions and human misery in New York State's Willowbrook Hospital for the mentally retarded. Public opinion forced construction of the Bronx Developmental Center, an expensive, futuristic complex that would permit the children to experience trees, people, activity. But in 1977, when it came time to open the new facility, critics of the institutional approach in treating the mentally retarded went to court to block its use. They argued that these patients are best treated in "environments that take as their design theme the images of conventional houses."[5] A story fraught with public relations problems.

More showmanship, less fear-mongering is emerging in social work. An example is the showmanship of Detroit's "Torch Drive." The Detroit Community Fund, at its annual lead-off, stages a parade worth seeing, one that brings out millions of Detroiters.

Fear and showmanship can sometimes be successfully blended to produce an effective educational effort in these emotion-laden fields—to wit, the campaign against cigarette smoking waged by the American Cancer Society and other health groups. The Cancer Society has been innovative and imaginative in many ways. Conscious that it had to reach young people, it enlisted poster artist Peter Max, whose colorful antismoking poster quickly became a collector's item. Other agencies have enlisted young people in their campaigns. High school students in California, Minnesota, New York, and other states have written and taped their own radio spots to fight smoking for the American Lung Association. The Heart Association encouraged young people to create posters for the heart cause in Maryland. In its many-faceted information campaign against drug abuse, the National Institute of Mental Health has recruited young talent from the ghetto to develop radio and poster messages for ghetto audiences. The Texas Health Careers program holds the attention of its high school assemblies with music and humorous audiovisual presentations.

The problems

There are many problems peculiar to this field. For one thing, there is the unflattering, untrue stereotype of the social worker. For another, there is social-work jargon, full of clichés and meaningless abstractions. As one editor commented, "Trying to catch such phrases as 'intergroup consciousness,' 'the weaving of the profession of social work into the community fabric,' *ad infinitum*, is like trying to catch a jellyfish in a net." There is also the fuzzy notion in some quarters that these agencies are tax-supported. This is caused by the blurring lines between voluntary work and government programs.

There is the language problem—what to call the person the agency is trying to help: "client," "patient," "customer," what? The very term "client" or "patient" connotes a difference in hierarchy. One social worker who raised this question added, "People who are so categorized are placed in a seeking, supplicant role, which implies a superiority on our part and a more dependent role on theirs." She answers the question, "Why don't we call them people? Perhaps this is one very important key to meaningful communication. People must be able to talk across the table in a free and sharing relationship, in which both participate with dignity and mutual respect. . . ."

Another problem is an overemphasis on publicity. This field pours out an endless flow of it. The national headquarters of such agencies as the United Way, Girl Scouts, Red Cross, Boy Scouts, Camp Fire Girls, and the health foundations have strong, competent publicity staffs that promote national coverage in the news media. At the local level, publicity is handled more often than not by volunteers with purely amateur standing. Many agencies could profit by putting more emphasis on the communication of ideas and less on getting publicity.[6]

The Camp Fire Girls, Inc., offers an example of how the headquarters public relations staffs can assist local units. Each year, the organization's small staff at New York City headquarters has developed a newsworthy theme for its annual birthday. One year it was "Make Mine Democracy," an economic-education program. Another year it was "Discovery Unlimited—An Adventure in Creative Living," a program devoted mainly to better understanding of crafts and arts. For each birthday program, the headquarters group has provided guidance kits to all the local councils, promoted the theme in its magazine, *Camp Fire Girls,* and climaxed the event with a network radio broadcast on the birthday date. The press is fully briefed on the details. The Camp Fire Girls stepped up this program for their fiftieth birthday with a Golden Jubilee Celebration, which had four goals: (1) to increase public understanding of the organization, (2) to update and enrich the program, (3) to render an outstanding service to the nation, and (4) to pay tribute to the vast body of dedicated volunteers across the nation. These goals were attained with a public relations staff of five professionals, two of them part-time, and four clerical assistants.

Leadership from national and state headquarters, coupled with follow-through at the local level, makes an unbeatable combination. The California division of the American Cancer Society brought out more than 186,000 California women to see showings of a film, "Breast Self-Examination," during a seven-week period. The success of this project was attributed to planning and local follow-through.[7]

Although the problems may differ from the United Fund to Family Welfare Service to Red Cross to National Council on Crime and Delinquency to Girl Scouts, the principles of programming are the same. In large cities, it is economical and effective to have one agency serving many of these volunteer groups. The pattern for this has been set by the Minneapolis Communications Center, a service funded primarily through Community Development Sharing Funds. The center was originally one of the 26 Model City programs. It provides public relations and related services to nonprofit organizations and community groups in the Twin Cities area.

Among the difficult problems facing health and welfare agencies is that of building a communications bridge between the black and white communities, the inner city and the outer city. Harold N. Weiner, a veteran practitioner in this field, has laid down the following plan to improve relationships and communications between social agencies and inner-city residents:

I. *Why New Efforts Are Needed*
   A. "Come-and-get-it" services fail to reach inner city adequately.
      1. Inner-city social disabilities and rates of mortality and morbidity from disease are far higher than in white urban and suburban communities.
      2. Most agencies lack service or information centers in inner city.
      3. Services that exist there are frequently second class.
      4. Interests of inner-city residents are not directly represented on boards of directors or staffs of most traditional agencies.
      5. Uncoordinated "marketing" of agency services compounds the difficulties of the poor in obtaining needed services.
   B. Traditional communication methods and messages rarely reach inner city.
      1. "White" mass media are unreliable routes to inner city.
      2. Pamphlets and other traditional materials are largely created by persons not in touch with inner-city needs, interests, language, etc.

3. Distribution of materials frequently stops short of inner city.

4. Competition of messages from a host of agencies creates confusing static.

5. Lack of involvement in inner-city problems has estranged many established agencies from that part of the community.

II. *What Kinds of Efforts Can Alter the Situation?*

A. Greater involvement of inner-city residents in affairs of social agencies.

1. As aides, staff members, committee and board members.

2. As advisors on agency communications and as communicators to and from the inner city.

3. As staff and volunteers in agency branch offices in inner-city neighborhoods.

4. As partners in developing training programs in inner city for civic leadership, for employment in social agencies.

B. Coordinated approaches by groups of agencies.

1. Establishment of inner-city health and welfare councils, staffed by local residents.

2. Creation of "supermarkets" of services and information to make available one-stop centers in inner-city neighborhoods.

3. Reallocation of agency services and budgets to make sufficient resources available to coordinated enterprises.

4. Development of coordinated social action programs by groups of agencies to help fill expressed inner-city needs.

C. Use of varied communication methods.

1. Work through inner-city organizations and institutions.

2. Enlist paid and volunteer workers from the inner city to help shape and deliver agency messages.

3. Reallocate agency public relations budgets to defray costs of communication research in inner city.

4. Allocate public relations resources to joint communication action with other agencies to make services better known and used.

5. Use black, Spanish-oriented media.

More effective communication with all sectors of society is imperative for nonprofit agencies. There is a growing public impatience with all inflexible, bureaucratic, and impersonal enterprises, and increased demand for straight talk from those in social agencies.

The years ahead

Welfare agencies must tightly link their programs to educating the public to accept enlightened social concepts in fields such as poverty, mental health, crime and correction, child welfare, and the problems of aging. *Planned, consistent programs* are required to break the barriers of public apathy, superstition, and the deadweight of indifference on these fronts. For example, only enlightened opinion will bring acceptance of sound rehabilitation and parole procedures in the field of crime and corrections. To counter opinions blended of vengeance and sloppy sentimentality, corrections leaders must persuade the public of the value of modern prisons and the supervised return of prisoners to society.[8] What can be accomplished is dramatically illustrated in the progress made in mental health since World War II.

The expanded range of activity and the mounting public bill for philanthropy have been financed in an inflated economy. In an economic headwind, social agencies are hard hit. The demand for their services multiplies in time of financial depression, but sources of funds shrink. Even with all the gains made, the pull on the citizen donor is still none too strong. Even in an economy loaded with cheap money, there is a strong tendency to "let George do it."

The tab for this vast range of social work can no longer be paid by the rich. It is from the upper and middle income groups that donor-supported agencies must get the bulk of their budgets. It is in the middle income group that a strong sense of responsibility must be built. The alternative is to transfer the burden to government; then all will pay, through compulsory contributions in the form of taxes. The donor-supported, volunteer-manned agency has an important innovative function. It must be maintained in the years ahead. *Leaders of these agencies must strive even harder to muster public support through public relations, support that will endure in good times or bad.*

Public relations for hospitals

The perspective

Hospitals, caught in the vise of rising public demands and escalating costs, are thrust more and more into public scrutiny. From 1950 to 1977, hospital costs rose 1,000 percent, far above costs for other goods and services. These rising costs are compounded of advances in medical technology and the cost of specialists to implement them. One clever way of depicting these costs is shown in Figure 21–1.

The complex problems involved in health care and in paying for it pose difficult public relations problems. As a consequence, doctors and health administrators are slowly becoming sensitive to this function's importance. A consultant, F. Gordon Davis, sees hospital administrators caught "in a sticky web of administrative uncertainty" because the hospital is "essentially an irrational concept." He sorts out the roots of today's major hospital public relations issues:

1. Perennially rising operating costs
2. Creeping nationalization
3. Popular insistence on all-encompassing health services
4. Third-party purchasing and fourth-party payment
5. Political vulnerability
6. Trend toward centralized planning of facilities
7. An outmoded charitable heritage
8. Distribution according to available dollars rather than geographic need
9. A product that is as feared and essential as it is costly[9]

Despite these difficult problems, hospital administrators are slow to employ professionally qualified practitioners. A recent survey on hospital public relations activities by the American Hospital Association's Bureau of Research Services found that 8.3 percent have none at all, and of the 91.7 percent that do, only 30 percent have an organized program. *Only one hospital in ten employed a full-time public relations officer.* Another 10 percent limp along with a part-time officer. Of those reporting organized programs, half dump this work on the administrator or his assistant as an additional duty. In terms of budgets, 80.2 percent (4,443 hospitals) allocate less than 1 percent of their expense budget to public relations. By way of contrast, the drug industry spends more than 8 percent of its budget on public relations.[10]

The Indiana Hospital Association followed up the AHA survey a year later. It found that 30 percent of Indiana's hospitals responding to the survey had some sort of an organized program. Some 4 percent reported no activities at all. A veteran Indiana practitioner says that of the 112 short-term acute-care hospitals in that state, only 20 employ public relations professionals. State university hospitals have led the way in public relations. Most of these have staffs of two or more professionals, large budgets, audiovisual departments, and so on. As hospital costs mount, as government constraints multiply, and as health consumerism intensifies, hospital administrators will have to confront their public relations problems and respond to them with professional counsel. Consequently, hospitals will provide an expanding area of employment for public relations graduates of the future.

FIGURE 21-1
One hospital found a clever way to demonstrate rising costs to its employees, visitors, and ambulatory patients. It set up a "store" and staged a "spring sale," attaching price tags to many of the items used in the hospital. Courtesy the Kennestone Hospital, Marietta, Georgia.

Medical men and hospital administrators, once coldly aloof and sternly professional, are developing a "public opinion consciousness" under pressure of mounting costs and criticism. Stung by such adjectives as "indifferent," "complacent," "smug," and even "arrogant," medical professionals, assisted by specialists, are coming to accept public relations as an essential part of medical practice. When charges against hospitals are catalogued in a widely sold book, *The Plot against the Patient,* major newspapers editorialize on "The Crisis in Health Care," and patients protest skyrocketing costs, only the obtuse would fail to see public relations' role in this vital field. Impetus is being provided by the American Society for Hospital Public Relations Directors. The American Hospital Association's *Public Relations Newsletter* stimulates innovation.

Public relations for medicine is also spearheaded by the growing number of practitioners serving the American Medical Association, the American Hospital Association, the American Nursing Association, Blue Cross, and similar groups at the national, state, and local levels. There is still too much effort expended, however, in justifying rather than correcting the irritants. Medical public relations needs to be more concerned with the "diseases" that blight relationships than with their "symptoms." There is also need for closer coordination of the several active programs in the health field.

On an average day, you can find in U.S. hospital beds more people than the combined populations of Boston and Cincinnati, plus some 45,000 newborn infants. The odds are that each of these infants will be confined in a hospital at least four times during its lifetime. More and more people are requiring and getting hospital care. The public is "hospital-conscious" as never before.

People do not have to be sold on the hospital; they want more hospital care. They do not have to be sold on doctors; they only want more of them and more opportunity to use them. What worries people most is the problem of financing their health needs. Unless this problem is met, the rest will not matter very much. Despite shorter average patient stays in hospitals, bills are up. And this problem of costs is the central one facing hospitals, too. Hospital deficits are swelling as the average deficit per patient is multiplied by an ever-growing stream of people entering hospitals. These deficits must be made up by either contributions or taxes.

Hospitals receive much criticism from state insurance commissioners, labor unions, employers, legislators, and other public spokesmen, principally because of hospital charges. For example, a General Motors official said that GM paid out $825 million in one recent year for hospital, medical, prescription-drug, and dental expense for its employees and their families—more than it paid for steel. And even though three-fourths of the population has some kind of hospital insurance, many millions of Americans do not. Nationalized health insurance appears probable for the 1980s.

Demand for broader-based support comes in the face of the highest patient rates in history. Alden Mills wrote:

> The voluntary hospitals have been expected to care for a larger number of free patients or patients who pay less than cost. . . . Increasing costs of operation have been particularly marked in the voluntary hospitals. These institutions have always been regarded as the pacemakers in hospital administration. . . . This country needs the leadership that they can provide. . . . To the voluntary hospital, adequate understanding, good will, and respect are today vital. . . . Lack of public support and generous respect may be fatal to voluntary institutions.[11]

The tax-supported municipal and state hospitals are likewise confronted with multiplying demands for treatment and the provision of new and expensive facilities. In either type of hospital, public support determines the answer to these problems. The sum of all this is that hospitals, from the smallest to the largest, need continuing programs directed by trained practitioners. The medical profession needs the intermediary in dealing with the public more than most groups do.

The program

In no field is painstaking attention to detail and bird-dogging of loose ends more important. A stay in the hospital is charged with emotion. The opportunities for irritations and ill will abound; but on the other hand, the hospital's opportunity to gain everlasting devotion is unequaled. On an average, every citizen is reached by the service of his community hospital at least once in every eight years. The basic requisite is considerate hospital service at reasonable rates. This means good medical care and efficient administration.

In many hospitals, there is a broad gap between "public relations" and patient care. Hospitals, like others, must learn that good performance should precede the news of it. Couple this principle to a planned program, and the hospitals have the means to meet their problems. Essentials of such a program are given in one planned for the Lancaster, Pennsylvania, General Hospital:

EMPLOYEE RELATIONSHIPS. Orienting an employee in the initial interview, providing a tour of the hospital, and giving him a personnel brochure. Informing employees through weekly publication, movies, bulletin boards, panel discussions, and pep talks in pay envelopes. Providing employee incentives and understanding through a clearly established wage scale, a vacation policy, a security program and an employee council as a channel of communication between management and staff, and plans for a termination interview. Using employees to tell the public the hospital story includes placing employee's family on mailing lists, hospital tours for families, and use of employees as speakers.

VOLUNTEER GROUPS. Informing members of the board of directors by providing full orientation, putting them on all mailing lists, and utilizing them as speakers and hospital representatives before public groups. Also providing appropriate recognition for their service. Keeping the volunteer auxiliaries thoroughly oriented, informed, and imbued with a sense of participation in hospital projects. Seeing that "Gray Ladies" are likewise given orientation, receive all hospital information, and are rewarded for their services.

MEDICAL STAFF. A contented staff essential to the best service and growth of the hospital. Definite and sound staff organization with working liaison between staff and hospital board. New staff men thoroughly oriented. Staff stimulated to help create means for the patient to better bear costs. Staff members continually made aware of variety of hospital problems. Staff, internes, and residents kept fully informed and educated as to importance of public relations consequences of their work.

PATIENTS. A voluntary hospital is a public utility. Patients are part of the society which owns and controls that utility. Demand the best of service. . . . Enter the hospital with a "combat mission" attitude. Their hospital experience a highly emotionalized one. Utilize this advantage. Admission interview to allay fears of hospitalization and financial worries. Understanding and appreciation of patient concept by all employees essential. The hospital interpreted to the patient, and convalescence is proper time to begin. Patient and visitors provided. Preadmission contacts also opportunity to win patient's understanding and goodwill.

Gordon McLean, director of public relations for St. Mary's Hospital, Evansville, Indiana, agrees with this kind of program. He writes, "In terms of priorities, I place employee relations first. As hospitals grow larger and employ more and more people, the lines of communication become very strained. In hospitals we have a wide disparity in educational levels and professional interests. We have many specialists, and specialists find it difficult to talk to one another."[12] Hospitals, once close-knit groups working for the well-being of humanity, have been forced by technology and public demand to become large business enterprises. Adjustment is difficult. Internal lines of communication must be kept open.

Norman Cousins, editor of the *Saturday Review,* in recounting his miraculous recovery from a near-fatal illness, wrote:

> I had a fast-growing conviction that a hospital is no place for a person who is seriously ill. The surprising lack of respect for basic sanitation; the rapidity with which staphylococci and other pathogenic organisms can run through an entire hospital; the extensive and sometimes promiscuous use of X-ray equipment; the seemingly indiscriminate administration of tranquilizers and powerful pain-killers, more for the convenience of hospital staff in managing patients than for therapeutic needs; and the regularity with which hospital routine takes precedence over the rest requirements of the patient (slumber, when it comes for an ill person, is an uncommon blessing and is not to be wantonly interrupted)—all these and other practices seemed to me to be critical shortcomings of the modern hospital.
>
> Perhaps the hospital's most serious failure was in the area of nutrition. It was not just that the meals were poorly balanced; what seemed inexcusable to me was the profusion of processed foods, some of which contained preservatives or harmful dyes. White bread, with its chemical softeners and bleached flour, was offered with every meal. Vegetables were often overcooked and thus deprived of much of their nutritional value. No wonder the 1969 White House Conference on Food, Nutrition, and Health made the melancholy observation that the great failure of medical schools is that they pay so little attention to the science of nutrition.

In response to vociferous patient criticism, many hospitals are junking the custom of 5 A.M. reveille, speeding admission procedures, dropping the requirement of payment in advance, providing tastier food and a choice of menus, and creating more pleasant surroundings. More medical people are coming to agree with Dr. Anthony J.J. Rourke, former president of the American Hospital Association, that "hospital rules must be set up for the benefit of the patient, not for the hospital or the doctor or the nurse." A writer found, in a 100-hospital survey, that those most affectionately regarded treated their customers as human beings, not as "symptoms with relatives attached."

One of the urgent problems facing hospital practitioners is that of building two-way communication with the minority and poverty communities. This starts with listening to angry demands for equal care in equal surroundings for these disadvantaged citizens. Michela Robbins Reichman, of San Francisco's Mount Zion Hospital and Medical Center, urges fellow practitioners, "We must identify

FIGURE 21-2   Patient-information literature.

I want to tell you about our operation at

VIRGINIA BAPTIST HOSPITAL

principles of patient care

Restoring your health involves the services of many
spital personnel; good communication is of utmost
portance while you are a patient at Madison General
pital.
ese "Principles

PATIENT QUESTIONNAIRE

tel-med tape library

a public service of st. mary's hospital and university health service

DON'T BE AFRAID OF HOSPITALS

by Norma Lee Browning
Chicago Tribune Staff Writer

the real issues behind the rhetoric, instead of responding emotionally to the rhetoric."

Patient relationships are more difficult in this era of consumerism. One result of this movement in the health field is the demand for a "Patient Bill of Rights." Although many hospitals try to steer clear of this term, because the hospital cannot control the relationships between patient and physician but, in a sense, provides only the "hall," some states have legislated a Patient Bill of Rights that health-care facilities must follow. Consumer groups are pressing hospitals and legislative leaders for this kind of law in other states. Another patient demand is the right to see and obtain copies of one's own medical record. This poses all sorts of problems for those involved in the care of the patient.

Typical of the new approach in hospital public relations is the attention given expectant mothers by Chicago's Michael Reese Hospital. Two months prior to expected delivery, the hospital sends the expectant mother (1) a letter confirming her room reservation; (2) a pre-admission registration form, which keeps admission delays to a minimum; (3) information about a special birth-announcement service sponsored by the hospital's Women's Board; (4) general hospital instructions, policies, and services; and (5) a folder about the availability of radio and TV sets with earphones. This is the positive approach.

To take the fright out of a child's first visit to the hospital, the St. Joseph Hospital, Albuquerque, New Mexico, organized pre-admission pediatric parties, scheduled on the second and fourth Saturdays every month. Parents accompany the future patients to the parties, and other children in the family are invited if they have not recently been exposed to a communicable disease. The parties include introduction to personnel of the pediatrics unit, a tour, a visit to the playroom, and a slide show. Visiting regulations are explained to parents.

Hospitals and the press

Doctors and hospitals are a vital news source. Direct, daily relationship with news media holds great potential and poses equally great problems. Hospital administrators who maintain cordial cooperation with the press are virtually assured of access to the community through these media. A hostile newspaper or radio station can blast a hospital's reputation by the factual reporting of an unfortunate mistake that cost a life. Such things do happen. Take the case of a Woonsocket, Rhode Island hospital. The newspaper, using subtlety and restraint, told with devastating effect the story of how a missing oxygen-tank wrench cost the life of a prematurely born baby.

As acknowledged in one hospital-doctor-press code:

It is mutually agreed that the primary interest and consideration of the physician and the hospital are the care and welfare of the patient. It is also agreed that newspapers, radio and television exist for the common good and function to bring matters of general interest to the public quickly and correctly, and therefore, the final decision of what is news remains with news personnel. . . . All significant events at a community hospital should be available to the public.

Each hospital should have available at all times an authorized spokesperson to answer inquiries from the media. The names of these designated persons, with telephone numbers and hours of availability, should be made known to telephone operators, admitting personnel, the information desk, nursing supervisors and nursing units, emergency rooms and other hospital personnel likely to receive calls from the news media. These names also should be made available to all news and information agencies in the community service area. Information requested, when duly authorized, should be provided to the media as rapidly as possible.[13]

Health care is a major news topic. But there is a gap between what the press wants for publication about personal injuries and illnesses and what the medical profession feels it can ethically reveal. The same is true in the matter of medical research and hospital innovations. The press demands for news run smack into the medical profession's code of ethics and the private relationship of doctor and patient. Hospitals, in turn, are circumscribed by doctors' attitudes and ethics. Leaders in both groups have been striving to gain agreement on mutually satisfactory procedures. The problems are that hospitals and their activities are complicated and technical, that the doctor–patient relationship must be a confidential one, that doctors have their own language, and that reporters are stretched too thin, with too little time to research a story. There has been some liberalization of what can be published and some relaxation in this medical–press relationship in recent years. *The public relations officer can speed this trend by preparing medical personnel for press interviews and by providing adequate background information to reporters.*

A number of codes have been worked out at state and local levels over the past few years. These codes are more guides than rigid rules. Such agreements recognize the press's obligation to report medical news adequately and accurately, and the related obligation of hospitals to serve as a cooperative news source. Both should be guided by three major considerations:

1. To safeguard the private rights of the individual, so that no hospital patient will be caused unnecessary embarrassment or discomfort, or be made the object of scorn or ridicule.
2. To report the news accurately, authoritatively, promptly.
3. To cooperate sincerely in all relationships.

Two trends of note

Multiplying controls: When President Carter asked Congress to impose a 9 percent limit on increase in costs per year, to halt construction of new facilities, and to limit investment in new technology, he symbolized the growing public constraints on hospital decision making that add to an already difficult public relations task. Federal legislation has granted great power to health-systems agencies, and working with them requires public relations skills. Once, when a hospital wanted to build a new wing or add a new service, it did so. No longer. For example, St. John's Hospital in Pittsburgh wanted to erect a $26 million building to replace its crumbling nineteenth-century structure. Its trustees were incensed when an area health-planning agency rejected the plan. After a futile appeal to the statewide health-planning agency, St. John's shelved its expansion plan.[14] Public justification for new additions and equipment must be gained through public relations. This underscores Charles Perrow's "Valley Hospital" study, which showed the need for public relations to control dependence by building a favorable reputation with salient publics.[15]

Marketing: One means of holding hospital costs down is to make maximum use of available facilities and beds. As of 1977, there was an excess of 100,000 hospital beds in the United States. As a consequence, there is renewed competition for patients, a competition that compels the practitioner to market a hospital's services. Position announcements for Director of Marketing for hospitals were beginning to appear in the late 1970s. This marketing concept has significance in a city such as Minneapolis, where there are more than 30 hospitals and low occupancy.

Marketing will become increasingly a part of the hospital public relations function. The fact is that all health organizations have been engaged in nonprofit marketing, but in an unorganized, ineffective manner. The marketing task is often found within the domain of the executive, the public relations director, or, in some cases, the development director. Each usually has a piece of the action, with no one in control of an integrated marketing plan.

Hospital marketing begins with the basic stance of the organization. Philip Kotler categorizes these as (1) *The Unresponsive Organization*—one that does nothing to measure the needs, perceptions, preferences, or satisfaction of its constituent publics; (2) *The Casually Responsive Organization*—one that shows an interest in learning about consumer needs and encourages inquiries and complaints; (3) *The Highly Responsive Organization*—one that relies on systematic information-collection procedures, such as formal opinion surveys and consumer panels. Kotler holds that marketing is the key to whether a hospital has a high or low bed census.[16]

A trend related to marketing is the increased demand that hospitals take an active role in public education for preventive health. Surely practitioners have the tools, experience, and knowledge of consumer behavior to aid in such outreach programs.

Public relations for churches

The perspective

An increasing number of the 240 church bodies in the United States are embracing the practice of public relations. In 1977, there were more than 131 million people, nearly 62 percent of the population, enrolled as church members. Communicating with this membership, reaching the public on social issues, and raising the funds to keep church work going require the aid of specialists. Caught between inflation on the one hand and declining support from local churches on the other, many major Protestant denominations were forced to reduce the size of staffs and missions in the early 1970s. This financial squeeze has underlined the importance of public relations.

Nonetheless, there is still some tendency among the clergy and lay leaders to shy clear of anything as "modern" and "secular" as public relations. Such churchmen ignore the past. From the earliest recorded history, religion has been spread by missionaries and travelers, hymns and sermons, parchment scrolls and books. The first book printed was Gutenberg's *Holy Bible*. The term *propaganda* originated in the Catholic Church in 1622 to describe the act of propagating the faith. Public relations is in reality but a new name for activities centuries old in the churches. It was St. Matthew who long ago said, "Let your light so shine among men that they may see your good works and glorify your Father which is in Heaven." And it was St. Paul who wisely advised those who would communicate with their fellow man, "Except ye utter by the tongue words easy to be understood, how shall it be known what is spoken? For ye shall speak into the air."

The major religious bodies have large staffs in their national headquarters, spending sizable sums on films and other media. Adoption of public relations techniques to bring the church to the people and the people to the church is dramatized by evangelist Billy Graham, who gets a good press. The *Wall Street Journal* reports, "A Billy Graham crusade is based on public relations, meticulous attention to detail and almost down-to-the-minute advance planning." More and more churches and religious agencies are determined to regain communion with those who have strayed. This trend will broaden and deepen. Religion's problems are born of the sense of "lost community," the intense competition for acceptance of ideas, and competition for membership. Typical of the increased use of public relations and advertising to promote a religion or a church was the national "I Found It" campaign in the 1970s. Bumper stickers, billboards, newspaper ads, and broadcast spots were used to publicize the slogan of the "Here's Life in America" mass-media campaign to stimulate evangelism at the local level.

The church can make a choice in the matter of continuing publicity, but it has no choice in the matter of relationships with society. Everything about a church is open to public view—its attitudes, needs, purposes, deficiencies, mistakes, and achievements. Each contributes to collective opinion. Churches are not immune to the power of public opinion. They must participate in public debates on moral issues. Also, they must effectively communicate their position and their principles. The president of the World Council of Churches in North America told members of that body, "Our biggest problem is our image." Said President Cynthia Wedel, "When people don't understand what we're doing, they resent the money their churches put in."

The program

So that "the whole Gospel might be brought to the whole world," churches are making increasing use of the mass media to express their spiritual message and views on social issues. In its public relations tasks, the church faces obstacles peculiar to it. These are the main ones:

1. The intangible nature of many religious activities.
2. The sacred nature of many activities, which demands a dignified approach.
3. The problem of showing the practical worth of religious values.
4. The problem of interpreting a program that follows a more or less traditional pattern.
5. The difficulty of knowing at which level to project ideas so that they will appeal to people of all ages.

There has been a rather distant and sometimes strained relationship between pulpit and press. Much of the current stress centers on improving the relations by telling the story of religion within the framework of standard news values. In the nineteenth century, the church relied mainly on the religious press to carry its message to the public. It has been estimated that in 1840, three-fourths of all the reading by the American people was religious. A century later, it was safe to say that the religious press's impact—in terms of copies published—was closer to one-tenth that of the secular press.[17] As the consequences of this shift in reading finally dawned on the clergy, they got busy. News media are responding.

A reexamination of news values is giving religion increased news value. The field of religious journalism is widening. As the mass media shed their traditional concept of religious news as church announcements, so must the clergy. As one newspaper editor once wrote, "Our newspaper, and I think it is generally true of

FIGURE 21–3 Photography can add greatly to the appeal of a message. Courtesy Religious Public Relations Council.

others, is trying to improve its religious news. But, as in any venture, it is the old story of cooperation. The church news is measured in terms of cooperation between newspaper and clergymen." Religious news has moved from the obituary or church page to the front page. Organized religion has not escaped the vortex of change, crisis, and confrontation, so it has become top news, often to a church's discomfiture.

This pressure for change and relevance in the church, and its present-day response, are vividly illustrated in William Jersey's exciting film, *A Time for Burning,* made for Lutheran Film Associates. This is a *verité* study of what happened to a midwestern congregation when racial integration was introduced by its young minister. Many church bodies have modernized their communications programs by utilizing the power of film and TV to bring their message to media-oriented audiences. For example, a group of Roman Catholic Franciscan religious communities, the Lutheran Church, the Southern Presbyterians, and the Mennonites, have all produced TV spot messages for national distribution. *Time* has observed, "It's a bit of a secret. Only those who on Sunday are not in church nor asleep nor buried in the papers know it: Religious TV is more varied, skilled, sophisticated, and imaginative than ever before."

A case study in promotion

Typical of the utilization of public relations to promote faith and support was promotion of a Holy Year program for Catholic children in an eastern city. The children, in grades 1–4, prepared for the "pilgrimage" for several weeks in advance. Overall coordination for the program was the responsibility of a committee of nuns from the faculties of five schools. This committee, following the basic steps outlined earlier in this book, identified their audiences, identified the messages they wished to communicate to those audiences, and utilized a variety of media for communicating those messages to those audiences.

The first and most important audience was the children themselves. The second was the children's teachers. A third audience was the parents of the children, who were informed that their children were taking part in an imaginative religious and educational program. Other audiences were the general Catholic public in the community and the public at large. News releases were sent to the daily newspapers, to the Catholic diocesan paper, to neighborhood weeklies, and to the local broadcast stations. Personal visits were made to religious writers. Because of the visual interest of the "pilgrimage" and the liturgy, special efforts were made to obtain photographic and TV coverage. Substantial press coverage resulted, although the TV stations did not cover this event.[18]

Fundraising

The big effort

There is a strong thread running through the warp and woof of all these fields. It is the eternal problem of raising sufficient funds to enable the agency, church, or hospital to keep going, one year to the next. Fund raising dominates the practice in all these areas. Sometimes it dominates the agency itself. Much of the thinking, planning, and publicizing in social, health, and religious agencies is tied to the coin container and the collection box. Competition is fierce. For example, in 1977 California's United Way was sued in state court by a smaller charity competing for payroll deductions on the grounds that the United Way was guilty of "monopolistic practices." As the *New York Times* headlined it, "Religious Fund-Raising Can Be Less Than a Lofty Calling."[19]

Philanthropy is big business in the United States, one of the biggest. To raise the money required takes a lot of publicity, promotion, organization, committee hours, and door-to-door canvassing. John Price Jones taught us, "Fund-raising is public relations, for without sound public relations no philanthropy can live long. . . . It takes better public relations to get a man to give a dollar than it does to convince him to spend a dollar. Favorable public opinion is the basis upon which American philanthropy has been built."[20]

Some of this giving is spontaneous; but by far most of it is in response to carefully organized and promoted campaigns, directed by professionals. Professional fund raising, a field closely allied with public relations, developed in the wake of World War I, when the potential of American philanthropy was realized for the first time.[21] It has been estimated that, year in and year out, professional fund-raising agencies help raise 25 cents of every philanthropic dollar. The professional fund raisers may serve as counselors to an organization's staff or they may fully staff and direct the campaign. Ethical fund raisers work only on a fixed-fee basis, not on percentage of money raised. Generally, the professional fund raiser is brought in for one-time capital fund drives, although some agencies retain them on a continuing advisory basis. The professional brings with him the accumulated experience of many drives.

Professional or amateur?

There is no pat answer to whether a fund-raising drive should be conducted by professionals or amateurs. There are advantages and disadvantages either way. The decision will depend on the organization and its environment. The professional can furnish expert know-how, skilled personnel, carefully screened donor lists, large libraries, and proved procedures. On the other hand, the fact that an outside firm is sharing in the proceeds can hurt the cause among prospective donors. The local, indigenous staff, sparked by zeal and enthusiasm, if expertly counseled, can often do an equally good job.

The most generally used adjunct in either case is the volunteer solicitor.[22] Volunteer fund raising has the advantage of broadly extending individual participation and thus increasing the opportunities for goodwill. There is a simple formula for raising money: Ask enough people to ask a lot of other people to ask for money.

Costs

A recurrent source of criticism for some of the national health groups is that campaign costs eat up as much as one-fourth of the money contributed. It is difficult to make broad generalizations about the ratio of campaign costs to total funds raised. Two axioms of business apply in most cases: (1) The ratio of costs to receipts gets smaller as the campaign goal gets larger; (2) a noncontinuing operation costs more per dollar raised than a continuing one. The professionals pretty well agree that it is impossible to run a campaign for funds at a cost of less than 5 percent of the total goal, and they regard 12 percent as a safe maximum. If costs appear to run over 15 percent, it is time to take another look. Most experts agree that publicity and promotion should be allocated at least one-fourth of the total campaign budget.

The Philanthropic Advisory Services of the Council of Better Business Bureaus has found that "there is no general agreement as to an 'acceptable' percentage for fund raising. Individual states differ in their definition of 'reasonable costs.' In nineteen states, there are no laws regulating the amount of money an organization can spend on fund raising. For the 36 states that do regulate charitable organizations, there is no consensus as to acceptable fund-raising costs." In the state of Washington, for example, an organization cannot spend more than 20 percent of its direct income; in Pennsylvania, the ceiling is 35 percent.

The Filer Commission recommended that "all larger tax-exempt charitable organizations except churches and church affiliates be required to prepare and make readily available detailed annual reports on their finances, programs, and priorities." Such reporting requirements now apply only to private foundations. Uniform accounting measures are also needed.

The principles

Whether the campaign is directed by a professional firm or the internal staff, the principles are the same. In most cases, however, it is unwise to leave the public relations planning and the publicity to amateurs, however zealous they may be. John Price Jones said, "Fully 50 percent of all the time and effort in the average fund-raising enterprise is in the field of public relations. Public relations in fund-raising demands a greater proportion of the entire effort than is required in industry." A successful campaign is compounded of a good cause, thorough fact-finding, careful planning, and skillful communication.

The American Association of Fund-Raising Counsel advises that before there can be a successful fund drive, these steps must come first:

1. *The house should be put in order*: the service program tested for effectiveness and efficiency; business management checked; investment policies scrutinized; governing boards and officers reviewed; the family assayed.
2. *The needs should be studied and documented*: what the institution proposes to "sell."
3. *The public relations should be "right"*: a clear indication of favorable opinion is an essential prerequisite.
4. *The governing board should lead the way*: support given the cause within the family.
5. *The area to be served should be defined.*
6. *Some estimate of total cost should be drafted.*

Common forms of fund-raising appeals include direct mail; sale of seals; benefits such as bazaars, balls, and dinners; radio and TV appeals and marathons; newspaper promotions; and direct door-to-door canvass. An effective use of the door-to-door method has been the March of Dimes porch-light campaign. Another fund-raising device, employed by the Red Cross, chambers of commerce, and others, is the membership campaign with various classes of membership. The annual membership drive is the backbone of several agency public relations fund-raising programs. It brings a sense of "belonging" and participation. This is why many organizations are reluctant to give up their separate drives and merge into united appeals.

The John Price Jones Company, one of the pioneer firms in the field, developed 25 principles of successful fund raising:[23]

Principles of preparation

1. The five essentials of a successful campaign are a strong case, effective leadership, conscientious workers, prospects willing and able to give, and sufficient funds to finance the campaign during the preliminary period. These five essentials should be weighed with scrupulous care before outlining a plan of campaign.
2. Committee work and publicity work should be mapped out in advance. The correlation of these two lines of activity, all designed toward bringing a trained and enthusiastic worker face to face with a sympathetic and well-informed prospect, is fundamental to the success of any fund-raising effort.
3. The cost of a campaign, within reasonable limits, should be estimated in advance.
4. All campaign activities should be given a time limit. Dates provide the only insurance for a proper correlation of committee work, list work, publicity, and canvassing.

Principles of committee work

1. The originating group, whether a committee or a board of trustees, should be a representative body.
2. The necessity for strong leadership is inversely proportional to the strength of the appeal.
3. The effectiveness of the group is conditioned by the degree to which individuals will accept personal responsibility.
4. The activity of the originating group determines the activity of all subordinate groups: The originating group is the inevitable yardstick both for giving and for working.
5. Committees are more responsive critically than creatively. In asking any group for ideas on a plan of action, for suggestions on a list of prospects . . . give each member of the group a copy of a plan.

Principles of public relations

1. The case must be bigger than the institution. The first object of publicity is to sell an idea; the second, to sell the means for its accomplishment.
2. Printed material should appeal both to the emotions and to the intellect.
3. Publicity must have continuity.
4. Publicity should proceed from the general to the specific. Interest in an idea proceeds from an appeal of general application.
5. Cheap publicity material is expensive. Quality in publicity pays dividends.
6. Publicity should be positive and not negative. Effective publicity always plays up elements of strength.

Principles of operation

1. A campaign should not only solve immediate financial need, but should lay a firm foundation for the future.
2. Solicitation should proceed in six steps: listing, rating, assignments, cultivation, canvassing, and the follow-up.
3. Effective canvassing answers five questions—why, where, who, what, and how.
4. Campaigns should periodically reach a climax point. The climax is essential in arousing concentrated interest.

5. All canvassing, even for special gifts, should be conducted in an atmosphere of universality. "What are others doing?" is the common query of all prospects, large and small.
6. Campaigns should be conducted under a steady and constant pressure.
7. The time to be spent on a campaign varies directly with the size of the goal and inversely with the popularity of the appeal.
8. The direct appeal for help should be made when the interest is at its peak.
9. Ask for ideas, not for money. The canvasser should first interest his prospect in an idea.
10. There are four tests of the effective operation of a campaign: quality, quantity, cost, and time.

Even a cursory scanning of this blueprint will indicate the hours upon hours of planning and preparation and the amount of energy required. Such a well-organized campaign for a good cause will get members—and money. In planning the public relations part of the campaign, keep these objectives in mind: (1) Appeal to the broad general public to create an atmosphere of universality, and (2) endeavor to reach individuals for a direct response.

Case problem

For many years now, University City's United Givers Fund has followed the conventional pattern of concentrating its publicity on the annual fund drive, which takes place the last two weeks of October. This fund embraces 30 nonprofit welfare agencies. Reliance for year-round educational efforts has been placed on the volunteer publicity chairmen in each of the 30 agencies. Because last year's fund appeal fell slightly short of the announced quota, fund officers have done considerable probing to determine the possible reasons. Among other things, they found a lack of public understanding of the needs of the individual agencies and of the relationship of the United Fund to such institutions as the local YMCA. The new chairman appointed a year-round public relations committee.

The purpose of the committee is "to evaluate public opinion and develop a program of activities that will create better understanding, goodwill, and acceptance by both the general public and special publics—agency boards, agency staffs, clergy, clients, givers, government leaders, labor leaders, business leaders, media personnel, etc." You have been called in as the public relations consultant to this committee of laymen. After the necessary fact-finding, including a study of the United Way, draft a year-round public relations program for the fund and its constituent agencies that will utilize available manpower and be most economical. The fund employs one person to handle its publicity at present.

ADDITIONAL READINGS

SPENCER ALBERT, "Lenox Hill's Outreach Program: Exhibit, Publications Inform Community about Health Hazards, Health Care," *Hospitals,* Vol. 46 (December 16, 1972).

J.A. BAIRD, JR., "Three Fund-Raising Myths Which Hinder Competition for Funds," *Fund Raising Management,* Vol. 4 (November/December 1972).

DON BATES, "Non-Profit Health and Social Welfare Public Relations Comes of Age," *Public Relations Journal,* Vol. 32 (August 1976).

ROBERT L. BISHOP, "Anxiety and Readership of Health Information," *Journalism Quarterly,* Vol. 51 (Spring 1974).

BEE F. BLOCK and M. ELLIOTT TAYLOR, "Bridging the Public Relations Gap between Hospital Provider and Consumer," *Public Relations Journal,* Vol. 28 (August 1972).

ROBERT BRUSTEIN, "Can the Arts Go On?" *New York Times Magazine,* July 10, 1977.

ABEL A. HANSON, *Guides to Successful Fund Raising.* New York: Columbia University Bureau of Publications, 1961.

B.F. JACKSON, ed., *Television-Radio-Film for Churchmen.* Nashville, Tenn.: Abingdon, 1969. How to use the electronic media effectively to further church work.

HAROLD P. KURTZ, *Public Relations for Hospitals.* Springfield, Ill.: Charles P. Thomas, 1969. A handbook for beginners.

WILLIAM A. MINDAK and H. MALCOLM BYBEE, "Marketing's Application to Fund Raising," *Journal of Marketing,* Vol. 35 (July 1971).

WILLARD PLEUTHNER, *More Power for Your Church.* New York: Farrar, Straus & Giroux, 1952.

BETTY RICE, *Public Relations for Public Libraries: Creative Problem Solving.* New York: H.W. Wilson, 1972.

FRANCES SCHMIDT and HAROLD N. WEINER, eds., *Public Relations in Health and Welfare.* New York: Columbia University Press, 1966.

HAROLD J. SEYMOUR, *Designs for Fund Raising.* New York: McGraw-Hill, 1966.

SUSAN SHEEHAN, *A Welfare Mother.* Boston: Houghton Mifflin, 1976. A close-up view of one welfare recipient that makes the "mess" comprehensible.

POLLY J. TOYNBEE. *Patients,* New York: Harcourt Brace Jovanovich, 1977.

LEONARD A. WOOD, "How the Public Views Voluntary Health and Social Welfare Organizations," *Public Relations Journal,* Vol. 33 (March 1977).

FOOTNOTES

1. Commission on Private Philanthropy and Public Needs, *Giving in America, Toward a Stronger Voluntary Sector* (Washington, D.C., 1975). This 240-page report is essential reading for practitioners in the nonprofit sector. Leonard L. Silverstein was executive director of the study. The commission later became known as the Filer Commission, from the name of its chairman, John Filer of Aetna Life & Casualty Co.

2. Data from *Giving USA,* published annually by the American Association of Fund-Raising Counsel, Inc., 500 Fifth Avenue, New York City 10036. For what agencies qualify for tax-deductible gifts under federal law, see Internal Revenue Code, sections 501(c)(3) through 501(c)(18) and section 501(d).

3. Letter to the authors, dated April 27, 1976.

4. *Donee Group Report,* Committee for Responsive Philanthropy, 1000 Wisconsin Avenue N.W., Washington, D.C. 20007. This report was published in 1976 in response to the Filer Commission report published in 1975.

5. *New York Times,* May 3, 1977, pp. 43 and 46.

6. For a case study in national organizations, see Harold P. Levy, *Building a Popular Movement* (New York: Russell Sage Foundation, 1944).

7. Publicity generated by the voluntary health agencies occasionally comes under fire for being less than candid. For example, see Daniel S. Greenberg, "A Critical Look at Cancer Coverage," *Columbia Journalism Review,* Vol. 13, January/February 1975.

8. For illustration, see James F. Donohue, "Social Action Makes a Prison Break," *Public Relations Journal,* Vol. 25 (October 1969).

9. F. Gordon Davis, "Public Relations Dilemma of an Unwanted Service," *Public Relations Journal,* Vol. 28 (August 1972).

10. In *Channels'* "Communication Forum," January 1977, a discussion of the hospital budget by Jerry Stremel, Poudre Valley Memorial Hospital, Fort Collins, Colorado.

11. Alden Mills, *Hospital Public Relations Today* (Berwyn, Ill.: Physicians Record Co., 1964). A pioneer book in this field.

12. In a letter to the authors, December 14, 1976. Mr. McLean was most helpful in revising this section.

13. State Medical Society of Wisconsin and Wisconsin Hospital Association, *A Guide for Physicians, Hospitals, and News Media,* rev. ed. (Madison, Wis.: The Society, 1977).

14. Gay Sands Miller, "Agencies Act to Lower Health Bills by Saying No to Bigger Hospitals," *Wall Street Journal,* May 5, 1977.

15. "Organizational Prestige: Some Functions and Dysfunctions," *American Journal of Sociology,* Vol. 66, pp. 335–41. A highly theoretical study of a hospital's public relations.

16. Philip Kotler, *Marketing for Nonprofit Organizations*

(Englewood Cliffs, N.J.: Prentice-Hall, 1975). A helpful book for health communicators. Kotler tends to equate marketing with public relations.

17. For a close look, see Martin E. Marty and others, *The Religious Press in America* (New York: Holt, Rinehart & Winston, 1963).

18. Condensed from *Religious Public Relations Handbook,* p. 7. This is a how-to-do-it manual for local churches, published by the Religious Public Relations Council, 475 Riverside Drive, New York, N.Y. 10027.

19. For one example, Paul N. Williams, "Boys Town: An Exposé without Bad Guys," *Columbia Journalism Review,* Vol. 13, January/February 1975. Another questionable fund-raising campaign, that of the Pallottine Fathers of Baltimore, was exposed in 1975. Between 1970 and 1975, this group spent less than $800,000 out of $62 million raised for its avowed purpose of aiding needy missions abroad. The Fund's director was indicted Jan. 6, 1978. (*New York Times,* Jan. 7, 1978, p. 8).

20. John Price Jones, in *The Engineering of Consent,* ed. Edward L. Bernays (Norman: University of Oklahoma Press, 1955), p. 159.

21. For the full story, see Scott M. Cutlip, *Fund Raising in the United States: Its Role in America's Philanthropy* (New Brunswick, N.J.: Rutgers University Press, 1965). This comprehensive history illustrates the impact of public relations on America's institutions.

22. For a scholarly study of the volunteer, his or her role and motivation, see David L. Sills, *The Volunteers: Means and Ends in a National Organization* (New York: Free Press, 1957). Also helpful: Gordon Manser and Rosemary Higgins Case, *Voluntarism at the Crossroads* (New York: Family Service Association of America, 1977). The authors examine problems confronting the voluntary sector and find voluntarism and philanthropy are in trouble.

23. In an undated pamphlet published a few years ago by the Jones firm. It has since merged with the George Brakeley fund-raising firm.

Citizens are increasingly disenchanted with their government
because they know so little about what it is doing, distrust
much of the information they do receive, and doubt their ability
to have input on large decisions.

CARLTON E. SPITZER

The Practice: governments and citizens

As the impact and extent of government increase, the need for adequate communication between public official and citizen becomes more urgent. Yet inescapable forces tend to drive them farther and farther apart. This problem is being met, to some degree, by public relations.

Government has become increasingly a matter of administration. A vast machinery of commissions, boards, bureaus—*bureaucracy*—has grown up to meet the complex problems of a nation mobilized to discharge its leadership in a divided world and to deal with its mounting energy, urban, and racial problems at home. There are some 86,000 separate units of government in America. One of the crucial problems is to handle today's issues without destroying popular government. Central to this problem is communication from government to citizen, citizen to government. As William Rivers notes, "Information policy has been at the very center of governing the United States from the beginning."

Government today—federal, state, and local—is so complex and often so remote that citizens tend to become apathetic and bewildered. Who can determine the exact number of billions of dollars and kinds of weapons required to provide adequate military security? Who can assert with confidence the solution for difficult problems in foreign relations? Who can devise a solution to the welfare problem, or come up with a plan for an effective health-care delivery system? It is hard for the busy, self-centered citizen to become interested in things he cannot easily understand. Relentlessly, the problems and pressures of society are putting increasing strains on the conventions of government.

The gulf between the citizen and his government tends to widen as decision making moves away from him. Centralization and concentration of government produce a vitiating sense of remoteness. *Government often appears to the citizen as just a bundle of entanglements among special-interest groups.* Urban renewal, for example, seems to be more a private fight between the real estate interests and the low-income groups than a significant public issue. Public apathy, well termed the "loss of citizenship," is sharply etched in each election by the millions of Americans who do not vote. For example, in the 1976 presidential election, only 53.3 percent of the nation's 150 million eligible voters voted, a decline from 55.4

percent in 1972. There are other evidences of default in citizenship and other reasons for it. Central to this problem is "the simple fact that the stuff of public life eludes the grasp of the ordinary man."[1]

The necessity and complexity of the government information task is clearly seen when a secretary of agriculture says that one reason people go hungry in America is their ignorance of food stamps. The difficulty of diffusing government information was underscored by a Health, Education and Welfare Department official who spent three days living in the poverty area of Baltimore: "Judging by observation and conversation with health and welfare clients—confirmed by workers—publications, newspapers, radio and TV do not reach the Baltimore poor. Word-of-mouth from a neighbor, minister, or block leader is the common channel."[2]

The breakdown of communication between citizens and a government they see as unresponsive is reflected in the low esteem in which government generally and the Congress, White House, and executive agencies are held. In the view of the Thirty-Second American Assembly:

> Millions of Americans view government as distant and unresponsive, if not hostile. Though often the targets of the resentment which ensues, government officials are usually not the cause of remoteness, but sometimes its victims. Dehumanized government derives from the impersonality of modern mass society. . . . There is a need in today's large and complex government for mechanisms devoted solely to receiving, examining, and channeling citizens' complaints, and securing expeditious and impartial redress.[3]

President Jimmy Carter sensed this in his two-year campaign for the White House. Once in office, he quickly set about putting American citizens in touch with their government again. He did this with fireside chats, first used effectively by President Franklin D. Roosevelt; telephone call-ins to the White House, which brought the president millions of calls and hard questions; attendance at town meetings; regional White House conferences; the mailing of questionnaires on a large scale; and easy accessibility to the news media. He sought to give ordinary citizens a sense of being in communication with the president and other officials. He set the pace for increased use of "Main Street" techniques—town-hall meetings, "accountability" sessions, walks along the city streets, toll-free call-in lines, TV shows with questions and answers, and frequent news conferences.[4] Such techniques rely in the end on media coverage for their reach and effectiveness, underscoring the prime role the media play in government.

The maze of government needs to be explained, interpreted, and clarified. Each person has only a small amount of time and attention to give to his government. Today's citizen needs a system of communications that will give him the same voice and understanding that his forefathers acquired in the town meeting. By the same token, today's administrators need the face-to-face relationships that their predecessors of years ago had. They dare not lose the common touch. The bureaucrat must guard himself or herself against isolation and insulation from the people of Punxsutawney and Prairie du Sac whose lives he or she so profoundly affects. This is an age-old problem, but one greatly magnified by the accelerating changes of the Space Age.

Effective administration must grow out of the lives and problems of the people rather than being imposed from above. Skilled, conscientious practitioners can contribute much to solving these problems. Zechariah Chafee, Jr., said, "Government information can play a vital part in the cause of good administration by exploring the impact of new social forces, discovering strains and tensions before they become acute, and encouraging a positive sense of unity and national direction."[5]

Reasonable people, in government and out, agree that there is real need and ample justification for a more effective transmission belt. In the words of one practitioner, *"Democracy will live where there is free communication of dependable information"* (italics ours). This problem raises anew and with fresh urgency a question posed by Aristotle centuries ago: "The environment is complex and man's political capacity is simple. Can a bridge be built between them?" In a real sense, as one observer points out, "while we Americans are many times as numerous as we once were and necessarily confront vastly more complex problems, our source of information and means for popular participation in the democratic dialogue are being ever more limited." This writer, John Cogley, asked, "Do our growing bureaucracies, our galloping technology, our bigness, and the headlong advance of science make government of the people, by the people, and for the people irrelevant?"

Much of the meaningful dialogue required to make democracy work today is shaped and phrased by the public relations practitioner. This imposes a civic obligation on him as he becomes, increasingly, the intermediary between the candidate or the public official and the citizens.

Public relations' role in politics

As political campaign costs skyrocket and the skills of persuasive communication become more specialized, the practitioner is playing an ever more important role in campaigns and in government. Political publicity is one of the oldest phases of the practice, but it never had the scope, shape, and reach that it has today. The 1976 campaigns for President and the Congress cost $177 million.

The public dialogue begins with the political campaign. Stanley Kelley observes:

> Political campaigns are the principal institution in which this interaction between politician and electorate occurs, and the most striking role of the public relations man is that of a campaigner. The particular kind of campaign activity with which he is most often concerned has, in terms of the theory . . . of democratic government, an importance all its own. For the public relations man is occupied with directing the course of public discussion as it relates to the selection of government officials and the settlement of controversial issues of public policy.[6]

The role of public relations in political campaigns and in government—the two are inextricably interrelated—is expanding, and public relations' impact is under scrutiny. Leon Epstein, a political scientist, thinks that the increased use of mass-media publicity and of behavioral research permits a direct appeal to the voter that is making our political parties *"relatively* less important." He notes the increased criticism of the public relations role: "Much of the criticism of the newer techniques is centered about the enterprise of public relations as such. The idea of selling candidates like soap is offensive to all those who . . . believe in the capacity of the voters to absorb information and make reasoned decisions. . . . Using the professional skills of public relations in political communication seems to involve an unusually frank rejection of rationalist assumptions about political behavior." [7]

Public relations' role in government

Certainly, the foundation stones of Aristotle's bridge must be *informative, candid, continuous reporting by government,* and more *accessible channels to government for all citizens,* not just those with an "in." The rise of the service state has had many profound implications, some of which were sketched in Chapter 5. Two are of special concern here.

First, governmental power has steadily ebbed from the community to the statehouse to the federal government. Important decision making has likewise shifted from the more responsive legislative bodies to less accessible regulatory and administrative agencies. The result is to make government increasingly remote from the voter's reach. Trying to get a piece of information, to have a problem solved, or to make a need known, the frustrated citizen often gives up in despair. He fulminates against "red tape." Or else he turns to a lawyer, lobbyist, legislator, public relations man, or political "fixer." That this new relationship is not satisfactory is demonstrated by widespread suspicion and distrust of government, attacks on bureaucrats (the word itself has a derogatory connotation), protests against the ever-mounting tax bill, and finally, default of citizenship by millions. It also breeds, inevitably, influence peddlers who gnaw at the vitals of government.

Second, the news media are grappling with the task of reporting under the heavy hand of news values fashioned in frontier days and with too few reporters. In days gone by, news of government was a relatively simple matter of personalities, oratorical political campaigns, trust-busting, and the like. It was entirely different from reporting world affairs, atomic energy, mental health, space travel, controversies over matters affecting equal opportunity, the environment, and other complex subject matter. *Interpreting the complexities of government requires trained specialists and often takes more time than deadlines permit.*

Much progress has been made by the media in government reporting. But there is still need for government to strengthen and supplement today's reporting by the media. *Time* has observed, "The shortcomings in coverage [of Washington] are not always the fault of the reporters; they are due to the size of the job." This is more true today than in 1939 when James L. McCamy observed, "The glut of occurrences each day in the vast and chaotic web of federal administration simply could not be followed by news staffs unless they were enlarged by many times their present size." Howard K. Smith acknowledged in the 1970s that "the number of P.R. men has grown to double the number of reporters in this city." All this was underlined when a National Press Club Committee criticized President Ford's press secretary, Ron Nessen: ". . . a press secretary must probe within the White House to learn what is going on, and we are not persuaded that Nessen has done all that he could in this regard."

Government activities embraced by the term "public relations" have developed naturally. They are part of the administrative system evolving to bridge the gap between popular and bureaucratic government. The objectives are *active cooperation in action programs* (for example, soil conservation); *compliance in regulatory programs* (for example, public-health laws); and *voter support for the incumbent administration's policies* (for example, foreign aid). The justification for government public relations rests on two premises; that (1) a democratic government is obliged to report to its citizens, and (2) effective administration requires citizen participation and voter support.

The White House's Office of Management and Budget defines government public relations as "those activities which serve to publicize or promote the objectives, operations, facilities or programs for which the agency has responsibility or in which it has an interest. These include but are not limited to activities concerned with press contacts, broadcasting, advertising, exhibits, films, publications and speeches." This OMB definition reflects the narrow, one-way concept that has been imposed on the function in government by strong forces of opposition and citizens' fear of "government propaganda."[8]

A more enlightened concept of the function emerges from Mordecai Lee's functional analysis of administrative public relations in government. He sees government public relations as contributing to:

1. The implementation of public policy.
2. Assisting the news media in coverage of government.
3. Reporting to the citizenry on agency activities.
4. Increasing the internal cohesion of the agency.
5. Increasing the agency's sensitivity to its publics.
6. Mobilization of support for the agency itself.[9]

The objectives

These are the objectives for a planned, continuing program in government:

1. To win consent for new laws and new reforms dictated by the needs of an ever-changing, technological society. This involves a deep, fundamental shift in our theory of government and has dangerous implications.
2. To overcome apathy and bewilderment toward new and complex functions of government; also, to provide reliable information for the voter seeking to make an intelligent decision at the polls.
3. To keep the citizen informed of the services and the functions provided, so that he may participate and gain full benefit from them.
4. To provide the citizen with usable devices for relaying his views and opinions to the administrator without employing intermediaries.
5. To interpret public opinion to the law-enforcement agencies so that regulations will be realistic and acceptable.
6. To crystallize public sentiment and pave the way for noncoercive compliance. This requires persuading the citizen of the need for the administrative rules and assisting him in understanding them.
7. To build a reservoir of support for an agency that it may tap when the going gets rough, so it may have friends in time of need when a conflict develops with other agencies, with the legislature, or with the public.

These objectives involve debatable practices when viewed within the framework of a government of checks and balances. McCamy points out, "Administrative publicity in the past and now has been useful in the process of administrative leadership. Presidents and their assistants have gone to the public on many important issues, sometimes to enlist public pressure on Congress and sometimes to explain to the public the program advocated by Congress and the executive leaders." [10] Actually, most of the impetus for public relations programs in government agencies comes from the need to marshal public support for the money and measures that must be voted in the legislative branch. Bureaucrats engage in lobbying just as surely as businessmen do, despite the myth that government bureaucracy is neutral. Peter Woll, who made a study of American bureaucracy, writes:

> . . . through what might be called undercover devices, the bureaucracy engages in extensive lobbying and propaganda activities. . . . Administrative agencies function to a considerable extent as freewheeling interest groups, and in their use of propaganda activities they are no exception. They not only seek to apply pressure at critical points in the political process, but also strive to maintain a favorable image of themselves before the public generally and before specific groups which they consider important in the battle for political survival. [11]

Hostility to the function

The public relations function has been established longer in government than in any other field of practice. Yet it has never been totally effective. Government practitioners face more hosility and suspicion than most other practitioners do. *This hostility stems from four fundamental and long-standing conflicts of interest embedded in our democratic government:*

1. The continuing struggle between the press, fighting for "the people's right to know," and the officials of government, who insist upon discretion in deciding what public business should be exposed to public scrutiny.
2. The unrelenting struggle for balance of power between the legislative and executive branches of government. This contest is present whether it is between mayor and council, governor and legislature, or president and Congress.
3. The continuing struggle for power between the major political parties. The "out" party fears the power of an army of "propagandists" in keeping the "ins" in and the "outs" out.
4. The protests of industries, institutions, and other vested interests when threatened by proposed legislation or government regulation. They often disparage the use of public funds and government machinery to carry the day against them.

These sources of opposition narrow and limit the function at all levels of government. At the federal level, Congressman Henry Reuss asserts, "The Defense Department cannot be relied upon to police itself. The propaganda machine moves inexorably on." In a state capital, a newspaper reports, "What may become known as 'The Great Public Relations Purge of 1971' began in state government Monday. The Legislative Audit and Fiscal Bureaus sent detailed questionnaires to all state departments with requests to identify all public relations personnel and activities within their areas." At the local level, creation of a public-information activity is almost always accompanied by a degree of political trauma. In Madison, Wisconsin, vehement media opposition blocked the city's plan to establish a public-information office. In Sacramento County, California, both administrators and elected officials agreed upon the need for such an office; but political opposition to the expenditure of tax dollars for "propaganda," coupled with press opposition, delayed its inception for years. Little wonder that the press secretary to the Governor of Georgia, whose office spends more than $110,000 a year on public relations, insists he is not involved in public relations, but rather deals only in "straight information."

Beyond these conflicts there is the inevitable association of government information programs with that dirty word, *propaganda*. Americans have long been deeply suspicious of anything with that label, and particularly so since this power device has been used in other countries to gain and hold despotic control. Thus, public suspicion of information as "nothing but propaganda" is especially strong when the information comes from government. This is reflected in former Senator William Fulbright's belief that "there is something basically unwise and undemocratic about a system which taxes the public to finance a propaganda campaign aimed at persuading the same taxpayers that they must spend more tax dollars to subvert their independent judgment." This is a difficult, age-old question. To quote Jacques Ellul, "To distinguish exactly between propaganda and information is impossible."[12]

Also involved in this opposition is the double standard that many citizens have for government and for private enterprise. The public generally accepts the right and propriety of business to publicize and advertise even though the customer pays for it. On the other hand, many people regard government information work as a waste of tax dollars; they see no need for government to hawk its wares. There is no way of telling just how deep-seated and widespread this citizen attitude is, but some politicians think they win votes when they flay "government propaganda."

From the press

It is the continuing task of the press to ferret out and publicize the actions of public officials, despite the insistence by officials that not all acts should be open to public view. One day, a metropolitan newspaper will assert that "the amount of federal money and manpower devoted to publicizing government . . . has reached staggering proportions." Another day, a New York State newspaperman will join in a "move to tear apart the paper curtain which shields government officials at Albany from inquiring reporters." And on still another day, a Florida weekly editor will announce "a boycott of all state agency handouts." Periodically there are magazine articles about "How Government Pressure Boys Squander Your Money," and blasts from TV commentators. This historic conflict runs from the village school board to the statehouse to the federal government. It has reached a new level of intensity in the past three decades.

The conflict stems from the growth of government at all levels and from the uneasy tensions and recurring crises throughout the world. Decreasing access to news of government is thought by many newsmen to be the major threat to freedom of the press today; they frequently and stridently sound the alarm in their meetings and in their journals. Three professional groups—the American Society of Newspaper Editors, the Society for Professional Journalists (Sigma Delta Chi), and the Associated Press Managing Editors—have given much attention to reporting of government by making studies and issuing reports. At the federal level, the attack has been on the abuse of security classification to hold back news. At the state and local level, the campaign has been to get laws put through requiring all agencies to hold open meetings and to maintain open records. The complexity of this problem and its meaning for freedom of the press have been well defined.[13]

The conflict between the media and government often revolves around the question of secrecy and the government's misuse of classification of information. This battle has raged and ebbed throughout the postwar era.[14] Although skirmishes have been won and lost and the generals change, the campaign goes on. In the mid-1950s, Cong. John Moss, then head of the House Subcommittee on Government Information, launched a war against secrecy in government. Moss argued that the "major cause of the restrictive situation is a 'papa knows best' attitude in federal agencies." More realistic are the reasons inherent in human nature and in the realities of politics. Executives find it more comfortable to do their jobs without the public looking over their shoulders. Subordinates find it safer to suppress information than to incur the boss's wrath. The media's "freedom of information" groups and the American Bar Association joined forces with the Moss Committee to get an effective "public records law" and a Freedom of Information Act, discussed in detail in Chapter 12.

The revised Freedom of Information Act has greatly increased the work load and the headaches of public relations officials in the federal government. Veteran officials concur that the act has had "a significant effect on all public affairs activities." In many agencies, a special office—such as the Freedom of Information Office in the Department of Defense—has been created to handle requests for release of information. In others, these are handled in the public-affairs or public-information office, adding to an already heavy work load. Quite often these requests result in exposure of agency skeletons and thus multiply the "crises" or "flaps" with which PAOs must deal. The act has served to bolster the responsible public-affairs officer in his demands for full and prompt disclosure of nonclassified information—in sum, to increase the pressures and strengthen the importance of the function.

Pressure on federal agencies to provide information more freely and conduct business in the open was further increased by passage of the "Government in the Sunshine" act. This measure, which became effective March 12, 1977, stipulates that each agency have rules establishing a policy of openness. Considering the different ways in which agencies conduct their proceedings, it is likely that meetings will not be opened uniformly by this act. Thus far, the act has had little impact.

In these clashes between journalists and government agencies, the public relations official is inevitably caught in the crossfire. Typical of this conflict is the battle over "management of the news" that boiled up in the wake of the Cuban crisis and reached new levels of bitterness in the traumas of Vietnam and Watergate. Still hotly debated is the assertion of a Defense Department official that "in the kind of world we live in, the generation of news by the government becomes one weapon in a strained situation." This statement fueled the news-management controversy through the Nixon years, and its echoes were heard early in the Carter administration when Press Secretary Jody Powell admitted, "There might be a time—an extreme circumstance, where people's lives or the security of the country is in danger—when you might have to flat-out tell a lie. . . . But to misrepresent the truth is, at the very best, an evil to avoid."[15] The "news as a weapon" debate, in Pierre Salinger's view, "illustrates once again the fundamental chasm that exists between the interests of the press and the government in a crisis situation."

Countless charges and countercharges have been hurled back and forth in this debate. Many newsmen concur with Britain's Lord Shawcross that "the tendency of governments is to shield themselves behind a curtain of secrecy in which the only window is controlled by a public relations official trained in the art of conveying a minimum of information with a maximum of self-righteousness." Hovering over press and public relationships with government have been the "crises in credibility" that began in the Eisenhower administration with the U–2 incident, gained intensity in the Kennedy administration's "Bay of Pigs" fiasco, escalated to a crescendo of charges and countercharges in the Johnson administration's deceptions on Vietnam, and came to a rancid climax in the Nixon administration's commission and coverup of the Watergate crimes. In the mid-1970s, there emerged what the Associated Press Managing Editors termed "the Post-Watergate Syndrome" of gag rules, privacy bills, official-secrets acts, subpoenas, closed meetings, closed records, jailed reporters. This syndrome was reflected in "efforts to subject reporters to criminal action for publication of a broad range of vaguely defined 'national security information' and, at the state level, . . . poorly drawn bills designed to protect the privacy of the individual but [that] may also protect the inept or corrupt public official from public scrutiny."[16]

As the APME report indicates, journalists hold that there is an equally strong trend toward suppression of government information at the state and local levels. Closed meetings of state and local boards are a frequent item of editorial protest. Efforts to break down the news barriers by the media have been more successful at these levels, where no national security matters are involved. Sigma Delta Chi's Freedom of Information Committee has spearheaded a campaign to get open-meetings and open-records laws passed in the states. As of 1976, most states had adopted both, but the laws are far from uniform. In no state are all public records and meetings open at all times. Those states still without adequate protection for public access, in the committee's view, give "ample proof that American politicians across the country still have an abiding love of secrecy."

The press lacks the resources to report comprehensively and constructively all the affairs of government. *First,* there is lack of manpower to cover the multiplying agencies and activities in government at all levels. A press service attempts to cover a state government of more than 60 separate agencies with a two- or three-man staff on a 40-hour week. Obviously, this is an impossible task if the reporters are to dig sufficiently to get the real news. *Second,* there is the outmoded set of news values that puts the spotlight on the negative, controversial, and wrongful aspects of government. For example, the press will quickly mobilize to report in detail a state prison riot; but the lack of an effective parole program, the lack of adequate penal facilities, and the mismanagement that led to the riot are not reported prior to the outbreak. Joseph Kraft thinks the improvement in public-affairs reporting must come from the media. "The central requirement is that the press and TV find and promote more intelligent and better trained people. . . . The chief danger of a kept press lies in the intellectual poverty of the press itself."

A veteran Washington reporter once said, "By and large, government information agencies have been invaluable to the Washington newsgatherers and therefore to the public. Without them, the comprehensive coverage of government affairs would be impossible." The working press in city hall, state capital, and Washington know that government information officials are essential; reporters seldom share the sometimes bombastic views of editors. As one veteran public relations man in Washington put it, "I have never found the working press to be hostile. The publishers and editors sometimes talk hostile, but reporters, correspondents, and commentators want and ask for and use the public information services of the agencies." The relationships of government and media represent an untidy accommodation at best. In the view of the longtime public-affairs officer of the Department of State, Ambassador Robert J. McCloskey, "The government information officer seeks to find the tolerable area of compatibility even though the two institutions are as separate as church and state."

Whatever the conflicts, the media put great reliance on government public relations staffs for their coverage of public affairs.

From legislators

Almost from the beginning, the public relations function in government has been handicapped by the opposition of legislators, which prevents maximum effectiveness and an accurate accounting of the function's cost. Attacks on public relations by legislators are less frequent than those of the press, but perhaps more damaging.

Legislative opposition is often stimulated by other sources of hostility. The Roosevelt-Pinchot campaign for land conservation soon brought congressional reaction from the spokesmen of lumbermen, mine operators, and cattle grazers who had been exploiting the nation's public lands. Cong. Franklin Mondell of Wyoming, a spokesman for sheepmen and stockmen, won adoption in 1908 of an amendment to the Agricultural Appropriation Bill dealing with the Forest Service, which read:

> That no part of this appropriation shall be paid or used for the purpose of paying for in whole or in part the preparation of any newspaper or magazine articles.[17]

Thus, the first effective use of public relations to promote acceptance of an administration's policies brought congressional restriction to the function in the executive branch.

Congressional ire next erupted in 1910 when Rep. Joseph T. Robinson, Arkansas, demanded an investigation of the Census Bureau for its employment in 1909 of a special agent at $8 per day to explain to the public the purpose of the 1910 census. The director of the Census Bureau, E. Dana Durand, insisted that it was essential, if the census was to be complete, that all citizens and aliens be reached—through newspapers, the foreign-language press, and agricultural weeklies—and assured that their replies would not be used for taxation purposes. The committee, after hearing this, tacitly approved.

By 1912, the number of publicity agents employed by executive departments was growing, and some campaigns were not beyond reproach. In May 1912,

Cong. John Nelson of Wisconsin gained passage of a House resolution to investigate meat inspection in the Department of Agriculture's Bureau of Animal Industry. Early in the hearings, Nelson was angered by a circular criticizing the resolution and defending the department; the pamphlet had been published before the hearings opened. He charged that the department was using publicity to discredit one of its accusers, and he introduced a House resolution to investigate "the expenditure of public moneys for press bureaus, postage, stationery, and employees by the Department of Agriculture and by other departments; and that said committee be directed to make recommendation to the House as to what steps are necessary to protect public funds from newspaper exploitations."[18] This resolution did not pass.

A year later, the Civil Service Commission advertised for "a press agent to help boom the good roads movement" in the Office of Public Roads. The circular called for a "publicity expert" whose "affiliations with newspaper publishers and writers is extensive enough to secure publication of items prepared by him." This triggered an amendment to an appropriations bill, by Rep. Frederick H. Gillett, providing that no money could be spent for publicity unless specifically authorized by Congress. The 1913 Gillett Amendment became embedded in law to hamper the function from that day to this.

Opposition comes from both the legislator engaged in a struggle for power with the executive branch, and the legislator of the minority political power seeking majority control. Legislative investigations are not frequent, but they are effective in intimidating government information officials or driving them underground. This conflict is born in our government of checks and balances. The legislative body cannot view calmly the skillful use of public relations by the executive to achieve his legislative goals. On the other hand, the executive cannot dispense with PR and do his job. Congress would do far better to recognize the facts and make intelligent and integrated provision for the proper function of publicizing government activity than to incessantly try to bottle up government publicists.

Four restrictions on the function have been written into U.S. codes. These laws cloud and confuse the practice in the federal government:

1. An act of Congress, passed in 1913, forbids spending for "publicity experts" any part of an appropriation unless that money is specifically appropriated by Congress. (See 38, U.S.C. 3107.)
2. The "gag law" of July 11, 1919, prohibits using any part of an appropriation for services, messages, or publications designed to influence any member of Congress in his attitude toward legislation or appropriations. (See 18, U.S.C. 1913.)
3. A law, also passed in 1919 but not strictly enforced until 1936, requires that all duplicating of material, including multilith and multigraph, must be done by the Government Printing Office, or at least farmed back to the department for reproduction by the G.P.O. (See 44, U.S.C. 501.)
4. Restrictions on the privilege of executive departments and independent establishments in use of the free-mail frank prohibit any executive department from mailing material without a request. (See Title 39, U.S.C.A. Sec. 321n.)

Congress's hostility to public relations in executive agencies, especially the White House, flared anew in the political battles of a Democratic Congress and

Republican Richard Nixon. Alarmed by Nixon's expansion of the White House public relations staff and creation of the Office of Communication, fears that heightened in a presidential election year, Congress voted to reaffirm that:

> No part of any appropriation contained in this or any other Act, or of the funds available for expenditure by any corporation or agency, shall be used for publicity or propaganda purposes designed to support or defeat legislation pending before the Congress. (Pub. Law 92–351, Sec. 608 [a], Enacted July 13, 1972.)

This reaffirmation of the 1919 law did not add greatly to the restrictions but did raise the troublesome question of defining "publicity or propaganda purposes." The new measure suffered from vagueness. But not for long.

In an effort to mobilize public opinion in support of his 1973 budget, President Nixon's public relations staff prepared and distributed to key executives and Republican leaders a public relations kit, "The Battle of the Budget, 1973." The kit included detailed instructions as to how government press releases and speeches were to be written, listing major themes, key facts, sample speech material, one-liners, and anecdotes. In giving examples of how "Horror Stories Might Be Used" in speeches and canned editorials, the kit stated, "Each day the Congress persists in its efforts to foist on the American public a gaggle of runaway spending schemes . . . and boondoggling programs which fuel inflation."

Nixon's White House public relations staff put heavy pressure on departmental information officers to write these "horror stories" and thus work to kill programs they were employed to promote and explain. The public-affairs bureaucracy was coerced by both implicit and overt threats to their jobs or threats of transfer, and by putting political appointees over them. At one time early in 1973, HEW had ten political appointees in its Office of Public Affairs. For the most part, these appointees were loyal to the White House, not to their departments. Nixon saw the public-affairs machinery as the cutting edge of the bureaucracy and tried to blunt it at every turn.

This "Battle of the Budget" kit, assembled by Ken W. Clawson, then deputy director of the Office of Communication, brought quick and heated reaction from Congress and from Ralph Nader's Public Citizen, Inc. The latter filed a civil action against Clawson in the U.S. District Court for the District of Columbia on April 20, 1973. The suit sought to enjoin the White House "from continuing to carry out at public expense a massive publicity campaign designed to influence the passage of certain legislation pending before the Congress."[19] Such litigation appeared to offer a chance to determine the legality of the public relations function in government. This opportunity soon vanished.

Faced with the suit and the darkening storm of Watergate, President Nixon and Clawson recalled the publicity kits in mid-May. They were also mindful of a report of the General Accounting Office to Sens. Hubert Humphrey and Edmund Muskie that the 1919 law had been broken but that it would be up to the Justice Department to take action. The suit was dismissed as moot on July 30.[20]

To correct the vagueness of the 1972 restriction, Senator Humphrey and his colleagues, in July 1973, spelled out the restrictions on what an agency cannot do to influence Congress:

No part of any appropriation contained in this or any other Act, or of the funds available for expenditure by any corporation or agency shall be used, other than for normal and recognized executive-legislative relationships, for publicity or propaganda purposes, for the preparation, distribution, or use of any kit, pamphlet, booklet, publication, radio, television, or film presentation designed to support or defeat legislation pending before the Congress, except for the presentation to Congress itself. (Pub. Law 93–50, Sec. 305, enacted July 1, 1973).[21]

Reflective of the congressional view was Senator Humphrey's assertion: "I believe that the Congress must be constantly on guard over the use of public funds to engage in propaganda or publicity. It must constantly watch over the public relations part of the executive branch. And it must insist on a strict accounting of public funds used for public information purposes."[22]

On the state level, a senator will slap an expensive booklet on the desk of a department head and ask, "What right do you have to spend the taxpayer's money to pressure us into spending more of his money for you?" In Michigan, the governor was called "in and down" by a legislative committee because he was "sending political propaganda to local newspapers in order to put the legislators on the spot." As a result, "the Michigan civil service put some sugar coating on this pill by making 'publicists' into 'public information specialists.' . . . Hiding these publicists has been facilitated by a regulation which allows each state agency two unclassified positions."[23] The effect of this legislative opposition is seen in this reply from a Michigan department in response to a query: "We do not have any PR unit or budget. Public relations is a dirty term in state government—we avoid it entirely. . . . We are not really in the image-making business." Not only does this title dodge blur the function's purpose, it hurts the status of the practitioner. One in the federal government writes, "We have brought this confusion about our job on ourselves through use of ambiguous terminology. It is a waste of effort and manpower; even worse, it confuses the public."

Yet legislators utilize public relations to advance their own political careers. Virtually every member of Congress has at least one public relations aide on his staff, and state legislative leaders are coming to recognize the value of such aides. Less often do legislators see the need for a systematic public relations program for the legislative body, but this is changing. For example, a 1966 Utah Legislative Study Committee concluded, "A legitimate expenditure of modest public funds for a report to the people is in order. . . . Total inaction . . . carries with it . . . penalty—a continuation of the decline of the Legislature as a branch of government." Since then, a number of state legislatures have employed public relations staffs. In 1969, the Wisconsin legislature authorized information officers for the majority and minority caucuses in both houses. As a result, media coverage of the Wisconsin legislators increased markedly.

This struggle for power—and thus for the weapons of power—does not handicap the function as much in local government as it does at the state and federal levels. In most local governing bodies, the legislative and executive functions are combined in one body. Boards of supervisors or commissioners exercise both powers in most of America's 3,000 counties. Exceptions are a few counties that employ a county executive—Westchester, New York, for example. Similarly, in most general-law cities, the mayor is elected by fellow councilmen and does little more than attend ceremonies and preside at council meetings. City managers and county administrators usually operate under tight controls of the city council or county board. Other handicaps beset the function at the local level. Nonetheless, the function does not escape attack at that level. For example, a Minnesota senate committee attacked a study manual distributed to schools by the Metropolitan Transit Commission as "appalling" and "manipulative." The senators were angry because the commission "was attempting to sway public opinion in favor of building a rapid transit system."

Legislative opposition to the function at all levels has led to legal restriction, circumvention of budgetary procedures, and wasteful under-the-table practices. Much of the waste and ineffectiveness that can be justly ascribed to government public relations is directly attributable to legislative hostility. This opposition causes many competent people to shy away from government practice. *Public relations should be a legitimate, aboveboard function in government if government is to be responsive to the citizens it was created to serve.*

Underneath the editorial bombasts and legislative scrutiny are solid questions of public policy that must be kept in mind. *Public relations, as a staff function, must be justified on the grounds that it will not give undue power to the executive branch of government and that it will provide the public with useful information.* Most vital of all is that the programs do not interfere in the slightest degree with freedom of speech and freedom of information. The opposition must have full opportunity to oppose, counter, and criticize. As long as all sides have equal access to the citizen, there can be no real danger to freedom from the government propagandist.

From vested interests

It is natural that those interests that are the object of government regulation or legislation that they deem hurtful would protest the use of the government's public relations machinery to promote such legislation. This was first illustrated by the efforts of the lumbermen and cattlemen to deprive Gifford Pinchot of funds for public information in 1908. This source of opposition is most dramatically illustrated in the long fight of the American Medical Association against what it termed "socialized medicine." This struggle, lasting two decades, cost the AMA and its affiliates some $50 million and a somewhat tarnished public reputation. Repeatedly in this long fight, the AMA decried the expenditure of public funds for "government propaganda."[24] It was influential in initiating the Harness Committee investigation of government public relations in the Eightieth Congress. Given the AMA ammunition, it is not surprising that the Harness Committee found, "At least six agencies in the executive branch are using Government funds in an improper manner for propaganda activities supporting compulsory national health insurance, or what certain witnesses and authors of propaganda refer to as socialized medicine in the United States."[25]

The function matures

The necessary emphasis here on the hostility and restrictions surrounding government public relations may present a distorted picture. *Despite this opposition, the field has steadily grown in concept, in ethics, and in practices.* The media continue to use the information and services provided.

Public relations in government has grown at the pace of the practice in other fields. Its necessity and usefulness in government make this inevitable. Congress, state legislatures, and city councils recognize and accept the function by their annual appropriation of large sums for public relations. For example, when Congress passed the National Aeronautics and Space Act, it provided that NASA make all information available to the public except that limited by national security. In the 1960s, a Senate Appropriations Committee directed the National Institutes of Health "to undertake a more vigorous and imaginative public information program dedicated to the public understanding of their activities." In another instance, Congress established in the Commerce Department a National Technical Information Service to make available to the public the information output of government. The wage-price freeze of 1971 and the energy crisis beginning in 1973 illustrated dramatically the need for machinery to quickly disseminate information to citizens via the media.

Public officials are using public relations increasingly to obtain compliance with administrative policies and the host of government regulations required to maintain stability in our society. In 1973, the state of New York revised its drug-abuse laws. This required a statewide information campaign; the state employed an advertising agency to supplement the work of its information staff. The former insurance commissioner of Pennsylvania, Herbert S. Dennenberg, thinks the most effective way to regulate insurance companies is through widespread publicity. He used his information staff to tell the public about "best buys" and "worst buys" in insurance as a way of getting reforms in rates and practices. He replied to critics, "I'm accused of being a publicity hound, but my job is to get publicity, to communicate." Administrators have come to see public relations as one of the important variables that affect their ability to accomplish their objectives. Today's government official, with an occasional exception, sees the "necessity for dealing with public relations as an inherent and continuing element in the managerial process."[26]

Maturation and acceptance of the function in government will be speeded by (1) repeal of the restrictive federal and state laws that cloud the function with illegitimacy and enforce a narrow "information-officer" concept on practitioners; and (2) the establishment of public affairs as a top-management responsibility in government. An effort to legislate such a top position for the information officer in the federal government was made, unsuccessfully, in 1973 by Rep. William Moorhead. His bill (H.R. 7268) would have provided: ". . . the chief public information officer appointed . . . shall be an assistant to such head [of the agency] and in case . . . of an executive department, such officer shall be Assistant Secretary." Given the congressional opposition, this bill had the chance of the proverbial snowball.

Numbers employed

No accurate figures are obtainable on the number of practitioners employed in government, especially at the federal and state levels. The camouflaging of titles and hiding of expenditures in government—owing to legislative and media hostility—make it impossible to get accurate data in the federal government and in most state governments. The Office of Management and Budget, expert in measuring most federal programs, made an attempt to measure public relations manpower and expenditures in the early 1970s but eventually gave up for lack of reliable information.

In 1967, the Associated Press asserted that there were 6,868 federal employees working full- or part-time in public information, and that the government was spending $425 million a year on information programs. The accuracy of these figures was hotly disputed by government officials. In 1976, the *Washington Star* surveyed twelve large U.S. agencies and found they employed 3,990 in public relations capacities at a cost of $92,836,927 a year. The *Star* admitted that the latter figure was only an estimate of the true costs involved, because of "the art of disguising publicity."[27] Neither of these journalistic exposés included the U.S. Communication Agency, which as of 1977 employed 8,840 and had an annual budget of more than $266 million. Of these ICA employees, some 3,000 are employed in the headquarters in Washington, the others in 104 overseas posts.[28] Before 1978, the ICA functioned as the United States Information Agency.

The nation's two most populous states lead the way in public relations programs. As of 1973, the state of New York was spending $4,250,000 on public relations, California some $2,000,000. The Associated Press found, "Although accurate figures are hard to come by, it is estimated that New York has about 300 fulltime employees working in public relations, and California has about 120 working for state agencies, and considerably more if one counts aides to the state's 120 legislators and the governor's eight-member public information staff."[29] In 1975, Rex Granum, then an *Atlanta Constitution* reporter and now deputy White House press secretary, estimated that the State of Georgia was spending more than $3 million a year on public relations. His figures are no more reliable than the others; there are few reliable data in this area, suggesting (1) caution in accepting such figures, and (2) research opportunities for the scholar.

Federal-government practice

The practice of public relations in government varies widely. It is a far cry from a city's explaining to voters where its tax dollar comes from and where it goes, to the U.S. Department of Agriculture's information system, radiating from Washington to 3,000 county agents. The range in government is from the one-person-plus-secretary operating on a simple publicity basis to the complex, far-flung mission of the U.S. Agency for International Communication, which serves as America's public relations arm around the world.

The magnitude of the federal government's public-information programs is reflected in these facts: The U.S. government's expenditures on public information exceed the total budgets of the nation's two major press associations—AP and UPI—and three TV networks—ABC, CBS, and NBC. The federal government is the nation's tenth largest advertiser and largest producer of films and TV programs. In 1975, the Department of Defense alone spent $76 million on advertising, about the same as Procter & Gamble's advertising budget. According to *Advertising Age,* the U.S. government spent $110.8 million on advertising in 1974—three times the amount spent by the Joseph Schlitz Brewing Company.[30] Most of this went to recruit young men and women for the armed forces. In 1976, the General Services Administration reported that the cost of audiovisual services was approximately $500 million annually. An intergovernmental task force found that in 1972, the government produced 593 films and 2,339 television programs in its own studios. The Department of Defense alone operates 45 audiovisual facilities in the Washington area, including 23 motion picture studios and 17 TV studios, manned by 3,072 employees.[31]

The International Communication Agency

The necessity, potential, and difficulties inherent in government practice are sharply illustrated in the 35-year history of the USIA, now the International Communication Agency.

From World War II on, the United States, as leader of the free world, has been concerned with the problems of international communication, particularly with getting the people of other nations to understand our way of life and our desire for peace. America's overseas public relations program has two main objectives: (1) countering opponents' propaganda and bringing other countries to a fuller and more friendly understanding of American policies; (2) making technical knowledge available to assist underdeveloped countries. The ICA has the responsibility of presenting to the world "a full and fair picture" of the United States. In its efforts to accomplish this, the agency has been subjected to several reorganizations, repeated budget cuts, sharp congressional attacks, and undercutting from inside and outside government. The ICA has no lobby to defend it from its critics.

Under the late Edward R. Murrow and Carl Rowan in the early 1960s, the USIA achieved a stature and stability commensurate with its mission. It was at Murrow's urging that President Kennedy broadened that mission to embrace "advising the President, his representatives abroad, and the various departments and agencies on the implications of foreign opinion," thus bringing to the agency the mature concept of public relations. But evidence suggests that the advisory role lessened under Presidents Johnson, Nixon, and Ford even though the 1963 mission statement was still in effect.

This agency suffers from a "split personality," because it is continually caught between demands for credibility abroad and domestic political demands that it erase America's blemishes in foreign countries. It also suffers from an atmosphere of uncertainty caused by frequent demands for its reorganization or for its return to the State Department. In February 1968, the U.S. Advisory Commission on Information called for an "in-depth critique . . . of what USIA does well and what poorly," and repeated this call in subsequent years. In May 1973, the Senate Foreign Relations Committee recommended a redistribution of the functions performed by the USIA and the State Department's Bureau of Educational and Cultural Affairs. Out of these demands came a panel headed by Frank Stanton, former president of CBS, which studied the agency in 1974–75.[32] The panel recommended that "policy information and advice would be folded into the Department of State, general information and exchange of persons would be integrated into a new agency, Information and Cultural Affairs Agency, and that the Voice of America would be established independently." These recommendations went unheeded in the waning days of the Ford administration, but the demands for dismantling the USIA as an independent agency were renewed after President Carter took office.[33]

To achieve its purposes, the ICA employs all the conventional techniques of modern mass communications: press, radio, film, television, libraries, books, the arts, exhibits, and, most important, personal contact by its officers overseas. At 239 posts in 104 countries throughout the world, some 1,000 agency officers serve as American spokesmen. The ICA operates an international wireless file, which carries some 10,000 words daily in several languages to these overseas posts, where they are adapted for local use. This wire news is used to supplement and balance that transmitted around the world by AP and UPI. Similarly, a constant flow of photos—some 750,000 prints and 160,000 copy negatives a year—is kept moving to the field for use in local publications. The agency produces four major magazines in 25 languages, as well as 20 newspapers, other periodicals, and wall posters. It operates libraries and distributes American books by the millions of copies. Best known of the programs is the Voice of America, the radio broadcasts carrying America's message in 34 languages, 774 hours weekly, to an overseas audience numbered in the millions. It also makes and widely distributes films and exhibits to tell our story. Professional practitioners have assisted the agency through participation in its "People to People" program.

Late in 1977, President Carter consolidated the functions of the USIA and the Department of State's Bureau of Educational and Cultural Affairs into the International Communication Agency. The new agency took over the USIA's international communication programs, including the Voice of America, and cultural exchange activities formerly handled in the State Department. The President explained: "The purpose of this reorganization is to broaden the nation's informational, educational, and cultural intercourse with the world, since this is the major means by which our government can inform others about our country, and inform ourselves about the rest of the world." He saw the new agency building "two way bridges of understanding between our people and the other peoples of the world."

The Department of Agriculture

On the domestic front, the U.S. Department of Agriculture is one of the government's oldest and most skilled users of public relations. As of 1976, the department employed 650 people in public affairs at a cost of $11,467,300. The USDA director of information told a Senate committee that in one year, his staff issued 3,600 news releases—more than ten a day, not counting Sundays and holidays. The staff that year also produced 600 different printed publications, distributing more than 34 million copies, supplied radio and TV stations with program material weekly, and sent out 6,000 photographs to the media. Other Agriculture Department divisions also employ information staffs, and the USDA has people stationed in field offices across the country. An increasing part of the USDA's assignment is to win public understanding of agriculture and the pricing of food among the now-predominant urban population. This extensive information-education program has contributed to America's unequaled agricultural production and to the quality of life for her farm families.

The armed forces

For their common defense, the people of the United States support a large and costly military establishment. The armed forces, with their expensive weaponry and all-volunteer structure, drain heavily the nation's wealth, manpower, and natural resources. Since World War II, taxpayers have paid out more than $1 trillion for national security. Each year, the federal government spends more than 26 cents of every dollar on the Defense Department, and similar expenditures are anticipated for the foreseeable future. So taxpayers must be persuaded of the need to pay heavy taxes for armaments; and young people must be persuaded to volunteer for military duty if manpower needs are to be met. It is mandatory, therefore, that the armed forces win public understanding of their mission. This calls for a giant-sized public relations and advertising program.

In the words of a great general, Omar Bradley, "No organization so directly concerned with the public interest can hope to escape the effects of popular opinion, nor can personnel do their best work without adequate knowledge of where they fit in." In that quote is the key to the military public relations mission—to maintain public support and to maintain adequate internal communications over a large organization spread around the world. To do this, the defense establishment employs some 3,000 people in public relations tasks and spends upwards of $50 million a year on public relations and advertising. In 1976, the *Washington Star* estimated that the Department of Defense had 1,486 public-affairs officers and was spending $24,508,000 in this function. Not only are these figures on the low side; they do not include the time and expense put into public relations by commanders and other non-PR officers, the cost of military aircraft used for PR purposes, and other overhead costs.[34]

Today's top military men provide a leadership responsive to public opinion. Consequently, they are keenly aware of the place and purpose of public relations. This trend represents a sharp break from the insulation that largely prevailed until World War II. And the attitude at the top is gradually permeating the whole establishment.

The unpopularity of the Vietnam conflict intensified the need for a sensitive understanding of public opinion. The military's public relations task has been made difficult in a day when the U.S. military budget totals more than $100 billion, while pressing social and educational needs go unmet. Dissents and dissatisfactions born of the Vietnam War left a bitter legacy inside and outside the armed forces. The acrimonious fight against the Safeguard antiballistic missile system, revelations of faulty weapons, recurring charges of cost overruns, and fears of "the military-industrial complex" are examples of problems facing military practitioners.

It should also be apparent that the military has a unique problem in the area of disasters or accidents. No matter how severe or how routine a mishap may be, it always involves taxpayers' investment and often the lives of citizens serving in the armed forces. Either of these factors increases public attention when circumstance, mismanagement, or misunderstanding create crisis: A number of Marines drown in a routine training exercise; a congressional committee claims that a new army tank costing millions to develop catches fire too easily; an American destroyer collides with an Australian aircraft carrier, costing nearly 100 lives; an air-force bomber carrying nuclear weapons crashes on foreign soil. These and countless other incidents create the necessity for immediate factual information to Congress, the press, and the people. The sensitivity of all segments of American society to such problems compels a recognition of the role and responsibility of those directly responsible for moving information from the military establishment into the public domain.

In the military, "public affairs" is the title used for the function. For many years, the practitioner was called an information officer (IO). Some commands still use IO and PIO (public-information officer) to indicate officers dealing specifically with the media, because these neutral titles appear to attract less flack from Congress and the media. In large commands, the public-affairs officer has public-information officers and command-information officers serving under him. Direction and impetus for the work these officers do is centered in the Department of Defense. The Office of the Assistant Secretary of Defense (Public Affairs) provides overall direction of the military's far-flung, costly public relations programs.

The army's organization is typical of the services. The army centers its program of public and command information in the Office of the Chief of Public Affairs. The mission is to discharge "Army staff responsibility for all matters pertaining to public and command information, and for Department of the Army Information plans and programs in support of Army basic plans and programs." In plain language, the chief of public affairs advises the army leadership, military and civilian, on public relations. The army and all other services and commands operate under policy guidance from the secretary of defense. But in their rivalry for weapons, budget, and manpower, the services find ways around those directives when it suits their need.[35] Army public affairs embraces two distinct programs: (1) those steps taken by the army to keep the public informed; and (2) community relations, encompassing all the actions taken by the army that are related to the public, whether international, national, regional, state, or local in scope, and whether an open house, a speakers' program, an aerial demonstration, or a band to march in a parade.

By the mid-1950s, all services had developed systems to identify and place officers with special talent and training for public relations duties. While the navy and air force provide for their exclusive employment in information functions, the army operates on a dual specialization system whereby a PAO is also skilled and employed in another field, such as infantry, artillery, or logistics management, and receives alternating assignments in his two specialties. The philosophy is that a public-affairs officer must know intimately and be easily identifiable with his or her organization—in this case, the army.

Shortcomings in government public relations

The missing link—feedback

Most government programs emphasize information dissemination and neglect fact-finding and feedback. The failure of government agencies to provide adequate channels for citizen input into programs and policies is at the root of the public's attitudes toward their government at every level. What citizens view as a lack of concern and responsiveness in their government not only exists at the remote federal level but extends down to the smallest village. Grafton is a small bedroom suburb of Milwaukee where "everybody knows everybody else." Some 50 of its residents picketed the village trustee's home for days to protest a plan to put in sidewalks. Said the leader of the protest, "Sidewalks are the symptom, not the real sickness. The trouble is that many board members are just out of touch with the obvious desires of the new people moving in." Little progress in providing channels for an inflow of information and ideas from the public has been made since Donald Krimel wrote in 1955 that "the agencies of the Federal Government . . . are almost entirely lacking in systematic, modern means for opinion measurement." An exception is shown in Figure 22–1.

Unfortunately, government practice is too often guided by such "realistic" directives as these:

1. The public affairs officer of the Office of Education in HEW issues a memo to his staff, entitled, "Illuminating Affirmatively," and directs: "Under the Operational Planning System, the Office of Public Affairs has one 'objective' which is to be tracked by the Deputy Commissioner for External Relations. The title of the objective is 'Affirmative Illumination of Success of Education.' With critics continually emphasizing what's wrong with education, the Commissioner wants to counterbalance that by highlighting what's right with education."[36]
2. Harry Treleaven, Jr., onetime media advisor to President Nixon, was hired by Secretary of the Interior Rogers Morton in 1971 to "streamline" Interior's public relations and "improve the image of the department." In his report, Treleaven defined the objectives of the public relations office as "to play a key role in helping develop new programs to mold public opinion in support of the Secretary and the administration . . . and to head off or counteract adverse publicity. . . ."[37]

The same forces—press and legislative critics—that compel government agencies to camouflage their work as to costs and numbers employed also *hinder full utilization of the research tools.* Despite criticisms, several agencies, including the

Figure 22-1 The Postal Service asks for feedback.

UNITED STATES POSTAL SERVICE
Washington, DC 20260
OFFICIAL BUSINESS

PENALTY FOR PRIVATE USE TO AVOID PAYMENT OF POSTAGE, $300

U.S. MAIL

POSTMASTER
U.S. POST OFFICE

City/Town State ZIP

CONSUMER SERVICE CARD

Date: ____ mo day year

B0653894

Name Address City State ZIP Day Phone

- Is this: Information request ☐ Suggestion ☐ Complaint ☐ Other ☐
- If this is a problem with a specific mailing, please complete following:

Was it: ☐ Letter ☐ Regular Parcel Post ☐ Air Parcel Post ☐ Newspaper/Magazine ☐ Advertisement

Was mailing: ☐ 1st Class ☐ Airmail ☐ Special Delivery ☐ Certified ☐ Registered ☐ Insured

Did it involve: ☐ Delay ☐ Non-receipt ☐ Damage

Please give information on the other person involved in this mailing:
Name ____
Address ____
City ____
State ____ ZIP ____
Was the above person ☐ Sender ☐ Receiver

- If not specific mail problem, is it: ☐ Self Service Postal Equipment ☐ Money Order ☐ Postal personnel
- Please give essential facts: ____

PS Form 4314-July 1975

Thank you. You will be contacted soon.

armed services, use surveys, but not enough do. Information sections in many agencies regularly provide their colleagues with editorial-opinion digests, with the result that many officials tend to think that press opinion *is* public opinion. By and large, however, government agencies rely on political channels to bring in the people's views. This is unwise. In contrast to government practice in the United States, the British government has long utilized public opinion research to guide its programs. Britain's survey unit was born in May 1941, as part of the wartime Ministry of Information. It was made an independent agency in 1967. Its longtime director, Louis Moss, states, "The basic techniques of survey research are democratic in every sense of the word. They are rooted in representativeness, personal involvement, and consultation." Dr. Rensis Likert, who first used opinion research in the U.S. Department of Agriculture, concurs: "Fundamentally sound programs have failed because of misinformation and ignorance on the part of the public."

The value of public opinion surveys as a means of making government responsive to the views of its citizens was recognized by Canada when Prime Minister Trudeau reorganized that government's public relations machinery in 1970. Based on recommendations of a Task Force on Information report, significantly titled *To Know and Be Known*,[38] he established a central public relations agency, Information Canada. The feedback innovations of the agency were fruitful and held the potential of making Canada's government more efficient and more responsive. A nationwide inquiry system operating out of regional centers and using mobile information officers had begun to balance the effects and limitations of traditional one-way public relations with an access system that delivered information on request.

Unfortunately, five years and nine months later, Trudeau abolished Information Canada as the result of continuing criticism from members of Parliament, the civil-service establishment, the press, and some information officers in executive departments. This short-lived program is the only experiment we know of in attuning national communication of government information to the convenience and specific needs of citizens. For democracy to work, it must possess a dynamic element to enable it to adjust to social change. Government agencies lag well behind legislative and executive officials in responding to change. Bureaucrats need the sharp prod of feedback to make them more responsive to citizens' needs.

Carlton E. Spitzer, who once served in government, observes:

> Neither the public nor the bureaucracy is well served by public information officials whose total reference is to the specialized needs of some subdivision whether located in the Executive Office Building or in some remote corner of HEW. The public affairs people must face outward, and they cannot retain that orientation if they are dispersed and isolated among masses of specialists in any bureaucracy. *They must know the sweep of their mission and operate at the top, with the support of regular, unfiltered information from the field.*[39]

A lack of planning

In government practice, there are wide disparities in planning. In many agencies, the information official is a strong and able personality who earns an influential voice in the agency's policy making. But more frequently, the information officer is relatively remote from the policy level. He or she is thus hampered in effectively interpreting the public to the agency and vice versa.

Informational programs in government generally take the form of (1) a campaign on particular topics—for example, revision of the state's deer-season law; (2) a steady play on a central theme for a long period of time—for example, conservation of natural resources; or (3) issuing of news without any specific objectives—for example, a personnel change. There is a tendency to place too much stress on formalized communications and not enough on actual face-to-face communications. One state highway commission takes great effort to prepare an attractive, readable annual report, but does nothing about a red-tape licensing procedure that irritates large numbers of citizens.

The public relations deficiencies that plagued the 1976 swine-flu immunization program provide dramatic proof of the dangers of hastily launching a public-information campaign without adequate planning and governmentwide coordination. A national committee assessing this campaign singled out these factors as contributing to its failure:

1. Failure to involve adequately the representatives of ethnic, minority, and low-income groups in decision making, planning, organization, and implementation of the program, from its earliest stages.
2. Failure to budget, fund, and clearly fix responsibility for the public-information component of the program, and to provide adequate lead time for the planning and implementation of that vital component of the program.
3. Failure to gauge adequately, and then to meet directly, the diminished credibility of government in the nation at large, and especially among the ethnic, minority, and low-income constituencies.
4. Failure to inform the public in advance of possible imperfections in understandable terms, so that Americans could make their own risk–benefit analyses on an informed basis.[40]

These *failures in fact-finding, planning, and communication* are lamentable when placed alongside the national need for immunization programs required to protect the public's health. As the committee observed, the swine-flu fiasco also demonstrated that "the public health field has not escaped the corrosive effect of the diminished confidence of Americans in established authority."

Participation in agency planning enables the public relations officer to help solve or prevent problems that bring criticism. For example, Herm Sittard, the public-information director of Hennepin County, Minnesota, proposed to the county welfare director that welfare services be decentralized as a way of blunting public criticism. Sittard and a group of colleagues were put to work on the problem and came up with a new concept of delivering social services—on a team basis, in neighborhoods—Project Vista. Such urgently needed services as counseling on drugs, aid to delinquents, and marriage counseling are now accessible, visible, and tailored to the needs of a particular neighborhood.[41]

Need for plain talk, not jargon

A major weakness overall in government information programs is the continued use of gobbledegook, still the trademark of the bureaucrat despite all the fun that has been poked at it. There is urgent need for plain English and conversational writing in government correspondence and communications. Government jargon is a real obstacle to meaningful communication. Stripping it away involves more than clarity of writing: It is equally a matter of attitude. Agencies tackle the problem periodically. Several years ago, the Internal Revenue Service brought in Dr. Rudolf Flesch. More recently, the General Services Administration hired a former college English teacher to show the government's 750,000 letter writers how to write less like government letter writers.

Government's communications suffer from the twin faults of too many words and too little substance. John Bitter, *Montgomery Advertiser* columnist, has little doubt about why the Postal Service is in financial difficulty: "Probably 50 percent of its workload is trashy news releases from governmental agencies that say nothing in far too many words." Take the question of volume: The *Federal Register,* on an average day, contains about a million words of regulations and notices—all written in bureaucratese. These regulations, which average about 25,000 words in length, cover everything from almonds to bubble-bath products. Early in his term, President Carter promised, "We will cut down on Government regulations and make sure that those that are written are in plain English." Others before him have tried and failed. President Ford appointed a Commission on Federal Paperwork (of course, it started its work by issuing a 16-page press kit), which found that there were 237,960,480 government forms in circulation.

In the matter of gobbledegook, much decried but still overused, here's a classic from Eliott Richardson when he was HEW secretary: "The food stamp notch has been flattened by the 'cash-out' provisions which eliminate food stamps eligibility for those eligible for cash payments." Such verbiage would be amusing if government communication to citizens weren't so vital. For example, countless taxpayers were puzzled and misled by the confusing and, in places, erroneous instructions in a recent Internal Revenue Service instruction book.

On the other hand, publications can be *too* readable—at least, in the eyes of Congress and bureaucrats. In the Johnson administration, HEW put out a 54-page pamphlet that was catchy, colorful, and crammed full of presidential photographs and Johnsonian wisdom. One hundred thousand copies were sent to places like government clinics, doctors' waiting rooms, and Social Security offices. The *Wall Street Journal* reported that old-line bureaucrats feared that the "Madison Avenue methods" would destroy public confidence in HEW.

The government practitioner uses the conventional tools of personal contact, annual reports, bulletins, films, publicity, education, consultation, and demonstrations—of which more emphasis is needed on personal contacts, consultation, and educational programs. Not to be overlooked in the dissemination of government information is the practice of "leaking" information to get it into public debate without revealing its source. "Leaks" through press officers, and "plants" at informal breakfasts or dinners with a few chosen Washington correspondents, are being used increasingly in the capital. Legislators as well as administrators use this technique. But it can backfire badly, and frequently does.

Because of the increasing complexity of public affairs, public officials, usually at the urging of their advisors, use the background conference with increasing frequency. The "backgrounder" is very useful; but it is fraught with peril—for the practitioner and for the public. One who is protected by anonymity can, if the press cooperates, grind an axe, float a balloon, or denigrate another department and still protect himself by fuzzing the source. Another danger is public confusion—how can the public judge the validity of information that comes from "a reliable source," or a "high government official"?

A typical task

Recruiting

Typical of the tasks assigned to public relations in government is that of assisting in recruitment of competent personnel. In promoting interest in government jobs, the practitioner runs head-on into the unflattering stereotype of a "government worker" or "bureaucrat": He's "a drone who comes to work late and leaves early. He got his job through pull and does as little each day as he can to get by. He's interested only in a big fat pension. He was probably a failure before he latched on to the public payrolls."[42] Such generally unfounded charges affect both the quantity and the quality of applicants. Information officials serving personnel agencies find themselves defending a sector of government that is in great need of public understanding. Unless candidates of competence and character are recruited to the increasingly complex tasks of government, no amount of subsequent management or "reorganization" will bring us quality public service. The task calls for something more than routine posters.[43]

The Illinois Civil Service Commission uses "career" stories to attract candidates. Just before a hospital-attendant examination was to be given, personnel and hospital officials selected some outstanding employees—all of whom had begun state service as attendants—for public recognition. In California, the U.S. Civil Service Commission and the California State Employment Service jointly sponsor a half-hour weekly TV program, "Help Wanted." Miami, Florida, and the state of Wisconsin greatly increased the number of applicants for city and state jobs by using brightly colored posters with art work that makes these announcements stand out alongside the conventional dull, mimeographed postings of many personnel agencies. In recent years, the U.S. Civil Service Commission has been using films such as, "What About Me?" mainly in high school civics courses, to attract young people to careers in government.

This task of promoting recruitment of manpower is crucial for the U.S. armed forces, which now depend on volunteers. When Congress ended the military draft and put the defense forces on a volunteer basis, it was compelled to recognize the necessity for a greatly enlarged military public relations and advertising budget. For example, using TV, radio, films, billboards, and glossy magazine spreads, the Department of Defense is spending some $400 million a year on advertising to push such slogans as "After High School, a Bright Future," "Travel is Part of Your Life," and "Now You'll Have Your Own Home." These themes are reiterated in a heavy flow of publicity from the several recruiting commands. Whether this public relations effort will succeed remains to be seen.

Other examples

There are many examples of skilled programs and useful techniques to be found in government—some borrowed, some homegrown. Many of these revolve around the effort of administrators to break out of their insulated environment and take government to America's Main Street. The innovative John F. Kennedy initiated the Regional White House Conference, which took federal officials to key cities of the nation for public conferences on current government problems. This useful idea lapsed in the Johnson and Nixon years but was used by President Ford. Ford, given the monumental task of restoring public faith in government, set up an Office of Public Liaison to promote citizen access to the White House. He set this as the mission of the new office: "To ensure effective two-way communication with all elements of the private sector, by bringing people to the White House and bringing the White House to the people." The latter was carried out by a series of "town-hall" meetings staged in major cities of the nation. These were day-long conferences with from 700 to 1,200 invited participants representing a public cross section of the particular region.

President Carter has continued the Ford-created office and is striving to maintain access of citizens to his government in a number of ways. As governor of Georgia, he kept in touch with the people through radio call-in shows, frequent speeches at service clubs and in churches, weekly news conferences, and several fact-finding commissions. For example, he set up a commission on "Goals for Georgia" that held hearings in all parts of the state to ascertain what services Georgians wanted and what they thought of their state government. Such out-of-the-office meetings serve the double purpose of publicizing the administration's policies and subjecting top officials to public opinion in lively give-and-take discussion.

The State of New York has borrowed industry's open-house idea. One year, the state held Open House Week, putting out the welcome mat for its 17 million residents to visit some 500 state offices and institutions. Employees provided guided tours, showed films, gave talks, and provided literature on their work. Some years ago, the Kentucky Department of Revenue used an information program to pave the way for a needed overhaul of its 55-year-old tax laws. Another good example is the story of Ralph Gates, who, as governor of Indiana, took "the state capitol to the people" in the manner of a corporation taking its annual meeting to the stockholders. John Reynolds, when governor of Wisconsin, borrowed and modified this idea by holding his budget hearings in the various state institutions as a way of dramatizing the needs of Wisconsin's colleges, mental hospitals, and penal institutions. When he was New York's governor, Nelson Rockefeller developed the practice of holding "town meetings" in various parts of the state. In such meetings, the governor "parried the complaints of New Yorkers disturbed about crime, narcotics, pornography, insurance rates, airplane noise, and migrant workers."

Typical of the way in which the function is maturing in state government is the program of the Oklahoma State Department of Health. Its public relations program, directed by a coordinator of public affairs, has these objectives:

1. To establish a system whereby newsworthy information on public health may be disseminated through all appropriate channels of communication.
2. To develop a capability for technical assistance, advice, and consultation to line programs within the State Department of Health, and to local health units on informational materials, public relations, and other appropriate aspects of informational activities.
3. To provide a focal point, or clearinghouse, for both the mass media and departmental staff on consistency of information to be released and policy statements representing the department's overall posture and attitude.
4. To effectively measure trends, attitudes, needs, and reactions of the general and specialized public on their acceptance of departmental programs and objectives, in order to meet these changes.

At no level of government is citizen understanding and cooperation more essential than at the local level, where government provides schools, fire and police protection, safe streets and expressways, recreation facilities, urban renewal to combat inner-city decay, low-rent housing, and a host of other services. Today our cities are in crisis, and their administrators are caught in the vortex of conflict: taxpayers demanding a halt in rising property taxes one moment, demanding more services the next; municipal employees, now organized into unions, demanding higher wages and more fringe benefits; the needy demanding more adequate welfare payments; policemen frustrated by their inability to cope with the new tactics of confrontation and protest. Yet it is at the local-government level that public relations has developed most slowly. A 170-city national survey conducted by the American Municipal Association discovered little agreement on the role of public relations. This survey found that in four out of every ten cities over 50,000 in population, no one had been assigned to public relations on a full-time basis. It also found excessive reliance on such timeworn gimmicks as presenting a key to the city, and student government days. Regardless of city size, the AMA survey showed, the four most needed improvements are (1) employee training in public relations techniques, (2) more effective communication of the municipal story, (3) a trained staff, and (4) better press relations.

In the view of one practitioner, "The news media are local government's first and most effective line of communication with the taxpayers . . . and the news media can provide local government with information on the effects of its policies so that mistakes can be corrected and needed city government improvements supported." This Lincoln, Nebraska, official observes, "The simple fact is that much of the misunderstanding arises because many city officials, mayors to meter readers, don't know how news-media representatives operate, how to work with them, or the importance of good press–government relations."[44]

Beyond this, the media, because of outmoded news values, limited manpower, and limitations of space or time, cannot fully perform the government information function—especially at the local level. Information regarding the time and location of 35 animal vaccination clinics throughout a 4,000-square-mile county will wind up in agate type near the classifieds in the daily newspaper, and won't be carried at all by either radio or TV. One county practitioner comments, "More and more, it is becoming essential to government to aim its message at a specific audience carefully and precisely. Messages sent through the media get filtered, filtered by the reporter's experience and knowledge, filtered by the rewrite man, by the copydesk and headline writer. There is a need for alternative channels in local government public relations."[45] These include newsletters, speakers' bureaus with strong audiovisual support, front-line or storefront information centers, public relations training for employees who deal with the public, ombudsmen, and call-in complaint or referral centers.[46]

How public relations can be utilized to assist local government was shown by the city of Birmingham, Alabama, and a construction company, which jointly put on a public relations campaign to get motorists' cooperation in closing a busy intersection for nine days, thus lopping off a full year's time in building a major expressway. Employment of practitioners to smooth the stormy relationships between police and civilians has brought calm to many cities. Yet many chiefs resist this development, insisting rather naively that "community relations is a task for the whole department."

Case problem

You are public relations director for the State Department of Public Welfare. Its division of corrections long ago decided that the state boys' school was grossly inadequate and a dangerous firetrap. Three years ago, the State Board of Public Welfare launched a public relations campaign to win legislative support for a new facility in a better location. Finally, the state legislature has appropriated $6 million for a new reformatory. The Board of Public Welfare, in collaboration with the governor, has decided to locate it in a state forest. This would provide attractive surroundings, isolation from cities, and constructive work for the boys. But when this decision is announced, conservation groups, headed by the Izaak Walton League and Sierra Club, issue vehement protests and threaten court action to block the move. The community in which the present reformatory is located organizes a committee to keep it there. Conservation groups start a public campaign to force the governor and welfare board to reverse the decision. The much-needed new reformatory appears to be in jeopardy. The director of public welfare and the head of the corrections division turn to you and ask, "How do we head this thing off?"

What are your recommendations?

ADDITIONAL READINGS

MELVYN H. BLOOM, *Public Relations and Presidential Campaigns: A Crisis in Democracy.* New York: Crowell, 1973. A study of modern campaign methods from 1952 to 1968, with a postscript on 1972.

DAVID H. BROWN, "Information Officers and Reporters: Friends or Foes?" *Public Relations Review,* Summer 1976.

WILLIAM O. CHITTICK, *State Department, Press, and Pressure Groups.* New York: John Wiley, 1970. Examination of an information officer's relationship with the press and with fellow bureaucrats—quite illuminating.

TIMOTHY CROUSE, *The Boys on the Bus: Riding with the Campaign Press Corps.* New York: Random House, 1973. A readable, insightful book; President Carter studied it with profit before he launched his campaign in 1974.

DELMAR D. DUNN, *Public Officials and the Press.* Reading, Mass.: Addison-Wesley, 1969. Examines the relationships of Wisconsin government officials and the press.

ROBERT E. ELDER, *The Information Machine: The United States Information Agency and American Foreign Policy.* Syracuse, N.Y.: Syracuse University Press, 1968.

WILLIAM H. GILBERT, ed., *Public Relations in Local Government.* Washington, D.C.: International City Management Association, 1975. Useful, up-to-date handbook for local practitioners.

PHIL G. GOULDING, *Confirm or Deny: Informing the People on National Security.* New York: Harper & Row, 1970. Series of mini-cases from the Kennedy and Johnson years.

CALVIN W. GOWER, "Conservatism, Censorship and Controversy in the CCC, 1930s," *Journalism Quarterly,* Vol. 52 (Summer 1975).

MALCOLM D. MacDOUGALL, *We Almost Made It.* New York: Crown, 1977. By the director of President Ford's 1976 advertising campaign.

HAROLD C. RELYEA, "The Freedom of Information Act: Its Evolution and Operational Status," *Journalism Quarterly,* Vol. 54 (Autumn 1977).

WILLIAM RIVERS, *The Adversaries: Politics and the Press.* Boston: Beacon Press, 1970. The conflict between press and government, examined in several readable essays.

MARTIN SCHRAM, *Running for President 1976.* New York: Stein & Day, 1977. Account of how Carter won the presidency.

LEON V. SIGAL, *Reporters and Officials: The Organization and Politics of Newsmaking.* Lexington, Mass.: Heath, 1973. Insight on how "the news" is defined.

DAVID WISE, *The Politics of Lying: Government Deception, Secrecy, and Power.* New York: Random House, 1973. Explains why citizens lost faith in their government in the '60s and '70s.

1. Joseph Kraft, *Profiles in Power* (New York: New American Library, 1966), p. 92.
2. Wilbur J. Cohen, "Communication in a Democratic Society," in *Voice of Government*, eds. Ray E. Hiebert and Carlton Spitzer (New York: Wiley, 1968), p. 20. A useful book of essays on government practice.
3. *Final Report of the Thirty-Second Assembly*, Columbia University, 1968, issued by the Assembly.
4. "New Breed of Governors Tries the Mainstreet Approach," *U.S. News & World Report*, Vol. 79 (August 18, 1975).
5. In *Government and Mass Communications*, Vol. II (Chicago: University of Chicago Press, 1947), p. 736. These two volumes, by-products of the Commission on Freedom of the Press, provide helpful background reading. This commission recommended strongly that "the government, through the media of mass communication, inform the public of the facts with respect to its policies and of the purposes underlying those policies. . . ."
6. Stanley Kelley, Jr., *Professional Public Relations and Political Power* (Baltimore: Johns Hopkins Press, 1956), p. 3. Recommended reading.
7. Leon D. Epstein, *Political Parties in Western Democracies* (New York: Praeger, 1967), pp. 240–41.
8. Quoted from Gordon L. Harris, *Selling Uncle Sam* (Hicksville, N.Y.: Exposition Banner, 1976), p. 25. A veteran IO provides "A Firsthand Look at the Public Relations behind U.S. Space Program."
9. Mordecai Lee, "A Descriptive Theory of Administrative Public Relations," manuscript prepared at Brookings Institution, 1973.
10. James L. McCamy, *Government Publicity* (Chicago: University of Chicago Press, 1939). A landmark book, now out of print.
11. Peter Woll, *American Bureaucracy* (New York: Norton, 1963), pp. 134–35.
12. Jacques Ellul, *Propaganda, Formation of Men's Attitudes* (New York: Knopf, 1971).
13. For helpful background reading, see Harold L. Nelson and Dwight L. Teeter, *Law of Mass Communications;* Harold L. Cross, *The People's Right to Know;* James Russell Wiggins, *Freedom or Secrecy,* 2nd ed.; Douglass Cater, *The Fourth Branch of Government;* Francis E. Rourke, *Secrecy and Publicity;* Herbert Brucker, *Freedom of Information;* and William L. Rivers, *The Opinion Makers.* It was Brucker who introduced the concept "managed news" in this context.
14. The conflict started in September 1951, when President Truman issued Executive Order 10290 giving civilian agencies authority to classify information. President Eisenhower, in Executive Order 10964, reduced the number of agencies granted such power, but this did little to diminish the conflict. President Nixon issued an order effective June 1, 1972, that limited the power to classify material "top secret" to twelve agencies. Nonetheless, the issue remains.
15. Sanford J. Ungar, "Washington," *The Atlantic,* April 1977, p. 13.
16. APME Freedom of Information Committee, *Annual Report 1975* (New York: APME, 1975). Also see Society of Professional Journalists, Sigma Delta Chi, "Report of the Advancement of Freedom of Information Committee, 1976."
17. *Congressional Record,* 60th Cong., 1st sess., 1908, Vol. 42, 4137. Historical data was provided by Felice Michaels Levin, a former student.
18. U.S. Congress, House, Rules Committee, *Hearing on H. Res. 545, Department Press Agents,* 62nd Cong. 2d sess., 1912, 3–4.
19. *Public Citizen, Inc.* v. *Ken W. Clawson,* Civil Action No. 759–73, U.S. District Court for the District of Columbia, Complaint for Declaratory and Injunctive Relief, filed April 20, 1973.
20. The case was heard by U.S. Judge Barrington D. Parker.
21. For debate on this measure, see *Congressional Record,* May 31, 1973, S10129–31.
22. *Ibid.* Senator Humphrey died in 1978.
23. Gerald J. Keir, "Government Public Relations and the Press in Michigan," *Journalism Quarterly,* Vol. 43 (Autumn 1966).
24. This epic pressure group–government struggle was fully chronicled by Richard Harris in *A Sacred Trust* (New York: The New American Library, 1966).
25. U.S. House of Representatives, 80th Cong. 1st sess., Committee on Expenditures in the Executive Departments, *Investigation of the Participation of Federal Officials in the Formation and Operation of Health Workshops* (1947), p.1.
26. "They Are All Afraid of Herb the Horrible," *Time,* July 10, 1972, p. 50.
27. John J. Fialka, "$92.8 Million Cost but No 'Publicity Experts,'" *Washington Star,* April 12, 1976, p. 1.
28. USIA, *44th Report to the Congress, July 1, 1975 to June 30, 1976* (Washington, D.C.: U.S. Information Agency).

29. Associated Press dispatch, April 24, 1973.

30. John J. Fialka, "Federal Advertising: Not Yet Ready for Prime Time?" *Washington Star,* April 15, 1976.

31. John J. Fialka, "Our 'Hollywood on Potomac' Subsidy," *Washington Star,* April 13, 1976. Also see Office of Telecommunications Policy, Executive Office of the President, *Audio-Visual Communications in the Federal Government,* a report dated January 1974.

32. Georgetown University Center for Strategic and International Studies, *International Information Education and Cultural Relations, Recommendations for the Future* (Georgetown University, 1975).

33. Graham Hovey, "New Effort Under Way to Dismantle U.S. Information Agency," *New York Times,* January 16, 1977.

34. Fialka, "$92.8 Million Cost." In 1969, Senator Fulbright got from the Department of Defense and the military services a detailed accounting of their expenditures and personnel assignments for public relations. He put these in the *Congressional Record.* See issues December 1, 1969 (S15144–S15157), December 2, 1969 (S15306–S15333), December 4, 1969 (S15649–S15674), and December 5, 1969 (S15804–S15845).

35. For an example, see Harris, *Selling Uncle Sam,* p. 23.

36. Memo dated September 27, 1972, issued by Jack Billings.

37. Copy of Treleavan's report to the secretary of interior, in author's possession. Matter investigated in Hearings of House Committee on Government Operations, Foreign Operations and Government Information Subcommittee in May 1972.

38. *To Know and Be Known,* The Report of the Task Force on Government Information, Vol. 1, Panorama; Vol. II, Research Papers (Ottawa: The Queen's Printer, 1969). Still useful.

39. "Three Ways to Improve Government Information," *Public Relations Journal,* Vol. 29 (August 1973).

40. Report, National Immunization Work Group on Health Information, *Health Information and Public Awareness,* March 1977, multilithed. Also see David M. Rubin, "Remember Swine Flu? The Press Was Not in a Critical Condition," *Columbia Journalism Review,* Vol. 16, July–August 1977, pp. 42–46.

41. "The Real Public Relations Pro Is a Staffer for the News Media," *Public Relations Journal,* Vol. 29 (June 1973).

42. Eleanor R. Ruhl, *Public Relations for Government Employees* (Chicago: Civil Service Assembly, 1952), p. 5.

43. See F. Arnold McDermott, *The Recruitment of Manpower: A Guide for Practitioners* (Public Personnel Association: Public Personnel Brief No. 26).

44. Leo Scherer, "Better Press–Government Relations," *Wisconsin Counties,* September 1969.

45. Quoted from a helpful letter from Fred Christenson, formerly San Diego County, California, information officer, dated May 3, 1976.

46. Another use of the function is to attract industry and tourists. See Daniel Machalaba, "Municipalities Step Up Image Building Aimed at Firms and Tourists," *Wall Street Journal,* October 4, 1977.

23

The progress of the school as an institution of democracy
depends upon the support of the public it serves.

The Practice:
public schools

In this era of unsettling change, the nation's public schools are caught in a web of difficult relationships. News of public education has moved from the inside of the paper to the front page. Headlines tell the story: "Desegregate Schools at Once, Court Rules," "In Ten Years, Americans Double School Spending," "Sex Education Banned," "School Bond Issue Defeated," "Rulings on Student Dress Anger School Officials," "Parents Oppose School Shifts," "Teachers Strike in Florida," "Controversy over Testing Flares Again," "Staff Opposes Principal as Editor," "New Trier Bans Huck Finn," "Police in Schools Plan Modified," "He Was Handed a Diploma He Can't Read," "Supreme Court Upholds Students' Right to a Hearing," "Students Down, Costs Rise 10%."

The growth in news coverage of education reflects in part the public's increased awareness of schools and their impact on society. With the rapid evolution of protests in the streets, the discovery of the poor, the rise in industrial technology, and swiftly changing social patterns, the social urgency of public education has been firmly established in the public mind. These developments have brought a broadly supported revolution in education, which has increased its costs, broadened its role, and made it the object of much criticism.

Schools, once sheltered in the tranquillity of tradition, have been thrust into the vortex of society's turbulence. Problems of violence, sex, and drug and alcohol abuse, for example, divert educators from their basic tasks. A U.S. Senate committee found recently that "violence and vandalism has reached a level of crisis" in the nation's schools. Columnist James J. Kilpatrick found the report "sickening." The Associated Press summarizes the context of school public relations:

> Golden rule discipline is gone, vandalism is on the rise. Teachers want more money, citizens don't want higher taxes. Enrollment declines, neighborhoods fight the closing of their schools. Educators expect more vandalism, teacher militancy and fiscal troubles and more difficulties over busing and racial integration in the years ahead.

Little wonder that a New York City school official calls for a campaign to give schools "a better public image." The vice-president of New York's board of education exhorts, "It's time to fight back. I'm sick and tired of teachers and supervisors, the board and community school boards constantly being put in a negative light."

The 1970s saw a national drop in school population as the post–World War II "baby boom" ended. This decline, expected to continue for several more years, caught many educational planners by surprise even though the decline in birthrate had become obvious several years earlier. The number of students in U.S. public schools, kindergarten through grade 12, in 1970 totaled 45.9 million. By 1975, it had dropped to 44.8 million and is projected to drop further to 41.1 million by 1980.

Education is a major enterprise that touches the life of virtually every citizen. There are roughly 3 million teachers and administrators employed by public schools. Because state and federal aid has decreased in some areas and stayed relatively the same in others, despite inflation and mandated programs such as those for the handicapped, the proportion of local taxes spent for schools in the nation had risen sharply to an estimated 57.4 percent by the mid-1970s.[1] This trend is expected to continue.

The relations between education and the people are many, direct, and diverse. Opportunities abound for friction, misunderstandings, and communications breakdowns. The need for understanding and support of education is urgent in a time when demands for freedom and equal rights have penetrated the schools, when the generation gap has widened, and when school dollars have been shrunk by inflation. Consequently, education public relations is expanding in scope and concept. The problems in the 1980s loom large.

The problems

Accountability

Growing public dissatisfaction with the performance and cost of schools has led to widespread demands for more *accountability* on the part of educators. In the 1960s, both educators and laymen put forth the heretical notion that it would be appropriate to examine education in terms of outcomes. Citizens were asking with increasing stridency why costs for elementary and secondary schools were rising as enrollments were falling, and why achievement scores were declining at the same time that staff/pupil ratios were being reduced. This idea of accountability has exposed many of the chronic problems that perplex educators. Accountability now comes in many forms, and more than 30 states have laws bearing on the question. Accountability demands have moved far beyond student assessment.[2]

Accountability requires keeping good records and making actions public. Taxpayers and legislators today reject the notion that schools will improve if they are better funded. Robert E. Stake defines an *accountable school* as one that (1) discloses its activities, (2) makes good on staff promises, (3) assigns staff responsibility for each area of public concern, and (4) monitors its teaching and learning.[3] Other writers suggest including in the list (5) gathers evidence of making good on public expectations, and (6) discovers through research the causes of strengths and weaknesses. *Educators' responses to these new and stricter demands for accountability will require more adequate information programs on the part of most school systems.*

Performance

Basic to effective public relations is *performance* that the public deems satisfactory. Central to the difficult task facing public-school officials is widespread evidence that the money American taxpayers have poured into their schools has not been effectively used. The resulting disillusionment is reflected in headlines and in parental grumbling. Under the headline, "Drop in Student Skills Unequalled in History," the *Los Angeles Times* asserts:

> After edging upward for apparently more than a century, the reading, writing, and mathematical skills of American students from elementary school through college are now in a prolonged and broadscale decline unequalled in U.S. history.
>
> The downward spiral, which affects many other subject areas as well, began abruptly in the mid-1960s and shows no signs of bottoming out. By most measures, student achievement is now below the national average of a decade ago. . . .
>
> And yet, paradoxically, in the face of strong evidence that students are doing poorer, they are receiving higher and higher grades for their classroom work.[4]

This trend was affirmed in the 1976–77 test year, when Scholastic Aptitude Test results dropped for the fourteenth consecutive year. These worsening scores, along with a sag in several other indicators of student progress, have brought widespread criticism of schools and an avalanche of possible explanations from educators. Controversy over the validity and fairness of tests and over causes of declining performance of secondary-school students creates a difficult and complex problem for practitioners and administrators alike.

Although educators argue with some validity that test scores are at best a dubious measure of student achievement, they are a measure that is watched closely by parents. The requirement in many states that test scores be released on a school-by-school as well as on a systemwide and statewide basis has naturally led to comparisons that are sometimes embarrassing. School principals in many districts are required to explain to parents the individual and school test scores and actions to be taken to overcome weaknesses.

Educators—from the kindergarten to the university—are being hauled into court with increased frequency as dissatisfied students and parents turn to litigation to express criticism. Two examples: (1) A U.S. district-court jury in Pennsylvania awarded $6,000 in damages to a 6-year-old who had flunked kindergarten and thus had had "his constitutional rights violated." The suit was brought by the child's irate mother; she had appealed first to the school board, which had denied her appeal. Her attorney said of the verdict, "It says that in order to hold a child back, the school must have valid reasons and let the parents know what these reasons are." (2) The parents of a graduate of Copiague (N.Y.) High School sued the Copiague Union Free Schools for $5 million on the ground of "educational malpractice" because their son was graduated even though he could not read a menu in a hamburger stand. These parents insist, understandably, that the schools should have paid more attention to diagnosing and treating their son's learning problems. The son said, "When I realized that they were going to pass me anyway I didn't do any more work."

Costs

Taxpayer revolts have led to one school-bond and tax defeat after another, and the closing of many schools when money has run out. For example, the voters of Rockford, Illinois, rejected by a margin of two to one a referendum that would have raised the school property tax, even though this meant that Rockford's public-school students would have to do without all extracurricular activities, including athletics. The only organization that had fought the tax increase openly was a "Committee of Citizens Against the Tax Hike," a group with few resources.[5]

That same year, schools from Oregon to Ohio were shut down when public funds ran out. In Oregon, school financing is made particularly difficult by state laws that give local taxpayers nearly complete control of it. *Newsweek* reported, "In district after district, the voters turned down school levies, and the impact has been devastating. Nearly 10,000 Oregon children have had no public education for a good part of the school year."[6] In Ohio that year, at least ten districts, out of money, closed early for the Christmas holidays. These ranged from small districts to Toledo's 50,900-pupil system. This education-crippling situation was repeated the following year.

Not all school enrollments are declining, and this compounds the problem for some administrators. For example, many school districts, particularly those in suburban rings around central cities, are coping with expanding enrollments while other systems are retrenching. While some districts are trying to close surplus buildings, others are operating overcrowded schools on double sessions. Still other districts have both problems, with declining enrollments and empty classrooms in areas of declining population, and overcrowding in growth areas of the district. It is difficult indeed to explain the need for new schools while at the same time closing schools with low enrollment.

Consequently, bond referendums are taking place in a climate that is, unlike the 1960s, no longer supportive of expansion. Inflation and resultant higher taxes complicate the problem. As a result, referendums are frequently defeated. For example, the approval of school-bond issues in the United States dropped from a high of 74.7 percent in the fiscal year ending June 30, 1965, to 46 percent in the fiscal year ending June 30, 1975.[7]

Persuasive public relations has taken on increased importance as officials try to persuade taxpayers to raise school levies to cope with inflation, or pass bond issues for new buildings because of shifting enrollment patterns. Also, the failure of bond and tax elections has made it more apparent to school boards that they can no longer depend on volunteer "citizen committees" to conduct the campaigns. Where referendums are successful, the school public relations practitioner has had to assume a central role in the campaign information effort.

A recent poll of school public relations practitioners resulted in overwhelming identification of the financing of public education as the issue that will present the greatest communications problem during the next five years. Other major issues identified were discipline, accountability, pupil performance, and negotiations.[8]

TABLE 23-1 Number of public elementary and secondary school bond elections held and number and percent approved: United States, fiscal years 1964–1975

Fiscal Year Ending June 30	Number of Elections		Approved (in percent)
	Held	Approved	
1964	2,071	1,501	72.5%
1965	2,041	1,525	74.7
1966	1,745	1,265	72.5
1967	1,625	1,082	66.6
1968	1,750	1,183	67.6
1969	1,341	762	56.8
1970	1,216	647	53.2
1971	1,086	507	46.7
1972	1,153	542	47.0
1973	1,273	719	56.5
1974	1,386	779	56.2
1975	929	430	46.3

Source: *Bond Sales for Public School Purposes, 1974–75.* (Washington, D.C.: Government Printing Office, 1976), p. 2.

Education—a job for all

Adequate financing and cooperation in education depend on sound public relationships. The key to such relationships is development of the idea that education is the job of all citizens. In achieving this, *educators must take the public into partnership.* Responsibility rests primarily with administrators and teachers, and they are coming to sense this.

Unfortunately, many educators are often arbitrary, inflexible, and sometimes discriminatory as they pursue their educational function. Too many still reflect a "papa knows best" attitude.[9] A few examples:

- In Macon, Ga., a 16-year-old black youngster was expelled for the three-month remainder of the school term because he could not pay $5 to replace a ruler that he had broken accidentally during shop class.
- In New Bedford, Mass., a 17-year-old white boy was suspended for two days when he left the school grounds to help an old man change a flat tire. His mother demanded an explanation. She was told her son had done a good deed, but the rule of suspension for leaving the school grounds could not be broken.
- A Madison, Wis., principal suspended a high school student of 15 for growing a mustache, and thereby precipitated a prolonged controversy that eventually forced the principal to resign.
- Richard Brimly, a teacher in East Hartford (Conn.) High School, was ordered by his principal to wear a tie as prescribed by the teacher's dress code. Brimly challenged the constitutionality of the dress code in federal court—and won. The U.S. Circuit Court of Appeals suggested that a teacher might, in fact, be more effective in an open-necked sport shirt or a turtleneck sweater.

529

Surveys repeatedly show that education ranks among the most valued symbols in American life. In fact, there have been disturbing signs that many Americans expect too much from education, presuming it to be the panacea for all the ills that beset the nation. They tend too easily to turn to schools for relief from weaknesses, for protection against feared enemies. If the accident rate zooms up, people demand safe-driving courses. If juvenile delinquency breaks out in a community, people insist that the schools do something about it. Feeling threatened from without and within by Communism, people demand that the schools give courses in "Americanism." They join forces with extremists to advocate loyalty oaths for teachers, and probe feverishly into the content of textbooks. Those concerned with the rising rate of illegitimate births press for sex education in the classroom, a movement spearheaded by the Sex Information and Educational Council of the United States (SIECUS). Those who fear such instruction coalesce in protest groups—the Concerned Parents Committee, the Movement to Restore Decency, and so on. And yet, with all their high expectations, Americans remain ambivalent toward education. Schools are a microcosm of society—reflecting its weaknesses and its potential.

A task force on building public confidence in education, sponsored by the National School Public Relations Association, recently concluded:

> The public is losing the feeling that it is responsible for the education of its children—the feeling that schools are *public* institutions. The public feels shut out of the decision-making process by local educators who are unresponsive and lack the desire to work with them, by an increasing influence from state and federal agencies, and by school consolidation and reorganization, which has removed an important communication link.[10]

A survey in 1976 by the National Opinion Research Center at the University of Chicago asked people about the amount of confidence they had in those running various institutions. Only 37 percent said they had a "great deal of confidence" in education. As recently as 1974, the same survey showed 49 percent with a "great deal of confidence."

Evidence of the need for and value of effective two-way communication between schools and taxpayers supporting them abounds, as shown in several exhaustive studies carried out by Stanford University under the sponsorship of the U.S. Office of Education. Two of these studies, directed by Richard F. Carter, were based on interviews with community leaders in 82 school districts in the nation and with a representative sample of voters in four widely spread cities. These studies found, among other things:

1. The voter thinks schools are good in general, but he criticizes them in particular areas: frills, too much play, curriculum, and discipline.
2. The voter thinks the most important tasks of schools are to teach the fundamentals—reading, writing, spelling, arithmetic, and speaking—and to instill loyalty to the United States. He also thinks that these are the jobs done best.
3. The voter thinks the least important tasks of the schools are to teach about the local region, to afford enjoyment of cultural activities—art and music—and to provide industrial-arts education.
4. The voter's evaluation of the local schools, his evaluation of school costs, and his

pride in the schools are most closely associated with the likelihood of his voting and voting favorably.

5. *About half the voters show no evidence of any participation in school affairs and no interest in such participation.* About a third of the voters participate actively. The more the voter participates, the more knowledge he has of school performance.[11]

The requirements

Essential aspects of a school–community relations program are these:

1. Commitment to public partnership on the part of school board, administrators, and teachers.
2. Competence in the school–community relations staff.
3. Centralization of community relations policy making.
4. Free-flowing communication from and to publics—up, down, and across.
5. Coordination of all efforts to ensure accomplishment of predetermined goals.

Dr. John H. Wherry, executive director of the National School Public Relations Association, suggests that school boards and superintendents ask themselves the following questions. He says that unless the answer is "yes" to at least four of the five questions, the system's PR program needs attention.

1. Do you have a board policy statement about public relations?
2. Does some top-level administrator have responsibility for coordinating your PR program?
3. Do you have an organized program of *internal* communication with your staff?
4. Do you have an organized program of *external* communication with the community?
5. Are you using individual school building units as the *basis* for your public relations program?

Commitment of the administrators is essential. The community relations function will be as large and useful or as inconsequential and ineffective as the administrators will it.[12] Even today, there is disturbing evidence that many school boards and administrators do not recognize the need for a planned program to build public support.

Such a program starts with the state department of education. Even though education represents a major expenditure of state funds and has profound importance for the progress of a state, many state education offices still lack the support of a professional public relations staff. The same lack can be found at the local level, where recognition of the value of the professional comes slowly. In Wisconsin, for instance: A study made in that state in 1963 found that few districts followed a predetermined information policy and that only three districts employed full-time practitioners. Many used high school teachers on a part-time basis to prepare news releases. By 1975, only nine districts employed full-time specialists; half the Wisconsin superintendents surveyed said they handled public relations themselves.

School districts without full-time school–community relations officials may get help from their state department of education. Most state superintendents' offices have experts available. Texas, for example, has 100 people in its state department with school–community relations experience. Most state offices are willing to help in continuing or one-shot problem areas. And some districts can get help through the federal ESEA IV-C Innovation and Support for projects such as parent-education seminars and the like.

The magnitude of the problem is becoming clearer as educators step up their efforts. Nationally, advances are being spearheaded by the field's political and educational leaders—the National Education Association and its onetime affiliate, the National School Public Relations Association, which split with the NEA in 1972 and established its own headquarters across the Potomac in Rosslyn, Virginia. Founded in 1935 to further public understanding of the public schools, the NSPRA has grown rapidly and has done much to clarify and elevate the status of the practitioner. It conducts an annual seminar and provides other assistance to school practitioners. But even with the gains of recent years, this progress is neither broad enough nor fast enough to meet the challenge confronting educators today.

Educators' influence in improving education rests upon their ability to guide public opinion and to be guided by it in meeting society's needs. Failure to establish this cooperative partnership frequently results in defeats of needed bond issues, and it is also the source of much of the unbridled criticism of teaching methods and curricula content.

Public disputes repeatedly demonstrate that the public does not fully understand modern educational methods and objectives. Too much attention has been focused on the sideshows—athletics, baton-twirling, school plays, social events—and too little attention on the show in the main tent.

The role of the school board

Boards of education occupy a strategic position in the public relations program. They determine the educational policies upon which the program must be based. Composed of lay citizens who have accepted responsibility for public education in their communities, the board is the intermediary between the public and the professional administrators. It is essential that a board agree on an adequate statement of public relations policy. The board must serve its function of interpreting the community to the school staff and, in turn, interpreting staff ideas and policies to the community. Influential, articulate board members can be a valuable asset to a school system. Self-seeking, opinionated members can be harmful.[13] The superintendent of the Madison, Wisconsin, schools says that many board members are disruptive in school management because they take on the role of adversaries and "sleuths," instead of accepting their role as "partners in management." All superintendents want a supportive board.

Many school boards draw suspicion, criticism, and ill will by insisting on a "closed door" at board meetings. Conversely, they fail to utilize the open meeting as a newsworthy means of focusing public attention on school policies and problems. A veteran news editor once advised school-board members, "Maybe if you really had debate on some of these problems . . . if you would invite in citizens to debate out the issues, it might be beneficial. It would be painful . . . but it is the only way in which to educate the American people in such a way that they can form an enlightened and intelligent public opinion." Newspapers are increasingly insistent on this point.

Able school executives realize that they must often go against popular opinion to serve the best interest of the pupils, and if the decisions are for the welfare of the children, they will be the right decisions over the long pull. *But the public must be persuaded that they are the right decisions.*

The use of advisory committees

Under the pressure of federal and state laws and to meet particular needs, school boards are gradually seeing the value of advisory committees. Many boards have resisted creation of such committees in the past because they saw them as threats to the board's power. Reflective of the new trend is the South Carolina State Board of Education's directive to its State Department of Education to utilize advisory committees at the local level. Such committees are usually created in response to:

1. Federal program requirements.
2. State legislative or board requirements.
3. A particular need or needs.
4. The board's and/or administration's desire for better communication with and involvement of the community.
5. Parent/citizen demand for better communication with and involvement in the school system.[14]

The "generating authority" for the advisory committee should be responsible for determining its composition. However, the composition of some committees is federally mandated, as in the cases of ESEA or Title 1 advisory committees. Generally, members should be chosen who are interested in education, have influence in the community, have the time to devote to their tasks, and are broadly representative of the whole public. In addition to these desirable criteria, school boards or superintendents may find these hints helpful in organizing a representative advisory group:

1. *Develop new sources.* There should be some attempt to get "new faces" on the committees.
2. *Involve community leaders.* There should be some attempt to identify community leaders in all various racial or ethnic communities. Opposition leaders should be included.
3. *Involve parents of students.* There should be an effort to recruit parents of children in the schools.
4. *Develop diversity of opinion.* Persons should be selected who are representative of their particular group, but also an effort should be made to avoid selecting persons who are rigidly committed to a particular position. A "rubber stamp" committee will have little public relations clout in the community over time.[15]

The size of the committee should be determined by the task assigned to it. Generally, the more informal the selection process, the less substantial is the committee's contribution to the school district. Once an advisory committee has been created, it should assume the responsibility for creating the structure in which it will operate, subject to review by the appointing authority. For such committees to function effectively, they must have free access to the board and administrators and they must be provided with adequate information to use in their deliberations and in interpreting the schools to the community. Such committees are especially helpful in providing community feedback. The value of this two-way bridge in school community relations is plain if it is properly utilized.

For example, the Pasadena, California, school system set up a number of citizen–staff advisory committees to deal with particular problems or issues. One was created to deal with the system's multimillion-dollar building program; another, to advise on how best to develop a vocational-education program. These citizen–staff committees have also been used on the problems of equitable districting, release time for religious education, and programs for the retarded. In this way, many fresh ideas are obtained, possible criticisms are eliminated beforehand, and two-way communication is firmly established with the community's influentials.[16]

The Columbus, Ohio, school district took another approach to this objective of closer citizen–school ties when it instituted a series of successful neighborhood seminars. These seminars were an outgrowth of a series of Saturday morning conferences held the year before by the school-board president and carefully chosen Columbus civic leaders. The neighborhood seminars, sponsored by a City-Wide Seminar Committee, were devoted to discussions of the Columbus schools' program and financial needs. Study guides were prepared and distributed ahead of time to serve as the basis of the discussions. When the series was announced the first time, some 4,000 Columbus citizens signed up; when the seminars were held, another 3,000 turned out. Columbus officials found these neighborhood ideas highly productive.

Typical of the tasks confronting the school practitioner is that of gaining public acceptance of new courses and new patterns of education. An example is Cooperative Vocational Education, commonly referred to as a work-study program. Because it breaks from traditional high school patterns, the concept has been hampered by misinformation and misunderstanding on the part of traditional-minded educators and parents. In such a program, state and federal guidelines must be met, and parents, students, and school administrators must be persuaded that this alternative form of education is as useful as older, traditional programs—*a task that requires public relations solutions.*

Such a program must target messages for school administrators who must approve and support new programs, teachers outside the program whose cooperation and coordination are required, parents who must give their consent for those enrolling in the work-study program, and local employers who must provide the on-the-job training opportunities. Advisory committees are an effective means of getting employers involved in the program. Such a committee would:

1. Serve as a communications channel between schools and community occupational groups.
2. List specific skills and suggest related and technical information for a course.
3. Recommend competent personnel from business and industry as potential instructors.

4. Help evaluate the program of instruction.

5. Assist in recruiting students, in providing work training stations, and in placing qualified graduates in appropriate jobs.

6. Keep the school informed about changes in the labor market, specific needs, and surpluses.

7. Provide means for the school to inform the community of programs.

8. Assess program needs in terms of the entire community.

9. Suggest ways of improving the public relations program of the school.[17]

Another reason for the increase in importance of advisory committees has been a decline in the effectiveness of parent–teacher associations. Although the National Congress of Parents and Teachers argues with justification that PTAs can be a formidable force in lobbying for education at local, state, and national levels, an increasing number of local schools are forming "Parent–Teacher Organizations" instead of PTAs. While some of this is the result of lack of parent interest, principals must also share the blame for attempting to restrict the role of the PTA to fund raising as a supplement to school-system funding. This led one superintendent to say:

> If the PTA is to survive, if it is to continue as a potent force in support of public education, it must avoid strangling itself with spaghetti dinners. The PTA cannot be a rubber stamp of the administration, but must represent the watchdog of the community—applaud when successful, chastise when unsuccessful. If the PTA doesn't do it, there will be other groups—civic associations, parents' unions, concerned citizen's groups—which will fill the vacuum. And their efforts are not always favorable to public education.[18]

Fact-finding, feedback

Educators have repeatedly said, "The community should be so organized that citizen control of its public-school policies is respected in principle and facilitated in practice." One of the surest ways to facilitate citizen control is through periodic surveys of community opinion. The Denver public schools have made such surveys at three-year intervals, with profitable results. Through these polls, in the words of the superintendent, Denver's administrators and teachers "obtain a sort of group concept of what parents want and what citizens of this community want—their concept of what good schools are." The results of these surveys, fully reported to staff and the community, serve as guides for Denver schools in their program and public relations planning.

Ned Hubbell, a consultant, stresses that it is necessary to get information before one can give information. This doesn't have to be a formal opinion poll, he says, it could even be an inventory of information obtained by teachers in conferences with parents or other groups.

The public's increasing demand for school accountability requires a shift of emphasis away from publicity in school public relations. There is need for *representative, nonintuitive feedback* in contrast to the present unrepresentative feedback from students, friends, simple news stories, and firsthand observations of officials and teachers. Wynne says that a nonintuitive-feedback system requires researchers (including public relations officers) committed to public accountability and sympathetic, informed disseminators.[19] Practitioners have to deal with the fact that feedback is costly and often brings unpleasant truths to their bosses.

Publics and programs

The chief executive of a school system needs skilled assistance in planning and directing the program. In too many systems, public relations is left to individual schools with no central direction and coordination. A public relations program requires direction, and the superintendent must provide it.[20] He must:

1. Accept personal responsibility for planning and coordinating the public relations program.
2. Adapt leadership activities to his ability and personality and to community expectations.
3. Merit community recognition and acceptance by performance and competence.
4. Delegate the proper public relations functions and commensurate authority to staff assistants without relinquishing his own responsibility.
5. Make effective use of available technical assistance from staff members and laymen in the community and assign specific responsibility to specific people.
6. Encourage and expect the staff of each school in his system to maintain good public relations in its own service area.

The public relations responsibility of boards and superintendents is taken for granted. However, a powerful new leadership force has emerged in the form of teacher and student activism. More and more, when school boards and administrators fail, the teachers are stepping in, using their own resources, to "tell it like it is" to the community. Teachers are seeking a voice in selecting their administrators; high school students are vigorously demanding more say in shaping their school programs. The Council of the Great City Schools—a body representing 30 urban school districts—has recommended active student participation in public-school operations. Some boards of education have seated high schoolers as ex officio members to establish better rapport with students.

The professional association or teachers' union is the spokesman for teachers. They have mustered the courage and clout to stand united for quality education—"fighting city hall" if necessary to accomplish needed reforms, working tirelessly on school-bond campaigns, becoming politically active on issues concerning the schools, and seeking a voice in the development of policies affecting their profession and the students they teach. Teacher militancy has been a prime force in bringing new emphasis to the public relations function. The ideal climate exists when the board, superintendent, teachers, and students work together as a team, but this seldom happens these days.

The publics

The starting point of any program is the careful determination of the publics involved, channels of two-way communication with them, and agreement on objectives. There are various publics in school relations that must be reached:

536

Internal		External
School board	Parents	Churches
Teachers	Taxpayer groups	Alumni
Children	Service clubs	Athletic boosters
Staff employees	Patriotic groups	Labor unions
	Civic groups	Legislators
	Industry	Government administrators
	School neighbors	Teachers' union

Teachers: First, there should be rapport between the school hierarchy and the teachers. That such a relationship is often lacking is made evident, however, by legislation making it mandatory for school boards to negotiate with teachers. The necessity for enacting such laws is indicative of administrative and communications breakdowns. A sound program cannot be built if the teacher is excluded.

Many teachers spend vacations and holidays in workshops and university courses to enhance their skills. If they are allowed a voice, this training can be shared for the benefit of the entire system. But most important, the teacher in his day-to-day activities is in a position to relate effectively to students, parents, and others—and, in turn, to provide valuable feedback to those responsible for the program.

In bridging the gulf between administrators and teachers, which grows as districts increase in size, one useful approach is a requirement that superintendents and principals take frequent turns as substitute teachers, enabling them to see the teacher's problems in a fresh way.

Children: Children are perhaps the most influential of a school's publics. Much of the information and the attitudes held by the general public are transmitted from pupil to parent to public on the community grapevine. There is no surer route to a person's heart—or resentment—than through his or her child. When the program of a school system rests on a foundation of classroom accomplishment, it is a house built upon a rock. Ill-founded criticism will not overwhelm it. The pupil's role as an intermediary is a strategic one. *Public relations truly starts in the classroom.* In a public opinion survey conducted by Ned S. Hubbell for the Fairfax County (Virginia) Public Schools, parents said they rely most on their children for information about the schools.

The school executive should determine whether students are enthusiastic boosters. He or she should see that pupils are well informed about policies, that courses satisfy their needs and challenge their abilities, that individual attention is provided for those who need it, and that the overall atmosphere engenders pupil and parent pride in the school. Proud, satisfied parents will ring doorbells to win a school-bond vote.[21]

Parents: It is important that both pupil and parent get off on the right foot, starting with kindergarten. Many schools have effective programs for introducing parent and child to the school. A typical one starts with preregistration in the spring before the child starts school. It includes enrollment by the principal so that he can get acquainted, a visit by the mother and child to the room the child will enter in September, and a leisurely cup of coffee with the principal and other teachers who may be free that hour. This is followed in August by mailing the parents a kindergarten handbook that tells them what is expected of the budding pupil. Informality, information, and consideration are the keys to a pleasant introduction.

Schools dare not rely upon the child's often twisted reports to keep parents fully, accurately informed. Good parent relationships are built by frequent, frank communication between teacher and parent. Although they share the same goals, there are many blocks to communication, so care must be used in report cards and in parent conferences. Many schools continue to use old-fashioned, dull, and uninformative report cards. There's no law that says report cards have to be printed on a drab yellow stock. Bright colors and a gay illustration, coupled with meaningful comments to the parent, can do wonders.

In a study of parent-teacher conferences, it was found that standard practices boomeranged unless the teachers were well prepared in interpreting data about the child.[22] Communication means conferences, encouragement of parent observation of normal classroom situations, special programs for parents, and home visits by the teachers to handle ticklish problems. PTA meetings with a purpose—not just excuses for a social hour—are a tool of proved worth in school-parent communication. Too many PTAs fail to serve this need.

Constructive relationships with parents are best built on annual parent-teacher conferences. In this connection, a ticklish problem has developed concurrently with our schools' extensive testing programs: To what information are parents entitled? Paul Woodring comments, "Parents in several American communities have charged that the schools are withholding important information about their children. Some have taken legal action to require that the full record on each child be made available to his parents. Teachers and administrators are troubled and frightened by these demands because they have compiled a great deal of . . . information about each student and many school systems have no clear policy regarding what may be released to parents."[23] The only prudent course is to develop carefully thought-out, clearly stated policies in this matter and enforce them. Such policies must be in accord with federal laws and U.S. court decisions. The Buckley Amendment (Family Education Rights and Privacy Act) gives parents and students the right of access to their personnel records. In 1975, in a landmark decision, the U.S. Supreme Court ruled in *Goss* v. *Lopez* that students have a constitutional right to a hearing before they can be suspended from school. The hearing may be informal, but a student's case must be heard.

An effective way to build school–parent understanding is to hold special night courses for parents. In recent years, many high schools have instituted such courses to introduce parents to new concepts and new teaching methods. Such courses have met with an enthusiastic response in most cities. Parents are anxious to know the content of their sons' and daughters' courses and thus to be able to assist the students with their homework. Smart school personnel capitalize on this parental interest.

Staff: Too often in the past, the emphasis on internal communication has been toward educational staff only. Each member of the school staff, from principal and teachers to bus driver to custodian to school nurse, must be brought into the program. This can best be accomplished through a continuing in-service training program. Also, the qualities and attitudes of a person should be given due weight in staff recruitment. Finally, it should be remembered that the happy, satisfied teacher or employee is the one who generally makes the best ambassador. Many superintendents have found it highly desirable to organize, and meet on a regular basis with, advisory councils representing all categories of employees (teacher advisory council, food-service advisory council, and so on).

Residents: A given school district's residents, who foot the bill, provide the children, and shape the school's environment, must be the ultimate targets. This public is composed of many groups—parents, taxpayers, and other citizens with positive ideas about "what our schools ought to be teaching." The public can be reached through the pupil, PTA, press, service clubs, and church groups, and in countless other ways. Community influentials can be involved most effectively through consultation on school matters.

Changes in school policy, organization, and curricula and plans for new schools should be cleared with key public groups. The counsel of lay leaders should be sought as often as possible and practicable. Location of new schools directly involves city government, real estate developers, businessmen, bankers, and others. Cooperative planning can be coordinated through councils, committees, and commissions. It should be based on a continuous process of self-analysis. Broadly based planning makes available a wealth of good ideas. It also serves to clear the path for important changes. Public hearings on major issues can be a profitable, if at times uncomfortable, procedure.

A new problem—the school paper

Typical of the new and more complex problems confronting school practitioners is that of the freedom of the scholastic newspapers—a "no-win" proposition. School authorities' traditional practice of controlling high school newspapers is being challenged. In an era charged with controversy and litigation, a number of school systems have been haled into court on this issue. For example, Lauren Boyd, editor of the Hayfield, Virginia, secondary-school paper, decided to publish an article headlined, "Sexually Active Students Fail to Use Contraception." The school principal ordered the students not to publish this article.

The students appealed the principal's decision to the Fairfax County superintendent, who in turn referred it to his Advisory Board on Student Expression. The board upheld the principal, and this decision was affirmed by the superintendent and the school board. The students, aided by the Student Law Center headquartered in nearby Washington, D.C., took the school authorities to court. The case was heard in the U.S. District Court for Northern Virginia, Alexandria, early in 1977, and the judge ruled in favor of the students. The judge held that the newspaper "was conceived, established, and operated as a conduit for student expression on a wide variety of topics. It falls clearly within the parameters of the First Amendment" *Gambino v. Fairfax,* 45 L.W. 2414 (E.D. Va. [1977]). This decision was upheld in October 1977, in a 2-1 ruling of the Court of Appeals for the Fourth Circuit (3 Med. L. Rptr. note Oct. 25, 1977). The board did not appeal further.

In a historic decision on students' First Amendment rights, *Tinker* v. *Des Moines,* 393 U.S. 503 (1969), the Supreme Court stated:

Students in school as well as out of school are "persons" under our Constitution. . . . In our system, students may not be regarded as closed-circuit recipients of only that which the state chooses to communicate. They may not be confined to the expression of those sentiments that are officially approved. In the absence of a specific showing of constitutionally valid reasons to regulate their speech, students are entitled to freedom of expression of their views.[24]

The *Tinker* decision has been applied to students producing official school newspapers where those papers have been established as forums for the expression of student views. In *Bayer* v. *Kinzler,* 383 F. Supp. 1164 (E.D.N.Y. 1974), high school students produced a "sex information supplement" as part of the official school newspaper. The supplement was primarily composed of articles dealing with contraception and abortion. School officials refused to allow distribution. The court ruled that the students' First Amendment rights had been violated, stating:

> The newspaper staff's attempt to educate their fellow students by means of a number of thoughtfully written articles seems at least equally deserving of protection under the First and Fourteenth Amendments as the symbolic wearing of an armband, the protected activity in *Tinker.*[25]

School officials in *Bayer* argued that censorship was "reasonable because publication of the supplement constituted an unauthorized intrusion into an area of secondary school curriculum." The court disagreed. Thus, school officials are caught between the rock of parental outrage when such articles are published and the hard place of the courts' grant of freedom to the scholastic press.

Communications

Objectives of public information for schools are primarily these: (1) to build the public support necessary to obtain adequate funds, (2) to gain public acceptance and cooperation in making educational changes, (3) to fully report school news and thus head off misinformation and rumor, and (4) to build amicable working relationships with news executives and reporters.

For years, press coverage of schools has emphasized athletics, student activities, and collective-bargaining disputes. Beyond this, the coverage has been largely restricted to hard news, much of it unfavorable. There is little prospect for an improvement in this situation, given tight newsholes, traditional news values, and the attitudes of newspaper executives, particularly with metropolitan daily papers. Suburban dailies and weeklies attempt better coverage, but their effectiveness is hampered by small, overworked staffs.

In a survey of a cross section of the nation's newspaper publishers, editors, and education reporters, James B. Dickson found that "a majority of the publishers and editors and half of the education reporters did not think that their newspapers' readers desired more coverage of educational programs in their regions. The newspersons tried to put much of the blame on educators. A majority of the publishers, editors, and education reporters asserted that interesting, newsworthy stories took place in their local schools, but educators failed to communicate them to the newspapers."[26]

The bottom line in Dickson's survey of 606 news executives and reporters is that the majority of publishers and editors are satisfied for the most part with their coverage of local education and wire-service coverage of education generally. Also, Dr. Dickson found that a majority of publishers, editors, and education writers believe that increased distribution of news releases by educators would not necessarily mean a corresponding increase in education coverage by their newspaper. Yet a majority of respondents in all three categories suggested that educators ought to strive for more balanced emphasis in school news coverage! In a contradictory expression, a majority of the publishers and editors thought "it would not be in the best interests of their newspaper to give local coverage of education equal emphasis with coverage of sports activities."[27]

In another survey—this one of more than 300 education writers—Harvey Jacobson found agreement on these ways of improving education coverage: (1) Increase the number of staff assigned to cover education in the mass media; (2) increase the salaries for education writers in the mass media; (3) conduct seminars for education writers; (4) offer college courses to prepare specialists in education reporting; (5) conduct research on problems of education reporting; and (6) offer college courses to educate school administrators in communication.[28] On the last point, these education writers saw as "a major handicap to improved news coverage" the failure of educators to understand newsmen. For example, the respondents asserted that they are interested in "accuracy" and stories "of interest to our readers," while educators are predominantly concerned about "usefulness to the source."

George Gerbner made a study of education news for the U.S. Office of Education and concluded, "The celebrated 'Boom on the School Beat' appears to have been limited to metropolitan dailies and to have been more a sign of recognition than a rise in the proportion of all special editorial employees holding school news assignments on American daily papers. . . . Mobility on the job is still generally high. The 'hard news, local angle' policy sets the style of reporting on most papers. The local orientation of the American daily paper assures a fair amount of community school news."[29]

The press is slowly revising its news values to include more news of positive educational developments. This trend, started some years ago by the news magazines, needs to be speeded. The local newspaper is the primary means of informing the public of what the schools are trying to do and what they contend with in doing it. This requires continuous reporting, so the schools must take the initiative with a planned information program directed by a trained practitioner.

The dependence of the media on school public relations personnel and the resulting payoff for systems employing competent information officers is shown in a study by Robert L. Rings. Rings selected from Ohio's 165 city school districts a sample of 35 districts with public-information officers and 35 without, and matched the two samples. He found:

> The school districts with public relations personnel did receive significantly more news coverage than the districts without public relations directors. This included the number of different stories as well as the amount of space. Likewise, the majority of coverage in the public relations directors' districts was of non-sports articles. In contrast, the majority of the coverage in the non-director districts was devoted to athletic activities.[30]

Further, Rings found persuasive evidence that public relations programs pay off. He continues:

. . . financial records indicated that the director systems' current average operating millage was two mills above the state mean, whereas the non-director systems' average operating millage was four mills below the state mean. In local support per pupil, the director sample averaged $375 to the non-director sample of $275.[31]

The lesson of the Rings study and similar studies is that the press will cover administrative changes, school conflicts, and school sports, but will not provide the manpower for the more time-consuming reportage of curriculum changes, educational policies, and the like. The situation is even less promising with the electronic media. Radio is useful primarily for spot news, and television is interested in human-interest stories that can be covered quickly and effectively. Thus, school systems must, in their own self-interest, provide broad, constructive coverage of education at the local level.

News—disseminated through the school paper and community papers, over radio and TV, through personal contact, and in public meetings—forms the hard core of the informational program. In Bedford, Michigan, the teachers bridged a credibility gap between the school system and the community by converting their own association membership newsletter into an open letter to the township citizens.

Many schools use American Education Week to stage open houses, exhibits, and student performances in shopping centers to gain the community's attention. Education–Business Days represent another effective adaptation of a tool by educators. Filmstrips and motion pictures, which need not be expensive, are another effective tool. One administrator, an amateur photographer, took a series of pictures of the school day, starting with the bus pickup and showing every school activity. The slides were grouped according to grade levels and extracurricular activities. No planned script was used for narration, and this informality and lack of education jargon strengthened the presentation.

An imaginative way of reaching the public by using its channels of communication was a daily radio program initiated by Lindley J. Stiles when he was dean of the University of Wisconsin School of Education. For several years, Professor Stiles's 15-minute program mixed relaxed comments about education with music. The program was first carried on a radio station appealing primarily to devotees of rock 'n' roll, jazz, and folk music.

The Fairfax County, Virginia, public-school system has for several years produced a 15-minute "Radio Report Card." Tapes featuring school news and interviews are delivered weekly to the nine stations that carry the program as a community service.

One year, the Milwaukee school board, responding to strong criticism of a budget that would sharply increase property taxes, authorized an advertising campaign using newspapers, TV, and radio to build support for its budget. Ironically, at the same meeting, the board turned down a plan to increase parental involvement in the schools.

One way of overcoming superficial and spotty news coverage is to get a readable annual report into the hands or homes of parents or community leaders. However, many school districts have turned away from annual reports as being expensive to produce and having limited community interest. They are instead investing in brief, readable newsletters distributed on a regular basis through the mail, or, in the interest of economy, through the schools to parents. Recently, practitioners have seen the value of publishing the annual report as a supplement

FIGURE 23–1 Public-information literature from the schools.

in newspapers that reach the active citizens in a community. This is economical—the cost per impression is usually a few cents, while a glossy printed report runs several times that amount. Practitioners are also beginning to utilize TV to disseminate the annual report, a wise move. John A. Cone of the South Carolina School Boards Association lists these advantages of using TV for the annual report:

1. The cost of using television can be considered comparable to newspapers, though the two are like apples and oranges. In a medium-sized market, one might expect to pay $800 for a thirty-minute prime time program reaching 60,000 households.
2. Those who cannot or will not read your annual report can and probably will sit and listen to an attractive televised report. This can be maximized with advance publicity and an entertaining format.
3. Thousands of citizens have an opportunity to see and hear the superintendent as he presents the "state of the schools" address. They can evaluate what sort of man he is. Is he honest? Is he compassionate? Is he capable?
4. The viewer can look at a chart and have it explained to him or her. Nothing is more frustrating than seeing a graph in the written annual report and not being able to understand it.
5. Through the use of film shot on site, the viewer can actually see what is happening in the schools. He is reminded of how small a five-year-old child is. He sees for the first time how crowded a classroom can be. He sees enthusiastic teachers and motivated students.
6. Others can appear live on the air and question what the school spokesman has said. A team of newsmen, known throughout the community to be champions of "sunshine," can lend credibility to the report by interviewing the superintendent right on the air. This also brings about answers to questions which naturally arise in the minds of the viewers as the report progresses.
7. The programs can all be taped, stored, and reviewed year after year. What a sense of continuity when the spokesman can say to his constituents, "Here is what we promised you three years ago and here is what we have done." When excerpts of previous reports are used, it lends an atmosphere of long-range planning and commitment to openness and candor.[32]

The printed word has its advantages whether in the newspaper or in a more traditional annual report. However, none of the advantages mentioned above can be found in the printed report. Clearly, TV cannot be ignored by the school district interested in communicating with its publics.

Guides for planning

When planning to broadcast an annual report, the practitioner should observe some caution signs:

1. Don't pay to have the report published in the paper and then expect the television stations to donate air time.
2. Check the rating books to see which station or stations should broadcast your report, how much you should pay them, and when your audience is watching.
3. Don't ask several stations for a simulcast. They will probably refuse, and even if they agree, robbing the TV audience of a choice of programs may make your viewers angry.

The informational task cannot be assigned to any specific medium. The prime importance of personal contact between school personnel and public must be kept foremost. A survey of California educators showed that they regard personal contact as "the most important channel in keeping the general public informed about the schools." Those interviewed rated the daily newspaper and reports carried home by children next in importance. Further, it is essential that the relationship between the publicity objective and the base objective of wholesome two-way relationships of school and community be kept clearly in mind. The program should be developed so that there is direct contact with every home in the community.

The two-way communications task between school and patron is sufficiently important and demanding to deserve the full-time efforts of a trained practitioner. But many school districts insist they cannot afford this. Effective programs can be developed by part-time specialists if they get the cooperation of administrators and teachers.

The informational task must be indigenous to and modified by each school's environment needs, problems, and personnel available to do the job. It takes public relations–mindedness and planning more than it takes money.

Evaluation

Jerome C. Kovalcik, New York City assistant superintendent and former NSPRA president, gives the following checkpoints for evaluating a school public relations program:

Is the program child-focused? Is the child the primary client?

Is reporting accurate and truthful?

Is the program based upon what goes on in the schools—and not on window dressing?

Are weaknesses as well as strengths reported?

Is it a multimedia program?

Is it sensitive to various publics?

Is there in-service public relations training for all staff members?

Case problem

Last night, the Calhoun County school board decided to eliminate public comment from its regular board meetings. Board members had been stung by harsh comments from citizens at several recent meetings. Beginning in June, the chairman said, all comments for the board will have to be made at public-information meetings, held throughout the county on the Monday night following the board meeting. The decision was made by a majority of members in a closed caucus.

The chairman, Joe Wilson, explained, "The board does not have to take any official action to cut out the public-comment section of the board meeting." A board member supporting the action said, "I don't want to get in the position of being called 'stupid' and have no opportunity to reply." A dissenting member

EXHIBIT 23-1

A Case History from Charleston

The common problems confronting today's practitioner—sagging public confidence in schools, confusion over what test scores are and mean, and the need to effectively use TV—are illustrated in this case history from Charleston, South Carolina, provided by John A. Cone, then the public relations director:

During the summer and fall of 1972, it became clear that the Charleston County schools suffered from a chronic loss of public confidence. No less than eight indicators were used to show the board of trustees that the problem was a serious one.

Content analysis of editorials and "Letters to the Editor" revealed that citizens wanted much more information about their public-school system. The debriefing of the district's speakers' bureau showed that citizens often did not believe what they were told by school officials.

Further research showed that, contrary to popular belief, the district did reach a wide audience with its information programs. The informal studies also indicated that school officials had never given citizens any reason to doubt their honesty.

Before any plans could be laid, *it was necessary to understand why the district's information dissemination plan was not working.* An examination of past performance showed that the information sent out was almost always favorable to the district. In addition, the impact of this information was diminished because it was usually either too dull or too light in nature to draw much attention.

The school administration had to devise a plan to combat two closely related public relations problems: (1) *present a body of pertinent information with such impact that it would be remembered by constituents,* and (2) *improve the credibility of the information being sent out.*

The district accepted the theory that "credibility increases when an organization becomes so open that it is willing to volunteer the bad news as well as the good." The strategy, based on this hypothesis, was to report to the public for the first time the results of the standardized test scores gathered over the past three years.

It was a bold idea. Few school districts anywhere in the country had ever voluntarily reported such scores. Even those school districts that reported their standardized scores did so because the scores were high and reflected positively upon the school district. In Charleston the scores were extremely low. It was inevitable that reporting them would stimulate much criticism of the system. But it would also improve the district's credibility.

In August 1973, the school district produced a 30-minute television broadcast that was aired on three VHF stations in the area. The broadcast was supported by an eight-page tabloid in the daily papers and by radio and television newscasts.

The format of the program allowed roughly ten minutes for an explanation of the test scores, ten minutes for a description of the "Bootstrap" programs to improve the schools, and ten minutes for questions by local newsmen. The last strengthened the credibility of the broadcast.

A critical part of this reporting system called for the continuation each year of televised accounting for student performance. The superintendent promised to come back again every year to tell what the scores were like. This he has done.

The prime-time audience for the three stations combined would normally have been in excess of 100,000 viewers. The only cost in the first year was

EXHIBIT 23-1 (CONT.)

some $400 to an advertising agency for filming and the preparation of visuals. The local stations provided air time and the production as a community service. In subsequent years, the air time was purchased.

The combination morning and evening papers reached some 105,000 readers with the special tabloid. The tabloid cost $4,000 and included vast amounts of material that had never before been made available.

This long-range public relations plan has done much to help the district meet its goals of providing more pertinent information in a more believable manner. Letters from constituents, phone calls, editorials, and the results of surveys have demonstrated that the public appreciates candor in its school officials.

Charges that the district withholds information have disappeared almost entirely. The statements of school-district officers are now viewed as reliable.

argued, "I believe the board should take every opportunity to hear citizens even if we don't like what they say."

The morning newspaper has a long story on this action, and a blistering editorial criticizing the board and demanding the public's right to be heard on school matters.

Your superintendent, visibly upset, calls you into his office as you arrive for work and says, "Now what in the blazes can we do about this?" You tell him not to push the panic button, and that you will need an hour or so to do some checking before you come back with a recommendation. What is it?

ADDITIONAL READINGS

ROBERT BYRNE and EDWARD POND, *Strengthening School-Community Relations.* Reston, Va.: National Association Secondary School Principals, 1976.

STEVEN H. CHAFFEE, "The Public View of the Media as Carriers of Information between School and Community," *Journalism Quarterly,* Vol. 44 (Winter 1967).

DON DAVIES, ed., *Schools Where Parents Make a Difference.* Boston: Institute for Responsive Education, 1976.

JOHN EDGERTON, *School Desegregation: A Report Card from the South.* Atlanta: Southern Regional Council, 1976.

GEORGE GERBNER, "The Press and the Dialogue in Education," *Journalism Monographs,* No. 5 (1967). Austin, Tex.: Association for Education in Journalism.

NAT HENTOFF, *Does Anybody Give a Damn?* New York: Knopf, 1977. A discussion of school problems that shows insight as well as vigor.

"High Schools under Fire, Even Outside the Big Cities There Is Trouble Everywhere," *Time,* November 14, 1977.

LESLIE KINDRED, DON BAGIN, and DONALD R. GALLAGHER, *The School and Community Relations.* Englewood Cliffs, N.J.: Prentice-Hall, 1976.

CARROLL G. LANCE, *Educators Meet the Press: A Communication Gap at the State Capital.* Madison, Wis.: U.S. Office of Education, Project Public Information, 1968. A survey of newsmen at 35 state capitals.

MARC LIBARLE and TOM SELIGSON, eds., *The High School Revolutionaries.* New York: Random House, 1970.

GORDON McCLOSKEY, *Education and Public Understanding,* 2nd ed. New York: Harper & Row, 1967.

PHILIP K. PIELE and JOHN STUART HULL, *Budgets, Bonds and Ballots.* New York: Heath, 1973.

DIANE RAVITCH, *The Great School Wars.* New York: Basic Books, 1975. Turbulent history of New York City schools, 1805–1973.

LOUISE SAUL, "School Boards Turning to Public Relations Experts to Keep Parents Informed," *New York Times,* September 1, 1974, NJ 11.

ADOLPH UNRUH and ROBERT A. WILLIER, *Public Relations for Schools.* Belmont, Calif.: Lear Sigler, 1974.

547

1. Figures obtained from Educational Research Service, Inc., Arlington, Va. See U.S. Department of Health, Education and Welfare, Education Division, *Projections of Education Statistics to 1984–85* (Washington, D.C., 1976).

2. See Edward Wynne, *The Politics of School Accountability* (Berkeley, Calif.: McCutchan, 1972), for implications for public information.

3. Robert E. Stake, "School Accountability Laws," *Journal of Educational Evaluation,* Vol. 4, February, 1973.

4. Article by Jack McCurty and Don Speich, in issue of August 15, 1976.

5. Calvin Trillin, "Schools without Money," *The New Yorker,* November 8, 1976.

6. *Newsweek,* December 13, 1976, p. 72.

7. Educational Research Service, Inc., *Voter Behavior and Campaign Strategies in School Finance Elections* (Arlington, Va.: ERS, 1977), p. 17.

8. Roy K. Wilson, "Communication Strategies for Dealing with Current Issues in American Education," Kingsley Address, NSPRA National Seminar, July 13, 1976, p. 3.

9. For many examples, see *Children out of School in America* (Cambridge, Mass.: Children's Defense Fund, 1975). Indicts a society that doesn't care about its children.

10. NSPA, "Summary of Task Force Meeting," Washington, D.C., November 9, 1976.

11. Richard F. Carter, *Voters and Their Schools* (Stanford, Calif.: Stanford University, Institute for Communication Research, 1960); findings summarized on pp. 4–16. Other studies in this long-term, fruitful research project include Richard F. Carter and William G. Savard, *Influence of Voter Turnout on School Bond and Tax Elections* (Washington, D.C.: Government Printing Office, 1961); Richard F. Carter, Bradley S. Greenberg, and Alvin Haimson, *Informal Communication about Schools* (1966); and Richard F. Carter and Steven H. Chaffee, *Between Citizens and Schools* (1966). The studies are summarized in Richard F. Carter and William R. Odell, *The Structure and Process of School-Community Relations: A Summary* (1966). The last three reports were published by the Stanford Institute for Communication Research.

12. For a case study showing the costs of a failure in public relations, see David Hulburd, *This Happened in Pasadena* (New York: Macmillan, 1951).

13. For details of a long-range, well-organized program for school innovation in Fullerton, Calif., see "No Surprises Wanted," *Trends in School Public Relations,* January 15, 1969.

14. National School Public Relations Association, *Citizens Advisory Committees* (Arlington, Va.: NSPRA, 1973), p. 10.

15. University of Miami School Desegregation Consulting Center, *Districtwide Advisory Committees* (Tampa, Fla.: University of Miami School Desegregation Consulting Center, 1974), p. 6.

16. For further guidance, see William F. Brievogel and Gordon Greenwood, *School Advisory Committees* (Gainesville, Fla.: Florida Educational Research and Development Council, 1973).

17. Calfrey Calhoun and Alton V. Finch, *Vocational and Career Education: Concepts and Operations* (Belmont, Calif.: Wadsworth, 1976), p. 385. Also helpful is Scott M. Cutlip, *Career Education: Communicating the Concept* (Columbus, O.: ERIC Clearinghouse on Vocational and Technical Education, Ohio State University, 1973).

18. Dr. John S. Davis, superintendent Fairfax, Va., County Schools, in speech to National Association of Elementary Principals, Atlantic City, N.J., April 26, 1976.

19. Wynne, *Politics of School Accountability,* p. 8, for a chart of the process as he sees it.

20. American Association of School Administrators, *Public Relations for America's Schools* (Washington, D.C.: The Association, 1950), p. 254.

21. For "how to" booklet on school-bond campaigns, see *School Finance Campaign Handbook* (Washington, D.C.: National Education Association, 1969).

22. Claud E. Kitchens, "The Parent-Teacher Conference as an Instrument for Changing Perceptions of and Attitudes toward Schools and Teachers," Ph.D. thesis, University of South Carolina, 1961.

23. Paul Woodring, "The Parent's Right to Know," *Saturday Review,* November 19, 1961.

24. 393 U.S. at 511.

25. 383 F. Supp. at 1165. For elaboration, see *Bazaar et al v. Fortune,* 476 F. 2d 570 (1970) in which officials of the University of Mississippi were ordered not to interfere with a student literary magazine.

26. James Brian Dickson, "A Study of the Perceptions of Publishers, Editors, and Education Reporters Related to the Desirability and Feasibility of Three Approaches to Increasing Newspaper

Coverage of American Education," Ph.D. dissertation, Ohio University, 1975.

27. *Ibid.*

28. "Needed Improvements in Education News Coverage as Perceived by Media and Education Gatekeepers," *Journal of Educational Research,* Vol. 66 (February 1973).

29. "Newsmen and Schoolmen: the State and Problem of Education Reporting," *Journalism Quarterly,* Vol. 44 (Summer 1967).

30. "Public School News Coverage with and without PR Directors," *Journalism Quarterly,* Vol. 48 (Spring 1971).

31. *Ibid.*

32. "Televised Annual Report: More Bang for Your Buck!" paper prepared for NSPRA Annual Seminar, 1976.

24

The need for public understanding of the colleges has never been more urgent than it is today. For as the nation grasps the complex problems of colleges, so will the legislators who vote funds and the private donors react.

L.L.L. GOLDEN

The Practice: higher education

The backdrop

Institutions of higher learning were among the first to set about winning public favor on a systematic basis. The emergence of the strong public university, dependent upon taxpayer support, in the latter part of the nineteenth century brought with it increased need for popular support. The University of Michigan led the way when it established a publicity office in 1897. Increased competition for funds and students forced the private institutions to counter with similar programs.

Public relations' seedbed years brought innovative publicity programs to many colleges and universities, among them Harvard, Yale, Columbia, and Pennsylvania in the Ivy League; Chicago, Michigan, and Wisconsin in the Big Ten. As classical education gave way to curricula responsive to the needs of the twentieth century, as the demand for extension grew, and as the need for money increased sharply, the college administrator turned, sooner or later, to the use of publicity and, ultimately, to public relations.[1] "By 1900 the publicity-conscious administrator found himself generally in charge of the new American university. Effortlessly blending the once distinct concepts of academic purpose, he sought to unite his constituents by providing them with the rhetoric of agreeable and uplifting ceremony."[2]

The development of the professional association in this field is significant. Organized in 1917 as the American Association of College News Bureaus, in 1930 it became the American College Publicity Association and in 1946 the American College Public Relations Association. At the start of the 1970s, this association had a membership of 1,244 institutions and some 3,650 men and women, professionals responsible for their institutions' public relations, financial support, and development programs. The institutional membership had nearly trebled since 1939–40, reflecting the growth in this field over the years.

Meanwhile, in 1959, Donald Smith, then president of the American Alumni Council, had said, "The efforts and expenditures of the American Alumni council and the American College Public Relations Association in serving programs of institutional advancement must be coordinated." Thus the first call for merger was sounded. Occasional negotiations between the two groups con-

551

tinued off and on until 1973, when a joint study committee was set up. The merger was voted in 1974 and became effective in January 1975, under the leadership of President Alice L. Beeman, the first woman to head a national public relations organization. She retired in 1978.

The three functions of public relations, alumni relations, and fund raising, now commonly called development, were brought together at the national level with this merger of the AAC and the ACPRA into the Council for Advancement and Support of Education (CASE). The three fields have much in common, but they also have competing interests, which are striving for accommodation under the CASE umbrella; the merger is not without stresses and strains.

Through publications, regional and national conferences, seminars, and publications, CASE strives to advance the fields of public relations and development. It publishes *CASE Currents* which replaced ACPRA's *College and University Journal.* As of 1977, approximately 1,800 colleges, universities, two-year colleges, and independent schools, represented by 7,000 individuals, were members.

The assignment

These organizational changes reflect to a small degree the vastly changed and more difficult assignment facing collegiate practitioners. The course of higher education has been profoundly altered during the past decade. Caught in recurring crises of confrontation, protest, distorted media images, and declining public confidence, colleges face public relations tasks unparalleled in the history of higher education. The student revolts that erupted so violently in the 1960s and continued into the 1970s, as well as growing public disenchantment with higher education, brought changes and recurring crises to the once-tranquil campus. The public opinion backlash from these conflicts also brought lessened support and vehement criticism. Even the worth of a college education, once taken for granted, is now hotly debated. But *the essentiality of the public relations function in higher education is no longer debated.* The hard question asked by today's college president is, "Can our public relations staff measure up to its assignment?"

As they reshape their institutions in the late 1970s to meet contemporary needs in instruction, research, and public service, college administrators must grapple with the diminished support of the sponsoring society. This is writ large in the failure of state appropriations, federal funding, and private gifts to keep pace with increased demands and the attrition of inflation. For example, in the late 1970s, state appropriations in 22 states fell behind the rate of inflation over a two-year period. In this same period, education fell to ninth place in the amount of research and development funds appropriated by the federal government.

Administrators' efforts will also be working upstream against the loss of confidence in collegiate institutions—a loss shared with most other institutions. A survey of professors by Everett C. Ladd, Jr., and Seymour M. Lipset in the mid-1970s found *two out of three* professors expressing the opinion that "the status of the academic profession" had decreased. A 1976 Harris poll found that even though higher education ranked second only to medicine in public confidence, only 31 percent of the public expressed "a great deal of confidence" in it—a slippage of 30 percentage points from a 1966 poll. A 1976 Gallup poll found college teachers ranking behind medical doctors and engineers in maintaining high standards, in the public's opinion. A survey by the market research division of Procter & Gamble, also made in 1976, found that colleges, in which 46 percent of the respondents expressed "a great deal of confidence," ranked below the military, established religion, religious leaders, TV news, network TV news, and TV commentators.[3] Columbia's Prof. Robert Nisbet attributes the disenchantment to "an alien spirit of pride, even arrogance" among social scientists and to their failure to fulfill many of the promises they have made to society.

Fred M. Hechinger has succinctly summarized this loss of public confidence and support:

> America is in headlong retreat from its commitment to education. Political confusion and economic uncertainty have shaken the people's faith in education as the key to financial and social success. This retreat ought to be the most pertinent issue in any examination of the country's condition. At stake is nothing less than the survival of American democracy.
>
> Let us have no illusions about an American future with declining confidence in universal education and diminished access to higher learning. A slowdown in the escalator of upward mobility constitutes a break with the most fundamental American ideals. The consequence will be a stratified, classbound society ruled by a self-perpetuating power elite of economic and social privilege. It would be the end of the road that was opened by Thomas Jefferson when he called for a new aristocracy of talent to replace the old aristocracy of inherited power.
>
> The threat of such a course is all the more serious because it is virtually universally ignored. None of those who are monitoring the nation's problems are paying attention to the far-reaching implications of the retreat from education.[4]

In recent years, university practitioners have faced a new challenge in public communications—the arguments of publicists, politicians, and researchers that a college education is not worthwhile. This notion was given wide currency by Caroline Bird's widely sold *The Case against College.*[5] In the mid-1970s, two M.I.T. researchers published an analysis of college as an investment. They asserted that "the economic status of college graduates is deteriorating" and that "the rate of return on college fell from about 11–12 percent in 1969 to 7–8 percent in 1974."[6] This study also was widely publicized—without the necessary qualifications. These and other works gave substance to the often-heard clichés, "College isn't worth it anyway," and, "Too many graduates are driving cabs."

Such studies play into the hands of political leaders who are anxious to cut spending for budgetary or political reasons. State governments each year confront increased demands for money for welfare, public-school aid, higher education, more highways, more recreational facilities, more health aid, and astronomical Medicaid bills. These demands come from sectors of society with heavier political clout than colleges and universities possess. As a result, many states are cutting back financial support for colleges in terms of constant dollars per student. Some are placing ceilings on enrollment and tightening up admissions. Many are raising tuition. These and other factors led to a downturn in college enrollment in the late 1970s. *A major public relations task for the foreseeable future will be to persuade the public to reorder its priorities.*

Since the 1960s, when funds were ample and public support strong, the fortunes of higher education have thus skidded to a serious state. This situation has alarmed and bewildered educators. They have made countless studies to define themselves and ascertain the reason for this turn of opinion. For example, the Carnegie Commission on Higher Education issued more than 60 volumes of critical essays, research studies, and reports in the 1970s. Prof. Cameron Fincher suggests that "we study more carefully the public and the roots of public attitudes toward higher education." He elaborates: "Pressures for accountability, a continuing managerial revolution, and a financial crisis have combined to impress on academic administrations that theirs is a rapidly changing role. In all this, we must recognize and make known to the public the contradictions of its expectations for higher education and the costs of the services it demands."[7]

The patriarchial college president is gone. Today's president must lead—not direct—faculties, students, and governing boards. Today's president or chancellor is caught in the crunch of conflicting values and demands from his constituent-claimant publics. To thread his way through these conflicts, he must be an effective communicator and mediator. The role is difficult. Clark Kerr has ruefully observed, "This mediator is always subject to some abuse. He wins few clear-cut victories; he must aim at avoiding the worst rather than seizing the best. He must find satisfaction in being equally distasteful to each of his constituencies; he must reconcile himself to the harsh reality that successes are shrouded in silence while failures are spotlighted in notoriety." College presidencies are not the nation's most desirable jobs.

The two-way communications task confronting colleges and universities is difficult and demanding, one that does not permit glibness. A sociologist suggests the complexity of the task:

> With [its] sizes, purposes, and duties, the university campus becomes an extremely complicated social arrangement of the relations of men at work. The formal structure is bound to be full of overlap, gap, and contradiction. It becomes somewhat like a confederation of tribes that have wandered into the same campgrounds. Bureaucracy enforced from the center is, at the level of the professoriate, not fully in control, since the centrifugal forces of profession and discipline are strong. . . . The campus is a setting for a hundred, several hundred, distinctive clusters of experts. With this as its primary nature, it is fractured rather than integrated.[8]

The colleges face communications breakdowns of equal magnitude with external publics—with communities crowded by campus growth and congested by student cars, with legislators angered by student protest and student mores, with alumni whose sons and daughters cannot be admitted, with taxpayers grown weary of the mounting bill for higher education. This breakdown in communications has had and will continue to have serious consequences. Allen H. Barton asserts, "The effect of alienating a generation of students and a large section of intellectuals from normal political channels can be very serious, both for universities and for nations, as demonstrated in other countries as well as in the United States."[9] On the positive side, these problems have done much to reinvigorate and freshen educational thinking, to bring education to the disadvantaged, and to make colleges and universities more relevant to society's needs.

New, more effective channels are needed to provide an inflow of information from students, faculty, townspeople, taxpayers, and other constituent-claimant publics. A trustee, John C. Corson, says, *"What an institution needs to cope with this new condition is an organizational capacity to listen."* (Italics ours.) Also, new and more imaginative ways must be found to facilitate communication between community and college. One example is the Dialogue Center set up at San Fernando Valley State College to provide a place where students, faculty, and residents of Northridge can get together for informal and frank discussion. Formal programs are also held in this center.

Morris B. Abram, formerly president of Brandeis University, observed that university administrators have been compelled to move from talking about the need for communication to actually communicating with their publics. He said, "Communication alone will not provide the solution to our problems. . . . I think that on our campuses today there is so much distrust and suspicion that most [communication] is rendered sterile." Speaking from a campus wracked by conflict, a Cornell vice-president observed that one effect of the recurring crises on campuses has been to place "universities and colleges under the lens of public scrutiny with an intensity that is relatively rare in their long history." Faced with a strong expression of discontent from the faculty, another university president saw the major problem as "communication, one of enormous proportions."

The new problems impose a heavy burden on the function. The dimensions of the task in higher education have been outlined by one veteran practitioner, Michael Radock of the University of Michigan:

> Today's educational administrator must deal with all echelons of government, with trade unions and professional associations, with virtually every kind of staff member, with a conglomerate of autonomous units, with private donors, with alumni, with parents, with vendors, with a governing board which may be publicly elected or politically appointed, with recruiters of the students and competitors for his staff. *And* he's working with society's most highly volatile and precious resource—talented youth.[10]

There is still too much emphasis on publicity in college practice. And much of the publicity smacks of press-agentry—the spotlight on the college sideshows of beauty queens, athletics, and contrived gags. A picture of a pretty coed throwing books and legs in the air to celebrate the end of exams does little to tell what higher education is all about.

Many institutions still have their "public relations offices" in some remote temporary setup instead of in the administrative suite. And some college practitioners, prodded by professional journals and association discussions, spend themselves on the barricades of faculty and administrative resistance. Scope and skill of performance, not the place on the organization chart, will decide the ultimate role.

The professors' cooperation is essential. Yet many faculty members remain aloof, others merely indifferent, and a few plainly hostile. For many younger faculty members, public relations is a weapon of "the Establishment." To some of the faculty, the function smacks of flacking or press-agentry. The coldness of a few stems from their distaste or hostility for the news media, a common attitude among intellectuals. Sometimes it is the result of overzealousness on the part of the practitioner: One university director admits, "Publicity people occasionally overextend themselves, even against the conservative background of a university. Inadvertently, a few unsteady practitioners assault the basic rights of the professor without the professor's knowing it." An example of such an assault is the occasional misguided effort to "centralize" or "coordinate" all faculty expressions through the central information office. This is especially irritating in a day of vocal faculty dissent.

EXHIBIT 24–1

A Profile of One Public Relations Department, by Alvo E. Albini

The public relations department of Loyola University of Chicago consists of a director, a news specialist, a writer, and two secretaries. The department services, and is the promotional arm of, the Office of Development, the Offices of the President and Chancellor, the Alumni Office, Student Personnel, the Undergraduate and Graduate Schools of Business, the Institute of Industrial Relations, the Institute of Futures Trading, the College of Arts and Sciences, the School of Social Work, the School of Nursing, University College, Correspondence Study, Summer Sessions, Continuing Education, the Graduate School, the School of Education, and the School of Law. It also services numerous administrative and nonacademic offices, such as the Admissions Office and the Institute of Urban Life. The production of catalogs for all professional schools and the integrated catalog of the six undergraduate schools and colleges is under the direction of the public relations department.

It is difficult to quantify the amount of time each member spends on a particular project; it varies from a half-hour on a news release to several months' preparations for Founders' Day. *Our objective is to render the finest professional service at the lowest possible cost in the quickest time possible.* We also strive to do any type of communication that is requested. For example, the Theology Department wanted a portable window display that could be exhibited in the lobby of Lewis Towers and at conventions and meetings. The result was a pictorial display of Theology's graduate brochure, which public relations produced.

Because of its small size, the public relations department at Loyola carries out a multitude of assignments; usually as many as a half-dozen projects are in process simultaneously. As an illustration, a PR professional in the department may be working on a *Loyola Report,* an academic brochure; editing a newsletter; handling advertising; carrying out the production work of a catalog; working on a special event; taking pictures; and writing news releases—all during the course of one or two days, two or three weeks, or several months.

The best way to win the faculty's cooperation is through patient internal education and through the provision of help when the professor needs it.

Emanuel Goldberg suggests ways in which the public relations department can serve the professor:

It can serve as a buffer between a potentially articulate and socially useful scholar and the raw press; that is, it can at least prepare a release in a manner satisfactory to the professor's wishes, even though there is never a guarantee that newspapers or broadcasting media will cast it in the same form, or even use it. Whenever a faculty member takes the trouble to document and deliver a speech . . . the news bureau can reach a larger and more general public. Books, articles, travel, papers, institutes, research, pet projects, civic and governmental service—all these are grist. They can be turned nicely to the professor's, the University's, and the community's advantage.[11]

The practitioner must strive ceaselessly to clear away faculty and administrator misconceptions. One of the strongest misconceptions is the idea that to have a strong program is to pander to public opinion and thus undercut a university's true purpose. The late Robert Hutchins reflected on this:

The most dangerous aspect of public relations work is its reflex action: We find that the public does not like something about the University; our temptation is to change this so that the public will like us. Our duty is to change public opinion so that the public will like what the University does, and, if this cannot be immediately accomplished, to hold out against the public until it can be. Public relations work in a university is a phase of its efforts in adult education.

Overall, the public relations function is generally accepted on the campus and, where it is competently practiced, is demonstrating its worth. One university president observes:

The importance of an informed public opinion about the individual institution and higher education in general is now quite widely accepted among educators. The hostility toward the lay adviser has disappeared; the resentment of the journalistic interpretation of science is nearly gone; the isolation of the academic community is no longer celebrated as a major virtue.

Freedom, funds, federalism, freshmen

Higher education faces four continuing problems: Its academic freedom is frequently in question, if not in danger, from within and from without. Its financial support is insufficient and precarious. The competition for qualified students is spirited, their selection difficult. And—a fourth problem, which has emerged in recent years—growing constraints that make university administration difficult and costly are being imposed by agencies of the federal government.

Clark Kerr has listed ten problems facing higher education, which illustrate:

1. The problem of public control and influence over public institutions, which are threatened by a loss of autonomy to legislators, governors, and federal agencies.
2. The problem resulting from neglect of undergraduates the past two decades.
3. The problem resulting from excessive pressure now put upon students.
4. Excessive specialization in curriculum and in research.
5. The geographic imbalance in higher education.
6. Financing higher education in a time of high taxes, competing social needs.
7. Adjusting to and accommodating the New Left.
8. The increasing gulf between the intellectual and society.
9. Equal access to education throughout the United States.
10. The problems posed by the new technology, which can bring changes as far-reaching as those brought by the printed book.

These problems are complicated and poorly understood. Not only have they been inadequately defined but too frequently they are discussed in a fragmentary, oversimplified way.

The need is clear; the task, formidable; the progress, slow. In an exhaustive survey of attitudes, *Fortune* magazine found unbounded faith in collegiate institutions but little real understanding of their function; great interest in education, but little information on it. It found great faith in education's ability to enable a person to earn more money, but little concern for its objective of enabling a person to live a fruitful, enjoyable life. The *Fortune* survey concluded that "the subject of higher education is very little understood by the American people generally." More recent public opinion polls only serve to emphasize the same inadequate understanding of education.

The need for freedom

Free inquiry as the fundamental of scholarship has long been recognized and generally observed. The teacher must have freedom to teach, not merely for his own sake or for the sake of his students, but for the future of mankind. Yet the freedom of the student to learn and of the teacher to teach comes under frequent attack. It is sometimes abridged, frontally or indirectly. *Protecting and defending intellectual freedom is a continuing task.*

The defense becomes doubly difficult in periods of internal tensions fed by threats of external aggressions, when fear and hysteria break loose. In an emotionally tense social climate, all ideas that diverge from the status quo become "dangerous" and open to suspicion—and pressure. In the years just after World War II, there were numerous legislative committee investigations, requirements of loyalty oaths for teachers, and similar incursions on academic freedom. Periodically the political extremes, the Far Right and the Far Left, assault it.

These limitations on free inquiry take a variety of forms. "Their net effect," as the *New York Times* points out, "is a widening tendency toward passive acceptance of the status quo, conformity, and a narrowing area of tolerance in which students, faculty, and administrators feel free to speak, act, and think independently." The consequences pose a grave threat to education. Such attacks must be repulsed. A president of the University of Kentucky once said that the most important activity a president has to perform is to keep the university free.

This has become increasingly difficult with the eruption of conflict on campuses across the land and the resulting backlash by legislators, trustees, and the public. Maintenance of a rule of law on the campus is essential not only to preserve the rights of all but to fend off external threats. President Robben Fleming of the University of Michigan put it plainly: "If the university community, including both faculty and students, is unwilling to face the responsibility which internal discipline requires, it is clear that the public will insist that order be imposed from the outside." Angry public demand resulted in much restrictive legislation enacted in the late 1960s and early 1970s, stiffer federal requirements on loans and grants, and congressional tax restrictions on philanthropic foundations. One practitioner observed that "threats by alumni and donors are rampant."

The college or university that is fearlessly seeking the truth out of the conflict of ideas cannot escape pressure. To reckon with such pressure, it must have the backing of an informed public that cherishes free inquiry. Education cannot, like the ostrich, hide its head in the sands of the past. Such a position is both undignified and vulnerable. It is the public relations function to persuade the people that "on this campus, all books, all expressions, all opinions are free." *An institution of learning cannot dispense with controversial ideas and live.* Research and teaching cannot be bland.

The task is also to demonstrate the vital necessity of freedom not only for the teacher to teach but for the student to learn and for the scholar to search for the truth without restriction. Too often, college men tend to claim academic freedom as merely a special license for the professor. The emphasis needs to be placed more on the by-products of the denial of academic freedom. Citizens need to be reminded forcefully that as academic freedom has disappeared in other countries, so also has the freedom of all citizens. Freedom is indivisible.

College practitioners man the front lines in the defense of academic freedom. Defending a professor's staging of a "teach-in" as a matter of principle is no easy task. The state can abolish freedom of learning only if the people are uninformed and inert. Loyalty-oath controversies and protest backlash, painful though they are, do provide an opportunity to dramatize these fundamentals.

For many institutions, political pressures bear most heavily on the problem of providing education for the disadvantaged. John A. Griffin, of the Southern Education Foundation, pointed out:

> Whether or not we have so far admitted it, colleges and universities have responsibilities in race relations, both on the campus and in the communities. . . . Thus for urban institutions and for many nonurban colleges and universities, North and South, race relations is increasingly a fact of life. This means that the colleges and universities, like the armed services, need staff persons who are specialists in race relations. . . . The problems that need attention range all the way from accreditation to football. . . . Public relations and development people need to give thoughtful attention to their responsibilities of sensitizing their institutions in regard to their responsibilities and their opportunities in race relations.[12]

The need for funds

It is almost trite to speak of the financial crisis facing collegiate institutions. This has been a pat phrase since Harvard held its first fund-raising lottery in the 1700s. Yet the years ahead pose problems of truly critical proportions. The facts are simple, their impact staggering. Today's college enrollment of some 12 million students is expected to reach nearly 13 million by 1980 and then to stabilize near that figure. John Leslie summarizes the problem:

> A dollar pinch is developing for higher education. The 1970s will bring larger student bodies, . . . greater demand for services and research, and continued rapidly rising costs. Competition for the education dollar will become acute. Budgets will be squeezed and all aspects of higher education will have to become more effective and efficient. The challenge to programs and personnel devoted to the furtherance of understanding and financial support will be equally as great. Interpretation of the educational program will be increasingly difficult as institutions grow more complex and the public more sophisticated. Added demands are being placed on the tax dollar, and education will find other agencies competing strongly for funds in the state house and on Capitol Hill. . . . Just to stay even, the management of educational fund raising and public relations programs will have to be improved greatly.

The seriousness of the financial crunch can be seen in the diminished support of research—research that must provide urgently needed answers to the energy crisis, the food problem, and nagging social problems. Two scholars, after an exhaustive study, concluded that the present-day quality of university research masks a deterioration that is rapidly spreading through the entire scientific enterprise. This conclusion is based on an 18-month survey that included visits to 36 universities and consultations with some 750 administrators.[13] An American

Association of Universities executive concurs: "The recent decay of the system will not be clearly manifest for several years."

This new crisis is compounded of three trends converging on the campus: (1) the increase in enrollments and in scientific research, (2) the mounting burden of educational costs, and (3) the drying up of traditional sources of support. The U.S. Office of Education estimates that colleges and universities will have to spend close to $1 billion per year *in new money* over the next decade. Where will this money come from? There are only three major sources: tuition fees, the federal government, and gifts and bequests.

Privately endowed and sectarian colleges are especially hard hit. Gifts and incomes from endowments fail to keep pace with the inflationary costs of frogs, footballs, and faculty members. America needs the strong, independent college, free of political control and influence. These colleges have already raised their tuitions to the limit—if not beyond. Some have been forced to shift investments from safer securities to common stocks. Others have dipped into reserves to keep going. The Carnegie Commission on Higher Education found, at the end of the last decade, that costs were rising faster than income for the private universities. The cost per student was then rising at a rate of about $7\frac{1}{2}$ percent each year. Private institutions are leaning more and more on gifts from corporations and annual alumni fund drives. Success in these efforts has enabled private higher education (with the exception of the "low-prestige" colleges) to maintain its competitive position over the past decade, despite rising costs and the growth of public colleges. Overall, there were more private institutions in 1975–76 than in the "prosperity" years of the 1960s.[14]

State-supported colleges are finding the going tougher all the time as their costs go up. They are faced with strong competition for the taxpayers' dollars. Consequently, state universities are putting more emphasis on voluntary support and are intensively promoting alumni giving. Such private support is increasing markedly for state universities.

In a time of increased demands on government resources, private support is seen as more critical than ever by leaders of public institutions. Howard R. Bowen, former Iowa University president, observed, "Legislators do not look with favor on the extras that will make the difference between adequacy and excellence. The public institutions, which wish to strive for exceptional performances, are therefore forced to look to private sources for the funds needed to lift them above the commonplace." Similarly, private institutions campaign hard for increased help from public funds. In fact, the line between private and public colleges and universities has become quite blurred. Both rely increasingly on the federal government. In fiscal 1978, for example, the federal government provided more than $4 billion in support of higher education, a sum that public and private institutions divided nearly equally. Federal funds have become the second most important source of private-university revenue. *Thus, the competition for the donor's dollar and for the tax dollar has intensified in both sectors of the higher-education establishment.*

The solution cannot be found in higher tuition fees. These fees have trebled in the past decade. And a number of studies show that reduced tuition increases college-going, that increased tuition has the opposite effect. A survey by the U.S. Office of Education a few years ago confirmed that the "nation's loss of talented, potential college students is due primarily to lack of money." Today, many qualified young people are excluded from the benefits of higher education—in some instances by sex, race, or religion, but mostly by the costs of college. By the end of the 1970s, more high school students were graduating each year, but fewer of them were going to college. Rates of college-going have dropped precipitously among dependent students from families with incomes of $15,000 or less. From 1970 to 1977, total costs of college (not counting pocket money) climbed more than 70 percent, to a median of $2,790 a year at state-run schools and $4,568 at private colleges.

Dr. Alvin C. Eurich, of the Fund for the Advancement of Education, warns that the competition for the federal and local tax dollars is such that we cannot expect anything like a sufficient flow of tax money to diminish the pressure on institutions to build more financial support. *Developing mass public support for mass giving on a regular basis seems to be one of the hopeful trends in this situation. It certainly spells more emphasis on public relations.*

Federalism and higher education

The federal government emerged in the Johnson years as a major source of funds for higher education. It spent $343 million on education at all levels in 1940; 35 years later, it was spending nearly $10 billion in this category. In 1966, the United States spent $538 million on higher education; a decade later, this sum had climbed to $2.6 billion. Most major universities get about one-third of their income from the federal government; the University of California, for example, gets $275 million for its nine campuses.

Building support in the executive agencies—mainly HEW—in the Congress, and in the voter public for increased support has become a major task. Many universities and state systems now maintain full-time or part-time public relations officers in Washington, where their tasks are fact-finding, troubleshooting, and lobbying. Most institutions continue to rely on their national organizations and on their communications with their representatives in Congress.

With this federal money has come a never-ending stream of rules and regulations that make administration increasingly difficult. These regulations challenge the university's autonomy and are costly to administer. The American Council on Education has found that compliance with a dozen federal programs costs $9 to $10 million a year at six representative schools, and consumes 1 to 4 percent of operating budgets. The University of Georgia estimated that in 1976, the costs of compliance and administration of federal requirements was about $4 million a year. President Fred C. Davison said, "We have become so bogged down in trying to cope with this morass of paperwork that sometimes we feel as though we are losing sight of what we're supposed to be doing—teaching and inquiring into the nature of things." And institutions must spend these sums at a time when they can't keep faculty salaries even with inflation, when they have to cut back on library book purchases and deny teachers, researchers, and students equipment and materials needed for their pursuits.

These controls can be far-reaching. The Buckley Amendment to the U.S. Education Act, designed to protect a student's privacy, has made it difficult to publish student directories, because any student can insist that his presence at a university not be disclosed publicly. This amendment also makes it difficult to post student grades and to get professors to provide written recommendations to prospective employers. Kingman Brewster, when president of Yale, saw the federal government's threat to the freedom of higher education as far more serious than the costs it imposes. He perceived a serious constitutional threat in the government's attaching of conditions to its support of higher education in order to achieve other social purposes. Assisting university administrators in getting more federal funds with one hand and fending off increased controls that raise costs and impair autonomy with the other will be an important part of college public relations in the years ahead.

Federalism has also brought increased burdens to the internal communications system. The University of Iowa has three components for its internal information system on federal programs: (1) an up-to-date, constantly monitored resource information library, (2) a not-so-structured but effective intelligence network to get word of new sources, and (3) a series of communications mechanisms to alert faculty members to sources of support and inform them of administrative changes.

What freshmen?

In years past, much of the college PR effort was on recruiting students. Often these campaigns used the techniques of advertising more than those of information and interpretation. They placed too much emphasis on getting students and too little on the social responsibility involved. The intense promotional publicity to get new students is responsible, in part at least, for the questionable notion that to get ahead in the world, one must go to college. The public no longer wholly believes this.

In student recruitment we have a paradox. On the one hand, colleges are worried about their overcrowded classrooms, On the other, they are trying to persuade still more students to enter. But there is an explanation. College officials know that something like 250,000 gifted high school graduates do not go on to college each year, half of them because of lack of money. Educators want to encourage and finance the talented students because they know that this nation requires more *educated manpower* than is available to meet America's postindustrial-society needs.

To bring quality and diversity to their student bodies, most colleges and universities now have special recruitment programs for National Merit Scholars, National Achievement Scholars, and minority students. Such programs include personal letters, visits from college officials and alumni, telegrams, specialized brochures, and offers of visits to the campus—much as star athletes are recruited. These programs, usually directed by a full-time person in admissions, require a strong public relations backup. An education writer observes, "The country's formerly staid higher educational establishment, in an effort to sell its product in an ever more competitive marketplace, has turned to the kinds of strategies once reserved for peddling toothpaste, dog food, beer and cigarettes." [15]

The recruitment program and its supporting public relations effort require *careful fact-finding and planning*. Great care must be exercised to ensure that no discriminatory practices creep into the process, however unintended. The combination of court action, laws and implementing regulations, private pressure, and public opinion has made it imperative that colleges admit all those who are qualified. Special efforts are required to redress the historic pattern of discrimination against blacks. A decade after the civil-rights revolution, only 7 to 8 percent of the blacks of college age were going to college (most of these to black colleges), yet the proportion of blacks in this age group in the United States was 12 percent.

Under pressure from students, parents, the courts, and the federal government, colleges are being compelled to tell prospective applicants more about themselves and to be more candid about their shortcomings. This demand for "truth in advertising" on the part of collegiate institutions has been spearheaded by the National Task Force on Better Information for Student Choice, a federally funded project involving eleven secondary schools and four education organizations. Its purpose is to determine the information needs of students and develop models for providing accurate information. The responsible practitioner should do these things without prodding.

There has long been a wide gap between the college campus in the brochure and campus reality. For example, a college in upper New England included in its promotional material an enticing photograph of a student couple relaxing at the shore of a lake. There is no lake on the campus. Sandra Willett, director of consumer education in HEW, asserts, "Some of the abuses of the economic marketplace are now present in the educational marketplace." Example of the new trend: Barat College, Lake Forest, Illinois, advised prospective students in a brochure, "Studio art, theater and dance and few other areas are outstanding enough to be a basis alone for choosing Barat. An exceptionally talented student musician or mathematician, on the other hand, might be advised to look further for a college with top faculty, students, and facilities in that field." The University of California at Irvine is another that has put credibility into its literature: Included in Irvine's prospectus is a short report on a survey of students who chose *not* to return to the university. These students listed three main objections to Irvine—impersonality of the campus community, inadequate social life, and a sense of social isolation. Irvine's vice-chancellor, John C. Hoy, believes, "The sooner institutions really tell what's going on, the better off they will be."

In the decade ahead, the student problem will not be one of recruiting numbers but the far more thorny tasks of deciding who should go to college and of financing the talented poor. The recruitment problem is complicated by vocal demands that admission to a college or university is a right, not a privilege. Increasing demands for waiver of requirements for the disadvantaged pose another problem. Solution of these problems will take statesmanship, not salesmanship.

The publics

The pitch and emphasis to the different publics of a collegiate institution vary according to the size, base of support, and philosophy of the institution.

Students

Foremost of the public relations agents are the students—first as students, later as alumni. Student attitudes and conduct are powerful factors in determining public attitudes. Students come from the farms and the mining camps, from the metropolitan city and the village, from all parts of the nation. They become authoritative interpreters of their college in their hometowns. If they have pride in it and enthusiasm, these will be mirrored. If they have an unhappy educational experience, that too will be reflected—and for years to come.

The student's role in shaping public attitudes was amply demonstrated in the late 1960s and early 1970s when student protests brought public anger and legislative retribution. In the course of these protests, students brought down college presidents, erased outmoded student regulations, and gained effective voices on faculty committees and on the governing board.

Although the issues change over time, the technique of the student protest is now a part of academic life. Although the number of sit-ins and picketings has dwindled, dealing with student outrage remains a recurring problem. For example, the students at Stanford, at Wisconsin, and at other universities periodically protest their schools' ownership of stock in companies doing business in South Africa. In other instances, ugly and sometimes violent protests have been staged to oust a president, to fight for retention of a discharged professor, or to protest censorship of the campus paper. Colleges remain the target of youthful discontent, sometimes in terms of legitimate complaints about the deficiences of the institution, sometimes as a convenient tactic for assault upon the general society.

Given the news values and methods of media reporting, dealing with these activities is difficult. The public is heavily influenced by the news media, which spotlight protest and neglect quiet academic achievement. The public record must be balanced by examples of students' public service, and by representation of the college in a constructive way.[16]

A university must develop an enthusiastic, responsible body of students as goodwill ambassadors. And because of the fast turnover of the student body, this is difficult. The surest way to develop the student's appreciation of his responsibility is to bring him into active participation in the program. Personable college students are the most effective public symbol a college can have. Students can be involved in the program through organizing of campus host and guide groups; High School Day, Legislator Day, or Parents' Weekend; touring college choirs, glee clubs, or drama groups; and in many other ways. College administrators, faculty members, and student leaders must guide the student in this responsibility. The University of Maryland, Baltimore County (UMBC), established a staff of student tour guides as a means of advertising itself as an "intimate and friendly institution." Since its beginnings, the UMBC tour staff has answered requests from thousands of prospective students, curious parents, high school counselors, senior classes from high schools, and others. Such tours should be available year-round, not just at orientation time.

A student may be in school from one to four years, but he is an alumnus for his life. Too many institutions wait until a student is graduated before they start to woo him. *The student who has good teachers, who is given wise counsel and helpful individual attention, generally becomes a loyal alumnus.* An educational program revealing the sources of educational support could do much in developing a sense of responsibility in future alumni.

Fundamental to effective student relationships is to maintain, regardless of the institution's size, free-flowing channels between the administrator and the student. Too often, with bigness, these break down. A study by the National Association of State Universities and Land Grant Colleges suggests greater student involvement in university policy and curriculum decisions as an effective way of dampening student protest and alienation. It listed these reforms of recent years: membership of students on committees, including those to select new presidents or chancellors; more effective communication with students; appointment of a university ombudsman; and enactment of student suggestions.

Among public universities, Kentucky led the way in giving students a vote on the governing board. Then the Universities of Connecticut and Maine followed suit. In the subsequent decade, many other universities adopted this means of getting student views to policy makers. In the words of one administrator, "Now, from Harvard to Salem State, from Stanford to Azuza Pacific, the role of the student both as a participant in the process of education and as the object of its intent is receiving widespread attention."[17]

For the large university, a President's Council of student leaders, meeting informally in the president's home, has worked well on many campuses where presidents have been willing to listen—although the danger is that such students may be labeled "Uncle Toms." In some instances, a minority group has got control of the campus newspaper and shut out other points of view, particularly the administration's. Therefore, many universities have started official newspapers aimed at getting administration views across to the student body. Effectiveness of these internal communications channels depends on the existence of a climate of credibility.

Hometown news stories of student accomplishments please both students and parents. This staple of college public relations has been made easy and economical by the computer, a capacity that most institutions possess. The computer center can provide tailor-made lists for such stories and can even type them. Honor lists that once took many man-hours of clerical time and typing can now be zipped through in a matter of minutes.

Faculty and staff

The college or university president and the custodian each play an important role. People think in terms of people, the personal symbol, the concrete. The personalities of people identified in the public mind with an institution largely determine the kind of confidence and support the institution has. The personal symbol is particularly important for a college, whose leaders and teachers are constantly in the public spotlight, free to speak out as they see fit.

College presidents and professors are a prolific source of news. Developing the staff of an institution into an effective team is the starting point for the program. *The college or university president, by reason of his position and prestige, must be the leader.* The president personifies the institution. A strong personality can bring prestige, stature, and public confidence. *A president whose mental radar is sensitive to public relations can contribute much to developing this awareness.*

The faculty member can contribute most by inspired teaching, by counseling his students, by research accomplishments, and by lending his talents to public service. Faculty members, especially those of the younger generation, are increasingly aware of their responsibilities. Members of the university's housekeeping staff, the secretaries, the telephone operators, the policemen, must be imbued with the spirit of friendly service. The important thing is that these staff members be kept adequately informed of the university's policies, programs, and problems. This requires a continuing internal information program. The college staff must be gently but *persistently* reminded of its public relations responsibilities.

Today, faculty members insist upon a voice in college policy making. If this participation is to be meaningful, they must be kept informed by the administration so that they can take informed positions. Without a steady flow of information from those who have it to those who need it, cooperative decision making can never amount to much.

Frustrated by their inability to gain a voice in the college's government and/or to get pay raises to keep up with inflation, many faculties have unionized in recent years. As of 1977, 544 institutions had recognized a union as the collective-bargaining agent for their faculty. Of this number, 208 were four-year colleges, 336 two-year colleges. Seventy-four other faculties rejected unionization in this same period. The coming of unions and collective bargaining has changed what was once a professional relationship on these campuses. It has also brought to the public relations office the task of dealing with the press in periods of negotiation. To prevent unionization, universities must keep channels of communication open to the administration and must provide adequate pay and research opportunities for teachers.

Members of the governing board constitute an important internal public that functions as the official intermediary between key publics and the college. An effective board serves as a heat shield. A strategic group, generally recruited from opinion leadership, trustees must be convinced of the need for giving consideration to public relations aspects of policy making. Consistent but subtle pressure is required to prompt the board to give full and sympathetic consideration to public opinion. This key group must be kept adequately informed of the university's aims and problems so that its members may interpret these aims correctly. Informing the board is primarily a task of the president. It is one of his two key publics. The faculty is the other.

The community

Next, in planning a program, come the important external publics to be reached and influenced. "Town-grown" relationships provide the environment. These relationships have been made difficult and sometimes abrasive in recent years by institutions' needs to expand and by the police problems posed by student protest and campus drug traffic. Colleges and universities are lagging well behind industry in recognizing the importance of good community relations. Support can be won by giving the citizens a voice and a sympathetic hearing, through consultation, on college matters directly affecting the community. There are a number of natural irritations that may develop if town-grown relations are neglected: For example, the tax-exempt status of educational institutions may appear as a sign of partiality. Municipalities are increasingly hard pressed to find adequate revenues to pay for their expanding services. Many institutions have wisely taken steps to dramatize their recognition of this problem. One state university, for example, arranged to buy a new fire truck for its community and to employ one-third of the firemen. In 1974, Harvard committed itself to pay $300,000 annually to the city of Boston for 40 years in lieu of property taxes, something it was not legally obligated to do. The payment was volunteered to cover a housing project.

Another problem is faced by metropolitan institutions that must expand in already built-up areas. This growth, although ultimately of great benefit to the community, means just one thing to the taxpayer: removal of property from the tax rolls and, hence, higher taxes. It also means dislocation to the residents. Such moves should not be suddenly thrust upon a surprised community; the college must properly explain them to its neighbors. Traffic congestion created by university facilities or activities, among many examples, has caused harsh irritations in some college towns.

Another example: Columbia University aroused the ire of the residents of the Riverdale section of the Bronx when it decided to sell for $1.2 million an estate it had received as a gift under an agreement that the land was to be preserved as a botanical garden. A Columbia public relations official said the university had to sell the land with its mansion and greenhouses because no suitable use could be found for the property. Residents, fighting a townhouse project to be built upon the estate, accused the university of acting in bad faith. Responding to these critics, President William J. McGill told them that the property was suitable only for a president's residence and that he preferred "the harshness of life on Morningside Heights" to the "imperial splendor in Riverdale." He ended his letter, "Now come off it," which the recipients found offensive. One professed shock at the president's "brawling street language."[18]

On the other hand, there are many positive advantages that the college can and does offer the community. Townspeople need to be reminded of these, lest they take them for granted.

Robert G. Miller, vice-mayor of San Jose, California, expressed the relationship between the university and community this way:

> A broad and comprehensive goal should be to integrate the campus both physically and socially with the surrounding area and the downtown, rather than to isolate itself from the city it serves. The campus should make efforts to relate itself to the large community in terms of the special skills available from the sub-community of the scholar. In the broadest sense, this means assisting the city in its search for a better and more meaningful life.
>
> In return, the city can offer support to its college or university in a myriad of ways, and a new spurt of growth is started as industry and capital, attracted to the university centers of the nation, locate and make available their resources for further support of the university.

The complexity of today's practice is sharply illustrated in the task of gaining the public's confidence in "moderate-risk recombinant DNA research." In recent years, scientists have begun to experiment with gene transplants, which offer both great promise to medical research and the potential for biological catastrophe. Near the end of the decade, nearly 100 universities were doing DNA research. This has created great public anxiety, leading to municipal ordinances, state laws, and federal regulations in an effort to prevent such research from getting out of hand.

In 1975, Cambridge, Massachusetts, refused to grant a building permit to Harvard to build a laboratory for this purpose—something unheard of in the history of Harvard–Cambridge relations. Cambridge ultimately agreed to permit the research under stringent guidelines devised by a citizens' panel. The Madison city council authorized a committee to deal with the implications of DNA research on the University of Wisconsin campus. Governments in Ann Arbor, Michigan, Palo Alto, California, and New Haven, Connecticut, among others, manifested similar concerns. In 1976, the National Institutes of Health issued rules setting strict laboratory standards and banning dangerous experiments, but these apply only to laboratories supported by NIH funds. Scientists agree on the need for strict regulation but insist that this should be enacted at the federal level, not controlled by a city government. Resolution of the conflict in the interest of science and of the public will require skilled communications in a controversial, complex matter.

Parents

Parents of students are a ready-made nucleus of support. They have a vital stake in the institution. They can be welded into an effective group of allies. Providing a good home away from home and giving sons and daughters kindly, personalized attention win parental support. But this potential goodwill needs to be activated and reinforced. Parents' Weekend, frequent letters from president to parent, and parents' clubs bring parents closer to the school, and spot newsletters are in order when trouble breaks out on campus.

Alumni

Maintaining the interest of the alumni has long been given emphasis—with varying degrees of success. Too often, the alumni interest centers almost exclusively on the fortunes of the football team rather than education. But this is changing, and can be further changed by strong, imaginative leadership in the alumni office. Many universities today bring their alumni to the campus for stimulating seminars in subjects of current interest. Others are involving alumni in educational tours and overseas trips. The key to alumni support is to get the alumni involved in campus life.

Practically every college has a going alumni association. Often its sole concern is keeping alive the flames of loyalty. Sometimes the alumni influence can be—and is—mobilized to override sound educational policy. Sometimes alumni associations tend to become vested interests, ends in themselves. The alumni association must be kept harnessed to its basic objective—support of the alma mater through organized effort.

The critical problems faced by higher education make it essential that alumni groups and universities forge a stronger bond. Informed alumni can be a strong base of support; uninformed, they can represent a disturbing interference in the conduct of the college. Those irresistible drives to fire the coach have led many faculties and administrators to fear alumni influence. There is a real need to do a better job of keeping alumni informed of more than merely their classmates' doings and the football statistics. Alumni magazines reach millions of people annually, but many of them contain little intellectual meat along with the traditional chroniclings.

The objective should be to get more than dollars. Colleges should strive to gain loyalty, interest, and counsel from their alumni. Win those, and the dollars will follow. Charles P. McCurdy, a former president of the American Alumni Council, has said, "I do not believe that we can continue to beseech our alumni or anybody else to contribute for *things*. We will have to begin asking them to contribute for *principles*."

Few institutions mobilize the full potential of political and philanthropic support of their alumni scattered across the nation. With the advent of the computer, alumni records constitute a broad marketing system. It is helpful to view this record data base as a commercial firm does when it uses its data base to check customer analyses and to gain its share of various markets. Ohio State University uses its Alumni Information Center to respond to a number of needs: preparing newsletters and announcements; locating prominent alumni to assist the placement office or to represent the university at inaugurations; conducting personalized fund appeals; identifying prestigious scholarship recipients; helping to find qualified department-chairman candidates; soliciting specific interest groups; and providing analyses of resources to and from certain markets, such as gifts, contracts, and grants.

To keep up to date with the changing needs of the alma mater, the alumni association should periodically evaluate its work and its worth. Charles Lang of State University College, Brockport, New York, suggests these questions:

1. Are short- and long-term objectives clearly stated?
2. For what percentage of the alumni do you have records?
3. Can you readily identify, isolate, and communicate with specialized groups?
4. How closely does the faculty and staff of your institution identify with alumni?
5. How does what you offer alumni compare with what you ask them to do or give?

John B. Fullen says the function of the alumni director is to see that the alumnus is appreciated rather than exploited, cultivated rather than coerced, frankly informed rather than party-lined, and, above all, interested in and organized for much besides money-raising.

One imaginative way to get alumni involved in the life of their alma mater is to engage them in a self-study of the college. Concerned about the state of alumni relations and about the impact the merger of Brown and Pembroke would have on them, Brown's president set up a committee to study these relations. A device was needed to effectively bring together two old and distinguished alumni organizations. A self-study committee was it. The unspoken agenda was Brown University's concern that "in age, sex, and minority groups, in geography and specialized intellectual concerns, alumni programs and the majority of Brown's alumni quietly passed each other in the night." In its 16 months of work—at a cost of less than $1,000—this committee brought "profound changes in the manner in which the university and its alumni relate to each other." For example, the university's first alumni center was planned, completed, and paid for out of special contributions that did not detract from the university's other needs.

When a college is caught up in the vortex of a crisis or controversy, it is imperative that it get the full story to its alumni and other publics as quickly as possible. For example, when Cornell University had a crisis, it arranged to reprint the news stories in the *Ithaca Journal* and quickly mail 115,000 copies to alumni and other key publics. In this era, the alumni magazine can and must become a channel of candid communication between an institution and its alumni. The day of the bland, rah-rah magazine, carrying college puffs, sports, and class notes, is dying. Typical of the new day was the Ohio State alumni magazine's campaign against the trustees' outside-speakers rule until it was rescinded. This represents, says Charles Helmken of the American Alumni Council, "a revolution that has not been easy." Emory's Virgil Hartley says, "Many alumni don't welcome candor." A mild understatement.

FIGURE 24-1   A checklist such as this can be the basis of a self-study.

Self-Evaluation Checklist
for College and University Relations

By **Dr. A. Westley Rowland,** *vice-president for university relations, State University of New York at Buffalo*

	Yes	No
1. Does your college or university have a clear-cut written statement of institutional objectives?		
2. Does your institution have a statement in writing of institutional relations goals?		
3. Does your institution allocate from one-half to one percent of its operating budget to institutional relations?		
4. Do you periodically review your institutional relations goals and modify them as necessary?		
5. Is your president committed to a viable institutional relations program?		
6. Is your president willing to allocate an adequate budget to institutional relations activities?		
7. Does your president give a significant amount of his time to institutional relations activities?		
8. Does your institution have a top-level institutional relations administrator at the vice-presidential or equivalent level who sits at the highest policy levels of your college or university?		
9. Does he have an important voice in all decisions that affect the institutional relations of a college or university?		
10. Do you systematically analyze the needs of your various publics and develop programs to meet their needs?		
11. Do you have a built-in mechanism for monitoring and evaluating how programs in institutional relations are achieving their goals?		
12. Are all segments of your institution deeply involved in institutional relations activities—administration, faculty, students, and staff?		
13. Do you have an advanced academic degree?		
14. Does your institution belong to the American College Public Relations Association?		
15. Does your institution belong to the American Alumni Council?		
16. Do you attend the district and/or national conferences of ACPRA and/or AAC every year?		
17. Do you read at least three books a year related to the crucial issues in higher education?		
18. Do you read at least one book a year related to the field of college and university relations?		
19. Do you regularly attend state institutional relations meetings?		
20. Do you accept assignments offered you in the institutional relations field at the local, state, and national levels?		
21. Do you have an effective information services program?		
22. Do you have an effective publications program?		
23. Do you have an effective program of alumni relations?		
24. Do you have an effective program of fund raising (annual giving, deferred giving, corporate giving, foundation giving)?		
25. Do you have an effective program of governmental/community relations?		
26. Do you have a balanced program of special events?		
27. Do you have an effective program of internal relations?		
28. Do you have a speakers' bureau which is functioning effectively?		
29. Do you have a community advisory council?		

Rating Scale

If you checked 26-29 questions "yes," your rating is: OUTSTANDING.
If you checked 21-25 questions "yes," your rating is: EXCELLENT.
If you checked 16-20 questions "yes," your rating is: GOOD.
If you checked 11-15 questions "yes," your rating is: FAIR.
If you checked 1-10 questions "yes," your rating is: POOR.

Other publics

Other publics include prospective students, parents of prospective students, present and prospective donors, opinion leaders, the various philanthropic foundations, sister educational institutions, legislators and state officials for the state-supported school, the armed forces, and various agencies of the federal government—particularly those with research programs.

The outlook

Institutions of higher learning face many difficult but not insoluble problems in the foreseeable future. These problems can be fundamental, such as definite decisions concerning the true function and purpose of the college and university. They can be specific, such as developing a sound relationship between the main function of education and the extracurricular athletics for men and women. The evils of proselytizing, commercialism, gambling, and overemphasis, which cloud intercollegiate athletics from time to time, represent a tough but typical problem for the practitioner.

For years ahead, institutions of higher learning must grapple with other problems. Funds must be raised to pay professors, to build buildings, and to buy expensive research equipment. Emotional attacks on teachers and doctrines by the Far Right and New Left must be beaten back. The right of faculty and student dissent must be preserved, however angry certain elements of the public become.[19] There will be the squeeze of doing more and more research and public service—particularly, continuing education to enable society to cope with the escalating technological and social changes in America. An increasing number of applicants will be denied admission to colleges, especially private ones. The demand that colleges do more for disadvantaged young people will grow. The fierce competition for public and philanthropic funds will increase, not lessen. This adds up to a need for all the confidence and support that can be mustered through effective public relations. Never has the task confronting the college practitioner been as difficult as it is today; never has his or her opportunity to serve and advance society been greater.

Case problem

Monday, seven black students, representing the Black Student Union, demanded an appointment with the president of the college. He was out of town, but the vice-president for student affairs met with them and heard these demands: (1) that the college sell immediately all its stocks held in companies doing business with South Africa because of that nation's racist policies; (2) that the college provide support for a black students' conference to be held next month; (3) that black athletes be assured of financial support for their college careers whether they continue to play or not; (4) that at least 500 black students be admitted next September whether they meet admission requirements or not. The students set a deadline of 1 P.M. Tuesday for answers to these demands, described by a spokesman as "nonnegotiable."

The president met with the group at 1 P.M. Tuesday. He made clear that actions were under way in the college to meet demands 1 and 2, but that demands 3 and 4 were unreasonable and could not be met. The students left peaceably, although protesting that their demands were not being met. Then they entered the bursar's office and office of records on the first floor of the administration building and established a blockade. Occupation continued all night. During the night, the occupiers did $11,000 worth of damage to building and equipment.

571

University administrators sought to seek settlement by negotiation Wednesday and Thursday, but without avail. College trustees, when interviewed by newsmen, criticized the administration for being "soft and too permissive." One said, "I'll be damned if we let students tell us how to invest our endowment. This is our business." A state senator lambasted the president, saying the college suffers from "a limp hand on the tiller."

Campus militants take up the cause of the black students. A campus strike is proposed. Sporadic fights occur among students and campus police. Four are arrested. Tension mounts. Parents of students begin phoning the college to ascertain whether their sons and daughters are safe.

Prepare a communications plan to get the college's position and policies in this crisis to key publics as promptly as possible and to maintain open channels of communication.

ADDITIONAL READINGS

Carnegie Foundation for the Advancement of Teaching, *More Than Survival: Prospects for Higher Education in a Period of Uncertainty.* San Francisco: Jossey-Bass, Inc., 1975. Essays by trustees of the foundation.

JOHN EGERTON, *State Universities and Black Americans.* Southern Education Foundation, 811 Cypress St. NE, Atlanta, GA. 1969. An inquiry by the Southern Education Reporting Service into desegregation and equity for negroes in 100 public universities.

LEWIS S. FEUER, *The Conflict of Generations: The Character and Significance of Student Movements.* London: Heinemann Educational Books, 1969.

MARGARET GORDON, *College Graduates and Jobs.* New York: McGraw-Hill, 1973. Contains an excellent essay by Richard S. Eckhouse, rebutting those who define the worth of an education in strictly economic terms.

DOUGLAS M. KNIGHT, ed., *The Federal Government and Higher Education.* Englewood Cliffs, N.J.: Prentice-Hall, 1960.

SEYMOUR MARTIN LIPSET, *The Berkeley Student Revolt.* Garden City, N.Y.: Doubleday, 1965.

MICHAEL V. MILLER et al., *A Campus Divided: Revolution at Berkeley.* New York: Dial Press, 1965.

MICHAEL RADOCK, "University of Michigan's 150th Birthday Observance," *College & University Journal,* Vol. 7 (Winter 1968).

DAVID RIESMAN and VERNE A. STADTMAN, eds., *Academic Transformation: Seventeen Institutions under Pressure.* New York: McGraw-Hill, 1973. Case studies in the campus revolt of the '60s.

A. WESTLEY ROWLAND, ed., *Handbook of Institutional Advancement.* San Francisco: Jossey-Bass, Inc., 1977. A useful guide to college and university relations, fund raising, alumni relations, and government relations. The authors are professionals.

STEPHEN WITHEY, *A Degree and What Else?: Consequences and Correlates of a College Education.* New York: McGraw-Hill, 1971.

DANIEL YANKELOVICH, *The New Morality: A Profile of American Youth in the '70s.* New York: McGraw-Hill, 1974.

FOOTNOTES

1. For the early history of the practice in higher education, see Scott M. Cutlip, "'Advertising' Higher Education: The Early Years of College Public Relations," Part I, *College & University Journal,* Vol. 9 (Fall 1970); Part II, Vol. 10 (January 1971). Also see Cutlip, *Fund Raising in the United States* (New Brunswick, N.J.: Rutgers University Press, 1965), "The 1920s . . . Cash for Colleges and Cathedrals."

2. Laurence R. Veysey, *The Emergence of the American University* (Chicago: University of Chicago Press, 1965), p. 382.

3. Seymour Martin Lipset, "The Wavering Polls," *The Public Interest,* Spring 1976, p. 83.

4. Fred M. Hechinger, "Murder in Academe: The Demise of Education," *Saturday Review,* March 20, 1976, pp. 11–18. Hechinger, education writer, is on the editorial staff of the *New York Times.*

5. Caroline Bird, *The Case against College* (New York: David McKay, 1975). For one rebuttal, see Fred C. Davison, "A College Education Is Worth Your Time and Money," *The Presbyterian College Report,* Vol. 30 (August 1977).

6. Richard Freeman and J. Herbert Hollomon, "The Declining Value of Going to College," *Change,* Vol. 7 (September 1975). Freeman published a book, *The Overeducated American* (New York: Academic Press, 1976), espousing this same point of view.

7. Cameron Fincher, "The Paradox and Counterpoint of Public Expectations for Higher Education," *Educational Record,* Vol. 55, No. 2 (1974), 107.

8. Burton R. Clark, "The New University," *American Behavioral Scientist,* Vol. 11 (May–June 1968), 2.

9. Allen H. Barton, "The Columbia Crisis, Vietnam and the Ghetto," *Public Opinion Quarterly,* Vol. 32 (Fall 1968).

10. Michael Radock, "Behind the Ivy Curtain," *Public Relations Journal,* Vol. 24 (October 1968).

11. Emanuel Goldberg, "The Professor and the Press," *College & University Journal,* Vol. 2 (Summer 1963), 57 and 59.

12. John A Griffin, "Higher Education and Race Relations," speech to American College Public Relations Association, June 25, 1963. His message unhappily remains valid in 1978.

13. Bruce L.R. Smith and Joseph J. Karlesky, *The State of Academic Science: The Universities in the Nation's Research Effort* (New York: Change Magazine Press, 1977). The study was financed by the National Science Foundation.

14. Jack Magarrell, "Private Universities Found Maintaining Their Competitive Position," *The Chronicle of Higher Education,* May 31, 1977, p. 3. For enrollment trends, see tables, "20-Year Trends in Higher Education," *Chronicle of Higher Education,* September 19, 1977.

15. Gene I. Maeroff, "Colleges Now Are Recruiting for More Than Athletic Reasons," *New York Times,* November 28, 1976, Section IV.

16. Janet Rich and D.C. Tork, *Student Power and How to Use It* (New York: Notre Dame College of Staten Island, 1969). A survey of student involvement in development and public relations in a cross section of colleges. Today many student groups, for example, are involved in fund raising for the college and other good causes.

17. Wallace Roberts, "Patterns of Reform," in a symposium on the "Academic Revolt," *Saturday Review,* October 18, 1969.

18. Judith Cummings, "Plan by Columbia to Sell Old Estate in Bronx Opposed," *New York Times,* December 4, 1977, p. 37.

19. One example: In the fall of 1977, Jane Fonda spoke on the campus of Central Michigan University and denounced Dow Chemical Co. as a part of a "new group of rulers, tyrants." Dow notified Central Michigan that it would get no more gifts from Dow until something was done about balancing "what your students hear." The year before, Dow had given Central Michigan $73,000. For elaboration of the problem, see Jack Magarrell, "Colleges Seen Threatening Capitalism," *Chronicle of Higher Education,* November 7, 1977.

25

I hold every man a debtor to his profession; from which men of course do seek to receive countenance and profit, so ought they of duty to endeavor themselves by way of amends to be a help and ornament thereunto.

FRANCIS BACON

Toward a Profession

Not only have the past four decades seen a phenomenal growth in public relations; this period has brought greater acceptance of the mature concept in practice and increased signs of professionalism. As an organized calling, public relations has come a long way since the days of Ivy Lee, Arthur Page, and Pendleton Dudley, but it still has some distance to go before it matures into a profession. The problem of effecting controlled access to its practice may long deny the field the true status of a profession.

Events of the postdepression period awakened widespread interest in and increased acceptance of the public relations concept. World War II brought new opportunities, new demonstrations of utility, and new techniques and channels of communication. The tensions and problems of the uneasy years of transition to a postindustrial society accentuated and extended these developments. National prosperity underwrote the expansion of old programs and the birth of new ones. Expanding world trade and political conflict extended the practice abroad. After two generations of rapid expansion, public relations is in the process of stabilization. Its necessity in today's interdependent, segmented society is seldom questioned.

Contemporary practice has been highlighted by these developments:

1. Steady growth in the number of programs in industries, institutions, social agencies, government bureaus, and trade associations. Already-established programs have tended to mature and to move beyond publicity.
2. Stabilization in the number of independent counseling firms, especially in the communications hubs of New York, Washington, Chicago, and Los Angeles.
3. A tremendous spurt in the number of books, articles, and journals devoted to the practice and its philosophy, problems, and techniques. The literature is voluminous, although somewhat repetitive.
4. Organization of new associations for practitioners, and redirection or consolidation of those already established. Many of these are now mature.
5. Growth in the number of college courses and students, and in the breadth and depth of the courses. Increased support for collegiate preparation from practitioners, and greater acceptance of young graduates in the job market.
6. Internationalization of the practice and its standards.

Reflecting on these and like developments, Pimlott observed, "As is illustrated by the literature, the growth of the associations, and the state of university training, the public relations group has made dramatic progress since the war, but its evolution is still in a fluid phase."[1] In the years since Pimlott made his study, the function has gained wider acceptance, become more secure within organizations, and strengthened its competence. The practice is steadily moving toward maturity as it shifts its emphasis to counseling and communication. Today, few debate the function's *essentiality* in a society in desperate need of clarifying communications and skillful mediation. Today, the questions focus on the *ethics* and *competence* of practitioners.

Public relations has come to occupy an important role in society, and consequently, it is coming under closer public scrutiny. This is proper. Irwin Ross argues, rightly, in his *Image Merchants,* "We should all gain, in sum, if the PR man were edged out of the shadows and subjected to the glare of attention normally reserved for his clients. These days he is important enough to warrant continual scrutiny."[2]

The counselor is primarily an advocate of a cause, a client, a company, an institution. Much of the confusion in the public's minds about the field is due to the refusal of many practitioners to face the fact that they are special pleaders. Their double-talk about their role as "interpreters" and as "reporters" confuses them—and others. If practitioners recognized their *advocacy* role and did not give those with whom they deal a false impression, part of this problem would be solved. The late John W. Hill said, "Public relations can't cover up mistakes— and shouldn't. However, no one's going to put the worst face on anything. *We're primarily advocates and we draw on a deep reservoir of experience in advocating our clients' causes.*"

To illustrate: When the giant retailer Sears was tried before a Federal Trade Commission administrative-law judge in Chicago on charges of systematically engaging in bait-and-switch selling tactics, the Sears public relations staff did nothing to publicize the testimony. That is not public relations' responsibility. The press did little to cover the trial until it ended when Sears abandoned its emphatic denial and sought a consent order. The Sears spokesman shrugged it off: "The story wasn't a big-ticket item around here." *The failure here was that of the media, not of the Sears public relations staff.*[3]

The practice was given a black eye in the mind of the public by Richard Nixon's preoccupation with his misshapen concept of the function. He and his aides *confused the shadow of "image" with the substance of performance.* Nixon's typical response to each new revelation of wrongdoing in his administration was, "Let's PR it." For example, in September 15, 1972, when Nixon and his coconspirators were trying to halt a House probe of the Watergate breakin, the president said that Republican members of Congress "really ought to blunderbuss in the public arena." When aides H.R. Haldeman and John Dean agreed, Nixon said, *"That's what this is, public relations."* President Nixon built the largest, most expensive White House public relations organization in history, yet it came to naught because it was built on dishonesty and incompetence. Only a few public relations practitioners were caught in the shadows of Watergate, and most of these on the outside. Yet the stigma lingers.

This is what we conceive to be the social justification of the public relations function in a free society: *to ethically, effectively plead the cause of a client or organization in the forum of public debate.* It is a basic democratic right that every idea, individual, or institution shall have a full and fair hearing in the public forum—that its merit is determined by its ability to get accepted in the public opinion marketplace. *To obtain such a hearing today, the individual, idea, or institution needs the expertise of a skilled advocate. The advocate is essential to make modern democracy work.*

Public relations' impact on society

Of much more importance than headline-making incidents involving practitioners is the *fundamental question of the function's impact on society.* The proponent of public relations can document many values of its work to society. The critic can cite, with equal validity, many harmful effects. These do not damn the function or vitiate its essentiality; they stand as a challenge to those who would make this a constructive calling. The greatest virtue and the greatest sin of public relations are identical: its chameleon nature. Practitioners can adapt easily from fund raising for a hospital to rousing public opinion against Medicare. When they do this, their "sin" is appearing to have no convictions of their own, of serving the master who pays them. But public relations is not based on a *morality* of its own, but rather on the possession of technical skills in communications and advocacy.

The practitioner's position is much like that of the lawyer. Central to this matter is the fact that the practice is shaped by the desires of employers or clients and the opportunism of practitioners. Ivy Lee's onetime partner, William W. Harris, noted this long ago: "If the public relations man is superfluous or useless, that is a matter for the corporation he serves." Raucher thinks public relations lacks "its own goals of social responsibility."

Ultimately, public relations must be judged on the basis of its social utility. Yardsticks for such judgment could be these:

1. The social utility of public relations rests in its promotion of free, ethical competition of ideas, individuals, and institutions in the marketplace of public opinion.
2. Social utility is diminished to the extent that competition of ideas, individuals, and institutions is suppressed in campaigns.
3. Social utility is served to the extent that the goals underlying influence attempts are revealed.
4. Social utility is diminished to the extent that public opinion is not permitted to come to bear on issues once they are made public.
5. Social utility is diminished when the origins of public relations are hidden or ascribed to other than their true source.

Two large minuses can be written against the practice: (1) Public relations has cluttered our already choked channels of communication with the debris of pseudoevents and phony phrases that confuse rather than clarify; and (2) public relations has corroded our channels of communication with cynicism and "credibility gaps." Too often, the thrust is to obfuscate and obscure rather than to clarify—and in a day when complex public issues must be made clear. Stage and film director Mike Nichols asserts, "Modern liberalism has become a process of public relations, changing the name of things."

Robert Heilbroner recognizes public relations as a social force and charges it with a major part "in the general debasement of communications from which we suffer." He wrote:

> No one can quarrel with the essential function that public relations fills as a purveyor of genuine ideas and information. No one denies that many public relations men, working for corporations as well as for colleges or causes, honestly communicate things which are worth communicating. Nor can anyone absolve public relations for loading the communications channels with noise. We read the news and suspect that behind it lies the "news release." We encounter the reputation and ascribe it to publicity. Worst of all, we no longer credit good behavior with good motives, but cheapen it to the level of "good public relations."[4]

When a large corporation announces a scholarship program for deserving youths or makes a big gift to a hospital drive, we cynically shrug it off as "smart public relations." Typical is this reaction of the *Milwaukee Journal* in commenting on an oil company's giving away cardboard bluebird houses: "Perhaps some crafty public relations man is behind the scheme." Awarding a plaque or citation is a standard gimmick that has reached the point where it is difficult to distinguish the award for achievement from the award for publicity purposes. Eric Sevareid notes wryly:

> For some time now, Gresham's Law has been operating with wild abandon—bad honorary degrees, scrolls, plaques, medals, and guilt-painted zinc trophies have been driving out the good ones, exactly as "celebrity" has been driving out the precious word, "fame," and as the serried rows of Publicity Saints have been taking over the field from Great Men.

Practitioners also stand indicted, with some validity, for loading our channels of communication with noise and clogging them with the clutter of manufactured stories. In his book, *The Image,* historian Daniel Boorstin introduces a useful term, *pseudoevents,* and argues that these serve to blur, rather than clarify, public issues. Boorstin writes:

> The disproportion between what an informed citizen needs to know and what he can know is ever greater. The disproportion grows with the increase of the officials' power of concealment and contrivance. The news gatherers' need to select, invent, and plan correspondingly increases. Thus inevitably our whole system of public information produces always more "packaged" news, more pseudoevents.[5]

Although Boorstin primarily blames journalists for this, *practitioners are the major producers of pseudoevents.* An event planned to promote a cause in the public interest and in keeping with the character of the sponsor has a legitimate place in public relations. This no one will deny. It is the phony event to promote a dubious product or cause that comes under fire. Precious news space or time given to Miss Universe cannot be used in explaining the complex energy situation. *Ethical public relations contributes to clarification of public issues, not to their distortion or obfuscation.*

Even after the practitioners representing competing parties have served their roles as advocates by providing the public with a persuasive presentation of each party's position, there remains a nagging doubt about whether the public is

EXHIBIT 25-1

Finger-lickin' Good Publicity

Typical of the pseudoevents that characterize much of today's practice is the National Chicken Cooking Contest—probably copied from Pillsbury's Annual Bakeoff. A writer describes the opening:

> It is the moment of truth. The top chicken cookers from each of the fifty states and the District of Columbia are assembled in the Exhibit Hall of San Antonio's Convention Center, awaiting the Parade of States.
>
> The Air Force Band of the West strikes up "Cook Your Chicken with a Tender Touch." Then, fifty-one finalists, accompanied by flag-bearing Boy Scouts and Cub Scouts, march through the hall to their Westinghouse ranges and their chicken-preparation tables, where two quarts of Mazola and a large shaker of Ac'cent await them.
>
> The Air Force Band plays the national anthem. Then the contest chairman, a Texas chicken man, announces: "Now is the time you all have been waiting for. I call the contestants to their Westinghouse ranges to do their thing with their chickens."[6]

---

adequately informed as a result. Typical of today's public relations battles was one waged between the advocates of the nation's steel companies and those of the United Steelworkers' Union. Both sides spent millions of dollars presenting their case before and during a long steel strike, but with little noticeable result. A special committee of the National Council of Churches of Christ, which made an exhaustive study of the implications of this dispute, said, "Both sides in this dispute indulged in one of the most spectacular utilizations of mass communications media to be employed in an industrial conflict, involving advertisement, radio and television programs, and direct mailings." The Council of Churches committee raises a basic question:

> The methodology for influencing public opinion is full of ethical issues and it is to be noted that during the steel dispute no way was available whereby the public could obtain an objective evaluation of the claims which were being pushed so energetically by both sides.[7]

Similarly, a study of the press's treatment of scientific findings linking cigarette smoking to lung cancer, made by editors of the *Columbia Journalism Review,* concluded, "Coverage has been sufficiently fragmented, uneven, and affected by publicity efforts on both sides to cause confusion."[8] The news media depend in large measure on the American Cancer Society and public-health agencies for the news on cancer. The public relations output from these sources has led to an unwarranted optimism about the progress being made against this deadly disease. An American Cancer Society theme is, "Cancer is one of the most curable of the major diseases in this country." But hard statistics won't support such a view.[9]

Presenting all sides of an issue and providing an objective, balanced appraisal of the merits of conflicting views is a responsibility of the news media, not the practitioner. The Council of Churches Committee recognized this: "When the media of mass communications are used by great power groups to try to win the American public to accept their point of view, there is an open necessity for some objective evaluation of the disputed facts. We feel that the newspapers and magazines did not serve the public adequately in this regard and that the radio and television networks did little better. . . ." The editors of the *Columbia Journalism Review* made the same point: "An important place for clarifying confusing news—the editorial page—has been little used."

The large pluses are these: (1) *By stressing the need for public approval, practitioners improve the conduct of organizations they serve.* (2) *Practitioners serve the public interest by making all points of view articulate in the public forum.* (3) *Practitioners serve our segmented, scattered society by using their talents of communication and mediation to replace misinformation with information, discord with rapport.*

Much constructive good can be accurately ascribed to the ethical practice—on behalf of our nation, our colleges and united funds, our corporations, and our conservation, mental health, and professional associations. Opportunities for serving the public have been stressed throughout this book. Public relations' benefits are displayed in sound economic enterprises providing profit for investors, jobs for employees, and goods for consumers; in the billions raised to build buildings, endow professorships, and provide scholarships in our nation's colleges; in campaigns for eradication of disease; in the lessening of racial and religious discrimination; and in broader understanding of our national and international problems. *The potential good inherent in ethical, effective public relations is limitless.*

A search for standards

As public relations has gained stability, and as public debate about its social role has mounted, the search by practitioners for ethical standards has intensified. There has been a great sensitivity to "public relations for public relations" in this period. This sensitivity has brought some pious platitudes and some self-serving rationalization; but it has also brought some honest soul-searching and sincere effort to enforce ethical standards within the craft, and this has resulted in self-imposed standards.

One serious effort being made by practitioners jointly is to surround performance of the function with the status and methods of a profession—in short, *to qualify functionally.* A second is concern for the behavior of individual practitioners—the effort *to qualify morally.* A third aspect relates to the calibre and kind of training required for recruits and the need for more basic communications research. This represents an effort *to qualify through knowledge and expertness.* These standards tend to fuse with each other in this period.

Much of the craft's discussion of ethics and standards is akin to whistling one's way through a graveyard. Counselor David Finn says bluntly, "Unfortunately, it is a subject not being discussed openly and straightforwardly in business circles, which in itself is not a good sign. Rationalizations, self-righteousness, and platitudes do not get rid of discerning challenges—nor do untalked-about skeletons in the closet make for well-adjusted consciences."[10]

It ought to be kept in mind that, as a noted legal historian has pointed out, "no abstract logic has created the concept of the professions." Rather, "practice and experience in making society function have led to the definition of some occupations as professional, and have from time to time determined which ways of earning a living should fit the professional category." Many callings have striven for the status of profession. Few have won it. Much of this effort is self-serving; some of it is public-spirited. Willard Hurst goes to the nub of the matter: "Neither ambition, social snobbery, nor self-assertion will serve to create a profession or define its area of autonomy; these will in the long run be determined by the function fulfilled."[11]

A former president of the Carnegie Corporation observed, "While this pressure toward professionalism might in one sense be labeled selfish, the results are beneficent for society as a whole. Professionalizing any activity tends to institutionalize the best ways of doing the job, and to create standards of quality which serve the public interest. This extension of the professional idea has by and large brought us safer bridges, better houses, higher standards in business, banking, and other fields."

To measure the advance of the contemporary practice toward the much-sought goal of professionalism, *there must be yardsticks*. Professor John Marston lists these characteristics as distinguishing professions from skilled occupations:

1. A defined area of competence.
2. An organized body of knowledge of some consequence.
3. Self-consciousness.
4. Competence of entrants determined by controlled access.
5. Continuing education.
6. Support of research.
7. Aid in the education of competent replacements.
8. Independence.[12]

Overall, there must be professional competence, recognition of obligations to others in the profession, and a dedication to serve, not injure, the public welfare.

Even though practitioners continue to be beset with all sorts of complexes and doubts as to their own worthiness, movement in these professional directions is apparent. Many stabilizing influences are at work. Much progress has been recorded. The trend toward professionalism can be seen in these assets: (1) a large national society, supplemented by several strong specialized associations; (2) a code of ethics clearly spelled out; (3) a National Judicial Council, created to enforce its standards upon PRSA members, and the beginnings of such enforcement in the early 1960s; (4) fairly stiff eligibility standards for membership in the PRSA; (5) training, education, and research in many universities and colleges, a small part of which is supported by the PRSA; (6) a large and growing body of technical books, papers, and journals; (7) organizational status for the practitioner; and (8) increasing contributions to the public service by practitioners.

The 1970s saw most of the foundation stones for a professional structure in place. When this foundation is complete, an enduring profession can be built upon something more substantial than self-pleading. Professional recognition cannot be a simple case of practitioners' lifting themselves by telling one another that they are professionals. Public opinion determines what is a profession—a fact that practitioners ought to know better than most. *The task of the practitioner is to earn the status*. Many are doing that.

A new frontier beckons

Public relations around a fast-shrinking world is the bright new frontier, beckoning young people with ability and a sense of adventure. International practice will accelerate to meet the needs born of a hotly competitive world market and of a spirited economic and political struggle in a world linked by rapid international telecommunication and transportation. In a day of satellite-relayed worldwide radio and television, of supersonic jetliners that make intercontinental trips a matter of a few hours and world travel commonplace, international public relations is bound to grow at a fast pace. In the prophetic words of a British pioneer practitioner, Sir Stephen Tallents, "If we are to play our part in the new world order, we need to master every means and every art by which we can communicate with other peoples."

Advances in telecommunications and transportation have brought people into the closest contact in the history of civilization. Never before have ideas and information had such rapid and far-reaching impact. The same ecological factors that compelled the development of public relations in the United States are operating to bring it about on a global scale—only more quickly. Public relations is being adapted to the needs of business firms, nonprofit institutions, and nations of the world at a breathtaking rate. Our business firms and the International Communications Agency are leading the way in spreading the practice to what once were far corners of the world.

In ever-growing numbers, U.S. companies are operating abroad through subsidiaries, branches, and distributors, and in partnership with local and multinational corporations. Firms doing business across national boundaries and in different cultures find public relations more imperative abroad than at home. Corporations abroad have to buck the onus of absentee ownership, avert the threat of expropriation, combat the hatreds bred by political and business opponents, and deal with different cultures. The dimensions of international practice and problems are seen in the far-flung operations of International Telephone & Telegraph, Royal Dutch Shell, Unilever, Phillips of the Netherlands, and Exxon. International public relations emerged in the 1950s, primarily as a marketing tool in Europe and Latin America, and as a means of fending off expropriation in the developing nations. Most firms emphasized product publicity in the early years; the large extractive companies, understandably, were more concerned with public relations in the broad sense.

Governments, too, employ countless practitioners to win world support for political objectives, to promote tourism, and to establish a nation's identity in the world community. Much of today's international news flow is provided by governments and their public relations agencies. There were some 560 agents of foreign principals registered with the U.S Department of Justice in the mid-1970s. Most of these were public relations agents, and 75 percent represented foreign governments. World political struggles and worldwide television have intensified these programs to inform and influence people in other lands. The idea is not new—only the channels, the volume, and the intensity of competition. Since ancient times, political leaders have supplemented diplomacy and force with communications to weaken an enemy's will, to gain allies, or to bring about cooperation and trade. In addition to governments and corporations, this international practice is also being extended by private organizations. Davison notes, "Many of these organizations are concerned with economic matters:

promoting trade, investment, or tourism. Others are concerned with humanitarian, educational, or religious affairs. A substantial number have political aims."[13]

Robert L. Bliss sees these as the reasons for the swift growth: (1) governmental programs of new nations and nations establishing independent identities out of colonial status; (2) movement of industries overseas, either in joint-venture establishment or in their own foreign-based production and sales expansion; (3) tourism; (4) changes in the government or political philosophy of nations, and movement from more traditional, isolated roles toward identification with activities in world interest; and (5) broadened transportation programs by air, sea, and land from national to international patterns.

The past decade saw a perceptible shift in emphasis from marketing to nonmarketing problems in public relations practice abroad. The nonmarketing problems include making absentee ownership acceptable in a world of rising nationalism, in which "takeover" and "Americanization" arouse angry political passions; making the mammoth size of multinational corporations acceptable to the public, which fears bigness and cartels; the competition for local capital and labor; and the consumer protest movement circling the world. As a consequence, there is a definite, discernible increase in international practice.

Toward a code of ethics

A basic requirement for a profession is adherence to a set of professional norms. As self-consciousness and a sense of cohesiveness have developed, there has been increasing concern for standards of professional responsibility. *Many practitioners are making an earnest effort to qualify morally. Others see codes of ethics as so much window dressing.* Exertions to advance the ethics in this field are reflected in a number of codes of professional standards for public relations practice. The principal code is that of the Public Relations Society of America. The PRSA's first Code of Professional Standards was adopted in 1954, and revised in 1959, in 1963, and in 1977. The 1963 revisions were designed to toughen the ethics of financial practices in response to an investigation by the Securities and Exchange Commission, which, as a climax to the several years' investigation, had issued a biting indictment of the malpractices of a handful of practitioners.[14] The 1977 revision of the code was in response to the threat of antitrust litigation against the PRSA by the Federal Trade Commission. The commission's Bureau of Competition had decided that the provisions of the code barring contingency fees and banning one member's encroaching upon another member's clients were in violation of free competition. These were the provisions of the code that were in contention:

13. A member shall not propose to a prospective client or employer that the amount of his fee or other compensation be contingent on or measured by the achievement of specified results; nor shall he enter into any fee agreement to the same effect.
14. A member shall not encroach upon the professional employment of another member. Where there are two engagements, both must be assured that there is no conflict between them.

The latter provision has long been a source of debate inside and outside the PRSA because it did not ban encroachment upon the employment of the 85 percent of practitioners who were not in the PRSA. Thus it appeared to be a protection only for counselors who were PRSA members, making fair game of those who were not. In fact, the provision was never meaningfully enforced. Frank Wylie, 1978 PRSA president, said, "An ethic which protects the club-members is really no ethic at all."

Although the PRSA membership did not accept the validity of the FTC's charges, the provisions above were eliminated in the code adopted in Chicago April 29, 1977, but PRSA leaders made it clear that the society still does not condone pirating accounts or contingency fees. The Federal Trade Commission, on October 27, 1977, accepted from the PRSA an agreement containing a consent order that prohibits the society from "promulgating rules that affect fee arrangements or business solicitations." Thus the FTC approved the society's code revisions.

The revised code also removed "sexist concepts and language," but it did retain another hotly debated provision:

3. A member shall adhere to truth and accuracy and to generally accepted standards of good taste.

The phrase "generally accepted standards" is the bone of contention among thoughtful practitioners. Its elasticity permits more than one unethical practice to go unpunished. Rea Smith, vice-president of the PRSA, defends this on the grounds that "good taste is subject to changing attitudes in society." Your authors think that "exemplary standards of good taste" would be more binding.

The PRSA's code follows:

PUBLIC RELATIONS SOCIETY OF AMERICA
Code of Professional Standards
for the Practice of Public Relations
Adopted and Effective April 29, 1977

(This Code, adopted by the PRSA Assembly, replaces a similar Code of Professional Standards for the Practice of Public Relations previously in force since 1954 and strengthened by revisions in 1959)

Declaration of Principles

Members of the Public Relations Society of America base their professional principles on the fundamental value and dignity of the individual, holding that the free exercise of human rights, especially freedom of speech, freedom of assembly and freedom of the press, is essential to the practice of public relations.

In serving the interests of clients and employers, we dedicate ourselves to the goals of better communication, understanding and cooperation among the diverse individuals, groups and institutions of society.

We pledge:

To conduct ourselves professionally, with truth, accuracy, fairness and responsibility to the public;

To improve our individual competence and advance the knowledge and proficiency of the profession through continuing research and education;

And to adhere to the articles of the Code of Professional Standards for the Practice of Public Relations as adopted by the governing Assembly of the Society.

Articles of the Code

These articles have been adopted by the Public Relations Society of America to promote and maintain high standards of public service and ethical conduct among its members.

1. A member shall deal fairly with clients or employers, past and present, with fellow practitioners and the general public.

2. A member shall conduct his or her professional life in accord with the public interest.

3. A member shall adhere to truth and accuracy and to generally accepted standards of good taste.

4. A member shall not represent conflicting or competing interests without the express consent of those involved, given after a full disclosure of the facts; nor place himself or herself in a position where the member's interest is or may be in conflict with a duty to a client, or others, without a full disclosure of such interests to all involved.

5. A member shall safeguard the confidence of both present and former clients or employers and shall not accept retainers or employment which may involve the disclosure or use of these confidences to the disadvantage or prejudice of such clients or employers.

6. A member shall not engage in any practice which tends to corrupt the integrity of channels of communication or the processes of government.

7. A member shall not intentionally communicate false or misleading information and is obligated to use care to avoid communication of false or misleading information.

8. A member shall be prepared to identify publicly the name of the client or employer on whose behalf any public communication is made.

9. A member shall not make use of any individual or organization purporting to serve or represent an announced case, or purporting to be independent or unbiased, but actually serving an undisclosed special or private interest of a member, client or employer.

10. A member shall not intentionally injure the professional reputation or practice of another practitioner.

However, if a member has evidence that another member has been guilty of unethical, illegal or unfair practices, including those in violation of this Code, the member shall present the information promptly to the proper authorities of the Society for action in accordance with the procedure set forth in Article XIII of the Bylaws.

11. A member called as a witness in a proceeding for the enforcement of this Code shall be bound to appear, unless excused for sufficient reason by the Judicial Panel.

12. A member, in performing services for a client or employer, shall not accept fees, commissions or any other valuable consideration from anyone other than the client or employer in connection with those services without the express consent of the client or employer, given after a full disclosure of the facts.

13. A member shall not guarantee the achievement of specified results beyond the member's direct control.

14. A member shall, as soon as possible, sever relations with any organization or individual if such relationship requires conduct contrary to the articles of this Code.

Enforcement of the PRSA code on the practices of its members has been uneven over the years. The first penalty for violation was meted out in 1962, when a member was censured for attempting to take away the account of another member. Two members were censured in 1963, and another was suspended in 1964 in the wake of the Fulbright Committee's investigation of counselors representing foreign governments. In a five-year period, 1965 through 1969, 21 cases involving apparently unethical practices came before the PRSA grievance board. In the six of these cases that were filed with the judicial panels, one member was suspended, one was reprimanded, one was censured, and three cases were dismissed.

In the 1970s, 46 complaints were filed with the grievance board, of which four cases were tried by judicial panels and one filed with a panel but not tried, because the member resigned and thus removed himself from the society's jurisdiction. (This resignation from the PRSA by an officer of a counseling firm to avoid trial illustrates the weakness of the PRSA—it cannot police the practitioners who do not belong to it.) One of the four cases was withdrawn by the complainant almost in midproceedings. In another case, the evidence did not support the claim of code violation, so it got in effect a verdict of not guilty. A third resulted in the suspension of a member for flagrant account piracy. In the fourth case, also a charge of encroachment, the facts were so fuzzy that it, too, was thrown out of court.[15]

Of the three PRSA members identified with the corruption of Watergate, two soon resigned. The third was still being investigated in 1978. There have also been instances when powerful counselors were able to refute charges. Members often escape scrutiny because no one files a complaint. Public relations is one major segment of mass communications making some effort to police its behavior.

Practical people know that adoption of a code of ethics does not automatically bring morality to a calling, but such codes do reflect a concern among the leaders for raising the ethical levels, and they provide yardsticks of measurement. Also, like a New Englander's conscience, a code can make a practitioner "durned uneasy." A distinguished Canadian counselor points out, "Unfortunately, these codes have little real value unless they are accepted in turn by the employers of practitioners and applied to the conduct of the business itself."[16] Frank Wylie, who has long crusaded for higher ethics in public relations, says, "We shouldn't allow ourselves to accept the lowest common denominator of behavior—the negative and retrogressive 'it won't really hurt anyone' philosophy. We must aspire to a better level of ethics, and we must persevere to achieve that goal."[17]

The skill, ethics, and concepts used by the wide variety of practitioners vary greatly. In appraising the ethics, it is well to remember that there is no watertight bulkhead between the practitioners and the society in which they operate. Moreover, they are generally found at the foci of power. And power is not always gained and held by playing according to the rules. When a university scholar can assert that "graft, crime, corruption, 'the fix,' are embedded in the very fabric of our highly competitive society," there is no reason to presume that all practitioners will be immune. When the four horsemen of calumny—fear, ignorance, bigotry, and smear—gallop madly about, it is natural to find a few of those skilled in communications and propaganda riding with them. Practitioners will be found to be representative of the institutions and causes they serve.

The question of licensure

Codes of behavior will lack wholly effective means of enforcement until there is legal certification of practitioners. Controlled access is the *sine qua non* of a recognized profession. We believe that there must be controlled access, through licensing, to the title of "certified public relations counselor." This is the only way that the frauds and flacks can be separated from legitimate practitioners.

Licensing should be done to protect society as well as to advance the cause of professionalism. Voluntary codes do not do this. Edward L. Bernays, pioneer counselor, was among the first to advocate licensure. In 1953 he argued, "In the entire history of professions, licensing standards and criteria and finally codes of ethics in public conduct have been necessary . . . to exclude those who are not properly qualified."[18] The indefatigable Bernays was still thumping the same drum in 1975: "If we want public relations to gain public understanding, recognition, and the support it deserves, we can follow precedents of law and medicine. We can demand licensure."[19] Even so, licensure has few champions in public relations.

The legal aspects

The issue of occupational licensure, the permission granted by the state to engage in a specific occupation, raises three basic constitutional issues: (1) *the right of freedom of expression*, (2) *the right of the states to regulate occupations*, and (3) *the right of individuals to pursue occupations without unjustified state interference*. Licensure must be justified on the grounds that it is *crucial* to the well-being and preservation of society. The right of the states to regulate occupations is based on the Tenth Amendment, which gives states all powers not specifically delegated to Congress.

There are two serious legal questions involved in the matter of licensing. One is the problem of demonstrating a compelling state interest; the other is safeguarding the practitioner's freedom of expression.

Compelling state interest: In recent years, the courts have raised the lower limits of what is defined as "compelling state interest." The two broad reasons generally given for public relations licensure—protection of society and professionalization of practitioners—must be considered carefully in the light of "compelling state interest."

The *first* of these reasons, that public relations can harm society by "corrupting the public channels of communications," is the stronger of the two, yet it is weak in the eyes of the courts. Although public relations has the potential for abuse, its actions are no more potentially dangerous to society as a whole than would be those exercised directly by the person for whom the practitioner might act. And although public relations may be controversial, the courts have argued in cases such as *Adams* v. *Tanner,* 244 U.S. 590 (1917), and *Baker* v. *Daly,* 15F. Supp. 2d 881, that controversy is not sufficient cause to regulate. The argument that licensing would protect society is directly refuted in law. The courts have consistently found that even abusive communication merits protection.

The *second* of these reasons, that licensure would professionalize the practice, also gets short shrift in the law. It may be a powerful *professional* argument, but it has no legal basis. In no case have the courts suggested that because licensing would be beneficial, it would be justifiable. Licensing cannot be imposed simply for the benefit of those in an occupational group, either to raise standards or to fence out competition.

Freedom of expression: Nor can the question of infringement of freedom of expression be easily dismissed. If the state did engage in the nondiscretionary licensing of practitioners, the exact degree of infringement of the practitioner's right of expression would most likely be minimal. What is at issue here is the right to the title, "certified public relations counselor." The Supreme Court stated, in *Time* v. *Hill,* 385 U.S. 374, that constitutional guarantees of free speech and press are not so much for the benefit of those concerned "as for the benefit of the citizens generally." In developing a measure of fitness that involves the competence to communicate, the state would be recognizing different competencies in individuals. Yet the right to freedom of expression is accorded to all, as contrasted with the privilege of practicing medicine, which is not guaranteed in the Constitution. On the whole, the law seems unready to grapple with the licensure of this vocation. The legal obstacles, together with the entrenched opposition of the public relations Establishment, ensure that licensure will not soon provide a means of elevating the ethics and competence of practitioners.

Given the weakness of voluntary codes that don't cover the majority of practitioners, and the little likelihood of state licensing, some advocate a Public Relations Council as an intermediate step. One proponent of this idea suggests:

> The council's purposes would include maintaining the character of the public relations practice in accordance with the highest professional and commercial standards, keeping under review developments likely to lead to abrogations of those standards, considering complaints about the conduct of PR practitioners and that of organizations relating to their public relations dealing with complaints in a systematic, orderly manner.[20]

Such councils would be organized and supported much in the manner of the National News Council and local press councils.

Professional organizations

The growth of professional associations reflects the serious efforts being made by many practitioners to surround the function with status and to advance its competence. Although these associations include only roughly half the people in public relations, they exert considerable influence through their publications, conferences, seminars, awards programs, and central office activities. The largest of these is the Public Relations Society of America, which as of January 1978 had 8,500 members, 3,000 of whom were accredited. The society is an amalgam of three older associations organized to win public recognition for this emerging vocation.

The PRSA was formed February 4, 1948, by the merger of the National

Association of Public Relations Counsel and the American Council on Public Relations. The former group was first organized in 1936 as the National Association of Accredited Publicity Directors. It was composed largely of New York City counselors; the words *national* and *accredited* were used in a very loose sense. It changed its name in 1944 to reflect the shift in emphasis to public relations. The American Council on Public Relations was started in San Francisco in 1939 as an association for West Coast practitioners.

The goal of forward-looking practitioners and educators for one strong national association, serving all fields of practice, was finally realized July 1, 1961, when the American Public Relations Association merged into the PRSA. The APRA, headquartered in Washington, D.C., and dominated by trade-association practitioners, had been organized in 1944 after some seven years' effort among Washington practitioners. At the time of the merger in 1961, the PRSA had 3,359 members and the APRA 826; 100 practitioners held membership in both organizations.

The APRA made two contributions to the advancement of its craft—its Silver Anvil Awards to recognize successful programs, and its *Quarterly Review of Public Relations,* later retitled in turn *PR Quarterly* and *Public Relations Quarterly.* The PRSA has continued the Silver Anvil Awards program. The PRSA does much to foster the exchange of ideas through its publications and meetings, to promote a sense of professionalism, to provide opportunities for continuing education, and to remind practitioners of the need for more ethical behavior. Its strength and scope were greatly enhanced when the National Communication Council for Human Services, the organization of practitioners serving the health and welfare fields, voted to consolidate its membership and services with those of the PRSA. This consolidation was completed in 1977.

The counselors in the Public Relations Society organized a "counselors' section" in 1960 as a means of dealing more effectively with the problems of special concern to public relations agencies. This section studied counseling fees, issued a booklet defining the role of the counselor, and in 1963 gained the PRSA's approval of a voluntary plan of self-accreditation, based on character, experience, and examination. PRSA members who were engaged in association work followed suit in 1963 when they won approval for a "business and professional association section." A "government section" was formed in 1970, and other interest groups have since organized. There are sections for practitioners in health work, education, corporations, transportation, utilities, and investor relations.

Several specialized national organizations have also served as spurs for solidarity and professional growth. The broad membership embraced in these vertical groups indicates this field's growth. It reflects a sense of common interests and an emerging *esprit de corps* of professionalism. Typical of these specialized groups is the young National Association of Government Communicators. It was organized in January 1976 as an amalgam of the Government Information Organization and the Federal Editors Association. A year after its founding, the NAGC had nearly 1,000 members. The goal is to gain professional recognition for government information officers and to advance members' skills through workshops, seminars, and annual meetings. It works with the Civil Service Commission to update and write meaningful job standards. One of this organization's goals is to get Congress to repeal the laws that restrict and hobble the public relations function in government. These were discussed in Chapter 22.

Other such specialized organizations are those listed below:

Title	Date Organized
Agricultural Relations Council	1953
American Society for Hospital Public Relations Directors	1964
CASE (Council for Advancement and Support of Education)	1975
Chemical Public Relations Association	1952
Bank Marketing Association (formerly Financial Public Relations Association)	1915
Library Public Relations Council	1939
National School Public Relations Association	1935
Railroad Public Relations Association	1952
Religious Public Relations Council	1929

In addition to the principal professional groups listed above, a number of informal "inside" groups have developed over the years, with varying degrees of impact in shaping the practice. These include the Wise Men, begun by John W. Hill, Pendleton Dudley, and T.J. Ross in 1938; the Public Relations Seminar, started in 1951 as an outgrowth of the National Conference of Business Public Relations Executives; Pride and Alarm, founded in 1957 by New York–based practitioners who style themselves "junior Wise Men"; Shop Talk, started in 1965 by twelve New York agencies; and PR Counselors Roundtable of Chicago, also established in 1965. Such groups function informally and hold their meetings in private. Exclusivity for the "in group" is their hallmark. The Public Relations Seminar annually holds a week-long seminar in some posh resort. Its history has been chronicled by Harold Brayman.[21] Some members of the PRSA fear that the proliferation of such groups will drain talent and funds from the field's main general association.

Professional literature

Related somewhat to associational developments has been the growth in the number of journals devoted to this field, increased space in established periodicals, and a growing number of books. An important advance came with public relations' first scholarly journal, *Public Relations Review,* launched in 1975 under the auspices of the Foundation for Public Relations Research and Education. This journal provides both encouragement to scholarly research and a bridge across the gulf that tends to separate scholar and practitioner. The oldest publication in the field, started in 1944 by Rex F. Harlow, PRSA's *Public Relations Journal* emphasizes professionalism, presents case histories, and provides a forum for debate on practice and ethics. *PR Quarterly,* started in 1954 as the publication of the American Public Relations Association, is similar to the *Journal* in purpose and content, although its articles are somewhat longer. Privately published since 1961 when APRA merged with PRSA, *Public Relations Quarterly* has been edited by Howard P. Hudson since its inception.

There are also four newsletters reporting current news and offering mini-case studies and how-to information:

Name	Year Started	Frequency
Public Relations News	1944	Weekly
PR Reporter	1958	Weekly
Practical Public Relations	1958	Twice monthly
Jack O'Dwyer's Newsletter	1967	Weekly

The first comprehensive bibliography of book and periodical literature was published in 1957 under the auspices of the PRSA. The second edition, published in 1965, carried nearly 6,000 entries of books or articles about or relevant to the practice. Two supplements have brought the bibliography through 1974.[22]

Other publications that contribute to the expanding knowledge of public opinion, survey research, communications, and public relations are:

Advertising Age

American City

A–V Communication Review

Broadcasting

CASE Currents

Channels (now published by PRSA)

Columbia Journalism Review

Editor & Publisher

Fortune

Harvard Business Review

Human Relations

It Starts in the Classroom

Journal of Advertising

Journal of Applied Psychology

Journal of Communication

Journal of Broadcasting

Journal of Personality and Social Psychology

Journal of Marketing

Journalism Quarterly

Marketing/Communications

MORE

Nieman Reports

Public Opinion Quarterly

Quill

Trends in School Public Relations

Television Quarterly

Professional education

University-level instruction in public relations dates from 1920. Concurrent with the beginning of the publicity boom of the 1920s, Jos. F. Wright introduced a publicity course at the University of Illinois, frankly admitting that the course was created to bring prestige to his new calling. Two years later, in 1922, Frank R. Elliott introduced a publicity course at Indiana University. Both Wright and Elliott organized the first publicity programs for their institutions and taught these courses on a part-time basis. Teaching such courses gave these pioneers faculty status, something they needed in order to earn support among faculty men who looked askance at "propagandists."[23]

The first public relations course was offered in 1923 by Edward L. Bernays, who had just written his *Crystallizing Public Opinion*. Bernays taught the one-semester-credit course for two years in the Department of Journalism of New York University's School of Commerce, Accounts, and Finance. Typical of the growing demand for skilled publicists was that found in the new fields of social work and philanthropic fund raising. Evart and Mary Swain Routzahn, pioneers of social-work public relations, first offered a course in social-work publicity in the New York School of Social Work in 1923.

The past three decades have brought phenomenal growth in public relations education, growth commensurate with the expansion of the practice in those years. A 1946 survey found 30 collegiate institutions offering 47 courses.[24] In 1956, the PRSA, under the leadership of Hale Nelson, made the first comprehensive survey of public relations education and found that the number of colleges offering courses had tripled in a decade.[25] Fourteen years later, another survey, financed by PRSA and directed by Prof. Ray Hiebert, reported 303 institutions offering one or more courses, with increased depth in instruction and much more scholarly research to support it.[26]

A survey five years later, directed by Prof. Albert Walker of Northern Illinois University, found "little change in direction, organization, and structure . . . the major difference is in growth."[27] Walker reported, "Public relations education is still very much an integral part of journalism education where it is treated as one of the journalistic career fields. . . . Substantial growth in the past five years in numbers of sequences and major programs has resulted in few new courses and certainly no proliferation. Growth primarily has been in students and faculty, and organizing related courses into sequences." Walker's survey indicated that nearly 80 percent of public relations instruction is in journalism or communication units, 10 percent in business schools. These findings strongly suggest a maturation in public relations education after three decades of rapid growth.

Walker also concluded, "Professors appear to be well schooled in practice and teaching, and have ample academic credentials." Two other researchers who made a more probing study of the qualifications of public relations teachers were more critical. They concluded tentatively, "First, it seems clear that PR instructors do have backgrounds which emphasize either academics or theory, but not necessarily public relations academics or theory. Some amount of public relations experience appears to be evident in most cases. Secondly, the backgrounds, activities, and associations of instructors do tend to correlate with the courses they teach but in some instances this correlation is minimal." They added, "There are several major areas where apparent deficiencies appear." In sum, these scholars answer a cautious "yes" to the question, "Are today's teachers well qualified?"[28]

A benchmark in education was established in 1976 when a commission of practitioners and educators agreed on the fundamentals of a public relations curriculum. This commission, sponsored by the Public Relations Division of the AEJ and PRSA, was set up because of the conviction that after "some thirty years of public relations education, there is urgent need for a thorough examination and review of the educational process in respect to preparing persons for the practice of public relations, and for managerial and administrative positions, so that they will have an appropriate understanding of public relations practice and its values."[29] The guiding principle in designing the model curriculum was "that the student should receive a well-rounded education in the liberal arts and humanities, with appropriate emphasis on education in communications and public relations."

This commission also agreed "that, since public relations practice is to a considerable extent concerned with effective communication (although certainly not to the exclusion of social analysis, management counseling and planning), the appropriate academic milieu for public relations education is a school or department of communications or journalism."[30] The majority of offerings in public relations—sequences or majors—are taught in schools of journalism and/or communications. The dominance of communications–centered education squares with the tasks assigned practitioners. However, many practitioners, especially those in business fields, question the journalism orientation, mainly in the mistaken notion that journalism education means only education in publicity techniques. The PRSA and the Public Relations Division of the AEJ have made little headway in persuading colleges of business to introduce courses for future business executives.

Education and recruitment have been greatly strengthened by the development of the Public Relations Student Society of America (PRSSA) under the auspices of the PRSA. The PRSA's interest in organizing student chapters first surfaced in 1950, but it was not until April 1967 that such an organization was proposed to the PRSA Assembly by Prof. Walter Seifert of Ohio State University. The proposal won quick approval, and the first chapter of the PRSSA was chartered in 1968. By January 1978, 75 chapters were functioning. The PRSSA's purpose is "to cultivate a favorable and mutually advantageous relationship between students and professional public relations practitioners." To ease the graduating student's way into the field, the PRSA has established a Pre-Associate Membership for PRSSA members.

The advance toward professionalism has been supported by the Foundation for Public Relations Research and Education, a nonprofit organization established by the PRSA in 1956 to foster and conduct basic research. In 1959, the foundation initiated a fellowship program that enables teachers to spend a few weeks working in counseling firms or corporations. A decade later, it set up a graduate scholarship award to a college student working for an advanced degree. In 1961, the foundation began sponsoring a series of annual lectures. It also contributed to the literature by subsidizing Morton J. Simon's *Public Relations Law*, Edward J. Robinson's *Public Relations and Survey Research*, the *Public Relations Review*, and the bibliographies.

Research required

To earn the title of professional, the practitioner must accept the obligation to work for the advancement of knowledge in the profession. Theodore Roosevelt said, "Every man owes some part of his time to the building up of the industry or profession of which he is a part." *A profession must be built upon a specialized body of knowledge and be devoted to the public interest above the private interest.* Using this yardstick, we should examine this calling's claims to professional status. First, these questions: How much specialized knowledge have practitioners contributed to the art of human relations and communication? Aren't the scientific methods and procedures of public relations borrowed from the social sciences of psychology, sociology, economics, history, and journalism? Can practitioners be hitchhikers and still lay claim to the title of professional?

One of the sure signs of advancement toward the professional horizon is the increasing demand for research and for critical examination of old theories.

Awareness is growing of the need for reexamination and redirection. Factual foundations will serve to dispel the idea of the practitioner as a sort of witch doctor. In today's world, the public relations problems in industry, for example, are every bit as tough and complicated as the problems of engineering, production, or distribution. Practitioners must approach them as methodically and as thoroughly prepared with facts as engineers, production men, and marketers approach their own. Such an approach can come only through extensive research. *Practitioners should strive for certainty in their work.*[31]

In a critical review of research in this field, Prof. James Grunig and Ronald Hickson found that "a great deal of research has been done in other disciplines which relates to public relations, but little of it has been done by public relations educators themselves, and few researchers or theorists have attempted to integrate this theory into a unified theory for one or more of the types of organizational and public behavior relevant to public relations."[32] These researchers suggested these areas as fruitful ones to explore in developing a unified theory for this practice: (1) organizational structure, (2) consumer and public behavior, (3) communications networks in organizations, (4) internal–external communications, (5) persuasive communication, (6) behavior in organizations, (7) human relations, (8) systems theories, (9) coorientation research, and (10) operations research.

Research is not a matter of putting a quarter in the slot, pulling a lever, and then picking up the answers in a tray below. Research takes time and sweat, as well as money. Research in any field is the laborious placing of one little brick on another until the structure is finished. It takes lots of bricklayers to build a building. If enough people work at it, it gets built. *Research is simply the act of searching for information—accurate, reliable, useful information—and organizing this information so that sound conclusions can be drawn.* Research is as much attitude as method. Research requires an itch and a scratch. The itch is the curiosity to know; the scratch, the will to satisfy the itch.

Toward new horizons

At midcentury, a practitioner was described this way:

> The public relations counsel is a specialist in verbal symbols. He has been well trained by his home environment and school career in the art of phrase-making. He is prosperous, on the whole, but nevertheless tends to be somewhat more nonconformist, in a political and economic sense, than do his clients. He has been mobile in an upward direction economically, and has often experienced geographic and social mobility as well. He has thus been sensitized to the outlook of people from many social strata. . . . The job of the public relations man is to keep open a two-way channel of communication so that no "misunderstandings" can arise to disturb the true harmony of interests between the publics and management. . . . His is an ideology of defense.[33]

Despite the considerable progress recorded in this generation, public relations still stands short of public acceptance as a true profession. The field lacks maturity, effective regulation, full-fledged devotion to the public interest, and a research program of its own. The 1970s did bring a consensus, shared by interested practitioners, on a fairly standardized course of preparation in the nation's schools and departments of journalism and communications. But public relations continues to be plagued with press agents parading as counselors, and with those who are more interested in manipulating the opinions of others than in understanding them. There is still evidence that the function is not fully and widely understood. The field still has those who cannot qualify *functionally, morally, or through knowledge and expertness.* Many can. But more are needed.

A start has been made toward deserving the professional status that practitioners seek. But it is only a start. As public relations practitioners demonstrate a sense of social responsibility and build a specialized body of knowledge that they can properly claim as their own, they will surround the function with the status and prestige its exponents desire. Practitioners know, better than most, that the way to gain public confidence is to deserve it. This they tell their employers. The practitioner cannot be content merely to let professional organizations adopt codes of ethics and express his views.

A publisher once remarked, "Morality is a highly personal matter; it is not to be found in the majority vote of the board of directors of a trade association, or in public expressions of association executives. . . ." Counselor Earl Newsom left this legacy to his fellow practitioners:

> I suggest that sober self-examination at this point requires that we come to an understanding of ourselves and what it is we really want to accomplish. This is not a problem that can be resolved by our Society or by any committees thereof. It is purely a personal matter. Each of us lives but once, and each of us wants to spend his life constructively. . . . I am as certain as can be that if each one of us establishes the highest of standards for his own conduct, we shall eventually earn the status of profession.[34]

The future looks promising. The public relations calling has become an important link in the free communications network upon which this nation depends for its culture, cohesion, and solidarity. *This profession has an important role to play in a nation that needs unity, a communion of purpose, and understanding and support among its people—in short, a sense of community.* In the sustaining of unity and the achievement of it where it does not now exist, the role of public relations is potentially a vital one. If practitioners as a group measure up, they will have to practice positive public relations. They will have to stand *for* things. Community will not be achieved by singing hymns of hate.

Hofstadter suggested that conflict may be contained and consensus reached when "those enlisted in society's contending interests have a basic minimal regard for each other: One party or interest seeks the defeat of an opposing interest on matters of policy, but at the same time seeks to avoid crushing the opposition or denying the legitimacy of its existence or values."[35] In achieving and sustaining unity, practitioners should carefully weigh their role.

Today's practitioners and the recruits now in training will largely determine the course this calling will take. Public relations can move on to accept John Dewey's challenge of "a responsive art of communication" that will "take possession of the physical machinery of transmission and circulation and breathe life into it." *As public relations serves to articulate and inform public opinion, it serves the public good; as it serves to confuse and mislead the public, it damages society.*

It can accomplish these things in the best interests of all. Or it can accomplish them for a greedy minority at the expense of the whole public. *Public relations as a technique is a power device. It can be used for good or evil.* It can steadily advance toward a mature, responsible profession that contributes to the unity, progress, and public welfare. Or it can decline into what philosophy professor William Earnest Hocking has described as a "conscienceless publicity racket" that brings the premiums of advancement to those who have "learned to surround their doings with a cackle of ignorant noise." *Those skilled in its techniques will have to decide which way it will go.*

A case in ethics: Marion Javits and Iran

Marion B. Javits is the wife of Sen. Jacob Javits of New York, a power in the U.S. Senate and member of the Senate Foreign Relations Committee. For some years she worked as a consultant for a Ruder & Finn subsidiary, buying art or making design studies. In this period, she was also president of Broadside Art, Inc., a company started in partnership with Clay Felker, then editor of *New York*.

On January 19, 1976, a *Village Voice* headline read, "Senator Javits Sleeps with Agent for Iran." The *Voice* had learned that Mrs. Javits had registered with the Justice Department in August 1975 as an agent for a foreign government to represent Iran (a story missed by the Washington press corps!). The next week, the *Village Voice* published the registration certificate, under a headline, "Mrs. Javits is being paid $67,500 to help Iran . . . one of the most brutal tyrannies on the planet." From the *Village Voice,* the story spread to the nation's media. A *New York Times* headline of January 16, 1976, read, "Javits Unhappy as Wife Decides to Continue Airline Work."

The Justice Department registration stated that Mrs. Javits was receiving a fee of $67,500 "plus secretarial fees" as a "consultant" to Ruder & Finn on its Iranian National Airlines account. At the time, the airline and the Iranian government had a one-year, $507,500 contract with Ruder & Finn to contact "prestigious organizations" to promote travel to Iran and general "goodwill." The contract stated that the agency was to act as spokesman to "professional men and women" and "topnotch businessmen" while making "approaches to such publications as the *New York Times, Time, Harper's,* and the *Washington Post* with a goal toward publicizing articles on Iran." It also stated that Ruder & Finn would seek to set up "small elite meetings," some of which would be held under the cosponsorship of such organizations as the Aspen Institute or the Brookings Institution and others who would be willing to cooperate. Ruder & Finn, when brought into the limelight, said Mrs. Javits was to become a senior vice-president of Ruder & Finn International.

On January 29, 1976, Marion Javits resigned her $67,500-a-year public relations consultantship, caving in to public criticism. Members of Senator Javits's staff had urged this course after the *New York Times* editorialized, ". . . for the spouse of a senator—especially one in Senator Javits' position—to be registered as a foreign agent clearly exceeds the limits of propriety."

Among those amazed to learn of the Javits/Ruder & Finn/Iran connection were executives of another major agency, Carl Byoir & Associates. Byoir had been representing Iran Air since March 1975, under a contract signed two months before the airline began service between New York and Teheran. David Finn acknowledged that his contract on top of the Byoir one was an unusual situation. "We are doing broader cultural and information work to build travel, while the other firm was concentrating on the airline." A Byoir executive rejoined, "We haven't seen any evidence of R&F's long-range work so far."

Ruder & Finn maintained that its actions did not violate the PRSA Code of Ethics. However, in an internal memo, one Ruder & Finn executive protested:

> Some business is not worth all the money in the world, if it affects our genuine credibility. A respected friend of mine had a comment which is typical: "For Lockheed or Gulf or United Brands to do the things which resulted in such terrible press indicates that top management was insensitive. For Ruder & Finn International to get involved in incidents which result in a disastrous press, one wonders if they have an understanding of public attitudes and political sensitivities to which press are responding. I can't understand the so-called 'pros' being insensitive to an obviously super-sensitive issue." Personally, I do not have a good answer for him.

In December 1975, Mrs. Javits and Ruder & Finn had proposed a public relations program to the Mexican National Tourist Council, aimed at ending Mexico's difficulties with American Jewish groups that were urging a travel boycott against Mexico because of its UN vote for an anti-Zionism resolution. The Ruder & Finn proposal followed the lines of its Iranian contract. The Mexican government turned down the bid. At the time, Mexico had a $60,000-a-year contract to promote tourism with Lawrence, Patterson & Farrell, Inc. The Ruder & Finn bid was obviously another effort to utilize the prestige and power of Senator Javits. It also raised the question of encroachment.[36]

ADDITIONAL READINGS

BERTRAND R. CANFIELD and H. FRAZIER MOORE, *Public Relations Principles, Cases, and Problems,* 7th ed. Homewood, Ill.: Dow Jones–Irwin, 1977.

ALLEN H. CENTER, *Public Relations Practices: Case Studies.* Englewood Cliffs, N.J.: Prentice-Hall, 1975.

JODY DONOHUE, *Your Career in Public Relations.* New York: Julian Messner, 1967. Outlines rewards and requirements of a career in public relations.

RONALD GOODMAN, "Excellence—An Urgent Need for Public Relations Counselors," *Public Relations Quarterly,* Vol. 11 (Winter 1967).

ARLENE HERSHMAN, "Public Relations Goes Public," *Dun's Review,* September 1977, pp. 62–66.

HILL and KNOWLTON EXECUTIVES, *Critical Issues in Public Relations.* Englewood Cliffs, N.J.: Prentice-Hall, 1975.

OTTO LERBINGER and ALBERT J. SULLIVAN, *Information,* *Influence, and Communication: A Reader.* New York: Basic Books, 1965. A book of readings.

PHILIP LESLY, *The People Factor: Managing the Human Climate.* Homewood, Ill.: Dow Jones–Irwin, 1974.

DOUG NEWSOM and ALAN SCOTT, *This Is PR: The Realities of Public Relations.* Belmont, Calif.: Wadsworth, 1976.

DAVID RICKS, MARILYN Y.C. FU, and JEFFREY S. ARPAN, *International Business Blunders.* Columbus, O.: Grid, 1974.

RAYMOND SIMON, *Public Relations: Concepts and Practices.* Columbus, O.: Grid, 1976.

———, ed., *Perspectives in Public Relations.* Norman: University of Oklahoma Press, 1966. A book of readings.

ALBERT J. SULLIVAN, "The Value Systems of Public Relations," *Public Relations Quarterly,* April, July, and October 1963.

1. J.A.R. Pimlott, *Public Relations and American Democracy* (Princeton, N.J.: Princeton University Press, 1951), p. 21. A British view of American practice at midcentury.

2. Irwin Ross, *Image Merchants* (New York: Doubleday, 1959). Ross's book is a critical look at the practice a decade later than Pimlott's. It offers illuminating insights that still apply.

3. Michael Hirsh, "The Sins of Sears are Not News in Chicago," *Columbia Journalism Review*, July/August 1976.

4. Robert Heilbroner, "Public Relations: The Invisible Sell," in Reo M. Christenson and Robert O. McWilliams, *Voice of the People*, 2nd ed. (New York: McGraw-Hill, 1967), p. 485.

5. Daniel Boorstin, *The Image* (New York: Atheneum, 1962), p. 17. A provocative if somewhat peevish book, still pertinent.

6. Francis Pollock, "The National Chicken Cooking Contest," *Columbia Journalism Review*, November/December 1975.

7. "In Search of Maturity in Industrial Relations," Report of a Special Committee of the National Council of the Churches of Christ in the U.S.A., 1960. See Part IV.

8. "Smoking and News Coverage of a Decade of Controversy," *Columbia Journalism Review*, Vol. II (Summer 1963), 12.

9. Daniel S. Greenberg, "A Critical Look at Cancer Coverage," *Columbia Journalism Review*, January/February 1975.

10. David Finn, "Struggle for Ethics in Public Relations," *Harvard Business Review*, Vol. 37 (January/February 1959), 30. For an example of a struggle involving Finn, see the case history at the end of this chapter.

11. Willard Hurst, "The Professions of American Life," *Public Relations Journal*, Vol. 13 (August 1957).

12. John Marston, "Hallmarks of a Profession," *Public Relations Journal*, Vol. 24 (July 1968).

13. W. Phillips Davison, *International Political Communication* (New York: Praeger, 1965), Chap. 8, "The Structure of International Communication Programs."

14. Securities and Exchange Commission, *Report of Special Study of the Securities Markets*, Parts I and III, 1963. Discussed in Chapter 12.

15. Letter from Rea W. Smith, executive vice-president of PRSA, dated April 8, 1977.

16. Leonard Knott, *Plain Talk about Public Relations* (Toronto: McClelland and Steward, 1961). A book of good sense by one who pioneered and shaped the practice in Canada.

17. Frank Wylie, "Professionalism, Ethics and Other Misconceptions," address before the Publicity Club of Chicago, April 20, 1977.

18. Edward L. Bernays, "Should Public Relations Counsel Be Licensed?" *Printers Ink*, December 25, 1953.

19. Edward L. Bernays, "Needed: An Ombudsman for Public Relations," *Public Relations Quarterly*, Vol. 21 (Winter 1976).

20. Neil A. Lavick, "Public Relations Council: An Alternative to Licensing?" *Public Relations Quarterly*, Vol. 20 (Spring 1975). See Bernays's response in the Summer 1975 issue.

21. Harold Brayman, *Developing a Philosophy for Business Action: A History of the Public Relations Seminar*, published in a limited edition of 500 in 1969 by the seminar.

22. *A Public Relations Bibliography*, compiled by Scott M. Cutlip (Madison: University of Wisconsin Press, 1957 and 1965). The second edition is still in print. The first supplement is *Public Relations, a Comprehensive Bibliography* (Ann Arbor: University of Michigan Press, 1974). The second was published as Winter Supplement, 1975–76, of *Public Relations Review*. The latter two were prepared by Robert L. Bishop, The University of Michigan.

23. Scott M. Cutlip, "History of Public Relations Education in the United States," *Journalism Quarterly*, Vol. 38 (Summer 1961).

24. Alfred McClung Lee, "Trends in Public Relations Training," *Public Opinion Quarterly*, Vol. 11 (Spring 1947).

25. "Training for Public Relations," *Public Relations Journal*, Vol. 12 (September 1956).

26. Ray Eldon Hiebert, *Trends in Public Relations Education, 1964–1970* (New York: Foundation for Public Relations Research and Education, 1970). Also see "PR in Classroom," *Public Relations Journal*, Vol. 26 (September 1970).

27. "Education Survey: Few Changes, Much Growth," *Public Relations Review*, Vol. 2 (Spring 1976), 31–43.

28. Thomas B. Johnson and Kenneth Rabin, "PR Faculty: What Are Their Qualifications?" *Public Relations Review*, Vol. 3 (Spring 1977), 38–48.

29. *A Design for Public Relations Education*, Report of the Commission on Public Relations Education,

1975. The commission was chaired by J. Carroll Bateman and Scott M. Cutlip. A summary may be found in *Public Relations Review,* Vol. 1 (Winter 1975).

30. *Ibid.,* p. 5.

31. The value, uses, and methods of research in public relations are set out in Edward J. Robinson, *Public Relations and Survey Research* (New York: Appleton-Century-Crofts, 1969). Includes six case studies.

32. James E. Grunig and Ronald H. Hickson, "An Evaluation of Academic Research in Public Relations," *Public Relations Review,* Vol. 2 (Spring 1976).

33. Leila A. Sussman, "The Personnel and Ideology of Public Relations," *Public Opinion Quarterly,* Vol. 12 (Winter 1948–49). Also see Ross, *Image Merchants,* "The P.R. Life."

34. Earl Newsom, "Business Does Not Function by Divine Right," *Public Relations Journal,* Vol. 19 (January 1963). In the same issue, see Scott M. Cutlip, "A Re-Examination of Public Relations Platitudes."

35. Richard Hofstadter, *The Progressive Historians: Turner, Beard, Parrington* (New York: Knopf, 1968).

36. References for this case study are the following: Jack Newfield, "Politics Makes Strange Bedfellows," *Village Voice,* January 19, 1976, p. 13; Newfield, "The Javits–Iran Connection," *Village Voice,* January 26, 1976, p. 11; "Marion Javits Registered as Agent on Behalf of Iran," *New York Times,* January 15, 1976, p. 4; "Getting Publicity No Problem for Marion Javits, Iran Air," *Advertising Age,* January 26, 1976, p. 19; Enid Nemy, "Feminists Are Critical of Mrs. Javits' Stand," *New York Times,* January 29, 1976, p. 29; Marylin Bender, "Marion Javits Issue Focuses Unwelcome Spotlight on Publicizing Foreign Clients," *New York Times,* February 27, 1976, p. 6; and Stanley Penn, "Role of Ruder & Finn in Iran–Javits Contract Shows PR's Influence," *Wall Street Journal,* March 25, 1976, p. 1.

index

index

Swados, Harvey, 104
Symbols, communication and, 207–209

Taft-Hartley Act (1947), 272, 275, 294, 404
Tarbell, Ida, 76
Tawney, R. H., 123
Team membership, 30
Technology, the audience and, 201
Telephone newslines, 248–249
Television, 71, 102, 249, 251, 252, 355, 356, 359, 371–377
  access to, 266–269
  advertising, 242
  audience research, 225–228
  cable, 253, 377
  closed-circuit, 253
  number of stations (1977), 372
Thinking, strategic, 168–169
Thoreau, Henry David, 162
Thurston, Robert, 59
Timing as a key element, 181–184
Toffler, Alvin, 100
Trade associations, 452–458
Transportation, predictions for the 1980s, 107
Two-step flow theory, 193–195
Tyler, Bessie, 87

Udrey, J. Richard, 199
Underdelivery, 14–15
United Press International (UPI), 361–362, 371
U.S. Bureau of Labor, 27, 28
U.S. Census Bureau, 19, 28, 98
U.S. Civil Rights Commission, 115
U.S. Constitution, 69
  the First Amendment, 260–263, 539–540
  the Fourteenth Amendment, 261, 540
U.S. Department of Agriculture, 66, 197, 209, 511
U.S. Department of Commerce, 20
U.S. Department of Labor, 19, 36
U.S. Information Agency, 45, 90
U.S. Internal Revenue Service, 281
U.S. Public Health Service, 114
U.S. Supreme Court, 261–283, 538
Urbanization, 98–99, 107
Utilities, 81–82

Vail, Theodore N., 74–75, 77, 82, 338
Value, cost and, 175–179
Vietnam War, 67, 205–206, 336, 409, 512
Virgil, 66

Vocational guidance survey, 22
Volunteer activities, 324–326

Walker, Albert, 147
Ward, Charles Sumner, 82–83
Warren, Joseph, 68
Watergate episode, 336, 412, 576
Webb, James E., 101
Weinberger, Casper, 126
Weiner, Harold N., 473–474
Welfare, 88, 206, 469–475
  business and, 437
Werner, Wm. G., 231
Westinghouse, George, 73–74
Wherry, Dr. John H., 531
Whitaker, Clem, 90
White, E. B., 392–393
White, Justice Bryon, 259
White, Theodore, 123
Whitney, Harry Payne, 73
Wilson, Woodrow, 84
Wire services, 361–365
Wittner, Fred, 234–235
Women, 333–335
  Equal Rights Amendment, 333, 335
  predictions for the 1980s, 107
  statistics on, 36–37
  suffrage movement, 85
Women Executives in Public Relations, 37
Wood, Leonard, 78
Words That Won the War (Mock and Larson), 84, 85
World War I, 67, 74, 84–85, 193
World War II, 67, 74, 90–91
Wright, Hamilton Mercer, 78
Wright, Joseph F., 591
Writing, description of activities of, 22
Wylie, Frank, 173

Xerox Corporation, 392–393, 437

Year Book of Railway Literature, 74
Young, Andrew, 341
Young Men's Christian Association, 89, 111, 166, 358
Young Women's Christian Association, 89
Youth, 335–340
  special programs for, 338–340

Zack, Albert, 463
Zumwalt, Elmo, 155